Windows™ Network Programming

How to Survive in a World of Windows, DOS, and Networks

RALPH DAVIS

Andrew Schulman
Series Editor

Addison-Wesley Publishing Company

Reading, Massachusetts   Menlo Park, California
New York   Don Mills, Ontario   Wokingham, England
Amsterdam Bonn Sydney Singapore Tokyo Madrid
San Juan Paris Seoul Milan Mexico City Taipei

Many of the designations used by manufacturers and sellers to distinguish their products are claimed as trademarks. Where those designations appear in this book and Addison-Wesley was aware of the trademark claim, the designations have been printed in initial capital letters.

The author and publisher have taken care in preparation of this book, but make no expressed or implied warranty of any kind and assume no responsibility for errors or omissions. No liability is assumed for incidental or consequential damages in connection with or arising out of the use of the information or programs contained herein.

Library of Congress Cataloging-in-Publication Data

Davis, Ralph, 1947-
    Windows network programming : how to survive in a
world of Windows, DOS, and Networks / Ralph Davis
        p.   cm.
    Includes index.
    ISBN 0-201-58133-7
    1. Microsoft Windows (Computer file) 2. Computer networks.
3. NetWare (Computer file)   I. Title.
QA76.76.W56D38 1993
004.6--dc20   92-34185
                                             CIP

Series Editor: Andrew Schulman
Managing Editor: Amorette Pedersen
Production Editor: Andrea G. Mulligan
Line drawings: Jennifer Noble
Set in 11-point ITC Galliard by Benchmark Productions

7 8 9 10 11-CRW-0099989796
Seventh printing, January 1996

Addison-Wesley books are available for bulk purchases by corporations, institutions, and other organizations. For more information please contact the Corporate, Government and Special Sales Department at (800) 238-9682.

To Bill Gates, for making the future look fun and exciting
To my daughter Lauren Michelle, for giving me such a large stake in the future
And to Mikhail Gorbachev, for making the future look possible again

contents

Acknowledgments

It would not have been possible for me to write as ambitious a book as this one without the help of many other people, and the generosity of a number of software companies. In particular, I would like to thank: Rose Kearsley and Margaret Lewis of Novell, Inc., Tim McCaffrey and Tanya Van Dam of Microsoft Corporation, and Jill Pembrooke of the Wagner Group, Gretchen Bilsson of Microsoft Systems Journal, Bill Cohn of FTP Software, Ted Bailey and Jackie Wah of Banyan Systems, Inc., Boris Yanovsky of NetManage, Anne Finkler of Frontier Technologies, and Christine Apap-Bologna of Distinct Corporation.

I am also grateful to the following people who have contributed to the production of the book: Andrew Schulman, for his thorough and exacting technical edits, Mike Shiels for his valuable technical advice and input, Andrea Mulligan, Chris Williams, and Amy Pedersen of Benchmark Productions, for their thoroughly professional production work, and for being, as always, a pleasure to work with. And, of course, Sandy Moore for her fine copy edits.

Finally, I want to especially thank Paul Funk of Funk Software, Inc., for everything he has taught me.

CHAPTER ■ 1

Introduction

Network Programming Under Windows

It is my intention in this book to explore some of the issues and problems involved in writing networked applications under Microsoft Windows. I also plan to develop a framework on which larger applications can be built.

Having used the word "problems," I should state at once that there are fewer problems now, with Windows 3.1 and Windows for Workgroups (WFW), than there were when Windows 3.0 was first released. Microsoft and vendors of network operating systems have had time to make their software work better together. This has important implications for us: it is no longer necessary to build networked applications from the ground up. Stable foundations are available, so we can concentrate on developing distributed applications.

However, networking APIs (Application Program Interface) still present a confusing potpourri. Although there are several rich vendor-specific network APIs, there is no standard Windows API for accomplishing network-related tasks. The Windows 3.1 API and the Windows network driver provide a few WNet functions that perform rudimentary tasks. By comparison with the vendor-specific APIs, however, these APIs are very lean. (See Chapter 9 for a discussion of these functions.) Windows NT and the Win32 API do offer some real enhancements, but these too do not replace the proprietary APIs (see Chapter 13).Windows for Workgroups expands the API set, but still falls far short of the vendor-specific APIs (see Chapter 14). One of the things I will do in this book is try to correct this deficiency by developing a full-featured, network-independent API for Windows.

The Ideal Situation

If things were truly ideal, we would have one great big protected-mode operating system. It would boot when we turned on our computer; it would not run on top of another operating system.

This operating system would also be a full-featured network operating system, and would provide its network services transparently. Users would see all their logged-in drives identically; it would not matter a whit to them whether drive H was on a local hard disk, in Chicago, in Paris, or in Afghanistan. To be sure, there would be differences in response time, but there would be no other difference in behavior.

The Real Situation

Of course, this is not the world we are confronted with. The jungle is still full of lions and tigers and creatures that make eerie sounds in the middle of the night. Three salient facts have dictated this:

- DOS is here to stay
- NetWare is here to stay
- Windows is here to stay

DOS   Several years ago, many of us were hopeful that OS/2 would supplant DOS as the operating system on everyone's desktop. The whole world would then run in protected mode. Of course, this has not happened; OS/2 has been a market bust, and DOS has proven very resilient.

NetWare   For a while, it seemed that every year would begin with analysts heralding the arrival of the network operating system of the future, and prophesying NetWare's doom. By the end of the year, they had all sat down, and Novell's market share had increased. Novell has shown itself to be a highly adaptable and well-managed company; it seems likely that it will continue to dominate the market. Its acquisition of Digital Research (makers of DR-DOS) and Excelan (developers of the TCP/IP LAN Workplace) should serve to further strengthen its position.

The biggest threat to NetWare was probably Microsoft's LAN Manager, but that has been hobbled by its association with OS/2. OS/2 is superior to NetWare as a platform for server-based applications; in NetWare, a wayward NetWare Loadable Module (NLM) can bring the server down for an entire workgroup. Nevertheless, NLMs are gaining legitimacy. The appearance of Oracle and SQL Server in NLM implementations confirms this.

It appears from Microsoft's marketing literature that they intend for Windows NT to become a new host for LAN Manager. This will undoubtedly boost its acceptance, but it still seems unlikely that it will supplant NetWare. There is too much money already invested in NetWare LANs, and it is, after all, a good product.

Windows for Workgroups, which is shipping as this book goes to press, enhances Windows' network awareness. However, Microsoft does not seem to anticipate that it will replace NetWare, either. It offers some interesting functionality—most important, distributed OLE and DDE—but it is more in the peer-to-peer genre of products like NetWare Lite and Artisoft's LANtastic.

Windows   Windows became a real operating system with the release of 3.0, and its market acceptance has been extraordinary. The investment in Windows-based software will soon make Windows a permanent fixture as well (if it is not already).

Coping with the Real Situation

As developers, it does us little good to complain about the world we are faced with. These market realities determine the kinds of tasks we are likely to be presented with. An understanding of how to deal effectively with our tasks (and some handy tools) will be essential in the next few years.

As we will see, most of the problems that we will face derive ultimately from the hybrid DOS-NetWare-Windows environment. We start with a primitive operating system,

DOS, that runs in real mode, thereby sacrificing most of the power of the Intel chips it runs on. This means that other software written for this environment—like network operating systems—must support this lowest common denominator of functionality. That is, it must also run at least partially in real mode, though fortunately only at the point where it communicates with DOS.

On top of this, we put a sophisticated protected-mode operating system, Windows. It must be able to mediate between the protected-mode software that it runs and the real-mode world that exists underneath it. Where standards exist, Windows can provide this service transparently. Thus, it provides a bridge between Windows applications and DOS system services, ROM-BIOS functions, and NetBIOS. Windows programs can access these services just as they do under DOS, and rest assured that Windows will have set up the proper environment by the time the real-mode interrupt takes control.

This brings us to the second problem: the absence of standards for local-area network APIs.

No Standards for Network Services

It is an exaggeration to say that there are *no* standards for network services, but not a flagrant one. DOS was not originally designed with networking in mind. DOS 3.1 added some networking support, but by then it was too late to establish a standard, since NetWare was already firmly entrenched. Even DOS 5 offers only a handful of functions for manipulating network resources. DOS alone cannot possibly serve as the basis for powerful networked applications.

Obtaining Network Services   Windows achieves device independence—and standardization—by having device drivers handle all device-dependent functions. The device drivers are called from Windows by means of a published interface, and this provides standardization. But while the network drivers do indeed provide a handful of calls (see Chapter 9), they do not offer much beyond the DOS networking functions.

If you want to write Windows programs that do things like:

- Talk to Windows programs on other machines
- Add users and user groups
- Change users' access rights
- Report on network traffic or configuration
- Determine how network resources are being used

you must sacrifice network independence and write to a specific vendor's API. Windows for Workgroups' Messaging API gives you some ability to exchange data between machines. But the contrast between the minimal built-in DOS and Windows network functions and the best vendor-specific APIs is still striking. The latter are rich and complex, containing hundreds of functions.

In this book, we will examine some of these APIs, decide what functionality should be standardized, and develop a network-independent interface for Windows applications on top of the proprietary APIs. We will keep the naming convention used in the Windows 3.1 and Win32 APIs, and preface all function names with WNet. For example, WNetAddUser() will add a new user to the network. In cases where it may be unclear whether a particular WNet() function is a Windows API or one of mine, I will spell it out explicitly.

Peer-to-Peer Protocols   Peer-to-peer communications are somewhat better standardized than network services; there are several protocols that have achieved acceptance.

Named pipes, originally developed in OS/2, are also supported under NetWare and VINES. TCP/IP, which enjoys considerable support in the world of wide-area networking, is rapidly gaining in the LAN world as well. It is presently being standardized for the Windows environment by the Windows Sockets specification (see Chapter 6). NetBIOS is well standardized in the PC world, and is the only protocol for which Windows offers built-in support. (I cover NetBIOS in Chapter 3.)

As with the network service APIs, I will develop a protocol-independent set of peer-to-peer functions that can then serve as building blocks for distributed applications under Windows. Here too I will use the WNet naming convention. WNetSendMessage(), for instance, will send a message to a window on a remote workstation.

Network Design

The move to graphical user interfaces (GUIs) poses new challenges for network designers. The transfer of graphic images across networks places significantly higher data transfer demands on them, even if the images are compressed before transmission. Thus, networks that were fast enough in a primarily text-based environment may cease to provide adequate performance in a graphical environment. On token-ring LANs, this means greater delay for users accessing network resources, as there is more competition for use of the token. On EtherNet LANs, it can conceivably cause LAN traffic to exceed the threshold where LAN throughput grinds to a halt, as almost all the LAN traffic becomes retransmissions after collisions.

There are two aspects of LAN design that will need reevaluation: data transfer rates previously thought to be fast enough now may not be, and LANs may need to be broken up into more segments, with each segment supporting fewer users. This may require bridges to connect the new segments.

There are no hard and fast rules, and no simple formulas. Network administrators and designers will need to carefully monitor their LAN traffic and performance, and should develop benchmark tests to see what their thresholds are. Particular attention to a couple of points is appropriate.

First, EtherNet LANs can be brought to their knees by heavy loads. Token-passing LANs, on the other hand, will continue to be usable, but users will experience longer delays.

Second, data transfer rates less than ten megabits per second may not provide adequate performance except under light loads.

It is an obvious truth, but nonetheless worth restating: a network's data-transfer rate refers to its *total* load. A four-megabit-per-second token-ring LAN does not move four megabits *per user* per second. If it has ten users, it moves 400,000 bits per user per second. And this is only its *nominal* rate. The actual throughput is likely to be no more than 65-80 percent of the nominal rate, because of factors like queuing delay and propagation time.

EtherNet is at the low end of this spectrum. If our four-megabit-per-second token-ring LAN is operating at 75 percent efficiency, then its actual data-transfer rate is three megabits—only 375,000 bytes—per second. If it has 50 active users, the per-user bandwidth is a mere 7,500 bytes per second. On a 16-megabit-per-second token ring, this increases to 30,000 bytes per second. On a 100-megabit-per-second fiber optic ring, it becomes 187,500 bytes per second.

I want to reemphasize that no precise formula applies to every situation. After all, network workstations spend most of their time interacting with end users; that is to say, they are idle as far as the network is concerned. Two-megabit-per-second Arcnet, four-megabit-per-second token ring, or ten-megabit-per-second EtherNet may be sufficient for most networks. However, it is a good idea to try to quantify how the move to Windows and Windows-based graphical applications will increase network traffic, and to leave room for future growth.

Structure of This Book

Following this introduction, this book is divided into three parts. Part I deals with "horizontal" applications, where software running on different machines communicates over the network. Part II deals with "vertical" applications, those where software on the end-user level communicates with lower-level network software (like the network shell) on the same machine. The network software in turn communicates over the network with file servers and other kinds of servers. The material covered in Part I is not required to understand Part II. Part III covers new developments in Windows network programming, specifically Windows for Workgroups and Win32.

Programming Tools and Conventions

The Win32 API specifications have been published, and they include suggestions for building portability into C programs now. The Windows 3.1 Software Development Kit (SDK) includes tools that allow us to plan for the future. The code in this book has been written to maximize portability to Win32. Specifically:

- It uses constants defined in WINDOWS.H and WINDOWSX.H as much as possible. Thus, instead of saying

  ```
  long FAR PASCAL
  ```

  it says

  ```
  LRESULT WINAPI
  ```

  or

  ```
  LRESULT CALLBACK.
  ```

  (WINAPI and CALLBACK are both #define'd as FAR PASCAL in WINDOWS.H.)
- It uses the STRICT type-checking offered in the Windows 3.1 SDK.

- It uses message-cracking macros.

The development tools and platforms I used are:

- Microsoft C/C++ 7.0, but only using C
- Microsoft Windows SDK 3.1
- Windows for Workgroups
- Win32 SDK
- Microsoft Macro Assembler 6.0 (when necessary)
- CodeView for Windows, version 4.00
- Microsoft LAN Manager SDK, version 2.1
- Novell's NetWare C Interface for Windows, version 1.3
- Banyan's Windows Developer's Toolkit, version 5.00 (5), and pre-release software provided by Banyan Systems

My operating system platforms are:

- MS-DOS version 5.0
- Windows 3.1
- Windows NT beta
- Novell NetWare version 3.11
- Banyan VINES 5.00 (5)
- Microsoft LAN Manager version 2.1 running on MS OS/2 version 1.3

Source Code Available

If you need the source code contained in this book, contact me via CompuServe at 71161,1060, or call me at (703) 720-6909.

Part I:

CHAPTER ■ 2

Horizontal Applications

General Discussion

In Part I, we will be dealing with what I refer to somewhat imprecisely as "horizontal" applications. I use the word "horizontal" because in applications of this kind, software running on workstation A talks to a similar program, perhaps even a copy of itself, on workstation B. The defining characteristic is that there is communication across the network. A frequently used term for this type of software is "distributed application." I prefer "horizontal" because it distinguishes these kinds of programs from vertical applications, which execute (or at least appear to execute) within a single workstation. A typical example of a horizontal application is a file-transfer program. System-administration programs like Novell's SYSCON, on the other hand, are vertical.

Horizontal applications include both client-client and client-server programs. The principal difference between these two is that under the client-server architecture, one machine (the server) offers services, and other machines (the clients) request them. The client-client model, on the other hand, involves a two-way exchange of services. In essence, client-client is two-way client-server.

To further narrow my working definition of these terms, I will use client-client to refer to at least two Windows applications on different workstations that cooperate to perform a single task. I will define client-server as a Windows application on a network workstation that requests services from a server-based application.

With these definitions, I have placed the client-server model beyond the scope of this book. There are many possible platforms for server-based applications: NetWare NLMs, LAN Manager services, VINES services, UNIX, to name some of the most important. Each one of these could occupy a book in itself. Our focus here will be on Windows programs talking to other Windows programs, and on building the foundation that enables them to do so.

Peer-to-Peer Protocols

Local-area networks are what is known as packet-switching networks. This means that all data transferred over the network is broken up into small pieces (packets). The actual size of the packets depends on a number of factors, but it is typically in the range of 512 to 4096 bytes. In addition to the data it contains, the packet must contain control information telling the network where to send it, how big it is, what place it occupies in the entire message, etc. The control information sent by one machine must be understood by any machines it wants to communicate with. This is called a *protocol*.

Peer-to-peer protocols are the basis of all horizontal programming. In order for software on different machines to exchange data, all participating machines must have agreed-upon packet formats and procedural conventions. The packet formats represent a common syntax; the procedural conventions determine the order in which actions are carried out.

In addition, data transferred over the network must be represented in a host-independent way. Different machines, for example, represent integers using different byte orders. A machine like an Intel 80x86 could not possibly talk to a Macintosh if the two did not pass integers in a common format. In the code I develop in this book, I make the simplifying assumption that all machines represent integers in Intel order. In a commercial-grade application designed to work with non-Intel machines, this is not a safe assumption.

The several protocols we will examine provide essentially the same services, but the programming interfaces vary widely. An API should shield the program that uses a protocol from the implementation of that protocol. Some of the interfaces we will look at provide a high degree of isolation. Others immerse the programmer in the details of the protocol.

There are three levels of service normally offered by peer-to-peer protocols:

- Unacknowledged connectionless (or datagram) service
- Acknowledged connectionless service
- Connection-oriented (or virtual circuit) service

Unacknowledged Connectionless (Datagram) Service

This is the least robust of the three types of service. It does not guarantee that packets will be delivered to their destination, or that they will arrive in the same sequence in which they departed. Packets sent at different times may travel different routes, depending on network traffic conditions. Packets may be discarded at any time without the sender being notified.

Datagram service is fast and lean. There are some applications where you do not need to know that the data actually arrives. For instance, you may be informing other stations that you have just joined the network. If they get the message, that's fine, but it won't stop the show if they don't. Local-area networks are highly reliable; the chances are pretty good that the data will actually reach its intended destination. However, if you require some assurance of delivery, either you will need to use a different level of service, or write code to handle acknowledgments and retransmissions.

Acknowledged Connectionless Service

Acknowledged connectionless service is more reliable; it involves a simple request-response protocol. The sender transmits a packet, and the receiver responds with an acknowledgment (perhaps piggybacked onto data). It operates strictly on a one-packet-at-a-time basis. Every packet transmitted must be acknowledged before another one can be sent.

Acknowledged connectionless service is very good for exchanges of small pieces of information. For example, interactions between workstation shells and file server operating systems frequently use this class of service. Unlike pure datagram service, it does guarantee delivery. Unlike connection-oriented service, it does not do packet sequencing; messages are assumed to consist of a single packet.

Both types of connectionless service need support only two operations in an API, sending a datagram and receiving a datagram.

Connection-Oriented Service

The most important peer-to-peer service is connection-oriented communication. Here, delivery of packets in the correct sequence is guaranteed. If a packet cannot be delivered, the sender will receive notification. The first packet sent will be the first delivered. To keep the receiver from being bombarded with more packets than it can handle, the sending and receiving stations agree on how many unacknowledged packets the sender will be permitted to transmit. The receiving station acknowledges packets as a group, which is more efficient than one-at-a-time acknowledgment.

Because the protocol does all this for you, connection-oriented service involves more overhead than connectionless service. Specifically, the protocol implementation on both communicating stations must internally maintain information on the state of the connection. For instance, each station must remember:

- What packet number it expects to receive next
- How many packets it is permitted to send
- The amount of time a group of packets has been outstanding without acknowledgment

The operations offered by connection-oriented APIs are somewhat more extensive than those provided for connectionless service. In addition to the send and receive operations, there must also be a way to call another station to initiate a connection; there must be a way for a station to indicate its willingness to accept connections; and there must be a way to terminate a connection. The sequence of operations differs, depending on whether a station is playing an active or a passive role. A single station can play both roles, and indeed that will be the norm in the software we develop in this book.

Sending and receiving packets of data over a network has many analogies to writing data to and reading it from a file. For the active side, the sequence of operations is:

1. Call the target station. Other names used for this operation are *connect* and *establish connection*. This is analogous to opening a file.
2. Send and receive data. These are analogous to writing and reading the file.
3. Terminate the connection. This corresponds to closing a file.

For the passive side, the operations are:

1. Listen for connection requests.
2. When a connection is established, send and receive data.
3. Terminate the connection.

Either partner may terminate the connection at any time; this is not exclusively the prerogative of the station initiating the conversation.

Specific Protocols

Before getting into a detailed discussion of the protocols, I would like to offer a few introductory remarks about each of them. The protocols I will be discussing in this book are:

- NetBIOS (originally from IBM PC-LAN) (Chapter 3)
- Novell's IPX/SPX (Chapter 4)
- VINES Sockets, from Banyan Systems (Chapter 5)
- Windows Sockets specification for TCP/IP (Chapter 6)
- Win32's mailslots and named pipes (Chapter 13)

NetBIOS

NetBIOS was introduced in IBM's PC-LAN program, and its Microsoft equivalent, MS-NET. It is now supported on all major networks.

NetBIOS provides good isolation between the interface to, and the implementation of, a protocol. Indeed, the NetBIOS programming interface is entirely independent of the underlying protocol. NetBIOS works the same under NetWare, VINES, LAN manager, and Windows for Workgroups, for instance. It thus provides a portable network API that shields programmers from the details of the non-portable protocols it runs on top of.

Stations on the network can be known by human-readable names, or you can use binary addresses. There are no protocol headers to deal with. The SEND command allows the transmission of up to 65,535 bytes, and CHAIN SEND can send twice that much.

NetBIOS offers an additional advantage: it is the only protocol that enjoys built-in support in the Windows environment. Instead of issuing INT 5CH, as you would in a DOS program, programs can call the Windows NetBIOSCall() function. Windows then handles all the translation between protected and real mode. (At present, NetBIOSCall() just issues an INT 5CH. However, using NetBIOSCall() shields you from future changes in its implementation.) NetBIOS is also supported in all the major network environments, and will continue to be supported in Win32.

IPX/SPX

Interret Packet Exchange (IPX) and Sequenced Packet Exchange (SPX) are important protocols for one reason: IPX/SPX is the native tongue of Novell's NetWare, which commands a comfortable majority of the LAN market. The protocols themselves are implementations of Xerox's Internet Datagram Protocol and Sequenced Packet Protocol. The IPX/SPX programming interface does not offer a high level of abstraction. As I noted above, it is desirable for an interface to a protocol to isolate the programmer from the way the protocol is implemented. Stated another way, the interface should not require the programmer to format protocol packets and ship them.

This is exactly what the IPX/SPX API obliges you to do. You must be aware of the protocol headers and fill in some of their fields. You must supply buffers for the drivers to use for incoming packets. You must deal with binary network addresses, rather than human-readable names. You are constantly reminded of the details of how the protocol is implemented.

However, because of NetWare's dominant market position, it is likely that you will have to program IPX and SPX. So a knowledge of how to use them, and of the particular pitfalls involved in using them with Windows, is imperative.

VINES Sockets

Banyan VINES is strongly oriented towards wide-area networking. For this reason, it supports several industry-standard protocols, including NetBIOS, TCP/IP, and X.25. It also has two native protocols, the Interprocess Communication Protocol (IPC) and the Sequenced Packet Protocol (SPP). IPC supports connectionless service, both acknowledged and unacknowledged. SPP, like Novell's SPX, is an implementation of Xerox's Sequenced Packet Protocol; it supports connection-oriented communications.

IPC and SPP are the protocols supported by Banyan's Windows DLL (VNSAPI-.DLL). TCP/IP and X.25 are primarily provided for use in server-based applications. However, Banyan also supports TCP/IP on workstations through an OEM version of FTP Software's TCP/IP.

The VINES Sockets API shields the developer from the implementation of the protocols. Banyan has taken the approach of condensing their API into a very small number of functions, and using bit flags to tell the functions what action they are to perform. For example, a send() function call is used to call another station, send a packet on a connection, terminate a connection, and send a datagram. A receive() call can listen for a connection request, receive a packet on a connection, or receive a datagram.

TCP/IP

TCP/IP is not native to any of the LAN operating systems we are discussing. Originally developed to support the U.S. Department of Defense's Internet, it offers many advantages. First, it is a mature, robust set of protocols, specifically designed to allow component networks that possess disparate characteristics to communicate. Second, it is very widely supported, and offers the best wide-area connectivity. Third, some very good programming interfaces have been developed to support it, specifically, Berkeley Sockets and AT&T's Transport Layer Interface (TLI). NetWare, VINES, and LAN Manager all support TCP/IP in one manner or another.

The programming interfaces available for Windows, however, have been late to standardize. The APIs mentioned above were developed originally for UNIX, a very different operating system from Windows. Thus, the ports to Windows come in several different vendor-specific flavors. We therefore find ourselves in the paradoxical situation of having no standard programming interface to the best-standardized protocol.

The Windows Sockets specification is being developed to address this problem, and to offer a standard that TCP/IP implementors can program to. As more products become available that support this standard, the programming situation with TCP/IP should greatly improve.

Mailslots and Named Pipes

LAN Manager and Win32 offer mailslots and named pipes for peer-to-peer communications, in addition to NetBIOS. Mailslots provide connectionless service. First-class mailslots offer acknowledged connectionless service, and second-class mailslots offer unacknowledged datagram service. Named pipes support full connection-oriented service.

Mailslots and named pipes are the most convenient programming interfaces of those we will discuss. Pipes and mailslots use Universal Naming Convention (UNC) filenames. For example, a pipe named WNET on the computer MYCOMPUTER would be accessed as \\MYCOMPUTER\PIPE\WNET. The name can also include pseudodirectories, so that a pipe or mailslot owned by one application can be distinguished from one owned by another. Thus, we could further expand WNET to be \\MYCOMPUTER\PIPE\WNET-BOOK\WNET. There is no actual directory path corresponding to this name; it is a virtual file name. Once a named pipe is opened, exchanges of data use standard file I/O calls. To send data, you do a write to the pipe or mailslot; to receive data, you read it.

Under LAN Manager, named pipes and first-class mailslots can only be used for client-server exchanges with OS/2 LAN Manager servers. Thus, NetBIOS is the protocol of choice for horizontal Windows applications under LAN Manager. However, Win32 supports the full named pipes/mailslot API. For this reason, and because it is such a good interface, it merits our attention.

Blocking Versus Non-blocking Operations

None of the protocols we will study originated in the Windows environment. NetBIOS and IPX/SPX started in the DOS world. TCP/IP and VINES Sockets came from UNIX, and named pipes are an OS/2 innovation. They have all been adapted to Windows, and the adaptation has not always been facile.

The most significant impediment has been blocking I/O. A function call is said to block if the program that issues it does not progress further until the function completes. Most of the functions you use in the course of a normal C program are blocking. For instance, when you write to a file under DOS using the C write() function, the function does not return until the data has been transferred from your program to operating system write buffers. All other activity ceases, except that generated by hardware interrupts.

This is not a problem under DOS; because your program owns the machine, it doesn't matter how long it takes for the function to complete. Your user may get bored, but you will not be holding up anyone else's program. Nor is it a problem under UNIX or OS/2. Because they are preemptive multitasking systems, write() will only appear to block. The operating system will preempt you and allow other programs to run while your operation is in progress.

In a sense, Windows gives us the worst of both worlds. You can no longer assume that you own the machine; there are other Windows applications running, and you cannot possibly anticipate what they will be. However, Windows 3.1 is non-preemptive; thus, a blocking call will tie up the machine for everybody else. Unlike UNIX or OS/2, a call that appears to block in Windows really does block.

A function that initiates a non-blocking operation, on the other hand, returns to your program immediately. You find out that the requested event has completed either by polling its status, or by receiving some kind of asynchronous notification. The Windows architecture is built on asynchronous notification: Windows passes you a message when something happens that you need to know about.

Clearly, the best way to do network I/O is with non-blocking operations that post a message when they are done. Indeed, it is almost correct to say that blocking operations are simply verboten. Even when we do a blocking operation, it should only appear to block, unless it can be safely assumed that it will finish quickly. Under the covers, it should execute a PeekMessage() loop to allow other applications to run, and to allow the calling application to respond to other input. You will see many examples of PeekMessage() loops throughout the code in this book.

The PeekMessage() loops actually call the routine MyPeekMessage(), presented in Listing 2-17. There is a serious problem with PeekMessage loops, described by Microsoft in several of its KnowledgeBase articles (see the bibliography). It is not enough to just call PeekMessage(), because it does not issue an MS-DOS idle interrupt. This may cause DOS TSRs and device drivers to time out. There are two ways to notify other software that you are in an idle loop. The old way is to call INT 28H. The new way is to issue an INT 2FH with AX set to 1689H. MyPeekMessage() does both, to make sure it notifies software that uses both the old and the new method. I will continue to refer to these loops as "PeekMessage() loops," rather than "MyPeekMessage() loops," to emphasize the fact that they use the Windows function PeekMessage().

You must use PeekMessage(), rather than WaitMessage() or GetMessage(), because those functions block if no message is available, and in Windows network software we simply cannot block.

A Network-Independent API for Peer-to-Peer Communications

In this chapter, we will develop a network-independent dynamic link library (DLL) to provide Windows programs the services normally associated with peer-to-peer protocols. As I said above, these are:

- Send datagram
- Receive datagram
- Initiate a conversation
- Express willingness to accept conversations
- Send data over a connection
- Receive data over a connection
- Terminate a connection

The goal of this DLL will be to provide an API that is fully portable from one network environment to another. It will provide this portability by loading a second, network-specific, DLL at runtime. (These additional DLLs are developed in Chapters 3 through 6.)

In addition to these basic services, we will need functions to initialize and shut down the DLL. One of the most important tasks performed at initialization will be determining which network-dependent DLL we need to link to. This in turn is done by loading the appropriate network driver supplied with Windows, or by the network vendor. The [boot] section of the SYSTEM.INI file has a setting

```
network.drv=
```

You can retrieve this by calling GetPrivateProfileString(). You have to use GetPrivate-ProfileString(), rather than GetProfileString(), because GetProfileString() reads WIN.INI.

```
char szNetworkDriver[128];
GetPrivateProfileString("BOOT", "NETWORK.DRV", "MSNET.DRV",
   szNetworkDriver, sizeof (szNetworkDriver), "SYSTEM.INI");
```

This asks Windows to get the network.drv setting from the [boot] section of SYSTEM.INI. The third argument ("MSNET.DRV") tells Windows what to return if there is no network.drv setting. (MSNET.DRV is the most generic network driver.)

Once we have obtained the name of the network driver file, we call LoadLibrary() to load it, then GetProcAddress() to obtain a pointer to the WNetGetCaps() function.

```
WORD (WINAPI *WNetGetCaps)(WORD wIndex);
HINSTANCE hNetLib;

hNetLib = LoadLibrary(szNetworkDriver);
if (hNetLib > HINSTANCE_ERROR)
   (FARPROC) WNetGetCaps = GetProcAddress(hNetLib, "WNetGetCaps");
```

WNetGetCaps() reports many of the capabilities of the network driver. What we are interested in here is the underlying network operating system. We pass WNetGetCaps() an argument of WNNC_NET_TYPE, and it returns a value telling us what network we are running on. We use this to determine which of our network-dependent DLLs to load (WNETNB.DLL, WNETIPX.DLL, or WNETVNS.DLL).

Here is a code fragment that does this:

```
char szNetworkDriver[128];
switch (WNetGetCaps(WNNC_NET_TYPE))
   {
   case WNNC_NET_None:     // No network
      return -1;
   case WNNC_NET_MSNet:
   case WNNC_NET_LanMan:
   case WNNC_NET_WFW:
      // Use NetBIOS for MS-Net, LAN Manager, or Windows for Workgroups
      lstrcpy(szNetworkDriver, "WNETNB.DLL");
      break;
   case WNNC_NET_NetWare:
      lstrcpy(szNetworkDriver, "WNETIPX.DLL");
      break;
   case WNNC_NET_Vines:
      lstrcpy(szNetworkDriver, "WNETVNS.DLL");
      break;
   default:
      // Non-supported network.
      return -1;
   }
```

WNetGetCaps( ) is discussed in more detail in Chapter 9. It is a crucial function, because it enables us to offer intelligent network independence, and, therefore, source-code portability. The network-independent DLL, which I am calling WNETLVL1.DLL, contains the API that we expose to other Windows programs. It in turn calls functions in the level 0 (network-specific) DLL to obtain the services. It accesses these functions through pointers that we initialize once we have loaded the library. For example:

```
DECLARE_HANDLE(HCONNECTION);
HCONNECTION (WINAPI *lpWNetCall)(int nNameIndex,
                LPVOID lpTargetStation);

(FARPROC) lpWNetCall =
   GetProcAddress(hNetLib, "_WNetCall");
```

Table 2-1 lists the functions that I will include in WNETLVL1.DLL. The functions in the network-specific DLL will have the same names, but begin with an underscore, as in the above example.

Table 2-1. Functions in the Network-Independent DLL (WNETLVL1.DLL)

Function Name	Purpose
Connection-oriented	
WNetCall( )	Attempt to connect to another station
WNetListen( )	Accept connection requests from another station
WNetSend( )	Send packet over connection
WNetReceive( )	Receive packet over connection
WNetHangup( )	Terminate connection
Datagram	
WNetSendDatagram( )	Transmit a datagram
WNetReceiveDatagram( )	Make buffers available for receiving incoming datagrams
General purpose	
WNetInit( )	Initialize DLL
WNetShutdown( )	Close down DLL
WNetGetName( )	Find out station name
WNetGetNameLength( )	Find out name length
WNetSetName( )	Set station name and name length
WNetShipData( )	Open connection, send packet, read response, terminate connection
WNetSetLastError( )	Remember a Windows network error [based on Win32 SetLastError( )]
WNetGetLastError( )	Get last error code remembered by WNetSetLastError( ) [based on Win32 GetLastError( )]

Remote Procedure Calls

The Windows environment consists of multiple Windows applications that respond to user-triggered events, such as keystrokes, mouse movement, menu selections, and so forth.

The affected applications respond by handling messages that Windows sends them. In addition, programs can communicate with each other either by using Dynamic Data Exchange (DDE) or by sending messages directly. It makes sense to extend this message-passing model to the network environment. To do this, we will develop functions that use those listed in Table 2-1 to implement a remote procedure call mechanism for Windows. They will enable a program running on one machine to call Windows functions on another machine. In particular, they will make it possible for applications to send Windows messages to each other over a network.

These functions will implement a higher-level protocol on top of the peer-to-peer operations. That is to say, they will use the functions provided by the network-independent DLL to pass both data and the control information they need. The control information will just look like data to the peer-to-peer functions.

To support distributed message passing, we need distributed versions of SendMessage() and PostMessage(), whose prototypes are:

```
BOOL    WINAPI PostMessage(HWND hWnd, UINT uMessage,
                           WPARAM wParam, LPARAM lParam);
LRESULT WINAPI SendMessage(HWND hWnd, UINT uMessage,
                           WPARAM wParam, LPARAM lParam);
```

The purpose of these functions is, of course, to deliver messages to windows. Clearly, to extend them to the network environment, we need to know the machine or station where the target window resides. Because the different network operating systems have their own conventions for naming stations, the function prototypes should make no assumption about the data type of this parameter. Thus, we will make it an LPVOID (void FAR *). The network-specific support routines will know how to interpret the address.

So the first expansion of the prototype is:

```
LRESULT WINAPI WNetSendMessage(LPVOID lpStation, HWND hWnd, UINT
               uMessage, WPARAM wParam, LPARAM lParam);
```

I will confine my discussion to WNetSendMessage(), not mentioning WNetPostMessage() except for the few places where it differs.

At least one additional extension is necessary. *lParam* is frequently a far pointer to data. It makes no sense to pass a pointer to local data to another station on the network; the pointer has no meaning in the remote environment. Thus, WNetSendMessage() must know when *lParam* is a far pointer so it can access the data on the sending station, transmit the data itself rather than the pointer, then allocate memory for it on the receiving station.

An easy way to handle this is to add a boolean argument indicating whether *lParam* is a pointer, and a DWORD argument giving the length of the buffer if it is a pointer. Hence:

```
LRESULT WINAPI WNetSendMessage(LPVOID lpStation, HWND hWnd,
               UINT uMessage, WPARAM wParam, LPARAM lParam,
               BOOL bIsLParamPtr, DWORD dwDataLength);
```

A much more sophisticated approach is to provide processing for all known Windows messages to determine which ones may take pointers in *lParam*. This approach imposes a little more complexity on WNetSendMessage(). However, it permits us to deal with the much more troublesome problem of passing handles to data, global atoms, or pointers to output buffers. This will be particularly important in the networked implementation of DDE that I will develop in this chapter.

By combining the two approaches, we can limit the number of messages we have to process. We also allow distributed applications to use private messages, which we cannot possibly know how to interpret. We will require them to pass pointers in *lParam*.

The algorithm I will use is:

1. If the message is a DDE message, ignore *bIsLParamPtr*. DDE packs atoms and handles into *wParam* and *lParam*. Like local pointers, local atoms and handles have no meaning on a remote machine. Therefore, we must expand atoms and handles, and encapsulate the data.

2. If *bIsLParamPtr* is TRUE, build a packet large enough to contain the data passed in. Also, look at the message to determine how much memory needs to be allocated for output data.

Because messages that expect return data are necessarily synchronous, only WNetSendMessage() will support them. WNetPostMessage() will process DDE messages and ship the data being passed. However, it will not make provisions for data coming back from the partner station, other than the return value of the remote PostMessage().

Data Structures

We need to encapsulate the WNetSendMessage() arguments in a data structure. An obvious element of this structure is the Windows MSG structure. After all, the parameters to SendMessage() are broken out of this structure by DispatchMessage(). We will simply put them back into the structure, then break them out again on the receiving end. To the receiving application, the incoming message will look like any other message. If the message was sent using WNetSendMessage(), the receiver will provide its answer through its return value, as it would to any SendMessage(). Indeed, our receiving software module, WNET.EXE, will dispatch the message using SendMessage(). If the message is sent using WNetPostMessage(), and the sender eventually expects a response, it can embed the information that the receiver needs in order to respond in *wParam* and *lParam*.

The structure also needs fields saying:

- Which function to execute on the receiving end [SendMessage(), PostMessage(), or some other function]
- Whether *lParam* is a pointer
- The number of bytes of input data being supplied
- The number of bytes of output data expected

Finally, the structure needs some kind of a signature to distinguish it from an undifferentiated data packet. Otherwise, we may unwittingly start to parse a packet that is not carrying remote procedure call information.

Our full structure has this format:

```
typedef enum tagWNetRequest
{
    POST_MESSAGE,
```

```
    SEND_MESSAGE
}
WNET_REQUEST;

typedef struct tagWNETMsg
{
    char szSignature[5];  // Long enough for null-terminated "WNET"
    WNET_REQUEST WNetRequest;
    MSG          Message;
    BOOL         bIsLParamPtr;
    DWORD        dwDataLength;
    DWORD        dwOutDataLength;
} WNET_MSG;
```

We will add other command codes to WNET_REQUEST soon.
Here is a first sketch of WNetSendMessage():

```
LRESULT WINAPI WNetSendMessage(LPVOID lpTargetStation,
                    HWND hWnd, UINT message,
                    WPARAM wParam, LPARAM lParam,
                    BOOL bIsLParamPtr, DWORD dwDataLength)
{
    // Build the data into a packet for shipping over
    // the network (including expansion of DDE atoms
    //    and handles).
    // Determine length of output data
    // Ship request and input data to the partner station--wait for
    // return code.
    // If there is any output data, copy it to the buffer
    // pointed to by lParam.
    // Return SendMessage() return code
}
```

Additional Remote Procedure Calls

We could expand the distributed message transmitter to be a complete remote procedure call mechanism for Windows. This would be highly desirable in a commercial release of this library, but it is somewhat too ambitious for this book, and does not illustrate additional basic principles.

There are, however, two more functions we must have to implement WNetSendMessage() and WNetPostMessage(). To send messages to remote windows, we need to be able to retrieve their window handles. For this, we want a distributed version of FindWindow(), which we will call WNetFindWindow(). We also need a function to determine what other stations are on the network. We will call it WNetEnumStations().

We add some elements to the WNET_REQUEST enumerated type:

```
typedef enum tagWNetRequest
{
    POST_MESSAGE,
    SEND_MESSAGE,
    FIND_WINDOW,
    ENUM_STATIONS,
```

```
        ENUM_STATION_RESPONSE
} WNET_REQUEST;
```

FIND_WINDOW will instruct WNET.EXE on the receiving station to execute Find-
Window() and return its value. ENUM_STATIONS announces the presence of a station, and
requests other stations to announce their presence. ENUM_STATION_RESPONSE stamps
the packet as a response to an ENUM_STATIONS request.

WNetFindWindow()   The prototype for FindWindow() is:

```
HWND WINAPI FindWindow(LPCSTR lpszClass, LPCSTR lpszWindow);
```

The arguments are the window class name and the window title. We need only add
the target station name:

```
HWND WINAPI WNetFindWindow(LPVOID lpStationName,
                           LPCSTR lpszClass,
                           LPCSTR lpszWindow);
```

We will transmit the class name and the window name as consecutive null-terminated
strings.

Here is a sketch of WNetFindWindow():

```
HWND WINAPI WNetFindWindow(LPVOID lpTargetStation,
                           LPCSTR lpszClass,
                           LPCSTR lpszWindow)
{
    // Build the data packet--signature string, request code,
    // followed by window class name and window title as
    // null-terminated strings. If either lpszClass or lpszWindow
    // is NULL, convert it to a zero-length string.

    // Ship data to target station, wait for response.
    // Return (HWND) response
}
```

WNetEnumStations()   Most Windows enumeration functions expect a pointer to a callback function that is called once for each object being enumerated. The enumeration function
returns when all objects have been enumerated, or when the callback function returns
FALSE. There is no good reason for deviating from this.

We might think to implement WNetEnumStations() like this:

```
// Broadcast ENUM_STATIONS datagram
// While new ENUM_STATION_RESPONSE packets received within timeout period
//      Invoke callback function for each new response
//      If callback function returns FALSE, return
```

The problem with this implementation is that the while loop could last a long time.
The way I have chosen to implement WNetEnumStations() is to keep a list of known stations, and enumerate the elements of that list when WNetEnumStations() is first called.
Then, WNetEnumStations() clears the list and broadcasts ENUM_STATIONS requests to
regenerate it. Each station calls WNetEnumStations() when it first loads the WNET software.

This has the dual effect of telling other stations that it is on-line, and of building its internal list of the stations that are already active. Here is the logic:

```
// Enumerate all elements in the station list
// Clear the list
// Broadcast ENUM_STATIONS request
// ENUM_STATION_RESPONSE packets come in asynchronously
//    Add reporting stations to the list
```

Architecture of the WNET System

Figure 2-1 shows the architecture of the WNET system. The foundation is the network communications drivers, and the Windows device drivers that mediate between them and the Windows environment. The next layer up is the network-dependent DLL. As I said, it contains functions with the same names as the functions in the network-independent DLL, but prefixed with an underscore. The network-independent DLL (implemented as WNETLVL1.DLL) is the programming interface that we expose to client applications.

FIGURE 2-1. WNET Architecture

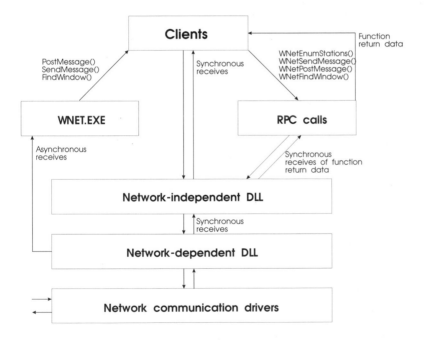

Though I include the remote procedure call functions in WNETLVL1.DLL for logistical simplicity, they are logically on a layer above the communications functions. WNetSendMessage(), WNetPostMessage(), and WNetFindWindow() are implemented using

WNetCall(), WNetSend(), WNetReceive(), and WNetHangup(). WNetEnumStations() uses WNetSendDatagram().

You will also notice that there is an executable Windows program, WNET.EXE, at the same level as the RPC calls. The user invokes this program to load the WNET system. It can also be loaded with a LOAD= line in WIN.INI, or client applications can run it using WinExec(). The sample program that I present in Appendix A does just that. As part of its WM_CREATE processing, WNET.EXE calls WNetInit(). This is the function that calls WNetGetCaps() in the network driver to determine which network is running. It then loads the appropriate bottom-level DLL. Next it calls _WNetInit() in the network-specific DLL to accomplish any initialization needed at the bottom level. Last, it obtains the addresses of all the low-level functions.

The primary responsibility of WNET.EXE is to handle incoming asynchronous (non-blocking) packets. To do this, WNET.EXE registers a global Windows message by calling the Windows function RegisterWindowMessage():

```
UINT WMU_PACKET_RECEIVED;

WMU_PACKET_RECEIVED = RegisterWindowMessage("WMU_PACKET_RECEIVED");
```

When a packet arrives, the lowest-level software posts a WMU_PACKET_RECEIVED message to its immediate superior. For the APIs that use assembly-language post routines (IPX/SPX and NetBIOS), the assembler function posts this message to a C handler, which then posts it to the main window procedure for WNET.EXE. APIs that do not need an assembler post routine (VINES Sockets and Windows Sockets) get a message from Windows, then post it to WNET.EXE.

When WNET.EXE receives a WMU_PACKET_RECEIVED message, it checks the request code in the packet header to see if it originated with WNetSendMessage(), WNetPostMessage(), WNetFindWindow(), or WNetEnumStations(). It unwraps the data encapsulated on the sending end, and invokes the appropriate Windows function. It then calls WNetSend() to ship the function return value, and output data, back over the network.

Synchronous reception of data will occur during a call to functions like WNetReceive(). As you will see, we will give the caller the option of telling us that we should not return from the function unless we have data in hand. In this case, data will not go through WNET.EXE; it will be received directly by WNetReceive(). (The situation is actually a little more complicated than that. Not all the protocols allow us to separate the asynchronous and synchronous data streams from each other. Thus, we may request a synchronous receive, only to find that the data has arrived in an asynchronous packet. We have to take precautions in our code to make sure the data doesn't slip in undetected.)

Figures 2-2 and 2-3 show the flow of execution and data transmission for synchronous and asynchronous reception.

On receipt of a WM_CLOSE or WM_ENDSESSION message, WNET.EXE calls WNetShutdown() to shut down the DLL.

FIGURE 2-2. WNet SendMessage()—Asynchronous Reception

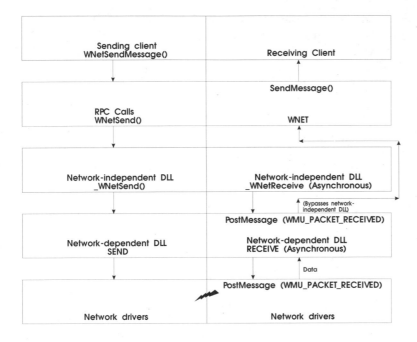

FIGURE 2-3. WNet SendMessage()—Synchronous Reception

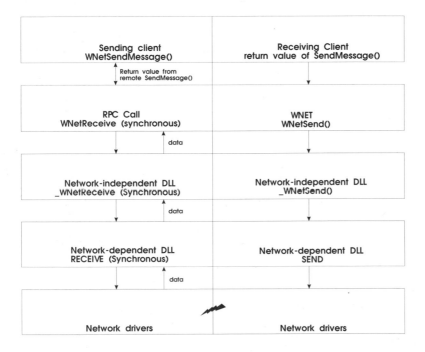

A Sample Client Application

Appendix A shows the full source code for an application, WNETINST.EXE, that uses the WNET system (in particular, distributed DDE) to install a group box, and icons for the programs presented in this book, on all other connected stations that are running WNET.EXE. This program runs as a hidden window, and does all of its processing in the WNetEnumStations() callback function. This function is invoked with the name of each station that has either broadcast its arrival on the network or responded to a previous WNetEnumStations() request. WNETINST calls WNetEnumStations() during processing of the WM_CREATE message.

Here is the WNetEnumStations() callback function, StationEnumProc().

```c
BOOL WINAPI StationEnumProc(LPBYTE lpStation)   // Called once
                                                // for each known station
{
    HWND hProgman;
    HCONNECTION hNewConnection = NULL;
    BOOL bReturnCode = TRUE;
    LPBYTE lpText = NULL;
    DWORD  dwTextLength;

    // Find Program Manager on the remote machine
    hProgman = WNetFindWindow(lpStation, "PROGMAN", NULL);

    if (hProgman != (HWND) 0xFFFF && hProgman != NULL)
        {
        // nNameIndex is the client identifier returned by
        // WNetInit()
        hNewConnection = WNetCall(nNameIndex, lpStation);
        if (hNewConnection == 0)
            {
            ++nFailed;
            goto End_StationEnum;
            }

        // Send WM_GETTEXTLENGTH to Program Manager on remote
        // machine to find out how much memory we need to allocate
        dwTextLength =
            WNetSendMessage((LPVOID) MAKELONG(hNewConnection, 0),
                hProgman, WM_GETTEXTLENGTH, 0, 0L,
                FALSE, 0L);
        if (dwTextLength != (DWORD) -1)
            {
            ++dwTextLength;  // For the null terminator
            lpText = GlobalAllocPtr(GHND, dwTextLength);
            if (lpText != NULL)
                {
                // Save remote Program Manager's current title bar
                if (WNetSendMessage((LPVOID) MAKELONG(hNewConnection, 0),
                        hProgman, WM_GETTEXT, (WORD) dwTextLength,
                        (LPARAM) lpText, TRUE, dwTextLength) ==
                        (LRESULT) -1)
```

```
            {
            ++nFailed;
            goto End_StationEnum;
            }
        }
    else
        {
        ++nFailed;
        bReturnCode = FALSE;      // Out of memory, terminate
                                  // enumeration
        goto End_StationEnum;
        }
    }
// Change Program Manager's title bar on remote machine
WNetSendMessage((LPVOID) MAKELONG(hNewConnection, 0),
    hProgman, WM_SETTEXT, 0,
    (LPARAM) (LPSTR) "Program Manager (Servicing Remote Request)",
    TRUE,
    lstrlen("Program Manager (Servicing Remote Request)") + 1);

// Restore Program Manager
WNetSendMessage((LPVOID) MAKELONG(hNewConnection, 0),
        hProgman, WM_SYSCOMMAND,
        SC_RESTORE, 0L, FALSE, 0L);

// Start DDE with remote Program Manager
if (WNetDDEInitialize("PROGMAN", "PROGMAN",
    (LPVOID) MAKELONG(hNewConnection, 0),
    (HINSTANCE) GetWindowWord(hTopWindow, GWW_HINSTANCE),
    HWND_BROADCAST))
    {
    WNetDDEExecute("[DeleteGroup(Windows Network Programs)]");
    WNetDDEExecute(
        "[CreateGroup(Windows Network Programs,winnet.grp)]");
    WNetDDEExecute(
        "[AddItem(wnet.exe, Windows Network Manager,wnet.exe)]");
    WNetDDEExecute(
        "[AddItem(wnetdemo.exe, Windows Network Driver Demo,wnetdemo.exe)]");
    WNetDDEExecute(
        "[AddItem(wnetnw.exe, Network Services for NetWare,wnetnw.exe)]");
    WNetDDEExecute(
        "[AddItem(wnetlm.exe, Network Services for LAN Manager,wnetlm.exe)]");
    WNetDDEExecute(
        "[AddItem(wnetvns.exe, Network Services for VINES,wnetvns.exe)]");
    WNetDDETerminate((LPVOID) MAKELONG(hNewConnection, 0));
    FlashWindow(hTopWindow, TRUE);
    ++nSuccess;
    }
else
    {
    ++nFailed;
    }
```

```
        // Restore original Program Manager title bar on remote machine
        if (lpText != NULL)
            WNetSendMessage((LPVOID) MAKELONG(hNewConnection, 0),
                hProgman, WM_SETTEXT,
                0, (LPARAM) lpText, TRUE, lstrlen(lpText) + 1);
        }
    else
        {
        ++nFailed;
        }
End_StationEnum:
    if (hNewConnection != NULL)
        WNetHangup(hNewConnection);
    if (lpText != NULL)
        GlobalFreePtr(lpText);
    return bReturnCode;
}
```

StationEnumProc() first calls WNetFindWindow() to get the window handle of the Program Manager on the other machine. If this is successful, it establishes a connection with the remote station by calling WNetCall(). These are both prerequisites for the rest of the program, which passes DDE messages to the remote Program Manager. Next, it retrieves the length of the Program Manager's title bar by passing a WM_GETTEXTLENGTH message. This message returns its answer through the SendMessage()—or, in this case, WNetSendMessage()—return value.

Now it allocates memory to hold the current title, then sends a WM_GETTEXT message to get the text. We want to save it so we can restore it later. This message returns the current text through the pointer in *lParam*. Next, we pass a WM_SETTEXT to change the title bar of the remote Program Manager to say "Program Manager (Servicing Remote Request)". This is a cue to the user on the remote machine that the Program Manager is not just going bananas (they are going to see a new group box emerge from the dust on their desktop). WM_SETTEXT uses *lParam* as a pointer to the new title.

The next thing WNETINST.EXE does is restore the Program Manager by sending a WM_SYSCOMMAND message with the wParam set to SC_RESTORE. Now the fun begins. The functions WNetDDEInitiate(), WNetDDEExecute(), and WNetDDETerminate() send WM_DDE_INITIATE, WM_DDE_EXECUTE, and WM_DDE_TERMINATE messages to the remote Program Manager. The end result is that the remote station has a new group box with generic application icons for the executable programs presented in this book, like the one in Figure 2-4.

I will defer a detailed discussion of distributed DDE until later, when I list the actual source files. What we have to do is create DDE agent windows on both stations that pretend to be the active participants in a DDE conversation. The DDE agents also communicate with each other to make sure the messages and data are delivered correctly.

A full discussion of the DDE protocol is beyond the scope of this book. I refer you to the Windows 3.1 SDK *Guide to Programming*, Charles Petzold's *Programming Windows*, and Jeffrey Clark's *Windows Programmer's Guide to OLE/DDE* for complete information.

Figure 2-4. Program Manager Group Box Created WNETINST.EXE

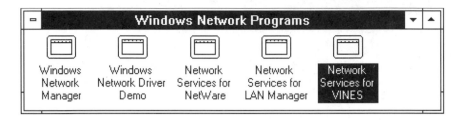

Source Code for the Network-Independent DLL

Without further ado, I will present the source code for the network-independent DLL. First, the header file, WNET.H. It will be included in the source files at all levels of the WNET hierarchy. It does these things:

- Includes WINDOWS.H and WINDOWSX.H, after #defining STRICT to force strict type-checking
- Defines all the constants and types we need
- Defines the message-cracking macros used in WNET.EXE
- Provides external references for global variables
- Gives prototypes of functions that need to be visible across all layers of the WNET system

```
/********
 *
 * Listing 2-1. WNET.H
 *
 * Copyright (c) 1992, Ralph P. Davis, All Rights Reserved
 *
 ********/


/*===== Includes =====*/

#define STRICT
#include <windows.h>
#include <windowsx.h>


/*===== Constants =====*/

#define WNET_DOMAIN                "WNET_DOMAIN"
#define MAX_STATION_NAME_LENGTH    25
#define MAX_NAMES                  256

/* BOOL Cls_OnPacketReceived(HWND hwnd, HCONNECTION hConn,
                        LPVOID lpData); */
#define HANDLE_WMU_PACKET_RECEIVED(hwnd, wParam, lParam, fn) \
    ((fn)((hwnd), (HCONNECTION)(wParam), (LPVOID) (lParam)))
```

```c
/* void Cls_OnDDEAdvise(HGLOBAL hDDEHandle, ATOM aItem,
            LPBYTE lpDataOut, LPDWORD lpdwDataLength,
            DWORD  dwOutBufferSize); */
#define HANDLE_WM_DDE_ADVISE(lParam, x, y, z, fn) \
   ((fn)((HGLOBAL) LOWORD(lParam), (ATOM) HIWORD(lParam), x, &y, z))

/* LPBYTE Cls_OnDDEDataPoke(HGLOBAL hDDEHandle, ATOM aItem,
            LPBYTE lpDataOut, LPDWORD lpdwDataLength,
            LPDWORD lpdwOutBufferSize, LPBYTE lpIn); */
#define HANDLE_WM_DDE_DATA_POKE(lParam, x, y, z, ptr, fn) \
   ((fn) ((HGLOBAL) LOWORD(lParam), (ATOM) HIWORD(lParam), x, &y, &z, ptr))

/* void Cls_OnDDEExecute(HGLOBAL hDDEHandle, LPBYTE lpDataOut,
         LPDWORD lpdwDataLength); */
#define HANDLE_WM_DDE_EXECUTE(lParam, x, y, fn) \
   ((fn) ((HGLOBAL) HIWORD(lParam), x, &y))

/* HWND Cls_OnDDEInitiate(ATOM aApplication, ATOM aTopic,
                          LPBYTE lpDataOut, LPDWORD lpdwDataLength,
                          DWORD  dwOutBufferSize); */
#define HANDLE_WM_DDE_INITIATE(lParam, x, y, z, fn) \
   ((fn) ((ATOM) LOWORD(lParam), (ATOM) HIWORD(lParam), x, &y, z))

/* void Cls_OnDDEAck(ATOM aApplication, ATOM aTopic, ATOM aItem,
                  HGLOBAL hDDEHandle, LPBYTE lpDataOut,
                  LPDWORD lpdwDataLength, DWORD  dwOutBufferSize); */
#define HANDLE_WM_DDE_ACK(lParam, x, y, z, fn) \
   ((fn) ((ATOM) LOWORD(lParam), (ATOM) HIWORD(lParam), \
       (ATOM) HIWORD(lParam), (HGLOBAL) HIWORD(lParam), \
       x, &y, z))

/* void Cls_OnDDERequestUnadvise(ATOM aItem, LPBYTE lpDataOut,
                          LPDWORD lpdwDataLength,
                          DWORD   dwOutBufferSize); */
#define HANDLE_WM_DDE_REQUEST_UNADVISE(lParam, x, y, z, fn) \
   ((fn) ((ATOM) HIWORD(lParam), x, &y, z))

/* Network device driver constants, defined in DDK files. */
#define WNNC_NET_TYPE      0x0002

#define WNNC_NET_None      0x0000
#define WNNC_NET_MSNet     0x0100
#define WNNC_NET_LanMan    0x0200
#define WNNC_NET_NetWare   0x0300
#define WNNC_NET_Vines     0x0400
#define WNNC_NET_WFW       0x8004

#define WNET_SIGNATURE     "WNET"
#define WNET_SIG_LENGTH  5

// Window long offsets for DDE agent windows
#define GWL_CONNECTION   0
#define GWL_REMOTE_HWND 4
#define GWL_LOCAL_HWND  8
#define GWL_LPARAM       12
```

```
/*===== Types =====*/

DECLARE_HANDLE(HCONNECTION);

typedef enum tagBlockState {NONBLOCKING, BLOCKING} BLOCK_STATE;

typedef enum tagWNetRequest
{
   POST_MESSAGE,
   SEND_MESSAGE,
   FIND_WINDOW,
   ENUM_STATIONS,
   ENUM_STATION_RESPONSE
} WNET_REQUEST;


typedef struct tagWNETMsg
{
   char          szSignature[5];  // "WNET"
   WNET_REQUEST  WNetRequest;
   MSG           Message;
   BOOL          bIsLParamPtr;
   DWORD         dwDataLength;
   DWORD         dwOutDataLength;
} WNET_MSG;

typedef BOOL (CALLBACK *STATIONENUMPROC)(LPSTR lpStationName);

// Used to concatenate asynchronous packets

typedef struct tagPacketTable
{
   HCONNECTION hConnection;
   LPBYTE      lpData;
   DWORD       dwDataSize;
} PACKET_TABLE;

typedef PACKET_TABLE FAR  *LPPACKET_TABLE;
typedef PACKET_TABLE NEAR *NPPACKET_TABLE;
typedef PACKET_TABLE      *PPACKET_TABLE;

typedef struct tagDDEInfo
{
   HCONNECTION hConnection;
   WNET_MSG FAR *lpMsgHeader;
} DDEINFO;

// This structure is used to queue packets received asynchronously
// that were requested synchronously

typedef struct tagPacketQueue
{
   LPBYTE lpPacket;
   HCONNECTION hConnection;
} PACKET_QUEUE;
```

```
/*===== Global Variables =====*/

extern HINSTANCE        hCurrentInstance;
extern HINSTANCE        hDLLInstance;
extern HWND             hTopWindow;
extern HCONNECTION (WINAPI *lpWNetCall)(int nNameIndex,
                                        LPVOID lpTargetStation);
extern BOOL (WINAPI *lpWNetListen)(int nNameIndex, HWND hWnd);
extern BOOL (WINAPI *lpWNetSend)(HCONNECTION hConnection, LPVOID lpData,
                            DWORD dwDataLength);
extern BOOL (WINAPI *lpWNetReceive)(HCONNECTION hConnection,
                                LPVOID lpData,
                                DWORD dwDataLength,
                                BLOCK_STATE BlockState,
                                int  nNameIndex,
                                HWND hWnd);
extern void (WINAPI *lpWNetHangup)(HCONNECTION hConnection);
extern void (WINAPI *lpWNetShutdown)(int nNameIndex);
extern BOOL (WINAPI *lpWNetSendDatagram)(LPVOID lpTargetStation,
                                LPVOID lpData,
                                WORD wDataLength,
                                int nNameIndex);
extern BOOL (WINAPI *lpWNetReceiveDatagram)(LPVOID lpBuffer,
                                    WORD wBufferSize,
                                    int  nNameIndex,
                                    HWND hWnd);
extern LRESULT (WINAPI *lpWNetShipData)(HWND hWnd,
                                LPVOID lpTargetStation,
                                LPVOID lpData,
                                DWORD dwDataLength,
                                LPVOID lpDataOut,
                                DWORD  dwOutDataLength);
extern void (WINAPI *lpNetYield)(void);

extern PACKET_QUEUE lpPackets[MAX_NAMES];
extern int    nPackets;


/*===== Functions =====*/

LRESULT WINAPI WNetSendMessage(LPVOID lpTargetStation,
                        HWND hWnd, UINT message, WPARAM wParam,
                        LPARAM lParam, BOOL bIsLParamPtr,
                        DWORD dwDataLength);
BOOL WINAPI WNetPostMessage(LPVOID lpTargetStation,
                        HWND hWnd, UINT message, WPARAM wParam,
                        LPARAM lParam, BOOL bIsLParamPtr,
                        DWORD dwDataLength);


LPVOID WINAPI WNetEncapsulateData(WNET_REQUEST WNetRequest,
                        HWND hWnd,UINT message,
                        WPARAM wParam, LPARAM lParam,
                        BOOL bIsLParamPtr,
```

```
                              DWORD dwDataLength);

LRESULT WINAPI WNetShipData(HWND hWnd,
                            LPVOID lpTargetStation,
                            LPVOID lpData,
                            DWORD  dwDataLength,
                            LPVOID lpDataOut,
                            DWORD  dwOutDataLength);
LRESULT WINAPI _WNetShipData(HWND hWnd,
                             LPVOID lpTargetStation,
                             LPVOID lpData,
                             DWORD  dwDataLength,
                             LPVOID lpDataOut,
                             DWORD  dwOutDataLength);


HCONNECTION WINAPI WNetCall(int nNameIndex,
                            LPVOID lpTargetStation);
HCONNECTION WINAPI _WNetCall(int nNameIndex,
                             LPVOID lpTargetStation);

BOOL WINAPI WNetListen(int nNameIndex, HWND hWnd);
BOOL WINAPI _WNetListen(int nNameIndex, HWND hWnd);

BOOL WINAPI WNetSend(HCONNECTION hConnection, LPVOID lpData,
                     DWORD dwDataLength);
BOOL WINAPI _WNetSend(HCONNECTION hConnection, LPVOID lpData,
                      DWORD dwDataLength);

BOOL WINAPI WNetReceive(HCONNECTION hConnection,
                        LPVOID lpData,
                        DWORD dwDataLength,
                        BLOCK_STATE BlockState,
                        int  nNameIndex,
                        HWND hWnd);
BOOL WINAPI _WNetReceive(HCONNECTION hConnection,
                         LPVOID lpData,
                         DWORD dwDataLength,
                         BLOCK_STATE BlockState,
                         int  nNameIndex,
                         HWND hWnd);

void WINAPI WNetHangup(HCONNECTION hConnection);
void WINAPI _WNetHangup(HCONNECTION hConnection);

int WINAPI WNetInit(HWND hWnd, LPVOID lpStationName,
                    HINSTANCE *phLibrary);
int WINAPI _WNetInit(HWND hWnd, LPVOID lpStationName);

void WINAPI WNetShutdown(HINSTANCE hLibrary,
                         int nNameIndex);
void WINAPI _WNetShutdown(int nNameIndex);

BOOL WINAPI WNetSendDatagram(LPVOID lpTargetStation,
                             LPVOID lpData, WORD wDataLength,
```

```
                              int nNameIndex);
BOOL WINAPI _WNetSendDatagram(LPVOID lpTargetStation,
                              LPVOID lpData, WORD wDataLength,
                              int nNameIndex);
BOOL WINAPI WNetReceiveDatagram(LPVOID lpBuffer,
                              WORD wBufferSize,
                              int  nNameIndex,
                              HWND hWnd);
BOOL WINAPI _WNetReceiveDatagram(LPVOID lpBuffer,
                              WORD wBufferSize,
                              int  nNameIndex,
                              HWND hWnd);

LPBYTE WINAPI WNetGetName(int nIndex);
WORD   WINAPI WNetGetNameLength(int nIndex);
void   WINAPI WNetSetName(int nIndex,
                          LPBYTE lpMyName,
                          WORD wNameLength);

HWND WINAPI WNetFindWindow(LPVOID lpStationName,
                           LPCSTR lpszClass,
                           LPCSTR lpszWindow);

BOOL WINAPI WNetEnumStations(int nNameIndex,
                           STATIONENUMPROC lpStationEnumProc);
int WINAPI _WNetEnumStations(int nNameIndex);
BOOL WINAPI _WNetAddStationToList(LPSTR lpStationName,
                           WORD wNameLength);

void WINAPI WNetSetLastError(DWORD dwLastError);
DWORD WINAPI WNetGetLastError(void);
LPVOID WINAPI AllocPageLockedBuffer(DWORD dwBytes);
void WINAPI FreePageLockedBuffer(LPVOID lpBlock);

ATOM GlobalInit(LPSTR lpszClassName, HINSTANCE hInstance);
HWND InstanceInit(LPSTR lpszClassName, HINSTANCE hInstance);

LRESULT CALLBACK WNetWndProc(HWND hWnd,
                             UINT uMessage,
                             WPARAM wParam,
                             LPARAM lParam);

// Message-cracking functions.
BOOL WNet_OnCreate(HWND hWnd, CREATESTRUCT FAR *lpCS);
BOOL WNet_OnPacketReceived(HWND hWnd,
                           HCONNECTION hConnection,
                           LPVOID lpReceivedData);
void WNet_OnClose(HWND hwnd);
void WNet_OnEndSession(HWND hwnd, BOOL fEnding);
void WNet_OnDDEAdvise(HGLOBAL hDDEHandle, ATOM aItem,
                      LPBYTE lpDataOut, LPDWORD lpdwDataLength,
                      DWORD   dwOutBufferSize);
LPBYTE WNet_OnDDEDataPoke(HGLOBAL hDDEHandle, ATOM aItem,
                          LPBYTE lpDataOut, LPDWORD lpdwDataLength,
```

```
                              LPDWORD lpdwOutBufferSize, LPBYTE lpIn);
void WNet_OnDDEExecute(HGLOBAL hDDEHandle, LPBYTE lpDataOut,
                    LPDWORD lpdwDataLength);
HWND WNet_OnDDEInitiate(ATOM aApplication, ATOM aTopic,
                    LPBYTE lpDataOut, LPDWORD lpdwDataLength,
                    DWORD dwOutBufferSize);
void WNet_OnDDEAck(ATOM aApplication, ATOM aTopic, ATOM aItem,
                HGLOBAL hDDEHandle, LPBYTE lpDataOut,
                LPDWORD lpdwDataLength, DWORD dwOutBufferSize);
void WNet_OnDDERequestUnadvise(ATOM aItem, LPBYTE lpDataOut,
                        LPDWORD lpdwDataLength,
                        DWORD dwOutBufferSize);

void WNet_OnPostSendMessage(HCONNECTION hConnection,
                    WNET_MSG FAR *lpMsgHeader);
void WNet_OnFindWindow(HCONNECTION hConnection, LPBYTE lpPacket);
BOOL WNet_OnEnumStations(LPBYTE lPacket, int nNameIndex,
                    BOOL bResponseRequired);


// DLL formalities.
int WINAPI LibMain(HINSTANCE hInstance,
                WORD wDataSeg,
                WORD cbHeapSize,
                LPSTR lpszCmdLine);
int WINAPI WEP(int nParameter);

// Compute size of output buffer depending
// on message.
DWORD WINAPI WNetGetOutDataLength(LPVOID lpTargetStation,
                            HWND   hWnd,
                            UINT   uMessage,
                            WPARAM wParam,
                            LPARAM lParam);

// DDE handlers
LPVOID WINAPI WNetEncapsulateDDEData(WNET_REQUEST WNetRequest,
                            HWND hWnd, UINT message,
                            WPARAM wParam, LPARAM lParam,
                            DWORD FAR *lpdwDataLength,
                            HCONNECTION hConnection);
int WINAPI WNetUnwrapDDE(LPBYTE lpDataIn, HCONNECTION hConnection);
LRESULT CALLBACK DDEAgentWndProc(HWND hWnd,
                            UINT uMessage,
                            WPARAM wParam,
                            LPARAM lParam);
void PASCAL CreateDDEAgent(HCONNECTION hConnection,
                        WNET_MSG FAR *lpMsgHeader,
                        LPBYTE lpDataIn);
BOOL CALLBACK DDEWindowEnumProc(HWND hWnd, LPARAM lParam);
BOOL PASCAL SendDDEInitiate(DDEINFO FAR *lpDDEInfo);

void WINAPI WNetQueuePacket(LPBYTE lpPacket, HCONNECTION hConnection);
LPBYTE WINAPI WNetGetNextQueuedPacket(HCONNECTION hConnection);
```

```
void WINAPI WNetCopyQueuedPacket(LPBYTE lpIn, LPBYTE lpOut,
                                 DWORD dwDataLength);
void WINAPI NetworkDependentYield(void);
void WINAPI WNetClearAllNames(void);

BOOL WINAPI MyPeekMessage(MSG FAR *lpMsg, HWND hWnd, UINT uFirst,
                          UINT uLast, UINT uCommand);
```

WNETGLOB.C

Listing 2-2, WNETGLOB.C, contains the definitions of global variables used in the network-independent DLL. Most are pointers to the functions in the network-dependent DLL. We will set them up them in Listing 2-3, WNETINIT.C.

```
/********
*
* Listing 2-2. WNETGLOB.C
*
* Copyright (c) Ralph P. Davis, All Rights Reserved
*
* Global variables for network-independent DLL
*
********/

/*===== Includes =====*/

#include "wnet.h"

/*===== Global Variables =====*/

HINSTANCE hDLLInstance;

HCONNECTION (WINAPI *lpWNetCall)(int nNameIndex,
                                 LPVOID lpTargetStation);
BOOL (WINAPI *lpWNetListen)(int nNameIndex, HWND hWnd);
BOOL (WINAPI *lpWNetSend)(HCONNECTION hConnection, LPVOID lpData,
                          DWORD dwDataLength);
BOOL (WINAPI *lpWNetReceive)(HCONNECTION hConnection,
                             LPVOID lpData,
                             DWORD dwDataLength,
                             BLOCK_STATE BlockState,
                             int  nNameIndex,
                             HWND hWnd);
void (WINAPI *lpWNetHangup)(HCONNECTION hConnection);
void (WINAPI *lpWNetShutdown)(int nNameIndex);
BOOL (WINAPI *lpWNetSendDatagram)(LPVOID lpTargetStation,
                                  LPVOID lpData, WORD wDataLength,
                                  int nNameIndex);
LRESULT (WINAPI *lpWNetShipData)(HWND hWnd,
                                 LPVOID lpTargetStation,
                                 LPVOID lpData,
                                 DWORD  dwDataLength,
                                 LPVOID lpDataOut,
                                 DWORD  dwOutDataLength);
```

```
BOOL (WINAPI *lpWNetReceiveDatagram)(LPVOID lpBuffer,
                                     WORD wBufferSize,
                                     int  nNameIndex,
                                     HWND hWnd);
void (WINAPI *lpNetYield)(void);

PACKET_QUEUE lpPackets[MAX_NAMES] = {NULL};
int    nPackets = 0;
```

WNETINIT.C

WNETINIT.C, shown in Listing 2-3, contains the function WNetInit( ). This is the entry point into the DLL, and is called by WNET during WM_CREATE processing. It reads SYSTEM.INI to determine which network driver to load, using GetPrivateProfileString( ) as I described earlier:

```
char szNetworkDrive[128];

GetPrivateProfileString("BOOT", "NETWORK.DRV", "MSNET.DRV",
   szNetworkDriver, sizeof (szNetworkDriver), "SYSTEM.INI");
```

We also look for our own initialization file, WNET.INI. NetBIOS is only native to some of our supported environments, and TCP/IP is not native to any of them. We therefore allow the user to choose one of them instead of the native protocol by specifying one of the following settings in the [Network] section:

```
Protocol=TCP/IP
Protocol=NetBIOS
```

If WNetInit( ) finds a Protocol= string in WNET.INI, and recognizes either of these values, it will use the protocol specified there instead of the default protocol. At present, this is the only WNET.INI setting we respond to.

Next, WNetInit( ) loads the network-dependent DLL and, if this is successful, calls the low-level initialization routine, _WNetInit( ). Once this is complete, WNetInit( ) gets the addresses of the functions in the low-level library.

WNetInit( ) returns a name index assigned by the low-level DLL. This has different meaning with the different protocols. It will be used as an argument to subsequent calls, and also acts as a client identifier. This allows many top-level programs to use the services of the WNET DLLs.

The LibMain( ) routine included in WNETINIT.C registers the DDEAgent window class, which we will use for distributed DDE.

```
/********
*
* Listing 2-3. WNETINIT.C
*
* Performs device-independent initialization
* Also calls device-dependent initialization routine
*   (_WNetInit())
*
********/

/*===== Includes =====*/
```

```c
#include "wnet.h"

/*===== Function Definitions =====*/

int WINAPI LibMain(HINSTANCE hInstance,
                   WORD wDataSeg,
                   WORD cbHeapSize,
                   LPSTR lpszCmdLine)
{
    WNDCLASS wndClass;

    hDLLInstance = hInstance;

    // Register class for DDE agent window
    wndClass.lpszClassName = "DDEAgent";
    wndClass.lpfnWndProc = DDEAgentWndProc;
    wndClass.hInstance   = hInstance;
    wndClass.hCursor     = NULL;
    wndClass.hIcon       = NULL;
    wndClass.hbrBackground = NULL;
    wndClass.lpszMenuName = NULL;
    wndClass.style  = 0;
    wndClass.cbClsExtra = 0;
    wndClass.cbWndExtra = 16; // Room for four long integers
                              // GWL_CONNECTION
                              // GWL_REMOTE_HWND
                              // GWL_LOCAL_HWND
                              // GWL_LPARAM

    if (!RegisterClass(&wndClass))
        return 0;

    return 1;
}

int WINAPI WNetInit(HWND hWnd, LPVOID lpStationName,
                    HINSTANCE *phLibrary)
{
    char          szNetworkDriver[255];
    HINSTANCE     hNetLib;
    WORD (WINAPI *WNetGetCaps)(WORD wIndex);
    int  (WINAPI *lpWNetInit)(HWND hWnd, LPVOID lpStationName);
    int           nNameIndex;
    char          szProtocol[25];

    *phLibrary = NULL;

    GetPrivateProfileString("BOOT", "NETWORK.DRV", "MSNET.DRV",
        szNetworkDriver, sizeof (szNetworkDriver), "SYSTEM.INI");

    GetPrivateProfileString("NETWORK", "PROTOCOL", "",
        szProtocol, sizeof (szProtocol), "WNET.INI");

    if (lstrlen(szProtocol) > 0)
```

```
   {
   if (lstrcmpi(szProtocol, "NETBIOS") == 0)
      lstrcpy(szNetworkDriver, "WNETNB.DLL");
   else if (lstrcmpi(szProtocol, "TCP/IP") == 0)
      lstrcpy(szNetworkDriver, "WNETTCP.DLL");
   else
      szProtocol[0] = '\0';  // Unrecognized option, use default
   }

if (lstrlen(szProtocol) == 0)
   {
   hNetLib = LoadLibrary(szNetworkDriver);

   if (hNetLib > HINSTANCE_ERROR)
      {
      // Load function definitions
      (FARPROC) WNetGetCaps = GetProcAddress(hNetLib, "WNetGetCaps");
      if (WNetGetCaps == NULL)
         {
         WNetSetLastError(WN_DEVICE_ERROR);
         FreeLibrary(hNetLib);
         return -1;
         }
      }
   else
      {
      WNetSetLastError(WN_WINDOWS_ERROR);
      return -1;
      }

   // Find out what type of network we're running on.
   if (WNetGetCaps != NULL)
      {
      switch (WNetGetCaps(WNNC_NET_TYPE))
         {
         case WNNC_NET_None:    // No network
            FreeLibrary(hNetLib);
            WNetSetLastError(WN_NOT_CONNECTED);
            return -1;
         case WNNC_NET_MSNet:
         case WNNC_NET_LanMan:
         case WNNC_NET_WFW:
            // Use NetBIOS for MS-Net, LAN Manager, or Windows for Workgroups
            lstrcpy(szNetworkDriver, "WNETNB.DLL");
            break;
         case WNNC_NET_NetWare:
            lstrcpy(szNetworkDriver, "WNETIPX.DLL");
            break;
         case WNNC_NET_Vines:
            lstrcpy(szNetworkDriver, "WNETVNS.DLL");
            break;
         default:
            // Non-supported network.
```

```
                FreeLibrary(hNetLib);
                WNetSetLastError(WN_NOT_SUPPORTED);
                return -1;
            }
        }
        FreeLibrary(hNetLib);
        }

    hNetLib = LoadLibrary(szNetworkDriver);

    if (hNetLib <= HINSTANCE_ERROR)
        {
        WNetSetLastError(WN_NET_ERROR);
        return -1;
        }
    *phLibrary = hNetLib;

    (FARPROC) lpWNetInit = GetProcAddress(hNetLib, "_WNetInit");

    if (lpWNetInit == NULL)
        {
        WNetSetLastError(WN_NET_ERROR);
        return -1;
        }
    (FARPROC) lpWNetShutdown =
        GetProcAddress(hNetLib, "_WNetShutdown");

    if ((nNameIndex = lpWNetInit(hWnd, lpStationName)) == (-1))
        return -1;

    // Load all function pointers

    (FARPROC) lpWNetCall =
        GetProcAddress(hNetLib, "_WNetCall");
    (FARPROC) lpWNetListen =
        GetProcAddress(hNetLib, "_WNetListen");
    (FARPROC) lpWNetSend =
        GetProcAddress(hNetLib, "_WNetSend");
    (FARPROC) lpWNetReceive =
        GetProcAddress(hNetLib, "_WNetReceive");
    (FARPROC) lpWNetHangup =
        GetProcAddress(hNetLib, "_WNetHangup");
    (FARPROC) lpWNetSendDatagram =
        GetProcAddress(hNetLib, "_WNetSendDatagram");
    (FARPROC) lpWNetShipData =
        GetProcAddress(hNetLib, "_WNetShipData");
    (FARPROC) lpWNetReceiveDatagram =
        GetProcAddress(hNetLib, "_WNetReceiveDatagram");
    (FARPROC) lpNetYield =
        GetProcAddress(hNetLib, "_NetworkDependentYield");
    return nNameIndex;
}

int WINAPI WEP(int nParameter)
{
    return 1;
}
```

WNetSendMessage() and WNetPostMessage()

Now let's take a look at how WNetSendMessage() is implemented. I will list WNetPost-Message() later in this chapter, but I will not discuss it further, since it behaves in essentially the same way as WNetSendMessage(). Some messages require WNetSendMessage(), specifically, those that expect the called window to return data through a pointer.

The first thing WNetSendMessage() does is check to see if the message is a DDE message. If it is, it calls WNetEncapsulateDDEData(), which evaluates the message and the arguments, and creates a packet containing the data. If the message does not involve DDE, WNetSendMessage() calls WNetEncapsulateData(), which allocates a buffer to the data being sent to the target station. Next, if *bIsLParamPtr* is TRUE, WNetSendMessage() calls WNetGetOutDataLength(), which looks at the message to see if the target station will be returning any information. If it will, it sets *dwOutDataLength* to the size of the output data.

Finally, WNetSendMessage() calls WNetShipData() to transmit the data and collect return information.

In order to provide reasonable performance, we allow the calling program to first establish a connection with the target station. Then, it can call WNetSendMessage() with *lpTargetStation* containing the connection number in the low word, and zero in the high word. Thus:

```
HCONNECTION hConnection;

hConnection = WNetCall(<target station> ...);
WNetSendMessage((LPVOID) MAKELONG(hConnection, 0), ...)
```

This avoids the overhead of connection establishment and termination on every WNetSendMessage(). It is the technique used by WNETINST.EXE in Appendix A.

```
 /********
*
* Listing 2-4. WNSNDMSG.C
*
* Copyright (c) 1992, Ralph P. Davis, All Rights Reserved
*
********/

/*===== Includes =====*/

#include "wnet.h"
#include <dde.h>

/*===== Function Definitions =====*/

LRESULT WINAPI WNetSendMessage(
                    LPVOID lpTargetStation,
                    HWND hWnd, UINT message,
                    WPARAM wParam, LPARAM lParam,
                    BOOL bIsLParamPtr, DWORD dwDataLength)

{

    LPVOID lpData;
```

```
      LRESULT lResult = -1L;
      DWORD   dwOutDataLength;
      WNET_MSG FAR *lpMsgHeader;

      if (message >= WM_DDE_FIRST && message <= WM_DDE_LAST)
         {
         // We are specifying that distributed DDE must use
         // a pre-established connection, so the offset portion
         // of lpTargetStation is the connection number

         lpData = WNetEncapsulateDDEData(SEND_MESSAGE, hWnd, message,
            wParam, lParam, &dwDataLength,
            (HCONNECTION) OFFSETOF(lpTargetStation));
         bIsLParamPtr = FALSE;
         }
      else
         {
         lpData = WNetEncapsulateData(SEND_MESSAGE, hWnd, message,
            wParam, lParam, bIsLParamPtr, dwDataLength);
         dwDataLength += sizeof (WNET_MSG);
         }

      if ((lpData != NULL))
         {
         if (bIsLParamPtr)
            dwOutDataLength =
               WNetGetOutDataLength(lpTargetStation,
                  hWnd, message, wParam, lParam);
         else
            dwOutDataLength = OL;
         lpMsgHeader = (WNET_MSG FAR *) lpData;
         lpMsgHeader->dwOutDataLength = dwOutDataLength;

         lResult = WNetShipData(NULL, lpTargetStation,
            lpData, dwDataLength,
            (bIsLParamPtr ? (LPVOID) lParam : NULL),
            dwOutDataLength);
         FreePageLockedBuffer(lpData);
         }
      return lResult;
}
```

WNetEncapsulateData()

Before we look at how we process DDE messages, let's see how WNetEncapsulateData()
formats the outgoing packet. First, it constructs the WNET packet header, which contains
the following data:

- The signature string "WNET"
- The MSG structure, holding the SendMessage() arguments
- *bIsLParamPtr*, indicating whether the *lParam* field of the MSG structure is a
  pointer

- The length of the data
- The request type (in this case, SEND_MESSAGE)

It then allocates page-locked memory for the header and the data, and copies them both to the buffer it obtains. The memory is made page-locked because it will be passed to the network drivers to be transmitted to the partner station. If it is not page-locked, Windows in Enhanced mode may swap it out to disk. When the network drivers go to access it again, the Windows pager will need to be invoked, at interrupt level. Page-locking the memory makes sure it stays resident. (See Listing 2-17 later in this chapter for the implementation of AllocPage Locked Buffer.)

```
/********
*
* Listing 2-5. WNENCDAT.C
*
* Copyright (c) 1992, Ralph P. Davis, All Rights Reserved
*
********/

#include "wnet.h"

LPVOID WINAPI WNetEncapsulateData(WNET_REQUEST WNetRequest,
                    HWND hWnd, UINT message, WPARAM wParam,
                    LPARAM lParam, BOOL bIsLParamPtr,
                    DWORD dwDataLength)
{
    WNET_MSG     msgHeader;
    LPVOID       lpDataOut = NULL;
    LPBYTE       lpTemp;
    LPBYTE       lpDataIn;

    lstrcpy(msgHeader.szSignature, WNET_SIGNATURE);
    msgHeader.Message.hwnd = hWnd;
    msgHeader.Message.message = message;
    msgHeader.Message.wParam = wParam;
    msgHeader.Message.lParam = lParam;

    msgHeader.bIsLParamPtr = bIsLParamPtr;
    msgHeader.WNetRequest = WNetRequest;

    msgHeader.dwDataLength = dwDataLength;

    lpDataOut = AllocPageLockedBuffer(
                    dwDataLength + sizeof (WNET_MSG));
    if (lpDataOut != NULL)
        {
        DWORD i;

        lpTemp = (LPBYTE) lpDataOut;
        *((WNET_MSG FAR *) lpTemp) = msgHeader;
        lpTemp += sizeof (WNET_MSG);
        lpDataIn = (LPBYTE) lParam;
        for (i = 0L; i < dwDataLength; ++i)
            lpTemp[i] = lpDataIn[i];
```

```
    }
   return lpDataOut;
}
```

Intelligent Message Processing

WNetEncapsulateData() does not give us the functionality we need for a full-featured distributed message-passing system. While it packages data being passed to the partner station, we need two additional things, a way of converting the atoms and handles used with DDE into the original data, so we can pass it to the partner station; and a way of determining if the message will be returning data through *lParam*, and if so, how much.

By handling DDE messages, we provide the framework for a fully distributed version of DDE. On the sending end, we add WNetEncapsulateDDEData(), which packages the data. On the receiving end, WNetUnwrapDDE() converts it back into DDE format. WNetEncapsulateDDEData() builds the same packet header as WNetEncapsulateData(). The logic in WNetEncapsulateDDEData() uses the *message* argument to extract the atoms and handles from *lParam*, depending on the actual DDE message received.

In response to a WM_DDE_INITIATE message, I create a window of the DDEAgent class. The way I implement distributed DDE is to have two local DDE conversations: one between the client window and its DDE agent, and another between the server window and its DDE agent. These windows are invisible; they serve to supply valid window handles to be used in the DDE conversation, and to have window procedures to handle WM_DDE messages. The DDE agents communicate with each other over the network. Figure 2-5 shows how this works.

I originally thought that I could implement distributed DDE by just having a local agent window on the server side. My reasoning was that the server window does not know that the DDE requests it is getting are coming from a remote station, so it will try to send messages back to the window indicated in the *wParam*. If this window is on a remote station, the SendMessage() or PostMessage() will either fail or deliver the message to a random window, that just happens to have the same handle, on the server station. For this reason, the DDE agent has to masquerade as the DDE conversant on the server side, and reroute messages from the server window to the remote partner.

However, it turned out that I also had to have a DDE agent on the client side. The client, after all, knows that it is communicating with a remote window; it initiated the conversation in the first place by calling WNetSendMessage(). So it would know that the *wParam* that accompanied its DDE messages was on a remote station. However, I discovered that the client window never got any of its messages. It appears that Windows does some validity checking on the window handle passed in *wParam*. A valid window handle on the remote end is unlikely to be valid on the local end. When I created a DDE agent window on the client side, and substituted its handle for the original *wParam*, everything worked fine.

Here is the algorithm I implemented:

The client window sends its original WM_DDE_INITIATE using WNetSendMessage(). It can either use a specific remote window handle or the broadcast window handle HWND_BROADCAST. WNetEncapsulateDDEData() sees this, and creates a DDE agent window to serve as the local DDE representative. This window has space for four long integers in its window structure, requested when the window class was registered in WNETINIT.C:

Figure 2-5. Distributed DDE Conversation

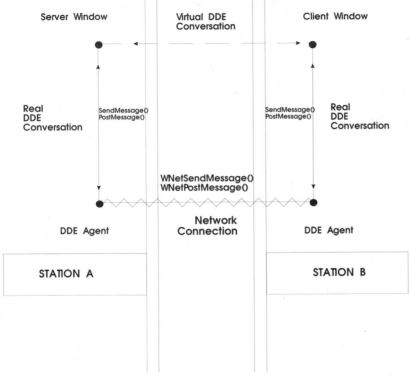

- GWL_CONNECTION, which remembers the connection number assigned by the network communications drivers. I require that distributed DDE use the technique I described above, where a network connection is established prior to beginning the DDE conversation.
- GWL_LOCAL_HWND, which records the window handle of the local DDE participant. This will be either the original client window or the server window.
- GWL_REMOTE_HWND. This keeps track of the DDE agent window on the partner station.
- GWL_LPARAM. This stores the *lParam* that the client window originally passed with WM_DDE_INITIATE. It has the atoms describing the application and topic on which a conversation is being requested. The DDE agent on the server station retrieves it when an application responds to WM_DDE_INITIATE with a WM_DDE_ACK accepting the request. It is then transmitted back to the client station.

On the server side, the WM_DDE_INITIATE percolates up to WNET.EXE, which looks at it in WNetUnwrapDDE(). In response to this message, WNetUnwrapDDE() calls CreateDDEAgent(), in WNETDDE.C (listed soon). This function creates a local DDE agent window and passes the request along to the server window. It replaces the *wParam* passed by WNetSendMessage() with the DDE agent window handle. Before SendMessage() returns, the window procedure for the local DDE agent [DDEAgentWndProc()] will receive an WM_DDE_ACK, assuming that there is an application willing to accept a conversation. In response to this, DDEAgentWndProc() sets the GWL_LOCAL_HWND window long to the handle of the server window.

Now, both the client and the server windows carry on a normal DDE conversation with their local DDE agent. The DDE agent on the sending side translates the PostMessage() call into a WNetPostMessage() directed to the DDE agent on the remote station. However, the DDE agent will never see it. WNET.EXE gets a WMU_PACKET-_RECEIVED message, discerns that the embedded message is a DDE message, and calls WNetUnwrapDDE(). WNetUnwrapDDE() in turn alters the target window and the *wParam* arguments. The target window becomes the local DDE conversant, saved as the GWL_LOCAL_HWND window long. The *wParam*, which describes the originating window, becomes the local DDE agent window—that is, the original target window. Here is the code that does this:

```
lpMsgHeader->Message.wParam = (WPARAM) lpMsgHeader->Message.hwnd;
lpMsgHeader->Message.hwnd =
        (HWND) GetWindowLong(lpMsgHeader->Message.hwnd,
                    GWL_LOCAL_HWND);
```

Termination of the conversation requires a small bit of special handling. The DDE documentation says that the conversant wishing to end a conversation should post, not send, a WM_DDE_TERMINATE message. The partner responds by also posting a WM_DDE_TERMINATE. It is important that the DDE agent windows respond to the WM_DDE_TERMINATE messages, and that they recognize when the conversation ends, so they can destroy themselves. It appears that posting the messages over the network caused some timing problems; when I used PostMessage() and WNetPostMessage(), I could not predictably obtain closure on my DDE conversations. Using SendMessage() and WNetSendMessage() instead cleared up these problems.

The next three listings are WNENCDDE.C, WNUNWDDE.C, and WNETDDE.C, which implement distributed DDE.

```
/********
*
* Listing 2-6. WNENCDDE.C
*
* Copyright (c) 1992, Ralph P. Davis, All Rights Reserved
*
********/

/*===== Includes =====*/

#include "wnet.h"
#include <dde.h>
#include <string.h>


/*===== Function Definitions =====*/
```

```
LPVOID WINAPI WNetEncapsulateDDEData(WNET_REQUEST WNetRequest,
                    HWND hWnd, UINT message, WPARAM wParam,
                    LPARAM lParam, DWORD FAR *lpdwDataLength,
                    HCONNECTION hConnection)
{
    WNET_MSG      msgHeader;
    LPBYTE        lpDataOut = NULL;
    LPBYTE        lpTemp;
    HWND          hDDEAgent;
    DWORD         dwDataLength, dwOutBufferSize;

    lstrcpy(msgHeader.szSignature, WNET_SIGNATURE);
    msgHeader.Message.hwnd = hWnd;
    msgHeader.Message.message = message;
    msgHeader.Message.wParam = wParam;
    msgHeader.Message.lParam = lParam;

    msgHeader.bIsLParamPtr = FALSE;
    msgHeader.WNetRequest = WNetRequest;
    msgHeader.dwOutDataLength = 0L;

    // Get a nice big buffer
    lpDataOut = GlobalAllocPtr(GPTR, 65535L);

    if (lpDataOut == NULL)
       return NULL;

    lpTemp = lpDataOut;
    lpDataOut += (sizeof (WNET_MSG));
    dwOutBufferSize = 65535L - (sizeof (WNET_MSG));
    dwDataLength = 0L;

    switch (message)
       {
       case WM_DDE_ACK:
          HANDLE_WM_DDE_ACK(lParam, lpDataOut, dwDataLength,
             dwOutBufferSize, WNet_OnDDEAck);
          break;
       case WM_DDE_ADVISE:
          HANDLE_WM_DDE_ADVISE(lParam, lpDataOut, dwDataLength,
             dwOutBufferSize, WNet_OnDDEAdvise);
          break;
       case WM_DDE_DATA:
       case WM_DDE_POKE:
          lpTemp = HANDLE_WM_DDE_DATA_POKE(lParam, lpDataOut, dwDataLength,
                dwOutBufferSize, lpTemp, WNet_OnDDEDataPoke);
          if (lpTemp == NULL)
             return NULL;
          break;
       case WM_DDE_EXECUTE:
          HANDLE_WM_DDE_EXECUTE(lParam, lpDataOut,
             dwDataLength, WNet_OnDDEExecute);
          break;
       case WM_DDE_INITIATE:
```

```
            hDDEAgent = HANDLE_WM_DDE_INITIATE(lParam, lpDataOut,
                dwDataLength, dwOutBufferSize,
                WNet_OnDDEInitiate);
            if (hDDEAgent == NULL)
                return NULL;
            else
                {
                SetWindowLong(hDDEAgent, GWL_LPARAM, lParam);
                SetWindowLong(hDDEAgent, GWL_LOCAL_HWND,
                    (LONG) msgHeader.Message.wParam);
                SetWindowLong(hDDEAgent, GWL_CONNECTION,
                    (LONG) hConnection);
                msgHeader.Message.wParam = (WPARAM) hDDEAgent;
                }
            break;
        case WM_DDE_REQUEST:
        case WM_DDE_UNADVISE:
            HANDLE_WM_DDE_REQUEST_UNADVISE(lParam, lpDataOut,
                dwDataLength, dwOutBufferSize,
                WNet_OnDDERequestUnadvise);
            break;
        default:
            dwDataLength = 0L;
            break;
        }

    lpTemp =
        (LPBYTE) GlobalReAllocPtr(lpTemp,
            dwDataLength + (sizeof (WNET_MSG)), GHND);
    if (lpTemp != NULL)
        {
        // Page lock--had to use GlobalAllocPtr() above
        // so we could call GlobalReAllocPtr()

        if (GetWinFlags() & WF_ENHANCED)
            GlobalPageLock((HGLOBAL) SELECTOROF(lpTemp));
        *lpdwDataLength = (dwDataLength + (sizeof (WNET_MSG)));
        *((WNET_MSG FAR *) lpTemp) = msgHeader;
        }

    return lpTemp;
}

void WNet_OnDDEAdvise(HGLOBAL hDDEHandle, ATOM aItem,
                      LPBYTE lpDataOut, LPDWORD lpdwDataLength,
                      DWORD  dwOutBufferSize)
{
    LPBYTE        lpDDE;

    // Structure of packet will be
    //    DDEADVISE structure
    //    followed by null-terminated string
    //    representing data item
```

```
        lpDDE = (LPBYTE) GlobalLock(hDDEHandle);
        _fmemcpy(lpDataOut, lpDDE, sizeof (DDEADVISE));
        GlobalUnlock(hDDEHandle);

        *lpdwDataLength = (sizeof (DDEADVISE));

        GlobalGetAtomName(aItem,
            &lpDataOut[*lpdwDataLength],
            (int) (dwOutBufferSize - *lpdwDataLength));
        *lpdwDataLength += (lstrlen(&lpDataOut[*lpdwDataLength]) + 1);
}

LPBYTE WNet_OnDDEDataPoke(HGLOBAL hDDEHandle, ATOM aItem,
                            LPBYTE lpDataOut, LPDWORD lpdwDataLength,
                            LPDWORD lpdwOutBufferSize, LPBYTE lpIn)
{
    LPBYTE lpOut = lpIn;
    DWORD  dwIndex;
    LPBYTE        lpDDE;

    // Structure of packet:
    //     DWORD length of data (OL if data handle is NULL)
    //     data
    //     Null-terminated string representing
    //     data item

    if (hDDEHandle != NULL)
        {
        *((DWORD FAR *) lpDataOut) =
            *lpdwDataLength = GlobalSize(hDDEHandle);
        }
    else
        *((DWORD FAR *) lpDataOut) =
            *lpdwDataLength = OL;
    *lpdwDataLength += (sizeof (DWORD));

    if (*lpdwDataLength > *lpdwOutBufferSize)
        {
        // Double size of out buffer
        lpOut =
            (LPBYTE) GlobalReAllocPtr(lpIn,
                2 * GlobalSize((HGLOBAL) SELECTOROF(lpIn)),
                GPTR);
        if (lpOut == NULL)
            return NULL;
        *lpdwOutBufferSize =
            GlobalSize((HGLOBAL)
                (LOWORD(GlobalHandle(SELECTOROF(lpOut)))))
            - (sizeof (WNET_MSG));
        lpDataOut = lpOut + (sizeof (WNET_MSG)) +
                    (sizeof (DWORD));
        }
    else
        lpDataOut += (sizeof (DWORD));
```

```
   if (hDDEHandle != NULL)
      {
      lpDDE = (LPBYTE) GlobalLock(hDDEHandle);

      for (dwIndex = OL; dwIndex < ((*lpdwDataLength)-4); ++dwIndex)
         lpDataOut[dwIndex] = lpDDE[dwIndex];
      GlobalUnlock(hDDEHandle);
      }

   GlobalGetAtomName(aItem,
      &lpDataOut[*lpdwDataLength],
      (int) (*lpdwOutBufferSize - *lpdwDataLength));
   *lpdwDataLength += (lstrlen(&lpDataOut[*lpdwDataLength]) + 1);
   return lpOut;
}

void WNet_OnDDEExecute(HGLOBAL hDDEHandle, LPBYTE lpDataOut,
                       LPDWORD lpdwDataLength)
{
   LPBYTE lpDDE;

   // Packet will just contain the command string.
   lpDDE = (LPBYTE) GlobalLock(hDDEHandle);

   lstrcpy(lpDataOut, lpDDE);
   *lpdwDataLength = (lstrlen(lpDDE) + 1);
   GlobalUnlock(hDDEHandle);
}

HWND WNet_OnDDEInitiate(ATOM aApplication, ATOM aTopic,
                        LPBYTE lpDataOut, LPDWORD lpdwDataLength,
                        DWORD dwOutBufferSize)
{
   HWND hDDEAgent;

   GlobalGetAtomName(
      aApplication,
      lpDataOut,
      (int) dwOutBufferSize);
   *lpdwDataLength = lstrlen(lpDataOut) + 1;
   GlobalGetAtomName(
      aTopic,
      &lpDataOut[*lpdwDataLength],
      (int) (dwOutBufferSize - *lpdwDataLength));
   *lpdwDataLength += (lstrlen(&lpDataOut[*lpdwDataLength]) + 1);

   // Create local DDE agent window
   hDDEAgent = CreateWindow("DDEAgent",
                            "DDE Agent Window",
                            WS_OVERLAPPEDWINDOW,
                            CW_USEDEFAULT,
                            CW_USEDEFAULT,
                            CW_USEDEFAULT,
                            CW_USEDEFAULT,
```

```
                                NULL,
                                NULL,
                                hDLLInstance,
                                NULL);

    return hDDEAgent;
}

void WNet_OnDDEAck(ATOM aApplication, ATOM aTopic, ATOM aItem,
                   HGLOBAL hDDEHandle, LPBYTE lpDataOut,
                   LPDWORD lpdwDataLength, DWORD  dwOutBufferSize)
{
    LPBYTE lpDDE;
    // See if we've got a valid application atom
    GlobalGetAtomName(
        aApplication,
        &lpDataOut[sizeof (UINT)],
        (int) (dwOutBufferSize - (sizeof (UINT))));
    *lpdwDataLength = (DWORD) lstrlen(&lpDataOut[sizeof (UINT)]);
    if (*lpdwDataLength == 0L)
        {
        // Not a valid atom, see if we're looking at
        // a WM_DDE_EXECUTE

        // aItem will be valid if not WM_DDE_EXECUTE

        GlobalGetAtomName(
            aItem,
            &lpDataOut[sizeof (UINT)],
            (int) (dwOutBufferSize - (sizeof (UINT))));

        *lpdwDataLength = (DWORD) lstrlen(&lpDataOut[sizeof (UINT)]);
        if (*lpdwDataLength != 0L)   // Not EXECUTE
            {
            // Flag packet to distinguish it from
            // WM_DDE_INITIATE and WM_DDE_EXECUTE
            *((UINT FAR *) lpDataOut) = WM_DDE_ACK;
            *lpdwDataLength += (sizeof (UINT));
            ++(*lpdwDataLength);   // For '\0'
            }
        else
            {
            // Structure of packet will be
            //     WM_DDE_EXECUTE
            //     followed by null-terminated command string.

            *((UINT FAR *) lpDataOut) = WM_DDE_EXECUTE;

            *lpdwDataLength = sizeof (UINT);

            // Get WM_DDE_EXECUTE commands
            lpDDE = (LPBYTE) GlobalLock(hDDEHandle);

            lstrcpy(&lpDataOut[*lpdwDataLength], lpDDE);
            *lpdwDataLength += (lstrlen(lpDDE) + 1);
```

```c
            GlobalUnlock(hDDEHandle);
            }
        }
    else
        {
        ++(*lpdwDataLength);  // For the null terminator

        // Application atom was valid, we're looking at
        // something besides a WM_DDE_EXECUTE

        // Structure of packet will be
        //    WM_DDE_INITIATE
        //    followed by null-terminated
        //    string identifying server application
        //    followed by null-terminated
        //    string identifying conversation topic

        *((UINT FAR *) lpDataOut) = WM_DDE_INITIATE;
        *lpdwDataLength += sizeof (UINT);

        // Get atom for topic
        GlobalGetAtomName(aTopic,
           &lpDataOut[*lpdwDataLength],
           (int) (dwOutBufferSize - *lpdwDataLength));
        *lpdwDataLength += (lstrlen(&lpDataOut[*lpdwDataLength]) + 1);
        }
}

void WNet_OnDDERequestUnadvise(ATOM aItem, LPBYTE lpDataOut,
                               LPDWORD lpdwDataLength,
                               DWORD   dwOutBufferSize)
{
    // Packet will contain null-terminated string
    // representing data item
    GlobalGetAtomName(aItem, lpDataOut,
       (int) dwOutBufferSize);
    *lpdwDataLength = lstrlen(lpDataOut) + 1;
}


/********
 *
 * Listing 2-7. WNUNWDDE.C
 *
 * Copyright (c) 1992 Ralph P. Davis, All Rights Reserved
 *
 ********/

/*===== Includes =====*/

#include "wnet.h"
#include <dde.h>
#include <string.h>
```

```
/*===== Function Definitions =====*/

int WINAPI WNetUnwrapDDE(LPBYTE lpDataIn, HCONNECTION hConnection)
{
    WNET_MSG FAR *lpMsgHeader = (WNET_MSG FAR *) lpDataIn;
    UINT        uDDEMessage;
    HGLOBAL     hDDEHandle;
    LPBYTE      lpDDE;
    ATOM        aApplication, aTopic, aItem;
    DWORD       i;

    lpDataIn += (sizeof (WNET_MSG));

    switch (lpMsgHeader->Message.message)
        {
        case WM_DDE_TERMINATE:
            lpMsgHeader->Message.wParam = (WPARAM)
                lpMsgHeader->Message.hwnd;
            lpMsgHeader->Message.hwnd =
                (HWND) GetWindowLong(lpMsgHeader->Message.hwnd,
                        GWL_LOCAL_HWND);
            SetWindowLong((HWND) lpMsgHeader->Message.wParam,
                GWL_LOCAL_HWND, OL);
            break;
        case WM_DDE_ACK:
            uDDEMessage = *((UINT FAR *) lpDataIn);
            lpDataIn += (sizeof (UINT));

            // See whether this is acknowledging a WM_DDE_EXECUTE,
            // a WM_DDE_INITIATE, or a data message
            // (like WM_DDE_DATA or WM_DDE_POKE)
            switch (uDDEMessage)
                {
                case WM_DDE_EXECUTE:
                    // Commands follow as null-terminated string.
                    // Convert to DDE handle
                    hDDEHandle = GlobalAlloc(GHND | GMEM_DDESHARE,
                        lstrlen(lpDataIn) + 1);
                    if (hDDEHandle == NULL)
                        {
                        WNetSetLastError(WN_OUT_OF_MEMORY);
                        return -1;
                        }
                    lpDDE = (LPBYTE) GlobalLock(hDDEHandle);
                    lstrcpy(lpDDE, lpDataIn);
                    GlobalUnlock(hDDEHandle);
                    lpMsgHeader->Message.lParam =
                        MAKELONG(LOWORD(lpMsgHeader->Message.lParam),
                        hDDEHandle);
                    lpMsgHeader->Message.wParam = (WPARAM)
                        lpMsgHeader->Message.hwnd;
                    lpMsgHeader->Message.hwnd =
                        (HWND) GetWindowLong(lpMsgHeader->Message.hwnd,
```

```
                            GWL_LOCAL_HWND);
           break;
       case WM_DDE_INITIATE:
           // Two strings to convert into atoms.
           aApplication = GlobalAddAtom(lpDataIn);
           lpDataIn += (lstrlen(lpDataIn) + 1);
           aTopic = GlobalAddAtom(lpDataIn);
           lpMsgHeader->Message.lParam =
               MAKELONG(aApplication, aTopic);
           SetWindowLong(lpMsgHeader->Message.hwnd,
               GWL_REMOTE_HWND, (LONG) lpMsgHeader->Message.wParam);
           lpMsgHeader->Message.wParam = (WPARAM)
               lpMsgHeader->Message.hwnd;
           lpMsgHeader->Message.hwnd =
               (HWND) GetWindowLong(lpMsgHeader->Message.hwnd,
                        GWL_LOCAL_HWND);
           break;
       default:
           // Only high word contains an atom.
           aItem = GlobalAddAtom(lpDataIn);
           lpMsgHeader->Message.lParam =
               MAKELONG(LOWORD(lpMsgHeader->Message.lParam),
               hDDEHandle);
           lpMsgHeader->Message.wParam = (WPARAM)
               lpMsgHeader->Message.hwnd;
           lpMsgHeader->Message.hwnd =
               (HWND) GetWindowLong(lpMsgHeader->Message.hwnd,
                        GWL_LOCAL_HWND);
           break;
       }
   break;
case WM_DDE_ADVISE:
   // First item in the packet is DDEADVISE structure
   hDDEHandle = GlobalAlloc(GHND | GMEM_DDESHARE,
       sizeof (DDEADVISE));
   if (hDDEHandle == NULL)
       {
       WNetSetLastError(WN_OUT_OF_MEMORY);
       return -1;
       }
   lpDDE = (LPBYTE) GlobalLock(hDDEHandle);
   *((DDEADVISE FAR *) lpDDE) = *((DDEADVISE FAR *) lpDataIn);
   GlobalUnlock(hDDEHandle);
   lpDataIn += (sizeof (DDEADVISE));

   // Next comes aItem atom.
   aItem = GlobalAddAtom(lpDataIn);
   lpMsgHeader->Message.lParam = MAKELONG(hDDEHandle, aItem);
   lpMsgHeader->Message.wParam = (WPARAM)
       lpMsgHeader->Message.hwnd;
   lpMsgHeader->Message.hwnd =
       (HWND) GetWindowLong(lpMsgHeader->Message.hwnd,
```

```
                        GWL_LOCAL_HWND);
        break;
    case WM_DDE_DATA:
    case WM_DDE_POKE:
        // First DWORD is size of data packet
        hDDEHandle = GlobalAlloc(GHND | GMEM_DDESHARE,
            *((DWORD FAR *) lpDataIn));
        if (hDDEHandle == NULL)
            {
            WNetSetLastError(WN_OUT_OF_MEMORY);
            return -1;
            }
        lpDDE = (LPBYTE) GlobalLock(hDDEHandle);

        // Next comes the data
        for (i = OL; i < (*((DWORD FAR *) lpDataIn)); ++i)
            lpDDE[i] = lpDataIn[(sizeof (DWORD)) + i];
        GlobalUnlock(hDDEHandle);

        // The next piece of information is the atom
        // describing the data item
        lpDataIn += (*((DWORD FAR *) lpDataIn)) + (sizeof (DWORD));
        aItem = GlobalAddAtom(lpDataIn);
        lpMsgHeader->Message.lParam = MAKELONG(hDDEHandle, aItem);
        lpMsgHeader->Message.wParam = (WPARAM)
            lpMsgHeader->Message.hwnd;
        lpMsgHeader->Message.hwnd =
            (HWND) GetWindowLong(lpMsgHeader->Message.hwnd,
                    GWL_LOCAL_HWND);
        break;
    case WM_DDE_EXECUTE:
        // Commands just come in as a string
        hDDEHandle = GlobalAlloc(GHND | GMEM_DDESHARE,
            lstrlen(lpDataIn) + 1);
        if (hDDEHandle == NULL)
            {
            WNetSetLastError(WN_OUT_OF_MEMORY);
            return -1;
            }
        lpDDE = (LPBYTE) GlobalLock(hDDEHandle);
        lstrcpy(lpDDE, lpDataIn);
        GlobalUnlock(hDDEHandle);
        lpMsgHeader->Message.lParam =
            MAKELONG(LOWORD(lpMsgHeader->Message.lParam),
            hDDEHandle);
        lpMsgHeader->Message.wParam = (WPARAM)
            lpMsgHeader->Message.hwnd;
        lpMsgHeader->Message.hwnd =
            (HWND) GetWindowLong(lpMsgHeader->Message.hwnd,
                    GWL_LOCAL_HWND);
        break;
    case WM_DDE_INITIATE:
```

```
         {
         LRESULT lResult = OL;

         if (IsWindow((HWND) hConnection) && InSendMessage())
            // Originated locally, ignore it
            return -1;
         WNetSend(hConnection, &lResult,
            sizeof (LRESULT));  // Thank you very much

         // Create local DDE agent window
         CreateDDEAgent(hConnection, lpMsgHeader, lpDataIn);
         return -1;  // Don't process any further upstairs
         }
      case WM_DDE_REQUEST:
      case WM_DDE_UNADVISE:
         // First piece of information is the atom
         // designating the data item
         aItem = GlobalAddAtom(lpDataIn);
         lpMsgHeader->Message.lParam =
            MAKELONG(LOWORD(lpMsgHeader->Message.lParam),
            aItem);
         lpMsgHeader->Message.wParam = (WPARAM)
            lpMsgHeader->Message.hwnd;
         lpMsgHeader->Message.hwnd =
            (HWND) GetWindowLong(lpMsgHeader->Message.hwnd,
                     GWL_LOCAL_HWND);
         break;
      default:
         return -1;    // Huh?
      }
   return 0;
}


/********
*
* Listing 2-8. WNETDDE.C
*
* Copyright (c) 1992 Ralph P. Davis, All Rights Reserved
*
********/


/*===== Includes =====*/

#include "wnet.h"
#include <dde.h>


/*===== Function Definitions =====*/

LRESULT CALLBACK DDEAgentWndProc(HWND hWnd, UINT uMessage, WPARAM wParam,
                                LPARAM lParam)
{
   DDEACK ddeAck;
```

```
WORD    FAR *lpDDEAck = (WORD FAR*) &ddeAck;
HCONNECTION hConnection =
   (HCONNECTION) GetWindowLong(hWnd, GWL_CONNECTION);
HWND    hLocalWindow = (HWND) GetWindowLong(hWnd, GWL_LOCAL_HWND);
HWND    hRemoteWindow = (HWND) GetWindowLong(hWnd, GWL_REMOTE_HWND);
DWORD   dwTickCount;

if (uMessage == WM_DDE_ACK)
   {
   if (IsWindow((HWND) wParam) && InSendMessage())
      {
      // Response to WM_DDE_INITIATE
      // Assume that respondent is polite enough to use
      // SendMessage(), as he is supposed to

      // Positive acknowledgement?
      *lpDDEAck = LOWORD(lParam);
      if (ddeAck.fAck)
         {
         // Remember this conversation
         SetWindowLong(hWnd, GWL_LOCAL_HWND, (LONG) (HWND) wParam);
         SetWindowLong(hWnd, GWL_LPARAM, lParam);
         }
      return OL;
      }
   }
if (uMessage >= WM_DDE_FIRST && uMessage <= WM_DDE_LAST)
   {
   // Response to all other messages
   // (including WM_DDE_ACK not in response to WM_DDE_INITIATE)
   // See if target window is local or remote
   // Also, make note of WM_DDE_TERMINATE by zeroing out the
   // appropriate window long
   if ((HWND) wParam == hLocalWindow || hLocalWindow == NULL)
      {
      // Sending to remote station
      if (uMessage == WM_DDE_TERMINATE)
         SetWindowLong(hWnd, GWL_REMOTE_HWND, OL);
      if (hRemoteWindow != NULL)
         WNetPostMessage((LPVOID) MAKELONG(hConnection, O),
            hRemoteWindow, uMessage, (WPARAM) hWnd, lParam, FALSE, OL);
      if (hLocalWindow == NULL || hRemoteWindow == NULL)
         DestroyWindow(hWnd);
      }
   }
else if (uMessage == WM_DESTROY || uMessage == WM_ENDSESSION ||
         uMessage == WM_CLOSE)
   {
   MSG msg;
   if (hLocalWindow != NULL)
      {
      PostMessage(hLocalWindow, WM_DDE_TERMINATE, (WPARAM) hWnd, OL);
```

```
            dwTickCount = GetTickCount() + 200; // Wait .2 seconds for response

            while (GetTickCount() <= dwTickCount)
                {
                if (MyPeekMessage(&msg, NULL, 0, 0, PM_REMOVE))
                    {
                    DispatchMessage(&msg);
                    if (msg.message == WM_DDE_TERMINATE)
                        break;
                    }
                }
            }
        if (hRemoteWindow != NULL)
            {
            WNetPostMessage((LPVOID) MAKELONG(hConnection, 0),
                hRemoteWindow, uMessage, (WPARAM) hWnd, lParam, FALSE, 0L);
            dwTickCount = GetTickCount() + 5000; // Wait 5 seconds for response

            while (GetTickCount() <= dwTickCount)
                {
                NetworkDependentYield();
                if (MyPeekMessage(&msg, NULL, 0, 0, PM_REMOVE))
                    {
                    DispatchMessage(&msg);
                    if (msg.message == WM_DDE_TERMINATE)
                        break;
                    }
                }
            }
        }
    else
        // All other messages
        return DefWindowProc(hWnd, uMessage, wParam, lParam);
    return 0L;
}

void PASCAL CreateDDEAgent(HCONNECTION hConnection,
                           WNET_MSG FAR *lpMsgHeader,
                           LPBYTE lpDataIn)
{
    ATOM         aApplication, aTopic;
    DDEINFO      ddeInfo;
    WNDENUMPROC  lpProc;

    if (*lpDataIn != '\0')
        aApplication = GlobalAddAtom(lpDataIn);
    else
        aApplication = NULL;
    lpDataIn += (lstrlen(lpDataIn) + 1);
    if (*lpDataIn != '\0')
        aTopic = GlobalAddAtom(lpDataIn);
    else
        aTopic = NULL;
```

```
    lpMsgHeader->Message.lParam =
       MAKELONG(aApplication, aTopic);

    ddeInfo.hConnection = hConnection;
    ddeInfo.lpMsgHeader = lpMsgHeader;

    if (lpMsgHeader->Message.hwnd == HWND_BROADCAST) // All windows?
       {
       // Have to create a new window for everybody
       (FARPROC) lpProc =
          MakeProcInstance((FARPROC) DDEWindowEnumProc, hDLLInstance);
       EnumWindows(lpProc, (LPARAM) (DDEINFO FAR *) &ddeInfo);
       FreeProcInstance((FARPROC) lpProc);
       }
    else
       SendDDEInitiate(&ddeInfo);
}

BOOL CALLBACK DDEWindowEnumProc(HWND hWnd, LPARAM lParam)
{
    DDEINFO FAR *lpDDEInfo = (DDEINFO FAR *) lParam;

    lpDDEInfo->lpMsgHeader->Message.hwnd = hWnd;
    return SendDDEInitiate(lpDDEInfo);
}

BOOL PASCAL SendDDEInitiate(DDEINFO FAR *lpDDEInfo)
{
    HWND hLocalWindow, hRemoteWindow;
    HWND hDDESender;

    if (lpDDEInfo->lpMsgHeader->Message.hwnd ==
        (HWND) lpDDEInfo->lpMsgHeader->Message.wParam)
       {
       // Window handles of local and remote windows are identical
       // We can't handle this, because we won't be able to tell
       // who to send WM_DDE_ACKs and WM_DDE_TERMINATEs to
       return TRUE;
       }
    hDDESender = CreateWindow("DDEAgent",
                             "DDE Agent Window",
                             WS_OVERLAPPEDWINDOW,
                             CW_USEDEFAULT,
                             CW_USEDEFAULT,
                             CW_USEDEFAULT,
                             CW_USEDEFAULT,
                             NULL,
                             NULL,
                             hDLLInstance,
                             NULL);
    if (hDDESender == NULL)
       return FALSE;

    SetWindowLong(hDDESender, GWL_CONNECTION,
```

```
              MAKELONG(lpDDEInfo->hConnection, 0));
      hRemoteWindow = (HWND) lpDDEInfo->lpMsgHeader->Message.wParam;
      SetWindowLong(hDDESender, GWL_REMOTE_HWND, (LONG) hRemoteWindow);

      SetWindowLong(hDDESender, GWL_LOCAL_HWND, OL);

      SendMessage(lpDDEInfo->lpMsgHeader->Message.hwnd, WM_DDE_INITIATE,
                 (WPARAM) hDDESender,
                 lpDDEInfo->lpMsgHeader->Message.lParam);

      // Now, check to see if the GWL_LOCAL_HWND is non-zero
      hLocalWindow =
         (HWND) GetWindowLong(hDDESender, GWL_LOCAL_HWND);
      if (hLocalWindow == NULL)
         {
         // Nobody responded to the message, destroy the agent window
         // First set remote window handle to OL so we don't send
         // him a WM_DDE_TERMINATE
         SetWindowLong(hDDESender, GWL_REMOTE_HWND, OL);
         DestroyWindow(hDDESender);
         return TRUE;
         }
      else
         {
         LPARAM lParam;

         lParam = GetWindowLong(hDDESender, GWL_LPARAM);

         // Send ack to partner station
         hRemoteWindow = (HWND) GetWindowLong(hDDESender, GWL_REMOTE_HWND);

         if (WNetSendMessage((LPVOID) MAKELONG(lpDDEInfo->hConnection, 0),
            hRemoteWindow, WM_DDE_ACK, (WPARAM) hDDESender, lParam,
            FALSE, OL) == -1L)
            {
            // Failure--blast this DDE conversation
            SetWindowLong(hDDESender, GWL_REMOTE_HWND, OL);
            DestroyWindow(hDDESender);
            return TRUE;
            }
         return FALSE;    // Stop the enumeration
         }
}
```

The second requirement for intelligent message processing is a routine that determines if any data is expected from the partner station. Listing 2-9 shows the routine WNetGet-OutDataLength(). WNetGetOutDataLength() is primarily an exercise in reading the SDK manual (*Programmer's Reference, Volume 3*).

Observe that some messages are multiply defined—that is, the same numeric code has two different meanings. We have no idea what the message-passing context is, so the best we can do is return the largest possible value. Also notice that to return the correct values for CB_GETLBTEXT and LB_GETTEXT, we have to make a recursive call to

WNetSendMessage(), passing the messages CB_GETLBTEXTLEN and LB_GETTEXT-
LEN. This is no problem; WNetSendMessage() is fully reentrant.

```c
/********
 *
 * Listing 2-9. WNETDLEN.C
 *
 * Copyright (c) 1992 Ralph P. Davis, All Rights Reserved
 *
 ********/


/*===== Includes =====*/

#include "wnet.h"
#include <commdlg.h>      // Common dialogs
#include <wfext.h>        // File-manager extensions


/*===== Function Definitions =====*/

DWORD WINAPI WNetGetOutDataLength(
                    LPVOID lpTargetStation,
                    HWND   hWnd,
                    UINT   uMessage,
                    WPARAM wParam,
                    LPARAM lParam)
{
    DWORD dwLength;
    LPBYTE lpTemp;

    switch (uMessage)
       {
       case EM_GETRECT:
       case LB_GETITEMRECT:
          return (sizeof (RECT));
       case CB_GETLBTEXT:
          dwLength =
             WNetSendMessage(lpTargetStation,
                hWnd, CB_GETLBTEXTLEN, wParam, OL, FALSE, OL);
          if (dwLength != CB_ERR)
             return dwLength  + 1;
          else
             return OL;
       case EM_GETLINE:
          // First byte has max characters to return.
          lpTemp = (LPBYTE) lParam;
          return ((*lpTemp) + 1);

       // File Manager extension messages.
       case FMEVENT_LOAD:
          return (sizeof (FMS_LOAD));
       case FM_GETDRIVEINFO:
          return (sizeof (FMS_GETDRIVEINFO));
       case FM_GETFILESEL:
```

```
    case FM_GETFILESELLFN:
       return (sizeof (FMS_GETFILESEL));

    case LB_GETSELITEMS:
       // LB_GETSELITEMS and CB_GETDROPPEDCONTROLRECT
       // have the same value in WINDOWS.H.
       // Return the maximum value required by either
       return (max(wParam * (sizeof (int)), (sizeof (RECT))));
    case LB_GETTEXT:
       dwLength =
          WNetSendMessage(lpTargetStation,
             hWnd, LB_GETTEXTLEN, wParam, OL, FALSE, OL);
       if (dwLength != LB_ERR)
          return dwLength  + 1;
       else
          return OL;
    case WM_ASKCBFORMATNAME:
       return wParam;
    case WM_CHOOSEFONT_GETLOGFONT:  // Defined in COMMDLG.H
       return (sizeof (LOGFONT));
    case WM_CREATE:
       return (sizeof (CREATESTRUCT));
    case WM_GETMINMAXINFO:
       return (sizeof (MINMAXINFO));
    case WM_GETTEXT:
       return wParam;
    case WM_MDICREATE:
       return (sizeof (MDICREATESTRUCT));
    case WM_MEASUREITEM:
       return (sizeof (MEASUREITEMSTRUCT));
    case WM_NCCALCSIZE:
       // NCCALCSIZE_PARAMS contains an embedded pointer.
       return (sizeof (NCCALCSIZE_PARAMS));
    case WM_NCCREATE:
       return (sizeof (CREATESTRUCT));
    case WM_PAINTCLIPBOARD:
       return (sizeof (PAINTSTRUCT));
    case WM_WINDOWPOSCHANGING:
       return (sizeof (WINDOWPOS));
    default:
       return OL;
    }
}
```

WNetShipData()

The last routine called by WNetSendMessage() and WNetPostMessage() is WNetShip-
Data(). WNetShipData() must use the resources of the network. However, it does so in a
completely network-independent way, by calling the routines we have provided for connection-oriented service.

What WNetShipData() does is very similar to the functionality provided by the named pipes functions DosCallNmPipe() and DosTransactNmPipe(). DosCallNmPipe() does the following things:

- Opens a named pipe
- Transmits data
- Reads the response
- Closes the connection

DosTransactNmPipe() transmits data and reads the response, assuming that the named pipe is already open and should remain so. WNetShipData() will work the same way. If the pointer to the target station name has a NULL selector, WNetShipData() will assume that the LOWORD() represents the ID of a connection that was previously established. Otherwise, it will open the connection itself by calling WNetCall().

WNetShipData() calls the other routines in the network-independent library to transmit the data. Specifically, WNetShipData()

1. Calls WNetCall() to open a connection to the target station (unless the connection is already established)
2. Calls WNetSend() to send the data
3. Calls WNetReceive() to get the return code of the operation as an LRESULT, and any output data expected
4. If it opened the connection to the target station, it closes it by calling WNetHangup()

The call to WNetReceive() is both blocking, because the higher-level software that calls WNetShipData() expects it to return with output data in hand.

```
/********
*
* Listing 2-10. WNETSHIP.C
*
* Copyright (c) 1992, Ralph P. Davis, All Rights Reserved
*
********/

/*===== Includes =====*/
#include "wnet.h"

/*===== Function Definitions =====*/

LRESULT WINAPI WNetShipData(HWND    hWnd,
                            LPVOID lpTargetStation,
                            LPVOID lpData,
                            DWORD  dwDataLength,
                            LPVOID lpDataOut,
                            DWORD  dwOutDataLength)
{
   HCONNECTION hConnection;
   LRESULT lResult = -1L;
```

```
LPBYTE   lpReceiveBuffer, lpTemp;
DWORD    i;

// See if there's a network-dependent version.  If so,
// use it.

if (lpWNetShipData != NULL)
   return lpWNetShipData(hWnd,
       lpTargetStation, lpData, dwDataLength,
       lpDataOut, dwOutDataLength);

lpReceiveBuffer = (LPBYTE) AllocPageLockedBuffer(dwOutDataLength +
                                             sizeof (LRESULT));
if (lpReceiveBuffer == NULL)
   {
   WNetSetLastError(WN_OUT_OF_MEMORY);
   return -1L;
   }

if (SELECTOROF(lpTargetStation) == 0)  // Connection already established
   hConnection = (HCONNECTION) OFFSETOF(lpTargetStation);
else
   hConnection = WNetCall(-1, lpTargetStation);

if (hConnection != NULL)
   {
   if (WNetSend(hConnection, lpData, dwDataLength))
       {
       if (!WNetReceive(hConnection, lpReceiveBuffer,
           sizeof (LRESULT) + dwOutDataLength, BLOCKING, -1, hWnd))
           lResult = -1L;
       else
           {
           lResult = *((LRESULT FAR *) lpReceiveBuffer);
           lpTemp = (LPBYTE) lpDataOut;
           lpReceiveBuffer += (sizeof (LRESULT));
           for (i = 0L; i < dwOutDataLength; ++i)
               lpTemp[i] = lpReceiveBuffer[i];
           }
       FreePageLockedBuffer(lpReceiveBuffer);
       }
   if (SELECTOROF(lpTargetStation) != 0)  // Temporary connection set up
       WNetHangup(hConnection);           // Terminate it
   }
   return lResult;
}
```

Communications Functions

All the communications functions in the network-independent DLL reside in the source file WNETFUNC.C, shown in Listing 2-11. These routines just call the corresponding routine in the low-level library, or set the network error code to WN_NOT_SUP-PORTED if the function pointer is NULL.

```c
/********
 *
 * Listing 2-11. WNETFUNC.C
 *
 * Copyright (c) 1992 Ralph P. Davis, All Rights Reserved
 *
 * High-level network-independent front end functions
 * Most call corresponding low-level function in the
 * network-dependent library.
 *
 ********/

/*===== Includes =====*/

#include "wnet.h"

/*===== Function Definitions =====*/

HCONNECTION WINAPI WNetCall(int    nNameIndex,
                            LPVOID lpTargetStation)
{
   if (lpWNetCall == NULL)
      {
      WNetSetLastError(WN_NOT_SUPPORTED);
      return 0;
      }
   return lpWNetCall(nNameIndex, lpTargetStation);
}

BOOL WINAPI WNetListen(int nNameIndex, HWND hWnd)
{
   if (lpWNetListen == NULL)
      {
      WNetSetLastError(WN_NOT_SUPPORTED);
      return FALSE;
      }
   return lpWNetListen(nNameIndex, hWnd);
}

BOOL WINAPI WNetSend(HCONNECTION hConnection,
                     LPVOID lpData,
                     DWORD dwDataLength)
{
   if (lpWNetSend == NULL)
      {
      WNetSetLastError(WN_NOT_SUPPORTED);
      return FALSE;
      }
   return lpWNetSend(hConnection, lpData, dwDataLength);
}
BOOL WINAPI WNetReceive(HCONNECTION hConnection,
                        LPVOID lpData,
                        DWORD  dwDataLength,
```

```
                        BLOCK_STATE BlockState,
                        int   nNameIndex,
                        HWND hWnd)
{
   if (lpWNetReceive == NULL)
      {
      WNetSetLastError(WN_NOT_SUPPORTED);
      return FALSE;
      }
   return lpWNetReceive(hConnection, lpData,
                        dwDataLength, BlockState, nNameIndex,
                        hWnd);
}

void WINAPI WNetHangup(HCONNECTION hConnection)
{
   if (lpWNetHangup == NULL)
      {
      WNetSetLastError(WN_NOT_SUPPORTED);
      return;
      }
   lpWNetHangup(hConnection);
}

void WINAPI WNetShutdown(HINSTANCE hLibrary, int nNameIndex)
{
   if (lpWNetShutdown == NULL)
      {
      WNetSetLastError(WN_NOT_SUPPORTED);
      return;
      }
   lpWNetShutdown(nNameIndex);
   FreeLibrary(hLibrary);
}

BOOL WINAPI WNetSendDatagram(LPVOID lpTargetStation,
                             LPVOID lpData, WORD wDataLength,
                             int nNameIndex)
{
   if (lpWNetSendDatagram == NULL)
      {
      WNetSetLastError(WN_NOT_SUPPORTED);
      return FALSE;
      }
   return lpWNetSendDatagram(lpTargetStation, lpData,
            wDataLength, nNameIndex);
}

BOOL WINAPI WNetReceiveDatagram(LPVOID lpBuffer,
                                WORD wBufferSize,
                                int  nNameIndex,
                                HWND hWnd)
{
```

```
   if (lpWNetReceiveDatagram == NULL)
      {
      WNetSetLastError(WN_NOT_SUPPORTED);
      return FALSE;
      }
   return lpWNetReceiveDatagram(lpBuffer,
            wBufferSize, nNameIndex, hWnd);
}
```

Other Remote Procedure Call Functions

There are three other remote procedure call functions in WNETLVL1.DLL: WNetPost-
Message(), WNetFindWindow(), and WNetEnumStations(). I list WNetPostMessage()
here for completeness; it does not differ substantially from WNetSendMessage().

```
/********
*
* Listing 2-12. WNPSTMSG.C
*
* Copyright (c) 1992, Ralph P. Davis, All Rights Reserved
*
********/


/*===== Includes =====*/

#include "wnet.h"
#include <dde.h>


/*===== Function Definitions =====*/

BOOL WINAPI WNetPostMessage(
                    LPVOID lpTargetStation,
                    HWND hWnd, UINT message,
                    WPARAM wParam, LPARAM lParam,
                    BOOL bIsLParamPtr, DWORD dwDataLength)
{

   LPVOID lpData;
   LRESULT lResult = -1L;
   WNET_MSG FAR *lpMsgHeader;

   if (message >= WM_DDE_FIRST && message <= WM_DDE_LAST)
      {
      // We are specifying that distributed DDE must use
      // a pre-established connection, so the offset portion
      // of lpTargetStation is the connection number

      lpData = WNetEncapsulateDDEData(POST_MESSAGE, hWnd, message,
         wParam, lParam, &dwDataLength,
         (HCONNECTION) OFFSETOF(lpTargetStation));
      bIsLParamPtr = FALSE;
      }
   else
      {
```

```
      lpData = WNetEncapsulateData(POST_MESSAGE, hWnd, message,
         wParam, lParam, bIsLParamPtr, dwDataLength);
      dwDataLength += sizeof (WNET_MSG);
      }

   if ((lpData != NULL))
      {
      lpMsgHeader = (WNET_MSG FAR *) lpData;
      lpMsgHeader->dwOutDataLength = 0L;

      lResult = WNetShipData(NULL, lpTargetStation,
         lpData, dwDataLength, NULL, 0L);
      FreePageLockedBuffer(lpData);
      }
   return (lResult != -1L);
}
```

Listing 2-13 shows WNetFindWindow(). It packages the class name and the window title as consecutive null-terminated strings, and tacks the header onto the packet. Listing 2-18 shows the routine WNet_OnFindWindow, which processes the request on the receiving end.

```
/********
 *
 * Listing 2-13. WNETFWND.C
 *
 * Copyright (c) 1992 Ralph P. Davis, All Rights Reserved
 *
 ********/

/*===== Includes =====*/

#include "wnet.h"

/*===== Function Definitions =====*/

HWND WINAPI WNetFindWindow(LPVOID lpTargetStation,
                           LPCSTR lpszClass,
                           LPCSTR lpszWindow)
{
   LRESULT lResult = 0L;
   LPBYTE  lpBuffer, lpTemp;
   DWORD   dwLength;

   dwLength = WNET_SIG_LENGTH +
              sizeof (WNET_REQUEST) +
              (lpszClass  == NULL ? 1 : lstrlen(lpszClass) + 1) +
              (lpszWindow == NULL ? 1 : lstrlen(lpszWindow) + 1);

   lpBuffer = (LPBYTE) AllocPageLockedBuffer(dwLength);
   if (lpBuffer != NULL)
      {
      lpTemp = lpBuffer;
      lstrcpy(lpTemp, WNET_SIGNATURE);
      lpTemp += WNET_SIG_LENGTH;
```

```
      *((WNET_REQUEST FAR *) lpTemp) = FIND_WINDOW;
      lpTemp += sizeof (WNET_REQUEST);
      if (lpszClass != NULL)
         {
         lstrcpy(lpTemp, lpszClass);
         lpTemp += (lstrlen(lpszClass) + 1);
         }
      else
         *lpTemp++ = '\0';

      if (lpszWindow != NULL)
         lstrcpy(lpTemp, lpszWindow);
      else
         *lpTemp = '\0';

      lResult = WNetShipData(NULL, lpTargetStation,
         lpBuffer, dwLength, NULL, OL);
      FreePageLockedBuffer(lpBuffer);
      }
   return ((HWND) lResult);
}
```

Listing 2-14 shows WNETENUM.C, which sends out a datagram requesting that other stations identify themselves. The receiving end is handled in Listing 2-18, in the function WNet_OnEnumStations.

```
/********
*
* Listing 2-14. WNETENUM.C
*
* Copyright (c) 1992 Ralph P. Davis, All Rights Reserved
*
********/

/*===== Includes =====*/

#include "wnet.h"
#include <string.h>


/*===== LOCAL Variables =====*/
static LPSTR lpStations[MAX_NAMES] = {NULL};
static int   nKnownStations = 0;


/*===== Function Definitions =====*/

BOOL WINAPI WNetEnumStations(int nNameIndex,
                             STATIONENUMPROC lpStationEnumProc)
{
   int  i;
   if (lpStationEnumProc != NULL)
      {
      for (i = 0; i < nKnownStations; ++i)
         {
```

```
            if (lpStations[i] != NULL)
               // Invoke the callback function
               if (!lpStationEnumProc(lpStations[i]))
                  break;
            }
        }

    // Regenerate station list
    for (i = 0; i < nKnownStations; ++i)
        {
        GlobalFreePtr(lpStations[i]);
        lpStations[i] = NULL;
        }
    nKnownStations = 0;
    return _WNetEnumStations(nNameIndex);
}

BOOL WINAPI _WNetEnumStations(int nNameIndex)
{
    WORD i, wNameLength;
    LPBYTE lpMyName, lpPacket;
    static BYTE byEnumStationPacket[WNET_SIG_LENGTH +
                                    sizeof (WNET_REQUEST) +
                                    sizeof (WORD) +
                                    MAX_STATION_NAME_LENGTH + 1];

    lpPacket = (LPBYTE) byEnumStationPacket;
    lstrcpy(lpPacket, WNET_SIGNATURE);
    lpPacket += WNET_SIG_LENGTH;
    *((WNET_REQUEST FAR *) lpPacket) = ENUM_STATIONS;
    lpPacket += sizeof (WNET_REQUEST);

    wNameLength = WNetGetNameLength(nNameIndex);
    *((LPWORD) lpPacket) = wNameLength;
    lpPacket += sizeof (WORD);
    lpMyName = WNetGetName(nNameIndex);

    for (i = 0;
         i < wNameLength && i < MAX_STATION_NAME_LENGTH;
         ++i)
        lpPacket[i] = lpMyName[i];

    // Null-terminate just in case this is a string
    lpPacket[i] = '\0';
    return
       WNetSendDatagram(WNET_DOMAIN,
          byEnumStationPacket, sizeof (byEnumStationPacket),
          nNameIndex);
}

BOOL WINAPI _WNetAddStationToList(LPSTR lpStationName, WORD wNameLength)
{
    int i;

    for (i = 0; i < MAX_NAMES && lpStations[i] != NULL; ++i)
```

```
   {
   if (_fmemcmp(lpStations[i], lpStationName, wNameLength) == 0)
      // Already in the list
      return TRUE;
   }
if (i == MAX_NAMES)
   return FALSE;
lpStations[i] = (LPSTR) GlobalAllocPtr(GHND, wNameLength);

if (lpStations[i] != NULL)
   {
   _fmemcpy(lpStations[i], lpStationName, wNameLength);
   ++nKnownStations;
   return TRUE;
   }
else
   return FALSE;
}
```

Additional General-Purpose functions

The general-purpose functions also include three that manipulate station names, two that set and get Windows network error codes, and two that allocate and free page-locked memory buffers. Listing 2-15 shows the name-related functions. We leave space for up to 256 names; this gives us more flexibility in implementing the NetBIOS-specific DLL, and permits multiple client applications to use our DLLs.

```
/********
*
* Listing 2-15. WNETNAME.C
*
* Copyright (c) 1992 Ralph P. Davis, All Rights Reserved
*
* Contains name-handling routines
*
********/

/*===== Includes =====*/

#include "wnet.h"

/*===== LOCAL Variables =====*/

LOCAL LPBYTE lpNames[MAX_NAMES];
LOCAL WORD   wMyNameLength[MAX_NAMES];

/*===== Function Definitions =====*/

LPBYTE WINAPI WNetGetName(int nIndex)
{
   if (nIndex >= 0 && nIndex < MAX_NAMES)
      return (lpNames[nIndex]);
   else
```

```
            return NULL;
    }

WORD    WINAPI WNetGetNameLength(int nIndex)
{
    if (nIndex >= 0 && nIndex < MAX_NAMES)
        return wMyNameLength[nIndex];
    else
        return 0;
}

void    WINAPI WNetSetName(int nIndex,
                            LPBYTE lpMyName,
                            WORD wNameLength)
{
    WORD i;

    if (nIndex >= 0 && nIndex < MAX_NAMES)
        {
        if (lpNames[nIndex] != NULL)
            GlobalFreePtr(lpNames[nIndex]);

        if (lpMyName == NULL || wNameLength == 0)
            {
            lpNames[nIndex] = NULL;
            wMyNameLength[nIndex] = 0;
            return;
            }
        lpNames[nIndex] =
            (LPBYTE) GlobalAllocPtr(GHND, (DWORD) (wNameLength + 1));
        if (lpNames[nIndex] != NULL)
            {
            for (i = 0; i < wNameLength; ++i)
                lpNames[nIndex][i] = lpMyName[i];

            // Force null-termination just in case
            lpNames[nIndex][i] = '\0';
            wMyNameLength[nIndex] = i;
            }
        }
}

void WINAPI WNetClearAllNames()
{
    int i;

    for (i = 0; i < MAX_NAMES; ++i)
        {
        if (lpNames[i] != NULL)
            {
            GlobalFreePtr(lpNames[i]);
            lpNames[i] = NULL;
            }
        }
}
```

Listing 2-16 shows the file WNETERR.C, with the routines WNetSetLastError() and WNetGetLastError(). These functions set and retrieve network-independent error codes. The codes used are the WN_ ones defined in WINDOWS.H. These are a very small subset of the kinds of error conditions that can occur, so our mapping is frequently not very precise.

WNetSetLastError() and WNetGetLastError() are modelled on the Win32 functions SetLastError() and GetLastError().

```
/********
 *
 * Listing 2-16. WNETERR.C
 *
 * Copyright (c) 1992 Ralph P. Davis, All Rights Reserved
 *
 ********/

/*===== Includes =====*/

#include "wnet.h"


/*===== LOCAL Variables =====*/

static DWORD dwLastError;


/*===== Function Definitions =====*/
void WINAPI WNetSetLastError(DWORD dwError)
{
    dwLastError = dwError;
}

DWORD WINAPI WNetGetLastError(void)
{
    return dwLastError;
}
```

Listing 2-17 shows the functions AllocPageLockedBuffer() and FreePageLockedBuffer(). These are used to allocate and free memory for submission to the network drivers. This memory must be fixed and page-locked. It will be passed along to the network drivers, and they will eventually attempt to access it in response to an interrupt. It is important that it still be resident in memory, and at the same location in memory, when this occurs.

In AllocPageLockedBuffer(), we allocate it using the GPTR flag, which includes GMEM_FIXED. We then call GetWinFlags() to determine if we're running in 386 enhanced mode, and if we are, we call GlobalPageLock() to prevent the memory from being paged to disk. In FreePageLockedBuffer(), we reverse the process, first calling GlobalPageUnlock() if we are in 386 enhanced mode, then calling GlobalFreePtr() to release the memory.

The functions WNetQueuePacket(), WNetGetNextQueuedPacket(), and WNetCopyQueuedPacket() deal with packets that are received asynchronously, but do not contain the "WNET" signature string. When this happens, we conclude that the packet is a response to a blocking receive, and queue it for retrieval by the network-dependent DLL routines.

The function NetworkDependentYield() is provided solely to support NetWare. The function IPXRelinquishControl() appears to be a requirement during PeekMessage() loops for IPX/SPX to function properly. NetworkDependentYield() allows us to call it in a network-independent way.

```
/********
 *
 * Listing 2-17. WNETMISC.C
 *
 * Copyright (c) 1992 Ralph P. Davis, All Rights Reserved
 *
 ********/


/*===== Includes =====*/

#include "wnet.h"


/*===== Function Definitions =====*/

LPVOID WINAPI AllocPageLockedBuffer(DWORD dwBytes)
{
   LPVOID lpPtr;

   lpPtr = GlobalAllocPtr(GPTR, dwBytes);

   if (lpPtr != NULL)
      if (GetWinFlags() & WF_ENHANCED)
         GlobalPageLock((HGLOBAL) SELECTOROF(lpPtr));

   return lpPtr;
}
void WINAPI FreePageLockedBuffer(LPVOID lpPtr)
{
   if (GetWinFlags() & WF_ENHANCED)
      GlobalPageUnlock((HGLOBAL) SELECTOROF(lpPtr));

   GlobalFreePtr(lpPtr);
}

void WINAPI WNetQueuePacket(LPBYTE lpPacket, HCONNECTION hConnection)
{
   if (nPackets < (MAX_NAMES - 1))
      {
      lpPackets[nPackets].lpPacket = lpPacket;
      lpPackets[nPackets++].hConnection = hConnection;
      }
   else
      FreePageLockedBuffer(lpPacket);
}

LPBYTE WINAPI WNetGetNextQueuedPacket(HCONNECTION hConnection)
```

```
{
   LPBYTE lpPacket;
   int    i;

   for (i = 0; i < nPackets; ++i)
      {
      if (lpPackets[i].hConnection == hConnection)
         {
         lpPacket = lpPackets[i].lpPacket;
         break;
         }
      }
   if (i == nPackets)
      // Nobody home
      return NULL;
   lpPackets[i].lpPacket = NULL;
   lpPackets[i].hConnection = 0;
   if (i == (nPackets - 1))  // Top entry
      --nPackets;
   return lpPacket;
}

void WINAPI WNetCopyQueuedPacket(LPBYTE lpIn, LPBYTE lpOut,
                                 DWORD dwDataLength)
{
   DWORD dwQueuedPacketSize;
   DWORD i;

   dwQueuedPacketSize = GlobalSize(GlobalPtrHandle(lpIn));
   if (dwQueuedPacketSize > dwDataLength)
      dwQueuedPacketSize = dwDataLength;

   for (i = 0L; i < dwQueuedPacketSize; ++i)
      lpOut[i] = lpIn[i];
   FreePageLockedBuffer(lpIn);
}

void WINAPI NetworkDependentYield(void)
{
   if (lpNetYield == NULL)
      return;
   lpNetYield();
}

BOOL WINAPI MyPeekMessage(MSG FAR *lpMsg, HWND hWnd, UINT uFirst,
                          UINT uLast, UINT uCommand)
{
   BOOL bPeek;
   static BOOL bSwitch;

   bPeek = PeekMessage(lpMsg, hWnd, uFirst, uLast, uCommand);

   if (!bPeek)
      {
```

```
    // We have to do either an INT 28H or an INT 2FH with AX = 0x1689.
    // This is the MS-DOS idle call, and it allows DOS device drivers
    // and TSRs to get a chance to bat.

    // According to the MS-DOS Programmer's Reference, INT 28H is
    // superseded, but there may be people out there who are looking
    // for it.
    // We'll do one one time, then the other the next time.

    if (bSwitch)
        {
        _asm mov ax, 0x1689
        _asm mov bl, 1    ; set mouse busy flag
        _asm int 0x2f
        }
    else
        _asm int 0x28

    bSwitch = !bSwitch;
    }
    return bPeek;
}
```

WNET.EXE

WNET.EXE resides on the same level of the WNET system as the remote procedure call functions. It runs as an iconized application, and does not allow itself to be restored or maximized.

The remote procedure calls are the sending side; WNET.EXE is the receiving side. When a remote station issues a WNetSendMessage(), WNetPostMessage(), WNetFind-Window(), or WNetEnumStations(), the window procedure for WNET.EXE receives a WMU_PACKET_RECEIVED message. It then breaks down the packet, and checks to see if it begins with our signature string ("WNET"). This marks it as having been generated by one of the RPC functions on another station. If it does, it examines the rest of the message header to determine the function that generated the packet. It then extracts the function arguments from the packet, allocates memory for any incoming or outgoing data, and calls the corresponding Windows function. Figure 2-2 shows the flow of data triggered by WNetSendMessage().

If WNET.EXE does not find the "WNET" signature at the front of the packet, it assumes that it is an asynchronous reception of a packet that was requested by a synchronous WNetReceive(). In this case, it calls WNetQueuePacket() to put it on a queue for WNetReceive() to pick it up. For blocking receives, WNetReceive() goes into a PeekMessage() loop, and periodically calls WNetGetNextQueuedPacket(), shown in Listing 2-17, to see if the packet arrived asynchronously.

The next listing is WNETMAIN.C. This file contains the window procedure for WNET.EXE, WNetWndProc, and the message-handling functions, of which the most important is WNet_OnPacketReceived().

By the way, the NetBIOS version expects the command line to include the network name of the station. Thus, you execute WNET.EXE by entering

WNET.EXE BLUEBOY

to run it on the machine named BLUEBOY. With the other protocols, it does not hurt anything to include an argument; it will be ignored.

WNet_OnPacketReceived()   WNet_OnPacketReceived() essentially reverses the action of WNetEncapsulateDDEData() and WNetEncapsulateData(). After checking the packet signature, one of the first things we do is determine if the message is a DDE message. If it is, we call WNetUnwrapDDE(), shown in Listing 2-7. If it is not, we fall into a case statement which checks the request code.

For SEND_MESSAGE and POST_MESSAGE, we extract the message number and the *wParam*, and, if appropriate, point *lParam* to the incoming data. We also provide memory for return data. Finally, we call SendMessage() or PostMessage().

For FIND_WINDOW, WNet_OnPacketReceived() parses out the class name and window title and calls FindWindow(). For ENUM_STATIONS, it adds the requesting station to the local station table by calling _WNetAddStationToList() (shown in Listing 2-14), then sends a datagram with an ENUM_STATION_RESPONSE command code. Finally, for an ENUM_STATION_RESPONSE, it calls _WNetAddStationToList(). The list that _WNetAddStationToList() populates is the one enumerated by WNetEnumStations().

```
/********
*
* Listing 2-18. WNETMAIN.C
*
* Copyright (c) 1992 Ralph P. Davis, All Rights Reserved
*
********/

/*===== Includes =====*/

#include "wnet.h"
#include <dde.h>
#include <string.h>

/*===== Constants =====*/

#define MAX_PM_BUFFERS 25

/*===== Global Variables =====*/

HINSTANCE       hCurrentInstance;
HWND            hTopWindow;
HINSTANCE       hNetLib;
int             nNameIndex;
LPVOID          lpPMBuffers[MAX_PM_BUFFERS];
int             nPMBufIndex = 0;

/*===== LOCAL Variables =====*/

static char szCmdLine[128] = "";
static UINT WMU_PACKET_RECEIVED;    // User-defined global message
/*===== FORWARD Functions =====*/
```

```
/*===== LOCAL Functions =====*/

LOCAL void NEAR PASCAL AddToStationTable(LPBYTE lpStationName,
                                         WORD   wNameLength);


/*===== External Functions =====*/

/*===== Function Definitions =====*/

int PASCAL WinMain(HINSTANCE hInst, HINSTANCE hPrevInstance,
                   LPSTR lpszCmdLine, int nCmdShow)
{
   MSG  msg;

   // Don't use hPrevInstance to determine if there's another
   // instance running.  In Win32, it will always return NULL.

   if (FindWindow("WNETMASTER", NULL) != NULL)
      return FALSE;

   if (GlobalInit("WNETMASTER", hInst) == 0)
      return FALSE;

   // Where appropriate, lpszCmdLine will be the name of the
   // station.

   if (lpszCmdLine != NULL)
      {
      while (*lpszCmdLine == ' ')   // Skip spaces
         ++lpszCmdLine;
      lstrcpy(szCmdLine, lpszCmdLine);
      }

   if ((hTopWindow = InstanceInit("WNETMASTER", hInst)) == NULL)
      return FALSE;

   hCurrentInstance = hInst;

   WMU_PACKET_RECEIVED =
      RegisterWindowMessage("WMU_PACKET_RECEIVED");

   while (GetMessage(&msg,NULL,NULL,NULL) )
      {
      // No need to do TranslateMessage()--we don't have
      // a keyboard interface
      DispatchMessage(&msg);
      }
   return(msg.wParam);
}

LRESULT CALLBACK WNetWndProc(HWND hWnd,
                             UINT uMessage,
                             WPARAM wParam,
                             LPARAM lParam)
```

```
{
    // We're only interested in a couple of messages.

    // WM_CREATE--triggers network initialization

    // WMU_PACKET_RECEIVED--parses and dispatches message

    // WM_CLOSE
    // WM_ENDSESSION--shut down network DLLs.

    if (uMessage == WMU_PACKET_RECEIVED)
        {
        // Returns TRUE if he processes the message,
        // FALSE otherwise
        return (HANDLE_WMU_PACKET_RECEIVED(hWnd, wParam, lParam,
                WNet_OnPacketReceived));
        }
    else
        {
        switch (uMessage)
            {
            HANDLE_MSG(hWnd, WM_CREATE, WNet_OnCreate);
            HANDLE_MSG(hWnd, WM_CLOSE, WNet_OnClose);
            HANDLE_MSG(hWnd, WM_ENDSESSION, WNet_OnEndSession);
            case WM_QUERYOPEN:
                MessageBeep(MB_ICONHAND);
                return FALSE;
            case WM_INITMENUPOPUP:
                if (HIWORD(lParam) != 0)
                    {
                    // It's the system menu
                    // We'll let the user close us and switch tasks,
                    // but that's all
                    EnableMenuItem((HMENU) wParam, SC_SIZE,
                        MF_GRAYED | MF_BYCOMMAND);
                    EnableMenuItem((HMENU) wParam, SC_MINIMIZE,
                        MF_GRAYED | MF_BYCOMMAND);
                    EnableMenuItem((HMENU) wParam, SC_MAXIMIZE,
                        MF_GRAYED | MF_BYCOMMAND);
                    EnableMenuItem((HMENU) wParam, SC_RESTORE,
                        MF_GRAYED | MF_BYCOMMAND);
                    }
                break;
            case WM_DESTROY:
                PostQuitMessage(0);
                break;
            default:
                break;
            }
        }
    return DefWindowProc(hWnd, uMessage, wParam, lParam);
}
BOOL WNet_OnCreate(HWND hWnd, CREATESTRUCT FAR *lpCS)
```

```
{
    if ((nNameIndex = WNetInit(hWnd, szCmdLine, &hNetLib)) == (-1))
        {
        MessageBeep(MB_ICONHAND);
        MessageBox(NULL, "WNet Server Initialization Failed",
            "WNet Error", MB_OK | MB_ICONHAND);
        WNetShutdown(hNetLib, nNameIndex);
        return FALSE;
        }
    else
        MessageBox(NULL, "WNet Server Initialization Successful",
            "WNet", MB_OK);

    // Pass NULL procedure pointer to set up list of
    // active stations
    WNetEnumStations(nNameIndex, NULL);

    return TRUE;
}


BOOL WNet_OnPacketReceived(HWND hWnd,
                           HCONNECTION hConnection,
                           LPVOID lpReceivedData)
{
    LPBYTE          lpPacket;
    WNET_MSG FAR *lpMsgHeader;
    BOOL            bRetcode;

    // Parse out the arguments.
    lpPacket = (LPBYTE) lpReceivedData;
    lpMsgHeader = (WNET_MSG FAR *) lpPacket;

    if (lstrcmp(lpMsgHeader->szSignature, WNET_SIGNATURE) != 0)
        {
        // Probably an asynchronous receive of a packet expected
        // in line
        WNetQueuePacket(lpPacket, hConnection);
        return FALSE;
        }

    if (lpMsgHeader->Message.message >= WM_DDE_FIRST &&
        lpMsgHeader->Message.message <= WM_DDE_LAST)
        {
        if (WNetUnwrapDDE(lpPacket, hConnection) != 0)
            return TRUE;
        else
            lpMsgHeader->bIsLParamPtr = FALSE;
        }

    switch (lpMsgHeader->WNetRequest)
        {
        case POST_MESSAGE:
        case SEND_MESSAGE:
            WNet_OnPostSendMessage(hConnection, lpMsgHeader);
```

```
            FreePageLockedBuffer(lpReceivedData);
            bRetcode = TRUE;
            break;
        case FIND_WINDOW:
            WNet_OnFindWindow(hConnection, lpPacket);
            bRetcode = TRUE;
            FreePageLockedBuffer(lpReceivedData);
            break;
        case ENUM_STATIONS:
            if (!(WNet_OnEnumStations(lpPacket, nNameIndex, TRUE)))
                // FALSE return means we didn't add it to the station list
                // Either it's the request coming from us
                // or the station list is full
                FreePageLockedBuffer(lpReceivedData);

            // TRUE return means it is in the station list, so
            // we can't release the memory for the packet

            // It will be freed when we call
            // WNetEnumStations() again.

            bRetcode = TRUE;
            break;
        case ENUM_STATION_RESPONSE:
            WNet_OnEnumStations(lpPacket, nNameIndex, FALSE);
            bRetcode = TRUE;
            FreePageLockedBuffer(lpReceivedData);
            break;
        default:
            // Starts with our signature, but an
            // unknown command code...chuck it
            bRetcode = FALSE;
            break;
        }
    return bRetcode;
}

/* void WNet_OnClose(HWND hwnd); */
void WNet_OnClose(HWND hwnd)
{
    // WM_CLOSE and WM_ENDSESSION are handled the same way.

    WNet_OnEndSession(hwnd, TRUE);
}

/* void WNet_OnEndSession(HWND hwnd, BOOL fEnding); */
void WNet_OnEndSession(HWND hwnd, BOOL fEnding)
{
    if (fEnding)
        {
        WNetShutdown(hNetLib, nNameIndex);
        DestroyWindow(hwnd);
        }
}
```

```c
void WNet_OnPostSendMessage(HCONNECTION hConnection,
                            WNET_MSG FAR *lpMsgHeader)
{
    LPBYTE         lpDataIn;
    BOOL           bError = FALSE;
    LRESULT        lResult;
    LRESULT FAR    *lplResult = (LRESULT FAR *) &lResult;
    LPBYTE         lpPacket = (LPBYTE) lpMsgHeader;

    // Allocate memory for incoming data
    if (lpMsgHeader->bIsLParamPtr)
        {
        DWORD i;

        lpDataIn = GlobalAllocPtr(GHND,
                        max(lpMsgHeader->dwDataLength,
                            lpMsgHeader->dwOutDataLength) +
                        sizeof (LRESULT));

        if (lpDataIn == NULL)
            {
            bError = TRUE;
            if (lpMsgHeader->WNetRequest == POST_MESSAGE)
                lResult = (LRESULT) FALSE;
            else
                lResult = -1L;
            lplResult = (LRESULT FAR *) &lResult;
            }
        else
            {
            lplResult = (LRESULT FAR *) lpDataIn;
            lpMsgHeader->Message.lParam =
                (LPARAM) (lpDataIn + sizeof (LRESULT));
            lpPacket += (sizeof (WNET_MSG));

            for (i = OL; i < lpMsgHeader->dwDataLength; ++i)
                lpDataIn[i + (sizeof (LRESULT))] = lpPacket[i];
            // Cycle through message buffers,
            // free previously used one.

            // We can't release the memory here, because we
            // don't know when we will be done listing it
            // So we use a pool of buffers

            if (lpPMBuffers[nPMBufIndex] != NULL)
                GlobalFreePtr(lpPMBuffers[nPMBufIndex]);
            lpPMBuffers[nPMBufIndex++] = lpDataIn;
            nPMBufIndex %= MAX_PM_BUFFERS;
            }
        }
    if (!bError)
        {
        if (lpMsgHeader->WNetRequest == POST_MESSAGE)
```

```
        {
        if (IsWindow(lpMsgHeader->Message.hwnd))
            *lplResult = (LRESULT) PostMessage(
                            lpMsgHeader->Message.hwnd,
                            lpMsgHeader->Message.message,
                            lpMsgHeader->Message.wParam,
                            lpMsgHeader->Message.lParam);
        else
            *lplResult = FALSE;
        }
      else
        {
        if (IsWindow(lpMsgHeader->Message.hwnd))
            *lplResult = SendMessage(
                        lpMsgHeader->Message.hwnd,
                        lpMsgHeader->Message.message,
                        lpMsgHeader->Message.wParam,
                        lpMsgHeader->Message.lParam);
        else
            *lplResult = -1L;
        }
    }
    // Return the result of the function call.
    WNetSend(hConnection, lplResult, sizeof (lResult)
        + lpMsgHeader->dwOutDataLength);
}

void WNet_OnFindWindow(HCONNECTION hConnection, LPBYTE lpPacket)
{
    LPSTR         lpszClass;
    LPSTR         lpszWindow;
    HWND          hFoundWindow;
    LRESULT       lResult;

    lpPacket += (WNET_SIG_LENGTH + sizeof (WNET_REQUEST));
    lpszClass = lpPacket;
    lpszWindow = lpPacket + lstrlen(lpszClass) + 1;
    if (lstrlen(lpszClass) == 0)
        lpszClass = NULL;
    if (lstrlen(lpszWindow) == 0)
        lpszWindow = NULL;
    hFoundWindow = FindWindow(lpszClass, lpszWindow);
    lResult = MAKELPARAM(hFoundWindow, 0);
    WNetSend(hConnection, (LPVOID) &lResult, sizeof (LRESULT));
}

BOOL WNet_OnEnumStations(LPBYTE lpPacket, int nNameIndex,
                        BOOL bResponseRequired)
{
    WORD          wNameLength;
    LPBYTE        lpSourceStation;
    static BYTE   byEnumStationResponse[
                    WNET_SIG_LENGTH +
```

```
                        sizeof (WNET_REQUEST) +
                        sizeof (WORD) +
                        MAX_STATION_NAME_LENGTH];

    lpPacket += (WNET_SIG_LENGTH + sizeof (WNET_REQUEST));
    wNameLength = *((LPWORD) lpPacket);
    lpPacket += sizeof (WORD);
    lpSourceStation = lpPacket;

    if (bResponseRequired)
      {
      _fmemcpy(byEnumStationResponse, WNET_SIGNATURE,
         WNET_SIG_LENGTH);
      lpPacket = (LPBYTE) &byEnumStationResponse[WNET_SIG_LENGTH];
      *((WNET_REQUEST FAR *) lpPacket) =
         ENUM_STATION_RESPONSE;
      lpPacket += sizeof (WNET_REQUEST);
      wNameLength = WNetGetNameLength(nNameIndex);
      *((WORD FAR *) lpPacket) = wNameLength;
      lpPacket += sizeof (WORD);
      _fmemcpy(lpPacket, WNetGetName(nNameIndex),
         wNameLength);
      if (_fmemcmp(lpPacket, lpSourceStation, wNameLength) != 0)
         // Don't answer our own broadcast.
         WNetSendDatagram(lpSourceStation, byEnumStationResponse,
                          sizeof (byEnumStationResponse),
                          nNameIndex);
      else
         return FALSE;
      }
   return _WNetAddStationToList(lpSourceStation, wNameLength);
}
```

WNETSTRT.C WNETSTRT.C contains initialization routines that WNET.EXE needs only
at startup. These register the window class WNETMASTER and create the window that handles WMU_PACKET_RECEIVED messages. We make WNETMASTER a global class by
setting the class style to CS_GLOBALCLASS. To determine if the DLL has already been
set up, the network-specific initialization function [_WNetInit()] checks to see if a window
of this class already exists. Thus, we want to make sure that no other applications confuse
us by using this window class name.

```
/********
*
* Listing 2-19. WNETSTRT.C
*
* Copyright (c) 1992 Ralph P. Davis, All Rights Reserved
*
* Contains WNET routines used only at startup
*
********/


/*===== Includes =====*/
```

```
#include "wnet.h"

/*===== Function Definitions =====*/
ATOM GlobalInit(LPSTR lpszClassName, HINSTANCE hInstance)
{
   WNDCLASS WndClass;

   WndClass.lpszClassName = lpszClassName;
   WndClass.lpfnWndProc   = WNetWndProc;
   WndClass.hInstance     = hInstance;
   WndClass.hCursor       = NULL;
   WndClass.hIcon         = LoadIcon(NULL, IDI_APPLICATION);
   WndClass.hbrBackground = NULL;
   WndClass.lpszMenuName  = NULL;
   WndClass.style         = CS_GLOBALCLASS;  // Our class will be
                                             // globally visible

   WndClass.cbClsExtra    = 0;
   WndClass.cbWndExtra    = 0;

   return RegisterClass(&WndClass);
}

HWND InstanceInit(LPSTR lpszClassName, HINSTANCE hInstance)
{
   HWND hWnd;

   hWnd = CreateWindow(
      lpszClassName,
      "Windows Network Manager",
      WS_OVERLAPPEDWINDOW,
      CW_USEDEFAULT,
      CW_USEDEFAULT,
      CW_USEDEFAULT,
      CW_USEDEFAULT,
      NULL,
      NULL,
      hInstance,
      NULL);

   if (hWnd != NULL)
      {
      ShowWindow(hWnd,SW_SHOWMINNOACTIVE);
      UpdateWindow(hWnd);
      }
   return hWnd;
}
```

Program Maintenance Files

The last two listings are the module definition files for WNET.EXE, WNETLVL1.DLL, and WNETLVL1.LIB. WNETLVL1.LIB is just the import library for WNETLVL1.DLL.

It is required for WNET.EXE and for the network-dependent DLLs. The full build procedure is:

1. Build the network-independent DLL.
2. Build WNET.EXE.
3. Build the network-dependent DLL.

Steps two and three are interchangeable.

```
;********
;
; Listing 2-20. WNETLVL1.DEF
;
; Copyright (c) 1992 Ralph P. Davis, All Rights Reserved
;
;********

LIBRARY    WNETLVL1

EXETYPE    WINDOWS

CODE       PRELOAD FIXED
DATA       PRELOAD FIXED SINGLE

HEAPSIZE   4096

EXPORTS
           WEP                      @1 RESIDENTNAME
           WNetSetLastError
           WNetGetLastError
           WNetEncapsulateData
           WNetEncapsulateDDEData
           WNetGetOutDataLength
           WNetEnumStations
           _WNetEnumStations
           _WNetAddStationToList
           WNetCall
           WNetListen
           WNetSend
           WNetReceive
           WNetHangup
           WNetShutdown
           WNetSendDatagram
           WNetReceiveDatagram
           WNetFindWindow
           WNetInit
           AllocPageLockedBuffer
           FreePageLockedBuffer
           WNetGetName
           WNetGetNameLength
           WNetSetName
           WNetClearAllNames
```

```
                WNetShipData
                WNetSendMessage
                WNetPostMessage
                WNetUnwrapDDE
                DDEAgentWndProc
                DDEWindowEnumProc
                WNetGetNextQueuedPacket
                WNetQueuePacket
                WNetCopyQueuedPacket
                NetworkDependentYield
                MyPeekMessage


;********
;
; Listing 2-21. WNETMAIN.DEF
;
; Copyright (c) 1992 Ralph P. Davis, All Rights Reserved
;
;********

NAME      WNET

EXETYPE   WINDOWS

CODE      PRELOAD MOVEABLE DISCARDABLE
DATA      PRELOAD MOVEABLE SINGLE

HEAPSIZE  8192
STACKSIZE 8192

STUB      'WINSTUB.EXE'

EXPORTS
          WNetWndProc
```

CHAPTER ■ 3

NetBIOS

Overview

NetBIOS is a widely supported communications protocol that has become a universal language for peer-to-peer communications on PCs. It is full-featured and relatively easy to use. It also represents a true interface, rather than a particular protocol; this is one reason for its wide acceptance.

NetBIOS has been implemented on top of a number of other protocols. The programmer writing for NetBIOS need not be concerned with the underlying protocol; NetBIOS takes care of packet assembly and disassembly. The NetBIOS programmer is only aware of exchanging data with other stations, which indeed is all he or she should be concerned with.

In addition to its generality, NetBIOS possesses another important advantage for the Windows programmer: Windows does all API translation for you. Thus, NetBIOS is an attractive option for Windows-based horizontal applications.

It has some disadvantages, however. Under NetWare and VINES, NetBIOS requires that an additional TSR be loaded. While their memory overhead (about 30K) is not that great in the protected-mode Windows environment, the burden of making sure that all users load the TSR is an additional headache for the network administrator. Furthermore, it consumes memory in the non-Windows environment where it may not be needed.

Also, under DOS, Windows 3.1, and Windows for Workgroups, there is no C language API for NetBIOS. (This is not the case under Windows NT, as we will see in Chapter 13.) The NetBIOS programming interface has been assembler-based since its inception. To issue a NetBIOS command, you populate the fields of a data structure called a Network Control Block (NCB), put its address in ES:BX, then issue an INT 5CH.

However, the advantages of NetBIOS mean that it is always a good choice for peer-to-peer Windows applications. Indeed, you can implement network-independent programs simply by using NetBIOS. However, it may not always be the *best* choice. Other protocols may perform better. For instance, IPX/SPX is faster than NetBIOS in the NetWare environment. After all, NetBIOS under NetWare is implemented on top of IPX/SPX. In his *LAN Manager Programmer's Guide*, Ralph Ryan presents benchmark test data showing that named pipes outperform NetBIOS under LAN Manager. Unfortunately, named pipes cannot be used for horizontal applications under Windows 3.X or Windows for Workgroups.

NetBIOS and Windows

The NetBIOS programming interface under Windows is the same as it is in any other environment. The commands are identical, and they use the same data structure—the Network Control Block. Table 3-1 lists the NetBIOS commands.

Table 3-1: NetBIOS Commands

Command Name	Numeric Code	Significance
General Commands		
RESET	32H	Clear all names and reconfigure station
CANCEL	35H	Cancel a previous request
ADAPTER STATUS	33H (blocking) 83H (non-blocking)	Get NetBIOS status and configuration
Name Support Commands		
ADD NAME	30H (blocking) B0H (non-blocking)	Register a unique network name
ADD GROUP NAME	36H (blocking) B6H (non-blocking)	Register a group name
DELETE NAME	31H (blocking) B1H (non-blocking)	Delete a registered name
Session Support Commands		
CALL	10H (blocking) 90H (non-blocking)	Attempt to establish connection
LISTEN	11H (blocking) 91H (non-blocking)	Make station available for connections
HANG UP	12H (blocking) 92H (non-blocking)	Terminate connection
SEND	14H (blocking) 94H (non-blocking)	Send data over a connection
CHAIN SEND	17H (blocking) 97H (non-blocking)	Send chained buffers over a connection
RECEIVE	15H (blocking) 95H (non-blocking)	Receive data over a specific connection
RECEIVE ANY	16H (blocking) 96H (non-blocking)	Receive data over any connection
SESSION STATUS	34H (blocking) B4H (non-blocking)	Retrieve session status

Table 3-1: NetBIOS Commands (Cont.)

Command Name	Numeric Code	Significance
Datagram Support		
SEND DATAGRAM	20H (blocking)	Send a datagram to a single station or a group of stations
	A0H (non-blocking)	
SEND BROADCAST DATAGRAM	22H (blocking) A2H (non-blocking)	Send a datagram to all stations
RECEIVE DATAGRAM	21H (blocking)	Receive a datagram sent to a name registered at this station
	A1H (non-blocking)	
RECEIVE BROADCAST DATAGRAM	23H (blocking) A3H (non-blocking)	Receive broadcast

The command codes are single-byte integers, with the high bit set to specify non-blocking mode. Non-blocking commands return immediately; the command essentially runs in the background and completes some time after the function has returned. Blocking commands do not return until the command completes, and tie up the entire Windows system in the meantime. Microsoft strongly recommends that you not use blocking commands. Even when the requirements of a particular situation dictate that you must appear to block (because the data is required synchronously), the preferred practice is to use non-blocking commands, then go into a PeekMessage() loop until they complete (or time out).

PeekMessage() loops have some complications; see the discussion of this in Chapter 2. I will actually call the function MyPeekMessage() that I developed in Chapter 2. However, to make it clear that PeekMessage() is the engine that drives these loops, I will continue to refer to them as "PeekMessage() loops."

The code in this chapter uses only non-blocking calls, except to cancel a command that has timed out. The CANCEL command does not have a non-blocking option.

Here is a typedef statement for the Network Control Block:

```
typedef struct
{
    BYTE byCommand;          // Command to execute
    BYTE byReturnCode;       // Immediate return code for non-blocking
                             // commands, final return code for blocking
                             // and non-blocking with non-NULL
                             // post routine
    BYTE byLocalSession;     // Local session number
    BYTE byNameNumber;       // Name number assigned by NetBIOS
                             // when name is registered
    LPVOID lpData;           // Data buffer
    WORD wDataLength;        // Size of data buffer
    char cRemoteName[16];    // Name of target station
                             // Space-padded, not null-terminated
    char cLocalName[16];     // Name of this station
    BYTE byReceiveTimeout;   // Receive time-out in 1/2 seconds
```

```
    BYTE bySendTimeout;      // Send time-out in 1/2 seconds
    FARPROC lpCallback;      // Callback function for non-blocking
                             // mode
    BYTE byAdapterNumber;    // LAN adapter--0 or 1
    BYTE byCompletionCode;   // Completion code for
                             // non-blocking commands with NULL lpCallback
                             // A value of 0xFF indicates that a non-blocking
                             // command is pending
    BYTE byReserved[14];     // The obligatory reserved bytes
} NCB;
```

The Windows-specific considerations for NetBIOS programming are:

- Buffers passed to NetBIOS, including NCBs, should be in fixed, page-locked memory. All buffers are allocated by calling AllocPageLockedBuffer(), which calls GlobalAlloc() with the GMEM_FIXED flag, then calls GlobalPageLock() if we are in 386 enhanced mode (see Listing 2-17).

- Callback functions must be procedure-instance addresses obtained from MakeProcInstance(). There is no need to use DPMI real-mode callbacks (see Chapter 7).

- In addition, callback functions must reside in fixed code segments. I declare the segment FIXED in the DLL's .DEF file (see Listing 3-17). If you are running in 386 enhanced mode, you also need to page lock them. They will be called at interrupt level; page locking them prevents the Windows swapper from being called during the servicing of the interrupt. Here's how you page lock an instance thunk:

```
FARPROC lpProc;

lpProc = MakeProcInstance(MyFunc, hMyInstance);
if ((GetWinFlags() & WF_ENHANCED) == WF_ENHANCED)
    GlobalPageLock((HGLOBAL) SELECTOROF(lpProc));
```

This is done during initialization, in the function _WNetInit(). See Listing 3-5.

- To repeat: don't use blocking commands.

NetBIOS Procedure

For a station to exchange messages with other stations, it must register a name with NetBIOS. This name can be either a group name, which need not be unique on the network, or an individual name, which must be. To participate in connection-oriented communications, a station *must* register an individual name. (You can use group names for connections, but the results may not be quite what you expect. When you try to connect to a station using a group name, NetBIOS will connect you to one of the stations that has that name registered, but there is no telling just *which* one.) Once a station has added its name, it can send datagrams to individual stations, groups of stations, or all stations. It can also receive datagrams from any other station on the network.

The LISTEN and CALL commands implement connection-oriented communications. A station willing to accept requests posts a LISTEN. A station wishing to initiate a conversation posts a CALL. Once a session is established, the stations can use SEND, CHAIN SEND, RECEIVE, and RECEIVE ANY to exchange data. HANGUP terminates a connection.

The Network-Dependent DLL for NetBIOS (WNETNB.DLL)

This section lists the code for the NetBIOS-specific DLL, and uses the code to demonstrate some of the specific issues mentioned above. As I stated in Chapter 2, the functions in the network-dependent layer have the same names as functions in the network-independent layer, prefixed with an underscore. These same functions will be included in all the network-dependent DLLs. The functions are shown in Table 3-2:

Table 3-2: Functions Called by Network-Independent DLL

Function	Operation Performed
_WNetCall	Establish a connection
_WNetListen	Listen for connection request
_WNetSend	Transmit packet over connection
_WNetReceive	Accept packet over connection
_WNetHangup	End connection
_WNetInit	Initialize the DLL
_WNetShutdown	Terminate the DLL
_WNetSendDatagram	Send a datagram packet
_WNetReceiveDatagram	Receive a datagram packet

Table 3-3 shows functions used internally by the NetBIOS-specific DLL.

Table 3-3: Functions Used Internally by the NetBIOS DLL

Function	Operation Performed
NetBios	Executes NetBIOS interrupt
NBWndProc	Window procedure for notification window. Separates data packet from NCB, passes it to higher-level software. Handles and forwards WMU_PACKET_RECEIVED message.
NetBIOSPostRoutine	Called by NetBIOS at interrupt level when an event completes. Generates WMU_PACKET_RECEIVED message.
MapNBToWinErr	Translates NetBIOS error to Windows WN_ error
NBAddName	Adds NetBIOS unique name
NBAddGroupName	Add NetBIOS group name
NBDropName	Deletes NetBIOS name

Header File—WNETNB.H
The first listing is the header file WNETNB.H.

```c
/********
 *
 * Listing 3-1. WNETNB.H
 *
 ********/

/*==== Includes =====*/

#include "wnet.h"

/*===== Constants =====*/

#define MAX_LISTEN_REQUESTS      2
#define RECEIVE_BUFFER_SIZE      512
#define MAX_SEND_BUFFER_SIZE     8192

#define CONCURRENT_CONNECTIONS   10

#define MAX_NETBIOS_NAMELEN      16

#define NB_NO_WAIT               0x80

#define NB_CALL                  0x10
#define NB_CALL_NO_WAIT          \
        (NB_CALL | NB_NO_WAIT)

#define NB_LISTEN                0x11
#define NB_LISTEN_NO_WAIT        \
        (NB_LISTEN | NB_NO_WAIT)

#define NB_HANGUP                0x12
#define NB_HANGUP_NO_WAIT        \
        (NB_HANGUP | NB_NO_WAIT)

#define NB_SEND                  0x14
#define NB_SEND_NO_WAIT          \
        (NB_SEND | NB_NO_WAIT)

#define NB_RECEIVE               0x15
#define NB_RECEIVE_NO_WAIT       \
        (NB_RECEIVE | NB_NO_WAIT)

#define NB_RECEIVE_ANY           0x16
#define NB_RECEIVE_ANY_NO_WAIT   \
        (NB_RECEIVE_ANY | NB_NO_WAIT)

#define NB_CHAIN_SEND            0x17
#define NB_CHAIN_SEND_NO_WAIT    \
        (NB_CHAIN_SEND | NB_NO_WAIT)

#define NB_SEND_DATAGRAM         0x20
#define NB_SEND_DATAGRAM_NO_WAIT \
        (NB_SEND_DATAGRAM | NB_NO_WAIT)

#define NB_RECEIVE_DATAGRAM      0x21
#define NB_RECV_DATAGRAM_NO_WAIT \
        (NB_RECEIVE_DATAGRAM | NB_NO_WAIT)
```

```
#define NB_SEND_BROADCAST          0x22
#define NB_SEND_BROADCAST_NO_WAIT \
        (NB_SEND_BROADCAST | NB_NO_WAIT)

#define NB_RECEIVE_BROADCAST       0x23
#define NB_RECV_BROADCAST_NO_WAIT \
        (NB_RECEIVE_BROADCAST | NB_NO_WAIT)

#define NB_ADD_NAME                0x30
#define NB_ADD_NAME_NO_WAIT        \
        (NB_ADD_NAME | NB_NO_WAIT)

#define NB_DELETE_NAME             0x31
#define NB_DELETE_NAME_NO_WAIT     \
        (NB_DELETE_NAME | NB_NO_WAIT)

#define NB_ADD_GROUP               0x36
#define NB_ADD_GROUP_NO_WAIT       \
        (NB_ADD_GROUP | NB_NO_WAIT)

#define NB_ADAPTER_STATUS          0x33
#define NB_ADAPTER_STATUS_NO_WAIT \
        (NB_ADAPTER_STATUS | NB_NO_WAIT)

// The following commands do not have a no-wait option
#define NB_RESET 0x32
#define NB_SESSION_STATUS 0x34
#define NB_CANCEL 0x35

// NetBIOS error return values
// See page 1-59 of the
//       IBM NetBIOS Application Development Guide

#define NB_SUCCESS                 0
#define NB_BAD_BUFFER_SIZE         1      // Invalid buffer length
#define NB_ERR_BAD_COMMAND         3      // Invalid command
#define NB_ERR_TIMEOUT             5      // Command timed out
#define NB_ERR_INCOMPLETE          6      // Message incomplete
#define NB_ERR_BAD_LSN             8      // Invalid local
                                          // session number
#define NB_ERR_NO_RESOURCE         9      // No resource available
#define NB_ERR_SESSION_CLOSED      0x0a   // Session closed
#define NB_ERR_CANCELLED           0x0b   // Command cancelled
#define NB_NAME_EXISTS_OK          0x0d   // Duplicate name in
                                          // local name table
                                          // (benign)
#define NB_ERR_NAME_TABLE_FULL     0x0e   // Name table full
#define NB_NAME_DEREGISTERED       0x0f   // Command completed
                                          // (name has active
                                          //  sessions and is now
                                          //  deregistered)
#define NB_ERR_SESSION_TABLE_FULL 0x11    // Local session table full
#define NB_ERR_SESSION_OPEN_REJ    0x12   // Session open rejected
#define NB_ERR_BAD_NAME_NUMBER     0x13   // Invalid name number
```

```
#define NB_ERR_BAD_CALLEE          0x14  // No answer (cannot find
                                         //  name called)
#define NB_ERR_BAD_NAME            0x15  // Invalid name
#define NB_ERR_NAME_IN_USE         0x16  // Name in use on remote node
#define NB_ERR_NAME_DELETED        0x17  // Name deleted
#define NB_ERR_SESSION_CRASHED     0x18  // Session ended abnormally
#define NB_ERR_NAME_CONFLICT       0x19  // Name conflict detected
#define NB_ERR_BUSY                0x21  // Interface busy
#define NB_ERR_SLOW_DOWN           0x22  // Too many commands
                                         // outstanding
#define NB_ERR_BAD_ADAPTER         0x23  // Invalid number in
                                         // lan adapter number field
#define NB_ERR_CANCEL_PENDING      0x24  // Command completed while
                                         // cancel pending
#define NB_ERR_CANT_CANCEL         0x26  // Command not valid to
                                         // cancel
#define NB_COMMAND_PENDING         0xff  // Command pending

// 0x40 and 0x50 to 0xf6 mean "adapter malfunction"

/*===== Types =====*/

typedef struct tagNCB
{
   BYTE     byCommand;
   BYTE     byReturnCode;
   BYTE     byLocalSession;
   BYTE     byNameNumber;
   LPVOID   lpData;
   WORD     wDataLength;
   BYTE     cRemoteName[16];
   BYTE     cLocalName[16];
   BYTE     byReceiveTimeout;
   BYTE     bySendTimeout;
   FARPROC  lpCallback;
   BYTE     byAdapterNumber;
   BYTE     byCompletionCode;
   BYTE     byReserved[14];
} NCB;

typedef NCB FAR  *LPNCB;
typedef NCB NEAR *NPNCB;
typedef NCB      *PNCB;

typedef struct tagXNCB
{
   NCB  ncbBase;
   HWND hWnd;
   WORD wOriginalDataLength;
} XNCB;           // Extended NCB

typedef XNCB FAR  *LPXNCB;
typedef XNCB NEAR *NPXNCB;
typedef XNCB      *PXNCB;
```

```
/*===== Global NetBIOS Variables =====*/

extern HINSTANCE hDLLInstance;
extern FARPROC   lpPostRoutine;
extern HWND      hMainWnd;
extern HWND      hNotifyWnd;
extern int       nMainNameIndex;
extern BYTE      byNameNumber;
extern BYTE      byGroupNameNumber;
extern UINT      WMU_PACKET_RECEIVED;
extern BOOL      bNameUnique[MAX_NAMES];
extern int       nRegistrations;
extern int       nClients[MAX_NAMES];
extern BYTE      byDatagramBuffers[MAX_LISTEN_REQUESTS]
                                 [RECEIVE_BUFFER_SIZE];
extern BYTE      byBroadcastBuffers[MAX_LISTEN_REQUESTS]
                                 [RECEIVE_BUFFER_SIZE];


/*===== Prototypes for NetBIOS-specific functions =====*/

WORD WINAPI NetBios(LPNCB lpNCB);
LRESULT WINAPI NBWndProc(HWND hNotifyWnd, UINT uMessage, WPARAM wParam,
                    LPARAM lParam);
void WINAPI NetBIOSPostRoutine(void);
DWORD PASCAL MapNBToWinErr(WORD wNBError);
WORD WINAPI NBAddName(LPSTR lpName, LPBYTE lpNameNumber);
WORD WINAPI NBAddGroupName(LPSTR lpGroupName,
                                 LPBYTE lpbyGroupNameNumber);
WORD WINAPI NBDropName(LPSTR lpName, int byNameNumber);
void PASCAL NBCancel(LPNCB lpNCB);
```

Post Routines—NetBIOSPostRoutine() and NBWndProc()

To do non-blocking I/O in NetBIOS, we use the no-wait version of the commands and include a post routine, this is a function we supply that NetBIOS will call when the no-wait command completes. In situations where we need to emulate blocking I/O, we pass a NULL address for the post routine, then poll the byCompletionCode field of the NCB. While the operation is in progress, this field will be set to 0xFF, which I have defined in WNETNB.H as NB_COMMAND_PENDING. When it completes, it will be set to some other value to indicate the status of the operation. This is the only situation in which *byCompletionCode* has meaning. In all other cases, *byReturnCode* reports the success or failure of an operation. Polling must include a PeekMessage() loop, and some reasonable timeout. Determining a "reasonable" timeout is as precise as determining "reasonable" doubt in court. I use five seconds for most of the code here.

The Assembler Post Routine—NetBIOSPostRoutine()   The assembler routine I use, shown here in Listing 3-2, does nothing but post a WMU_PACKET_RECEIVED message to the C handler, NBWndProc(), which is the window procedure for our notification window, *hNotifyWnd*. We create this window in the LibMain() routine that Windows calls when it first loads the DLL (see Listing 3-5).

Because the post routine is called through an instance thunk, Windows takes care of setting up its correct context. Posting a message to the C handler also ensures that it runs in its own context, rather than that of whatever task happened to be running when the past routine was invoked. I use exactly the same technique in Chapter 4 for the IPX/SPX post routine.

To reemphasize, the post routine address we actually pass to NetBIOS is an instance thunk for NetBIOSPostRoutine(). Like other callback functions, we must export NetBIOSPostRoutine() in the module definition file. The code segment for this routine, NBPOST_TEXT, is explicitly declared as FIXED in the .DEF file (see Listing 3-17). We also page lock the instance thunk to keep it from being paged to disk, then being reloaded at interrupt level.

```
;********
;
; Listing 3-2.  NBPOST.ASM
;
; Copyright (c) 1992, Ralph P. Davis, All Rights Reserved
;
;********

.286

memM EQU 1              ; medium model
?PLM      =      1      ; PASCAL calling convention
?WIN      =      1      ; Windows prologs and epilogs

INCLUDE CMACROS.INC

PUBLIC NetBIOSPostRoutine
EXTRN   POSTMESSAGE:FAR
EXTRN   _WMU_PACKET_RECEIVED:WORD
EXTRN   _hNotifyWnd:WORD

createSeg       NBPOST_TEXT,CODE1,BYTE,PUBLIC,CODE
sBegin          CODE1
                assumes CS, CODE1

cProc  NetBIOSPostRoutine,<FAR, PUBLIC>
cBegin NetBIOSPostRoutine
       PUSH _hNotifyWnd
       PUSH _WMU_PACKET_RECEIVED
       PUSH 0   ; wParam
       PUSH ES  ; lParam = Pointer to NCB
       PUSH BX
       CALL POSTMESSAGE
cEnd
sEnd            CODE1
END
```

To assemble this with Microsoft Macro-Assembler version 6.0, you must use the version of CMACROS.INC that comes with the assembler. It requires a small change. Line 1065 of CMACROS.INC reads

```
lea     sp,-2[bp]
```

This causes an assembler error, though it is a perfectly valid instruction. Change this to

```
lea     sp,[bp-2]
```

The C Handler—NBWndProc()   NBWndProc() is the window procedure for our notification window, and thus is prototyped like any window procedure:

```
LRESULT WINAPI NBWndProc(HWND hNotifyWnd, UINT uMessage, WPARAM wParam,
                         LPARAM lParam)
```

It is called with *wParam* set to zero and *lParam* pointing to the original NCB. Our asynchronous calls will actually use the extended NCB structure defined in WNETNB.H.

```
typedef struct tagXNCB
{
   NCB  ncbBase;
   HWND hWnd;
   WORD wOriginalDataLength;
} XNCB;          // Extended NCB

typedef XNCB FAR  *LPXNCB;
```

NetBIOS, of course, thinks it is pointing to an NCB. Because the NCB is the first part of the extended NCB, NetBIOS is right.

The additional fields of the extended NCB give NBWndProc() information it needs so it can dispatch the data and recycle the NCB. NBWndProc() allocates memory, extracts the data from the packet, and posts the WMU_PACKET_RECEIVED message to the window indicated by the *hWnd* field of the extended NCB, pointing *lParam* to the data. *hWnd* is the handle of a window belonging to a client application [the one that originally called one of our functions like WNetReceive()]. When the data has arrived over a connection, NBWndProc() passes the connection number (called the "local session number" or LSN in NetBIOS terminology) in *wParam*. Otherwise, *wParam* is irrelevant, and is set to zero.

If the NCB originated as one of the passive requests (LISTEN, RECEIVE, RECEIVE ANY, or RECEIVE DATAGRAM), NBWndProc() recycles it. NCBs for these events must be available at all times to handle asynchronous events. There is a limited pool of NCBs that can be outstanding at any one time, so we have to use a small number and recycle them (I use two LISTENs, two RECEIVEs, two RECEIVE DATAGRAMs for group broadcasts, and two RECEIVE DATAGRAMs for individual transmissions). The *wOriginalDataLength* field of the extended NCB tells NBWndProc() how big the data buffer originally was. When you submit an NCB, the *wDataLength* field holds the length of the input buffer. When NetBIOS receives data, it sets *wDataLength* to the actual number of bytes received. If we simply recycle it as is, we lose the original size of the buffer. By using *wOriginalDataLength* to remember the original size of the buffer, we make sure that we recycle it the way it was originally created, and so do not lose buffer space.

If the NCB came from an active request (SEND, CALL, SEND DATAGRAM, or HANGUP), it should not be recycled; these are one-time operations. In this case, NBWndProc() frees the memory originally allocated for the extended NCB; no one else will see it after this.

If the original command was LISTEN, NBWndProc() gets called when a request for a connection comes in from another station. It is not necessary to do anything else to accept the connection, but it is important to post buffers to receive incoming data. NBWnd-Proc() allocates memory for 8K buffers, then calls _WNetReceive(), shown in Listing 3-11, to make them available to NetBIOS.

When a session terminates or a name is deleted, any outstanding NCBs will come to NBWndProc() with *byReturnCode* set to the appropriate error code. These NCBs should also die here; their memory is released and they are not reposted.

We need to concatenate the receive buffers if the original transmission is too big to fit into a single one. As you will see, _WNetSend(), shown in Listing 3-10, expects the size of the input message as a DWORD, so it has to provide for transmitting it with several SEND operations. NetBIOS does not give you any way to tell the receiving station that a given message constitutes the end of a message. The way I solve this problem is to stipulate that no transmission will exceed 8,191 bytes unless it is serving as a flag that there is more data coming. Therefore, NBWndProc() checks to see if the amount of incoming data is less than or equal to 8,191. If it is, this is the last packet in the message, and we call RetrieveCompletePacket() to get the full message. Otherwise, we call AppendToPacket() to add it to whatever data has already been received.

This requirement is not unique to NetBIOS; it will be necessary with all the protocols we examine. The rest of the protocols, however, do give us ways to flag a given packet as the last one in a message.

```
/********
 *
 * Listing 3-3.   NBWND.C
 *
 * Copyright (c) 1992 Ralph P. Davis, All Rights Reserved
 *
 ********/

/*===== Includes =====*/

#include "wnetnb.h"
#include <string.h>

/*===== LOCAL Variables =====*/

static PACKET_TABLE PacketTable[CONCURRENT_CONNECTIONS] = {0};

/*===== FORWARD Functions =====*/

LPBYTE RetrieveCompletePacket(HCONNECTION hConnection, LPBYTE lpOldData,
          DWORD dwTotalBytes);
LPBYTE AppendToPacket(HCONNECTION hConnection, LPBYTE lpOldData,
                      DWORD dwTotalBytes);
void StopTrackingPacket(HCONNECTION hConnection);

/*===== Function Definitions =====*/

LRESULT WINAPI NBWndProc(HWND hNotifyWnd, UINT uMessage, WPARAM wParam,
                    LPARAM lParam)
{
```

```
LPXNCB lpXNCB = (LPXNCB) lParam;
WPARAM wOutParam;
LPVOID lpData, lpOldData;
BOOL    bRepost;
BOOL    bEndOfMessage;

if (uMessage == WMU_PACKET_RECEIVED)
    {
    switch (lpXNCB->ncbBase.byCommand & (~NB_NO_WAIT))
        {
        // Was it a passive command (listen, receive,
        // receive datagram)? If so, we'll repost it.
        case NB_RECEIVE:
        case NB_RECEIVE_ANY:
            switch (lpXNCB->ncbBase.byReturnCode)
                {
                case NB_ERR_SESSION_CLOSED:
                case NB_ERR_SESSION_CRASHED:
                case NB_ERR_BAD_LSN:
                case NB_NAME_DEREGISTERED:
                case NB_ERR_BAD_NAME_NUMBER:
                case NB_ERR_BAD_NAME:
                case NB_ERR_NAME_DELETED:
                case NB_ERR_CANCEL_PENDING:
                    // The above errors indicate that our
                    // NetBIOS support environment is no longer
                    // around, so don't recycle the request.
                    // If we do, we'll keep getting this error
                    // in an infinite cycle, or crash Windows
                    FreePageLockedBuffer(lpXNCB->ncbBase.lpData);
                    bRepost = FALSE;
                    break;
                default:
                    bRepost = TRUE;
                    break;
                }
            break;
        case NB_RECEIVE_DATAGRAM:
        case NB_LISTEN:
        case NB_RECEIVE_BROADCAST:
            switch (lpXNCB->ncbBase.byReturnCode)
                {
                case NB_NAME_DEREGISTERED:
                case NB_ERR_BAD_NAME_NUMBER:
                case NB_ERR_BAD_NAME:
                case NB_ERR_NAME_DELETED:
                case NB_ERR_CANCEL_PENDING:
                    // Don't repost if environment has gone away.
                    bRepost = FALSE;
                    break;
                default:
                    bRepost = TRUE;
```

```
            break;
         }
      break;
   default:
      bRepost = FALSE;
      break;
   }

// OK, evaluate the command to determine how to
// process the NCB
switch (lpXNCB->ncbBase.byCommand & (~NB_NO_WAIT))
   {
   case NB_LISTEN:
      if (lpXNCB->ncbBase.byReturnCode == NB_SUCCESS)
         {
         int i;
         LPBYTE lpBuffer;

         // Request for connection has come in from client station.
         // Post asynchronous _WNetReceive() requests.
         for (i = 0; i < MAX_LISTEN_REQUESTS; ++i)
            {
            lpBuffer = (LPBYTE) AllocPageLockedBuffer(
               MAX_SEND_BUFFER_SIZE);
            if (lpBuffer != NULL)
               {
               _WNetReceive(
                  (HCONNECTION) lpXNCB->ncbBase.byLocalSession,
                  lpBuffer, MAX_SEND_BUFFER_SIZE,
                  NONBLOCKING, 0, lpXNCB->hWnd);
               }
            }
         }
      break;
   case NB_CALL:
   case NB_SEND:
   case NB_RECEIVE:
   case NB_HANGUP:
   case NB_RECEIVE_ANY:
   case NB_CHAIN_SEND:
      // Connection-oriented operation.
      // byLocalSession field of NCB has the connection number,
      // which we'll pass along as the wParam
      wOutParam = (WPARAM) lpXNCB->ncbBase.byLocalSession;
      break;
   default:
      // Not a connection-oriented command, set wParam to 0.
      wOutParam = 0;
      break;
   }

// Make sure packet was not received in error,
// and that the extended NCB has a target window for
```

```
    // us to post a message to.
    if (lpXNCB->hWnd != NULL &&
        lpXNCB->ncbBase.byReturnCode == NB_SUCCESS)
      {
      // Copy the data

      if (lpXNCB->ncbBase.wDataLength <=
          (WORD) (MAX_SEND_BUFFER_SIZE - 1))
        {
        // If the wDataLength field of the NCB is less than
        // MAX_SEND_BUFFER_SIZE, then this is the last packet
        // in a message.

        bEndOfMessage = TRUE;
        }
      else
        {
        // Otherwise, it's a packet somewhere in the middle of a
        // message. The sending station will transmit the boundary
        // byte twice, so ignore it.
        lpXNCB->ncbBase.wDataLength =
            (WORD) (MAX_SEND_BUFFER_SIZE - 1);
        bEndOfMessage = FALSE;
        }

      lpData = GlobalAllocPtr(GHND,
          (DWORD) lpXNCB->ncbBase.wDataLength);

      if (lpData != NULL)
        {
        WORD i;

        // Move data from packet to our new buffer
        for (i = 0; i < lpXNCB->ncbBase.wDataLength; ++i)
          ((LPBYTE) lpData)[i] =
              ((LPBYTE) (lpXNCB->ncbBase.lpData))[i];
        if (bEndOfMessage)
          {
          // Pick up packets previously stored
          lpOldData = lpData;
          lpData = RetrieveCompletePacket(
              (HCONNECTION) wOutParam,
              lpData, lpXNCB->ncbBase.wDataLength);
          if (lpData != lpOldData)
            GlobalFreePtr(lpOldData);

          // And finally, post the WMU_PACKET_RECEIVED message
          // wParam is the connection number, if it's relevant,
          // and lParam points to the buffer we just allocated.
          if (lpData != NULL)
            PostMessage(lpXNCB->hWnd, WMU_PACKET_RECEIVED,
                        wOutParam, (LPARAM) lpData);
          }
        else
```

```
                     {
                     // Not the end of the message
                     // Store the packet for later retrieval
                     AppendToPacket((HCONNECTION) wOutParam,
                         lpData, lpXNCB->ncbBase.wDataLength);
                     GlobalFreePtr(lpData);
                     }
                 }
             }

         if (bRepost)
             {
             // Reset the wDataLength field of the NCB to the original
             // size of the buffer, which we've remembered in the
             // wOriginalDataLength field of the extended NCB
             lpXNCB->ncbBase.wDataLength =
                 lpXNCB->wOriginalDataLength;
             NetBios((LPNCB) lpXNCB);
             }
         else
             FreePageLockedBuffer(lpXNCB);
         }
     else
         return DefWindowProc(hNotifyWnd, uMessage, wParam, lParam);
}

LPBYTE RetrieveCompletePacket(HCONNECTION hConnection,
                              LPBYTE lpOldData, DWORD dwTotalBytes)
{
    LPBYTE  lpData;

    if (hConnection == 0)
        // Not a connection-oriented receive, no packet concatenation
        // takes place
        return lpOldData;

    lpData = AppendToPacket(hConnection, lpOldData, dwTotalBytes);
    StopTrackingPacket(hConnection);
    return lpData;
}

LPBYTE AppendToPacket(HCONNECTION hConnection, LPBYTE lpOldData,
                      DWORD dwTotalBytes)
{
    int    i;
    DWORD  j;
    LPBYTE lpData, lpTemp;
    DWORD  dwOriginalBytes;
    int    nFirstEmpty = -1;
    // See if we're keeping track of packets for this connection
    for (i = 0; i < CONCURRENT_CONNECTIONS; ++i)
        {
        if (nFirstEmpty == (-1) && PacketTable[i].hConnection == 0)
```

```
            nFirstEmpty = i;
        if (PacketTable[i].hConnection == hConnection)
            break;
        }

    if (i < CONCURRENT_CONNECTIONS)
        {
        // We've got a hit
        dwOriginalBytes = dwTotalBytes;
        dwTotalBytes += PacketTable[i].dwDataSize;
        lpData = GlobalReAllocPtr(PacketTable[i].lpData,
            dwTotalBytes, GHND);
        if (lpData == NULL)
            return NULL;
        lpTemp = &lpData[PacketTable[i].dwDataSize];

        for (j = 0; j < dwOriginalBytes; ++j)
            lpTemp[j] = lpOldData[j];
        PacketTable[i].dwDataSize = dwTotalBytes;
        PacketTable[i].lpData = lpData;
        return lpData;
        }
    else if (nFirstEmpty != (-1))
        {
        lpData = GlobalAllocPtr(GHND, dwTotalBytes);
        if (lpData != NULL)
            {
            for (j = 0; j < dwTotalBytes; ++j)
                lpData[j] = lpOldData[j];
            PacketTable[nFirstEmpty].hConnection = hConnection;
            PacketTable[nFirstEmpty].lpData = lpData;
            PacketTable[nFirstEmpty].dwDataSize = dwTotalBytes;
            }
        return lpData;
        }
    else    // No room in the table
        return NULL;
}

void StopTrackingPacket(HCONNECTION hConnection)
{
    int i;

    for (i = 0; i < CONCURRENT_CONNECTIONS; ++i)
        {
        if (PacketTable[i].hConnection -- hConnection)
            {
            // Just zero it out--memory gets released somewhere else.
            _fmemset(&PacketTable[i], '\0', sizeof (PACKET_TABLE));
            return;
            }
        }
}
```

Invoking NetBIOS—NetBios()

LAN Manager offers several functions for accessing NetBIOS under OS/2. These functions are not available in the MS-DOS or MS-Windows environment. The most relevant is NetBiosSubmit(), which submits an NCB to NetBIOS for processing. The same function exists in Win32 as NetBios(). These are C function calls, unlike the Windows NetBIOS-Call(). It is handy to have the equivalent function under Windows, so we will borrow the Win32 function name, and prototype it as follows:

```
WORD WINAPI NetBios(LPNCB lpNCB);
```

Listing 3-4 shows its implementation. Notice that after we have called NetBIOSCall(), we cannot access any of the fields in the NCB if the original command was of the no-wait variety. Our post routine may be called *during* Windows' NetBIOSCall() processing. The post routine posts a message to NBWndProc(). For some commands, NBWndProc() frees the memory that we originally allocated for the NCB. Surprisingly, therefore, NBWnd-Proc() may have released the memory by the time NetBIOSCall() returns! For this reason, we remember the command in DL, then check to see if it was a no-wait command. If it was, NetBIOS has already given us the immediate return code in AL, so we return that as the value of the function. Otherwise, we pull *byReturnCode* from the NCB and return that.

```
;********
;
; Listing 3-4. NETBIOS.ASM
;
; Copyright (c) 1992, Ralph P. Davis, All Rights Reserved
;
;*******

.286

OPTION OLDMACROS
memM EQU 1              ; medium model
?PLM      =      1      ; PASCAL calling convention
?WIN      =      1      ; Windows prologs and epilogs

INCLUDE CMACROS.INC

NB_NO_WAIT                EQU        000000080h

tagNCB       STRUCT 2t
byCommand                 BYTE       ?
byReturnCode              BYTE       ?
byLocalSession            BYTE       ?
byNameNumber              BYTE       ?
lpData                    DWORD      ?
wDataLength               WORD       ?
cRemoteName               BYTE       16t DUP (?)
cLocalName                BYTE       16t DUP (?)
byReceiveTimeout          BYTE       ?
bySendTimeout             BYTE       ?
lpCallback                DWORD      ?
```

```
byAdapterNumber                  BYTE      ?
byCompletionCode                 BYTE      ?
byReserved                       BYTE      14t DUP (?)
tagNCB      ENDS

NCB         TYPEDEF     tagNCB

PUBLIC           NetBios
externFP         NetBIOSCall

createSeg        NETBIOS_TEXT,CODE1,BYTE,PUBLIC,CODE
sBegin           CODE1
                 assumes CS, CODE1

cProc       NetBios, <FAR,PUBLIC>, <SI,DI,DS>
parmD NCBptr

cBegin           NetBios
                 LES  BX, NCBptr

                 ; Remember the command in DL
                 MOV  DL, (NCB PTR ES:[BX]).byCommand
                 PUSH DX
                 cCall NetBIOSCall

                 ; After this point, we cannot access
                 ; the original NCB pointer if it's a
                 ; no-wait command.  The memory may have
                 ; already been released  by NBWndProc.

                 POP  DX
                 TEST DL, NB_NO_WAIT

                 ; If it's the no-wait option, the
                 ; immediate return code is in AL.
                 JNZ  NetBios_Exit

                 ; Otherwise, get the final return code
                 MOV  AL, (NCB PTR ES:[BX]).byReturnCode
NetBios_Exit:
                 XOR  AH, AH
cEnd

sEnd             CODE1
END
```

Initializing the DLL

The NetBIOS initialization routine must handle several tasks. These include:

- Obtaining a procedure-instance address for the NetBIOS post routine. This is remembered in the global variable *lpPostRoutine*, and will be used by all the other non-blocking routines in this chapter.
- Making sure the code segment containing the post routine is page locked.
- Adding the station's name to the name table, and remembering it for later use.

- Remembering the window handle of the top-level window.
- Adding the WNET_DOMAIN group name for WNetEnumStations() broadcasts.
- Posting LISTEN requests so the station can receive calls from other stations.
- Registering the WMU_PACKET_RECEIVED message.

The first time _WNetInit() is called, it checks the global variable *hMainWnd*. If it is NULL, it calls FindWindow() to see if the window with class "WNETMASTER" exists (the window class registered by WNET.EXE in Chapter 2). If the window does not exist, it rejects the request. If the window does exist, _WNetInit() records its window handle in *hMainWnd*, and posts RECEIVE DATAGRAM NCBs to handle incoming WNetEnum-Stations() requests.

_WNetInit() returns the number that NetBIOS assigns to the name we register. This will be used subsequently by higher-level software as, in effect, a client ID. This allows more than one program to register as a client, using its own name. To enable more than one client to register using the same name, we keep track of how many clients are using a given name. When a client calls _WNetShutdown(), we do not delete the name until the number of clients using it falls to zero.

_WNETINI.C also includes WEP() and LibMain(), which are required in a DLL. LibMain() creates the notification Window and registers the WMU_PACKET_RE-CEIVED message.

```
/********
*
* Listing 3-5. _WNETINI.C
*
* Copyright (c) 1992 Ralph P. Davis, All Rights Reserved
*
* Contains NetBIOS-specific initialization
*
********/

/*===== Includes =====*/

#include "wnetnb.h"

#include <string.h>

/*===== LOCAL Functions =====*/

LOCAL BOOL IsNetBIOSInstalled(void);

/*===== Function Definitions =====*/

int WINAPI LibMain(HINSTANCE hInstance,
                   WORD wDataSeg,
                   WORD cbHeapSize,
                   LPSTR lpszCmdLine)
{
    WNDCLASS wndClass;

    WMU_PACKET_RECEIVED =
```

```
            RegisterWindowMessage("WMU_PACKET_RECEIVED");

    hDLLInstance = hInstance;
    wndClass.lpszClassName = "NetBiosNotify";
    wndClass.lpfnWndProc = NBWndProc;
    wndClass.hInstance   = hInstance;
    wndClass.hCursor     = NULL;
    wndClass.hIcon       = NULL;
    wndClass.hbrBackground = NULL;
    wndClass.lpszMenuName = NULL;
    wndClass.style  = 0;
    wndClass.cbClsExtra = 0;
    wndClass.cbWndExtra = 0;

    if (!RegisterClass(&wndClass))
        return 0;
    hNotifyWnd = CreateWindow("NetBiosNotify",
                              "NetBIOS Window",
                              WS_OVERLAPPEDWINDOW,
                              CW_USEDEFAULT,
                              CW_USEDEFAULT,
                              CW_USEDEFAULT,
                              CW_USEDEFAULT,
                              NULL,
                              NULL,
                              hInstance,
                              NULL);

    return (hNotifyWnd != NULL);
}

int WINAPI _WNetInit(HWND hWnd, LPVOID lpStationName)
{
    WORD    wNBReturnCode;
    char    szMyName[MAX_NETBIOS_NAMELEN + 1];
    int     i;

    // We assume that this routine can be called many times
    // by many different programs.

    WNetSetLastError(WN_SUCCESS);  // Clear error variable.

    // See if top-level software has been installed
    // (or if the caller is the top-level routine)
    // If not, return WN_NOT_SUPPORTED
    if (hMainWnd == NULL)
        {
        // Set up hMainWnd (window which will receive
        // incoming POST_MESSAGE, SEND_MESSAGE, FIND_WINDOW,
        // and ENUM_STATION packets).

        hMainWnd = FindWindow("WNETMASTER", NULL);
        if (hMainWnd == NULL || hWnd != hMainWnd)
            {
```

```
    // Either WNETMASTER not installed yet, or somebody
    // else got here first.
    WNetSetLastError(WN_NOT_SUPPORTED);
    return -1;
    }

// Better make sure NetBIOS is installed.
if (!IsNetBIOSInstalled())
    {
    WNetSetLastError(WN_NOT_SUPPORTED);
    return -1;
    }

lpPostRoutine = MakeProcInstance(NetBIOSPostRoutine,
                hDLLInstance);

if (lpPostRoutine == NULL)
    {
    WNetSetLastError(WN_WINDOWS_ERROR);
    return -1;
    }

if ((GetWinFlags() & WF_ENHANCED) == WF_ENHANCED)
    GlobalPageLock((HGLOBAL) SELECTOROF(lpPostRoutine));
if (NBAddGroupName(WNET_DOMAIN, &byGroupNameNumber) == NB_SUCCESS)
    {
    // Listen for ENUM_STATION broadcasts
    for (i = 0; i < MAX_LISTEN_REQUESTS; ++i)
        {
        if (!_WNetReceiveDatagram(byBroadcastBuffers[i],
            RECEIVE_BUFFER_SIZE, byGroupNameNumber, hMainWnd))
            return -1;
        }
    }
else
    {
    WNetSetLastError(WN_NET_ERROR);
    return -1;
    }
}
// If called with empty name, see if we have a main
// name.  If so, use it.

if (lpStationName == NULL ||
   *((LPSTR) lpStationName) == '\0')
    {
    if (nMainNameIndex == (-1))
        {
        WNetSetLastError(WN_BAD_LOCALNAME);
        return -1;
        }
    lstrcpy(szMyName, WNetGetName(nMainNameIndex));
    }
```

```
    else
        lstrcpy(szMyName, lpStationName);
    // Pad name with spaces on the right.
    while (lstrlen(szMyName) < MAX_NETBIOS_NAMELEN)
        lstrcat(szMyName, " ");

    wNBReturnCode = NBAddName(szMyName, &byNameNumber);

    if (wNBReturnCode != NB_SUCCESS &&
        wNBReturnCode != NB_NAME_EXISTS_OK)
        {
        WNetSetLastError(MapNBToWinErr(wNBReturnCode));
        return -1;
        }

    ++nRegistrations;           // Bump usage count

    if (nMainNameIndex == (-1))
        nMainNameIndex = byNameNumber;

    if (nClients[byNameNumber] == 0)
        {
        // Post LISTENs and RECEIVE DATAGRAMs.
        for (i = 0; i < MAX_LISTEN_REQUESTS; ++i)
            {
            if (!_WNetListen(byNameNumber, hWnd))
                return -1;
            if (!_WNetReceiveDatagram(byDatagramBuffers[i],
                    RECEIVE_BUFFER_SIZE, byNameNumber, hWnd))
                return -1;
            }
        }
    ++nClients[byNameNumber];
    return (int) byNameNumber;
}

LOCAL BOOL IsNetBIOSInstalled()
{
    // This uses the algorithm outlined in the IBM
    // NetBIOS Application Development Guide, pg. 2-9.

    // First it checks to see if an INT 5CH handler has been
    // installed by testing to see if the vector contains a
    // NULL pointer.

    // If the INT 5CH vector is not NULL,
    // it issues a bogus NetBIOS command (0xFF), and checks
    // to see if this returns an appropriate NetBIOS error code.

    BOOL bNBInstalled;
    WORD wNBRetcode;
    NCB  ncbTest;

    // See if there's a non-zero INT 5CH vector
    _asm
```

```
        {
        PUSH BX
        PUSH ES
        MOV  AX, 0x355c
        INT  0x21
        MOV  AX, ES
        OR   AX, BX
        JZ   NBVector_Exit
        MOV  AX, 1
NBVector_Exit:
        POP  ES
        POP  BX
        MOV  bNBInstalled, AX
        }

    if (!bNBInstalled)
        return FALSE;

    // Issue bogus command 0xFF, should return NetBIOS error code.
    ncbTest.byCommand = 0xFF;
    ncbTest.lpCallback = NULL;
    wNBRetcode = NetBios(&ncbTest);

    // The return codes 0x40 to 0x4f mean "unusual network condition"
    //                   0x50 to 0xfe mean "adapter malfunction"
    // These mean that NetBIOS is there

    if ((wNBRetcode >= 0x40 && wNBRetcode <= 0x4f) ||
        (wNBRetcode >= 0x50 && wNBRetcode <= 0xfe))
        bNBInstalled = TRUE;
    else
        {
        switch (wNBRetcode)
            {
            // We may also see the error codes meaning that we
            // have issued an invalid NetBIOS command (NB_ERR_BAD_COMMAND,
            // #define'd as 3), or NB_ERR_BAD_ADAPTER, #define'd as 0x23
            case NB_ERR_BAD_COMMAND:
            case NB_ERR_BAD_ADAPTER:
               bNBInstalled = TRUE;
               break;
            default:
               // Any other value means NetBIOS is not there
               bNBInstalled = FALSE;
            }
        }
    return bNBInstalled;
}

int WINAPI WEP(int nParameter) // Windows exit procedure
{
    return 1;
}
```

Global Variables

Listing 3-6 is the file _WNETGLB.C, which contains global variables for the NetBIOS DLL.

```
/********
 *
 * Listing 3-6. _WNETGLB.C
 *
 * Copyright (c) 1992 Ralph P. Davis, All Rights Reserved
 *
 * Global variables needed by NetBIOS-specific routines
 *
 ********/

/*===== Includes =====*/

#include "wnetnb.h"

/*===== Global Variables =====*/

HINSTANCE hDLLInstance;
FARPROC   lpPostRoutine = NULL;
char      szStationName[MAX_NETBIOS_NAMELEN + 1] = "";
HWND      hMainWnd = NULL;
HWND      hNotifyWnd = NULL;
int       nMainNameIndex = -1;
BYTE      byNameNumber;
BYTE      byGroupNameNumber;
UINT      WMU_PACKET_RECEIVED = 0;
BOOL      bNameUnique[MAX_NAMES];
int       nRegistrations = 0;    // Number of client apps upstairs
int       nClients[MAX_NAMES];
BYTE      byDatagramBuffers[MAX_LISTEN_REQUESTS]
                           [RECEIVE_BUFFER_SIZE];
BYTE      byBroadcastBuffers[MAX_LISTEN_REQUESTS]
                            [RECEIVE_BUFFER_SIZE];
```

NetBIOS Name-Related Commands

Listing 3-7 shows the file _WNETNAM.C, which includes the routines NBAddName(), NBAddGroupName(), and NBDeleteName(). NBAddName() keeps track of which names it succeeds in adding. When NetBIOS is implemented on top of a system that has named stations, such as MS-NET or LAN Manager, we may get a request to use a name which is already registered. If this is the case, we do not want to delete it at termination; doing so could destroy the station's ability to communicate. Thus, we use the global array *bNameUnique* to remember which names we created.

We use the no-wait version of the name commands, and pass a NULL pointer for the post routine. We then enter a PeekMessage() loop testing the *byCompletionCode* field of the NCB. However, we cannot include a timeout, because NetBIOS won't let us cancel any of the name commands. Thus, the command will still be outstanding if we do timeout, and freeing the memory will cause a general protection interrupt. We therefore call the function WaitForNBNameCommand(). It does a PeekMessage() loop until the command completes, as it eventually will, if NetBIOS is installed (and we have already verified that it is).

```c
/********
 *
 * Listing 3-7. _WNETNAM.C
 *
 * Copyright (c) 1992 Ralph P. Davis, All Rights Reserved
 *
 ********/

/*===== Includes =====*/

#include "wnetnb.h"
#include <string.h>

/*===== LOCAL Functions =====*/

static void NEAR WaitForNBNameCommand(LPNCB lpNCB);

/*===== Function Definitions =====*/
WORD WINAPI NBAddName(LPSTR lpName, LPBYTE lpNameNumber)
{
    LPNCB   lpNCB;
    WORD    wNBReturnCode;
    HCURSOR hOldCursor;

    lpNCB = (LPNCB) AllocPageLockedBuffer(sizeof (NCB));

    if (lpNCB == NULL)
        {
        WNetSetLastError(WN_OUT_OF_MEMORY);
        return NB_ERR_NO_RESOURCE;
        }
    _fmemset(lpNCB->cLocalName, ' ',
        sizeof (lpNCB->cLocalName));
    _fmemcpy(lpNCB->cLocalName, lpName, lstrlen(lpName));

    // Add station name and save name number assigned.
    lpNCB->byAdapterNumber = 0;
    lpNCB->lpCallback      = NULL;
    lpNCB->byCommand       = NB_ADD_NAME_NO_WAIT;

    // Put up hourglass cursor--this is a real snorer!
    hOldCursor = SetCursor(LoadCursor(NULL, IDC_WAIT));
    ShowCursor(TRUE);

    NetBios(lpNCB);

    WaitForNBNameCommand(lpNCB);

    SetCursor(hOldCursor);
    ShowCursor(TRUE);

    wNBReturnCode = (WORD) lpNCB->byCompletionCode;

    if (wNBReturnCode == NB_SUCCESS ||
```

```
          wNBReturnCode == NB_NAME_EXISTS_OK)
      {
      *lpNameNumber = lpNCB->byNameNumber;
      if (wNBReturnCode == NB_SUCCESS)
         WNetSetName(*lpNameNumber, lpName, MAX_NETBIOS_NAMELEN);

      if (wNBReturnCode == NB_SUCCESS)
         // New name--we'll delete it later.
         bNameUnique[*lpNameNumber] = TRUE;
      }

   FreePageLockedBuffer(lpNCB);
   return wNBReturnCode;
}

WORD WINAPI NBAddGroupName(LPSTR lpGroupName,
                                       LPBYTE lpGroupNameNumber)
{
   LPNCB lpNCB;
   WORD wNBReturnCode;
   HCURSOR hOldCursor;
   lpNCB =
      (LPNCB) AllocPageLockedBuffer(sizeof (NCB));

   if (lpNCB == NULL)
      {
      WNetSetLastError(WN_OUT_OF_MEMORY);
      return NB_ERR_NO_RESOURCE;
      }

   // Add group name, using no-wait option.

   lpNCB->byAdapterNumber = 0;
   lpNCB->lpCallback      = NULL;
   lpNCB->byCommand       = NB_ADD_GROUP_NO_WAIT;
   lpNCB->lpData          = NULL;
   lpNCB->wDataLength     = 0;

   _fmemset(lpNCB->cLocalName, ' ',
      sizeof (lpNCB->cLocalName));
   _fmemcpy(lpNCB->cLocalName, lpGroupName,
         lstrlen(lpGroupName));

   hOldCursor = SetCursor(LoadCursor(NULL, IDC_WAIT));
   ShowCursor(TRUE);

   NetBios((LPNCB) lpNCB);

   WaitForNBNameCommand(lpNCB);

   SetCursor(hOldCursor);
   ShowCursor(TRUE);
   wNBReturnCode = (WORD) lpNCB->byCompletionCode;

   if (wNBReturnCode != NB_SUCCESS)
```

```
        {
        FreePageLockedBuffer(lpNCB);
        WNetSetLastError(MapNBToWinErr(wNBReturnCode));
        }
    else
        *lpGroupNameNumber = lpNCB->byNameNumber;

    return wNBReturnCode;
}

WORD WINAPI NBDropName(LPSTR lpName, int nNameNumber)
{
    LPNCB lpNCB;
    WORD  wNBReturnCode;

    lpNCB =
        (LPNCB) AllocPageLockedBuffer(sizeof (NCB));

    if (lpNCB == NULL)
        {
        WNetSetLastError(WN_OUT_OF_MEMORY);
        return NB_ERR_NO_RESOURCE;
        }

    lpNCB->byAdapterNumber = 0;
    lpNCB->lpCallback      = NULL;
    lpNCB->byCommand       = NB_DELETE_NAME;

    _fmemset(lpNCB->cLocalName, ' ', sizeof (lpNCB->cLocalName));
    _fmemcpy(lpNCB->cLocalName, lpName,
            lstrlen(lpName));

    NetBios(lpNCB);

    WaitForNBNameCommand(lpNCB);

    wNBReturnCode = (WORD) lpNCB->byCompletionCode;

    if (wNBReturnCode == NB_SUCCESS)
        {
        if (nNameNumber >= 0 && nNameNumber < MAX_NAMES)
            {
            bNameUnique[byNameNumber] = FALSE;
            WNetSetName(byNameNumber, NULL, 0);
            }
        }
    FreePageLockedBuffer(lpNCB);

    return wNBReturnCode;
}

static void NEAR WaitForNBNameCommand(LPNCB lpNCB)
{
    MSG msg;

    // Note that we can't time out here--if we get a time out,
```

```
// we can't cancel the command (NetBIOS won't let you
// cancel any of the name commands).

// However, we also won't be able to free the memory, because
// the command will still be outstanding.

while (lpNCB->byCompletionCode == NB_COMMAND_PENDING)
   {
   while (MyPeekMessage(&msg, NULL, 0, 0, PM_REMOVE))
      {
      TranslateMessage(&msg);
      DispatchMessage(&msg);
      }
   }

}
```

Session-Oriented Commands

The NetBIOS session commands are CALL, LISTEN, SEND, RECEIVE, RECEIVE ANY, and HANGUP. SESSION STATUS retrieves data on the state of a given session.

Establishing a Session—_WNetCall()
Listing 3-8 shows _WNETCAL.C, containing the function _WNetCall(). Under NetBIOS, this issues a CALL to establish a session with a partner station. In order for CALL to succeed, the desired partner has to have posted a LISTEN. If _WNetCall() is successful, it returns the NetBIOS local session number as the connection handle. This will be used for any future activity over this connection.

The CALL command requires that the *cLocalName* field be filled with the name of the calling station, and *cRemoteName* with the station being called. The caller's name is retrieved using the *nNameIndex* argument to the function. This will be the value originally returned by _WNetInit(). The *bySendTimeout* and *byReceiveTimeout* fields of the NCB are used by the CALL command to specify the maximum amount of time NetBIOS will wait before timing out a blocking receive and send, specified in 500 millisecond intervals. I specify a receive timeout of ten seconds, and a send timeout of zero. Specifying a non-zero send timeout is risky, because if a send command does time out, NetBIOS will drop the connection to the partner station. We do not use blocking sends and receives, anyway; I set these fields as a defensive measure, to make sure I don't make a mistake and end up with a permanently blocking operation.

If a connection is established, _WNetCall() calls _WNetReceive() to enable reception of asynchronous packets, then returns the NetBIOS local session number. Otherwise, it returns zero.

Notice that _WNetCall() uses a no-wait CALL command with no post routine. The caller needs to be able to test the function return value to determine whether a connection was established or not. Therefore, after posting the NCB, we go into a PeekMessage() loop for five seconds. At the end of this loop, if *byCompletionCode* is still NB_COM-MAND_PENDING (0xFF), we cancel the request.

```
/*******
*
* Listing 3-8. _WNETCAL.C
*
* Copyright (c) 1992 Ralph P. Davis, All Rights Reserved
*
*******/

/*===== Includes =====*/

#include "wnetnb.h"
#include <string.h>

/*===== Function Definitions =====*/
HCONNECTION WINAPI _WNetCall(int nNameIndex,
                            LPVOID lpTargetStation)
{
    HCONNECTION hConnection;
    LPNCB       lpNCB;
    DWORD       dwStartTime;
    MSG         msg;
    WORD        wNBReturnCode;

    lpNCB = (LPNCB) AllocPageLockedBuffer(sizeof (NCB));

    if (lpNCB == NULL)
        {
        WNetSetLastError(WN_OUT_OF_MEMORY);
        return 0;
        }

    if (nNameIndex == (-1))
        nNameIndex = nMainNameIndex;
    _fmemcpy(lpNCB->cLocalName, WNetGetName(nNameIndex),
        WNetGetNameLength(nNameIndex));
    _fmemset(lpNCB->cRemoteName, ' ',
        sizeof (lpNCB->cRemoteName));
    _fmemcpy(lpNCB->cRemoteName, lpTargetStation,
        lstrlen(lpTargetStation));

    // Set receive timeout value to 10 seconds
    // No send timeout
    lpNCB->bySendTimeout = 0;
    lpNCB->byReceiveTimeout = 20;
    lpNCB->byAdapterNumber = 0;
    lpNCB->byCommand = NB_CALL_NO_WAIT;
    LpNCB->LpCallback=NULL;

    NetBios(lpNCB);

    dwStartTime = GetCurrentTime();

    while ((lpNCB->byCompletionCode == NB_COMMAND_PENDING) &&
           ((GetCurrentTime() - dwStartTime) < 5000L))
        {
        while (MyPeekMessage(&msg, NULL, 0, 0, PM_REMOVE))
            {
            TranslateMessage(&msg);
```

```
            DispatchMessage(&msg);
            }
        }

    wNBReturnCode = (WORD) lpNCB->byCompletionCode;

    if (wNBReturnCode == NB_COMMAND_PENDING)
        {
        // Timed out
        NBCancel(lpNCB);
        wNBReturnCode = NB_ERR_TIMEOUT;
        }

    if (wNBReturnCode == NB_SUCCESS)
        {
        int i;
        LPBYTE lpBuffer;

        hConnection = (HCONNECTION) lpNCB->byLocalSession;
        // Have to post some asynchronous receives

        for (i = 0; i < MAX_LISTEN_REQUESTS; ++i)
            {
            lpBuffer = (LPBYTE) AllocPageLockedBuffer(
                MAX_SEND_BUFFER_SIZE);
            if (lpBuffer != NULL)
                _WNetReceive(
                    hConnection,
                    lpBuffer, MAX_SEND_BUFFER_SIZE,
                    NONBLOCKING, 0, hMainWnd);
            }
        }
    else
        hConnection = 0;

    FreePageLockedBuffer(lpNCB);
    return hConnection;
}
```

Listening for Connections—_WNetListen()   _WNetListen() waits for calls to come in from other stations. The LISTEN NCB uses the *cRemoteName* field to specify the station or stations from which it will accept connection requests. Setting the first byte to '*', as we do, says that you will accept connections from any station.

   _WNetListen() is implemented using a non-blocking LISTEN, so when a call comes in, the post routine (shown in Listing 3-9) wakes up and passes the NCB to NBWndProc(). NBWndProc() then calls _WNetReceive() so the station can receive transmissions from the calling station. Finally, it reissues the LISTEN NCB to handle connection requests from other clients.

   Both the calling and the listening station must call _WNetReceive() to receive data asynchronously from the other station. Once a connection is established, neither side is active or passive; both stations play either role.

Although _WNetListen() allocates memory for the NCB, it does not free it. With all asynchronous operations that we develop here and in subsequent chapters, the memory will be released by the notification procedure—in this case, NBWndProc(). As long as an operation completes successfully, NBWndProc() just recycles it. Eventually, however, the command will report a fatal error, either because a connection terminates or the user shuts down the DLL (in other words, the error is perfectly normal). At this point, NBWndProc() frees the memory.

```c
/********
*
* Listing 3-9. _WNETLIS.C
*
* Copyright (c) 1992 Ralph P. Davis, All Rights Reserved
*
********/

/*===== Includes =====*/

#include "wnetnb.h"
#include <string.h>


/*===== Function Definitions =====*/
BOOL WINAPI _WNetListen(int nNameIndex, HWND hWnd)
{
   LPXNCB lpXNCB;
   WORD   wNBReturnCode;

   lpXNCB = (LPXNCB) AllocPageLockedBuffer(sizeof (XNCB));

   if (lpXNCB == NULL)
      {
      WNetSetLastError(WN_OUT_OF_MEMORY);
      return FALSE;
      }
   if (nNameIndex == (-1))
      nNameIndex = nMainNameIndex;
   lpXNCB->ncbBase.cRemoteName[0] = '*';  // Anybody

   _fmemcpy(lpXNCB->ncbBase.cLocalName,
      WNetGetName(nNameIndex),
      WNetGetNameLength(nNameIndex));
   lpXNCB->hWnd = hWnd;

   lpXNCB->ncbBase.byCommand = NB_LISTEN_NO_WAIT;
   lpXNCB->ncbBase.byReceiveTimeout = 20;
   lpXNCB->ncbBase.bySendTimeout = 0;
   lpXNCB->ncbBase.lpCallback = lpPostRoutine;
   lpXNCB->ncbBase.byAdapterNumber = 0;
   lpXNCB->wOriginalDataLength = 0;
   if ((wNBReturnCode = NetBios((LPNCB) lpXNCB)) == NB_SUCCESS)
      return TRUE;
   else
```

```
     {
     WNetSetLastError(MapNBToWinErr(wNBReturnCode));
     FreePageLockedBuffer(lpXNCB);
     return FALSE;
     }
  }
```

Sending a Packet—_WNetSend()   The routine _WNetSend() shown in Listing 3-10 transmits a packet over a previously established connection. The largest size buffer that you can send with one NetBIOS SEND is 65,535 bytes. This is already a high level of abstraction compared to a protocol like IPX/SPX, where packets are limited to around 540 bytes. _WNetSend() allows you to pass a buffer size expressed as a DWORD, and issues multiple sends to transmit all the data. We limit any individual send to 8,191 bytes so we do not have to allocate 64K RECEIVE buffers. If there is more data than this, we tell the receiving station that we are passing 8,192 bytes as a flag that there is more data to come.

Because we allow the length of the input buffer to be described by a DWORD, we have to use a _huge pointer (here, *lpTemp*) to step through it. Otherwise, when we would overflow a segment boundary, we will wrap back around to the beginning of the buffer. The same is true in _WNetReceive(), which follows _WNetSend().

```
/********
*
* Listing 3-10. _WNETSND.C
*
* Copyright (c) 1992 Ralph P. Davis, All Rights Reserved
*
********/

/*===== Includes =====*/

#include "wnetnb.h"

/*===== Function Definitions =====*/

BOOL WINAPI _WNetSend(HCONNECTION hConnection, LPVOID lpData,
                          DWORD dwDataLength)
{
   BYTE _huge *lpTemp;
   LPNCB  lpNCB;
   WORD   wNBReturnCode;
   DWORD  dwStartTime;
   MSG    msg;
   BOOL   bReturnCode = TRUE;

   lpNCB = (LPNCB) AllocPageLockedBuffer(sizeof (NCB));

   if (lpNCB == NULL)
      {
      WNetSetLastError(WN_OUT_OF_MEMORY);
      return FALSE;
      }
```

```
lpNCB->byLocalSession = (BYTE) hConnection;
lpNCB->byCommand = NB_SEND_NO_WAIT;
lpNCB->lpCallback = NULL;
lpNCB->byAdapterNumber = 0;

lpTemp = (BYTE _huge *) lpData;
do
    {
    lpNCB->lpData = lpTemp;

    // We won't transmit any more than MAX_SEND_BUFFER_SIZE - 1 bytes
    // If we have more than that, we'll lie and say we're transmitting
    // MAX_SEND_BUFFER_SIZE,
    // as a signal to the receiver that there is more to
    // this message.

    // This will actually cause the boundary byte to be transmitted
    // twice--the receiver will ignore it on the first reception.

    // Unlike NetWare and VINES, NetBIOS does not allow us to
    // pass protocol information (like end-of-message flags).

    if (dwDataLength > (MAX_SEND_BUFFER_SIZE - 1))
        {
        lpNCB->wDataLength = MAX_SEND_BUFFER_SIZE;
        }
    else
        {
        lpNCB->wDataLength = (WORD) dwDataLength;
        }

    NetBios(lpNCB);

    dwStartTime = GetCurrentTime();

    while ((lpNCB->byCompletionCode == NB_COMMAND_PENDING) &&
           ((GetCurrentTime() - dwStartTime) < 5000L))
        {
        while (MyPeekMessage(&msg, NULL, 0, 0, PM_REMOVE))
            {
            TranslateMessage(&msg);
            DispatchMessage(&msg);
            }
        }

    wNBReturnCode = (WORD) lpNCB->byCompletionCode;

    if (wNBReturnCode == NB_COMMAND_PENDING)
        {
        // Timed out
        NBCancel(lpNCB);
        wNBReturnCode = NB_ERR_TIMEOUT;
        }

    if (wNBReturnCode != NB_SUCCESS)
```

```
            {
            WNetSetLastError(MapNBToWinErr(wNBReturnCode));
            bReturnCode = FALSE;
            break;
            }
        if (dwDataLength >= (MAX_SEND_BUFFER_SIZE - 1))
            {
            dwDataLength -= ((DWORD) (MAX_SEND_BUFFER_SIZE - 1));
            lpTemp += ((DWORD) (MAX_SEND_BUFFER_SIZE - 1));
            }
        else
            dwDataLength = 0L;
        }
    while (dwDataLength > 0L);

    FreePageLockedBuffer(lpNCB);
    return bReturnCode;
}
```

Receiving Packets—_WNetReceive()   Listing 3-11, _WNETRCV.C, shows the function _WNetReceive(), which accepts packets sent by _WNetSend(). _WNetReceive() allows both blocking and non-blocking requests. It limits non-blocking requests to 8192 bytes, because this is the most _WNetSend() will transmit at any one time. For blocking requests larger than that, it steps through the buffer using a _huge pointer (*lpTemp*) and receives data into it. We cannot easily do this with a non-blocking receive, because there is no guarantee that the different portions of the buffer will be filled from bottom to top. We could end up with blocks 1, 2, 3, and 4 of the buffer being filled with blocks 1, 3, 4, and 2 of the message.

The life cycle of a non-blocking receive (or receive datagram) request is as follows:

1. _WNetReceive() issues a NetBIOS no-wait RECEIVE.

2. Sometime later, a packet arrives; NetBIOSPostRoutine(), the assembler routine shown in Listing 3-2, gets called.

3. NetBIOSPostRoutine() posts a WMU_PACKET_RECEIVED to the notification window. This activates NBWndProc() in Listing 3-3.

4. NBWndProc() extracts the incoming data from the packet, and the NetBIOS session number from the NCB. It then posts a WMU_PACKET_RECEIVED message to the window that originally called _WNetReceive(), as indicated by the *hWnd* argument to the function. *wParam* reports the session number, and *lParam* points to the data.

5. If no fatal error has occurred, NBWndProc() passes the NCB back to NetBIOS by calling the NetBios() function shown in Listing 3-4. This reissues the NetBIOS no-wait RECEIVE from step 1.

```
/*******
*
* Listing 3-11. _WNETRCV.C
*
* Copyright (c) 1992 Ralph P. Davis, All Rights Reserved
```

"localhost", so that we can retrieve the network address of the current station. A NULL pointer will also be set to "localhost".

Next we open two sockets, one for datagrams and one to listen for connections. Each of these will have a different local address, because we have to use a different port for datagram and connection-oriented communications. Our name table [the one accessed by the WNetGetName() function] has 256 entries; we therefore have room for 128 clients. In practice, we probably won't be able to service this many. The maximum number of sockets we can open is defined by the constant FD_SETSIZE, which defaults to 64. (It may, however, vary from one vendor's implementation to another's. It is returned in the *iMaxSockets* fields of the WSADATA structure when you call WSAStartup().)

We call the routine _WNetGetHostAddress() to get the correct Internet address and port numbers to bind the sockets to. It appears in Listing 6-11. After the binding, we call _WNetReceiveDatagram() to make the UDP socket ready for incoming data, and _WNetListen() so the TCP socket can accept incoming calls.

```
/********
 *
 Listing 6-1. _WNETINI.C
 *
 * Copyright (c) 1992 Ralph P. Davis, All Rights Reserved
 *
 ********/

/*===== Includes =====*/

#include "wnettcp.h"     // Includes WINSOCK.H
                         // See Listing 6-13

/*===== Function Definitions =====*/

int WINAPI LibMain(HINSTANCE hInstance,
                   WORD wDataSeg,
                   WORD cbHeapSize,
                   LPSTR lpszCmdLine)
{
   WNDCLASS wndClass;

   hDLLInstance = hInstance;
   wndClass.lpszClassName = "WinSockNotify";
   wndClass.lpfnWndProc = WinSockWndProc;
   wndClass.hInstance   = hInstance;
   wndClass.hCursor     = NULL;
   wndClass.hIcon       = NULL;
   wndClass.hbrBackground = NULL;
   wndClass.lpszMenuName = NULL;
   wndClass.style  = 0;
   wndClass.cbClsExtra = 0;
   wndClass.cbWndExtra = 0;

   if (!RegisterClass(&wndClass))
      return 0;
```

```
    hNotifyWnd = CreateWindow("WinSockNotify",
                              "Windows Sockets Window",
                              WS_OVERLAPPEDWINDOW,
                              CW_USEDEFAULT,
                              CW_USEDEFAULT,
                              CW_USEDEFAULT,
                              CW_USEDEFAULT,
                              NULL,
                              NULL,
                              hInstance,
                              NULL);

    return (hNotifyWnd != NULL);
}

int WINAPI _WNetInit(HWND hWnd, LPVOID lpStationName)
{
    SOCKADDR sa;

    WNetSetLastError(WN_SUCCESS);

    if (nMainNameIndex == (-1))  // Strictly a flag
        {
        nMainNameIndex = WNET_UDP_NAME;

        // Call WSAStartup(), ask for version 1.0
        if (WSAStartup(0x0001, &WSAData) != 0)
            return -1;
        hMainWnd = FindWindow("WNETMASTER", NULL);
        if (hMainWnd == NULL || hWnd != hMainWnd)
            {
            // Either WNETMASTER not installed yet, or somebody
            // else got here first.
            WNetSetLastError(WN_NOT_SUPPORTED);
            return -1;
            }
        WMU_PACKET_RECEIVED = RegisterWindowMessage("WMU_PACKET_RECEIVED");

        lpStationName = "localhost"; // For first-time initialization
        }
    else if (lpStationName == NULL || *((LPBYTE) lpStationName) == '\0')
        lpStationName = "localhost";

    if (nRegistrations == (MAX_WSA_NAMES - 1))
        {
        // Can't add any more names
        ++nRegistrations;  // Will be decremented by _WNetShutdown()
        WNetSetLastError(WN_ACCESS_DENIED);
        return -1;
        }
    // Open a UDP socket
    TCPClients[nRegistrations].sUDP =
        socket(PF_INET, SOCK_DGRAM, IPPROTO_UDP);
    if (TCPClients[nRegistrations].sUDP == INVALID_SOCKET)
```

```
        {
        WNetSetLastError(WN_NET_ERROR);
        return -1;
        }

    // Get UDP name and bind the socket to it
    if (_WNetGetHostAddress(lpStationName, "udp", &sa))
        WNetSetName(nRegistrations * 2, (LPBYTE) &sa,
            sizeof (SOCKADDR));
    else
        {
        WNetSetLastError(WN_BAD_LOCALNAME);
        return -1;
        }
    if (bind(TCPClients[nRegistrations].sUDP, &sa, sizeof (SOCKADDR)) != 0)
        {
        WNetSetLastError(WN_NET_ERROR);
        return -1;
        }

    if (!_WNetReceiveDatagram(NULL, 0, nRegistrations, hNotifyWnd))
        return -1;

    // Open a TCP socket
    TCPClients[nRegistrations].sTCP =
        socket(PF_INET, SOCK_STREAM, IPPROTO_TCP);
    if (TCPClients[nRegistrations].sTCP == INVALID_SOCKET)
        {
        WNetSetLastError(WN_NET_ERROR);
        return -1;
        }

    if (_WNetGetHostAddress(lpStationName, "tcp", &sa))
        WNetSetName((nRegistrations * 2) + 1, (LPBYTE) &sa,
            sizeof (SOCKADDR));
    else
        {
        WNetSetLastError(WN_BAD_LOCALNAME);
        return -1;
        }

    if (bind(TCPClients[nRegistrations].sTCP, &sa, sizeof (SOCKADDR)) != 0)
        {
        WNetSetLastError(WN_NET_ERROR);
        return -1;
        }

    if (_WNetListen(nRegistrations, hNotifyWnd))
        return -1;

    return nRegistrations++;
}

int WINAPI WEP(int nParameter)
```

```
{
    return 1;
}
```

_WNetReceiveDatagram() and _WNetListen()

_WNetReceiveDatagram() is very simple; it just calls WSAAsyncSelect() to request notification of FD_READ events. Note that it does not post any read or listen requests:

```
/********
*
Listing 6-2. _WNETRDG.C
*
* Copyright (c) 1992 Ralph P. Davis, All Rights Reserved
*
********/

/*===== Includes =====*/

#include "wnettcp.h"

/*===== Function Definitions =====*/

BOOL WINAPI _WNetReceiveDatagram(LPVOID lpBuffer,
                                 WORD wBufferSize,
                                 int  nNameIndex,
                                 HWND hWnd)
{
    // Buffer argument is irrelevant.  The WinSock DLL does
    // all the buffering for us.

    // The UDP socket is ready to start accepting datagrams
    // Force into non-blocking mode and ask for incoming data
    // notification

    if (WSAAsyncSelect(TCPClients[nNameIndex].sUDP, hWnd,
        WMU_PACKET_RECEIVED, FD_READ) != 0)
        {
        WNetSetLastError(WN_NET_ERROR);
        return FALSE;
        }
    return TRUE;
}
```

_WNetListen() is only slightly more complex. The first thing it does is make sure the socket is not already in the listening state. It does this by calling the function getsockopt():

```
int WINAPI getsockopt(SOCKET s, int level, int optname,
                      char FAR *optval, int FAR *optlen);
```

getsockopt() retrieves information on the current state and configuration of a socket. The *level* argument must be SOL_SOCKET. *optname* can be a number of things; the value we are interested in is SO_ACCEPTCONN. *optval* and *optlen* are output variables; when the call returns, *optval* will contain the setting, and *optlen* will contain its length.

SO_ACCEPTCONN returns a BOOL, with TRUE indicating that the socket is already in the listening state.

Next, _WNetListen() initializes the client's TCPCLIENT structure by allocating memory for an array of FD_SETSIZE sockets, and setting the socket count to zero. It then calls WSAAsyncSelect() to request notification of FD_ACCEPT events. Finally, it calls listen() to ready the TCP socket for incoming connection requests.

```
/********
*
Listing 6-3. _WNETLIS.C
*
* Copyright (c) 1992 Ralph P. Davis, All Rights Reserved
*
********/

/*===== Includes =====*/

#include "wnettcp.h"

/*===== Function Definitions =====*/
BOOL WINAPI _WNetListen(int nNameIndex, HWND hWnd)
{
   BOOL bListening;
   int  nSize = sizeof (BOOL);

   if ((getsockopt(TCPClients[nNameIndex].sUDP, SOL_SOCKET,
      SO_ACCEPTCONN, (char FAR *) &bListening, &nSize) == 0) && bListening)
      {
      // Socket is already in listening state, disregard
      return TRUE;
      }
   TCPClients[nNameIndex].nAccepts = 0;

   // FD_SETSIZE is the maximum number of sockets that can be
   // open, period.
   TCPClients[nNameIndex].lpSockets =
      (SOCKET FAR *) GlobalAllocPtr(GHND, FD_SETSIZE * sizeof (SOCKET));

   if (TCPClients[nNameIndex].lpSockets == NULL)
      {
      WNetSetLastError(WN_OUT_OF_MEMORY);
      return FALSE;
      }

   // Set the TCP socket into non-blocking mode and
   // ask for FD_ACCEPT notification
   if (WSAAsyncSelect(TCPClients[nNameIndex].sTCP, hWnd,
      WMU_PACKET_RECEIVED, FD_ACCEPT) != 0)
      {
      WNetSetLastError(WN_NET_ERROR);
      return FALSE;
      }
```

```
    // Set him listening
    return (listen(TCPClients[nNameIndex].sTCP, MAX_LISTEN_REQUESTS) == 0);
}
```

_WNetCall()

To initiate a conversation, _WNetCall() calls the Windows Sockets routine connect(). It must first retrieve the network address of the target station. Berkeley Sockets uses human-readable names to refer to stations and services. The routines gethostbyname() and get-servbyname() convert the human-readable forms into their binary Internet addresses and port numbers, which are required for Windows Sockets function calls.

Next, it opens a new TCP socket, then promptly calls connect(). "Promptly" means specifically that it does not bind the socket to the local machine's address, and it does not force the socket into non-blocking mode. It is not necessary to bind the socket to a local address; the Windows Sockets DLL will assign a unique address if no binding was previously performed. We can retrieve it by calling getsockname(), but we don't need it.

If the socket is opened successfully, and the connect() call succeeds, we remember the new socket number in the *lpSockets* array of the *TCPClients* table. Now, we set the socket into non-blocking mode by calling WSAAsyncSelect(). At this point, we are interested in incoming data, so the significant events are FD_READ, FD_OOB, and FD_CLOSE. (We look for the socket to be closed so we can remove it from the table.)

_WNetCall() returns the socket number as the value of the function. Unlike the other APIs we have looked at, Windows Sockets have no concept of a connection number. Because a socket used to send and receive data is only used for that purpose, the socket number alone serves to uniquely identify the connection. Thus, we use it as the *hConnection* argument to all our subsequent connection-oriented functions [_WNetSend(), _WNetReceive(), and _WNetHangup()].

```
/********
*
Listing 6-4. _WNETCAL.C
*
* Copyright (c) 1992 Ralph P. Davis, All Rights Reserved
*
********/

/*===== Includes =====*/

#include "wnettcp.h"

/*===== Function Definitions =====*/

HCONNECTION WINAPI _WNetCall(int nNameIndex,
                            LPVOID lpTargetStation)
{
    HCONNECTION hConnection;
    SOCKADDR RemoteAddress;
    SOCKET   s;

    if (_WNetGetHostAddress(lpTargetStation, "tcp", &RemoteAddress) != 0)
        {
        WNetSetLastError(WN_BAD_NETNAME);
```

```
   return 0;
   }

// Open a new socket
s = socket(PF_INET, SOCK_STREAM, IPPROTO_TCP);
if (s == INVALID_SOCKET)
   {
   WNetSetLastError(WN_NET_ERROR);
   return 0;
   }
// Don't need to bind the socket

if (connect(s, &RemoteAddress, sizeof (SOCKADDR)) == 0)
   {
   AddToSocketList(nNameIndex, s);
   // Ask to be notified of FD_READ, FD_OOB, and FD_CLOSE events
   WSAAsyncSelect(s, TCPClients[nNameIndex].hWnd, WMU_PACKET_RECEIVED,
      FD_READ | FD_OOB | FD_CLOSE);
   hConnection = (HCONNECTION) s;
   }
else
   {
   WNetSetLastError(WN_NET_ERROR);
   closesocket(s);
   hConnection = 0;
   }
return hConnection;
}
```

Sending and Receiving Data Over Connections

Having initialized the sending and receiving sides, we can exchange data. The simplicity of the source code stands out here especially, because we do not have to allocate memory for incoming buffers. All the buffering is handled behind the scenes by WINSOCK.DLL.

A connection-oriented send [_WNetSend()] offers only one complication, the need to step through the incoming buffer and transmit it with multiple sends if it is too big to send all at once. The send() and sendto() functions use an int variable to describe the length of the buffer being transmitted. _WNetSend() uses a DWORD. Under Windows 3.1, if we are sending more than 65,535 bytes, we have to do it in multiple operations. Under Windows NT, an int and a DWORD are the same size. In WNETTCP.H, shown in Listing 6-13, you will see that I have defined the maximum buffer size (RECEIVE-_BUFFER_SIZE) so that it depends on the size of an int.

If _WNetReceive() gets a request for a blocking receive, we need to force the connection temporarily into blocking mode by calling ioctlsocket(); otherwise, we will receive an asynchronous notification when the data arrives. However, to prevent ourselves from blocking indefinitely, we call ioctlsocket() to make sure there is data available, and do not issue the recv() unless there is.

If no data becomes available within five seconds, we time out. If there is more data available than will fit in the buffer space provided, we call WNetSetLastError() to set the error code to WN_MORE_DATA, and return FALSE.

When we are done receiving the data, we put the socket back into non-blocking mode by calling WSAAsyncSelect().

A non-blocking receive does not need to post any actual receive request; it just calls WSAAsyncSelect().

```c
/********
*
Listing 6-5. _WNETSND.C
*
* Copyright (c) 1992 Ralph P. Davis, All Rights Reserved
*
********/

/*===== Includes =====*/

#include "wnettcp.h"

/*===== Function Definitions =====*/
BOOL WINAPI _WNetSend(HCONNECTION hConnection, LPVOID lpData,
                      DWORD dwDataLength)
{
    int nBytesToSend;
    BYTE _huge *lpSendData = (BYTE _huge *) lpData;

    while (dwDataLength > 0L)
        {
        if (dwDataLength > RECEIVE_BUFFER_SIZE)
            dwDataLength -= (nBytesToSend = RECEIVE_BUFFER_SIZE);
        else
            {
            nBytesToSend = (int) dwDataLength;
            dwDataLength = 0L;
            }

        if (send((SOCKET) hConnection, lpSendData, nBytesToSend, 0) != 0)
            {
            WNetSetLastError(WN_NET_ERROR);
            return FALSE;
            }
        lpSendData += nBytesToSend;
        }
    return TRUE;
}

/********
*
Listing 6-6. _WNETRCV.C
*
* Copyright (c) 1992 Ralph P. Davis, All Rights Reserved
*
********/

/*===== Includes =====*/
```

```c
#include "wnettcp.h"

/*===== Function Definitions =====*/

BOOL WINAPI _WNetReceive(HCONNECTION hConnection,
                         LPVOID lpData,
                         DWORD dwDataLength,
                         BLOCK_STATE BlockState,
                         int  nNameIndex,
                         HWND hWnd)
{
   u_long ulNonBlockState = OL;  // Not non-blocking
   u_long ulBytesToRead = OL;
   DWORD  dwStartTime;
   MSG    msg;
   DWORD  dwBytesRead = OL;
   BOOL   bReturnCode = TRUE;
   BOOL   bMoreData = FALSE;
   BYTE _huge *lpReceiveData = (BYTE _huge *) lpData;

   if (BlockState == NONBLOCKING)
      {
      // Request notification for FD_READ, FD_OOB, and FD_CLOSE
      if (WSAAsyncSelect((SOCKET) hConnection, hWnd, WMU_PACKET_RECEIVED,
              FD_READ | FD_OOB | FD_CLOSE) != O)
         {
         WNetSetLastError(WN_NET_ERROR);
         bReturnCode = FALSE;
         }
      }
   else
      {
      // A little more complicated for a blocking receive
      // We have to force the socket into blocking mode,
      // then see if there is any data waiting
      // We also do multiple reads to fill the buffer

      ioctlsocket((SOCKET) hConnection, FIONBIO, &ulNonBlockState);

      dwStartTime = GetCurrentTime();

      // See if there's anything to read--loop for five seconds
      while ((GetCurrentTime() - dwStartTime) < 5000L)
         {
         while (MyPeekMessage(&msg, NULL, O, O, PM_REMOVE))
            {
            TranslateMessage(&msg);
            DispatchMessage(&msg);
            }
         ioctlsocket((SOCKET) hConnection, FIONREAD, &ulBytesToRead);
         while (ulBytesToRead > OL)
            {
            if ((ulBytesToRead + dwBytesRead) > dwDataLength)
               {
```

```
                    // Not enough buffer space
                    bMoreData = TRUE;  // Otherwise, we may never read this
                                       // data
                    ulBytesToRead = (dwDataLength - dwBytesRead);
                    }
                if (recv((SOCKET) hConnection, &lpReceiveData[dwBytesRead],
                    (int) ulBytesToRead, 0) != 0)
                    {
                    bReturnCode = FALSE;
                    break;
                    }
                if (ulBytesToRead == dwDataLength)
                    break;
                dwBytesRead += ulBytesToRead;
                ioctlsocket((SOCKET) hConnection, FIONREAD, &ulBytesToRead);
                }
            }
        // Set the socket back into non-blocking mode
        if (WSAAsyncSelect((SOCKET) hConnection, hWnd, WMU_PACKET_RECEIVED,
                FD_READ | FD_OOB | FD_CLOSE) != 0)
            {
            WNetSetLastError(WN_NET_ERROR);
            bReturnCode = FALSE;
            }
        }
    if (bMoreData)
        {
        WNetSetLastError(WN_MORE_DATA);  // Set flag to say, there's more
                                         // here
        bReturnCode = FALSE;
        }
    else if (!bReturnCode)
        WNetSetLastError(WN_NET_ERROR);

    return bReturnCode;
}
```

Sending and Receiving Datagrams

The exchange of datagrams is even simpler, because all datagram operations are non-blocking, and it is illegal to transmit more than one bufferful of information. When we called WSAStartup() at initialization, one of the items of information it returned was the maximum size of a datagram. This is the *iMaxUdpDg* field of the WSADATA structure. In _WNetSendDatagram(), we reject the request if the input buffer size exceeds this amount. It is a misuse of datagrams to send a single contiguous buffer as multiple datagrams. There is no guarantee that each piece of the buffer will be received in the same order in which it was sent, so the buffer may be reassembled incorrectly on the receiving station.

We also check to see if the request is for a broadcast, such as might be invoked by WNetEnumStations(), for example. If it is, we use the special destination address INADDR_BROADCAST, and include the port number corresponding to the WNET service using the UDP protocol. We also call setsockopt() to make sure the socket is capable of handling broadcast requests. It is the inverse of getsockopt():

```
int WINAPI setsockopt(SOCKET s, int level, int optname,
                      char FAR *optval, int optlen);
```

The arguments are the same as they are for getsockopt(). The only difference is that the last argument is strictly an input argument. In this case, the *optname* is set to SO_BROADCAST. It expects a boolean value at *optval*.

_WNetReceiveDatagram() is shown in Listing 6-2.

```
/********
*
Listing 6-7. _WNETSDG.C
*
* Copyright (c) 1992 Ralph P. Davis, All Rights Reserved
*
********/


/*===== Includes =====*/

#include "wnettcp.h"
#include <string.h>


/*===== Function Definitions =====*/

BOOL WINAPI _WNetSendDatagram(LPVOID lpTargetStation,
                              LPVOID lpData, WORD wDataLength,
                              int nNameIndex)
{
    SOCKADDR_IN sin;

    if (wDataLength > (WORD) WSAData.iMaxUdpDg)
        {
        WNetSetLastError(WN_NOT_SUPPORTED);
        return FALSE;
        }
    if (lstrcmp(lpTargetStation, WNET_DOMAIN) == 0)  // Broadcast?
        {
        BOOL bBroadcast = TRUE;

        _fmemcpy(&sin, WNetGetName(WNET_UDP_NAME * 2),
            sizeof (SOCKADDR_IN));
        sin.sin_addr.s_addr = INADDR_BROADCAST;
        setsockopt(TCPClients[nNameIndex].sUDP, SOL_SOCKET,
            SO_BROADCAST, (char FAR *) &bBroadcast, sizeof (BOOL));
        }
    else
        _fmemcpy(&sin, lpTargetStation, sizeof (sin));

    if (sendto(TCPClients[nNameIndex].sUDP, lpData, (int) wDataLength,
        0, (LPSOCKADDR) &sin, sizeof (sin)) != 0)
        {
        WNetSetLastError(WN_NET_ERROR);
        return FALSE;
```

```
    }
  return TRUE;
}
```

Termination

_WNetHangup() terminates a conversation by calling closesocket(). It does not need to do anything else. Remember that one of the events we asked to be notified about was FD_CLOSE. In response to this message, we remove the socket from the internal table. Either side can terminate the connection, though it is usually the client side that knows when the conversation is finished. When you are notified of an FD_CLOSE event, you do not need to acknowledge it; by this time, you are past the point of no return anyway.

```
/********
*
Listing 6-8. _WNETHGP.C
*
* Copyright (c) 1992 Ralph P. Davis, All Rights Reserved
*
********/

/*===== Includes =====*/

#include "wnettcp.h"

/*===== Function Definitions =====*/

void WINAPI _WNetHangup(HCONNECTION hConnection)
{
    closesocket((SOCKET) hConnection);
}
```

_WNetShutdown() closes down the DLL. It first closes the UDP and TCP sockets for the indicated client, then goes through the list of connected sockets and closes each one. It also cancels notification of all events on these sockets by calling WSAAsyncSelect() with a message number and event code of zero. This is important, because we are going to free the memory for the *lpSockets* list here. If there is an asynchronous notification of the FD_CLOSE event, we may try to access the memory after we have freed it.

If this is the last connected client (*nRegistrations* falls to a number less than or equal to zero), we also call WSACleanup() to break the connection to the Windows Sockets DLL.

```
/********
*
Listing 6-9. _WNETSHD.C
*
* Copyright (c) 1992 Ralph P. Davis, All Rights Reserved
*
********/

/*===== Includes =====*/

#include "wnettcp.h"
```

```
/*===== Function Definitions =====*/

void WINAPI _WNetShutdown(int nNameIndex)
{
    int i;

    // Close all our open sockets
    // These two guys will be removed from the TCPClients
    // table by the asynchronous notification of the FD_CLOSE event,
    // and this is OK.
    closesocket(TCPClients[nNameIndex].sUDP);
    closesocket(TCPClients[nNameIndex].sTCP);

    if (TCPClients[nNameIndex].lpSockets != NULL)
        {
        for (i = 0; i < TCPClients[nNameIndex].nAccepts; ++i)
            {
            // We first call WSAAsyncSelect() with the last two arguments
            // (the message number and the event code) set to zero.
            // This cancels notification for the socket.  We don't
            // want asynchronous stuff happening here, because if it is,
            // we can't release the memory for the lpSockets list.

            WSAAsyncSelect(TCPClients[nNameIndex].lpSockets[i],
                TCPClients[nNameIndex].hWnd, 0, 0L);
            closesocket(TCPClients[nNameIndex].lpSockets[i]);
            }
        GlobalFreePtr(TCPClients[nNameIndex].lpSockets);
        }

    if (--nRegistrations <= 0)
        {
        WSACleanup();      // Nos vemos al rato...
        DestroyWindow(hNotifyWnd);
        hNotifyWnd = NULL;
        hMainWnd = NULL;
        nMainNameIndex = -1;
        nRegistrations = 0;

        // Release memory in name table
        WNetClearAllNames();
        }
}
```

The Asynchronous Notification Handler--WinSockWndProc()
The notification handler is the engine that drives the Windows Sockets implementation of the network-dependent DLL. It responds to several events:

- FD_ACCEPT, telling us that another station wants to establish a connection
- FD_READ and FD_OOB, telling us that there is data to read
- FD_CLOSE, telling us that the socket is being closed—most likely because a connection is being terminated

The *wParam* identifies the socket that we passed to WSAAsyncSelect(). We use the WSAGETSELECTEVENT() and WSAGETSELECTERROR() macros to parse the *lParam*.

When the event is FD_ACCEPT, the original socket is the one we are listening on. Remember that in Berkeley Sockets, as opposed to the other protocols we have looked at, a listening socket never does anything but listen. The actual exchange of data uses a new socket created by the accept() function. We call accept() in response to the FD_ACCEPT notification. Ordinarily, this would block, but since we issue it following the FD_ACCEPT, we know it will not. If accept() is successful, we call the function FindNameOfSocket() to retrieve the client ID (name index) associated with the original socket. It appears in the source file _WNETMIS.C, shown in Listing 6-11. We then add it to the *lpSockets* list by calling AddToSocketList(), also in _WNETMIS.C, then call _WNetReceive() to post a non-blocking receive (see Listing 6-6). The only thing _WNetReceive() does is ask for notification of FD_READ, FD_OOB, and FD_CLOSE events.

If the event is FD_READ or FD_OOB, there is data to read, and ioctlsocket() tells us exactly how much data. So we allocate memory to retrieve the data, then call recvfrom(). recvfrom() works with both UDP and TCP sockets, so it doesn't matter if the FD_READ was triggered by an incoming datagram or a packet arriving on a connection. If the retrieve was successful, we post a WMU_PACKET_RECEIVED message to the original calling window. Because we have no control block to get information from, we have to look the window handle up in the *TCPClients* table, again by calling FindNameOfSocket(). This function returns the index into the table where it finds the socket passed in *wParam*.

Finally, an FD_CLOSE event requires only that we remove the socket from the *lpSockets* list. The function RemoveFromSocketList() does this (see Listing 6-11).

Listing 6-10 shows the file WSAWND.C. The routines AppendToPacket() and StopTrackingPacket() are the same as in Listing 3-3, and are not repeated here. Listing 6-11 presents _WNETMIS.C, which contains miscellaneous TCP/IP support functions.

```
/********
 *
 Listing 6-10. WSAWND.C
 *
 * Copyright (c) 1992 Ralph P. Davis, All Rights Reserved
 *
 ********/

/*===== Includes =====*/
#include "wnettcp.h"
#include <string.h>

/*===== LOCAL Functions =====*/

LPBYTE AppendToPacket(HCONNECTION hConnection, LPBYTE lpOldData,
                      DWORD dwTotalBytes);
void StopTrackingPacket(HCONNECTION hConnection);
void HandleAccept(SOCKET sListen, HWND hWnd);
void HandleRead(SOCKET s, WORD wEvent);
```

```
/*===== LOCAL Variables =====*/

static PACKET_TABLE PacketTable[CONCURRENT_CONNECTIONS] = {0};

/*===== Function Definitions =====*/

LRESULT CALLBACK WinSockWndProc(HWND hWnd, UINT uMessage, WPARAM wParam,
                                LPARAM lParam)
{
   WORD     wEvent, wError;
   int      nNameIndex;

   if (uMessage != WMU_PACKET_RECEIVED)
      return DefWindowProc(hWnd, uMessage, wParam, lParam);

   wError = WSAGETSELECTERROR(lParam);

   if (wError != 0)
      // Problem, can't do any more
      return 0L;

   wEvent = WSAGETSELECTEVENT(lParam);

   switch (wEvent)
      {
      case FD_ACCEPT:
         // Connection request has come in
         HandleAccept((SOCKET) wParam, hWnd);
         break;
      case FD_READ:
      case FD_OOB:
         HandleRead((SOCKET) wParam, wEvent);
         break;
      case FD_CLOSE:
         // Find socket and remove it
         nNameIndex = FindNameOfSocket((SOCKET) wParam);
         RemoveFromSocketList(nNameIndex, (SOCKET) wParam);
         break;
      default:
         break;
      }
   return 0L;
}

void HandleAccept(SOCKET sListen, HWND hWnd)
{
   int      nNameLen;
   SOCKET   s;
   SOCKADDR sa;
   int      nNameIndex;

   nNameLen = sizeof (SOCKADDR);
   s = accept(sListen, &sa, &nNameLen);

   if (s != INVALID_SOCKET)
```

```c
        {
        // Add him to the table
        nNameIndex = FindNameOfSocket(sListen);
        if (nNameIndex == -1)
            {
            closesocket(s);
            return;
            }
        if (AddToSocketList(nNameIndex, s) != 0)
            {
            closesocket(s);
            return;
            }
        if (!_WNetReceive((HCONNECTION) s, NULL, 0L, NONBLOCKING,
            nNameIndex, hWnd))
            {
            RemoveFromSocketList(nNameIndex, s);
            closesocket(s);
            }
        }
}

void HandleRead(SOCKET s, WORD wEvent)
{
    u_long   ulBytesToRead;
    LPBYTE   lpData;
    int      nNameIndex;

    // Data is available for reading
    // We'll use recvfrom(), because it will work with both
    // TCP and UDP sockets

    if (ioctlsocket(s, FIONREAD, &ulBytesToRead) == 0)
        {
        while (ulBytesToRead > 0L)
            {
            lpData = (LPBYTE) GlobalAllocPtr(GHND, ulBytesToRead);
            if (lpData == NULL)
                {
                WNetSetLastError(WN_OUT_OF_MEMORY);
                return;
                }
            if (recvfrom(s, lpData, (int) ulBytesToRead,
                (wEvent == FD_OOB ? MSG_OOB : 0), NULL, NULL) <= 0)
                {
                // Error
                WNetSetLastError(WN_NET_ERROR);
                GlobalFreePtr(lpData);
                return;
                }
            lpData = AppendToPacket((HCONNECTION) s,
                lpData, ulBytesToRead);
            if (ioctlsocket(s, FIONREAD, &ulBytesToRead) ==
```

```
                 SOCKET_ERROR)
              break;
         }
      StopTrackingPacket((HCONNECTION) s);
      nNameIndex = FindNameOfSocket(s);

      if (nNameIndex != -1)
         PostMessage(TCPClients[nNameIndex].hWnd, WMU_PACKET_RECEIVED,
            (WPARAM) s, (LPARAM) lpData);
      }
}

/********
*
* Listing 6-11. _WNETMIS.C
*
* Copyright (c) 1992 Ralph P. Davis, All Rights Reserved
*
* Contains miscellaneous TCP/IP support functions
*
********/

/*===== Includes =====*/

#include "wnettcp.h"
#include <string.h>

/*===== Function Definitions =====*/

// _WNetGetHostAddress() populates a SOCKADDR structure with the
// Internet address of the local machine, and the port number of
// our WNET process

int WINAPI _WNetGetHostAddress(LPSTR lpszHost, LPSTR lpszProto,
                               LPSOCKADDR lpAddr)
{
   LPHOSTENT lpHost;
   LPSERVENT lpServ;
   SOCKADDR_IN sin;

   lpHost = gethostbyname(lpszHost);
   if (lpHost != NULL)
      {
      sin.sin_family = PF_INET;
      _fmemcpy(&sin.sin_addr, lpHost->h_addr_list[0],
               lpHost->h_length);
      lpServ = getservbyname("wnet", lpszProto);
      if (lpServ != NULL)
         {
         sin.sin_port = lpServ->s_port;
         _fmemset(sin.sin_zero, '\0', sizeof (sin.sin_zero));
         _fmemcpy(lpAddr, &sin, sizeof (SOCKADDR));
         return TRUE;
         }
```

```
      }
   return FALSE;
}

// FindNameOfSocket() returns the index of a given socket number
// into the table of applications that we are servicing.
// This corresponds to the name index returned
// by WNetInit()

int PASCAL FindNameOfSocket(SOCKET s)
{
   int i, j;

   for (i = 0; i < MAX_WSA_NAMES; ++i)
      {
      if (TCPClients[i].sUDP == s || TCPClients[i].sTCP == s)
         return i;
      else
         {
         for (j = 0; j < TCPClients[i].nAccepts; ++j)
            {
            if (TCPClients[i].lpSockets[j] == s)
               return i;
            }
         }
      }
   return -1;
}

// AddToSocketList() puts a new socket number into the list of
// sockets for a given client application (identified by
// nNameIndex)

int PASCAL AddToSocketList(int nNameIndex, SOCKET s)
{
   if (TCPClients[nNameIndex].nAccepts == (FD_SETSIZE - 1))
      return -1;

   TCPClients[nNameIndex].lpSockets[TCPClients[nNameIndex].nAccepts++] = s;
   return 0;
}

// RemoveFromSocketList() pulls a socket from the client table
// The client is identified by nNameIndex

void PASCAL RemoveFromSocketList(int nNameIndex, SOCKET s)
{
   int i, nTop;

   if (TCPClients[nNameIndex].sUDP == s)
      {
      TCPClients[nNameIndex].sUDP = 0;
      return;
      }
   if (TCPClients[nNameIndex].sTCP == s)
```

```
        {
        TCPClients[nNameIndex].sTCP = 0;
        return;
        }
    nTop = TCPClients[nNameIndex].nAccepts;
    for (i = 0; i < nTop; ++i)
        {
        if (TCPClients[nNameIndex].lpSockets[i] == s)
            {
            TCPClients[nNameIndex].lpSockets[i] = 0;
            if (i < (nTop - 1))
                // Bring down the top guy
                {
                TCPClients[nNameIndex].lpSockets[i] =
                    TCPClients[nNameIndex].lpSockets[nTop - 1];
                }
            --TCPClients[nNameIndex].nAccepts;
            }
        }
}
```

Additional Source Listings

The final listings are _WNETGLB.C, which defines global variables; WNETTCP.H, the header file; and WNETTCP.DEF, the module definition file.

```
/********
*
Listing 6-12. _WNETGLB.C
*
* Copyright (c) 1992 Ralph P. Davis, All Rights Reserved
*
********/


/*===== Includes =====*/

#include "wnettcp.h"


/*===== Global Variables =====*/

HWND        hNotifyWnd = NULL;
HWND        hMainWnd = NULL;
int         nMainNameIndex = -1;
HINSTANCE   hDLLInstance;
UINT        WMU_PACKET_RECEIVED = 0;
TCPCLIENTS  TCPClients[MAX_WSA_NAMES];
int         nRegistrations = 0;
WSADATA     WSAData;
```

```
/********
*
Listing 6-13. WNETTCP.H
*
* Copyright (c) 1992 Ralph P. Davis, All Rights Reserved
*
********/

/*===== Includes =====*/

#include "wnet.h"
#define _INC_WINDOWS // Keep WINDOWS.H from being included twice
#include <winsock.h>

/*===== Constants =====*/

#define MAX_LISTEN_REQUESTS        5
#define MAXINT                     (sizeof (int) == 2 ? 0x7FFF : 0x7FFFFFFFL)
#define MAXUINT                    (sizeof (int) == 2 ? 0xFFFF : 0xFFFFFFFFL)
#define RECEIVE_BUFFER_SIZE        MAXINT

#define WNET_UDP_NAME              0
#define WNET_TCP_NAME              1

#define MAX_WSA_NAMES              128

#define CONCURRENT_CONNECTIONS     FD_SETSIZE

/*===== Types =====*/

typedef struct tagTCPClients
{
    SOCKET sUDP;
    SOCKET sTCP;
    int    nAccepts;
    SOCKET FAR *lpSockets;
    HWND   hWnd;
} TCPCLIENTS;

/*===== Global Variables =====*/

extern HWND        hNotifyWnd;
extern HWND        hMainWnd;
extern int         nMainNameIndex;
extern HINSTANCE   hDLLInstance;
extern UINT        WMU_PACKET_RECEIVED;
extern TCPCLIENTS  TCPClients[];
extern int         nRegistrations;
extern WSADATA     WSAData;

/*===== Function Prototypes =====*/

int WINAPI _WNetGetHostAddress(LPSTR lpszHost, LPSTR lpszProto,
                               LPSOCKADDR lpAddr);
LRESULT CALLBACK WinSockWndProc(HWND hWnd, UINT uMessage, WPARAM wParam,
```

```
                              LPARAM lParam);
int PASCAL FindNameOfSocket(SOCKET s);
int PASCAL AddToSocketList(int nNameIndex, SOCKET s);
void PASCAL RemoveFromSocketList(int nNameIndex, SOCKET s);

;********
;
; Listing 6-14. WNETTCP.DEF
;
; Copyright (c) 1992 Ralph P. Davis, All Rights Reserved
;
;********

LIBRARY    WNETTCP

EXETYPE    WINDOWS

CODE    PRELOAD MOVEABLE DISCARDABLE
DATA    PRELOAD FIXED SINGLE
HEAPSIZE  4096

EXPORTS
            WEP                   @1 RESIDENTNAME
            _WNetInit
            _WNetCall
            _WNetHangup
            _WNetListen
            _WNetReceive
            _WNetReceiveDatagram
            _WNetSendDatagram
            _WNetShutdown
            _WNetSend
            WinSockWndProc
```

Conclusion

The Windows Sockets specification is an important step towards developing a standard Windows networking API. Right now, it only standardizes TCP/IP under Windows; in the future, it may serve as a truly protocol-independent programming interface. There are many advantages to standardizing TCP/IP, which is a solid protocol suite that has been around for many years, and it is the most important platform for wide-area networking. The continued importance of UNIX, with which TCP/IP is closely associated, makes it likely that there will be considerable interest in linking Windows stations into TCP/IP networks. A standardized programming interface will bring order into what is now a somewhat confusing situation, and thereby accelerate the development of TCP/IP-based Windows applications.

CHAPTER ■ 7

API Translation and DPMI

Overview

This chapter explores the mechanism that underlies the APIs we have studied in the last three chapters. Underneath APIs that are visible to a Windows program, there has to be a layer that maps from protected-mode Windows to real-mode network drivers. When your network vendor provides a usable Windows API, you are shielded from this software layer. For most of your programming, you probably won't have to worry about the material presented in this chapter. But if you are ever in a situation where there is no Windows-level API available for network programming, you can create your own using the DOS Protected-Mode Interface (DPMI) and a few special-purpose Windows functions. This chapter will show you how to do that.

For example, early in 1991 I was developing a large networked application for NetWare. At the time, Novell had not completed their *NetWare C Interface for Windows*, so there was no support for protected-mode Windows applications. I had to use DPMI to do my own mapping between Windows and the IPX/SPX system calls. Today, the *NetWare C Interface for Windows* takes care of this for us, using the same DPMI mechanism.

API Translation

API translation is a term that describes what must happen behind the scenes for Windows applications running in protected mode to access real-mode TSRs and drivers. Pointers in protected mode consist of a selector and an offset; the selector is an index into the local descriptor table (LDT). The corresponding table entry maps the selector to its actual memory address. In real mode, an address consists of a segment and an offset; the segment is multiplied by 16 and added to the offset to compute the physical memory address. These two addressing modes are totally incompatible. Moreover, a protected-mode address can be anywhere in the total memory space of the machine; a real-mode address must be in the lower megabyte. When there are two sets of software inside the same machine, one running in protected mode, the other in real mode, it is almost the same as if there were two completely different machines communicating over a LAN.

Suppose there is a real-mode INT 42H handler that requires a pointer to an input buffer in DS:SI and to an output buffer in ES:DI. To issue this interrupt in protected mode, a program must:

1. Obtain memory in the lower megabyte of RAM for both the input and output buffers.
2. Generate protected-mode descriptors for those memory areas, and obtain selectors for those descriptors.
3. Using the selector for the input buffer, move the input data into the lower megabyte.
4. Switch the CPU into real mode.
5. Load DS:SI and ES:DI with the real-mode segment:offset addresses of the buffers.
6. Issue the interrupt.
7. Load DS:SI and ES:DI with the protected-mode selector:offset addresses of the buffers.
8. Switch the processor back into protected mode.
9. Process the output data.

Fortunately, you don't have to go through this process every time you want to issue a system interrupt. Windows handles ROM-BIOS interrupts and the standard DOS INT 21H calls for you. The Novell driver for Windows (NETWARE.DRV) contains the function NetWareRequest. Most Novell system services are requested through extensions to INT 21H, and many of them want a pointer to an input buffer in DS:SI and an output buffer in ES:DI. Instead of calling INT 21H directly, set up the registers as you normally would, then call NetWareRequest:

```
EXTRN NETWAREREQUEST:FAR

; Put function number in AH, set up DS:SI and ES:DI
CALL NETWAREREQUEST
```

In the IMPORTS section of your .DEF file, add the line:

```
NetWare.NetWareRequest
```

Using DPMI for API Translation

The DOS Protected-Mode Interface (DPMI) is a set of software services that. First, it allows software running in a DOS window and starting up in real mode to obtain protected-mode memory management by switching into protected mode. DOS extenders run under Windows by requesting DPMI services. The Microsoft C/C++ compiler, version 7.0, for example, runs in a DOS window and uses DPMI. Second, DPMI allows Windows programs running in protected mode to call real-mode software, access physical memory, and so on.

In protected mode you request DPMI services by loading AX with the function number, loading other registers as appropriate, then issuing an INT 31H. First, though, you must issue an INT 2FH with AX equal to 1686H, to see if DPMI is present. On return, AX will be zero if it is.

For our purposes, the second set of functions is what interests us. There is a good discussion on using DPMI for DOS extension in Chapter 9 of the second edition of Ray Duncan's *Extending DOS* (Addison-Wesley, 1992).

As of this writing, there are two versions of DPMI, 0.9 and 1.0. As you can learn by asking Windows (using DPMI function 0400H), Windows 3.1 supports DPMI 0.9. (The *Programmer's Reference, Volume 1: Overview* incorrectly states that it supports 1.0.) Some vendors extend DPMI 0.9 with virtual device drivers (VxDs), producing a sort of DPMI "0.95." Although DPMI supports some 49 functions, only seven of them are officially blessed by Microsoft for use in Windows programs (though several other DPMI functions are in fact useful). The approved subset is shown in Table 7-1:

Table 7-1: DPMI Functions of Interest under Windows

AX Value	Service

InterruptManagement Services

0200H	Get Real Mode Interrupt Vector
0201H	Set Real Mode Interrupt Vector

Note: To set and get protected-mode interrupt vectors, use INT 21H functions 25H and 35H.

Translation Services

0300H	Simulate Real Mode Interrupt
0301H	Call Real Mode Procedure with Far Return Frame
0302H	Call Real Mode Procedure with Interrupt Return Frame
0303H	Allocate Real Mode Callback Address
0304H	Free Real Mode Callback Address

Many of the other DPMI calls are unnecessary because they have equivalent Windows 3.1 functions, which are shown in Table 7-2:

Table 7-2: Windows Functions Offering Equivalents to DPMI Functionality

Function Name	Service
AllocDStoCSAlias	Creates executable alias for data segment descriptor
AllocSelector	Copies an existing selector or allocates a new selector
FreeSelector	Frees selector allocated by AllocSelector() or AllocDStoCSAlias()
GetSelectorBase	Returns base address of selector
GetSelectorLimit	Returns size of segment associated with selector
Global32CodeAlias	Creates executable alias for 32-bit memory object
Global32CodeAliasFree	Frees selector created by Global32CodeAlias()

Table 7-2: Windows Functions Offering Equivalents to DPMI Functionality

Function Name	Service
GlobalDosAlloc	Allocates memory in the first megabyte
GlobalDosFree	Frees memory allocated by GlobalDosAlloc()
GlobalPageLock	Prevents memory block from being paged out or moved
GlobalPageUnlock	Releases page lock
PrestoChangoSelector	Creates executable alias for data segment descriptor or vice-versa
SetSelectorBase	Sets base address of a selector
SetSelectorLimit	Sets size of segment associated with a selector

Note: See Undocumented Windows by Andrew Schulman, Matt Pietrek, and David Maxey (Addison-Wesley, 1992) for more information on some of these functions (which until recently were undocumented).

Calling Real-Mode Software

The DPMI calls you need to create your own API translation layer are all in the Translation Services group. They are:

- 0300H: Simulate Real Mode Interrupt
- 0301H: Call Real Mode Procedure with Far Return Frame
- 0302H: Call Real Mode Procedure with Interrupt Return Frame
- 0303H: Allocate Real Mode Callback Address
- 0304H: Free Real Mode Callback Address

The first three allow you to call real-mode software. Simulate Real Mode Interrupt invokes an interrupt handler. The second two execute a FAR CALL to real-mode software. 0301H is used with routines that return with a RETF, 0302H with those that terminate with an IRET.

All three expect ES:(E)DI to point to a structure containing the values that should be loaded into the real-mode registers before the call is issued. For 0301H and 0302H, this structure will include the real-mode address of the function you want to invoke. When you execute INT 31H, DPMI saves the contents of the protected-mode registers, switches the processor into real mode, then loads the registers from the structure. After the INT 31H, DPMI places the new contents of the registers in the structure. It then reloads the registers with the saved protected-mode values, switches back to protected mode, and issues an IRET to return to you.

For example, to get the IPX/SPX entry address, load 7A00H into AX, then issue an INT 2FH. The value is returned in ES:BX. Here is how you would do that with a DPMI call:

```
// Put 7A00H into the AX field of the real-mode register structure
// Point ES:DI to the structure
// Put interrupt number (2FH) in BX
// Zero out CX (cx tells DPMI how many bytes of data to copy
// from the protected-mode stack to the real-mode stack)
// Put 0300H in AX
// Issue an INT 31H
// The real-mode entry point will be returned in the fields of
// the real-mode register structure corresponding to ES and BX
```

Once you have obtained the IPX entry point, you can make IPX system calls. IPX returns with a RETF, so you need to use DPMI function 0301H, Call Real-Mode Procedure with Far Return Frame. Place an IPX function number in BX and a pointer to an ECB in ES:SI (3 is the function number to send an IPX packet). Here's how to do it:

```
// Put 3 into the BX field of the DPMI real-mode register structure
// Put the IPX entry address retrieved by the call above into
// the CS and IP fields
// Put the real-mode address of the ECB in the ES and SI fields
// Load AX with 0301H, CX with 0
// Point ES and DI (the actual registers) to the register structure
// Issue an INT 31H
```

Here is a typedef for the DPMI register structure. The 32-bit registers are defined as DWORDs. To use them as 16-bit registers, set the high word to zero:

```
typedef struct tagDPMIRegs
{
    DWORD dwEDI;        // DI or EDI
    DWORD dwESI;        // SI or ESI
    DWORD dwEBP;        // BP or EBP
    DWORD dwReserved;
    DWORD dwEBX;        // BX or EBX
    DWORD dwEDX;        // DX or EDX
    DWORD dwECX;        // CX or ECX
    DWORD dwEAX;        // AX or EAX
    WORD  wFlags;
    WORD  wES;
    WORD  wDS;
    WORD  wFS;
    WORD  wGS;
    WORD  wIP;
    WORD  wCS;
    WORD  wSP;
    WORD  wSS;
} DPMI_REGS;
```

Memory Allocation

As I said, you make an IPX system call by placing the address of the ECB in the ES and SI
fields of the register structure. Of course, this cannot be a protected-mode address; it must
be a real-mode address. But your program needs to address the ECB with a protected-
mode pointer. The Windows function GlobalDosAlloc() allocates memory that you can
look at from either point of view:

```
DWORD WINAPI GlobalDosAlloc(DWORD dwBytes);
```

dwBytes is the number of bytes to allocate. GlobalDosAlloc() returns a real-mode segment
in its high word and a protected-mode selector in its low word. This union is a convenient
way of looking at the return value:

```
typedef union tagDOSBlock
{
   DWORD dwBlock;
   struct
      {
      WORD wSelector;
      WORD wSegment;
      } Pointers;
} DOSBLOCK;

#define RealSegment        Pointers.wSegment
#define ProtectedSelector  Pointers.wSelector
```

The two words returned by GlobalDosAlloc() can each be converted to far pointers
using the WINDOWS.H macro MAKELP(). The buffer begins at offset zero. Depending
on what you are using DPMI for, it may also be advisable to page-lock the memory by
passing GlobalPageLock() its protected-mode selector. This prevents it from being paged
to disk when you are in 386 enhanced mode. To free the memory, call GlobalDosFree(),
also passing it the selector. For instance:

```
LPSTR    lpReal, lpProtected;
DOSBLOCK DosBlock;

DosBlock.dwBlock = GlobalDosAlloc((DWORD) 576);

if (DosBlock.dwBlock != 0L)
   {
   lpReal = (LPSTR) MAKELP(DosBlock.RealSegment, 0);
   lpProt = (LPSTR) MAKELP(DosBlock.ProtectedSelector), 0);
   if ((GetWinFlags() & WF_ENHANCED) == WF_ENHANCED)
      GlobalPageLock(DosBlock.ProtectedSelector);
   }
else
   // Memory not available, issue error.

/* Use the memory here. */

if ((GetWinFlags() & WF_ENHANCED) == WF_ENHANCED)
   GlobalPageUnlock(DosBlock.ProtectedSelector);
GlobalDosFree(DosBlock.ProtectedSelector);
```

Here is a more extended code sample that shows how to allocate memory for an IPX/SPX ECB, retrieve the IPX entry point, then issue an IPX send packet:

```
ECB FAR  *lpECBReal, *lpECBProt;
LPBYTE     lpbyPacketReal, lpbyPacketProt;
DosBlock  DosECB, DosPacket;
DPMI_REGS DPMIRegs;
void (FAR *IPXEntry)(void);

if ((DosPacket.dwBlock = GlobalDosAlloc(576)) == OL)
   return;
lpbyPacketReal = (LPBYTE) MAKELP(DosPacket.RealSegment), O);
lpbyPacketProt = (LPBYTE) MAKELP(DosPacket.ProtectedSelector), O);

// Set up IPX header and data
if ((DosECB.dwBlock = GlobalDosAlloc(sizeof (ECB))) == OL)
   {
   GlobalDosFree(DosPacket.ProtectedSelector);
   return;
   }
if ((GetWinFlags() & WF_ENHANCED) == WF_ENHANCED)
   {
   GlobalPageLock(DosPacket.ProtectedSelector);
   GlobalPageLock(DosECB.ProtectedSelector);
   }
lpECBReal = (ECB FAR *) MAKELP(DosECB.RealSegment), O);
lpECBProt = (ECB FAR *) MAKELP(DosECB.ProtectedSelector), O);

// Use protected-mode pointer to set up fields of ECB.
lpECBProt->fragmentCount = 1;
lpECBProt->fragment[O].size = 576;

// However, put real-mode address in packet address field
// IPX will take this address out of the ECB
lpECBProt->fragment[O].address = lpbyPacketReal;

// Now, get the IPX entry point
DPMIRegs.dwEAX = 0x00007A00L;

// Set SS and SP of DPMIRegs to zero to ask DPMI to allocate
// the real-mode stack.
DPMIRegs.wSS = DPMIRegs.wSP = 0;
_asm
   {
   // The flags will be pushed and popped--make sure
   // they're valid.
   PUSHF
   POP  DPMIRegs.wFlags
   PUSH DI
   PUSH ES
   MOV  AX, 0x0300   // Simulate Real Mode Interrupt
   MOV  BX, 0x2F     // Interrupt number
```

```
    XOR  CX, CX        // Nothing to put on real-mode stack
    PUSH DS
    POP  ES            // Point ES to our data segment, assuming that
                       // DPMIRegs is a static variable.
    LEA  DI, DPMIRegs
    INT  0x31
    POP  ES
    POP  DI
    }

// The entry point can now be constructed from
// DPMIRegs.wES and DPMIRegs.dwEBX
IPXEntry = MAKELP(DPMIRegs.wES, LOWORD(DPMIRegs.dwEBX));

// Put real-mode address of ECB into DPMI register structure
DPMIRegs.wES = DosECB.RealSegment;
DPMIRegs.dwESI = 0L;

// Put the IPX entry point in the CS and IP fields of the
// DPMI register structure
DPMIRegs.wCS = HIWORD(IPXEntry);
DPMIRegs.wIP = LOWORD(IPXEntry);

// Put the IPX send packet code (3) in the BX field
DPMIRegs.dwEBX = 3;
_asm
    {
    MOV  AX, 0x0301   // Call Real Mode Procedure with
                      // Far Return Frame
    XOR  BH, BH       // Reserved
    XOR  CX, CX       // No arguments on stack
    PUSH DS
    POP  ES           // Assume DPMIRegs is in our data segment
    LEA  DI, DPMIRegs
    INT  0x31
    }
```

IPX places all return values in the ECB, which can now be examined through the protected-mode pointer *lpECBProt*.

Real-Mode Callbacks

Many APIs for peer-to-peer communications allow you to specify a routine that will be called when an event occurs. As we have seen, these have several names: post routines, callback routines, and event service routines. As you would expect, any callback address provided to real-mode software must be a real-mode address. But your program is running in protected mode. DPMI function 0303H, Allocate Real Mode Callback Address, creates a real-mode stub for a protected-mode callback function. You invoke it by placing 0303H in AX, putting the address of the protected-mode callback in DS:(E)SI, and a pointer to a DPMI register structure in ES:(E)DI. DPMI will use this structure to report the contents of the real-mode registers at the time the real-mode stub is triggered. The callback address is returned in CX:DX. This is what you will use as, for instance, your NetBIOS post routine or your IPX/SPX event service routine. It is also what you pass to function 0304H to free the callback when you no longer need it.

When the real-mode stub is called, it switches the CPU into protected mode, then invokes the protected-mode routine. When it is entered, the registers contain the following information:

DS:(E)SI   selector:offset address pointing to the real-mode stack
ES:(E)DI   selector:offset pointing to the DPMI register structure that you passed
                originally to function 0303H. It contains the real-mode registers when
                the stub was invoked.

The callback function can then examine the contents of the real-mode registers and do any appropriate processing. In the Windows environment, this will probably mean posting a message, as we have seen. With most network drivers, the real-mode software passes the callback function the address of the data structure that triggered the original event. For example, NetBIOS passes the original NCB in ES:BX, and IPX/SPX passes the ECB in ES:SI.

Because this will be an address obtained from GlobalDosAlloc( ), you can translate it to its protected-mode equivalent by looking it up in your own tables. Using the sample code I presented above, this would involve a scan of an array of *DosBlock* unions. When you find the real-mode segment you are looking for, the protected-mode selector is available in *ProtectedSelector*. Pass this, and an offset of zero, to your notification function. The following assembler fragment posts a WMU_PACKET_RECEIVED message, and points *lParam* to the original control block:

```
EXTRN POSTMESSAGE:FAR

PUSH hNotifyWnd      ; Saved in global variable
PUSH WMU_PACKET_RECEIVED
PUSH 0               ; wParam
PUSH <Protected-mode selector>
PUSH 0               ; Offset is zero
CALL POSTMESSAGE
```

To return from the callback routine, you must pull the real-mode return address off the real-mode stack and update the DPMI register structure accordingly. This can be done without difficulty. Recall that DS:(E)SI points to the real-mode stack as of the time the DPMI stub was called, and ES:(E)DI points to the structure. Thus, ES:(E)SI will be pointing to the return address, whether the real-mode software issues a far call, like IPX, or an interrupt, like NetBIOS. The code is as follows:

```
MOV  AX, [SI]        ; AX <= IP of return address
MOV  ES:[DI].wIP, AX
MOV  AX, [SI+2]
MOV  ES:[DI].wCS, AX
```

You must also adjust the real-mode stack, since you have just effectively popped the return address off of it.

```
ADD  ES:[DI].wSP, 4
```

The callback function exits by issuing an IRET.

You may also want to have your callback function execute within a Windows critical section. This can be particularly important with network software; it prevents the callback from being reentered. To start a critical section, issue INT 2FH as follows:

```
MOV  AX, 1681H
INT  2FH
```

Here's how you end a critical section:

```
MOV  AX, 1682H
INT  2FH
```

Real-mode callbacks, like DOS memory blocks, are limited global resources and should be released when you no longer need them. Do this by calling DPMI function 0304H, loading CX:DX with the callback address that function 0303H returned in those same registers.

Listing 7-1 shows a real-mode callback version of the IPX event service routine I presented in Chapter 4.

```
;********
;
; Listing 7-1. DPMIESR.ASM
;
; Copyright (c) 1992 Ralph P. Davis, All Rights Reserved
;
; Real-mode callback implementation of
; IPX Event Service Routine
;
;********

        .386

memM equ 1
?PLM = 1
?WIN = 1

INCLUDE cmacros.inc

PUBLIC IPXEventServiceRoutine
EXTRN   POSTMESSAGE:FAR
EXTRN   _WMU_PACKET_RECEIVED:WORD
EXTRN   _hNotifyWnd:WORD

DGROUP      GROUP       IPXESR_DATA
IPXESR_DATA SEGMENT WORD PUBLIC 'IPXESR_DATA'
ASSUME DS:DGROUP

tagDPMIRegs     STRUCT
dwEDI           DWORD        ?
dwESI           DWORD        ?
dwEBP           DWORD        ?
```

```
dwReserved      DWORD           ?
dwEBX           DWORD           ?
dwEDX           DWORD           ?
dwECX           DWORD           ?
dwEAX           DWORD           ?
wFlags          WORD            ?
wES             WORD            ?
wDS             WORD            ?
wFS             WORD            ?
wGS             WORD            ?
wIP             WORD            ?
wCS             WORD            ?
wSP             WORD            ?
wSS             WORD            ?
tagDPMIRegs     ENDS

DPMI_REGS       TYPEDEF         tagDPMIRegs

IPXESR_DATA     ENDS

createSeg IPXESR_TEXT, DPMI_CODE, PARA, PUBLIC, CODE
sBegin      DPMI_CODE

IPXEventServiceRoutine PROC FAR
        PUSHA
        PUSH DS
        PUSH ES

        PUSH DS
        MOV  AX, SEG _hNotifyWnd      ; Pick up data segment
        MOV  DS, AX
        PUSH _hNotifyWnd
        PUSH _WMU_PACKET_RECEIVED
        POP  DS
        PUSH 0                        ; wParam
        MOV  BX, DI                   ; BX <== Pointer to real mode register
                                      ;        structure
        ; Pick up segment address of ECB
        MOV  DI, ES:[BX].DPMI_REGS.wES
        PUSH DI                       ; lParam = Pointer to ECB
        ; Pick up offset address of ECB
        MOV  EDI, ES:[BX].DPMI_REGS.dwESI
        PUSH DI
        CALL POSTMESSAGE

        ; Set up real-mode registers for return to IPX
        MOV  AX, SI
        ADD  AX, 4                    ; Clear return address off stack
        MOV  ES:[BX].DPMI_REGS.wSP, AX
        MOV  AX, [SI]                 ; Pick up return address
        MOV  ES:[BX].DPMI_REGS.wIP, AX
        MOV  AX, [SI + 2]
        MOV  ES:[BX].DPMI_REGS.wCS, AX
```

```
        POP  ES
        POP  DS
        POPA
        IRET
IPXEventServiceRoutine ENDP
sEND    DPMI_CODE
END
```

Summary of DPMI Translation Services Function Calls

The Translation Services calls expect the function number in AX and a pointer to the real-mode register structure in ES:(E)DI—except for 0304H, which does not need the registers.

Function 0300H: Simulate Real Mode Interrupt

To execute a real-mode interrupt, set up the registers as follows:

AX: 0300H
BL: the number of the interrupt you want to invoke
BH: clear to zero (reserved)
CX: the number of words to copy from the protected-mode to the real-mode stack. This permits you to pass arguments by pushing them
ES: (E)DI: the address of the real-mode register structure

Note that:

- If the *wSS* and *wSP* values in the register structure are non-zero, DPMI will use the memory they point to for the real-mode stack. Setting them to zero causes DPMI to allocate the real-mode stack. This is true for functions 0301H and 0302H as well.

- The *wFlags* field must be initialized. Whatever value is in this field will be pushed onto the stack when the real-mode interrupt is invoked. This also applies to function 0302H.

- Any pointers placed in the real-mode register structure must be real-mode pointers.

Next, issue an INT 31H. On return, if the carry flag is clear, the function was successful, and the register structure will have been modified to show the contents of the registers on return from the interrupt. If the carry flag is set, AX reports one of the following errors:

8012H: unable to allocate linear memory for the stack
8013H: unable to allocate physical memory for the stack
8014H: unable to obtain backing store (virtual memory) for the stack
8021H: the value in the CX register is too large

Function 0301H: Call Real Mode Procedure with Far Return Frame

This DPMI function makes a far call to real-mode software that returns by issuing a RETF. Its usage is identical to function 0300H, with these exceptions:

- Load AX with 0301H
- The address of the real-mode procedure goes in the *wCS* and *wIP* fields of the register data structure, using a real-mode pointer
- The *wFlags* field does not get pushed onto the stack

Function 0302H: Call Real Mode Procedure with IRET Frame

DPMI function 0302H makes a far call to real-mode software that returns with IRET. It has similarities to functions 0300H and 0301H. Like 0300H, the *wFlags* field of the register data structure will be pushed before making the far call, so it must be initialized. Like 0301H, the *wCS* and *wIP* fields must contain the entry point for the real-mode routine, using a real-mode pointer.

Function 0303H: Allocate Real Mode Callback Address

The syntax for function 0303H is:

AX: 0303H
DS:(E)SI: address of protected-mode callback (using protected-mode address)
ES:(E)DI: protected-mode address of DPMI register structure. When the protected-mode routine is invoked, this structure will show the state of the real-mode registers

If the function succeeds, the carry flag will be clear and CX:DX will contain the segment:offset address of the real-mode callback. If the function fails, the carry flag will be set and AX will contain the error code. The only documented error code is 8015H, which means that no more callbacks are available.

Function 0304H: Free Real Mode Callback Address

The syntax for function 0304H is:

AX: 0304H
CX:DX   The real-mode callback address returned by function 0303H

DPMI will return error code 8024H in AX and set the carry flag if the address is CX:DX is not a valid callback.

CHAPTER ■ 8

Overview of Vertical Applications

General Discussion

In Part II, we move on to consider vertical applications. This is a different kind of networked application. With the horizontal applications we saw in Part I, all stations on the network are equal; terms like "file server" and "workstation" are meaningless. In vertical applications, different stations on the network begin to play different roles.

With vertical applications, we move up the OSI layers and create applications that use the data-moving services of the network transparently. They do so by requesting services from the network operating system. This is what gives them their appearance of being vertical: they obtain services from lower-level software, such as a workstation shell, and all interactions appear to be on a top-to-bottom and back-to-top basis. Any horizontal communications are handled by the network operating system.

Some of the services that are pertinent here are:

- Mapping drives to file server directories, or local devices to shared network devices
- Obtaining a list of logged-in users
- Adding and deleting users and user groups
- Submitting print jobs
- Obtaining network operation, configuration, and performance statistics
- Assigning users rights to files and directories

Network Service APIs

There are fewer standards for these services than for the peer-to-peer protocols that we examined in Part I. NetBIOS is a true standard; applications which use NetBIOS will run on any network platform, as long as the user loads the appropriate driver. TCP/IP, as we saw, is moving towards full standardization. There is no such promise of portability in the network services arena. The Windows network drivers offer some callable functions, and provide a foundation on which a full-featured standard can be built. There are several excellent vendor-specific APIs. Our task here will be to extend the model offered by the Windows network drivers and create a network-independent layer between Windows and the vendor-specific APIs.

The Network-Driver Functions

The only API that constitutes anything like a standard is the set of functions included in the Windows network drivers. These are primarily intended to give Control Panel, Print Manager, and File Manager some network awareness. When the user selects an option in one of those programs where network support is needed, the program calls the driver routines that are responsible for handling the request. There is a different network driver for each network operating system, but they are all required by the Microsoft device driver specification to implement a core set of functions.

There is no reason why other application programs cannot call these functions as well. We had occasion to do so in Chapter 2, when we called WNetGetCaps() to determine the underlying network software. The calling procedure is somewhat roundabout. First, you call GetPrivateProfileString() to get the NETWORK.DRV setting from SYSTEM.INI. This is the appropriate section:

```
[boot]
network.drv=netware.drv
```

Having obtained the name of the driver, you call LoadLibrary() to bring it into memory, or to obtain a handle to access it with (Windows has probably loaded it already). Then you call GetProcAddress() to get the address of WNetGetCaps(). Finally, you can call the function itself.

Here is a code extract from Chapter 2:

```
char          szNetworkDriver[255];
HINSTANCE     hNetLib;
WORD (WINAPI *WNetGetCaps)(WORD wIndex);

GetPrivateProfileString("BOOT", "NETWORK.DRV", "MSNET.DRV",
   szNetworkDriver, sizeof (szNetworkDriver), "SYSTEM.INI");

hNetLib = LoadLibrary(szNetworkDriver);

if (hNetLib > HINSTANCE_ERROR)
   // Load function definitions
   (FARPROC) WNetGetCaps = GetProcAddress(hNetLib, "WNetGetCaps");

if (WNetGetCaps != NULL)
   {
   switch (WNetGetCaps(WNNC_NET_TYPE))
```

The fact that these functions reside in the network drivers has a couple of implications. First, they are documented only in the manuals for the Windows Device Driver Kit, so they are not widely known. Second, if you want to be network-independent, you have to go through the sequence shown above to get to the functions. If portability is not a concern for you, you can name them in the IMPORTS section of your .DEF file. To import WNetGetCaps() from NETWARE.DRV, your IMPORTS section would look like this:

```
IMPORTS
    NetWare.WNetGetCaps
```

You can also use IMPLIB to create an import library from the driver file, as follows:

```
IMPLIB NETWARE.LIB NETWARE.DRV
```

Then you can include the library in your linker commands.

Surprisingly, there are stubs for all the WNet driver functions in USER.EXE, but you cannot link to them through LIBW.LIB because they aren't there. These stubs go through steps similar to those I have described. You can also create an import library from USER.EXE:

```
IMPLIB USERW.LIB USER.EXE
```

For a more complete discussion, see Chapter 6 of *Undocumented Windows* by Andrew Schulman, et al. I will discuss only the documented API in the rest of this book.

It appears that Microsoft does not really intend these functions to be used as a general-purpose API. Only three of them have been promoted to the Windows 3.1 above-ground API, and one more makes it into Win32. Also, the driver functions are rather narrowly focused. When you compare them with the API sets offered by NetWare, LAN Manager, and VINES, which contain hundreds of functions, you realize the bare-bones aspects of the network-driver APIs. They cannot possibly serve as a true network-independent API for the simple reason that they do not offer a great deal of functionality. Nevertheless, they do provide a basis and a model for building a full-featured API.

Table 8-1 lists the categories of functions in the network drivers.

Table 8-1: Categories of Functions in the Windows Network Drivers

Category	Services Provided
Network Capabilities	Reports on characteristics and capabilities of underlying network.
Connection Functions	Map local devices to network resources. (Part of Windows 3.1 documented API)
Printing Functions	Print to network print queues, report on status of print queues.
Dialog Functions	Display dialog boxes for user interaction.
Administrative Functions	Get type of directory (network or local). Inform driver of impending action by File Manager. Get name of logged-in user. (In Win32 API)
Long-filename Functions	Support filenames that do not conform to MS-DOS naming conventions (LAN Manager HPFS-386, for example).
Error-Handling Functions	Retrieve information on network errors.

The network driver functions are indeed network-independent, but they are narrowly specialized. There are 40-plus functions in the driver; as you will see in Chapter 9, only eight of them are of real use to application programs. To develop full-featured vertical applications, you must turn to the vendor-specific APIs. Our goal through the rest of Part

II will be to take the vendor-dependent interfaces and create a portable API that accomplishes some of the important tasks that vertical applications are normally responsible for.

Novell NetWare

NetWare offers a comprehensive set of APIs that enable applications to exercise a high level of control over the network environment. Table 8-2 shows the function categories and gives a brief description of what each one does. (I omit those categories having to do with horizontal communications.)

Table 8-2: NetWare Function Categories

Category	Description
Accounting	Allows charging for services and tracking of resource usage.
AFP	Permits access to Macintosh format files from DOS workstations.
Bindery	Manipulation of users and user groups.
Connection	Attachment and login to servers, information about logged-in users.
Diagnostic	Generation and collection of network configuration, operation, and performance statistics.
Directories	Manipulation of drives and directories. Assignment of user rights.
File Server	Control file server configuration. Real-time monitoring of resource usage. Remote file copy. Get and set file server date and time.
File	Specialized file services (does not include standard file I/O operations).
Message	Simple system for sending and receiving bottom-line messages.
Name Spaces	Allows multiple naming of files to support different file systems (Macintosh, OS/2, UNIX, FTAM).
Print Server	Configure print server software.
Print	Control network printing.
Queue	Manage NetWare Queue Management System (for asynchronous job submission).
Service Advertising	Advertise presence of a specialized server. Find out what servers are present.
Synchronization	File and record locks and semaphores.
Transaction Tracking	Provides data protection through rollback recovery.
Workstation	Manage local environment including attached servers.

Chapter 10 will explore NetWare. See also my books on NetWare programming, *NetWare Programmer's Guide* and *NetWare/386 Programmer's Guide* (Addison-Wesley, 1990 and 1992).

LAN Manager

LAN Manager has an equally rich API set. Many of the function categories overlap those offered by NetWare. Table 8-3 lists the LAN Manager API categories. I leave out functions pertaining to communications, or those only available under OS/2.

Table 8-3: LAN Manager Function Categories

Category	Description
Access Permissions	Assign rights to files and directories.
Auditing	Track network events, read audit records (only OS/2 programs can write audit trail records).
Character Device	Control shared communications devices, such as modems and faxes.
Configuration	Reads configuration information from LANMAN.INI.
Connection	Lists mapping of local devices to network. (Mapping is handled by the *Use* category.)
Domain	Retrieves information on logged-in users in the domain.
	Retrieve name of server acting as domain controller.
Error Logging	Reads information logged in LAN Manager error log (only OS/2 programs can write error log records).
File	Gets information on usage of server files. Does not include standard file I/O functions.
Group	Create and delete user groups, add and delete group members.
Handle	Get and set buffering parameters for named pipes.
Message	Simple user-to-user messaging system.
Print Destination	Manage routing of print jobs to server print queues.
Print Job	Get and set info on currently scheduled print jobs.
Printer Queue	Create, delete, and manage server print queues.
Remote Utility	Remote file copy and move.
	Remote program execution only under OS/2.
	Get file server time.
Server	Execute "NET ..." commands on a server.
	Get server disk information.
	Get and set detailed server configuration.
	Find out what servers are available.
Service	Manage LAN Manager services (server-based LAN Manager applications).
Session	Force disconnection of user from a server.
	Get information on users accessing server resources.
Share	Make server resources available for shared use. Resources include disks, printers, communications devices, and named pipes.
Statistics	Retrieve operating and performance statistics.
Use	Programmatic implementation of NET USE commands.
	Redirect local devices to network.
User	Add and delete users.
	Assign users to groups.
	Control login behavior.
Workstation	Log user on to a workstation, configure the workstation.

I will discuss LAN Manager in detail in Chapter 11. See also Ralph Ryan's *LAN Manager Programmer's Guide.*

The LAN Manager API is of heightened interest now, because some of the functions have been added to the Windows for Workgroups API (see Chapter 14).

Banyan VINES

The VINES API set is also extensive. As befits VINES's particular specialty, many of its API groups deal with wide-area communications. Of greatest interest to us is the Street-Talk distributed database.

StreetTalk is the distributed directory of network resources which VINES maintains. A user on a VINES network is not aware of logging onto a server; he sees only a network. By sharing StreetTalk information, VINES servers are able to provide this virtualization of the network. This is a direction that we are likely to see other vendors moving in. Novell, for instance, is saying that NetWare 4.0 will eliminate the bindery, and go to a distributed, global naming service.

Table 8-4 lists the VINES API categories (once again omitting those having to do with communications).

Table 8-4: VINES API Categories

Category	Description
StreetTalk	Management of users and user groups. Find out what servers are present.
Security	Validation of user's identity and access rights.
NetRPC	Automatic generation of C code for remote procedure calls in client-server applications.
Messaging	Simple bottom-line messaging system.
Internationalization	Conversion of strings between ANSI and ASCII representations.
Service	Query and control VINES server-based applications.
Network Management	Collect statistics on network configuration, operation, and performance.
Network Mail Client	Electronic mail handling.

I will discuss VINES in Chapter 12.

Achieving Network Independence with Vertical Applications

Defining a set of network-independent operations is not as easy with vertical applications as it was with horizontal ones. The set of services offered by peer-to-peer communications protocols has been standardized over the course of a couple of decades. Network service APIs, on the other hand, are relatively new. The Windows network device-driver functions begin to describe a standard, but cannot by any stretch of the imagination be considered full-featured. The proprietary APIs have some areas of overlap, and some vendor-specific enhancements. In the areas where they do overlap—which are obvious candidates for standardization—their implementations differ widely.

Because of the large number of functions available in the several environments, it is not possible to do an exhaustive analysis of each vendor's API in this book. There are full-length books dealing with the NetWare and LAN Manager APIs, including the two of my own that I alluded to earlier. My intention is rather to develop a standardized group of WNet() functions that implement some centrally important APIs, building on those already provided in the Windows network drivers.

In Chapter 9, I explore the Windows network driver functions in some detail. Chapters 10, 11, and 12 present the NetWare, LAN Manager, and VINES versions of the additional functions. Appendix B presents a sample application, WNETSVCS.EXE, that uses the functions we develop here to list and select servers, add and delete users and user groups, and add and remove users from groups.

Additional APIs

As I stated earlier in this chapter, as we move up the OSI ladder from the transport layer, the specialization of machines on the network becomes important. Whereas Part I dealt exclusively with workstations, here the concern becomes file servers, print servers, job servers, database servers, modem servers, FAX servers, mail servers, etc., etc., etc. One of the most important things in harnessing the power of the network is being able to locate servers. For this, we will develop a function WNetEnumServers(). One of its arguments will specify the type of server, and it will allow a wildcard argument to request all server types.

It is also important to protect server resources from use by unauthorized people. To grant specific sets of rights, we need to maintain a database of known users, and we need functions to add and delete users. We will call these functions WNetAddUser() and WNetDeleteUser(). We will also need to enumerate current users; for this, we develop a WNetEnumUsers() function.

On a large network, it is very inconvenient to implement a complex security scheme on a user-by-user basis. It is much more common to use some kind of indirect assignment of rights. The most common way of doing this is to define groups of users, then grant rights to the groups. To do this, we need to be able to create and delete groups, add and delete group members, and check for a user's membership in a group. We will call the corresponding functions WNetAddGroup(), WNetDeleteGroup(), WNetAddGroupMember(), WNetDeleteGroupMember(), and WNetIsUserGroupMember(). We also want to be able to enumerate groups, group members, and groups to which a user belongs. These functions will be WNetEnumGroups(), WNetEnumGroupMembers(), and WNetEnumMemberGroups().

Finally, we need functions to grant, revoke, and modify user rights to network objects. We will develop two functions for this, WNetGrantRights() and WNetRevokeRights(). We also need a function to retrieve the user's (or group's) current rights; we will call it WNetGetRights().

Function Syntax

Here are the prototypes for these functions, and a description of the arguments. Note that the function names use the same WNet prefix as the functions in the network drivers, to emphasize that we are expanding the interface already provided, not replacing it.

WNetEnumServers()

```
typedef BOOL (CALLBACK *SERVERENUMPROC)(LPSTR lpszServerName, WORD wServerType);
BOOL WINAPI WNetEnumServers(SERVERENUMPROC lpServerEnumProc, WORD wServerType);
```

WNetEnumServers() invokes the callback function once for each server of the given type, as long as the callback function returns TRUE. A *wServerType* of 0xFFFF is interpreted to mean all types.

The callback function is passed the server name and type:

```
BOOL CALLBACK ServerEnumProc(LPSTR lpszServerName, WORD wType);
```

WNetAddUser()

```
BOOL WINAPI WNetAddUser(LPSTR lpszServerName, LPSTR lpszUserName,
                        LPSTR lpszPassword, BOOL bAdmin);
```

The user *lpszUserName* is added to the user database on the server *lpszServerName*, and given the password *lpszPassword*. If *lpszPassword* is NULL, or points to a null string, the user will not have a password. If *bAdmin* is TRUE, the user is given administrative privileges.

WNetDeleteUser()

```
BOOL WINAPI WNetDeleteUser(LPSTR lpszServerName, LPSTR lpszUserName);
```

Reverses the action of WNetAddUser().

WNetEnumUsers()

```
typedef BOOL (CALLBACK *USERENUMPROC)(LPSTR lpszServerName, LPSTR lpszUserName);
BOOL WINAPI WNetEnumUsers(LPSTR lpszServerName, USERENUMPROC lpUserEnumProc);
```

WNetEnumUsers() calls *lpUserEnumProc* for every user known on the designated server. The syntax for the callback function is:

```
BOOL CALLBACK UserEnumProc(LPSTR lpszServerName, LPSTR lpszUserName);
```

WNetAddGroup()

```
BOOL WINAPI WNetAddGroup(LPSTR lpszServerName, LPSTR lpszGroupName);
```

This creates the group *lpszGroupName* on the server *lpszServerName*.

WNetDeleteGroup()

```
BOOL WINAPI WNetDeleteGroup(LPSTR lpszServerName, LPSTR lpszGroupName);
```

The opposite of WNetAddGroup().

WNetAddGroupMember()

```
BOOL WINAPI WNetAddGroupMember(LPSTR lpszServerName, LPSTR lpszGroupName,
                               LPSTR lpszUserName);
```

Adds user *lpszUserName* to group *lpszGroupName* on server *lpszServerName*.

WNetDeleteGroupMember()

```
BOOL WINAPI WNetDeleteGroupMember(LPSTR lpszServerName, LPSTR lpszGroupName,
                                  LPSTR lpszUserName);
```

Deletes user *lpszUserName* from group *lpszGroupName* on server *lpszServerName*.

WNetIsUserGroupMember()

```
BOOL WINAPI WNetIsUserGroupMember(LPSTR lpszServerName, LPSTR lpszGroupName,
                                  LPSTR lpszUserName);
```

Determines whether user *lpszUserName* belongs to group *lpszGroupName* on server *lpszServerName*.

WNetEnumGroups()

```
typedef BOOL (CALLBACK *GROUPENUMPROC)(LPSTR lpszServerName, LPSTR lpszGroupName);
BOOL WINAPI WNetEnumGroups(LPSTR lpszServerName, GROUPENUMPROC lpGroupEnumProc);
```

Calls *lpGroupEnumProc* for every group on the given server. The syntax for the callback is:

```
BOOL CALLBACK GroupEnumProc(LPSTR lpszServerName, LPSTR lpszGroupName);
```

WNetEnumGroupMembers()

```
typedef BOOL (CALLBACK *GROUPMEMBERENUMPROC)(LPSTR lpszServerName,
                                             LPSTR lpszGroupName,
                                             LPSTR lpszUserName);
BOOL WINAPI WNetEnumGroupMembers(LPSTR lpszServerName,
                                 LPSTR lpszGroupName,
                                 GROUPMEMBERENUMPROC lpMemberEnumProc);
```

Invokes the callback function for each group member, and passes it the server name, the group name, and the user name.

```
BOOL CALLBACK GroupMemberEnumProc(LPSTR lpszServerName,
                                  LPSTR lpszGroupName,
                                  LPSTR lpszUserName);
```

WNetEnumMemberGroups()

```
typedef BOOL (CALLBACK *MEMBERGROUPENUMPROC)(LPSTR lpszServerName,
                                             LPSTR lpszUserName,
                                             LPSTR lpszGroupName);
BOOL WINAPI WNetEnumMemberGroups(LPSTR lpszServerName,
                                 LPSTR lpszUserName,
                                 MEMBERGROUPENUMPROC lpGroupEnumProc);
```

Invokes callback for each group to which *lpszUserName* belongs.

```
BOOL CALLBACK MemberGroupEnumProc(LPSTR lpszServerName,
                                  LPSTR lpszUserName,
                                  LPSTR lpszGroupName);
```

WNetGrantRights()

```
BOOL WINAPI WNetGrantRights(LPSTR lpszServerName,
                            LPSTR lpszUserOrGroupName,
                            LPSTR lpszResource,
                            WORD  wRights);
```

Gives the user or group *lpszUserOrGroupName* the rights to the resource *lpszResource* specified by *wRights*. *lpszUserOrGroupName* is identified as a group instead of a user by the WNET_GROUP_ACCESS flag in *wRights*. *wRights* is a network-independent bitmask, whose bits are defined as shown in Table 8-5:

Table 8-5: WNET Network-Independent Rights

Value	Meaning
WNET_READ_ACCESS (0x01)	Read permission
WNET_WRITE_ACCESS (0x02)	Write permission
WNET_CREATE_ACCESS (0x04)	Create permission
WNET_EXECUTE_ACCESS (0x08)	Execute permission
WNET_DELETE_ACCESS (0x10)	Delete permission
WNET_ATTRIB_ACCESS (0x20)	Permission to modify the object's attributes
WNET_VIEW_ACCESS (0x40)	File is visible on directory scan
WNET_PERM_ACCESS (0x80)	User has permission to grant other users access to the object
WNET_ADMIN_ACCESS (0x100)	User has administrative rights to the file (includes all other rights)
WNET_ALL_NORMAL_ACCESS (0x200)	User has all non-administrative rights to the object
WNET_ALL_ACCESS (0x400)	User has all rights to the object, including administrative rights
WNET_GROUP_ACCESS (0x800)	Access is being granted to a group, not an individual user

These flags are a union of all the permissions that LAN Manager, NetWare, and VINES support. The network-specific implementations will examine each bit and construct the bitmask that is appropriate for the host network operating system.

WNetRevokeRights()

```
BOOL WINAPI WNetRevokeRights(LPSTR lpszServerName,
                             LPSTR lpszUserOrGroup,
                             LPSTR lpszResource,
                             BOOL  bUser);
```

Deletes *lpszUserOrGroup* as a trustee of *lpszResource* on the server *lpszServerName*. If *bUser* is TRUE, *lpszUserOrGroup* designates a user; otherwise, *lpszUserOrGroup* is a group.

WNetGetRights()

```
BOOL WINAPI WNetGetRights(LPSTR lpszServerName, LPSTR lpszUserOrGroupName,
                          LPSTR lpszResource,
                          LPWORD lpwRights);
```

Returns user's or group's rights to the given resource through *lpwRights*. This points to a word with the same format as the *wRights* argument to WNetGrantRights(). The WNET_GROUP_ACCESS bit will be set if *lpszUserOrGroupName* designates a group.

Source Code

Listing 8-1 shows the header file WNETAPI.H, which includes the #defines, typedefs, and function prototypes for our network services API. It is included by all the network-specific implementations that we develop in Chapters 10 through 12.

```
/********
*
* Listing 8-1. WNETAPI.H
*
* Copyright (c) 1992 Ralph P. Davis, All Rights Reserved
*
********/

/*===== Includes =====*/

#include "wnet.h"

/*===== Constants =====*/

#define WNET_FILE_SERVER      1
#define WNET_PRINT_SERVER     2
#define WNET_JOB_SERVER       3
#define WNET_WORKSTATION      4
#define WNET_SQLSERVER        5
#define WNET_DOMAIN_CTRL      6
#define WNET_DOMAIN_BKUP      7
#define WNET_TIME_SOURCE      8
#define WNET_AFP_SERVER       9
#define WNET_NETWARE          10
#define WNET_DOMAIN_MEMBER    11
#define WNET_DIALIN_SERVER    12
#define WNET_UNIX_SERVER      13
#define WNET_VINES_SERVER     14
#define WNET_ST_SERVER        15     // VINES StreetTalk service
#define WNET_MAIL_SERVER      16     // VINES Mail service
#define WNET_UNKNOWN      0xFFFE
#define WNET_ALL_SERVERS  0xFFFF

#define WNET_READ_ACCESS       0x01  // read permission
#define WNET_WRITE_ACCESS      0x02  // write permission
#define WNET_CREATE_ACCESS     0x04  // create permission
#define WNET_EXECUTE_ACCESS    0x08  // execute permission
#define WNET_DELETE_ACCESS     0x10  // delete permission
#define WNET_ATTRIB_ACCESS     0x20  // permission to modify
                                     // the object's attributes
#define WNET_VIEW_ACCESS       0x40  // file is visible on
```

```
                              // directory scan
#define WNET_PERM_ACCESS      0x80  // user has permission to
                                    // grant other users
                                    // access to the object
#define WNET_ADMIN_ACCESS     0x100 // user has administrative
                                    // rights to the file
                                    // (includes all other rights)
#define WNET_ALL_NORMAL_ACCESS 0x200 // user has all non-administrative
                                     // rights to the object
#define WNET_ALL_ACCESS       0x400 // user has all rights to the object,
                                    // including administrative rights
#define WNET_GROUP_ACCESS     0x800 // access is being granted to a group,
                                    // not an individual user

#define WNNC_NET_DualNet      0xF000 // LAN Manager/NetWare
                                     // dual network

/*===== Types =====*/

typedef BOOL (CALLBACK *SERVERENUMPROC)
                (LPSTR lpszServerName, WORD wServerType);
typedef BOOL (CALLBACK *USERENUMPROC)(LPSTR lpszServerName,
                                      LPSTR lpszUserName);
typedef BOOL (CALLBACK *GROUPENUMPROC)(LPSTR lpszServerName,
                                       LPSTR lpszGroupName);
typedef BOOL (CALLBACK *GROUPMEMBERENUMPROC)(LPSTR lpszServerName,
                                             LPSTR lpszGroupName,
                                             LPSTR lpszUserName);
typedef BOOL (CALLBACK *MEMBERGROUPENUMPROC)(LPSTR lpszServerName,
                                             LPSTR lpszUserName,
                                             LPSTR lpszGroupName);

/*===== Function Prototypes =====*/

BOOL WINAPI WNetEnumServers(SERVERENUMPROC lpServerEnumProc,
                            WORD wServerType);
BOOL WINAPI WNetAddUser(LPSTR lpszServerName, LPSTR lpszUserName,
                        LPSTR lpszPassword, BOOL bAdmin);
BOOL WINAPI WNetDeleteUser(LPSTR lpszServerName, LPSTR lpszUserName);
BOOL WINAPI WNetEnumUsers(LPSTR lpszServerName,
                          USERENUMPROC lpUserEnumProc);
BOOL WINAPI WNetAddGroup(LPSTR lpszServerName, LPSTR lpszGroupName);
BOOL WINAPI WNetDeleteGroup(LPSTR lpszServerName,
                            LPSTR lpszGroupName);
BOOL WINAPI WNetEnumGroups(LPSTR lpszServerName,
                           GROUPENUMPROC lpGroupEnumProc);
BOOL WINAPI WNetAddGroupMember(LPSTR lpszServerName,
                               LPSTR lpszGroupName,
                               LPSTR lpszUserName);
BOOL WINAPI WNetDeleteGroupMember(LPSTR lpszServerName,
                                  LPSTR lpszGroupName,
                                  LPSTR lpszUserName);
BOOL WINAPI WNetIsUserGroupMember(LPSTR lpszServerName,
```

```
                                    LPSTR lpszGroupName,
                                    LPSTR lpszUserName);
BOOL WINAPI WNetEnumGroupMembers(LPSTR lpszServerName,
                                 LPSTR lpszGroupName,
                                 GROUPMEMBERENUMPROC lpMemberEnumProc);
BOOL WINAPI WNetEnumMemberGroups(LPSTR lpszServerName,
                                 LPSTR lpszUserName,
                                 MEMBERGROUPENUMPROC lpGroupEnumProc);
BOOL WINAPI WNetGrantRights(LPSTR lpszServerName,
                            LPSTR lpszUserOrGroup,
                            LPSTR lpszResource,
                            WORD  wRights);
BOOL WINAPI WNetRevokeRights(LPSTR lpszServerName,
                             LPSTR lpszUserOrGroup,
                             LPSTR lpszResource,
                             BOOL  bUser);
BOOL WINAPI WNetGetRights(LPSTR  lpszServerName,
                          LPSTR  lpszUserOrGroup,
                          LPSTR  lpszResource,
                          LPWORD lpwRights);
```

## CHAPTER 9

Windows Built-In Network Services

Overview

Windows 3.0 was the first version of Windows to offer any network awareness. That awareness was provided by the addition of network drivers that support a small set of standardized functions, mostly focusing on mapping local devices to network resources and on printing to network print queues. The Windows 3.1 drivers add a number of new functions; three of the most important functions in 3.0—WNetAddConnection(), WNetCancelConnection(), and WNetGetConnection()—are now part of the standard Windows API, and are included in USER.EXE.

The network services offered by Windows are still quite limited. There are 40-some functions in the network driver. By contrast, the LAN Manager API offers over 100 functions; the VINES Application Toolkit has around 200; and *NetWare C Interface for Windows* has close to 400. Nevertheless, Windows 3.1 does offer some useful and interesting network services, plus some common dialog boxes.

The inclusion of WNetAddConnection(), WNetCancelConnection(), and WNetGetConnection() in USER.EXE does not change the situation much. All it means is that you can now call those functions from a Windows application without owning the Windows Device Driver Kit (DDK). To use any of the other functions, you need the header files included with the DDK, specifically, WINDOWS.H and WINNET.H. The version of WINDOWS.H that comes with the DDK is slightly different from the one shipped with the SDK.

The User's View of the World

As we explore the Windows network services, we will have a glimpse of what the world looks like from the user's point of view. The purpose of the network driver, after all, is not to provide a general-purpose network services API; it is to give Windows a device-independent way of providing network services to the end user. The functions in the driver are called by File Manager, Print Manager, and Control Panel to handle network-specific situations. For example, when you click on the Networks icon in Control Panel, Windows calls WNetDeviceMode(). When you click the Network... button on the Control Panel Printer Setup screen, Windows calls WNetConnectDialog().

The Driver Specification

The specification for the network driver functions is published in Chapter 5 of the *Device Driver Adaptation Guide*, one of the manuals for the Windows 3.1 DDK. This specification could provide the basis for a standardized interface; in the functions that are supported by all networks, it does indeed do that. The problem with the network driver specification (besides its spartan set of services) is that the functions are not consistently *not* supported. The specification states, "The network driver *must* support all the functions defined in this chapter..." (emphasis added). Each function is supposed to return a WN_NOT_SUPPORTED error code if the driver does not implement it. This makes sense, and our job would be easier if all the driver implementations worked this way.

But they don't. Some of the drivers do indeed return WN_NOT_SUPPORTED for *some* unsupported functions. Other unsupported functions are simply omitted, causing errors if you try to link to the driver. For example, the NetWare driver (NET-WARE.DRV), the LAN Manager driver (LANMAN21.DRV), the VINES driver (VINES.DRV), and the generic MS-Net driver (MSNET.DRV) don not support WNetViewQueueDialog(). NetWare and MS-Net, however, include the function and return WN_NOT_SUPPORTED when you invoke it. LAN Manager simply omits it. (Ironically, Novell's adherence to the specification is more faithful than Microsoft's. However, Novell omits the long filename functions.)

Calling the Functions

If you are only using WNetAddConnection(), WNetCancelConnection(), and WNetGet-Connection(), you can ignore the discussion in this section. You need do nothing special to call them; they are prototyped in WINDOWS.H, and you can link to them by way of LIBW.LIB in Microsoft C, or IMPORTS.LIB in Borland C++.

Using the functions in the driver is not quite as simple. Because of the inconsistency in the way functions are not implemented, programs that use them are not source-code compatible across all possible networks. If all network drivers included all the functions, then the driver could be given a standard name (how about NETWORK.DRV?) when you install Windows, and the SDK could provide an import library.

One option is to generate an import library from the driver by typing:

```
IMPLIB <network>.LIB <network>.DRV
```

You must then tailor your source code to the specific target network using #ifdef statements.

The most flexible way to call the driver functions is to use the technique I discussed in Chapters 2 and 8.

1. Get the name of the driver file by calling GetPrivateProfileString(). The [boot] section of SYSTEM.INI contains the parameter NETWORK.DRV=. Its value is the name of the actual network driver file, such as MSNET.DRV or NETWARE.DRV.
2. Call LoadLibrary() to load the driver. The call may fail; for instance, the user may not have the network software installed.
3. If the library loads successfully, initialize pointers to all the functions named in the driver specification by calling GetProcAddress(). It will return NULL for any functions that have been omitted.

To go one step further and provide full source-code compatibility, you need to write front-end routines with the same name as the driver functions. After going through the procedure outlined above to set up function pointers, these routines do one of three things:

1. If the pointer is not NULL, they invoke the driver function.
2. Otherwise, they flag the function as not supported.
3. If either of the above steps indicates that the function is not supported, either return WN_NOT_SUPPORTED, or provide default processing.

Once again, I should mention that similar front-end functions for the WNet() network driver functions are contained in USER.EXE, but not documented. You can link to these routines by generating an import library from USER.EXE. This eliminates the need for your own front end to the driver. I will not dwell on this approach, though, precisely because it is undocumented. In the future, it may end up being documented, but it may also change radically. That, after all, is always the problem with using undocumented features. In any case, these stubs in USER.EXE currently do something very similar to what I describe here.

Connection Functions in USER.EXE

There are four functions in the Connection group: WNetAddConnection(), WNetCancelConnection(), WNetGetConnection(), and WNetRestoreConnection(). Starting with Windows 3.1, the first three are included in USER.EXE, and can therefore be linked to through LIBW.LIB. As you might expect, these are just front-end routines for the corresponding routines in the driver. Their presence in USER.EXE makes them easier for Windows applications to access (and cheaper—you don't have to buy the DDK).

The most important network services offered by Windows are contained in WNetAddConnection() and WNetCancelConnection(). They map a local device to a network resource and reset the local mapping, respectively. Sharing network resources is, after all, one of the primary reasons for installing a LAN.

WNetAddConnection()

WNetAddConnection() connects a local device to a network resource. Here is the prototype from WINDOWS.H:

```
UINT WINAPI WNetAddConnection(LPSTR lpszNetPath, LPSTR lpszPassword,

                              LPSTR lpszLocalName);
```

WNetAddConnection() connects the local device *lpszLocalName* to the network resource *lpszNetPath*. *lpszLocalName* can be a drive from A: to Z:, or a print device like LPT1, LPT2, etc. *lpszPassword* is necessary only for servers running the equivalent of LAN Manager's share-level security. This includes workstations running the LAN Manager Basic workstation software, and most of the MS-Net compatible networks. On these networks, users do not log on to the network or a server. Instead, they are given access to individual shared resources by supplying a password.

WNetCancelConnection()

WNetCancelConnection() deletes a network mapping:

```
UINT WINAPI WNetCancelConnection(LPSTR lpszName, BOOL fForce);
```

lpszName can specify either the local or the remote name of the resource. If it is a remote name, all connections to the device will be closed. If *fForce* is TRUE, then any files or print jobs open on the device will be closed before the connection is canceled. If it is FALSE, WNetCancelConnection() will fail if there are open jobs, returning WN_OPEN_FILES.

WNetGetConnection()

WNetGetConnection() reports the current mapping of a local device:

```
UINT WINAPI WNetGetConnection(LPSTR lpszLocalName, LPSTR lpszRemoteName,
                          UINT FAR *lpcbBufferSize);
```

On input, *lpszLocalName* is the local device whose mapping you are asking about, and *lpcbBufferSize* points to an unsigned int indicating the initial size of the buffer. If the function is successful, the network name is returned in *lpszRemoteName*, and *lpcbBufferSize* is set to the number of bytes returned. If the function returns WN_MORE_DATA, the buffer pointed to by *lpszRemoteName* is too small, and *lpcbBufferSize* tells you how many bytes of memory you need.

There is a wrinkle that diminishes the value of WNetGetConnection(). Under NetWare, it does not correctly report any drives the user mapped before starting Windows, unless he mapped them as virtual roots using the MAP ROOT command. If you map a drive to a NetWare directory without specifying ROOT, the root of the mapped drive is the volume on which the directory resides. Thus, if drive F: is mapped to SYS:SYSTEM, when you change to drive F:, you will be in F:\SYSTEM. You can then type cd .. to back up to the root of the volume. If, on the other hand, you map drive G: as a virtual root to SYS:SYSTEM (MAP ROOT G:=SYS:SYSTEM), when you change to G:, you will be in the directory G:\. Now, you cannot go any further up the tree.

For any drives not mapped as roots, WNetGetConnection() returns only the server and volume names. So for the drive F: that I mapped to SYS:SYSTEM on my server NW3BOOK, WNetGetConnection() will return NW3BOOK/SYS:.

Figure 9-1 shows the dialog box presented by WNetConnectionDialog() (which I discuss shortly). Notice the strings enclosed in square brackets. These are the strings that WNetGetConnection() returns. It does correctly report all drives mapped by calling WNetAddConnection() within Windows, whether or not they are mapped as roots. This includes drives mapped using the driver dialog boxes.

**Figure 9-1. NetWare WNetConnectionDialog()
Driver Reported by WNetGetConnection()**

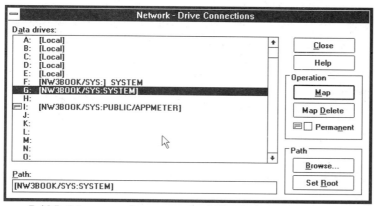

LAN Manager (or generic MS-Net) NET USE behavior mimics NetWare MAP ROOT. When you connect a drive to a shared server directory, the directory automatically becomes the root directory of the drive. So, for instance, if you type:

```
NET USE G: \\LMSERVER\PUBLIC
```

G:\ becomes an alias for \\LMSERVER\PUBLIC, and you cannot ascend the tree any further. If, for instance, you go to G:\ and type cd .., you will get the DOS message "Invalid directory." You will not move to \\LMSERVER\. WNetGetConnection() correctly reports the mapping of G: as \\LMSERVER\PUBLIC.

Connection Functions in the Network Driver

WNetAddConnection(), WNetCancelConnection(), and WNetGetConnection() also exist in the network driver. The routines in the driver provide the network-specific support for the top-level functions in USER.EXE. There is one additional connection function in the driver, WNetRestoreConnection().

WNetRestoreConnection() is a somewhat esoteric function; it is unclear to me what value it has for applications, if any. It is rooted in the concept of permanent, or persistent, connections. This is a feature built into LAN Manager whereby it remembers connections that you make during one session. Then, the next time you log on, it automatically restores them. You do not need to run a login script to make the connection. (This applies only to an Enhanced LAN Manager workstation.)

For networks that do not provide this feature (like NetWare, VINES, or MS-Net networks), Windows offers a convenient way to emulate it. The [Network] section of WIN.INI records any permanent drive mappings. Here is the [Network] section of my NetWare WIN.INI file:

```
[Network]
I:=[NW3BOOK/SYS:PUBLIC]
H:=[NETWARE_286/SYS:PUBLIC]
```

During its initialization, the NetWare driver scans the entries in WIN.INI and calls WNetAddConnection() to reconnect the drives. It may also ask the user for more information. For instance, if one of the drives is mapped to a server that the user is not attached to, it prompts for the user's login ID and password.

Here is the syntax for WNetRestoreConnection(), taken from WINNET.H:

```
WORD API WNetRestoreConnection(HWND hWndParent, LPSTR lpszDevice);
```

This is the first time we have seen the function type API. It is defined in the version of WINDOWS.H that comes with the DDK, and is a synonym for WINAPI. However, WINAPI is defined slightly differently in this version of WINDOWS.H. Here are the pertinent lines:

```
#ifdef BUILDDLL
#define WINAPI          _loadds _far _pascal
#define CALLBACK        _loadds _far _pascal
#else
#define WINAPI          _far _pascal
#define CALLBACK        _far _pascal
#endif
#define API             WINAPI
```

Because the DDK is used to build .DRV files, which are DLLs, the #define adds the keyword _loadds, which forces the loading of the DS register when the DLL function is entered.

The *hWndParent* argument to WNetRestoreConnection() is included because it is assumed that WNetRestoreConnection() may need to present dialog boxes to the user. *hWndParent* will serve as their parent window. *lpszDevice* specifies the device to redirect. There is no argument saying what to map *lpszDevice* to; it is assumed that the driver has some way of retrieving this information. If *lpszDevice* is NULL, the driver will restore all permanent connections. If it is one, WNetRestoreConnection() does any required device-specific initialization, then restores all drives.

The driver specification states that File Manager calls WNetRestoreConnection() "exactly once" with the argument one during its initialization, and never calls it with a NULL argument. It is unclear what this means, but experimentation yields some unexpected results. For example:

- To disconnect a LAN Manager drive that is a permanent connection, you have to select the Disconnect Network Drive option twice. The first time, the disconnection has no effect.

- Once you have disconnected a drive in File Manager (either a LAN Manager or a NetWare drive), it will not reappear in File Manager, even if you exit File Manager and start it up again. Furthermore, if you log off the LAN Manager server, then log on again as the same user, the drives no longer appear in File Manager.

It appears that after the first disconnection, LAN Manager immediately restores the drive. The second disconnection not only disconnects the drive, but removes it from the list of permanent connections.

I have never encountered a situation where I needed to call WNetRestoreConnection().

Dialog Boxes

I have termed the network driver dialogs "common dialogs" because they have some similarities to the Windows 3.1 Common Dialogs. They provide a standard way to offer network services to users of your software. For instance, if you want to allow a user to connect to a network drive, you can present a dialog box to gather the information you need, and then call WNetAddConnection(). You can also just call WNetConnectDialog() or WNetConnectionDialog(); they will handle all the interaction with the user, and do the drive mapping for you. Most of the network dialogs act like WNetConnectDialog(); that is, they do not return values. Instead, they collect information from the user, then carry out whatever action he or she has requested.

All the dialog box functions take a window handle as their first argument. In the prototypes, I show it as *hWndParent*. This serves as the parent window handle in the call the driver makes to the DialogBox() function.

Table 9-1 lists the dialog functions.

Table 9-1. Windows Network Driver Dialog Functions

Function Name	Supported By			
	NetWare	LAN Manager	VINES	MS-Net
WNetBrowseDialog	X	X		
WNetConnectDialog	X	X		
WNetConnectionDialog	X	X		
WNetDeviceMode	X	X	X	X
WNetDisconnectDialog	X	X		
WNetPropertyDialog	X			
WNetViewQueueDialog				

VINES has two dialog box functions of its own: VnsDlgStdaSelect() and VnsDlgStdaMultiSelect(). They are similar to WNetBrowseDialog(); they allow the user to browse the network resources that are available for her to connect to.

The most important of the dialog functions are WNetConnectDialog(), WNetConnectionDialog(), WNetDisconnectDialog(), and WNetDeviceMode().

The Connection Dialog Boxes

The driver specification states that the driver may choose to support connect and disconnect with separate dialogs [WNetConnectDialog() and WNetDisconnectDialog()], or support them both with WNetConnectionDialog(). Novell heeds this advice; WNetConnect-Dialog() and WNetDisconnectDialog() are implemented, but they both call WNetConnectionDialog(). LAN Manager implements all three functions: Control Panel calls WNetConnectionDialog() when you connect to a network printer; File Manager calls WNetConnectDialog() and WNetDisconnectDialog() when you select Connect Network Drive or Disconnect Network Drive from the Disk menu. Incidentally, you can tell how your network implements these dialogs by examining the File Manager Disk menu. If connect and disconnect are separate options (as under LAN Manager), WNetConnectDialog() and WNetDisconnectDialog() are implemented independently. If there is only one option (called Network Connections under NetWare), then connects and disconnects are handled by WNetConnectionDialog().

Here are the prototypes for these functions from WINNET.H:

```
WORD API WNetConnectDialog(HWND hWndParent, WORD wType);
WORD API WNetDisconnectDialog(HWND hWndParent, WORD wType);
WORD API WNetConnectionDialog(HWND hWndParent, WORD wType);
```

wType indicates the type of resource you are interested in, and can be one of the values shown in Table 9-2:

Table 9-2. Network Resource Types

Type	Meaning
WNTYPE_DRIVE	Disk drive
WNTYPE_FILE	File (not presently supported)
WNTYPE_PRINTER	Printer device
WNTYPE_COMM	Communications port (reserved, should not be used)

The type WNTYPE_FILE is a good example of how functions in the network driver are not consistently *not* supported. Neither NetWare nor LAN Manager support this as an argument to WNetConnectDialog() or WNetConnectionDialog(). LAN Manager returns WN_BAD_VALUE when you pass it a type of WNTYPE_FILE, which makes sense. NetWare returns WN_NET_ERROR. According to the driver specification, when a function returns WN_NET_ERROR, you should call WNetGetError() to get the error code, then WNetGetErrorText() to get the corresponding message. However, in this case, if you call WNetGetError() right after WNetConnectDialog() returns WN_NET_ERROR, it returns WN_NO_ERROR.

Figures 9-2 and 9-3 show the LAN Manager WNetConnectDialog() and WNetDisconnectDialog() screens for file resources.

Notice that the last drive in the listbox in Figure 9-3, drive Q:, is mapped to a NetWare server. I took this screen shot while running the LAN Manager dual network configuration, which allows you to connect to both LAN Manager and NetWare servers.

Figures 9-4 and 9-5 show the NetWare WNetConnectionDialog() screens for drive and printer resources.

Figure 9-2. LAN Manager WNetConnectDialog()

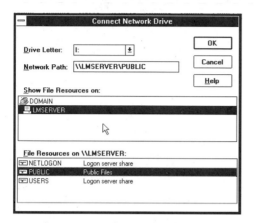

Figure 9-3. LAN Manager WNetDisconnectDialog()

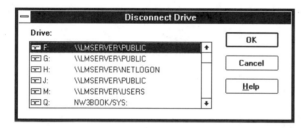

Figure 9-4. NetWare WNetConnectionDialog() for directories

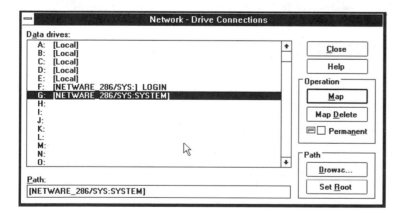

Figure 9-5. NetWare WNetConnectionDialog() for Print Queues

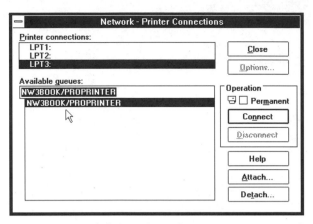

Figure 9-6 shows the LAN Manager WNetConnectionDialog() screen for connecting to network printers.

Figure 9-6. LAN Manager WNetConnectionDialog() for Print Queues

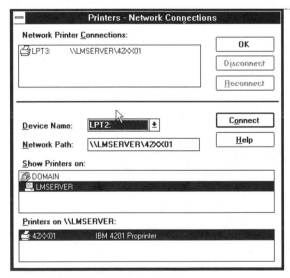

WNetBrowseDialog()

The Browse dialog box allows the user to select network drives and print queues from list boxes, much like the File Open common dialog box. It is the only dialog function that returns information. Here is its prototype:

```
WORD API WNetBrowseDialog(HWND hWndParent, WORD wType, LPSTR lpszPath);
```

wType has two possible values: WNBD_CONN_DISKTREE and WNBD_CONN_PRINTQ. WNBD_CONN_DISKTREE lets the user browse the directory structures of network disks. WNBD_CONN_PRINTQ browses network print queues. If the function returns WN_SUCCESS, *lpszPath* contains the resource selected by the user.

The NetWare driver invokes this function when the user selects the Browse push button on the connection dialog box (see Figure 9-4). LAN Manager supports the function, but does not give the user a hook to it.

The primary purpose of WNetBrowseDialog() is to support connecting to and disconnecting from network resources. Thus, the specification states that the string returned must be suitable for passing unchanged to WNetAddConnection(). For LAN Manager, it will be in the format \\<server name>\<share name>\<path name>. For NetWare, it will be <server name>/<volume name>:<path name>.

Figures 9-7 and 9-8 show the LAN Manager browse dialog boxes.

Figure 9-7. LAN Manager WNetBrowseDialog() for Directories

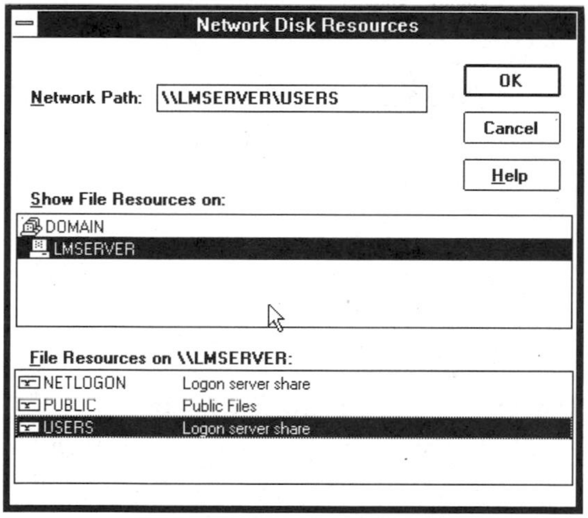

Figure 9-8. LAN Manager WNetBrowseDialog() for Print Queues

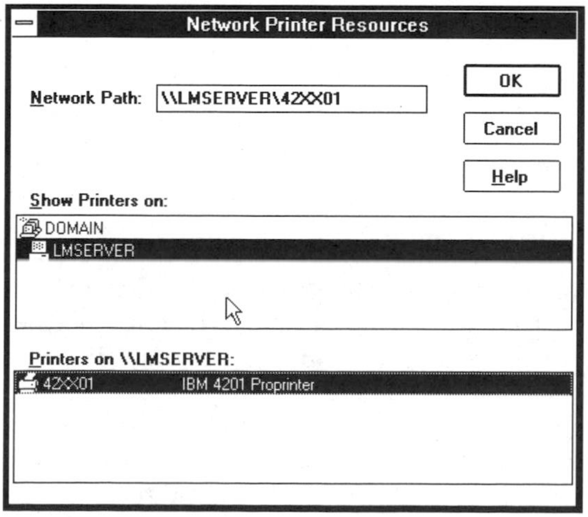

Figures 9-9 and 9-10 show the corresponding NetWare screens.

Figure 9-9. NetWare WNetBrowseDialog() for Directories

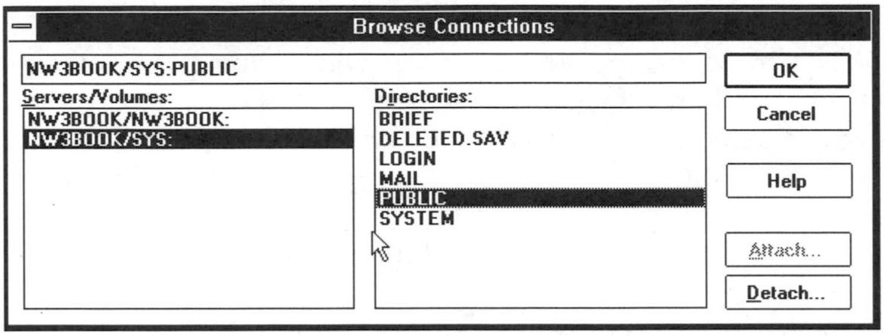

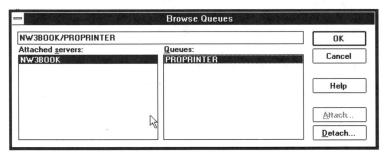

Figure 9-10. NetWare WNetBrowseDialog() for Print Queues

There is little reason to use WNetBrowseDialog() in a program. If your purpose is to connect or disconnect a network resource, you might as well use the connection dialogs, and let them do all the work.

WNetDeviceMode()

WNetDeviceMode() calls up a network-specific dialog box that allows you to set system-wide network parameters. It is activated when you double-click the Network icon in Control Panel:

```
WORD API WNetDeviceMode(HWND hWndParent);
```

This is the only dialog box supported by the VINES driver, VINES.DRV, and the generic MS-Net driver, MSNET.DRV.

NetWare   Figure 9-11 shows the NetWare device mode dialog box.

The NWShare handles setting, which is only relevant in 386 enhanced mode, controls the NWShareHandles setting in the [NetWare] section of SYSTEM.INI. This specifies whether the mapping of drives in one DOS virtual machine should affect only that VM (NWShareHandles=FALSE) or all other VMs (NWShareHandles=TRUE). By default, Windows maintains a separate set of drive mappings for each virtual machine. This is a sensible default; normally, you do not want drives mapped in one VM to affect the drives in use by another VM. However, users can change this if they need to for some reason, or if they just want to experiment with it. After seeing what it does, though, they will probably change it back. In fact, it seems to me that it would be reasonable to remove this as an option.

Figure 9-11. NetWare WNetDeviceMode()

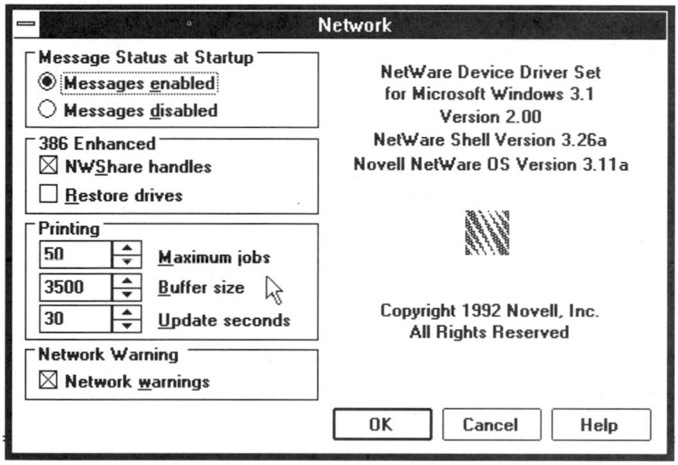

LAN Manager does not give you any choice in this matter, and it takes the counterintuitive (i.e., wrong) course of action by default. Any drives mapped in one VM (DOS or Windows) pollute all other VMs of both types.

Restore drives, which also pertains only to 386 enhanced mode, changes the RestoreDrives setting in the [NetWare] section of SYSTEM.INI. It is documented in a somewhat ambiguous manner. It is unclear whether it means restoring connections as discussed above, or restoring the drive mappings that existed before you ran Windows when you return to DOS. It means the latter. The default is RestoreDrives=TRUE.

The printing options determine the number of jobs Print Manager will display, the size of internal buffers used for printing, and the frequency with which NetWare will advise Print Manager to update its display by posting an SP_QUEUECHANGED message.

The network warning option determines whether NetWare will warn the user when she starts Windows without having loaded the workstation shell. When this happens, the network driver is not loaded, and no network services are available. It is saved in the [windows] section of WIN.INI under the setting NetWarn=.

LAN Manager   Figure 9-12 shows the LAN Manager WNetDeviceMode() screen.

Instead of using checkboxes, it offers a menu of options. The Account menu includes Logon, Logoff, Change Password, and Exit.

The Message menu has one option, Send, which presents the dialog box shown in Figure 9-13. It allows the user to send a message to a user on another station (or to herself, for that matter).

Figure 9-12. LAN Manager WNetDeviceMode()

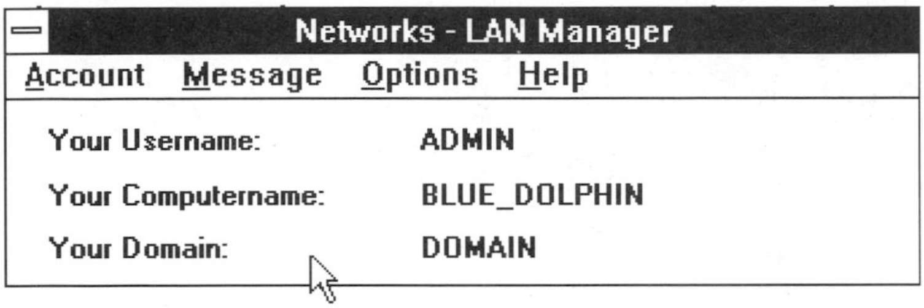

Figure 9-13. LAN Manager Send Message Dialog Box

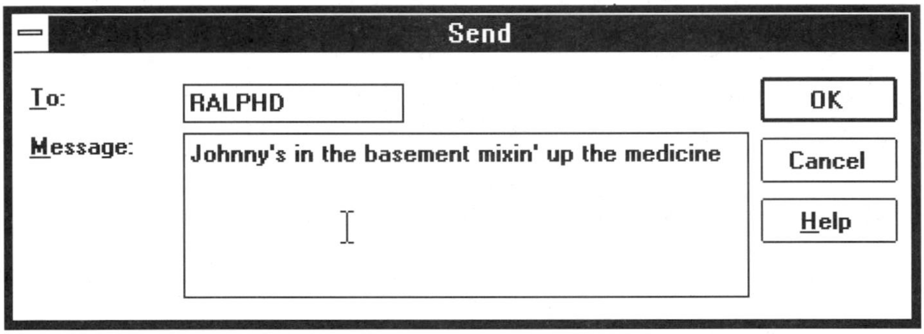

The Options menu has four items: Log On at Startup, Restore Connections at Log On, Save Changes to Connections, and Display Initial Warning Message.

These are each toggled items; selecting the menu item checks or unchecks it. The options *Log On at Startup* and *Restore Connections at Log On* are handy. They make it possible for you to go right into Windows when you boot your computer, and still end up logged on to the network when your Windows session starts. *Save Changes to Connections* is the same setting as the NetWare *RestoreDrives*, but reverses the logic. It defaults to TRUE. *Display Initial Warning Message* is the same as the NetWare network warning, and also sets the NetWarn parameter in WIN.INI.

MS-Net   Figure 9-14 (on the following page) shows the MS-Net device mode dialog box. This is the only dialog box it supports.

The network warning option is the same as for NetWare and LAN Manager, and, like them, it affects the NetWarn setting in WIN.INI. *Restore all connections at startup* influences whether Windows restores network drives remembered in the [network] section of WIN.INI. It also sets a boolean flag in that section, Restore=.

VINES   The VINES device mode dialog box is a read-only screen; it does not present any configurable options. The VINES driver displays it as a sign-on screen when it starts up.

Figure 9-14. MS-Net WNetDeviceMode()

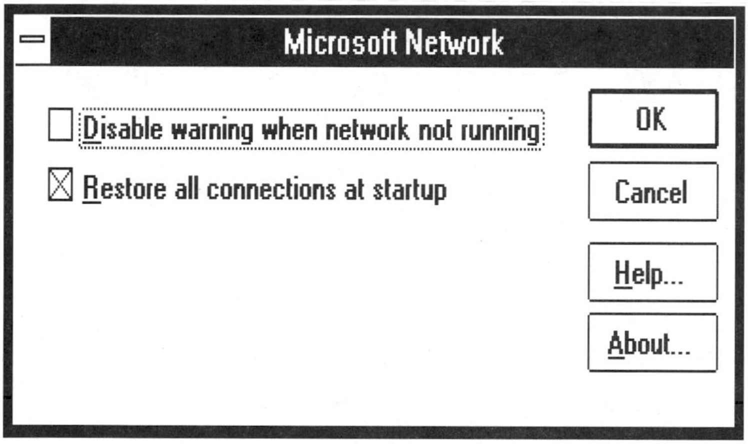

WNetGetPropertyText() and WNetPropertyDialog()

These functions provide network support for the File Properties dialog box in File Manager. They allow the network driver to add network-specific buttons to the screen, and activate a dialog box in the driver when the user selects one of them. At present, only NetWare supports them. Here are the prototypes:

```
WORD API WNetGetPropertyText(WORD wButton, WORD wPropSel,
                        LPSTR lpszName, LPSTR lpszButtonName,
                        WORD cbButtonName, WORD wType);
WORD API WNetPropertyDialog(HWND hWndParent, WORD wButton,
                        WORD wPropSel, LPSTR lpszName, WORD wType);
```

The *wButton*, *wPropSel*, *lpszName*, and *wType* arguments are common to both functions. *wButton* is an index from zero to five. File Manager calls WNetGetPropertyText() in a loop, starting *wButton* at zero. It terminates the loop when *wButton* reaches six, or the function returns a zero-length button name in *lpszButtonName*.

wPropSel and *wType* appear to be somewhat redundant. *wPropSel* can take the value WNPS_FILE, WNPS_DIR, or WNPS_MULT. NetWare only returns a value when *wPropSel* is WNPS_FILE. *wType*, for its part, can only be WNTYPE_FILE. You can select directories and multiple files in File Manager, then ask to view their properties. Figure 9-15 shows the Property dialog box that File Manager presents when you select multiple files.

When File Manager calls WNetGetPropertyText() with *wPropSel* set to WNPS_FILE, button zero gets the text Network.... Figure 9-16 shows the File Manager property dialog with this button.

When you press the Network... button, File Manager calls WNetPropertyDialog(), passing it a *wButton* of zero, a *wPropSel* of WNPS_FILE, an *lpszName* of DRWATSON.EXE, and a *wType* of WNTYPE_FILE. Figure 9-17 shows the dialog box that NetWare displays. It allows the user to set the extended attributes that NetWare associates with a file.

Figure 9-15. File Manager Property Screen for Multiple Files

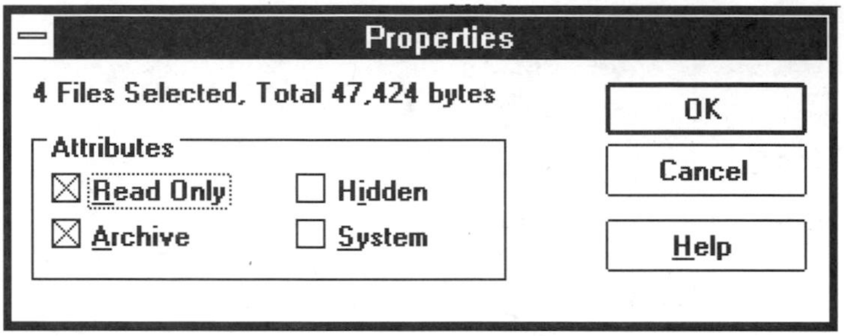

Figure 9-16. File Manager Property Screen for Single NetWare Files

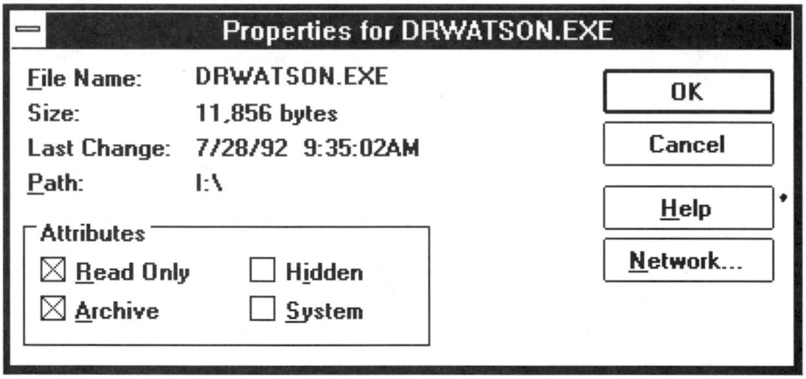

Figure 9-17. NetWare WNetPropertyDialog()

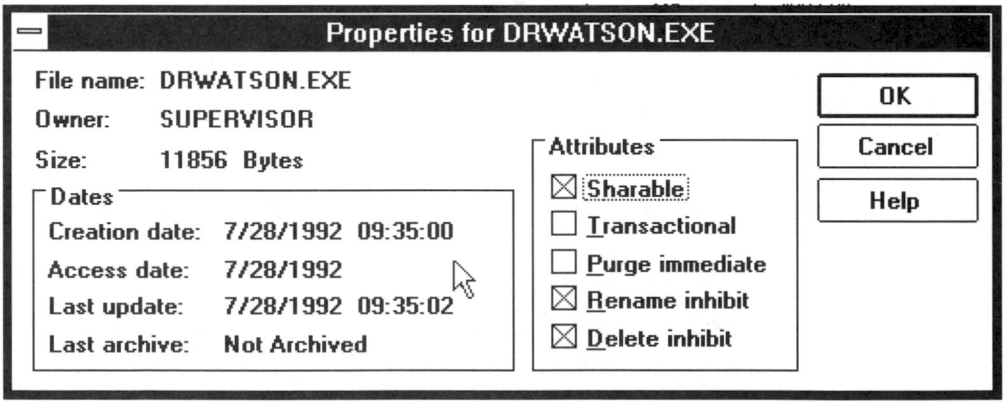

The sample program in Appendix C shows an example that calls WNetProperty-Dialog() to display the extended NetWare attributes of a file.

Monitoring Print Queues

There are four functions that you can use to monitor print queues: WNetWatchQueue(), WNetLockQueueData(), WNetUnlockQueueData(), and WNetUnlockData(). These are the functions Print Manager uses to provide queue status information. Figure 9-18 shows the Print Manager screen for NetWare.

Figure 9-18. Print Manager Monitor for NetWare

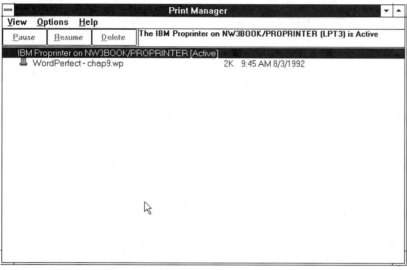

The sequence of steps in monitoring a queue are:

1. Call WNetWatchQueue(). Following this, the network driver will post SP_QUEUECHANGED messages to your window procedure. Messages will be posted at 30-second intervals, or whenever the queue status changes. NetWare allows you to change the notification interval on the WNetDeviceMode() dialog screen, which is accessed through Control Panel. SP_QUEUECHANGED is defined in WINNET.H as 0x0500. If you watch the message stream with SPY, it refers to it as WM_USER + 256.

2. In response to the SP_QUEUECHANGED message, call WNetLockQueueData() to get information on the jobs currently in the queue.

3. After you have read the queue information, call WNetUnlockQueueData().

4. When you are done monitoring the queue, call WNetUnwatchQueue() to cancel notification.

The driver demo program in Appendix C displays print queue information in a mode-less dialog box.

WNetWatchQueue() and WNetUnwatchQueue()

The prototype for WNetWatchQueue() is:

```
WORD API WNetWatchQueue(HWND hWnd, LPSTR lpszLocal, LPSTR lpszUser,
                    WORD wQueue);
```

This requests notification for the queue to which *lpszLocal* (LPT1, LPT2, etc.) is attached. If *lpszUser* is not NULL, only queue changes caused by that user will trigger notification. Otherwise, all jobs are reported. *wQueue* will be passed to *hWnd* as the *wParam* of the SP_QUEUECHANGED message, and can be used to identify the queue if you are watching more than one.

WNetWatchQueue() is documented to return the error WN_ALREADY_LOCKED if someone else is watching the queue. However, I have not noticed any problems here. You can watch a queue at the same time that Print Manager is capturing the queue status; the driver sends both of you SP_QUEUECHANGED messages.

WNetUnwatchQueue() cancels notification:

```
WORD API WNetUnwatchQueue(LPSTR lpszLocal);
```

lpszLocal is the same argument that you passed previously to WNetWatchQueue().

WNetLockQueueData() and WNetUnlockQueueData()

WNetLockQueueData() returns information on the jobs currently in a print queue. Its syntax is:

```
WORD API WNetLockQueueData(LPSTR lpszQueue, LPSTR lpszUser,
                    LPQUEUESTRUCT FAR *lplpQueueStruct);
```

lpszQueue gives either the local or the remote name of the queue. *lpszUser* has the same meaning as it does for WNetWatchQueue(); if it is not NULL, only jobs submitted by the indicated user will be reported. *lplpQueueStruct* is a pointer to a pointer to a QUEUESTRUCT, defined as follows in WINNET.H:

```
typedef struct _queuestruct    {
    WORD   pqName;       // Queue name
    WORD   pqComment;
    WORD   pqStatus;     // Queue status
                         // WNPRQ_ACTIVE: active
                         // WNPRQ_PAUSE: paused
                         // WNPRQ_ERROR: network error
                         // WNPRQ_PENDING: queue is being deleted. Current
                         //                jobs will run to completion,
                         //                but no new jobs may be submitted
                         // WNPRQ_PROBLEM: all printers stopped
    WORD   pqJobcount;   // Number of jobs in the queue
    WORD   pqPrinters;   // Number of printers servicing the queue
} QUEUESTRUCT;
```

The function sets the pointer designated by *lplpQueueStruct* to point to a buffer holding the returned information. In this buffer, a QUEUESTRUCT precedes an array of JOBSTRUCTs describing each individual job. The number of JOBSTRUCTs is indicated by the *pqJobcount* field in the QUEUESTRUCT.

```
typedef struct _jobstruct {
   WORD  pjId;          // Job ID
   WORD  pjUsername;    // Submitting user
   WORD  pjParms;       // Implementation string
   WORD  pjPosition;    // Position in the queue
   WORD  pjStatus;      // Combination of Queue Status and Device Status
                        // Queue Statuses
                        // WNPRJ_QS_QUEUED: job is queued
                        // WNPRJ_QS_PAUSED: job is paused
                        // WNPRJ_QS_SPOOLING: job is spooling
                        // WNPRJ_QS_PRINTING: job is printing
                        // Device Statuses
                        // WNPRJ_DS_COMPLETE: job is complete
                        // WNPRJ_DS_INTERV: intervention is required
                        // WNPRJ_DS_ERROR: printer error
                        // WNPRJ_DS_DESTOFFLIN: printer offline
                        // WNPRJ_DS_DESTPAUSED: printer paused
                        // WNPRJ_DS_NOTIFY: notify owner
                        // WNPRJ_DS_DESTNOPAPER: printer out of paper
                        // WNPRJ_DS_DESTFORMCHG: form change required
                        // WNPRJ_DS_DESTCRTCHG: cartridge change required
                        // WNPRJ_DS_DESTPENCHG: pen change required
   DWORD pjSubmitted;   // Time when job submitted (UNIX time)
   DWORD pjSize;        // Job size in bytes. If -1L, size is not available
   WORD  pjCopies;      // Number of copies. If zero, not available
   WORD  pjComment;     // Job comment
} JOBSTRUCT;
```

Any strings returned (*pqName*, *pqComment*, *pjUsername*, *pjParms*, and *pjComment*) are returned as offsets from the beginning of the QUEUESTRUCT. Thus, if *lpQueueStruct* points to the QUEUESTRUCT, you get the print queue name as (LPSTR) lpQueueStruct + lpQueueStruct->pjName. To find the user who submitted a particular job in the queue, first set a JOBSTRUCT pointer to the beginning of the JOBSTRUCT array, as follows:

```
JOBSTRUCT FAR *lpJobStruct;

lpJobStruct = (JOBSTRUCT FAR *) (&lpQueueStruct[1]);
```

The user who submitted the fifth job in the queue, for example, can then be fetched as:

```
(LPSTR) lpQueueStruct + lpJobStruct[4].pjUsername
```

See the demonstration program in Appendix C for an example of using these structures.

WNetUnlockQueueData() releases the block of information returned by WNetLock-QueueData():

```
WORD API WNetUnlockQueueData(LPSTSR lpszQueue);
```

lpszQueue is the queue name that you passed to WNetLockQueueData().

Other Useful WNet() Functions

There are a few other WNet() functions of varying value to application programs: WNet-GetUser(), WNetGetDirectoryType(), WNetGetError(), WNetGetErrorText(), and WNet-GetCaps().

WNetGetUser()
WNetGetUser() reports the login name of the user on the current workstation:

```
WORD API WNetGetUser(LPSTR lpszUser, LPINT lpnBufferSize);
```

This information is often useful. For instance, you might pass it to the queue-watching functions to limit the report to that user's jobs. WNetGetUser() has ascended to the documented API in Win32.

WNetGetDirectoryType()
This is a valuable function—or at least the service it theoretically provides is valuable. In my experience developing networked applications, I have often needed to know whether a drive is local or mapped to a network.

```
WORD API WNetGetDirectoryType(LPSTR lpName, LPINT lpType);
```

The type of the directory *lpName* is returned through *lpType*. If it is WNDT_NET-WORK, the drive is mapped to a network disk. A value of WNDT_NORMAL means it is local. The only documented error is WN_NET_ERROR.

At present, this function is only supported by NetWare. However, if it reports that the type is WNDT_NORMAL, it does not necessarily mean that the drive is local. It only means that NetWare never heard of it. The NetWare driver returns WN_SUCCESS whether the drive is a valid local drive, like C:, or just a drive that isn't currently mapped to the network.

Actually, Windows provides a function that does the same thing, GetDriveType():

```
UINT GetDriveType(int nDriveNumber);
```

It returns DRIVE_REMOVABLE for a removable drive, DRIVE_FIXED for a hard disk, DRIVE_REMOTE for a network disk, and zero for an unused disk.

Because this information can be useful, my front end for WNetGetDirectoryType() calls GetDriveType() if WNetGetDirectoryType() does not return a definitive answer (that is, it either returns WN_NOT_SUPPORTED or says that the drive is a local drive). It is probably a good idea to call WNetGetDirectoryType() if it exists, because the file name may be in some format that only the network driver understands. For instance, it could be a NetWare file name in the format SYS:PUBLIC/POOBAH.TXT.

Here is my front-end routine for WNetGetDirectoryType(). (See Appendix C for the complete source listing.)

```
WORD API WNetGetDirectoryType(LPSTR lpszName, LPINT lpnType)
{
    // We are going to support this guy if the driver doesn't
    // by using GetDriveType()

    // We will call the driver version if it exists, because
    // the file name may be in some format that only the
    // network driver will understand
    // For example, it could be a NetWare file name in the format
    // SYS:PUBLIC/POOBAH.TXT

    static WORD (API *lpWNetGetDirectoryType)(LPSTR,LPINT) = NULL;
    static BOOL bPointerValid = FALSE;
    WORD    wReturnValue;
    BYTE    byDrive;
    int     nDriveType = WNDT_NORMAL;

    if (hNetLib == (HINSTANCE) (-1))
        (FARPROC) lpWNetGetDirectoryType = CheckLib("WNetGetDirectoryType");
    else if ((hNetLib != 0) && (!bPointerValid))
        {
        (FARPROC) lpWNetGetDirectoryType =
            GetProcAddress(hNetLib, "WNetGetDirectoryType");
        bPointerValid = TRUE;
        }

    if (lpWNetGetDirectoryType != NULL)
        {
        wReturnValue = lpWNetGetDirectoryType(lpszName, lpnType);

        if (wReturnValue == WN_NOT_SUPPORTED)
            {
            // Set function pointer to NULL so we don't call the
            // driver function over and over again
            lpWNetGetDirectoryType = NULL;
            }
        else if (wReturnValue == WN_SUCCESS && *lpnType == WNDT_NORMAL)
            {
            // Meaningless--doesn't tell us anything except that
            // network (most likely NetWare) never heard of the drive
            wReturnValue - WN_NOT_SUPPORTED;
            }
        }
    else
        wReturnValue = WN_NOT_SUPPORTED;

    if (wReturnValue == WN_NOT_SUPPORTED)
        {
        if (lpszName[1] == ':')
```

```
            byDrive = (lpszName[0] - 'A');
        else
            {
            *lpnType = WNDT_NORMAL;    // Actually means I don't know
            return WN_SUCCESS;
            }
        switch (GetDriveType(byDrive))
            {
            case 0:
                wReturnValue = WN_NET_ERROR;
                break;
            case DRIVE_REMOTE:
                nDriveType = WNDT_NETWORK;
                wReturnValue = WN_SUCCESS;
                break;
            default:
                nDriveType = WNDT_NORMAL;
                wReturnValue = WN_SUCCESS;
                break;
            }
        *lpnType = nDriveType;
        }
    return wReturnValue;
}
```

WNetDirectoryNotify()

This function sounds useful as it is documented in the Microsoft specification. In practice, however, it does very little, and is only of marginal value. Only NetWare supports it.

The purpose of the function is to allow File Manager (or any other Windows program) to tell the network driver that it wants to perform some directory operation. The driver then has the option of performing the operation itself, requesting information from the user, or telling the calling program to go ahead with the operation.

Here is the syntax:

```
WORD API WNetDirectoryNotify(HWND hWndParent, LPSTR lpDir, WORD wOperation);
```

This tells the driver that you want to do *wOperation* to *lpDir*. Possible values for *wOperation* are WNDN_MKDIR (create the directory), WNDN_RMDIR (delete it), or WNDN_MVDIR (rename it). If the driver puts up a dialog box, *hWndParent* will be its parent window.

The driver can return these values:

- WN_CANCEL: the operation was canceled by the user. Don't do it.
- WN_CONTINUE: the driver took care of it. Don't do it.
- WN_NOT_SUPPORTED: the driver does nothing special with the operation. You do it.
- WN_SUCCESS: go ahead, you do it.

NetWare returns WN_SUCCESS when *wOperation* is WNDN_MKDIR or WNDN_RMDIR. The subsequent calls to mkdir() or rmdir() then succeed. It returns

WN_NOT_SUPPORTED when *wOperation* is WNDN_MVDIR, and the rename() call fails. Thus, WNetDirectoryNotify() is a no-op; it doesn't tell you anything you couldn't learn by just doing the operation and checking the return code. And neither LAN Manager nor VINES supports it.

WNetGetError() and WNetGetErrorText()

All of the driver functions return WN_NET_ERROR under some conditions. However, those conditions may vary widely from one network to another. The driver specification includes WNetGetError() and WNetGetErrorText() so a program can get more detailed information on the error that has occurred. WNetGetError() returns a network-specific numeric code for the error, and WNetGetErrorText() provides a message corresponding to the code.

```
WORD API WNetGetError(LPINT lpnError);
WORD API WNetGetErrorText(WORD wError, LPSTR lpszMessage,
                        LPINT lpnMessageLength);
```

For the results to be reliable, you must call the function as soon as you experience an error. The following code fragment shows how you might use it:

```
WORD wReturnCode;

wReturnCode = <some WNet() function>

if (wReturn == WN_NET_ERROR)
   DisplayNetError();
.
.
.
void DisplayNetError()
{
   WORD wNetErr;
   char szMessage[255];
   int  nBufSize;

   if (WNetGetError((LPINT) &wNetErr) != WN_SUCCESS)
      return 0;
   nBufSize = sizeof (szMessage);
   if (WNetGetErrorText(wNetErr, szMessage, &nBufSize) == WN_SUCCESS)
      MessageBox(NULL, szMessage, "Network Error", MB_OK);
}
```

WNetGetCaps()

WNetGetCaps() provides information about the capabilities and configuration of the underlying network. We used it in Chapter 2 to determine the network operating system in use. It also returns bitflags indicating what WNet() functions ("capabilities") the driver supports. Of course, this information can be determined just as well by calling GetProcAddress() to link to the function. If it returns NULL, the function isn't supported. However, a function may exist in the driver and still return WN_NOT_SUP-PORTED when it is called. In this case, GetProcAddress() will return a non-NULL pointer. WNetGetCaps( ) will correctly report whether the driver supports the function or not.

Here is its prototype:

```
WORD API WNetGetCaps(WORD wIndex);
```

I refer you to the demo program in Appendix C, which exercises WNetGetCaps( ) thoroughly.

Print-Job Functions

The print-job functions are not of great interest; all the functionality they provide comes for free without your having to call them directly. Print Manager handles all the details for you. However, the functions are available to use if you want to, so I want to say a few words about them here.

The print-job functions offer these basic services: open a print job, write to a print job, submit a print job, and control a print job after submission. There are also functions to abort a print job prior to submitting it [WNetAbortJob( )], to cancel it after submission [WNetCancelJob( )], and to pause or continue a job [WNetHoldJob( ) and WNetReleaseJob( )].

WNetOpenJob()

WNetOpenJob( ) starts a print job and returns a handle to the spool file that the network driver opens on your behalf. This handle can then be used to write to the file. Here is the prototype of WNetOpenJob( ):

```
WORD API WNetOpenJob(LPSTR lpszQueue, LPSTR lpszJobTitle, WORD wCopies,
                     LPWORD lpwFileHandle);
```

This starts a print job that targets *lpszQueue*. The queue name can specify either the full network name of the queue or a redirected local device. It has been my experience that it works better to use the local device name (LPT1, LPT2, etc.). This is not owing to any problems with WNetOpenJob( ), which does indeed accept either form. Under NetWare, however, WNetCloseJob( ) causes a general protection fault if you use the queue name, and works fine with the device name.

lpszTitle is any name you want to give the job. If you pass it as NULL, the driver will assign a default name. The job name is returned in the *pjComment* field of the JOBSTRUCT when you call WNetLockQueueData( ).

wCopies tells the driver how many copies you want to print. *lpwFileHandle* returns the handle of the spool file if the function succeeds.

WNetWriteJob()

According to the Microsoft specification, WNetWriteJob( ) is not used by Windows 3.1. Oddly enough, the only driver that supports it is MSNET.DRV, the plain vanilla network driver. It sends a block of data to the spool file. In its absence, you can write to the file using write( ) or _lwrite( ), using the handle returned by WNetOpenJob( ).

```
WORD API WNetWriteJob(HANDLE hSpoolFile, LPSTR lpData, LPINT lpcbData);
```

Notice that *hSpoolFile* is declared as a HANDLE, rather than as a WORD, which is the type of value returned by WNetOpenJob(). It can actually be any kind of 16-bit value that the driver wants to use. It is quite sufficient to cast the file handle to a HANDLE to satisfy the STRICT type-checking requirements. *lpData* points to the data. On input, *lpcbData* points to the number of bytes that should be written. On output, it contains the number actually written.

Here is my front-end routine for WNetWriteJob(). It calls _lwrite() if the network does not support WNetWriteJob().

```
WORD API WNetWriteJob(HANDLE hFile, LPSTR lpData, LPINT lpcbData)
{
    static WORD (API *lpWNetWriteJob)(HANDLE,LPSTR,LPINT) = NULL;
    static BOOL bPointerValid = FALSE;
    WORD   wReturnValue = WN_SUCCESS;
    UINT   nBytesWritten = 0;

    if (hNetLib == (HINSTANCE) (-1))
       (FARPROC) lpWNetWriteJob = CheckLib("WNetWriteJob");
    else if ((hNetLib != 0) && (!bPointerValid))
       {
       (FARPROC) lpWNetWriteJob =
          GetProcAddress(hNetLib, "WNetWriteJob");
       bPointerValid = TRUE;
       }

    if (lpWNetWriteJob != NULL)
       {
       wReturnValue = lpWNetWriteJob(hFile, lpData, lpcbData);

       if (wReturnValue == WN_NOT_SUPPORTED)
          {
          // Set lpWNetWriteJob to NULL so we don't keep calling
          // the driver function
          lpWNetWriteJob = NULL;
          }
       }
    else
       wReturnValue = WN_NOT_SUPPORTED;

    if (wReturnValue == WN_NOT_SUPPORTED)
       {
       // Do the write using _lwrite()
       nBytesWritten = _lwrite((HFILE) hFile, lpData, (UINT) (*lpcbData));
       if (nBytesWritten != (UINT) (*lpcbData))
          wReturnValue = WN_NET_ERROR;
       else
          wReturnValue = WN_SUCCESS;
       *lpcbData = (int) nBytesWritten;
       }
    return wReturnValue;
}
```

WNetCloseJob() and WNetAbortJob()

WNetCloseJob() tells the driver to close the print file and submit the job. It returns the ID assigned to the job. WNetAbortJob() cancels the job prior to submission. Notice that WNetAbortJob() takes the file handle as an argument. WNetCancelJob(), which we will look at in the next section, takes the job ID.

```
WORD API WNetCloseJob(WORD wFileHandle, LPINT lpnJobID, LPSTR lpszQueue);
WORD API WNetAbortJob(LPSTR lpszQueue, WORD wFileHandle);
```

If WNetCloseJob() is successful, it returns the newly assigned job ID in *lpnJobID*. It may be WN_NULL_JOBID, which means that the driver was unable to return the job ID. It does not necessarily indicate an error; the function return value will report a failure. The job ID is a required argument for all the functions covered in the next section.

The Job-Control Functions

The four functions in this group deal with print jobs after they have been submitted. The functions are WNetCancelJob(), WNetHoldJob(), WNetReleaseJob(), and WNetSetJob-Copies(). All these functions take the queue name (or the device name) and the job ID returned by WNetCloseJob() as arguments.

Here is the prototype for WNetCancelJob(). WNetHoldJob() and WNetReleaseJob() are identical.

```
WORD API WNetCancelJob(LPSTR lpszQueue, WORD wJobID);
```

WNetSetJobCopies() also expects the new value for the number of copies desired:

```
WORD API WNetSetJobCopies(LPSTR lpszQueue, WORD wJobID, WORD wCopies);
```

WNetCancelJob() removes the job from the queue. WNetHoldJob() and WNet-ReleaseJob() pause and resume the job, respectively.

The Long-Filename Functions

The long-filename functions are provided to support the OS/2 High Performance File System (HPFS). Where HPFS is installed, LAN Manager drives support filenames of up to 264 characters, and allow certain characters that DOS forbids (like spaces). They can also include periods anywhere in the filename, and can have more than one of them; there is no notion of file extensions. You cannot access these files from a Windows program with standard file I/O calls. The long-filename functions allow you to perform a limited set of operations on non-DOS files, such as:

- Scanning filenames (find first/find next)
- Copying, moving, and deleting files
- Getting and setting file attributes
- Determining if a filename conforms to DOS or HPFS naming conventions
- Determining if a drive supports long filenames
- Getting and setting a volume label

The long filename functions are listed in Table 9-3. If you are interested, the driver demo program in Appendix C gives examples of how to use these functions.

Table 9-3. Windows Network Driver Long-Filename Functions

Function	Action Performed
LFNCopy	Copies a file
LFNDelete	Deletes a file
LFNFindClose	Ends a scan initiated by LFNFindFirst
LFNFindFirst	Opens a file-scanning operation
LFNFindNext	Continues a file scan
LFNGetAttributes	Gets the attributes of a file
LFNGetVolumeLabel	Gets the volume label of a drive
LFNMKDir	Creates a directory
LFNMove	Move or rename a file
LFNParse	Determine if a filename conforms to DOS or HPFS conventions
LFNRMDir	Remove a directory
LFNSetAttributes	Set a file's attributes
LFNSetVolumeLabel	Change the volume label of a drive
LFNVolumeType	Determine if volume supports long filenames

## CHAPTER 10

NetWare Network Services API

NetWare INT 21H System Calls

The base NetWare network services API consists of extensions to the DOS INT 21H interface. The NetWare shell intercepts INT 21H calls, and determines if they need to be redirected to the network. This mechanism enables programs to use the standard DOS functions (or C library routines that call them) for I/O to network files. Another way for networks to do the same thing is to use the DOS network redirector, but NetWare does not use this, as it predates the redirector. (See *Undocumented DOS, by Andrew Schulman et al. for a discussion of the network redirector.*)

Many of the network service calls take two pointers as input arguments: a pointer to an input buffer (called a request packet) in DS:SI and to an output buffer (called a reply packet) in ES:DI. They are invoked by issuing an INT 21H with function numbers in AH that neither DOS nor the Windows DOS extenders—DOSX in standard mode, and DOSMGR in enhanced mode—know anything about. For this reason, they will not work unmodified in the protected-mode Windows environment. The Windows DOS extenders have no idea how to do API mapping for NetWare.

The NetWare driver (NETWARE.DRV) exports a function, NetWareRequest, that does API translation for the NetWare system calls. It is easy to use: just replace NetWare INT 21H system calls with a far call to NetWareRequest. Here is a code fragment illustrating this procedure:

```
EXTRN NETWAREREQUEST:FAR
; Load AH with the NetWare function number
; Load DS:SI with the address of the request packet.
; Load ES:DI with the address of the reply packet.
CALL NETWAREREQUEST      ; Instead of INT 21H
```

If you are using the Microsoft assembler CMACROS.INC, the corresponding lines are:

```
INCLUDE CMACROS.INC
externFP NetWareRequest
```

.
.
.

```
cCall NetWareRequest
```

You must also import NetWareRequest, either by mentioning it in your .DEF file, or by linking with an import library created from NETWARE.DRV. Here is the IMPORTS statement you would place in the .DEF file:

```
IMPORTS
     NetWare.NetWareRequest
```

NetWare C Interface for Windows

Though the direct invocation of NetWare system calls is certainly an option, the DLLs which Novell has developed are a better alternative in the Windows environment. First, they offer a function-call interface which is more in keeping with Windows conventions. Second, if all NetWare applications insist on writing their own interfaces to the NetWare system calls, each of them will be carrying around its own copy of nearly identical code, which will load DS:SI and ES:DI and call NetWareRequest. There is usually a one-to-one correspondence between a function in the *NetWare C Interface for Windows* DLLs and an underlying system call: all the DLL function does is load DS:SI and ES:DI and call Net-WareRequest! There aren't too many ways to do this, and loading memory with many copies of code, each of which does practically the same thing, makes no sense. By the same token, it is better to use Windows replacements for C runtime library functions than to have redundant copies of sprintf(), strlen(), open(), read(), write(), and all the others. Third, use of the DLLs makes programs more portable to other platforms on which Windows and NetWare may be supported in the future.

NetWare C Interface for Windows is a Windows derivative of the *NetWare C Interface—DOS*, which I discuss in my other books, *NetWare Programmer's Guide* and *NetWare/386 Programmer's Guide*.

NetWare Implementation of the WNet() Vertical APIs

Table 10-1 lists our WNet() extensions, and the NetWare function groups that we will implement them with.

Table 10-1: WNet() Extensions and Their Supporting NetWare API Groups

WNet() Function	NetWare Categories
WNetEnumServers	Bindery
WNetAddUser	Bindery, Workstation Environment
WNetDeleteUser	Bindery, Workstation Environment
WNetEnumUsers	Bindery, Workstation Environment
WNetAddGroup	Bindery, Workstation Environment
WNetDeleteGroup	Bindery, Workstation Environment

Table 10-1: WNet() Extensions and Their Supporting NetWare API Groups (cont.)

WNet() Function	NetWare Categories
WNetAddGroupMember	Bindery, Workstation Environment
WNetDeleteGroupMember	Bindery, Workstation Environment
WNetIsUserGroupMember	Bindery, Workstation Environment
WNetEnumGroups	Bindery, Workstation Environment
WNetEnumGroupMembers	Bindery, Workstation Environment
WNetEnumMemberGroups	Bindery, Workstation Environment
WNetGrantRights	Bindery, Directory, Workstation Environment
WNetRevokeRights	Bindery, Directory, Workstation Environment
WNetGetRights	Bindery, Directory, Workstation Environment

Bindery API

The bindery is a database of network resources. It keeps track of what objects exist on the network, specific attributes of those objects, and relationships among objects. Novell uses certain kinds of objects for its own administrative tasks. Some of the more important are users, user groups, file servers, print queues, and print servers. Applications can use the bindery for their own purposes by using private object types. Objects are known uniquely by either the combination of their name and object type, or by the NetWare-assigned object ID.

The attributes of bindery objects are referred to as properties in the Novell literature. These are stored in 128-byte segments, and can either be item or set properties. An item property is unformatted binary data. For instance, NetWare stores a user's full name as the property IDENTIFICATION. A set property is a list of bindery objects that belong to the set. They are stored in the segments as arrays of object IDs, which are represented as long integers in high-low order. All the entries in a single segment are compacted, with an object ID of 0L indicating the end of the segment. However, there is no compaction between segments. Thus, if a set member is saved in the second segment, it will always reside in the second segment, even if the first segment empties completely.

Set properties describe relationships among bindery objects. For example, NetWare maintains two set properties for users, SECURITY_EQUALS and GROUPS_I'M_IN. The first lists other users to whom the user is security-equivalent. The second lists groups that the user belongs to. Groups have the corresponding property GROUP_MEMBERS, which lists all objects that belong to the group.

To implement our WNet() extensions, we will need to perform these bindery operations:

- Create and delete objects (users and groups)
- Create properties
- Add and remove group members
- Verify group membership
- Enumerate objects (servers, users, and groups)
- Enumerate group members

Table 10-2 lists the Bindery Services functions that we will use to effect the operations.

Table 10-2: Bindery Services Functions Required for WNet() Extensions

Function

AddBinderyObjectToSet
ChangeBinderyObjectPassword
CreateBinderyObject
CreateProperty
DeleteBinderyObject
DeleteBinderyObjectFromSet
GetBinderyObjectID
GetBinderyObjectName
IsBinderyObjectInSet
ReadPropertyValue
ScanBinderyObject
WritePropertyValue

The bindery will disappear from NetWare 4.0, as Novell goes to a global naming service. However, bindery calls will be supported by emulation, so there is no danger of obsolescence.

Directory API

The NetWare Directory Services perform a number of operations on the NetWare directory system, such as creating, deleting, and renaming directories; mapping local drives to file server directories; managing user rights; and limiting the amount of disk space a user can consume.

To implement WNetGrantRights(), WNetRevokeRights(), and WNetGetRights(), we use the functions listed in Table 10-3. (The term "trustee" is NetWare jargon for a network object, like a user or user group, that has rights to access a file.)

Table 10-3: Directory Services Functions Required for WNet() Extensions

Function

DeleteTrustee
ScanEntryForTrustees
SetTrustee

NetWare supports the following set of rights. They can be assigned to both files and directories; some of them have a slightly different meaning in each context.

- READ: At the directory level, means that the user can open files in the directory for read access. At the file level, means that the user can open and read the file.
- WRITE: At the directory level, allows the user to open files in the directory for write access. At the file level, gives the user permission to open and write the file.
- CREATE: At the directory level, gives the user permission to create files and subdirectories in the directory. At the file level, allows the user to salvage the file after it has been deleted.

- ERASE: At the directory level, means that the user can delete the directory, provided that he also has permission to delete all the files in the directory. At the file level, gives him permission to delete the file.
- ACCESS CONTROL: Allows the user to grant and revoke other users' rights.
- FILE SCAN: At the directory level, makes files in the directory visible to a directory scan. At the file level, makes the file visible.
- MODIFY: Allows the user to rename the file or directory, or change its attributes.
- SUPERVISOR: Gives the user all rights. Furthermore, rights are inherited by all files and subdirectories regardless of more restrictive rights assigned at a lower level. This is a way of granting a user supervisor control over a portion of a disk without making her security-equivalent to the SUPERVISOR.

A user's rights are generated from the top of the directory tree. The inherited rights mask of files and directories at a lower level of the hierarchy determine how rights flow down. By default, all bits in this mask are set, which causes all rights to be automatically inherited. If bits in the inherited rights mask are cleared, then the corresponding right will not be granted unless it is explicitly assigned.

Furthermore, rights specifically granted at a lower level of the directory tree override any granted higher up. For instance, if a user JOE has read, write, modify, and file scan rights in SYS:PUBLIC, and the inherited rights mask for MYPROG.EXE allows all rights to be inherited, JOE will have read, write, modify, and file scan rights to MYPROG.EXE. If JOE is then specifically assigned read and file scan rights to MYPROG.EXE, he loses his write and modify rights.

A user's effective rights to a file or directory are a combination of rights explicitly assigned with those awarded indirectly, by virtue of inheritance or security equivalence. Continuing the above example, if the group EVERYONE has full rights to MYPROG.EXE, and JOE is a member of EVERYONE *and* security equivalent to it, then JOE will also have full rights, in spite of the more restrictive rights he was assigned originally. If EVERYONE has read, write, and file scan rights to MYPROG.EXE, and KAREN—to whom JOE is security-equivalent—has read, file scan, create, and modify, then JOE's full complement of rights will be read, write, file scan, create, and modify.

Group membership involves three relationships between a group and each individual member: the group is in the user's GROUPS_I'M_IN property; the user is in the group's GROUP_MEMBERS property; and the group is in the user's SECURITY_EQUALS property.

Note that group membership is a two-way relationship. Also, group membership by itself does not confer any rights. For a group member to gain access to files and directories that the group has rights to, the user must also be security-equivalent to the group. Security equivalence is a one-way relationship. If you belong to my SECURITY_EQUALS property, then any rights you have, I have. However, you do not inherit any rights from me unless I am also a member of your SECURITY_EQUALS property.

Workstation Environment API

All but one of our WNet() extensions take a server name as an argument. Unlike LAN Manager, most NetWare APIs do *not* include it. Instead, they target the current preferred server. Thus, we must use several functions from the Workstation Environment group to make sure we are addressing the correct server. Table 10-4 lists them.

Table 10-4: Workstation Environment
Services Functions Required for WNet() Extensions

Function

GetConnectionID
GetPreferredConnectionID
SetPreferredConnectionID

NetWare expects a server name to have no delimiting characters. LAN Manager, on the other hand, requires that it be preceded by two backslashes. To be fully network-independent, we allow the server name to be passed in either form, and adjust it to the appropriate format. [See NWSetServer() in Listing 10-2.]

WNetEnumServers()

Because the rest of the calls require the file server name as an argument, one of the first things we will need to do is find out what servers are available. When a NetWare file server detects a server advertising its presence on the network, it adds it to its bindery with the property NET_ADDRESS. Servers are required to broadcast their identity every 60 seconds. If a server has not broadcast for a certain length of time, the other servers assume it has terminated, and remove it from their binderies. Thus, we can query the bindery for servers.

The function that enumerates bindery objects is ScanBinderyObject():

```
WORD WINAPI ScanBinderyObject(LPSTR    lpszSearchObjectName,
                              WORD     wSearchObjectType,
                              LPDWORD  lpdwObjectID,
                              LPSTR    lpszObjectName,
                              LPWORD   lpwObjectType,
                              LPBYTE   lpbyObjectHasProperties,
                              LPBYTE   lpbyObjectFlag,
                              LPBYTE   lpbyObjectSecurity);
```

ScanBinderyObject() iterates over all objects matching *lpszSearchObjectName* and *wSearchObjectType*. Either one of these can be a wildcard. "*" is the wildcard for the name; OT_WILD is the wildcard object type. To begin with, you initialize the object ID to (DWORD) -1L; each call to ScanBinderyObject() will update it. The iteration stops when ScanBinderyObject() returns a non-zero value.

We use a search name of "*". The search type depends on the input argument. If it is WNET_FILE_SERVER, we use the NetWare equivalent, OT_FILE_SERVER. If it is WNET_ALL_SERVERS, we issue successive calls to ScanBinderyObject() for the most important kinds of servers: file servers, print servers, and job servers. We implement this logic by using an array of the possible server types, whose first element is OT_FILE-_SERVER. We set a variable to the number of array elements to iterate over, either one or the number of elements in the array, then call ScanBinderyObject() in a while loop contained within a for loop. For every server retrieved, we invoke the callback function passed to WNetEnumServers(). If the callback returns FALSE, we exit the function.

```c
/********
 *
 * Listing 10-1. WNETESRV.C
 *
 * Copyright (c) 1992 Ralph P. Davis, All Rights Reserved
 *
 ********/

/*===== Includes =====*/

#include "wnetapi.h"
#include <nwbindry.h>
#include <niterror.h>

/*===== LOCAL Variables =====*/

static const WORD wServerTypes[]    = {OT_FILE_SERVER,
                                       OT_PRINT_SERVER,
                                       OT_JOB_SERVER};
static const WORD wNetServerTypes[] = {WNET_FILE_SERVER,
                                       WNET_PRINT_SERVER,
                                       WNET_JOB_SERVER};

/*===== Function Definitions =====*/

BOOL WINAPI WNetEnumServers(SERVERENUMPROC lpServerEnumProc,
                            WORD wServerType)
{
    int   i, nServerTypes;
    char  szServerName[49];
    WORD  wFoundServerType;
    DWORD dwObjectID;
    BYTE  byPropertiesFlag;  // These three will be ignored,
    BYTE  byObjectFlag;      // but they're required by
    BYTE  byObjectSecurity;  // ScanBinderyObject()

    if (wServerType == WNET_FILE_SERVER)
      nServerTypes = 1;
    else
      nServerTypes = (sizeof (wServerTypes)) / (sizeof (wServerTypes[0]));

    for (i = 0; i < nServerTypes; ++i)
      {
      dwObjectID = (DWORD) -1L;
      while (ScanBinderyObject("*", wServerTypes[i], &dwObjectID,
                               szServerName, &wFoundServerType,
                               &byPropertiesFlag, &byObjectFlag,
```

```
                                &byObjectSecurity) == SUCCESSFUL)
     {
     // Invoke callback routine
     if (!lpServerEnumProc(szServerName, wNetServerTypes[i]))
         {
         i = nServerTypes; // To terminate for loop
         break;
         }
     }
  }
  return TRUE;
}
```

WNetAddUsers()

Adding a user involves creating a new bindery object with the object type OT_USER. This requires a call to CreateBinderyObject( ):

```
WORD WINAPI CreateBinderyObject(LPSTR lpszObjectName,
                                WORD  wObjectType,
                                BYTE  byObjectFlag,
                                BYTE  byObjectSecurity);
```

byObjectFlag can be either BF_STATIC or BF_DYNAMIC. A static object is permanent; that is, once it is created, it exists until it is explicitly deleted. A dynamic object is automatically deleted when the program that created it terminates. We want to create a permanent object.

byObjectSecurity specifies who will be aware of the user's existence and who will be allowed to add bindery properties. The five levels of read access are

- BS_BINDERY_READ: only NetWare itself can read the object information
- BS_SUPER_READ: only a user with SUPERVISOR rights can read the object information
- BS_OBJECT_READ: only the user can view the information
- BS_LOGGED_READ: any logged-in user can read the information
- BS_ANY_READ: anyone can read the data

Users who satisfy more restrictive criteria are included in less restrictive settings. BS_OBJECT_READ, for example, also allows the SUPERVISOR and NetWare to see the object.

There are five corresponding values for write access: BS_BINDERY_WRITE, BS_SUPER_WRITE, BS_OBJECT_WRITE, BS_LOGGED_WRITE, and BS_ANY-_WRITE.

When NetWare users are created using the SYSCON utility, they are given security access BS_SUPER_WRITE | BS_LOGGED_READ, so that is what we will use.

Setting the Target Server

As I mentioned above, the NetWare APIs do not take a server name as an argument. They assume that you have already targeted the correct server. Thus all the rest of the code listings in this chapter begin by calling the function NWSetServer(), and end by calling NWResetServer(). These change the target server and reset the original target server, respectively. We allow the server name to include leading backslashes. NWSetServer() strips them from the name, then sets the target server by converting the server name into a connection ID. It does this by calling GetConnectionID(), from the Workstation Environment group:

```
WORD WINAPI GetConnectionID(LPSTR lpszFileServerName,
                            LPWORD lpwConnectionID);
```

The connection ID is a number from one to eight that uniquely identifies servers to which the user is attached.

To target this server, we call SetPreferredConnectionID(). However, we first call GetPreferredConnectionID() to remember the current preferred server. NWSetServer() returns this to the caller, so he can pass it to NWResetServer(). Here are the prototypes for GetPreferredConnectionID() and SetPreferredConnectionID():

```
WORD WINAPI GetPreferredConnectionID(void);

void WINAPI SetPreferredConnectionID(WORD wConnectionID);
```

NWResetServer() calls SetPreferredConnectionID() with the connection ID that NWSetServer() retrieved.

```
/********
 *
 * Listing 10-2. NWCONNS.C
 *
 * Copyright (c) 1992 Ralph P. Davis, All Rights Reserved
 *
 ********/

/*===== Includes =====*/

#include "wnetnw.h"
#include <nwwrkenv.h>

/*===== Function Definitions =====*/

BOOL NWSetServer(LPSTR lpszServerName,
                 LPWORD lpwOldConnectionID)
{
   WORD wNewConnectionID;

   while (*lpszServerName == '\\')
      ++lpszServerName;

   if (GetConnectionID(lpszServerName, &wNewConnectionID) != SUCCESSFUL)
      return FALSE;

   *lpwOldConnectionID = GetPreferredConnectionID();
```

```
    SetPreferredConnectionID(wNewConnectionID);
    return TRUE;
}

void NWResetServer(WORD wOldConnectionID)
{
    SetPreferredConnectionID(wOldConnectionID);
}
```

Creating a User According to NetWare Standards

It is important to initialize the user's properties so they conform to NetWare's expectations. This will involve adding several properties and giving them default values. We will add the set properties SECURITY_EQUALS and GROUPS_I'M_IN, and add the group EVERYONE to both of them. We will also add the user to EVERYONE's GROUP-_MEMBERS list. If the user is to have administrative status [as indicated by the *bAdmin* argument to WNetAddUser()], we will add SUPERVISOR to her SECURITY_EQUALS set.

SYSCON creates three item properties as well: LOGIN_CONTROL, ACCOUNT-_BALANCE, and MISC_LOGIN_INFO. LOGIN_CONTROL contains information about login limitations. It is stored in a single segment, and formatted as follows:

```
typedef struct tagLoginControl
{
    BYTE byAccountExpires[3];   // Date account expires
    BYTE byAccountDisabled;     // Account disabled? OxFF = yes, 0 = no
    BYTE byPasswordExpires[3];  // Date password expires
    BYTE byGraceLogins;         // Number of logins allowed with
                                // expired password. OxFF = unlimited
    WORD wPasswordInterval;     // Number of days before user must
                                // change password.  O means never expires
    BYTE byGraceLoginReset;     // Initial value for byGraceLogins
                                // after password changes.
    BYTE byMinPasswordLength;   // Minimum length of password. 0 = no
                                // password required.
    WORD wMaxConnections;       // Maximum number of stations that a
                                // user can log in from at the same time.
                                // 0 = unlimited
    BYTE byLoginTimes[42];      // Bits corresponding to each half-hour
                                // period in the week. Bit set = user
                                // may log in, clear = user may not log in.
    BYTE byLastLogin[6];        // Date and time of last login
    BYTE byRestrictions;        // Bit 0: set = only SUPERVISOR can change
                                //               user's password
                                //        clear = anyone who knows the
                                //                password can change it
                                // Bit 1: set = unique passwords required
                                //              (used only by SYSCON)
    BYTE byUnused;
    long lMaxDiskBlocks;        // Max number of disk blocks allowed per
                                // user. Ox7FFFFFFF = no limit.
```

```
    WORD wBadLogins;              // Number of login failures since last
                                  // successful login
    LONG lNextResetTime;          // Time to unlock account in seconds since
                                  // January 1, 1985 (used when account is
                                  // locked because an intruder is detected).
    BYTE byBadLoginAddr[12];      // Station address where bad login occurred
} LOGIN_CONTROL;
```

The ACCOUNT_BALANCE property is used by the NetWare accounting system to determine if a user can afford a resource. It can also just monitor resource usage. It is structured as follows:

```
typedef struct tagAccountBalance
{
    long lBalance;        // Current account balance
    long lCreditLimit;    // Credit limit
} ACCOUNT_BALANCE;
```

lCreditLimit indicates the lowest balance the user is permitted to maintain. If it is set to 0x80000000, the user has unlimited credit.

Note that all numeric fields in both these structures are stored in high-low format, the opposite of normal Intel order.

The LOGIN_CONTROL and ACCOUNT_BALANCE properties take their initial values from the property USER_DEFAULTS, which belongs to the SUPERVISOR. It is stored in this format:

```
typedef struct tagUserDefaults
{
    BYTE byAccountExpiresYear;     // byAccountExpires[0] of LOGIN_CONTROL
    BYTE byAccountExpiresMonth;    // byAccountExpires[1] of LOGIN_CONTROL
    BYTE byAccountExpiresDay;      // byAccountExpires[2] of LOGIN_CONTROL
    BYTE byRestrictions;           // byRestrictions of LOGIN_CONTROL
    WORD wPasswordInterval;        // wPasswordInterval of LOGIN_CONTROL
    BYTE byGraceLoginReset;        // byGraceLoginReset of LOGIN_CONTROL
    BYTE byMinPasswordLength;      // byMinPasswordLength of LOGIN_CONTROL
    WORD wMaxConnections;          // wMaxConnections of LOGIN_CONTROL
    BYTE byLoginTimes[42];         // byLoginTimes of LOGIN_CONTROL
    long lBalance;                 // lBalance of ACCOUNT_BALANCE
    long lCreditLimit;             // lCreditLimit of ACCOUNT_BALANCE
    long lMaxDiskBlocks;           // lMaxDiskBlocks of LOGIN_CONTROL
} USER_DEFAULTS;
```

After creating the LOGIN_CONTROL and ACCOUNT_BALANCE properties, we retrieve the value of the SUPERVISOR's USER_DEFAULTS. We then transfer the fields to the appropriate C structures, and write the values of the LOGIN_CONTROL and ACCOUNT_BALANCE properties.

MISC_LOGIN_INFO is not given any initial value. It appears to be for user-defined information. Unlike the other properties, which only the supervisor can write, MISC_LOGIN_INFO has object-read/object-write access.

The steps to add a user, and the functions which carry them out, are as follows:

1. Set the current preferred server.

2. Create a bindery object of type OT_USER, having type BF_STATIC and security BS_LOGGED_READ | BS_SUPER_WRITE. The function we use is CreateBinderyObject(), whose prototype appears earlier in this chapter.

3. Assign the user's password by calling ChangeBinderyObjectPassword():

```
WORD WINAPI ChangeBinderyObjectPassword(LPSTR lpszObjectName,
                                        WORD  wObjectType,
                                        LPSTR lpszOldPassword,
                                        LPSTR lpszNewPassword);
```

In response to this call, NetWare creates the item property PASSWORD and assigns its value. It has NetWare-only security access (BS_BINDERY_READ | BS_BINDERY_WRITE), which means not even the SUPERVISOR can access it directly. This function (actually, its underlying system call) is the only way to change a password. It gives the SUPERVISOR what amounts to write-only access, so if you forget your password, she can't help you.

4. Create the property SECURITY_EQUALS with property flags BF_STATIC | BF_SET and security BS_SUPER_WRITE | BS_OBJECT_READ. (This is the security setting which SYSCON assigns.) The appropriate function is CreateProperty():

```
WORD WINAPI CreateProperty(LPSTR lpszObjectName,
                           WORD  wObjectType,
                           LPSTR lpszPropertyName,
                           BYTE  byPropertyFlags,
                           BYTE  byPropertySecurity);
```

lpszObjectName and *wObjectType* identify the bindery object that owns the property named in *lpszPropertyName*. *byPropertyFlags* specifies the flags (BF_STATIC | BF_SET, in this case); *byPropertySecurity* is the read and write access (BF_SUPER_WRITE | BS_OBJECT_READ).

5. Add the group EVERYONE to the SECURITY_EQUALS set. If the user is being given administrative status, also add the user SUPERVISOR. The appropriate function is AddBinderyObjectToSet():

```
WORD WINAPI AddBinderyObjectToSet(LPSTR lpszObjectName,
                                  WORD  wObjectType,
                                  LPSTR lpszPropertyName,
                                  LPSTR lpszMemberName,
                                  WORD  wMemberType);
```

lpszObjectName and *wObjectType* specify the owner of the set property. *lpszPropertyName* is the name of the property. *lpszMemberName* and *wMemberType* indicate the object being added to the set.

6. Create the property GROUPS_I'M_IN. Like SECURITY_EQUALS, its flags are BF_STATIC | BF_SET. However, its security is BS_LOGGED_READ | BS_SUPER_WRITE.

7. Add the group EVERYONE to the GROUPS_I'M_IN set, and add the new user to EVERYONE's GROUP_MEMBERS set.

8. Create the properties ACCOUNT_BALANCE, LOGIN_CONTROL, and MISC_LOGIN_INFO. They all have type BF_STATIC | BF_ITEM. ACCOUNT_BALANCE and LOGIN_CONTROL have BS_SUPER_WRITE | BS_OBJECT_READ security. MISC_LOGIN_INFO has BS_OBJECT_READ | BS_OBJECT_WRITE.

9. Retrieve the SUPERVISOR's USER_DEFAULTS property, and distribute the fields to the structures representing the LOGIN_CONTROL and ACCOUNT_BALANCE properties. The function that reads property information is ReadPropertyValue():

```
WORD WINAPI ReadPropertyValue(LPSTR lpszObjectName,
                              WORD  wObjectType,
                              LPSTR lpszPropertyName,
                              WORD  wSegmentNumber,
                              LPBYTE lpbyPropertyValue,
                              LPBYTE lpbyMoreSegments,
                              LPBYTE lpbyPropertyFlags);
```

It reads the property *lpszPropertyName* belonging to the object with the name *lpszObjectName* and object type *wObjectType*. *wSegmentNumber* specifies which 128-byte segment you want to read; the first segment is segment one, not segment zero. The segment contents are returned through *lpbyPropertyValue*, and the property's flags (BF_STATIC, BF_SET, BF_ITEM) through *lpbyPropertyFlags*. If there is more information to read, the byte at *lpbyMoreSegments* will be returned as 0xFF; otherwise, it will be set to zero.

10. Write the newly-assigned values of LOGIN_CONTROL and ACCOUNT_BALANCE to the bindery. The function is WritePropertyValue():

```
WORD WINAPI WritePropertyValue(LPSTR lpszObjectName,
                               WORD  wObjectType,
                               LPSTR lpszPropertyName,
                               WORD  wSegmentNumber,
                               LPBYTE lpbyPropertyValue,
                               BYTE   byMoreSegments);
```

The arguments are similar to ReadPropertyValue(). *wSegmentNumber* tells NetWare which segment you are writing. If you pass *byMoreSegments* as 0xFF, it tells NetWare that there are additional segments to follow the current one. If *byMoreSegments* is zero, you are writing the last segment.

Listing 10-3 shows the full coded version. The header file which it includes, WNETNW.H, is listed at the end of the chapter.

```
/********
*
* Listing 10-3. WNETAUSR.C
*
* Copyright (c) 1992 Ralph P. Davis, All Rights Reserved
```

```
*
*******/

/*===== Includes =====*/

#include "wnetnw.h"
#include <nwbindry.h>
#include <string.h>

/*===== Function Definitions =====*/

BOOL WINAPI WNetAddUser(LPSTR lpszServerName, LPSTR lpszUserName,
                        LPSTR lpszPassword, BOOL bAdmin)
{
   WORD wOldConnectionID;
   ACCOUNT_BALANCE AccountBalance, FAR *lpAccountBalance;
   LOGIN_CONTROL LoginControl, FAR *lpLoginControl;
   USER_DEFAULTS FAR *lpUserDefaults;
   BYTE bySegment[128];
   BYTE byMoreSegments, byPropertyFlags;
   WORD wCompletionCode;

   // Set the server
   if (!NWSetServer(lpszServerName, &wOldConnectionID))
      return FALSE;

   wCompletionCode =
       CreateBinderyObject(lpszUserName, OT_USER,
                           BF_STATIC,
                           BS_LOGGED_READ | BS_SUPER_WRITE);
   if (wCompletionCode != SUCCESSFUL)
      {
      NWCleanup(NULL, 0, wOldConnectionID);

      // OK if user already exists.
      return (wCompletionCode == OBJECT_ALREADY_EXISTS);
      }

   if (ChangeBinderyObjectPassword(lpszUserName, OT_USER,
                                   "", lpszPassword) != SUCCESSFUL)
      {
      NWCleanup(lpszUserName, OT_USER, wOldConnectionID);
      return FALSE;
      }

   if (CreateProperty(lpszUserName, OT_USER, "SECURITY_EQUALS",
      BF_STATIC | BF_SET, BS_SUPER_WRITE | BS_OBJECT_READ) != SUCCESSFUL)
      {
      NWCleanup(lpszUserName, OT_USER, wOldConnectionID);
      return FALSE;
      }

   if (AddBinderyObjectToSet(lpszUserName, OT_USER, "SECURITY_EQUALS",
```

```
       "EVERYONE", OT_USER_GROUP) != SUCCESSFUL)
    {
    NWCleanup(lpszUserName, OT_USER, wOldConnectionID);
    return FALSE;
    }

if (bAdmin)
    {
    if (AddBinderyObjectToSet(lpszUserName, OT_USER, "SECURITY_EQUALS",
      "SUPERVISOR", OT_USER) != SUCCESSFUL)
        {
        NWCleanup(lpszUserName, OT_USER, wOldConnectionID);
        return FALSE;
        }
    }

if (CreateProperty(lpszUserName, OT_USER, "GROUPS_I'M_IN",
    BF_STATIC | BF_SET, BS_SUPER_WRITE | BS_LOGGED_READ) != SUCCESSFUL)
    {
    NWCleanup(lpszUserName, OT_USER, wOldConnectionID);
    return FALSE;
    }

if (AddBinderyObjectToSet(lpszUserName, OT_USER, "GROUPS_I'M_IN",
    "EVERYONE", OT_USER_GROUP) != SUCCESSFUL)
    {
    NWCleanup(lpszUserName, OT_USER, wOldConnectionID);
    return FALSE;
    }

if (AddBinderyObjectToSet("EVERYONE", OT_USER_GROUP, "GROUP_MEMBERS",
    lpszUserName, OT_USER) != SUCCESSFUL)
    {
    NWCleanup(lpszUserName, OT_USER, wOldConnectionID);
    return FALSE;
    }

if (CreateProperty(lpszUserName, OT_USER, "LOGIN_CONTROL",
    BF_STATIC | BF_ITEM, BS_SUPER_WRITE | BS_OBJECT_READ) != SUCCESSFUL)
    {
    NWCleanup(lpszUserName, OT_USER, wOldConnectionID);
    return FALSE;
    }

if (CreateProperty(lpszUserName, OT_USER, "ACCOUNT_BALANCE",
    BF_STATIC | BF_ITEM, BS_SUPER_WRITE | BS_OBJECT_READ) != SUCCESSFUL)
    {
    NWCleanup(lpszUserName, OT_USER, wOldConnectionID);
    return FALSE;
    }

if (CreateProperty(lpszUserName, OT_USER, "MISC_LOGIN_INFO",
    BF_STATIC | BF_ITEM, BS_OBJECT_WRITE | BS_OBJECT_READ) != SUCCESSFUL)
    {
```

```
      NWCleanup(lpszUserName, OT_USER, wOldConnectionID);
      return FALSE;
      }

  if (ReadPropertyValue("SUPERVISOR", OT_USER, "USER_DEFAULTS",
                     1, bySegment, &byMoreSegments,
                     &byPropertyFlags) != SUCCESSFUL)
      {
      NWCleanup(lpszUserName, OT_USER, wOldConnectionID);
      return FALSE;
      }

  lpUserDefaults = (USER_DEFAULTS FAR *) bySegment;
  _fmemset(&LoginControl, '\0', sizeof (LOGIN_CONTROL));
  _fmemset(&AccountBalance, '\0', sizeof (ACCOUNT_BALANCE));

  // Move values from USER_DEFAULTS to user's LOGIN_CONTROL
  // and ACCOUNT_BALANCE.
  LoginControl.byAccountExpires[0] =
      lpUserDefaults->byAccountExpiresYear;
  LoginControl.byAccountExpires[1] =
      lpUserDefaults->byAccountExpiresMonth;
  LoginControl.byAccountExpires[2] =
      lpUserDefaults->byAccountExpiresDay;
  LoginControl.wPasswordInterval =
      lpUserDefaults->wPasswordInterval;
  LoginControl.byRestrictions =
      lpUserDefaults->byRestrictions;
  LoginControl.byGraceLoginReset =
      lpUserDefaults->byGraceLoginReset;
  LoginControl.byMinPasswordLength =
      lpUserDefaults->byMinPasswordLength;
  LoginControl.wMaxConnections =
      lpUserDefaults->wMaxConnections;
  _fmemcpy(LoginControl.byLoginTimes,
      lpUserDefaults->byLoginTimes, sizeof (LoginControl.byLoginTimes));
  LoginControl.lMaxDiskBlocks =
      lpUserDefaults->lMaxDiskBlocks;

  AccountBalance.lBalance =
      lpUserDefaults->lBalance;
  AccountBalance.lCreditLimit =
      lpUserDefaults->lCreditLimit;

  lpLoginControl = (LOGIN_CONTROL FAR *) bySegment;
  _fmemset(bySegment, '\0', sizeof (bySegment));
  *lpLoginControl = LoginControl;

  if (WritePropertyValue(lpszUserName, OT_USER, "LOGIN_CONTROL",
                     1, bySegment, FALSE) != SUCCESSFUL)
                  {
      NWCleanup(lpszUserName, OT_USER, wOldConnectionID);
      return FALSE;
      }
```

```
   lpAccountBalance = (ACCOUNT_BALANCE FAR *) bySegment;
   _fmemset(bySegment, '\0', sizeof (bySegment));
   *lpAccountBalance = AccountBalance;

   if (WritePropertyValue(lpszUserName, OT_USER, "ACCOUNT_BALANCE",
                       1, bySegment, FALSE) != SUCCESSFUL)
                    {
      NWCleanup(lpszUserName, OT_USER, wOldConnectionID);
      return FALSE;
      }

   return NWCleanup(NULL, 0, wOldConnectionID);
}

BOOL NWCleanup(LPSTR lpszUserName, WORD wUserType, WORD wOldConnectionID)
{
   if (lpszUserName != NULL)
      if (DeleteBinderyObject(lpszUserName, wUserType) != SUCCESSFUL)
         return FALSE;
   NWResetServer(wOldConnectionID);
   return TRUE;
}
```

WNetAddUser() is by far the most complicated routine in this DLL.

WNetDeleteUser()

WNetDeleteUser() admits of a much simpler implementation. The function that removes users from the bindery is DeleteBinderyObject(), which we used in NWCleanup() in the previous listing:

```
WORD WINAPI DeleteBinderyObject(LPSTR lpszObjectName,
                                WORD  wObjectType);
```

In fact, we can implement WNetDeleteUser() with two functions we've already written: one to NWSetServer() (Listing 10-2) to set the correct server, and one to NWCleanup() (Listing 10-3) to do everything else:

```
/********
*
* Listing 10-4. WNETDUSR.C
*
* Copyright (c) 1992 Ralph P. Davis, All Rights Reserved
*
********/

/*===== Includes =====*/

#include "wnetnw.h"
#include <nwbindry.h>
```

```
/*===== Function Definitions =====*/

BOOL WINAPI WNetDeleteUser(LPSTR lpszServerName,
                           LPSTR lpszUserName)
{
   WORD wOldConnectionID;

   if (!NWSetServer(lpszServerName, &wOldConnectionID))
      return FALSE;

   return NWCleanup(lpszUserName, OT_USER, wOldConnectionID);
}
```

WNetEnumUsers()

WNetEnumUsers() resembles WNetEnumServers(). It too uses ScanBinderyObject(), with an object type of OT_USER. For each user fetched, it invokes the callback function.

```
/********
 *
 * Listing 10-5. WNETEUSR.C
 *
 * Copyright (c) 1992 Ralph P. Davis, All Rights Reserved
 *
 ********/

/*===== Includes =====*/

#include "wnetapi.h"
#include <nwbindry.h>
#include <niterror.h>

/*===== Function Definitions =====*/

BOOL WINAPI WNetEnumUsers(LPSTR lpszServerName,
                          USERENUMPROC lpUserEnumProc)
{
   char  szUserName[49];
   WORD  wFoundUserType;
   DWORD dwObjectID;
   BYTE  byPropertiesFlag;
   BYTE  byObjectFlag;
   BYTE  byObjectSecurity;

   dwObjectID = (DWORD) -1L;

   while (ScanBinderyObject("*", OT_USER, &dwObjectID,
                            szUserName, &wFoundUserType,
                            &byPropertiesFlag, &byObjectFlag,
                            &byObjectSecurity) == SUCCESSFUL)
   {
      if (!lpUserEnumProc(lpszServerName, szUserName))
         break;
```

```
      }
   return TRUE;
}
```

WNetAddGroup()

WNetAddGroup(), like WNetAddUser(), uses CreateBinderyObject() to add a bindery object of type OT_USER_GROUP. Its security is BS_LOGGED_READ | BS_SUPER-_WRITE. Group objects get only one property, GROUP_MEMBERS, which is initially empty.

```
/********
*
* Listing 10-6. WNETAGRP.C
*
* Copyright (c) 1992 Ralph P. Davis, All Rights Reserved
*
********/

/*===== Includes =====*/

#include "wnetnw.h"
#include <nwbindry.h>

/*===== Function Definitions =====*/
BOOL WINAPI WNetAddGroup(LPSTR lpszServerName, LPSTR lpszGroupName)
{
   WORD wOldConnectionID;
   WORD wCompletionCode;

   if (!NWSetServer(lpszServerName, &wOldConnectionID))
      return FALSE;

   wCompletionCode =
      CreateBinderyObject(lpszGroupName, OT_USER_GROUP,
                          BF_STATIC,
                          BS_LOGGED_READ | BS_SUPER_WRITE);
   if (wCompletionCode != SUCCESSFUL)
      {
      NWCleanup(NULL, 0, wOldConnectionID);
      return (wCompletionCode == OBJECT_ALREADY_EXISTS);
      }

   if (CreateProperty(lpszGroupName, OT_USER_GROUP, "GROUP_MEMBERS",
      BF_STATIC | BF_SET, BS_SUPER_WRITE | BS_OBJECT_READ) != SUCCESSFUL)
      {
      NWCleanup(lpszGroupName, OT_USER_GROUP, wOldConnectionID);
      return FALSE;
      }

   return NWCleanup(NULL, 0, wOldConnectionID);
}
```

WNetDeleteGroup()

WNetDeleteGroup() is almost identical to WNetDeleteUser(). The only difference is that it deletes an object of type OT_USER_GROUP.

```
/********
 *
 * Listing 10-7. WNETDGRP.C
 *
 * Copyright (c) 1992 Ralph P. Davis, All Rights Reserved
 *
 ********/

/*===== Includes =====*/

#include "wnetnw.h"
#include <nwbindry.h>

/*===== Function Definitions =====*/

BOOL WINAPI WNetDeleteGroup(LPSTR lpszServerName,
                            LPSTR lpszGroupName)
{
   WORD wOldConnectionID;

   if (!NWSetServer(lpszServerName, &wOldConnectionID))
      return FALSE;

   return NWCleanup(lpszGroupName, OT_USER_GROUP, wOldConnectionID);
}
```

WNetEnumGroups()

WNetEnumGroups() is very similar to WNetEnumUsers(); it calls ScanBinderyObject() with the object type OT_USER_GROUP.

```
/********
 *
 * Listing 10-8. WNETEGRP.C
 *
 * Copyright (c) 1992 Ralph P. Davis, All Rights Reserved
 *
 ********/

/*===== Includes =====*/

#include "wnetapi.h"
#include <nwbindry.h>
#include <niterror.h>

/*===== Function Definitions =====*/

BOOL WINAPI WNetEnumGroups(LPSTR lpszServerName,
```

```
                    GROUPENUMPROC lpGroupEnumProc)
{
   char   szGroupName[49];
   WORD   wFoundGroupType;
   DWORD  dwObjectID;
   BYTE   byPropertiesFlag;
   BYTE   byObjectFlag;
   BYTE   byObjectSecurity;

   dwObjectID = (DWORD) -1L;

   while (ScanBinderyObject("*", OT_USER_GROUP, &dwObjectID,
                            szGroupName, &wFoundGroupType,
                            &byPropertiesFlag, &byObjectFlag,
                            &byObjectSecurity) == SUCCESSFUL)
      {
      if (!lpGroupEnumProc(lpszServerName, szGroupName))
         break;
      }
   return TRUE;
}
```

WNetAddGroupMember()

WNetAddGroupMember() relies on the NetWare function AddBinderyObjectToSet(),
calling it three times: once for the group's GROUP_MEMBERS, once for the user's
GROUPS_I'M_IN, and once for the user's SECURITY_EQUALS. We have to add the
group to the user's SECURITY_EQUALS property for him to acquire rights from the
group. This is, after all, the main reason for putting users into groups. It also imitates the
process performed by SYSCON when you add a user to a group.

```
/********
*
* Listing 10-9. WNETAMBR.C
*
* Copyright (c) 1992 Ralph P. Davis, All Rights Reserved
*
********/

/*===== Includes =====*/

#include "wnetnw.h"
#include <nwbindry.h>

/*===== Function Definitions =====*/

BOOL WINAPI WNetAddGroupMember(LPSTR lpszServerName,
                               LPSTR lpszGroupName,
                               LPSTR lpszUserName)
{
```

```
    WORD wOldConnectionID;
    WORD wCompletionCode;

    if (!NWSetServer(lpszServerName, &wOldConnectionID))
       return FALSE;

    wCompletionCode = AddBinderyObjectToSet(lpszGroupName, OT_USER_GROUP,
                                            "GROUP_MEMBERS",
                                            lpszUserName, OT_USER);
    if (wCompletionCode == SUCCESSFUL)
       {
       wCompletionCode = AddBinderyObjectToSet(lpszUserName,
                                               OT_USER,
                                               "GROUPS_I'M_IN",
                                               lpszGroupName,
                                               OT_USER_GROUP);
       if (wCompletionCode != SUCCESSFUL)
          DeleteBinderyObjectFromSet(lpszGroupName, OT_USER_GROUP,
                                     "GROUP_MEMBERS",
                                     lpszUserName, OT_USER);
       else
          {
          wCompletionCode = AddBinderyObjectToSet(lpszUserName,
                                                  OT_USER,
                                                  "SECURITY_EQUALS",
                                                  lpszGroupName,
                                                  OT_USER_GROUP);
          if (wCompletionCode != SUCCESSFUL)
             {
             DeleteBinderyObjectFromSet(lpszGroupName, OT_USER_GROUP,
                                        "GROUP_MEMBERS",
                                        lpszUserName, OT_USER);
             DeleteBinderyObjectFromSet(lpszUserName,
                                        OT_USER,
                                        "GROUPS_I'M_IN",
                                        lpszGroupName,
                                        OT_USER_GROUP);
             }
          }
       }
    NWResetServer(wOldConnectionID);
    return (wCompletionCode == SUCCESSFUL);
}
```

WNetDeleteGroupMember()

WNetDeleteGroupMember(), is very similar to WNetAddGroupMember(), but it uses
DeleteBinderyObjectFromSet() instead of AddBindaryObjectToSet()::

```
WORD WINAPI DeleteBinderyObjectFromSet(LPSTR lpszObjectName,
                                       WORD  wObjectType,
                                       LPSTR lpszPropertyName,
                                       LPSTR lpszMemberName,
                                       WORD  wMemberType );
```

The arguments are the same as those for AddBinderyObjectToSet().

```
/********
*
* Listing 10-10. WNETDMBR.C
*
* Copyright (c) 1992 Ralph P. Davis, All Rights Reserved
*
********/

/*===== Includes =====*/

#include "wnetnw.h"
#include <nwbindry.h>

/*===== Function Definitions =====*/

BOOL WINAPI WNetDeleteGroupMember(LPSTR lpszServerName,
                                  LPSTR lpszGroupName,
                                  LPSTR lpszUserName)
{
   WORD wOldConnectionID;

   if (!NWSetServer(lpszServerName, &wOldConnectionID))
      return FALSE;

   DeleteBinderyObjectFromSet(lpszGroupName, OT_USER_GROUP,
                              "GROUP_MEMBERS",
                               lpszUserName, OT_USER);
   DeleteBinderyObjectFromSet(lpszUserName, OT_USER, "GROUPS_I'M_IN",
                              lpszGroupName, OT_USER_GROUP);
   DeleteBinderyObjectFromSet(lpszUserName, OT_USER, "SECURITY_EQUALS",
                              lpszGroupName, OT_USER_GROUP);
   NWResetServer(wOldConnectionID);
   return TRUE;
}
```

WNetIsUserGroupMember()

WNetIsUserGroupMember() uses the function IsBinderyObjectInSet() to determine if the given user belongs to the given group:

```
WORD WINAPI IsBinderyObjectInSet(LPSTR lpszObjectName,
                                 WORD  wObjectType,
                                 LPSTR lpszPropertyName,
                                 LPSTR lpszNemberName,
                                 WORD  wMemberType );
```

IsBinderyObjectInSet() takes the same arguments as AddBinderyObjectToSet() and DeleteBinderyObjectFromSet(). It is counter-intuitive; it does not return TRUE or FALSE, as the name suggests it should. Instead, a return value of zero (#defined as SUCCESSFUL in NITERROR.H) means that the user does belong to the group. Any other value means he or she does not.

```
/********
 *
 * Listing 10-11. WNETIMBR.C
 *
 * Copyright (c) 1992 Ralph P. Davis, All Rights Reserved
 *
 ********/

/*===== Includes =====*/

#include "wnetnw.h"
#include <nwbindry.h>

/*===== Function Definitions =====*/
BOOL WINAPI WNetIsUserGroupMember(LPSTR lpszServerName,
                                  LPSTR lpszGroupName,
                                  LPSTR lpszUserName)
{
   WORD wOldConnectionID;
   BOOL bRetcode;

   if (!NWSetServer(lpszServerName, &wOldConnectionID))
      return FALSE;

   bRetcode = (IsBinderyObjectInSet(lpszGroupName, OT_USER_GROUP,
                                    "GROUP_MEMBERS",
                                    lpszUserName, OT_USER) == SUCCESSFUL);
   NWResetServer(wOldConnectionID);
   return bRetcode;
}
```

WNetEnumGroupMembers()/WNetEnumMemberGroups()

These enumeration functions are a bit more complicated than the ones we have previously encountered. Here, we have to do these steps:

1. Call ReadPropertyValue() until it says there is nothing more to report. For WNetEnumGroupMembers(), we will read the property GROUP_MEMBERS; for WNetEnumMemberGroups(), we will read GROUPS_I'M_IN.

2. Scan the array of object IDs in the return buffer. For each one, call GetBinderyObjectName() to get the object name and type:

```
WORD WINAPI GetBinderyObjectName(DWORD   dwObjectID,
                                 LPSTR   lpszObjectName,
                                 LPWORD  lpwObjectType);
```

The object IDs returned by ReadPropertyValue() are in network order (high byte at low address). They need to be converted to Intel order before we call GetBinderyObjectName(). The function LongSwap() accomplishes this nicely:

```
DWORD WINAPI LongSwap(DWORD dwSwapMe);
```

LongSwap() is part of the NetWare Miscellaneous Services group.

3. Call the enumeration function for each object. With WNetEnumGroupMembers(), we will only enumerate group members of type OT_USER. Although group members are not restricted to being users, that is the only type you can add with WNetAddGroupMember().

I include both routines in the same source file, WNETEMBR.C:

```
/********
*
* Listing 10-12. WNETEMBR.C
*
* Copyright (c) 1992 Ralph P. Davis, All Rights Reserved
*
********/

/*===== Includes =====*/

#include "wnetnw.h"
#include <nwbindry.h>
#include <nwmisc.h>

/*===== Function Definitions =====*/

BOOL WINAPI WNetEnumGroupMembers(
                      LPSTR lpszServerName,
                      LPSTR lpszGroupName,
                      GROUPMEMBERENUMPROC lpMemberEnumProc)
{
   WORD     wOldConnectionID;
   BYTE     bySegment[128];
   BYTE     byMoreSegments = 0xFF;
   BYTE     byPropertyFlags;
   int      nSegmentNumber = 1;
   char     szUserName[49];
   WORD     wUserType;
   LPDWORD  lpObjectIDs;

   if (!NWSetServer(lpszServerName, &wOldConnectionID))
      return FALSE;

   while (byMoreSegments == 0xFF)
      {
      if (ReadPropertyValue(lpszGroupName, OT_USER_GROUP,
          "GROUP_MEMBERS", nSegmentNumber++, bySegment,
          &byMoreSegments, &byPropertyFlags) != SUCCESSFUL)
         break;
```

```c
    for (lpObjectIDs = (LPDWORD) bySegment;
        *lpObjectIDs != OL;
        ++lpObjectIDs)
      {
      if (GetBinderyObjectName(LongSwap(*lpObjectIDs),
                              szUserName, &wUserType) != SUCCESSFUL)
        continue;
      if (wUserType == OT_USER)
        {
        if (!lpMemberEnumProc(lpszServerName, lpszGroupName, szUserName))
          {
          byMoreSegments = 0;
          break;
          }
        }
      }
    }
  NWResetServer(wOldConnectionID);
  return TRUE;
}

BOOL WINAPI WNetEnumMemberGroups(
                    LPSTR lpszServerName,
                    LPSTR lpszUserName,
                    MEMBERGROUPENUMPROC lpGroupEnumProc)
{
  WORD    wOldConnectionID;
  BYTE    bySegment[128];
  BYTE    byMoreSegments = 0xFF;
  BYTE    byPropertyFlags;
  int     nSegmentNumber = 1;
  char    szGroupName[49];
  WORD    wGroupType;
  LPDWORD lpGroupIDs;

  if (!NWSetServer(lpszServerName, &wOldConnectionID))
    return FALSE;

  while (byMoreSegments == 0xFF)
    {
    if (ReadPropertyValue(lpszUserName, OT_USER,
        "GROUPS_I'M_IN", nSegmentNumber++, bySegment,
        &byMoreSegments, &byPropertyFlags) != SUCCESSFUL)
      break;

    for (lpGroupIDs = (LPDWORD) bySegment;
        *lpGroupIDs != OL;
        ++lpGroupIDs)
      {
      if (GetBinderyObjectName(LongSwap(*lpGroupIDs),
                              szGroupName, &wGroupType) != SUCCESSFUL)
        continue;
      if (wGroupType == OT_USER_GROUP)
```

```
            {
            if (!lpGroupEnumProc(lpszServerName, lpszUserName, szGroupName))
                {
                byMoreSegments = 0;
                break;
                }
            }
        }
    }
    NWResetServer(wOldConnectionID);
    return TRUE;
}
```

WNetGrantRights()

WNetGrantRights() takes the network-independent rights mask passed to it and translates it into its NetWare equivalent. If the rights set is non-zero, it calls SetTrustee() to grant the user the request rights. Otherwise, it calls DeleteTrustee() to remove the user as a trustee. We use this behavior to implement WNetRevokeRights(). SetTrustee() has this prototype:

```
WORD WINAPI SetTrustee(WORD   wConnectionID,
                       BYTE   byDirHandle,
                       LPSTR  lpszPath,
                       DWORD  dwTrusteeObjectID,
                       DWORD  dwTrusteeRightsMask);
```

Notice that SetTrustee() takes the target server connection ID as an argument. We will still go through our standard initialization; we can get this argument by calling GetPreferredConnectionID(). *byDirHandle* and *lpszPath* specify the target file or directory; if *byDirHandle* is 0, then *lpszPath* specifies a full path from the volume root.

In order to be network-independent, WNetGrantRights() expects the server name as an argument. This argument is superfluous; we can determine it from the file or directory name by calling the function ParsePath() from the Miscellaneous Services group. It splits the filename into server name, volume name, and path name components.

```
WORD WINAPI ParsePath(LPSTR lpszPath, LPSTR lpszServerName,
              LPSTR lpszVolumeName, LPSTR lpszDirectories);
```

We use the server name reported by ParsePath().

Next, we call the function ConvertNameToFullPath(), also from the Miscellaneous Services group, to convert the path name to its full NetWare form (VOLUME:DIR1-/DIR2/DIR3/FILE):

```
WORD WINAPI ConvertNameToFullPath(LPSTR lpszFileName,
                                  LPSTR lpszPath);
```

lpszFileName is converted to full NetWare form in *lpszPath*. We pass it to SetTrustee() or DeleteTrustee() this way. Here is the prototype for DeleteTrustee():

```
WORD WINAPI DeleteTrustee(WORD  wConnectionID,
                          BYTE  byDirHandle,
                          LPSTR lpszPath,
                          DWORD dwObjectID);
```

The arguments are the same as they are for SetTrustee(), except that the rights mask is not included.

Rights can be, and frequently are, assigned to groups. Following LAN Manager usage, I have defined the flag WNET_GROUP_ACCESS, which indicates that rights are being given to a group, not a user. I determine the object type by testing this flag in the rights mask.

```
/********
*
* Listing 10-13. WNETGRNT.C
*
* Copyright (c) 1992 Ralph P. Davis, All Rights Reserved
*
********/

/*===== Includes =====*/

#include "wnetnw.h"
#include <nwbindry.h>
#include <nwdir.h>
#include <nwmisc.h>
#include <nwwrkenv.h>

// Note that ntt.h defines BYTE, WORD, and DWORD
// No problem, except that WORD is defined as an unsigned int,
// which it ain't--it's an unsigned short
#include <ntt.h>

/*===== LOCAL Functions =====*/

static void near MapWNetRightsToNW(LPWORD lpwRights);

/*===== Function Definitions =====*/

BOOL WINAPI WNetGrantRights(LPSTR lpszServerName,
                            LPSTR lpszUserOrGroup,
                            LPSTR lpszResource,
                            WORD  wRights)
{
    WORD  wUserType;
    char  szServerName[49];
    char  szVolumeName[17];
    char  szPath[255];
    WORD  wOldConnectionID;
    WORD  wCompletionCode;
    DWORD dwObjectID;

    if (wRights & WNET_GROUP_ACCESS)
        wUserType = OT_USER_GROUP;
```

```
   else
      wUserType = OT_USER;

   wRights &= (~WNET_GROUP_ACCESS);

   MapWNetRightsToNW(&wRights);

   ParsePath(lpszResource, szServerName, szVolumeName, szPath);

   if (szServerName[0] == '\0')  // Not a network path
      return FALSE;

   lpszServerName = (LPSTR) szServerName;

   if (!NWSetServer(lpszServerName, &wOldConnectionID))
      return FALSE;

   if (GetBinderyObjectID(lpszUserOrGroup, wUserType, &dwObjectID)
       != SUCCESSFUL)
      return FALSE;

   ConvertNameToFullPath(lpszResource, szPath);

   if (wRights != 0)
      wCompletionCode = SetTrustee(GetPreferredConnectionID(), 0,
                                   szPath, dwObjectID, (DWORD) wRights);
   else
      wCompletionCode = DeleteTrustee(GetPreferredConnectionID(), 0,
                                      szPath, dwObjectID);

   NWResetServer(wOldConnectionID);
   return (wCompletionCode == SUCCESSFUL);
}

static void near MapWNetRightsToNW(LPWORD lpwRights)
{
   WORD wNWRights;

   if (*lpwRights & WNET_ALL_ACCESS)
      {
      *lpwRights = TR_ALL;
      return;
      }
   if (*lpwRights & WNET_ALL_NORMAL_ACCESS)
      {
      *lpwRights = TR_NORMAL;
      return;
      }
   wNWRights = 0;
   if (*lpwRights & WNET_READ_ACCESS)
      wNWRights |= TR_READ;
   if (*lpwRights & WNET_WRITE_ACCESS)
      wNWRights |= TR_WRITE;
   if (*lpwRights & WNET_CREATE_ACCESS)
      wNWRights |= TR_CREATE;
   if (*lpwRights & WNET_DELETE_ACCESS)
```

```
        wNWRights |= TR_ERASE;
    if (*lpwRights & WNET_ATTRIB_ACCESS)
        wNWRights |= TR_MODIFY;
    if (*lpwRights & WNET_VIEW_ACCESS)
        wNWRights |= TR_FILE;
    if (*lpwRights & WNET_PERM_ACCESS)
        wNWRights |= TR_ACCESS;
    if (*lpwRights & WNET_ADMIN_ACCESS)
        wNWRights |= TR_SUPERVISOR;

    *lpwRights = wNWRights;
}
```

WNetRevokeRights()

WNetRevokeRights() calls WNetGrantRights() with a rights mask of zero. If the trustee being removed is a group, as indicated by the *bUserOrGroup* argument, the WNET_GROUP-_ACCESS in the rights mask is set.

```
/********
 *
 * Listing 10-14. WNETREVK.C
 *
 * Copyright (c) 1992 Ralph P. Davis, All Rights Reserved
 *
 ********/

/*===== Includes =====*/

#include "wnetnw.h"
#include <nwbindry.h>
#include <nwdir.h>
#include <nwmisc.h>
#include <nwwrkenv.h>
#include <ntt.h>

/*===== Function Definitions =====*/

BOOL WINAPI WNetRevokeRights(LPSTR lpszServerName,
                             LPSTR lpszUserOrGroup,
                             LPSTR lpszResource,
                             BOOL  bUser)
{
    return WNetGrantRights(lpszServerName, lpszUserOrGroup,
                   lpszResource, (bUser ? 0 : WNET_GROUP_ACCESS));
}
```

WNetGetRights()

NetWare has several functions for retrieving a user's rights. One of them, GetEffective-Rights(), returns the user's full set of rights, including those which he or she has received indirectly (by inheritance or security equivalence). Two others return the set of rights actually assigned. They are ScanEntryForTrustees() and ScanBinderyObjectTrusteePaths(). Both of these are cumbersome to use.

Which set of rights is of greatest interest? WNetGetRights() is based on the LAN Manager function NetAccessGetUserPerms(). This function returns the rights assigned to the user. However, if the user has no explicit rights, it returns those assigned to any groups the user belongs to. This is equivalent to what NetWare calls the effective rights. For this reason, I implement WNetGetRights() using GetEffectiveRights(). [I refer you to my books on NetWare programming for a discussion of ScanEntryForTrustees() and Scan-BinderyObjectTrusteePaths(). In particular, see Chapter 8 of my *NetWare/386 Programmer's Guide*.] Here is the prototype for GetEffectiveRights():

```
WORD WINAPI GetEffectiveRights(WORD  wConnectionID,
                               BYTE  byDirHandle,
                               LPSTR lpszPath,
                               LPWORD lpwRights);
```

wConnectionID is the connection ID of the target server. *byDirHandle* can be a handle representing part of the path where the file is found. If it is non-zero, then *lpszPath* is relative to this path. If *byDirHandle* is zero, then *lpszPath* contains the full path name of the file or directory. It may be expressed in NetWare format (SYS:PUBLIC/FILE-NAME.TXT) or DOS format (F:\PUBLIC\FILENAME.TXT). The user's effective rights are returned through *lpwRights*.

WNetGetRights() maps the rights returned by GetEffectiveRights() from NetWare format to the WNet network-independent representation. Just as we did with WNet-GrantRights(), we ignore the server name, and figure it out for ourselves.

WNetGetRights() expects the WNET_GROUP_ACCESS bit of *lpwRights* to be set on input. We use this bit to determine if *lpszUserOrGroup* is a user or a group.

```
/********
*
* Listing 10-15. WNETGRTS.C
*
* Copyright (c) 1992 Ralph P. Davis, All Rights Reserved
*
********/

/*===== Includes =====*/

#include "wnetnw.h"
#include <ntt.h>
#include <nwbindry.h>
#include <nwdir.h>
#include <nwmisc.h>
#include <nwwrkenv.h>
```

```
/*===== LOCAL Functions =====*/

static void near MapNWRightsToWNet(LPWORD lpwRights);

/*===== Function Definitions =====*/

BOOL WINAPI WNetGetRights(LPSTR   lpszServerName,
                          LPSTR   lpszUserOrGroup,
                          LPSTR   lpszResource,
                          LPWORD  lpwRights)
{
   WORD   wOldConnectionID;
   WORD   wUserType;
   char   szServerName[49];
   char   szVolumeName[17];
   char   szPath[255];
   DWORD  dwObjectID;
   WORD   wRights;
   WORD   wCompletionCode;

   ParsePath(lpszResource, szServerName, szVolumeName, szPath);

   if (szServerName[0] == '\0')
      return FALSE;

   lpszServerName = (LPSTR) szServerName;
   if (!NWSetServer(lpszServerName, &wOldConnectionID))
      return FALSE;

   if (*lpwRights & WNET_GROUP_ACCESS)
      wUserType = OT_USER_GROUP;
   else
      wUserType = OT_USER;

   if (GetBinderyObjectID(lpszUserOrGroup, wUserType, &dwObjectID)
      != SUCCESSFUL)
      return FALSE;

   ConvertNameToFullPath(lpszResource, szPath);

   wCompletionCode = GetEffectiveRights(GetPreferredConnectionID(), 0,
                                        szPath,
                                        &wRights);

   if (wCompletionCode == SUCCESSFUL)
      {
      MapNWRightsToWNet(&wRights);
      if (wUserType == OT_USER_GROUP)
         wRights |= WNET_GROUP_ACCESS;
      *lpwRights = wRights;
      }
   NWResetServer(wOldConnectionID);
   return (wCompletionCode == SUCCESSFUL);
}

static void near MapNWRightsToWNet(LPWORD lpwRights)
```

```
{
   WORD wRights = *lpwRights;

   if ((wRights & TR_ALL) == TR_ALL)
      {
      *lpwRights = WNET_ALL_ACCESS;
      return;
      }
   if ((wRights & TR_NORMAL) == TR_NORMAL)
      {
      *lpwRights = WNET_ALL_NORMAL_ACCESS;
      return;
      }
   if (wRights == TR_NONE)
      return;
   *lpwRights = 0;
   if (wRights & TR_READ)
      *lpwRights |= WNET_READ_ACCESS;
   if (wRights & TR_WRITE)
      *lpwRights |= WNET_WRITE_ACCESS;
   if (wRights & TR_CREATE)
      *lpwRights |= WNET_CREATE_ACCESS;
   if (wRights & TR_ERASE)
      *lpwRights |= WNET_DELETE_ACCESS;
   if (wRights & TR_ACCESS)
      *lpwRights |= WNET_PERM_ACCESS;
   if (wRights & TR_FILE)
      *lpwRights |= WNET_VIEW_ACCESS;
   if (wRights & TR_MODIFY)
      *lpwRights |= WNET_ATTRIB_ACCESS;
   if (wRights & TR_SUPERVISOR)
      *lpwRights |= WNET_ADMIN_ACCESS;
}
```

Miscellaneous Files

The last three listings are the file NWDUMMY.C, the header file WNETNW.H, and the
.DEF file. NWDUMMY.C contains the required DLL routines LibMain() and WEP().
These are just dummy routines; they do nothing but return one to indicate that they suc-
ceeded. Notice that the .DEF file exports all the network driver routines.

```
/********
 *
 * Listing 10-16. NWDUMMY.C
 *
 * Copyright (c) 1992 Ralph P. Davis, All Rights Reserved
 *
```

```
********/

/*===== Includes =====*/

#include "wnetnw.h"

/*===== Global Variables =====*/

HINSTANCE hDLLInstance;

/*===== Function Definitions =====*/

int WINAPI LibMain(HINSTANCE hInstance,
                   WORD wDataSeg,
                   WORD cbHeapSize,
                   LPSTR lpszCmdLine)
{
   hDLLInstance = hInstance;
   return 1;
}

int WINAPI WEP(int nParameter)
{
   return 1;
}

/********
 *
 * Listing 10-17. WNETNW.H
 *
 * Copyright (c) 1992 Ralph P. Davis, All Rights Reserved
 *
 ********/

/*===== Includes =====*/

#include "wnetapi.h"
#include <niterror.h>

/*===== Constants =====*/
```

```
/*===== Types =====*/

typedef struct tagLoginControl
{
   BYTE byAccountExpires[3];
   BYTE byAccountDisabled;
   BYTE byPasswordExpires[3];
   BYTE byGraceLogins;
   WORD wPasswordInterval;
   BYTE byGraceLoginReset;
   BYTE byMinPasswordLength;
   WORD wMaxConnections;
   BYTE byLoginTimes[42];
   BYTE byLastLogin[6];
   BYTE byRestrictions;
   BYTE byUnused;
   long lMaxDiskBlocks;
   WORD wBadLogins;
   LONG lNextResetTime;
   BYTE byBadLoginAddr[12];
} LOGIN_CONTROL;

typedef struct tagAccountBalance
{
   long lBalance;         // Current account balance
   long lCreditLimit;     // Credit limit
} ACCOUNT_BALANCE;

typedef struct tagUserDefaults
{
   BYTE byAccountExpiresYear;
   BYTE byAccountExpiresMonth;
   BYTE byAccountExpiresDay;
   BYTE byRestrictions;
   WORD wPasswordInterval;
   BYTE byGraceLoginReset;
   BYTE byMinPasswordLength;
   WORD wMaxConnections;
```

```
    BYTE byLoginTimes[42];
    long lBalance;
    long lCreditLimit;
    long lMaxDiskBlocks;

} USER_DEFAULTS;
/*===== Global Variables =====*/

extern HINSTANCE hDLLInstance;

/*===== Function Prototypes =====*/

BOOL NWSetServer(LPSTR lpszServerName,
                 LPWORD lpwOldConnectionID);
void NWResetServer(WORD wOldConnectionID);
BOOL NWCleanup(LPSTR lpszUserName, WORD wUserType, WORD wOldConnectionID);

;********
;
; Listing 10-18. WNETNW.DEF
;
; Copyright (c) 1992 Ralph P. Davis, All Rights Reserved
;
;********

LIBRARY    WNETNW

EXETYPE    WINDOWS

CODE    PRELOAD MOVEABLE DISCARDABLE
DATA    PRELOAD MOVEABLE SINGLE

HEAPSIZE  4096

EXPORTS
          WEP                   @1 RESIDENTNAME
          WNetAddUser
          WNetEnumUsers
          WNetDeleteUser
          WNetEnumServers
          WNetAddGroup
```

```
WNetEnumGroups
WNetDeleteGroup
WNetAddGroupMember
WNetDeleteGroupMember
WNetIsUserGroupMember
WNetEnumGroupMembers
WNetEnumMemberGroups
WNetGrantRights
WNetRevokeRights
WNetGetRights
```

CHAPTER ▪ 11

LAN Manager Network Services API

Overview

Like NetWare, Microsoft's LAN Manager offers a rich set of APIs for obtaining network services. The LAN Manager APIs show a consistent, logical design that is particularly well-suited to the Windows environment. Since the Windows and LAN Manager APIs were both developed by Microsoft, it is not surprising that the two blend so comfortably. But there is another important reason for this.

LAN Manager's preferred environment is OS/2. Thus, unlike NetWare, the LAN Manager APIs have always consisted of C function calls, not assembly language interrupts. They are also named systematically, and the names describe their function. In NetWare, the function names in the NetWare C Interface libraries describe the underlying assembler call. Thus, to create a new user under NetWare, you call CreateBinderyObject(), as we saw; under LAN Manager, you call NetUserAdd().

LAN Manager offers the exact same interface for programs that run under DOS, OS/2, and Windows. At present, NetWare has a different interface in all three environments. It is Novell's intention to offer a consistent interface across all these platforms in NetWare 4.0. Clearly, this is a better way to do things.

LAN Manager Naming Conventions

The LAN Manager functions are divided into approximately 20 groups. Most of the groups contain only a small number of closely related functions. The group with the largest number of functions, the User group, comprises 11 functions. The Connection "group" contains only one. By contrast, the NetWare Directory Services group has 50 functions.

LAN Manager function names consist of three obligatory, and one optional, component:

- The keyword Net or Dos. Net indicates a function that is particular to LAN Manager. Dos indicates a function intended for eventual inclusion in the base OS/2 API.

- The type of network object the function operates on. This is also the name of the category in which the function is included. Examples are Group, User, PrintQ, Server, and Wksta.
- A verb indicating the action performed on the object. Examples are: Add, Del, Enum, Get, Set, Read, Write. Thus, NetUserAdd() adds a new user; NetGroupDel() deletes a group; NetUserEnum() enumerates users.
- Optionally, a further object of the action. For example, NetGroupAdd() adds a new group; NetGroupAddUser() adds a user to that group.

Sometimes, a function name ends with the number 2. This indicates that the function is a second-generation function, usually introduced into LAN Manager in version 2.0, and that it supersedes an older function of the same name, without the 2 on the end.

Another consistent aspect of the interface is that all functions are defined to return the same type of value. All prototypes published in this chapter appear in the form:

```
API_FUNCTION NetFunctionName()
```

API_FUNCTION is defined in the LAN Manager header file LAN.H as unsigned far pascal. In all cases, the return value is a status code; any other return information is passed back through FAR pointers.

A number of LAN Manager functions enumerate network objects. For example, NetUserEnum() enumerates end users, NetGroupEnum() enumerates groups, and NetServerEnum2() enumerates servers. Almost all the enumeration functions take the same litany of arguments. To illustrate, here is the prototype for NetUserEnum():

```
API_FUNCTION NetUserEnum(LPCSTR lpszServerName,
                short   sLevel,
                LPSTR   lpBuffer,
                unsigned short cbBuffer,
                unsigned short far *lpcEntriesRead,
                unsigned short far *lpcTotalAvail);
```

The *sLevel*, *lpBuffer*, *cbBuffer*, *lpcEntriesRead*, and *lpcTotalAvail* arguments are common to almost all the enumeration functions, and are passed in the same order when they are all included. *sLevel* refers to the amount of detail desired. *lpBuffer* points to the buffer where you want the data returned. *cbBuffer* tells LAN Manager how big the output buffer is. *lpcEntriesRead* returns the number of entries deposited in the output buffer; *lpcTotalAvail* tells you the total number of entries available. All the enumeration functions allow you to initially pass *cbBuffer* as zero. LAN Manager will think it does not have enough room to pass any information, and the function will return the status code ERROR_MORE_DATA. At this point, *lpcTotalAvail* will tell you exactly how many array elements you need to allocate. After obtaining the memory, you call the function again to get the complete set of information. We will exploit this behavior on numerous occasions.

LAN Manager Port of the WNet() Vertical APIs

Because I like the way the LAN Manager APIs are designed, I have modeled the WNet() Network Services API after them. Thus, in most cases, one WNet() call will map to a single LAN Manager function.

Table 11-1 shows the WNet() extensions, the supporting LAN Manager group, and the corresponding function (or functions, where there is no one-to-one correspondence).

Table 11-1: WNet() Functions and their LAN Manager Mapping

Function Name	LAN Manager Category	LAN Manager Function	One-to-One Correspondence?
WNetEnumServers	Server	NetServerEnum	Yes
WNetAddUser	User	NetUserAdd	Yes
WNctDeleteUser	User	NetUserDel	Yes
WNetEnumUsers	User	NetUserEnum	Yes
WNetAddGroup	Group	NetGroupAdd	Yes
WNetDeleteGroup	Group	NetGroupDel	Yes
WNetEnumGroups	Group	NetGroupEnum	Yes
WNetAddGroupMember	Group	NetGroupAddUser	Yes
WNetDeleteGroupMember	Group	NetGroupDelUser	Yes
WNetIsUserGroupMember	User	NetUserGetGroups	No
WNetEnumGroupMembers	Group	NetGroupGetUsers	Yes
WNetEnumMemberGroups	User	NetUserGetGroups	Yes
WNetGrantRights	Access	NetAccessGetInfo	
		NetAccessSetInfo	No
WNetGetRights	Access	NetAccessGetUserPerms	Yes
WNetRevokeRights	Access	NetAccessGetInfo	
		NetAccessSetInfo	No

The User Category

Functions in the User category manipulate the LAN Manager User Accounts Subsystem (UAS). The UAS is a database that LAN Manager uses to verify users' rights to access network resources, such as server disks, print queues, modem queues, and named pipes.

The LAN Manager APIs use data structures containing varying levels of information. Level zero provides the least amount of detail, typically only the name of the object in question. Level one provides more detail, level two still more, and so on up to the highest level offered (usually two or three). Sometimes there are intermediate levels of detail, such as 10 or 11, which provide more detail than level one but less than level two. Typically, levels two and beyond require administrative privileges, whereas levels 10 and 11 do not. Higher levels of detail are supersets of lower levels; they include all the fields of the lower-level structures.

The user information that is stored in the User Accounts Subsystem is described by the *user_info_X* structures, where X takes on the values 0, 1, 2, 10, or 11. The complete information is encapsulated in the *user_info_2* structure, whose typedef follows. Comments indicate the meaning of each field; those which we use for our WNet() functions will be covered in more detail later in this chapter.

```
struct user_info_2
{
    char usri2_name[UNLEN + 1];             // User's name
    char usri2_pad_1;
    char usri2_password[ENCRYPTED_PWLEN];   // Password
    long usri2_password_age;                // Number of seconds since
                                            // password was changed

    unsigned short usri2_priv;              // Privilege--guest, user,
                                            // or admin
    char far *usri2_home_dir;               // User's home directory
    char far *usri2_comment;                // Account comment,
                                            // not interpreted
                                            // by LAN Manager

    unsigned short usri2_flags;             // Flags describing
                                            // account,discussed
                                            // later in this chapter

    char far *usri2_script_path;            // Location of user's
                                            // logon script
    unsigned long usri2_auth_flags;         // Specify whether
                                            // user has
                                            // print operator,
                                            // comm operator,
                                            // server operator,
                                            // or accounts
                                            // operator privileges
    char far *usri2_full_name;              // User's full name
    char far *usri2_usr_comment;            // User comment
    char far *usri2_parms;                  // Application-specific
                                            // info,
                                            // not used by LAN Manager

    char far *usri2_workstations;           // String containing names
                                            // of computers that the
                                            // user is
                                            // allowed to log in from
    long usri2_last_logon;                  // Time when user
                                            // last logged on
                                            // in UNIX time format
                                            // (number of
                                            // seconds since 01/01/1970)

    long usri2_last_logoff;                 // Time of last logoff, or
                                            // 0 if unknown
    long usri2_acct_expires;                // Time when account will
                                            // expire
                                            // TIMEQ_FOREVER means never
    unsigned long usri2_max_storage;        // Maximum amount of disk
                                            // space
                                            // user can consume
                                            // USER_MAXSTORAGE_UNLIMITED
                                            // means no limit
```

```
unsigned shortusri2_units_per_week;    // Constant, set to
                                       // UNITS_PER_WEEK
                                       // Specifies how many units
                                       // the following field is
                                       //  divided into
unsigned char far *usri2_logon_hours;  // String of 168 bits
                                       // representing each hour in
                                       // the week. Bit set
                                       // means user is allowed to
                                       // logon during that hour
unsigned shortusri2_bad_pw_count;      // Number of times logon failed
                                       // due to invalid password
unsigned shortusri2_num_logons;        // Number of successful
                                       // logons
char far *usri2_logon_server;          // Name of the server
                                       // that processes this
                                       // user's logon requests
unsigned short usri2_country_code;     // Specifies OS/2 country
                                       // code for user's language
                                       // of choice
unsigned shortusri2_code_page;         // Specifies OS/2 code
                                       // page for
                                       // user's language of choice
};
```

The user-to-group functions in the User category [NetUserGetGroups() and Net-UserSetGroups()] expect a *group_info_0* structure. It has only one field, the group name:

```
struct group_info_0
{
    char grpi0_name[GNLEN + 1];
};
```

As shown in Table 11-1, we will use four functions from this group to implement the LAN Manager Network Services DLL:

NetUserAdd()
NetUserDel()
NetUserEnum()
NetUserGetGroups()

All functions in the User category require you to #define INCL_NETERRORS and INCL_NETUSER, then #include LAN.H:

```
#define INCL_NETERRORS
#define INCL_NETUSER
#include <lan.h>
```

A discussion of these functions follows. Because the mapping to the corresponding WNet() function is straightforward, I include the code listing as well.

NetUserAdd()

```
API_FUNCTION NetUserAdd(LPCSTR lpszServer,
                        short   sLevel,
                        LPSTR   lpBuffer,
                        unsigned short cbBuffer);
```

This function adds a new user on server *lpszServer*. *sLevel* indicates whether *lpBuffer* points to a *user_info_1* or *user_info_2* structure. These are the only possibilities, so *sLevel* must be one or two. *cbBuffer* is the size of the structure.

The first level of detail is sufficient for WNetAddUser(). Thus we will pass NetUser-Add() a pointer to a *user_info_1* structure. Though it is a strict subset of the *user_info_2* structure listed above, I show the layout of the *user_info_1* structure here for easy reference:

```
struct user_info_1
{
   charusri1_name[UNLEN + 1];
   charusri1_pad_1;
   charusri1_password[ENCRYPTED_PWLEN];
   longusri1_password_age;
   unsigned shortusri1_priv;
   char far *usri1_home_dir;
   char far *usri1_comment;
   unsigned short usri1_flags;
   char far *usri1_script_path;
};
```

usri1_name is the user's name.

usri1_password will hold the user's password. The length of the string, ENCRYPTED_PWLEN, allows enough space for the encrypted version of the password to be transmitted over the network. We need to limit its length to PWLEN, which is less than ENCRYPTED_PWLEN.

usri1_password_age specifies the number of seconds since the user's password was changed. It is irrelevant to NetUserAdd(), and is ignored.

usri1_priv specifies the level of privilege that the user will enjoy. It can have one of three values: USER_PRIV_GUEST, USER_PRIV_USER, or USER_PRIV_ADMIN. LAN Manager automatically assigns the user to the group *guests*, *users*, or *admins* depending on the setting of this flag. These groups correspond to guest users, normal end users, and administrators.

usri1_home_dir specifies the user's initial working directory; *usri1_comment* is a comment describing the user; and *usri1_flags* sets certain characteristics of the account, as shown in Table 11-2.

Table 11-2: User Account Flags

Flag	Meaning
UF_SCRIPT	Execute logon script (must be set for LAN Manager 2.X)
UF_ACCOUNTDISABLE	Account is disabled
UF_DELETE_PROHIBITED	Deleting is prohibited

Table 11-2: User Account Flags (cont.)

Flag	Meaning
UF_HOMEDIR_REQUIRED	A home directory must be supplied
UF_PASSWORD_NOTREQD	If set, user is not required to have a password
UF_PASSWORD_CANT_CHANGE	If set, user cannot change her own password

usri1_script_path specifies the user's logon script file.

WNetAddUser()   WNetAddUser() translates easily into NetUserAdd(). Here is the prototype for WNetAddUser() again:

```
BOOL WINAPI WNetAddUser(LPSTR lpszServerName, LPSTR lpszUserName,
                LPSTR lpszPassword, BOOL bAdmin);
```

We pass the server name along to NetAddUser(), after first calling LMAdjustServerName(), shown in Listing 11-16, to make sure the server name is in its correct format. LAN Manager requires that the server name be preceded by two backslashes. We saw in Chapter 10 that NetWare wants the server name by itself. To preserve network independence, we allow the server name to be passed with or without the leading backslashes. In Chapter 10, we stripped off the backslashes, because NetWare does not want them. Here, LMAdjustServerName() adds the backslashes if they are not already there.

The other arguments serve to initialize the *user_info_1* structure. *lpszUserName* goes to the *usri1_name* field, if it is not too long. *lpszPassword* goes to the *usri1_password* field, again provided it is not too long. If *bAdmin* is TRUE, we set *usri1_priv* to USER_PRIV_ADMIN; otherwise, we set it to USER_PRIV_USER. We do not use *usri1_home_dir* or *usri1_script_path*, so we set them to NULL. We set *usri1_flags* to UF_SCRIPT (as required) and UF_PASSWORD_NOTREQD, so the user will not be required to have a password.

Listing 11-1 shows the implementation:

```
/********
*
* Listing 11-1. WNETAUSR.C
*
* Copyright (c) 1992 Ralph P. Davis, All Rights Reserved
*
********/

/*===== Includes =====*/

#define INCL_NETERRORS
#define INCL_NETUSER

#include "wnetlm.h"

/*===== Function Definitions =====*/

BOOL WINAPI WNetAddUser(LPSTR lpszServerName, LPSTR lpszUserName,
                LPSTR lpszPassword, BOOL bAdmin)
{
```

```
struct user_info_1 UserInfo;
API_RET_TYPE uReturnCode;
char         szFullServerName[NNLEN + 1];

WNetSetLastError(WN_SUCCESS);
if (lstrlen(lpszUserName) > UNLEN)
   {
   WNetSetLastError(WN_BAD_USER);
   return FALSE;
   }

lpszServerName = LMAdjustServerName(lpszServerName, szFullServerName);

if (lpszServerName == NULL)
   {
   WNetSetLastError(WN_BAD_NETNAME);
   return FALSE;
   }
if (lpszPassword != NULL && lstrlen(lpszPassword) > PWLEN)
   {
   WNetSetLastError(WN_BAD_PASSWORD);
   return FALSE;
   }

lstrcpy(UserInfo.usri1_name, lpszUserName);

if (lpszPassword != NULL)
   lstrcpy(UserInfo.usri1_password, lpszPassword);
else
   UserInfo.usri1_password[0] = '\0';

if (bAdmin)
   UserInfo.usri1_priv = USER_PRIV_ADMIN;
else
   UserInfo.usri1_priv = USER_PRIV_USER;
UserInfo.usri1_flags = UF_SCRIPT | UF_PASSWD_NOTREQD;
UserInfo.usri1_home_dir = UserInfo.usri1_comment =
   UserInfo.usri1_script_path = NULL;

uReturnCode = NetUserAdd(lpszServerName, 1, (LPSTR) &UserInfo,
   sizeof (UserInfo));
if (uReturnCode == NERR_Success || uReturnCode == NERR_UserExists)
   return TRUE;
else
   {
   WNetSetLastError(MapLMToWinErr(uReturnCode));
   return FALSE;
   }
}
```

NetUserDel()   NetUserDel() is a very simple function. It takes two arguments, the server name and the user name:

```
API_FUNCTION NetUserDel(LPCSTR lpszServer, LPSTR lpszUserName);
```

It makes the implementation of WNetDeleteUser( ) trivial.

```
/********
*
* Listing 11-2. WNETDUSR.C
*
* Copyright (c) 1992 Ralph P. Davis, All Rights Reserved
*
********/

/*===== Includes =====*/

#define INCL_NETERRORS
#define INCL_NETUSER

#include "wnetlm.h"

/*===== Function Definitions =====*/
BOOL WINAPI WNetDeleteUser(LPSTR lpszServerName, LPSTR lpszUserName)
{
    API_RET_TYPE uReturnCode;
    char        szFullServerName[NNLEN + 1];

    lpszServerName = LMAdjustServerName(lpszServerName, szFullServerName);

    if (lpszServerName == NULL)
        {
        WNetSetLastError(WN_BAD_NETNAME);
        return FALSE;
        }
    uReturnCode = NetUserDel(lpszServerName, lpszUserName);

    if (uReturnCode == NERR_Success || uReturnCode == NERR_UserNotFound)
        return TRUE;
    else
        {
        WNetSetLastError(MapLMToWinErr(uReturnCode));
        return FALSE;
        }
}
```

NetUserEnum()   LAN Manager enumeration functions work differently from Windows enumerators, which invoke a callback function for each instance of the object type in question. LAN Manager enumerators return an array of objects. Thus, our task in adapting LAN Manager enumerators for the WNet library will be to obtain the array of enumerated objects, then invoke a callback function once for each object.

As I mentioned earlier, the LAN Manager enumeration functions have a feature that we can use to our advantage. If the buffer we pass to them is not large enough to hold all the objects, it will return ERROR_MORE_DATA and set one of the output variables to the total number of objects. By calling the function once and telling it that we have no space available, we can find out exactly how much memory we need to allocate.

Here is the prototype for NetUserEnum():

```
API_FUNCTION NetUserEnum(LPCSTR lpszServer,
                         short   sLevel,
                         LPSTR   lpBuffer,
                         unsigned short cbBuffer,
                         unsigned short far *lpcEntriesRead,
                         unsigned short far *lpcTotalAvail);
```

sLevel can be zero, one, two, or 10. Levels one and two require admin or account operator privilege. Levels zero and 10 require no special privileges. We have seen the *user_info_1* and *user_info_2* structures. The *user_info_0* structure consists of nothing but the user name:

```
struct user_info_0
{
   char usri0_name[UNLEN + 1];
};
```

The level 10 structure contains one field available at level zero (the user name), two available at level one, and two available at level two.

```
struct user_info_10
{
   char        usri10_name[UNLEN + 1];   // Level 0
   char        usri10_pad_1;             // Level 1
   char far *usri10_comment;             // Level 1
   char far *usri10_usr_comment;         // Level 2
   char far *usri10_full_name;           // Level 2
};
```

The only one of these fields to which LAN Manager attaches meaning is the user name.

The *lpBuffer* argument to NetUserEnum() points to the output structure. *cbBuffer* is the size in bytes of the output buffer, and can be set to zero if you are telling NetUser-Enum() a little fib. *lpcEntriesRead* reports the number of users enumerated in *lpBuffer*. If NetUserEnum() returns ERROR_MORE_DATA, *lpcTotalAvail* reports the total number of users available for enumeration.

WNetEnumUsers()   Once again, the prototype for WNetEnumUsers() is:

```
BOOL WINAPI WNetEnumUsers(LPSTR lpszServerName,
                          USERENUMPROC lpUserEnumProc);
```

Here's how we express it in terms of NetUserEnum():

1. Call NetUserEnum() with an output buffer size of zero.
2. If NetEnumUser() returns ERROR_MORE_DATA, take the number of users passed back in *lpcTotalAvail* and GlobalAlloc() an array of *user_info_0* structures. Level zero is sufficient for our purposes; all we need are the user names.
3. Call NetUserEnum() again. This time it should succeed.

4. For every element in the array, call the enumeration function. If it returns FALSE, go to step 5.

5. Free the memory allocated and return to the caller.

```c
/********
 *
 * Listing 11-3. WNETEUSR.C
 *
 * Copyright (c) 1992 Ralph P. Davis, All Rights Reserved
 *
 ********/

/*===== Includes =====*/

#define INCL_NETERRORS
#define INCL_NETUSER
#include "wnetlm.h"

/*===== Function Definitions =====*/

BOOL WINAPI WNetEnumUsers(LPSTR lpszServerName,
                          USERENUMPROC lpUserEnumProc)
{
    struct user_info_0 FAR *lpUserInfo = NULL;
    DWORD        dwBytesNeeded;
    WORD         wEntriesRead = 0, wTotalAvail = 0;
    API_RET_TYPE uReturnCode;
    WORD         i;
    BOOL         bRetcode = TRUE;
    char         szFullServerName[NNLEN + 1];

    lpszServerName = LMAdjustServerName(lpszServerName, szFullServerName);

    if (lpszServerName == NULL)
        {
        WNetSetLastError(WN_BAD_NETNAME);
        return FALSE;
        }
    // Step 1
    uReturnCode = NetUserEnum(lpszServerName, 0, NULL, 0, &wEntriesRead,
                              &wTotalAvail);

    // Step 2
    // Should return ERROR_MORE_DATA or maybe NERR_BufTooSmall
    if (uReturnCode == ERROR_MORE_DATA || uReturnCode == NERR_BufTooSmall)
        {
        // We use wTotalAvail + 1 just in case wTotalAvail comes
        // back as zero
        dwBytesNeeded = (DWORD) (((DWORD) (wTotalAvail + 1)) *
                                 ((DWORD) sizeof (struct user_info_0)));
        lpUserInfo = (struct user_info_0 FAR *)
            GlobalAllocPtr(GHND, dwBytesNeeded);
        if (lpUserInfo == NULL)
            {
```

```
                WNetSetLastError(WN_OUT_OF_MEMORY);
                return FALSE;
                }
        // Step 3
        uReturnCode = NetUserEnum(lpszServerName, 0, (LPSTR) lpUserInfo,
            (WORD) dwBytesNeeded, &wEntriesRead, &wTotalAvail);
        }
    if (uReturnCode == NERR_Success)
        {
        // Step 4
        for (i = 0; i < wEntriesRead; ++i)
            {
            // In ANSI C, (*f)(x) is equivalent to f(x).
            // No need to say (*lpUserEnumProc)(...)
            if (!lpUserEnumProc(lpszServerName, lpUserInfo[i].usri0_name))
                {
                bRetcode = TRUE;
                break;
                }
            }
        }
    else
        {
        WNetSetLastError(MapLMToWinErr(uReturnCode));
        bRetcode = FALSE;
        }
    // Step 5
    if (lpUserInfo != NULL)
        GlobalFreePtr(lpUserInfo);
    return bRetcode;
}
```

NetUserGetGroups()   NetUserGetGroups() enumerates the groups to which a user belongs. Though it isn't named with the Enum verb like a standard LAN Manager enumerator, it functions in the same way. If the buffer initially passed to the function is too small, it returns ERROR_MORE_DATA and tells you how many groups the user belongs to.

```
API_FUNCTION NetUserGetGroups(LPCSTR lpszServer,
                              LPSTR  lpszUserName,
                              short  sLevel,
                              LPSTR  lpBuffer,
                              unsigned short cbBuffer,
                              unsigned short far *lpcEntriesRead,
                              unsigned short far *lpcTotalAvail);
```

The arguments are the same as for NetUserEnum(), with the addition of *lpszUserName*. *sLevel* must be zero; NetUserGetGroups() returns an array of *group_info_0* structures, which contain just the group name:

```
struct group_info_0
{
    char grpi0_name[GNLEN + 1];
};
```

WNetEnumMemberGroups()   Here is the prototype for WNetEnumMemberGroups():

```
BOOL WINAPI WNetEnumMemberGroups(LPSTR lpszServerName,
                                 LPSTR lpszUserName,
                                 MEMBERGROUPENUMPROC lpGroupEnumProc);
```

We follow the same steps here as we did with WNetEnumUsers(). We lie and say we don't have any buffer space available, then GlobalAlloc() the memory that LAN Manager tells us we need. We then call NetUserGetGroups() once more, and for every group returned, we call *lpGroupEnumProc*.

```
/********
*
* Listing 11-4. WNETEMGR.C
*
* Copyright (c) 1992 Ralph P. Davis, All Rights Reserved
*
********/

/*===== Includes =====*/

#define INCL_NETERRORS
#define INCL_NETGROUP
#define INCL_NETUSER

#include "wnetlm.h"

/*===== Function Definitions =====*/

BOOL WINAPI WNetEnumMemberGroups(LPSTR lpszServerName,
                                 LPSTR lpszUserName,
                                 MEMBERGROUPENUMPROC lpGroupEnumProc)
{
    struct group_info_0 FAR *lpGroupInfo = NULL;
    DWORD        dwBytesNeeded;
    WORD         wEntriesRead = 0, wTotalAvail = 0;
    API_RET_TYPE uReturnCode;
    WORD         i;
    BOOL         bRetcode = TRUE;
    char         szFullServerName[NNLEN + 1];

    lpszServerName = LMAdjustServerName(lpszServerName, szFullServerName);

    if (lpszServerName == NULL)
        {
        WNetSetLastError(WN_BAD_NETNAME);
        return FALSE;
        }
    uReturnCode = NetUserGetGroups(lpszServerName, lpszUserName,
                                   0, NULL, 0, &wEntriesRead,
                                   &wTotalAvail);

    if (uReturnCode == ERROR_MORE_DATA || uReturnCode == NERR_BufTooSmall)
        {
        dwBytesNeeded = (DWORD) (((DWORD) (wTotalAvail + 1)) *
```

```
                                ((DWORD) sizeof (struct group_info_0)));
      lpGroupInfo = (struct group_info_0 FAR *)
         GlobalAllocPtr(GHND, dwBytesNeeded);
      if (lpGroupInfo == NULL)
         {
         WNetSetLastError(WN_OUT_OF_MEMORY);
         return FALSE;
         }
      uReturnCode = NetUserGetGroups(lpszServerName, lpszUserName,
                                     0, (LPSTR) lpGroupInfo,
                                     (WORD) dwBytesNeeded,
                                     &wEntriesRead, &wTotalAvail);
      }
   if (uReturnCode == NERR_Success)
      {
      for (i = 0; i < wEntriesRead; ++i)
         {
         if (!lpGroupEnumProc(lpszServerName, lpszUserName,
                              lpGroupInfo[i].grpi0_name))
            {
            bRetcode = TRUE;
            break;
            }
         }
      }
   else
      {
      WNetSetLastError(MapLMToWinErr(uReturnCode));
      bRetcode = FALSE;
      }
   if (lpGroupInfo != NULL)
      GlobalFreePtr(lpGroupInfo);
   return bRetcode;
}
```

The Group API Category

The functions in the Group category allow programs to create and delete user groups, to add and delete group members, and to obtain information about existing groups.

As I discussed in Chapter 10, groups provide a more convenient way to assign user rights in a complex network environment. Rather than giving hundreds of individual users identical sets of rights, you grant rights to groups, then assign users to those groups.

LAN Manager uses three groups (*guests*, *users*, and *admins*) for its own purposes, and adds users to the appropriate group when they are created. Membership is determined by the user privilege field of the *user_info_X* structure passed to NetUserAdd(). You cannot add members to or delete them from these groups directly. You can only query LAN Manager for information about them.

The functions in this category that we will use are NetGroupAdd(), NetGroupDel(), NetGroupEnum(), NetGroupAddUser(), NetGroupDelUser(), and NetGroupGetUsers().

Programs using the Group APIs require this prologue:

```
#define INCL_NETERRORS
#define INCL_NETGROUP
#include <lan.h>
```

NetGroupAdd(), NetGroupDel(), and NetGroupEnum() use *group_info_X* structures at two levels, zero and one. The *group_info_0* structure appeared earlier in this chapter; it contains only the group name. The level one structure, besides a padding field, has a comment field:

```
struct group_info_1
{
    char grp1_name[GNLEN + 1];
    char grp1_pad;
    char far *grp1_comment;
};
```

NetGroupGetUsers() returns an array of *group_users_info_0* structures, defined as follows:

```
struct group_users_info_0
{
    char grui0_name[UNLEN + 1];
};
```

This is exactly the same format as the *user_info_0* structure we saw earlier.

NetGroupAdd()   The prototype for NetGroupAdd() is:

```
API_FUNCTION NetGroupAdd(LPCSTR lpszServer,
                         short  sLevel,
                         LPSTR  lpBuffer,
                         unsigned short cbBuffer);
```

sLevel is either zero or one, indicating that *lpBuffer* points to a *group_info_0* or *group_info_1* structure.

WNetAddGroup()   WNetAddGroup() maps to NetGroupAdd() in much the same way as WNetAddUser() does to NetUserAdd(). Here is the prototype of WNetAddGroup():

```
BOOL WINAPI WNetAddGroup(LPSTR lpszServerName,
                         LPSTR lpszGroupName);
```

We pass *lpszServerName* through to NetGroupAdd() and put the group name into a *group_info_0* structure, testing first to make sure it is not too long. A single call to NetGroupAdd() (along with our usual server-name adjustments and error handling) implements the function.

```
/********
*
* Listing 11-5. WNETAGRP.C
*
* Copyright (c) 1992 Ralph P. Davis, All Rights Reserved
*
```

```
*******/

/*===== Includes =====*/
#define INCL_NETERRORS
#define INCL_NETGROUP

#include "wnetlm.h"

/*===== Function Definitions =====*/

BOOL WINAPI WNetAddGroup(LPSTR lpszServerName, LPSTR lpszGroupName)
{
    struct group_info_0 GroupInfo;
    API_RET_TYPE uReturnCode;
    char          szFullServerName[NNLEN + 1];

    WNetSetLastError(WN_SUCCESS);
    if (lstrlen(lpszGroupName) > GNLEN)
        {
        WNetSetLastError(WN_BAD_USER);
        return FALSE;
        }

    lpszServerName = LMAdjustServerName(lpszServerName, szFullServerName);

    if (lpszServerName == NULL)
        {
        WNetSetLastError(WN_BAD_NETNAME);
        return FALSE;
        }
    lstrcpy(GroupInfo.grpi0_name, lpszGroupName);

    uReturnCode = NetGroupAdd(lpszServerName, 0, (LPSTR) &GroupInfo,
        sizeof (GroupInfo));
    if (uReturnCode == NERR_Success || uReturnCode == NERR_GroupExists)
        return TRUE;
    else
        {
        WNetSetLastError(MapLMToWinErr(uReturnCode));
        return FALSE;
        }
}
```

NetGroupDel()   The prototype of NetGroupDel() bespeaks its simplicity:

```
API_FUNCTION NetGroupDel(LPCSTR lpszServer, LPSTR lszGroupName);
```

WNetDeleteGroup(), in turn, is very close to NetGroupDel(); its listing needs no further comment.

```
/********
 *
 * Listing 11-6. WNETDGRP.C
 *
 * Copyright (c) 1992 Ralph P. Davis, All Rights Reserved
```

```
*
*******/

/*===== Includes =====*/
#define INCL_NETERRORS
#define INCL_NETGROUP

#include "wnetlm.h"

/*===== Function Definitions =====*/

BOOL WINAPI WNetDeleteGroup(LPSTR lpszServerName,
                            LPSTR lpszGroupName)
{
   API_RET_TYPE uReturnCode;
   char         szFullServerName[NNLEN + 1];

   lpszServerName = LMAdjustServerName(lpszServerName, szFullServerName);

   if (lpszServerName == NULL)
      {
      WNetSetLastError(WN_BAD_NETNAME);
      return FALSE;
      }
   uReturnCode = NetGroupDel(lpszServerName, lpszGroupName);

   if (uReturnCode == NERR_Success || uReturnCode == NERR_GroupNotFound)
      return TRUE;
   else
      {
      WNetSetLastError(MapLMToWinErr(uReturnCode));
      return FALSE;
      }
}
```

NetGroupEnum()   NetGroupEnum() behaves like the other LAN Manager enumeration functions:

```
API_FUNCTION NetGroupEnum(LPCSTR lpszServer,
                          short  sLevel,
                          LPSTR  lpBuffer,
                          unsigned short cbBuffer,
                          unsigned short far *lpcEntriesRead,
                          unsigned short far *lpcTotalAvail);
```

sLevel can be either zero or one to request a *group_info_0* or *group_info_1* structure in return.

We implement WNetEnumGroups() as we have WNetEnumUsers() and WNetEnum-MemberGroups(). That is, we tell LAN Manager we have no space available for the return data, then allocate the amount of memory we actually need. For each *group_info_0* structure in the array, we call the enumeration function.

```
/********
*
* Listing 11-7. WNETEGRP.C
*
```

```
 * Copyright (c) 1992 Ralph P. Davis, All Rights Reserved
 *
 ********/

/*===== Includes =====*/
#define INCL_NETERRORS
#define INCL_NETGROUP

#include "wnetlm.h"

/*===== Function Definitions =====*/

BOOL WINAPI WNetEnumGroups(LPSTR lpszServerName,
                           GROUPENUMPROC lpGroupEnumProc)
{
    struct group_info_0 FAR *lpGroupInfo = NULL;
    DWORD        dwBytesNeeded;
    WORD         wEntriesRead = 0, wTotalAvail = 0;
    API_RET_TYPE uReturnCode;
    WORD         i;
    BOOL         bRetcode = TRUE;
    char         szFullServerName[NNLEN + 1];

    lpszServerName = LMAdjustServerName(lpszServerName, szFullServerName);

    if (lpszServerName == NULL)
        {
        WNetSetLastError(WN_BAD_NETNAME);
        return FALSE;
        }
    uReturnCode = NetGroupEnum(lpszServerName, 0, NULL, 0, &wEntriesRead,
                          &wTotalAvail);

    if (uReturnCode == ERROR_MORE_DATA || uReturnCode == NERR_BufTooSmall)
        {
        dwBytesNeeded = (DWORD) (((DWORD) (wTotalAvail + 1)) *
                          ((DWORD) sizeof (struct group_info_0)));
        lpGroupInfo = (struct group_info_0 FAR *)
            GlobalAllocPtr(GHND, dwBytesNeeded);
        if (lpGroupInfo == NULL)
            {
            WNetSetLastError(WN_OUT_OF_MEMORY);
            return FALSE;
            }
        uReturnCode = NetGroupEnum(lpszServerName, 0, (LPSTR) lpGroupInfo,
            (WORD) dwBytesNeeded, &wEntriesRead, &wTotalAvail);
        }
    if (uReturnCode == NERR_Success)
        {
        for (i = 0; i < wEntriesRead; ++i)
            {
            if (!lpGroupEnumProc(lpszServerName, lpGroupInfo[i].grpi0_name))
                {
                bRetcode = TRUE;
```

```
                break;
                }
            }
        }
    else
        {
        WNetSetLastError(MapLMToWinErr(uReturnCode));
        bRetcode = FALSE;
        }
    if (lpGroupInfo != NULL)
        GlobalFreePtr(lpGroupInfo);
    return bRetcode;
}
```

NetGroupAddUser()

```
API_FUNCTION NetGroupAddUser(LPCSTR lpszServer,
                             LPSTR  lpszGroupName,
                             LPSTR  lpszUserName);
```

NetGroupAddUser() adds the user *lpszUserName* to the group *lpszGroupName* on the server *lpszServer*. WNetAddGroupMember() serves as an alias for it, taking the same arguments in the same order.

```
/********
*
* Listing 11-8. WNETAMBR.C
*
* Copyright (c) 1992 Ralph P. Davis, All Rights Reserved
*
********/

/*===== Includes =====*/

#define INCL_NETERRORS
#define INCL_NETGROUP

#include "wnetlm.h"

/*===== Function Definitions =====*/

BOOL WINAPI WNetAddGroupMember(LPSTR lpszServerName,
                               LPSTR lpszGroupName,
                               LPSTR lpszUserName)
{
    API_RET_TYPE uReturnCode;
    char         szFullServerName[NNLEN + 1];

    lpszServerName = LMAdjustServerName(lpszServerName, szFullServerName);

    if (lpszServerName == NULL)
        {
        WNetSetLastError(WN_BAD_NETNAME);
        return FALSE;
        }
```

```
   uReturnCode = NetGroupAddUser(lpszServerName, lpszGroupName,
                                 lpszUserName);

   if (uReturnCode == NERR_Success || uReturnCode == NERR_UserInGroup)
      return TRUE;
   else
      return FALSE;
}
```

NetGroupDelUser()   NetGroupDelUser() removes a group member, and mirrors NetGroupAddUser(). Similarly, WNetDeleteGroupMember() mirrors WNetAddGroup-Member().

```
/********
 *
 * Listing 11-9. WNETDMBR.C
 *
 * Copyright (c) 1992 Ralph P. Davis, All Rights Reserved
 *
 ********/

/*===== Includes =====*/

#define INCL_NETERRORS
#define INCL_NETGROUP

#include "wnetlm.h"

/*===== Function Definitions =====*/

BOOL WINAPI WNetDeleteGroupMember(LPSTR lpszServerName,
                                  LPSTR lpszGroupName,
                                  LPSTR lpszUserName)
{
   API_RET_TYPE uReturnCode;
   char         szFullServerName[NNLEN + 1];

   lpszServerName = LMAdjustServerName(lpszServerName, szFullServerName);

   if (lpszServerName == NULL)
      {
      WNetSetLastError(WN_BAD_NETNAME);
      return FALSE;
      }
   uReturnCode = NetGroupDelUser(lpszServerName, lpszGroupName,
                                 lpszUserName);

   if (uReturnCode == NERR_Success || uReturnCode == NERR_UserNotInGroup)
      return TRUE;
   else
      return FALSE;
}
```

NetGroupGetUsers()   NetGroupGetUsers() enumerates the members of a group:

```
API_FUNCTION NetGroupGetUsers(LPCSTR lpszServer,
                              LPSTR  lpszGroupName,
```

```
short   sLevel,
LPSTR   lpBuffer,
unsigned short cbBuffer,
unsigned short far *lpcEntriesRead,
unsigned short far *lpcTotalAvail);
```

sLevel must be zero; only *group_users_info_0* structures, containing just the user name, are returned.

WNetEnumGroupMembers()   By now, the technique for translating LAN Manager enumerators into Windows-style enumerators should be familiar to you. I list WNetEnum-GroupMembers(), which is based on NetGroupGetUsers(), without further ado.

```
/********
 *
 * Listing 11-10. WNETEMBR.C
 *
 * Copyright (c) 1992 Ralph P. Davis, All Rights Reserved
 *
 ********/

/*===== Includes =====*/

#define INCL_NETERRORS
#define INCL_NETGROUP

#include "wnetlm.h"

/*===== Function Definitions =====*/
BOOL WINAPI WNetEnumGroupMembers(LPSTR lpszServerName,
                                 LPSTR lpszGroupName,
                                 GROUPMEMBERENUMPROC lpGroupEnumProc)
{
   struct group_users_info_0 FAR *lpGroupUsersInfo = NULL;
   DWORD        dwBytesNeeded;
   WORD         wEntriesRead = 0, wTotalAvail = 0;
   API_RET_TYPE uReturnCode;
   WORD         i;
   BOOL         bRetcode = TRUE;
   char         szFullServerName[NNLEN + 1];

   lpszServerName = LMAdjustServerName(lpszServerName, szFullServerName);

   if (lpszServerName == NULL)
      {
      WNetSetLastError(WN_BAD_NETNAME);
      return FALSE;
      }
   uReturnCode = NetGroupGetUsers(lpszServerName, lpszGroupName,
                           0, NULL, 0, &wEntriesRead,
                           &wTotalAvail);

   if (uReturnCode == ERROR_MORE_DATA || uReturnCode == NERR_BufTooSmall)
      {
```

```
                dwBytesNeeded = (DWORD) (((DWORD) (wTotalAvail + 1)) *
                                  ((DWORD) sizeof (struct group_users_info_0)));
                lpGroupUsersInfo = (struct group_users_info_0 FAR *)
                    GlobalAllocPtr(GHND, dwBytesNeeded);
                if (lpGroupUsersInfo == NULL)
                    {
                    WNetSetLastError(WN_OUT_OF_MEMORY);
                    return FALSE;
                    }
                uReturnCode = NetGroupGetUsers(lpszServerName, lpszGroupName,
                                      0, (LPSTR) lpGroupUsersInfo,
                                      (WORD) dwBytesNeeded,
                                      &wEntriesRead, &wTotalAvail);
                }
        if (uReturnCode == NERR_Success)
            {
            for (i = 0; i < wEntriesRead; ++i)
                {
                if (!lpGroupEnumProc(lpszServerName, lpszGroupName,
                                lpGroupUsersInfo[i].grui0_name))
                    {
                    bRetcode = TRUE;
                    break;
                    }
                }
            }
        else
            {
            WNetSetLastError(MapLMToWinErr(uReturnCode));
            bRetcode = FALSE;
            }
        if (lpGroupUsersInfo != NULL)
            GlobalFreePtr(lpGroupUsersInfo);
        return bRetcode;
}
```

WNetIsUserGroupMember()   Unlike NetWare and VINES, LAN Manager does not
have a single function to determine group membership. However, we can take advantage
of the work we've already done. We call WNetEnumGroupMembers() to enumerate the
users belonging to the group in question. The callback function looks for the user being
inquired about, and sets a static variable (*bUserFound*) accordingly. When WNetEnum-
GroupMembers() returns, we return *bUserFound*.

```
/******
*
* Listing 11-11. WNETIMBR.C
*
* Copyright (c) 1992 Ralph P. Davis, All Rights Reserved
*
*******/

/*===== Includes =====*/
```

```
#define INCL_NETERRORS
#define INCL_NETGROUP

#include "wnetlm.h"

/*===== LOCAL Variables =====*/

static char szUserName[UNLEN + 1];
static BOOL bUserFound = FALSE;

/*===== FORWARD Functions =====*/

BOOL CALLBACK IsUserGroupMember(LPSTR lpszServer, LPSTR lpszGroup,
                                LPSTR lpszUser);


/*===== Function Definitions =====*/

BOOL WINAPI WNetIsUserGroupMember(LPSTR lpszServerName,
                                  LPSTR lpszGroupName,
                                  LPSTR lpszUserName)
{
    GROUPMEMBERENUMPROC lpProc;
    BOOL                bRetcode;

    (FARPROC) lpProc = MakeProcInstance((FARPROC) IsUserGroupMember,
        hDLLInstance);

    if (lstrlen(lpszUserName) > UNLEN)
        {
        WNetSetLastError(WN_BAD_VALUE);
        return FALSE;
        }

    lstrcpy(szUserName, lpszUserName);
    bUserFound = FALSE;

    bRetcode = WNetEnumGroupMembers(lpszServerName, lpszGroupName, lpProc);

    if (!bRetcode)
        return FALSE;

    FreeProcInstance((FARPROC) lpProc);
    return bUserFound;
}

BOOL WINAPI IsUserGroupMember(LPSTR lpszServer, LPSTR lpszGroup,
                              LPSTR lpszUser)
{
    if (lstrcmpi(lpszUser, szUserName) == 0)
        {
        bUserFound = TRUE;
        return FALSE;          // End enumeration
        }
    else
```

```
       return TRUE;
}
```

Access API Category

The Access API category contains functions for granting, revoking, and retrieving user rights.

LAN Manager Security Scheme   LAN Manager has two levels of security, share-level and user-level. Share-level security is an older implementation. Under this scheme, rights are not assigned on a global basis. Rather, they are granted on a per-resource basis. When a user maps a local device name to a shared network resource, he must supply a password (if the resource requires a password). This gives him rights to access that particular resource.

User-level security is a more advanced scheme, where rights are assigned globally. Users do not have to supply passwords to use a resource. Rather, LAN Manager determines by a somewhat complicated algorithm whether they have rights to the resource.

The Access functions require that the target server be running user-level security. Any function invoked for a server running share-level security will return ERROR_NOT_SUPPORTED.

Data Structures   The rights structure for a resource is stored in a data structure called an access control list (ACL). The C equivalent of this is the *access_info_1* structure, defined as follows:

```
struct access_info_1
{
    char far *acc1_resource_name;
    short acc1_attr;
    short acc1_count;
};
```

The *acc1_resource_name* names the resource. The format of the name determines the device type.

- If the name is in the format *drive:*, it refers to a server disk drive. This is not the same as assigning rights to the root directory of the drive. As we shall see, assignment of rights to drives plays an important role in the LAN Manager rights scheme. The drive must exist in order to grant rights to it. You cannot assign rights to a drive on a LAN Manager server that is running the High Performance File System (HPFS).

- If the name is in the format *\path*, with no drive letter, it refers to a path that is not relative to a disk, and the path is not required to exist.

- A name in the format *drive:\path* refers to either a file or a directory. The target entity must exist.

- The name can be a file or directory in Universal Naming Convention (UNC) format, which is *\\server\share\path*. For example, if the server MYSERVER is sharing C:\PUBLIC under the share name PUBLIC, the file MYFILE.TXT in that directory would be called \\MYSERVER\PUBLIC\MYFILE.TXT.

If the name is specified in UNC format, the indicated file or directory must already exist.

If a resource name is passed to an Access function in this format, the server portion of the UNC name will override the function's *lpszServer* argument.

- The name may also refer to a logical device, such as a named pipe, a printer queue, or a communications device queue. Names of devices appear thus:

\PIPE\pipename   (a named pipe)
\PRINT\queuename   (a printer queue)
\COMM\queuename   (a communications queue)

The *accl_attr* field is a bit mask specifying which operations on the resource are to be audited. The events are opens, writes, deletions, and changes to the access control list. Either successful or unsuccessful operations (or both) can be audited. When an audited event occurs, LAN Manager writes an entry to the audit file, NET.AUD. The log can be read from a Windows program by calling the NetAuditRead() function in the Auditing category. Only OS/2 programs can write to the audit file. For more information on the LAN Manager Audit APIs see Ralph Ryan's *LAN Manager Programmer's Guide*, and the Microsoft *LAN Manager Programmer's Reference*.

The third field in the ACL, *accl_count*, specifies the number of Access Control Entry (ACE) structures that follow the ACL. Each ACE specifies a single user (or group) and the rights she has to the resource.

The ACE is defined by this C structure:

```
struct access_list
{
    char acl_ugname[UNLEN + 1];
    char acl_ugname_pad_1;
    short acl_access;
};
```

acl_ugname is the user or group name. *acl_access* is a set of bits defining the user's rights. The bit flags are shown in Table 11-3.

Table 11-3: LAN Manager Access Rights

Bit flag	Significance
ACCESS_READ	Permission to read or execute the resource
ACCESS_WRITE	Permission to write to the resource
ACCESS_CREATE	Permission to create a specific resource (such as a named pipe)
ACCESS_EXEC	Permission to execute the resource
ACCESS_DELETE	Permission to delete the resource
ACCESS_ATRIB	Permission to change the resource's attributes
ACCESS_PERM	Permission to grant or revoke access to the resource
ACCESS_ALL	A bitwise OR of all the above permission flags
ACCESS_GROUP	Access is being assigned to a group

Windows NT also uses Access Control Lists and Access Control Entries for security management.

Scheme for Determining a User's Rights   Users who belong to the *admins* group on a server can access all resources on that server. If a user does not have administrative privileges, rights are determined by searching the ACEs for a resource. LAN Manager follows these rules for determining a user's permission set:

1. Permissions assigned at the file level take precedence over those assigned at the directory level.

2. Permissions assigned to individual users take precedence over group assignments. This is in marked contrast to NetWare, where group and individual permissions complement each other.

3. If a user does not have individually assigned rights, her rights are the combination of all rights she enjoys by dint of group membership.

4. If there is no ACE for the user or for any of her member groups, LAN Manager checks to see if there is an ACE for the *guest* user account. If so, she is given its rights.

5. If the above steps yield no rights, LAN Manager will then perform the same steps on the resource's parent. For a file or directory, this will be its containing directory. For pipes and queues, it will be the next pseudodirectory back in the device name. For example, if a pipe is called \PIPE\WINBOOK\NICEPIPE, its parent is \PIPE\WINBOOK.

6. If the search still has not produced an ACE for the user, her groups, or *guest*, LAN Manager will finally search the root of the resource. For files and directories, this is the drive where they reside, not the root directory of the drive. For devices, it is a backslash followed by the device type (\PIPE, \PRINT, or \COMM).

Note that the progression from parent to root is not recursive. It is a three-step process: resource, parent, root.

Access Functions Used to Implement the WNet() Extensions   We have three WNet() functions relating to rights assignment, WNetGrantRights(), WNetGetRights, and WNetRevokeRights(). LAN Manager does not offer a single function to assign or revoke a user's (or group's) rights. The functions NetAccessAdd() and NetAccessDel() add or delete an entire Access Control List, with all its concomitant Access Control Entries. Thus, we have to retrieve the current ACL and its ACE list and scan the list for the desired user. If he is in the list, we change his permission set accordingly, or delete him altogether. If he is not, we either create a new ACE for him and tell LAN Manager to update the list or, if he is being deleted, we do nothing.

The functions that read and change the ACL and ACEs are NetAccessGetInfo() and NetAccessSetInfo():

```
API_FUNCTION NetAccessGetInfo(LPCSTR lpszServer,
                    LPSTR   lpszResource,
                    short   sLevel,
                    LPSTR   lpBuffer,
                    unsigned short cbBuffer,
                    unsigned short far *lpcTotalAvail);
```

NetAccessGetInfo() varies somewhat from the other LAN Manager enumerator functions in that it does not include an *lpcEntriesRead* argument, and *lpcTotalAvail* reports the number of bytes of information available. The return information is not a simple array; it consists of an *access_info_1* structure followed by a potentially empty array of *access_list* structures. As with the other enumerators, calling it initially with *cbBuffer* set to zero will provoke an ERROR_MORE_DATA return code; here though, *lpcTotalAvail* will tell us how many *bytes* to allocate.

sLevel can be either zero or one. It is hard to imagine a use for level zero. Like most level zero structures, the *access_info_0* contains only the name of the resource. Presumably, you already know that, since you must supply it as an argument to the function.

Remember that if the resource name is expressed in UNC format, *lpszServer* will be ignored.

```
API_FUNCTION NetAccessSetInfo(LPCSTR lpszServer,
                              LPSTR  lpszResource,
                              short  sLevel,
                              LPSTR  lpBuffer,
                              unsigned short cbBuffer,
                              short  sParmNum);
```

sParmNum is a standard argument with LAN Manager functions that change a current setting. In general, it can either change all the settings or change a specific setting. With NetAccessSetInfo(), the possibilities are PARMNUM_ALL and ACCESS_ATTR_PARMNUM. With PARMNUM_ALL, *lpBuffer* points to an access control list followed by an array of access control entries. This completely rewrites the ACL and ACEs for the resource. If *sParmNum* is ACCESS_ATTR_PARMNUM, then *lpBuffer* points to an unsigned short variable that indicates the new setting of the audit bit mask.

The last Access category function that we need is NetAccessGetUserPerms(). This returns a user's effective rights to a resource—those he enjoys either directly or through group membership. We will use it to implement WNetGetRights().

```
API_FUNCTION NetAccessGetUserPerms(LPCSTR lpszServer,
                                   LPSTR  lpszUgName,
                                   LPSTR  lpszResource,
                                   unsigned short far *lpusPerms);
```

The permission set returned is a combination of the access bits discussed earlier in this chapter.

The Access functions require the prologue:

```
#define INCL_NETERRORS
#define INCL_NETACCESS
#include <lan.h>
```

WNetGrantRights()   In Listing 11-12, I implement WNetGrantRights() using NetAccessGetInfo() and NetAccessSetInfo(). The routine MapWNetRightsToLM() takes the network-independent rights mask passed in and converts it to LAN Manager format.

```
/*******
*
* Listing 11-12. WNETGRNT.C
*
* Copyright (c) 1992 Ralph P. Davis, All Rights Reserved
*
*******/

/*===== Includes =====*/

#define INCL_NETERRORS
#define INCL_NETACCESS

#include "wnetlm.h"

/*===== Function Definitions =====*/

BOOL WINAPI WNetGrantRights(LPSTR lpszServerName,
                            LPSTR lpszUserOrGroup,
                            LPSTR lpszResource,
                            WORD  wRights)
{
    struct access_info_1 FAR *lpACL;
    struct access_list   FAR *lpACE;
    LPBYTE                    lpBuffer = NULL;
    API_RET_TYPE              uReturnCode;
    WORD                      wTotalAvail;
    short                     i;
    BOOL                      bFound = FALSE;
    char                      szFullServerName[NNLEN + 1];

    MapWNetRightsToLM(&wRights);

    if (lstrlen(lpszUserOrGroup) > UNLEN)
        {
        WNetSetLastError(WN_BAD_USER);
        return FALSE;
        }
    lpszServerName = LMAdjustServerName(lpszServerName, szFullServerName);

    if (lpszServerName == NULL)
        {
        WNetSetLastError(WN_BAD_NETNAME);
        return FALSE;
        }
    uReturnCode = NetAccessGetInfo(lpszServerName,
                                   lpszResource,
                                   1, NULL, 0, &wTotalAvail);

    if (uReturnCode == ERROR_MORE_DATA || uReturnCode == NERR_BufTooSmall)
        {
        lpBuffer = (LPBYTE) GlobalAllocPtr(GHND, wTotalAvail);
        if (lpBuffer == NULL)
            {
            WNetSetLastError(WN_OUT_OF_MEMORY);
```

```
          return FALSE;
          }
      uReturnCode = NetAccessGetInfo(lpszServerName,
                                     lpszResource,
                                     1,
                                     (LPSTR) lpBuffer,
                                     wTotalAvail,
                                     &wTotalAvail);

      }

   if (uReturnCode == NERR_Success)
      {
      // Data is returned as an access control list (ACL)
      // followed by an array of access control entries (ACEs)
      lpACL = (struct access_info_1 FAR *) lpBuffer;
      if (lpACL->acc1_count > 0)
         {
         // Look at ACE array
         lpACE =
            (struct access_list FAR *)
            (lpBuffer + (sizeof (struct access_info_1)));

         // Look for our boy in the array of ACEs.
         for (i = 0; i < lpACL->acc1_count; ++i)
            {
            if (lstrcmpi(lpszUserOrGroup, lpACE[i].acl_ugname) == 0)
               {
               // Change the user's current rights
               bFound = TRUE;
               lpACE[i].acl_access = (short) wRights;
               break;
               }
            }
         if (!bFound)
            {
            // The user is being added
            // Increase the size of the array so it can hold
            // one more element
            wTotalAvail += (sizeof (struct access_list));
            lpBuffer = GlobalReAllocPtr(lpBuffer, wTotalAvail, GHND);

            if (lpBuffer == NULL)
               {
               WNetSetLastError(WN_OUT_OF_MEMORY);
               return FALSE;
               }

            // Reset the pointers--lpBuffer may have changed, since
            // we reallocated it
            lpACL = (struct access_info_1 FAR *) lpBuffer;
            lpACE =
               (struct access_list FAR *)
```

```
                (lpBuffer + (sizeof (struct access_info_1)));
            // Populate the new element in the array,
            // then bump the count
            lstrcpy(lpACE[lpACL->acc1_count].acl_ugname,
                lpszUserOrGroup);
            lpACE[lpACL->acc1_count++].acl_access = (short) wRights;
            }
        uReturnCode = NetAccessSetInfo(lpszServerName,
            lpszResource, 1, lpBuffer, wTotalAvail, PARMNUM_ALL);

        }
    }
    if (lpBuffer != NULL)
        GlobalFreePtr(lpBuffer);
    if (uReturnCode != NERR_Success)
        {
        WNetSetLastError(MapLMToWinErr(uReturnCode));
        return FALSE;
        }
    else
        return TRUE;
}

void WINAPI MapWNetRightsToLM(LPWORD lpwRights)
{
    WORD wLMRights = 0;

    if (*lpwRights == 0)
        return;

    if (*lpwRights & WNET_GROUP_ACCESS)
        wLMRights |= ACCESS_GROUP;

    if ((*lpwRights & WNET_ALL_NORMAL_ACCESS) ||
        (*lpwRights & WNET_ALL_ACCESS))
        {
        wLMRights |= ACCESS_ALL;
        *lpwRights = wLMRights;
        return;
        }

    if (*lpwRights & WNET_READ_ACCESS)
        wLMRights |= ACCESS_READ;
    if (*lpwRights & WNET_WRITE_ACCESS)
        wLMRights |= ACCESS_WRITE;
    if (*lpwRights & WNET_CREATE_ACCESS)
        wLMRights |= ACCESS_CREATE;
    if (*lpwRights & WNET_EXECUTE_ACCESS)
        wLMRights |= ACCESS_EXEC;
    if (*lpwRights & WNET_DELETE_ACCESS)
        wLMRights |= ACCESS_DELETE;
    if (*lpwRights & WNET_ATTRIB_ACCESS)
        wLMRights |= ACCESS_ATRIB;
    if (*lpwRights & WNET_PERM_ACCESS)
```

```
      wLMRights |= ACCESS_PERM;
   *lpwRights = wLMRights;
}
```

WNetRevokeRights()   WNetRevokeRights() uses a similar technique. It retrieves the
current access control list for the resource, then looks for the requested user in the access
control entry array. If it finds her, it removes her from the array and calls NetAccess-
SetInfo(). Otherwise, it does nothing.

```
/********
*
* Listing 11-13. WNETREVK.C
*
* Copyright (c) 1992 Ralph P. Davis, All Rights Reserved
*
********/

/*===== Includes =====*/

#define INCL_NETERRORS
#define INCL_NETACCESS

#include "wnetlm.h"

/*===== Function Definitions =====*/
BOOL WINAPI WNetRevokeRights(LPSTR lpszServerName,
                             LPSTR lpszUserOrGroup,
                             LPSTR lpszResource,
                             BOOL  bUser)
{
   struct access_info_1 FAR *lpACL;
   struct access_list   FAR *lpACE;
   LPBYTE                    lpBuffer = NULL;
   API_RET_TYPE              uReturnCode;
   WORD                      wTotalAvail;
   short                     i;
   BOOL                      bFound = FALSE;
   char                      szFullServerName[NNLEN + 1];

   if (lstrlen(lpszUserOrGroup) > UNLEN)
      {
      WNetSetLastError(WN_BAD_USER);
      return FALSE;
      }
   lpszServerName = LMAdjustServerName(lpszServerName, szFullServerName);

   if (lpszServerName == NULL)
      {
      WNetSetLastError(WN_BAD_NETNAME);
      return FALSE;
      }
   uReturnCode = NetAccessGetInfo(lpszServerName,
                                  lpszResource,
```

```
                                       1, NULL, 0, &wTotalAvail);
   if (uReturnCode == ERROR_MORE_DATA || uReturnCode == NERR_BufTooSmall)
       {
       lpBuffer = (LPBYTE) GlobalAllocPtr(GHND, wTotalAvail);
       if (lpBuffer == NULL)
           {
           WNetSetLastError(WN_OUT_OF_MEMORY);
           return FALSE;
           }
       uReturnCode = NetAccessGetInfo(lpszServerName,
                                      lpszResource,
                                      1,
                                      (LPSTR) lpBuffer,
                                      wTotalAvail,
                                      &wTotalAvail);

       }

   if (uReturnCode == NERR_Success)
       {
       lpACL = (struct access_info_1 FAR *) lpBuffer;
       if (lpACL->acc1_count > 0)
           {
           lpACE =
               (struct access_list FAR *)
               (lpBuffer + (sizeof (struct access_info_1)));

           // Look for requested user's ACE
           for (i = 0; i < lpACL->acc1_count; ++i)
               {
               if (lstrcmpi(lpszUserOrGroup, lpACE[i].acl_ugname) == 0)
                   {
                   bFound = TRUE;
                   // Pull down everybody else's ACEs
                   while (++i < lpACL->acc1_count)
                       lpACE[i - 1] = lpACE[i];
                   --lpACL->acc1_count;
                   wTotalAvail -= (sizeof (struct access_list));
                   break;
                   }
               }
           if (bFound)
               uReturnCode = NetAccessSetInfo(lpszServerName,
                   lpszResource, 1, lpBuffer, wTotalAvail, PARMNUM_ALL);
           }
       }
   if (lpBuffer != NULL)
       GlobalFreePtr(lpBuffer);
   if (uReturnCode != NERR_Success)
       {
       WNetSetLastError(MapLMToWinErr(uReturnCode));
       return FALSE;
```

```
      }
   else
      return TRUE;
}
```

WNetGetRights()   Listing 11-14 shows WNetGetRights() coded using NetAccessGet-UserPerms(). Here, we convert the rights mask from the LAN Manager format to the network-independent WNET format. The function MapLMRightsToWNet() does this:

```
/********
*
* Listing 11-14. WNETGRTS.C
*
* Copyright (c) 1992 Ralph P. Davis, All Rights Reserved
*
********/

/*===== Includes =====*/

#define INCL_NETERRORS
#define INCL_NETACCESS

#include "wnetlm.h"

/*===== Function Definitions =====*/

BOOL WINAPI WNetGetRights(LPSTR  lpszServerName,
                          LPSTR  lpszUserOrGroup,
                          LPSTR  lpszResource,
                          LPWORD lpwRights)
{
   API_RET_TYPE uReturnCode;
   WORD         wRights;
   char         szFullServerName[NNLEN + 1];

   lpszServerName = LMAdjustServerName(lpszServerName, szFullServerName);

   if (lpszServerName == NULL)
      {
      WNetSetLastError(WN_BAD_NETNAME);
      return FALSE;
      }
   uReturnCode = NetAccessGetUserPerms(lpszServerName,
                                       lpszUserOrGroup,
                                       lpszResource,
                                       &wRights);

   if (uReturnCode != NERR_Success)
      {
      WNetSetLastError(MapLMToWinErr(uReturnCode));
      return FALSE;
      }

   MapLMRightsToWNet(&wRights);
   *lpwRights = wRights;
```

```
      return TRUE;
}

void WINAPI MapLMRightsToWNet(LPWORD lpwRights)
{
   WORD wRights = 0;

   if (*lpwRights == 0)
      return;

   if (*lpwRights & ACCESS_GROUP)
      wRights |= WNET_GROUP_ACCESS;

   if ((*lpwRights & ACCESS_ALL) == ACCESS_ALL)
      {
      wRights |= WNET_ALL_NORMAL_ACCESS;
      *lpwRights = wRights;
      return;
      }
   if (*lpwRights & ACCESS_READ)
      wRights |= WNET_READ_ACCESS;
   if (*lpwRights & ACCESS_WRITE)
      wRights |= WNET_WRITE_ACCESS;
   if (*lpwRights & ACCESS_CREATE)
      wRights |= WNET_CREATE_ACCESS;
   if (*lpwRights & ACCESS_EXEC)
      wRights |= WNET_EXECUTE_ACCESS;
   if (*lpwRights & ACCESS_DELETE)
      wRights |= WNET_DELETE_ACCESS;
   if (*lpwRights & ACCESS_ATRIB)
      wRights |= WNET_ATTRIB_ACCESS;
   if (*lpwRights & ACCESS_PERM)
      wRights |= WNET_PERM_ACCESS;

   *lpwRights = wRights;
}
```

Server Category

The Server API category offers functions for getting and setting the configuration of servers in the network, for enumerating servers, and for enumerating server disk drives. Our only interest is in enumerating servers so that we can implement WNetEnumServers().

You can retrieve four levels of information on servers, described by the *server_info_0* through *server_info_3* structures. The enumeration function, NetServerEnum2(), reports only levels zero and one. Levels two and three return almost fifty fields of detailed configuration information. These levels can be retrieved using NetServerGetInfo(). Refer to the *LAN Manager Programmer's Reference* for more information.

The *server_info_0* structure has the server name. *server_info_1* includes the name and four other fields:

```
struct server_info_1
{
   char sv1_name[CNLEN + 1];
```

```
    unsigned char sv1_version_major;
    unsigned char sv1_version_minor;
    unsigned long sv1_type;
    char far *sv1_comment;
};
```

sv1_version_major ANDed with the mask MAJOR_VERSION_MASK (0x0F) returns the major version number of LAN Manager running on the server. *sv1_version_minor* returns the minor version number. *sv1_type* is the most interesting field; there are a number of distinct server types, as shown in Table 11-4.

Table 11-4: LAN Manager Server Types

Constant	Significance
SV_TYPE_WORKSTATION	Workstation
SV_TYPE_SERVER	LAN Manager file server
SV_TYPE_SQLSERVER	SQL Server
SV_TYPE_DOMAIN_CTRL	Primary domain controller
SV_TYPE_DOMAIN_BAKCTL	Backup domain controller
SV_TYPE_TIME_SOURCE	Time server
SV_TYPE_AFP	Apple FileTalk Protocol server
SV_TYPE_NOVELL	NetWare server
SV_TYPE_DOMAIN_MEMBER	Domain member
SV_TYPE_PRINTQ_SERVER	Print queue server
SV_TYPE_DIALIN_SERVER	LAN Manager Remote Access server
SV_TYPE_SERVER_UNIX	UNIX Server
SV_TYPE_ALL	All server types

NetServerEnum2()   NetServerEnum2() is the latter-day replacement for NetServer-Enum(), which did not allow the specification of a type of server to enumerate.

Here is the prototype for NetServerEnum2(). All functions in this category require that you #define INCL_NETSERVER and INCL_NETERRORS before including LAN.H:

```
#define INCL_NETERRORS
#define INCL_NETSERVER
#include <lan.h>

API_FUNCTION NetServerEnum2(LPCSTR lpszServer,
                            short   sLevel,
                            LPSTR   lpBuffer,
                            unsigned short cbBuffer,
                            unsigned short far *lpcEntriesRead,
                            unsigned short far *lpcTotalAvail,
                            unsigned long flServerType,
                            LPSTR lpszDomain);
```

NetServerEnum2() is a classic LAN Manager enumeration function. The *lpszServer* argument seems to be irrelevant; indeed, you can pass it as a NULL pointer or an empty string. Of the remaining arguments, only *flServerType* and *lpszDomain* are unfamiliar.

flServerType is a bitmask indicating which of the server types listed in Table 11-4 you want to enumerate. *lpszDomain* specifies the domain in which you want servers enumerated. (Domains in LAN Manager are logical groupings of networked computers.) It can be specified as NULL or "", and this is how we will use it.

WNetEnumServers()   WNetEnumServers() maps to NetServerEnum2() in much the same way as our other enumeration functions have. It first calls NetServerEnum2() with an output buffer size of zero to find out how many servers are available. Next, it allocates the memory and calls NetServerEnum2() again. Then, for every server retrieved, it invokes the callback function supplied by the caller, passing it the server name and type. We translate the server type from its LAN Manager representation to its WNet() form before passing it to the callback routine.

```
/********
*
* Listing 11-15. WNETESRV.C
*
* Copyright (c) 1992 Ralph P. Davis, All Rights Reserved
*
********/

/*===== Includes =====*/

#define INCL_NETERRORS
#define INCL_NETSERVER

#include "wnetlm.h"

/*===== Function Definitions =====*/

BOOL WINAPI WNetEnumServers(SERVERENUMPROC lpServerEnumProc,
                            WORD wServerType)
{
   API_RET_TYPE uReturnCode;
   struct server_info_1 FAR *lpServerInfo = NULL;
   WORD          wEntriesRead, wTotalAvail;
   DWORD         dwBytesNeeded;
   WORD          i;
   BOOL          bReturnCode;
   DWORD         dwServerType = (DWORD) wServerType;

   MapWNetServerToLM(&dwServerType);

   uReturnCode = NetServerEnum2(NULL, 1, NULL, 0, &wEntriesRead,
                                &wTotalAvail, dwServerType, NULL);

   if (uReturnCode == ERROR_MORE_DATA || uReturnCode == NERR_BufTooSmall)
      {
      dwBytesNeeded =
         (DWORD)
            (((DWORD) (wTotalAvail + 1)) *
             ((DWORD) (sizeof (struct server_info_1))));
      lpServerInfo = (struct server_info_1 FAR *)
         GlobalAllocPtr(GHND, dwBytesNeeded);
```

```
      if (lpServerInfo == NULL)
         {
         WNetSetLastError(WN_OUT_OF_MEMORY);
         return FALSE;
         }
      uReturnCode = NetServerEnum2(NULL, 1,
                                  (LPSTR) lpServerInfo,
                                  (WORD) dwBytesNeeded, &wEntriesRead,
                                  &wTotalAvail,
                                  dwServerType, NULL);
      }
   if (uReturnCode == NERR_Success)
      {
      bReturnCode = TRUE;
      for (i = 0; i < wEntriesRead; ++i)
         {
         MapLMServerToWNet(&lpServerInfo[i].sv1_type);

         if (!lpServerEnumProc(lpServerInfo[i].sv1_name,
            (WORD) lpServerInfo[i].sv1_type))
            break;
         }
      }
   else
      bReturnCode = FALSE;

   if (lpServerInfo != NULL)
      GlobalFreePtr(lpServerInfo);

   return bReturnCode;
}

void WINAPI MapWNetServerToLM(LPDWORD lpdwType)
{
   DWORD dwType = 0;

   if (*lpdwType == WNET_ALL_SERVERS)
      {
      *lpdwType = SV_TYPE_ALL;
      return;
      }
   if (*lpdwType & WNET_FILE_SERVER)
      dwType |= SV_TYPE_SERVER;
   if (*lpdwType & WNET_PRINT_SERVER)
      dwType |= SV_TYPE_PRINTQ_SERVER;
   if (*lpdwType & WNET_WORKSTATION)
      dwType |= SV_TYPE_WORKSTATION;
   if (*lpdwType & WNET_SQLSERVER)
      dwType |= SV_TYPE_SQLSERVER;
   if (*lpdwType & WNET_DOMAIN_CTRL)
      dwType |= SV_TYPE_DOMAIN_CTRL;
   if (*lpdwType & WNET_DOMAIN_BKUP)
      dwType |= SV_TYPE_DOMAIN_BAKCTRL;
```

```
    if (*lpdwType & WNET_TIME_SOURCE)
       dwType |= SV_TYPE_TIME_SOURCE;
    if (*lpdwType & WNET_AFP_SERVER)
       dwType |= SV_TYPE_AFP;
    if (*lpdwType & WNET_NETWARE)
       dwType |= SV_TYPE_NOVELL;
    if (*lpdwType & WNET_DOMAIN_MEMBER)
       dwType |= SV_TYPE_DOMAIN_MEMBER;
    if (*lpdwType & WNET_DIALIN_SERVER)
       dwType |= SV_TYPE_DIALIN_SERVER;
    if (*lpdwType & WNET_UNIX_SERVER)
       dwType |= SV_TYPE_SERVER_UNIX;

    *lpdwType = dwType;
}

void WINAPI MapLMServerToWNet(LPDWORD lpdwType)
{
    DWORD dwType = 0;

    if (*lpdwType == SV_TYPE_ALL)
       {
       *lpdwType = WNET_ALL_SERVERS;
       return;
       }
    if (*lpdwType & SV_TYPE_SERVER)
       dwType |= WNET_FILE_SERVER;
    if (*lpdwType & SV_TYPE_PRINTQ_SERVER)
       dwType |= WNET_PRINT_SERVER;
    if (*lpdwType & SV_TYPE_WORKSTATION)
       dwType |= WNET_WORKSTATION;
    if (*lpdwType & SV_TYPE_SQLSERVER)
       dwType |= WNET_SQLSERVER;
    if (*lpdwType & SV_TYPE_DOMAIN_CTRL)
       dwType |= WNET_DOMAIN_CTRL;
    if (*lpdwType & SV_TYPE_DOMAIN_BAKCTRL)
       dwType |= WNET_DOMAIN_BKUP;
    if (*lpdwType & SV_TYPE_TIME_SOURCE)
       dwType |= WNET_TIME_SOURCE;
    if (*lpdwType & SV_TYPE_AFP)
       dwType |= WNET_AFP_SERVER;
    if (*lpdwType & SV_TYPE_NOVELL)
       dwType |= WNET_NETWARE;
    if (*lpdwType & SV_TYPE_DOMAIN_MEMBER)
       dwType |= WNET_DOMAIN_MEMBER;
    if (*lpdwType & SV_TYPE_DIALIN_SERVER)
       dwType |= WNET_DIALIN_SERVER;
    if (*lpdwType & SV_TYPE_SERVER_UNIX)
       dwType |= WNET_UNIX_SERVER;

    *lpdwType = dwType;
}
```

Support Routines

Listing 11-16 shows the routine MapLMToWinErr(), which converts a LAN Manager error code into its nearest Windows equivalent. As you might expect, the Windows errors are derived from the LAN Manager errors. Though they are much less extensive, they do allow us to do a more accurate translation than we have been able to do in other chapters. The listing also contains LMAdjustServerName(), which adds double backslashes to the front of the server name if necessary. Other routines here are a dummy LibMain() and WEP().

```
/********
*
* Listing 11-16. _WNETMIS.C
*
* Copyright (c) 1992 Ralph P. Davis, All Rights Reserved
*
* Miscellaneous LAN Manager support routines
*
********/

/*===== Includes =====*/

#define INCL_NETERRORS

#include "wnetlm.h"

/*===== Global Variables =====*/

HINSTANCE hDLLInstance;

/*===== Function Definitions =====*/

DWORD PASCAL MapLMToWinErr(API_RET_TYPE uReturnCode)
{
    switch (uReturnCode)
        {
        case NERR_Success:
            return WN_SUCCESS;
        case ERROR_MORE_DATA:
        case NERR_BufTooSmall:
            return WN_MORE_DATA;
        case ERROR_NOT_SUPPORTED:
            return WN_NOT_SUPPORTED;
        case NERR_BadUsername:
        case NERR_UserNotFound:
            return WN_BAD_USER;
        case ERROR_BAD_NETPATH:
            return WN_BAD_NETNAME;
        case ERROR_NETWORK_ACCESS_DENIED:
            return WN_ACCESS_DENIED;
        case NERR_BadPassword:
        case NERR_PasswordTooShort:
        case NERR_PasswordExpired:
        case NERR_BadPasswordCore:
```

```
        case NERR_PasswordExpired:
        case NERR_BadPasswordCore:
        case NERR_PasswordMismatch:
            return WN_BAD_PASSWORD;
        default:
            return WN_NET_ERROR;
        }
}

LPSTR PASCAL LMAdjustServerName(LPSTR lpszIn, LPSTR lpszOut)
{
    if (lstrlen(lpszIn) > CNLEN)
        return NULL;
    lstrcpy(lpszOut, "\\\\");
    while (*lpszIn == '\\')
        ++lpszIn;
    lstrcat(lpszOut, lpszIn);
    return lpszOut;
}

int WINAPI LibMain(HINSTANCE hInstance,
                   WORD wDataSeg,
                   WORD cbHeapSize,
                   LPSTR lpszCmdLine)
{
    hDLLInstance = hInstance;
    return 1;
}

int WINAPI WEP(int nParameter)
{
    return 1;
}
```

Program Maintenance Files

The final listings are the LAN Manager-specific header file for the WNet library, WNETLM.H, and the .DEF file.

```
/********
*
* Listing 11-17. WNETLM.H
*
* Copyright (c) 1992 Ralph P. Davis, All Rights Reserved
*
********/
```

```
/*===== Includes =====*/

// #define INCL_ statements must come before WNETLM.H is included.

#include <lan.h>
#include "wnetapi.h"


/*===== Global Variables =====*/

extern HINSTANCE hDLLInstance;


/*===== Function Prototypes =====*/

DWORD PASCAL MapLMToWinErr(API_RET_TYPE uReturnCode);
void  WINAPI MapWNetRightsToLM(LPWORD  lpwRights);
void  WINAPI MapLMRightsToWNet(LPWORD  lpwRights);
void  WINAPI MapWNetServerToLM(LPDWORD lpdwType);
void  WINAPI MapLMServerToWNet(LPDWORD lpdwType);
LPSTR PASCAL LMAdjustServerName(LPSTR lpszIn, LPSTR lpszOut);
BOOL WINAPI IsUserGroupMember(LPSTR lpszServer, LPSTR lpszGroup,
                             LPSTR lpszUser);


;********
;
; Listing 11-18. WNETLM.DEF
;
; Copyright (c) 1992 Ralph P. Davis, All Rights Reserved
;
;********

LIBRARY    WNETLM

EXETYPE    WINDOWS

CODE    PRELOAD MOVEABLE DISCARDABLE
DATA    PRELOAD MOVEABLE SINGLE

HEAPSIZE  4096

EXPORTS
          WEP                 @1 RESIDENTNAME
          WNetAddUser
          WNetEnumUsers
          WNetDeleteUser
          WNetEnumServers
          WNetAddGroup
          WNetEnumGroups
          WNetDeleteGroup
          WNetAddGroupMember
```

```
WNetDeleteGroupMember
WNetIsUserGroupMember
IsUserGroupMember
WNetEnumGroupMembers
WNetEnumMemberGroups
WNetGrantRights
WNetRevokeRights
WNetGetRights
```

Banyan VINES Network Services API

Overview

Banyan's VINES Application Toolkit includes a network services API with a full set of calls to perform administrative functions, manage the network, send electronic mail, etc. Each of these groups of services is documented separately and most have their own Windows DLL. For example, VNSAPI.DLL includes the administrative services, VNSNM.DLL controls network management, and VNSMAIL.DLL supports electronic mail. All the services discussed here are contained in VNSAPI.DLL.

VINES Names

VINES uses a three-part naming scheme for network objects. The three parts of a name are the item, which refers to one unique individual object; the group; and the organization. The item can contain up to 31 characters; the group and organization are restricted to 15. Each part of a name is separated by an @. Here are several examples:

- RALPHD@users@MyOrg
- VFS@VNSSERVER@Servers
- AdminList@VNSSERVER@Servers
- AdminList@users@MyOrg

The item portion can designate several different types of objects. Most important for our purposes are users and lists (the VINES equivalent of what NetWare and LAN Manager call groups). In the above examples, RALPHD is a user; AdminList is a list. Some names are used internally by VINES. For example, AdminList keeps track of users who have administrative privileges. There are two levels of administration, the group and the server. Members of the AdminList for a particular group—like AdminList@users@MyOrg—have administrative control over members of that group. Members of the AdminList for a server—AdminList@VNSSERVER@Servers—have administrative rights for an entire server. A user can belong to more than one AdminList.

The group portion is used in several places. First, it plays a part in the VINES file access scheme. Second, it is the basic unit by which the VINES database is distributed. In addition, it stores server names, when combined with the organization name Servers. When we implement WNetEnumServers(), we will ask for all groups belonging to the organization Servers (indicated by the string "*@Servers"). For the most part, VINES attaches no semantics to the organization name. It is provided as a clarifier in network administration. Because VINES is strongly oriented towards wide-area networking, the item name and the group name may not always be enough to uniquely identify an object.

StreetTalk

VINES uses a distributed database, called StreetTalk, to keep track of network users, groups, services, and servers. Network objects are organized into groups, according to the group portion of their Street Talk name. Only one server stores information on the members of any one group. All the other servers know which server has information about which group.

The StreetTalk database is distributed by being partitioned. No one server needs to maintain a copy of the entire database, and the copies on each server differ from each other. When one server needs information kept by another server, it calls the other one to get it.

This process is invisible to both end users and applications. This has one very specific implication for us. You will recall that all of our WNet() network service functions except WNetEnumServers() include the server name as an argument. With VINES, this argument is irrelevant. We simply toss our requests out onto the network, and VINES takes care of figuring out where the information is.

The partitioning of the database does mean that if a server is not on-line, no other servers can get information about the groups maintained on that server.

I want to point out again (and I will do so often in the course of this chapter) that the word "group" differs in VINES from NetWare or LAN Manager. A VINES "list" corresponds exactly to a NetWare or LAN Manager group. A VINES group, on the other hand, behaves like a UNIX group—the VINES file server software is, after all, a version of UNIX. As in UNIX, a user can belong to only one VINES group. However, she can belong to any number of VINES lists. UNIX recognizes three levels of access rights: those assigned to a file's owner, those granted to a file's group, and those allowed everyone else. At each level, there are three possible permissions: read, write, and execute. VINES uses this same basic system, though with a set of rights more like those we have already seen.

VINES also allows the granting of rights to five additional users, groups, or lists. It uses a rather complicated scheme to determine a user's rights at runtime. In this context, too, groups and lists behave differently.

StreetTalk Directory Assistance

On top of the StreetTalk database sits the StreetTalk Directory Assistance (STDA) database. It consists of the local StreetTalk database (including information on groups stored on remote servers), and also tracks objects in foreign systems. It is rebuilt periodically—usually once a day—from the StreetTalk database and from so-called inclusion files, which contain the names of other known users on other systems. This is primarily used for electronic mail, but it also comes into play when users connect to network resources from Windows.

Unlike the StreetTalk database, which is partitioned, the STDA database is distributed by replication. In any system, there is one server that is designated the master STDA server. All the other servers are STDA satellites. The satellites periodically download the complete STDA database from the master.

The core database for network administration is StreetTalk. It is the one that we will be using to implement the WNet() functions. The only place I use STDA is in the network driver demo program shown in Appendix C. If it detects that the underlying network is VINES, it makes the VINES STDA dialog boxes available from the Dialogs menu. These are similar to the network driver WNetBrowseDialog() function (which VINES does not support), in that they allow the user to browse network resources. The StreetTalk API set is much more extensive than the STDA API. It is also much easier to program. This would not by itself be sufficient reason for using StreetTalk; I use StreetTalk because it is the critical element. You can run a VINES network without StreetTalk Directory Assistance. You cannot run it without StreetTalk.

API Groupings

As I said earlier, each VINES API group is documented in its own manual, and sometimes supported by its own DLL. All the services we will use reside in VNSAPI.DLL. They are documented as two API groupings: the Client API and the StreetTalk API.

The Client API

The Client API provides a wide cross-section of services. In Chapter 5, we used the socket functions to implement the VINES peer-to-peer DLL. It also includes functions to do things like map drives and assign user rights. We will cast a glance at the access rights functions, but we can do no more; the current version of VINES [5.00 (5)] does not support them under Windows. They will be supported in a future version. The code I present later for WNetGetRights(), WNetGrantRights(), and WNetRevokeRights() compiles, but always returns an error. I have not been able to test it beyond this. The VINES API for DOS does support these functions; you can access them under Windows using DPMI, as described in Chapter 7.

Table 12-1: VINES Access Functions

Function Name	Purpose
VnsDuplicateAccessRightsList	Copy list of trustees from one file or directory to another
VnsGetAccessRightsList	Retrieve list of file/directory trustees
VnsGetUserAccessRights	Retrieve user's effective rights to a file or directory
VnsSetAccessRightsList	Change list of file/directory trustees

The StreetTalk API

The StreetTalk API provides most of the functionality that we will build on. These include the functions that add, delete, and enumerate users; add, delete, and enumerate groups; enumerate servers; add users to groups; delete users from groups; enumerate group members; and check if a user belongs to a certain group.

The StreetTalk API is further subdivided in two ways: between session-implicit and session-explicit functions, and according to the service performed.

Session-Implicit Versus Session-Explicit Functions   All the StreetTalk functions act by establishing a session with the StreetTalk service running on a VINES server. (Services are background processes running under UNIX on the server.) In versions of the VINES API before 5.0, the session establishment was invisible to an application (i.e., implicit). In addition, all the functions used a single session that was globally visible.

VINES 5.0 introduces the session-explicit functions, where sessions are visible to application programs. Functions are provided for establishing and terminating a StreetTalk session, and the other calls refer to an explicit session, rather than using one implicit global session. Banyan recommends that all new code use the session-explicit functions, for several reasons. There is no longer a need for one global session, so code using explicit sessions is reentrant; you can have multiple concurrent StreetTalk sessions; and the session-implicit functions call the session-explicit functions anyway, so calling them directly is faster.

The session-implicit functions are still available, primarily for backward compatibility. Each session-implicit function has a corresponding session-explicit function. Generally, they differ in two ways. The session-explicit function adds an 'S' in the middle of the name (after the verb). Thus VnsAddStUser() becomes VnsAddSStUser(); VnsListStNames() becomes VnsListSStNames(). And the session-explicit functions add one argument, a pointer to a data structure that identifies the session. The rest of the arguments are the same.

Function Subgroupings   The StreetTalk functions are classified into eight subgroups:

- StreetTalk Record functions
- User Management functions
- Group and Organization Management functions
- Name Management functions
- List Management functions

- Security Management functions
- Session Management functions
- Service Management functions

The most important for our purposes are User Management and List Management. Session Management contributes functions to start and end StreetTalk sessions, and Name Management gives us one all-important enumeration function.

The StreetTalk Record functions manipulate specific information kept in the StreetTalk database. This information is stored as 1024-byte arrays referred to as "associated records." There are 1000 associated records for any network object; only those that have been specifically assigned a value actually exist. Some of them are used by VINES. Record zero, for instance, is the main record for all network objects. Its format depends on the type of object being described. As an example, record zero for a group tells VINES which server is keeping track of the group. Associated record one for a user stores her profile (login script). Record 700 is reserved for the configuration information of third-party server-based applications ("services"). Records 701-799 are available to applications for their own purposes.

VINES associated records are similar to NetWare bindery properties.

Table 12-2 lists the StreetTalk Record functions. Where there is both a session-implicit and a session-explicit version, I include only the session-explicit one.

Table 12-2: StreetTalk Record Functions

Function Name	Purpose
VnsAddSStAssocRecord	Add an associated record for an object
VnsDeleteSStAssocRecord	Delete an associated record for an object
VnsGetSStAssocRecord	Retrieve the current value of an associated record
VnsSetSStAssocRecord	Change the current value of an associated record
VnsSetSStDesc	Change the description of an object

The User Management functions allow applications to create new users, delete users, and manipulate user information. The specific information includes:

- The user's login script
- When the user last logged in, when her account expires, when she last changed her password, and whether her account is disabled

Table 12-3: User Management Functions

Function Name	Purpose
VnsAddSStUser	Add a new user
VnsDeleteSStUser	Delete a user
VNsGetSStProfile	Retrieve a user's profile
VnsGetStProfileEntry	Retrieve a specific entry from a user's profile
VnsGetStProfileEntryEx	Retrieve a specific entry from a user's profile
VnsGetSStUserAttrib	Retrieve user attributes
VnsGetUserName	Get name of user logged in on current station

Table 12-3: User Management Functions (cont.)

Function Name	Purpose
VnsSetSStProfile	Change user's profile
VnsSetSStUserAttrib	Change user attributes

We will revisit VnsAddSStUser() and VnsDeleteSStUser() when we develop WNet-AddUser() and WNetDeleteUser().

The Group and Organization Management functions allow you to create and delete groups, and to find out what server is maintaining a particular group. Remember that VINES groups are not the kinds of groups we are interested in for our network services API; those are lists in the VINES universe.

Table 12-4: Group and Organization Management Functions

Function Name	Purpose
VnsAddSStGroup	Create a new group
VnsDeleteSStGroup	Delete a group
VnsFormatSStGroup	Format a group name in its full VINES representation
VnsFormatSStOrg	Format an organization name in its full VINES representation
VnsGetSStGroup	Get the name of the server that owns a group

The Name Management functions offer a variety of miscellaneous services relating to the names of network objects. Most important for us, it provides a function to enumerate them, VnsListSStNames(). This function acts like NetWare's ScanBinderyObject(); it enumerates objects of all types. Recall from Chapter 11 that LAN Manager has one enumeration function for each class of object.

VINES also allows the creation of nicknames for users. A nickname is stored in the StreetTalk database as its own unique object type. The functions VnsAddSStNickname() and VnsDeleteSStNickname() create and delete a nickname. VnsListSStNicknames() enumerates all the nicknames for a given user.

Table 12-5: Name Management Functions

Function Name	Purpose
VnsAddSStNickname	Add a nickname for a user
VnsBreakStName	Parse a StreetTalk name into item, group, and organization components
VnsConvLatin1ToAscii	Converts a string containing 8-bit ANSI characters to 7-bit ASCII (Latin1 is the ISO standard name for what Windows calls the ANSI character set.)
VnsConvLatin1ToPcm	Converts a string from ANSI to IBM-PC representation
VnsConvLatin1ToUpAscii	Converts a string from ANSI to 7-bit ASCII, and also makes all characters upper-case
VnsConvPcmToAscii	Converts a string from 8-bit IBM-PC format to 7-bit ASCII
VnsConvPcmToLatin1	Converts a string from 8-bit IBM-PC format to 8-bit ANSI
VnsDeleteSStNickname	Delete a nickname

Table 12-5: Name Management Functions (cont.)

Function Name	Purpose
VnsFormatSStName	Formats a name in its original form
VnsHashStName	Generates a hash value for a StreetTalk name
VnsListSStNames	Enumerates StreetTalk objects
VnsListSStNicknames	Enumerates a user's nicknames
VnsSetUserName	Set the name of the logged-in user
VnsValidateStName	Checks to see if a name is a valid StreetTalk name (not necessarily representing an existing StreetTalk object)
VnsVerifySRouteRev	Checks to see if a name contains international characters, and if the target StreetTalk service supports international characters

The List Management group provides functions for creating and deleting lists, for adding objects to and deleting them from lists, for enumerating a list's members, and for checking to see if a user belongs to a list. We will exploit all the functions in this category in our VINES network services DLL.

Remember that VINES lists, not VINES groups, are analogous to NetWare and LAN Manager groups. Their principal importance is in assigning access to files and directories. VINES also allows rights to be assigned to VINES groups. The actual rights that the user will be given depends on the VINES security scheme.

VINES lists have one characteristic that we have not seen: lists can be made members of lists. In determining a user's effective rights, VINES will search lists recursively until it either finds the user or exhausts the search without finding him. As you might gather, abuse or accidental misuse of nested lists can degrade network performance.

Table 12-6: List Management Functions

Function Name	Purpose
VnsAddSStList	Create a new list
VnsAddSStMember	Add a new member to a list
VnsDeleteSStList	Delete a list
VnsDeleteSStMember	Remove a list member
VnsGetSStListMembers	Enumerate list members
VnsTestSStMembership	Check for list membership

The Security Management functions control settings like:

- The maximum numbers of stations that a user can login from
- Whether a user is allowed to login from a DOS, OS/2, or Macintosh station (or any combination thereof)
- Whether the user can change her own profile
- Whether the user may, or must, change her password
- The minimum length of a user's password
- The frequency with which a user is required to change her password
- Days and times when the user may login

- Specific stations that the user is allowed to login from
- The user's password

Table 12-7: Security Management Functions

Function Name	Purpose
VnsDeleteSStSecurity	Delete security restrictions
VnsDisableSLogin	Prevent a user from logging in
VnsEnableSLogin	Allow a user to login
VnsGetSStSecurity	Retrieve user's or group's security restrictions
VnsGetNonce	Get login data structure (called a "nonce" in VINES parlance) for current station
VnsGetSStWhenLogin	Retrieve user's or group's time restrictions
VnsGetSStWhereLogin	Retrieve user's or group's location restrictions
VnsGetSStWhereLoginCnt	Retrieve current number of login location restrictions, and maximum number of restrictions
VnsSetNonce	Sets login data structure (nonce) for current session
VnsSetSStWhenLogin	Set time restrictions on login
VnsSetSStWhereLogin	Set location restrictions on login
VnsSetSPassword	Change user's password
VnsSetSStSecurity	Change user's or group's security restrictions
VnsVerifyNonce	Verify login data structure (nonce)
VnsVerifySPassword	Check user's password

The Session Management functions control StreetTalk sessions between the workstation and the StreetTalk service on a VINES server. Release 5.0 of the VINES Application Toolkit adds session-explicit versions of older session-implicit functions. The most important service offered by the Session Management functions is to allow applications to start and end StreetTalk sessions.

Table 12-8: Session Management Functions

Function Name	Purpose
VnsEndStSession	Close a session
VnsGetImplicitStSession	Get the global session data structure used by the session-implicit functions
VnsGetSIntl	Check if session has international characters enabled
VnsGetIntlLoc	See which directory in the VINES file system is being used as the root of drive Z: (this is country-dependent)
VnsGetSActive	See if a session structure refers to an active StreetTalk session
VnsInitStSession	Initialize session structure without starting a session
VnsSetSIntl	Enable or disable conversions of characters to international (ANSI) representation
VnsStartStSession	Initialize a session structure and open a session

The Service Management functions allow a program to retrieve information on VINES services (server-based applications).

Table 12-9: Service Management Functions

Function Name	Purpose
VnsGetSStSvc	Get a service's description and location
VnsGetSvrName	Get name of server where a service is running
VnsGetSvrRev	Get service information from port address
VnsGetSvrLRev	Get service information from port address

The WNet() Network Services DLL for VINES (WNETVNST.DLL)

The port of our Windows Network Services API to VINES offers few surprises. The VINES API is on a level of abstraction somewhere between NetWare (the lowest) and LAN Manager (the highest). For the most part, we will see a one-to-one mapping between our WNet() functions and the underlying VINES functions. In some places, we will need to compensate for VINES default behavior.

StreetTalk Sessions

We will use the session-explicit functions, as Banyan recommends. This means that all of our functions will begin by starting a StreetTalk session, and end by closing it. The functions that do this are VnsStartStSession() and VnsEndStSession():

```
CallStatus VNSENTRY VnsStartStSession(LPIPCPORT lpPort,
                         BOOL bIntl,
                         LPVOID lpReserved,
                         VNS_ST_SESS FAR *lpSession);
```

lpPort is usually passed as a NULL pointer. Doing so causes VINES to locate a StreetTalk service on any server and connect to it. You can use a non-NULL argument to designate a specific StreetTalk service if you wish.

bIntl specifies whether you want to enable (TRUE) or disable (FALSE) international character-set conversions. VINES supports three character sets: the 7-bit ASCII set, as used by UNIX; the so-called PC multinational set (the 8-bit ASCII character set used on the IBM PC); and the so-called Latin1 set (the ANSI character set used by Windows). Under Windows, you will normally pass it as TRUE.

StreetTalk names consist of three parts: the item, the group, and the organization. If *bIntl* is set to TRUE, the item portion can include 8-bit characters from the ANSI character set. Otherwise, it is limited to the 7-bit ASCII set. Both the group and organization are restricted to 7-bit ASCII characters, no matter how you set *bIntl*.

lpReserved is reserved for future use, and must be passed as NULL.

lpSession points to a VNS_ST_SESS structure, shown here:

```
typedef struct {
    IPCPORT       stPort;      /* StreetTalk's port             */
    SessionHandle sessionId;   /* Active session handle         */
    Boolean       bIntl;       /* Returns are native or 7-bit ASCII */
    Boolean       bActive;     /* Is there an active ST Session? */
    void FAR*     pReserved;   /* For future use.               */
} VNS_ST_SESS;
```

VINES sets the fields of this structure to the appropriate values. There is no need to access them directly, and doing so is not considered good practice. All the other session-explicit functions take a pointer to this structure as their first argument.

```
CallStatus VNSENTRY VnsEndStSession(VNS_ST_SESS FAR *lpSession);
```

VnsEndStSession() terminates a session begun with VnsStartStSession(). *lpSession* points to the same structure that was passed to VnsStartStSession().

Server Name Is Irrelevant

All our WNet() Network Services functions, except WNetEnumServers(), take the target server name as an argument. Because StreetTalk is a distributed database, the server name is irrelevant. When you start a StreetTalk session, you connect to a specific service on a specific server. All requests for action or information are directed to that service. However, if the information you want is not on that server, it knows where it does reside, and finds it. This process is completely transparent to you. Thus, it is also invisible to our network services DLL; we simply ignore the server name argument.

WNetEnumServers()

As I mentioned, VINES provides a single function for enumerating StreetTalk objects, VnsListSStNames():

```
CallStatus VNSENTRY VnsListSStNames(VNS_ST_SESS FAR *lpSession, LPCSTR lpszPattern,
                        WORD wType, ObjectClass uClass,
                        Catselect FAR *lpCatsel,
                        LPWORD lpwPassnum,
                        STRecord FAR *lpStRecord);
```

lpSession is a VNS_ST_SESS structure that has been passed to VnsStartStSession().

lpszPattern is a string indicating the objects you want to enumerate. It can contain an asterisk as a wildcard. For example, the string "*@users@MyOrg" selects all objects belonging to the group *users* and the organization *MyOrg*.

wType indicates the type of object, and can be either ORGTYPE (organization), GRP-TYPE (group), or OBJTYPE (individual item or object). *uClass* specifies further classifications of the type. If passed as UNSPECCLASS, all objects of type *wType* matching *lpszPattern* are enumerated. Other possible values for *uClass* are USER, SERVICE, LIST, NICKNAME, or GROUPENTRY.

lpCatsel points to a *Catselect* structure. It applies only when you are enumerating services—that is, *wType* is OBJTYPE and *uClass* is SERVICE. It allows you to name individual services for inclusion in or exclusion from the search. Here is the typedef for the structure from the VINES header file STSTRUCT.H:

```
typedef unsigned short   Cardinal;
#define MAXCAT           5
typedef struct
{
   Boolean ExcludeFlag;
   struct
     {
```

```
        Cardinal length;
        Cardinal sequence[MAXCAT];
        } cats;
} Catselect;
```

The *Catselect* structure is ignored unless *cats.length* is non-zero. In that case, VINES' response depends on the setting of the *ExcludeFlag* field. If it is TRUE, the service categories named in *cats.sequence* will be excluded from the enumeration. If it is FALSE, *only* the service categories named will be enumerated. *sequence* is an array of unsigned short integers; possible values are SSCAT (the VINES Server service), STCAT (the StreetTalk service), BFSCAT (the VINES file service), BPSCAT (the VINES print service), and BMSCAT (the VINES electronic mail service). Numbers between 1,000 and 1,999 can also be used to designate third-party services.

The variable pointed to by *lpwPassnum* controls the iteration. It should be initialized to zero; VINES will update it on each subsequent call to VnsListSStNames().

All StreetTalk information on the object is returned through the last argument, *lpStRecord*. The *VINES StreetTalk and STDA Programming Interface* manual incorrectly calls this an *STRec* type. Because there is a wide variety of record types, *STRecord* is defined as a union.

```
typedef Cardinal RecordClass;
typedef struct
{
    RecordClass designator;
    union
        {
#define USER_case               u0.u_USER
#define SERVICE_case            u0.u_SERVICE
#define LIST_case               u0.u_LIST
#define ALIASENTRY_case         u0.u_ALIASENTRY
#define ENUM_case               u0.u_ENUM
#define LSTMEMB_case            u0.u_LSTMEMB
#define ASSOCREC_case           u0.u_ASSOCREC
#define DOMREC_case             u0.u_DOMREC
        User u_USER;
        Service u_SERVICE;
        List u_LIST;
        Alias u_ALIASENTRY;
        Enum u_ENUM;
        LstMemb u_LSTMEMB;
        AssocRec u_ASSOCREC;
        DomRec u_DOMREC;
        } u0;
} STRecord;
```

The members of the union (*u0*) are structures defining the record layouts for the various types of objects. The only kind we will use are the *Enum* and the *LstMemb* records. Here are their typedefs extracted from STSTRUCT.H:

```
#define ENUMSET         15
typedef struct
```

```
{
   Cardinal length;
   STNAME sequence[ENUMSET];
} Enum;
#define MAXLSTSET        10
typedef struct
{
   Cardinal length;
   STNAME sequence[MAXLSTSET];
} LstMemb;
```

In both cases, *sequence* returns an array of null-terminated StreetTalk names; *length* returns the number of elements in the array.

Server names are tracked as groups belonging to the organization *Servers*. To enumerate servers, we pass an object string of "*@Servers", and an object type (the *wType* argument) of GRPTYPE.

Be careful to distinguish between servers and services in VINES terminology. When we dealt with NetWare and LAN Manager, it was appropriate to speak of file servers and print servers, for example. In VINES, it is not. These are implemented as services, which are just server-based applications. I have chosen to have this function enumerate servers, rather than specific services.

```
/********
*
* Listing 12-1. WNETESRV.C
*
* Copyright (c) 1992 Ralph P. Davis, All Rights Reserved
*
********/

/*===== Includes =====*/

#include "wnetvnst.h"

/*===== Function Definitions =====*/

BOOL WINAPI WNetEnumServers(SERVERENUMPROC lpServerEnumProc,
                            WORD wServerType)
{
   // wServerType will be ignored

   Catselect   Categories;
   WORD        wPassnum = 0;
   VNS_ST_SESS VnsStSession;
   STRecord    ServerList;   // Incorrectly listed in the manual
                             // as an STRec
   Cardinal    i;
   LPSTR       lpTemp;

   Categories.cats.length = 0;

   if (VnsStartStSession(NULL, TRUE, NULL, &VnsStSession) != BYCALLOK)
      {
```

```
      WNetSetLastError(WN_NET_ERROR);
      return FALSE;
      }

   while (TRUE)
      {
      if (VnsListSStNames(&VnsStSession,
          "*@Servers", GRPTYPE, UNSPECCLASS, &Categories,
          &wPassnum,
          &ServerList) != BYCALLOK)
        break;
      for (i = 0; i < ServerList.ENUM_case.length; ++i)
         {
         // ServerList.ENUM_case.sequence is an array of
         // null-terminated strings
         // ServerList.ENUM_case.length tells us how many elements
         // ServerList.ENUM_case.sequence contains

         // Look for '@'
         lpTemp = ServerList.ENUM_case.sequence[i];
         while (*lpTemp != '@' && *lpTemp != '\0')
            ++lpTemp;
         if (*lpTemp == '@')
            *lpTemp = '\0';
         if (!lpServerEnumProc(ServerList.ENUM_case.sequence[i],
            WNET_FILE_SERVER))
            goto EndEnumServers;
         }
      }
EndEnumServers:
   VnsEndStSession(&VnsStSession);
   return TRUE;
}
```

WNetAddUser()

WNetAddUser() takes the user name as an argument. VINES names differ from NetWare and LAN Manager names in that they have three parts. Fortunately, we do not have to introduce any network-dependent behavior by requiring that names be passed in this form. If no group or organization is included in the name, VINES assigns the user to the group and organization of the user who creates him. For example, if I am user admin@users@MyOrg, and I add the user ralphd, VINES will give him the full name ralphd@users@MyOrg.

We can also retrieve the name of the current user by calling VnsGetUserName().

```
CallStatus VNSENTRY VnsGetUserName(LPSTR lpszUserName);
```

This enables us to expand a network-independent name into a full StreetTalk name, using the same algorithm that VINES itself uses. I have chosen to do this, because we need to know the user's group and organization. The function MakeFullStreetTalk-Name(), listed in WNETAUSR.C, is called from several other functions in this chapter, specifically WNetGrantRights() and WNetRevokeRights().

The function that creates a new user is VnsAddSStUser():

```
CallStatus VNSENTRY VnsAddSStUser(VNS_ST_SESS FAR *lpSession, LPCSTR lpszName,
                        LPCSTR lpszPassword, LPCSTR lpszDescription,
                        LPCSTR lpszProfile);
```

lpSession is the session identifier. *lpszName* is the user name; *lpszPassword* is his password. *lpszDescription* is an application-defined description of the user, and may be passed as a zero-length string. *lpszProfile* is the user's profile (known in other environments as a login script).

When you add a user with the VINES administration utility MUSER, it gives her the default profile

```
bprint /b:"<user name>"
use Sample Profile@<group name>@<organization name>
```

The first command says to use the user's name as the banner for all her print jobs. The second says to invoke the sample profile for the user's group. The sample profiles are provided with the VINES software, and can be accessed as StreetTalk objects with the name "Sample Profile". The embedded space is a valid character in a StreetTalk name. In the VINES implementation of WNetAddUser(), I mimic this behavior.

The *bAdmin* argument to WNetAddUser() specifies whether the user should have administrative privileges. There are two levels of administration in VINES, server-wide and group-by-group. Only VINES behaves this way, so to preserve network independence, I take the conservative approach and only give the newly created user administrative rights at the group level. I do this by adding him to the list AdminList. The full name is Admin-List@<group name>@<organization name>. The function that does this is VnsAddSSt-Member():

```
CallStatus VNSENTRY VnsAddSStMember(VNS_ST_SESS FAR *lpSession,
                        LPCSTR lpszMemberName,
                        LPCSTR lpszListName);
```

This function adds *lpszMemberName* to the list *lpszListName*. *lpszMemberName* can be either a user name or the name of another list.

```
/********
*
* Listing 12-2. WNETAUSR.C
*
* Copyright (c) 1992 Ralph P. Davis, All Rights Reserved
*
********/

/*===== Includes =====*/

#define INCL_WS
#include "wnetvnst.h"

/*===== Function Definitions =====*/
```

```
BOOL WINAPI WNetAddUser(LPSTR lpszServerName, LPSTR lpszUserName,
                        LPSTR lpszPassword, BOOL bAdmin)
{
    VNS_ST_SESS VnsStSession;
    static char szProfile[1024];
    char        szUserName[100];
    LPSTR       lpszUserTemp, lpszGroupName, lpszOrgName;
    CallStatus  nErr;
    BOOL        bRetval;
    char        szAdminListName[100];

    WNetSetLastError(WN_SUCCESS);

    if (lpszPassword == NULL)
        lpszPassword = "";

    if (VnsStartStSession(NULL, TRUE, NULL, &VnsStSession) != BYCALLOK)
        {
        WNetSetLastError(WN_NET_ERROR);
        return FALSE;
        }

    // User name is not required to be in full VINES format
    // (<user name>@<group name>@<organization name>

    // It can be entered as just the user name,
    // user name + group name, or the whole thing.

    // If only the user name is included, VINES assigns the user
    // to the group to which the currently logged-on user belongs.
    // That user must have administrative rights to that group.

    // We parse the user name, and if we find a group and
    // organization, we use the sample profile for that
    // group.

    // Passing just the user name is the only format that makes no
    // assumptions about the underlying network operating system.

    // MakeFullStreetTalkName() converts it to a full name based
    // on the user running this program, which is also what VINES
    // itself will do
    MakeFullStreetTalkName(lpszUserName, szUserName);

    // Isolate group and organization portions of name
    lpszUserTemp = szUserName;
    lpszGroupName = lpszUserTemp;
    while (*lpszGroupName != '@' && *lpszGroupName != '\0')
        ++lpszGroupName;
    if (*lpszGroupName != '\0')
        *lpszGroupName++ = '\0';
    else
        lpszGroupName = NULL; // This shouldn't happen, but let's be safe

    lpszOrgName = lpszGroupName;
```

```
    while (lpszOrgName != NULL && *lpszOrgName != '@' && *lpszOrgName != '\0')
        ++lpszOrgName;

    if (lpszOrgName != NULL && *lpszOrgName != '\0')
        *lpszOrgName++ = '\0';
    else
        lpszOrgName = NULL;   // This also shouldn't happen

    wsprintf(szProfile, "\tbprint /b:\"%s\"", lpszUserTemp);

    if (lpszGroupName != NULL && lpszOrgName != NULL)
        {
        wsprintf(&szProfile[lstrlen(szProfile)],
            "\n\tUSE Sample Profile@%s@%s",
            lpszGroupName, lpszOrgName);
        }

    if ((nErr = VnsAddSStUser(&VnsStSession, lpszUserName, lpszPassword,
            "", szProfile)) != BYCALLOK)
        {
        WNetSetLastError(MapVnsToWinErr(nErr));
        bRetval = FALSE;
        }
    else
        {
        if (bAdmin)
            {
            lstrcpy(szAdminListName, "AdminList");
            if (lpszGroupName != NULL)
                {
                lstrcat(szAdminListName, "@");
                lstrcat(szAdminListName, lpszGroupName);
                if (lpszOrgName != NULL)
                    {
                    lstrcat(szAdminListName, "@");
                    lstrcat(szAdminListName, lpszOrgName);
                    }
                }
            VnsAddSStMember(&VnsStSession, lpszUserName, szAdminListName);
            }
        bRetval = TRUE;
        }
    VnsEndStSession(&VnsStSession);
    return bRetval;
}

void MakeFullStreetTalkName(LPSTR lpszPartial, LPSTR lpszFull)
{
    char   szMyUserName[75];
    int    i;

    // Get name of user running this program
    VnsGetUserName(szMyUserName);
    lstrcpy(lpszFull, lpszPartial);
```

```
    for (i = 0; i < lstrlen(lpszFull); ++i)
        if (lpszFull[i] == '@')
            return;  // Name is already in full format

    // Now look for first '@' in current user's name
    for (i = 0; i < lstrlen(szMyUserName); ++i)
        if (szMyUserName[i] == '@')
            break;
    lstrcat(lpszFull, &szMyUserName[i]);
}
```

WNetDeleteUser()

We implement WNetDeleteUser() using VnsDeleteSStUser():

```
CallStatus VNSENTRY VnsDeleteSStUser(VNS_ST_SESS FAR *lpSession,
                                     LPCSTR lpszUserName);
```

WNetDeleteUser() has an additional complication. When you delete a user, VINES does *not* do two things: it does not remove the user from any lists to which he belongs, and it does not remove the user from the rights lists of any files or directories.

We can do the first easily; we call WNetEnumMemberGroups(), and have the callback function delete him from all enumerated groups. Notice that we have to do this before we call VnsDeleteSStUser(). If we do not, WNetEnumMemberGroups() does not report the user as belonging to any lists. This is a gotcha that should be fixed.

There is no way for us to determine what files and directories the user has rights to.

```
/********
 *
 * Listing 12-3. WNETDUSR.C
 *
 * Copyright (c) 1992 Ralph P. Davis, All Rights Reserved
 *
 ********/

/*===== Includes =====*/

#include "wnetvnst.h"

/*===== FORWARD Functions =====*/

BOOL CALLBACK EnumMyGroups(LPSTR lpszServerName, LPSTR lpszUserName,
                           LPSTR lpszGroupName);

/*===== Function Definitions =====*/

BOOL WINAPI WNetDeleteUser(LPSTR lpszServerName, LPSTR lpszUserName)
{
    CallStatus  nErr;
    VNS_ST_SESS VnsStSession;
    BOOL        bRetval;
    MEMBERGROUPENUMPROC lpProc;

    WNetSetLastError(WN_SUCCESS);
```

```
   if (VnsStartStSession(NULL, TRUE, NULL, &VnsStSession) != BYCALLOK)
      {
      WNetSetLastError(WN_NET_ERROR);
      return FALSE;
      }

   (FARPROC) lpProc = MakeProcInstance((FARPROC) EnumMyGroups,
      hDLLInstance);

   // Enumerate the groups (i.e., StreetTalk lists)
   // the user belongs to, and remove him as a member

   WNetEnumMemberGroups(NULL, lpszUserName, lpProc);
   FreeProcInstance((FARPROC) lpProc);

   if ((nErr = VnsDeleteSStUser(&VnsStSession, lpszUserName)) != BYCALLOK)
      {
      WNetSetLastError(MapVnsToWinErr(nErr));
      bRetval = FALSE;
      }
   else
      bRetval = TRUE;
   VnsEndStSession(&VnsStSession);
   return bRetval;
}

BOOL CALLBACK EnumMyGroups(LPSTR lpszServerName, LPSTR lpszUserName,
                           LPSTR lpszGroupName)
{
   // We'll use the session-implicit function; no point in starting
   // a session for each enumeration

   // We could also just call WNetDeleteGroupMember()
   VnsDeleteStMember(lpszUserName, lpszGroupName);
   return TRUE;
}
```

WNetEnumUsers()

We enumerate users in the same way that we enumerated servers: by calling VnsListSSt-Names(). This time, we pass it the object name "*@*@*," meaning all objects, a *wType* of OBJTYPE, and a *uClass* of USER. This limits the enumeration to users.

```
/********
 *
 * Listing 12-4. WNETEUSR.C
 *
 * Copyright (c) 1992 Ralph P. Davis, All Rights Reserved
 *
 ********/

/*===== Includes =====*/

#include "wnetvnst.h"
```

```
/*===== Function Definitions =====*/

BOOL WINAPI WNetEnumUsers(LPSTR lpszServerName,
                          USERENUMPROC lpUserEnumProc)
{
    VNS_ST_SESS VnsStSession;
    Catselect   Categories;
    WORD        wPassnum = 0;
    STRecord    UserList;   // Incorrectly listed in the manual
                            // as an STRec
    Cardinal    i;

    Categories.cats.length = 0;  // Enumerate all users

    if (VnsStartStSession(NULL, TRUE, NULL, &VnsStSession) != BYCALLOK)
        {
        WNetSetLastError(WN_NET_ERROR);
        return FALSE;
        }

    while (TRUE)
        {
        if (VnsListSStNames(&VnsStSession,
            "*@*@*", OBJTYPE, USER, &Categories, &wPassnum,
            &UserList) != BYCALLOK)
          break;
        for (i = 0; i < UserList.ENUM_case.length; ++i)
            {
            if (!lpUserEnumProc("", UserList.ENUM_case.sequence[i]))
                goto EndEnumUsers;
            }
        }
EndEnumUsers:
    VnsEndStSession(&VnsStSession);
    return TRUE;
}
```

Group Functions

WNetAddGroup() and WNetDeleteGroup() port easily to their VINES equivalents, VnsAddSStList() and VnsDeleteSStList(). WNetEnumGroups() calls VnsListSStNames() with the object name "*@*@" and a *wType* of OBJTYPE (just as we did to enumerate users), but specifies a *uClass* of LIST.

```
/********
*
* Listing 12-5. WNETAGRP.C
*
* Copyright (c) 1992 Ralph P. Davis, All Rights Reserved
*
********/

/*===== Includes =====*/
```

```c
#include "wnetvnst.h"

/*===== Function Definitions =====*/

BOOL WINAPI WNetAddGroup(LPSTR lpszServerName, LPSTR lpszGroupName)
{
    CallStatus  nErr;
    VNS_ST_SESS VnsStSession;
    BOOL        bRetval;

    WNetSetLastError(WN_SUCCESS);

    if (VnsStartStSession(NULL, TRUE, NULL, &VnsStSession) != BYCALLOK)
        {
        WNetSetLastError(WN_NET_ERROR);
        return FALSE;
        }

    if ((nErr = VnsAddSStList(&VnsStSession, lpszGroupName, "")) != BYCALLOK)
        {
        WNetSetLastError(MapVnsToWinErr(nErr));
        bRetval = FALSE;
        }
    else
        bRetval = TRUE;

    VnsEndStSession(&VnsStSession);
    return bRetval;
}

/********
*
* Listing 12-6. WNETDGRP.C
*
* Copyright (c) 1992 Ralph P. Davis, All Rights Reserved
*
********/

/*===== Includes =====*/

#include "wnetvnst.h"

/*===== Function Definitions =====*/

BOOL WINAPI WNetDeleteGroup(LPSTR lpszServerName, LPSTR lpszGroupName)
{
    CallStatus  nErr;
    VNS_ST_SESS VnsStSession;
    BOOL        bRetval;

    WNetSetLastError(WN_SUCCESS);

    if (VnsStartStSession(NULL, TRUE, NULL, &VnsStSession) != BYCALLOK)
        {
        WNetSetLastError(WN_NET_ERROR);
        return FALSE;
```

```
        }

    if ((nErr = VnsDeleteSStList(&VnsStSession, lpszGroupName)) != BYCALLOK)
        {
        WNetSetLastError(MapVnsToWinErr(nErr));
        bRetval = FALSE;
        }
    else
        bRetval = TRUE;

    VnsEndStSession(&VnsStSession);
    return bRetval;
}

/********
 *
 * Listing 12-7. WNETEGRP.C
 *
 * Copyright (c) 1992 Ralph P. Davis, All Rights Reserved
 *
 ********/

/*===== Includes =====*/

#include "wnetvnst.h"

/*===== Function Definitions =====*/
BOOL WINAPI WNetEnumGroups(LPSTR lpszServerName,
                           GROUPENUMPROC lpGroupEnumProc)
{
    VNS_ST_SESS VnsStSession;
    Catselect   Categories;
    WORD        wPassnum = 0;
    STRecord    GroupList;  // Incorrectly listed in the manual
                            // as an STRec
    Cardinal    i;

    Categories.cats.length = 0;  // Enumerate all groups

    if (VnsStartStSession(NULL, TRUE, NULL, &VnsStSession) != BYCALLOK)
        {
        WNetSetLastError(WN_NET_ERROR);
        return FALSE;
        }

    while (TRUE)
        {
        if (VnsListSStNames(&VnsStSession,
            "*@*@*", OBJTYPE, LIST, &Categories, &wPassnum,
            &GroupList) != BYCALLOK)
          break;
        for (i = 0; i < GroupList.ENUM_case.length; ++i)
            {
            if (!lpGroupEnumProc("", GroupList.ENUM_case.sequence[i]))
              goto EndEnumGroups;
```

```
            }
        }
EndEnumGroups:
    VnsEndStSession(&VnsStSession);
    return TRUE;
}
```

Group Membership Functions

WNetAddGroupMember() and WNetDeleteGroupMember() are implemented using
VnsAddSStMember() and VnsDeleteSStMember(), which we have already seen. WNetIs-
UserGroupMember() uses the function VnsTestSStMembership().

```
CallStatus VNSENTRY VnsTestSStMembership(VNS_ST_SESS FAR *lpSession,
                                         LPCSTR lpszUserName,
                                         LPCSTR lpszListName,
                                         BOOL   bClosure,
                                         BOOL FAR *lpIsMember);
```

The arguments *lpSession*, *lpszUserName*, and *lpszListName* should be obvious. *bClosure* tells VINES whether to search lists recursively for the requested user. If *bClosure* is
passed as TRUE and VINES does not find *lpszUserName* in the list itself, it will search any
lists that belong to the list, and any lists belonging to them. The result of the search is
returned through *lpIsMember*; TRUE means the user is a member.

```
/********
*
* Listing 12-8. WNETAMBR.C
*
* Copyright (c) 1992 Ralph P. Davis, All Rights Reserved
*
********/

/*===== Includes =====*/

#include "wnetvnst.h"

/*===== Function Definitions =====*/

BOOL WINAPI WNetAddGroupMember(LPSTR lpszServerName,
                               LPSTR lpszGroupName,
                               LPSTR lpszUserName)
{
    CallStatus  nErr;
    VNS_ST_SESS VnsStSession;
    BOOL        bRetval;

    if (VnsStartStSession(NULL, TRUE, NULL, &VnsStSession) != BYCALLOK)
        {
        WNetSetLastError(WN_NET_ERROR);
        return FALSE;
        }

    if ((nErr = VnsAddSStMember(&VnsStSession,
```

```
                      lpszUserName, lpszGroupName)) != BYCALLOK)
         {
         WNetSetLastError(MapVnsToWinErr(nErr));
         bRetval = FALSE;
         }
      else
         bRetval = TRUE;

      VnsEndStSession(&VnsStSession);
      return bRetval;
}

/********
*
* Listing 12-9. WNETDMBR.C
*
* Copyright (c) 1992 Ralph P. Davis, All Rights Reserved
*
********/

/*===== Includes =====*/

#include "wnetvnst.h"

/*===== Function Definitions =====*/

BOOL WINAPI WNetDeleteGroupMember(LPSTR lpszServerName,
                                  LPSTR lpszGroupName,
                                  LPSTR lpszUserName)
{
   CallStatus  nErr;
   VNS_ST_SESS VnsStSession;
   BOOL        bRetval;

   if (VnsStartStSession(NULL, TRUE, NULL, &VnsStSession) != BYCALLOK)
      {
      WNetSetLastError(WN_NET_ERROR);
      return FALSE;
      }

   if ((nErr = VnsDeleteSStMember(&VnsStSession,
                 lpszUserName, lpszGroupName)) != BYCALLOK)
      {
      WNetSetLastError(MapVnsToWinErr(nErr));
      bRetval = FALSE;
      }
   else
      bRetval = TRUE;
   VnsEndStSession(&VnsStSession);
   return bRetval;
}

/********
*
* Listing 12-10. WNETIMBR.C
```

```
*
* Copyright (c) 1992 Ralph P. Davis, All Rights Reserved
*
********/

/*===== Includes =====*/

#include "wnetvnst.h"

/*===== Function Definitions =====*/
BOOL WINAPI WNetIsUserGroupMember(LPSTR lpszServerName,
                                  LPSTR lpszGroupName,
                                  LPSTR lpszUserName)
{
    CallStatus  nErr;
    BOOL        bIsMember;
    VNS_ST_SESS VnsStSession;

    WNetSetLastError(WN_SUCCESS);

    if (VnsStartStSession(NULL, TRUE, NULL, &VnsStSession) != BYCALLOK)
        {
        WNetSetLastError(WN_NET_ERROR);
        return FALSE;
        }

    if ((nErr = VnsTestSStMembership(&VnsStSession,
                 lpszUserName, lpszGroupName,
                 TRUE, &bIsMember)) != BYCALLOK)
        {
        WNetSetLastError(MapVnsToWinErr(nErr));
        bIsMember = FALSE;
        }
    VnsEndStSession(&VnsStSession);
    return bIsMember;
}
```

WNetEnumGroupMembers() uses the VINES function VnsGetSStListMembers().

```
CallStatus VNSENTRY VnsGetSStListMembers(VNS_ST_SESS FAR *lpSession,
                              LPCSTR lpszListName,
                              LPWORD lpPassnum,
                              STRecord FAR *lpStRecord);
```

lpszListName is the list whose members you want to enumerate. The variable pointed to by *lpPassnum* should be set initially to zero; each call to the function will update it automatically. The list of members is returned in the *STRecord* structure pointed to by *lpStRecord*. Recall from the previous discussion of VnsListSStNames() that this structure is a union of structures, and that each component of the union describes the information returned for a particular type of StreetTalk object. In this case, the part we are interested in is the *LstMemb* structure, which I show again here for your convenience.

```
#define MAXLSTSET        10
typedef struct
{
    Cardinal length;
    STNAME sequence[MAXLSTSET];
} LstMemb;
```

The list members are returned in the *sequence* field as an array of null-terminated StreetTalk names.

```
/********
*
* Listing 12-11. WNETEMBR.C
*
* Copyright (c) 1992 Ralph P. Davis, All Rights Reserved
*
********/

/*===== Includes =====*/

#include "wnetvnst.h"

/*===== Function Definitions =====*/

BOOL WINAPI WNetEnumGroupMembers(LPSTR lpszServerName,
                                 LPSTR lpszGroupName,
                                 GROUPMEMBERENUMPROC lpMemberEnumProc)
{
    VNS_ST_SESS VnsStSession;
    WORD        wPassnum = 0;
    STRecord    MemberList;

    Cardinal    i;

    if (VnsStartStSession(NULL, TRUE, NULL, &VnsStSession) != BYCALLOK)
        {
        WNetSetLastError(WN_NET_ERROR);
        return FALSE;
        }

    while (TRUE)
        {
        if (VnsGetSStListMembers(&VnsStSession, lpszGroupName, &wPassnum,
            &MemberList) != BYCALLOK || wPassnum == 0)
          break;
        for (i = 0; i < MemberList.LSTMEMB_case.length; ++i)
            {
            // LSTMEMB_case.sequence contains the names of the list members
            if (!lpMemberEnumProc("",
                lpszGroupName, MemberList.LSTMEMB_case.sequence[i]))
                goto EndEnumMembers;
            }
        }
EndEnumMembers:
```

```
    VnsEndStSession(&VnsStSession);
    return TRUE;
}
```

We cannot implement WNetEnumMemberGroups( ) directly. We have to enumerate all StreetTalk lists and check the user's membership in each with VnsTestSStMembership( ).

```
/********
 *
 * Listing 12-12. WNETEMGR.C
 *
 * Copyright (c) 1992 Ralph P. Davis, All Rights Reserved
 *
 ********/

/*===== Includes =====*/
#include "wnetvnst.h"

/*===== Function Definitions =====*/

BOOL WINAPI WNetEnumMemberGroups(LPSTR lpszServerName,
                                 LPSTR lpszUserName,
                                 MEMBERGROUPENUMPROC lpGroupEnumProc)
{
    VNS_ST_SESS VnsStSession;
    Catselect   Categories;
    WORD        wPassnum = 0;
    STRecord    GroupList;
    Cardinal    i;
    BOOL        bIsMember;

    Categories.cats.length = 0;  // Enumerate all groups

    if (VnsStartStSession(NULL, TRUE, NULL, &VnsStSession) != BYCALLOK)
        {
        WNetSetLastError(WN_NET_ERROR);
        return FALSE;
        }

    while (TRUE)
        {
        if (VnsListSStNames(&VnsStSession,
            "*@*@*", OBJTYPE, LIST, &Categories, &wPassnum,
            &GroupList) != BYCALLOK)
          break;
        for (i = 0; i < GroupList.ENUM_case.length; ++i)
            {
            if ((VnsTestStMembership(lpszUserName,
                GroupList.ENUM_case.sequence[i],
                TRUE, &bIsMember) == BYCALLOK) && bIsMember)
                {
                if (!lpGroupEnumProc("", lpszUserName,
                        GroupList.ENUM_case.sequence[i]))
                  goto EndEnumMembers;
```

```
            }
        }
    }
EndEnumMembers:
    VnsEndStSession(&VnsStSession);
    return TRUE;
}
```

Access Functions

There are four access functions in the VINES API, documented as part of the Client API:

- VnsDuplicateAccessRightsList()
- VnsGetAccessRightsList()
- VnsGetUserAccessRights()
- VnsSetAccessRightsList()

None of them are available to Windows programs in the current release of VINES [5.00 (5)], but they will be supported in a future release. We can implement WNet-GetRights(), WNetGrantRights(), and WNetRevokeRights() using these functions; there are dummy functions in VNSAPI.DLL that return error codes. I have not been able to test the code I present in an environment where these functions are fully operative. These functions are supported by underlying DOS interrupt calls, so you can implement them using DPMI if you so desire.

The VINES Access Scheme

The VINES scheme for determining users' rights to files and directories is the most complicated of all those we have seen. Part of the reason for the complexity is that the VINES scheme is a hybrid between the UNIX way of doing things and the way in which access is determined in NetWare and LAN Manager. It is natural that VINES would resemble UNIX, since it is a specialized version of UNIX.

The UNIX aspect of the VINES scheme is the notion that files and directories have a base set of rights. These rights are those accorded the file's owner, the file's group, and the rest of the world. (We are using the term *group* now in the VINES sense—it is not a VINES *list*.) Absent any other rights, VINES decides a user's right to access a file as follows:

1. If the user is the file's owner, he gets all rights granted the owner.
2. If the user is not the file's owner, but belongs to the file's group, he receives the rights granted the group.
3. Otherwise, he is given the rest-of-the-world rights.

VINES departs from UNIX in adding an extended access list. This is an array of up to five additional grantees who are explicitly assigned rights to the file. They can be individual users, groups, lists, or organizations. Thus, even though the array can only contain five elements, these elements can encompass tens, hundreds, even thousands of individual users. The rights that can be assigned by way of the extended access list are limited by the maximum extended rights for the file.

Dual Sets of Rights

When a user is granted rights to directories, he actually receives two sets of rights. One is his rights to the directory. The other is the set of rights he will have to any files he creates in that directory. These are referred to as his initial rights. Thus, the base rights in a directory consist of the owner's, the group's, and the world's actual and initial rights. Files have only one set of rights.

When a user creates subdirectories in a directory, the rights of the parent directory propagate downward according to the propagation rule in effect for the parent. Possibilities are:

- No rights propagate (ARL_PROPAGATE_NONE)
- Rights propagate according to VINES rules (ARL_PROPAGATE_VINES)
- Rights propagate according to Macintosh rules (ARL_PROPAGATE_AFP)
- Rights propagate according to UNIX rules (ARL_PROPAGATE_UNIX)

Under Windows, we need only concern ourselves with VINES propagation, whereby the rights list of the parent directory is copied wholesale to new subdirectories.

Views and Rights

As the propagation principles I just mentioned would suggest, there are three ways of looking at a user's rights to a file or directory, called *views*. One is the VINES view (ARL_VINES_VIEW), one is the Macintosh Apple FileTalk Protocol view (ARL_AFP_VIEW), and one is the UNIX view (ARL_UNIX_VIEW). The Macintosh and UNIX views present rights compatibly with those operating systems. The VINES view presents them in a more abstract way that closely resembles NetWare and LAN Manager. For Windows, again, only the VINES view is relevant.

The set of rights available for files and directories is:

- ARL_VINES_READ: user may read the file or directory.
- ARL_VINES_WRITE: for a directory, allows the user to create, rename, or change the attributes of files in the directory. For a file, allows the user to write to the file.
- ARL_VINES_SEARCH: user may list files contained in the directory.
- ARL_VINES_DELETE: user may erase the file or delete the directory.
- ARL_VINES_EXECUTE: user may execute the file (either an executable program or a batch file).
- ARL_VINES_CONTROL: user can grant rights to other users.

Determining a User's Access Rights at Runtime

VINES uses the following priority scheme to determine what a user's full set of rights are at runtime:

1. If the user is the file's owner, he gets the rights assigned to the owner.
2. If there is a specific entry in the extended access list for the user, he gets those rights.

3. If the user belongs to the file's group, he gets those rights.

4. If the user belongs to a group or a list that has rights through the extended access list, he is given those rights.

5. If the user belongs to an organization included in the extended access list, he acquires the rights granted that organization.

6. If all the previous conditions fail, the user is given the rights that were granted to the rest of the world.

Note that these cases are mutually exclusive; the logic is if-else if-else if-else. Also, rights are not cumulative. Thus, if a user belongs to two lists that are in the extended access list, she will only acquire the rights granted to the first one.

Data Types

This scheme is represented with several C data types, which are also used with the four Access functions I mentioned above. The most basic type is the *AccessRights* type, an unsigned long integer that incorporates the user's rights as a bitmask.

The *BaseAccess* structure is built on top of the *AccessRights* bitmask. Here is its definition from VNSARL.H:

```
typedef struct
{
    STNAME ownerName;
    STNAME groupName;
    AccessRights ownerRights;
    AccessRights ownerInitialRights;
    AccessRights groupRights;
    AccessRights groupInitialRights;
    AccessRights worldRights;
    AccessRights worldInitialRights;
    unsigned short uReserved;
    unsigned short uPropagation;
    AccessRights maxExtendedRights;
    AccessRights maxExtendedInitialRights;
} BaseAccess;
```

The extended access list is an array of five *ExtendedAccess* structures, which are formatted as shown:

```
typedef struct
{
    AccessRights accessRights;
    AccessRights initialRights;
    unsigned short uObjectType;
    STNAME objectName;
} ExtendedAccess;
```

The *uObjectType* field indicates what type of StreetTalk object *objectName* is. Possible settings are ARL_USER (a user), ARL_GROUP (a group), ARL_ORG (an organization), and ARL_LIST (a list). *objectName* can include the '*' as a wildcard; it is not restricted to indicating only single objects.

Finally, all these structures are encapsulated in an *AccessRightsList* structure. This represents the entire permission set for the file or directory.

```
#define NUM_EXTENDED_ACCESS    5
typedef struct
{
   short sCurrentView;
   short sSavedView;
   BaseAccess acl;
   unsigned short uExtended;
   ExtendedAccess extArl[NUM_EXTENDED_ACCESS];
   unsigned short uErrorIndex;
} AccessRightsList;
```

sCurrentView tells us whether the rights should be interpreted according to Macintosh, UNIX, or VINES rules. *sSavedView* indicates how the rights were last saved. These are usually the same, and for our purposes will always be ARL_VINES_VIEW. However, they are not required to be the same. *acl* has the rights for the owner, the group, and the world, and the maximum rights that can be granted through the extended access list. *uExtended* tells how many entries are in the extended access list, represented by *extArl*. Finally, *uErrorIndex* points to any element in the extended access list that is in error. It is one-based, so a value of zero indicates that there is no error.

WNetGetRights()

We can now look at the WNet() access functions, and see how they map to the appropriate VINES functions. WNetGetRights() is the easiest function to implement. It uses VnsGetUserAccessRights():

```
CallStatus VNSENTRY VnsGetUserAccessRights(LPSTR lpszUserName,
                                           LPSTR lpszPathName,
                                           WORD  wView,
                                           AccessRights FAR *lpRights);
```

This function returns the rights *lpszUserName* has to *lpszPathName* in the variable pointed to by *lpRights*. The rights are expressed in the view indicated by *wView*— ARL_VINES_VIEW, ARL_AFP_VIEW, or ARL_UNIX_VIEW.

Here is WNETGRTS.C, which contains WNetGetRights(). The routine MapVnsRightsToWNet() translates the VINES-specific rights to our network-independent representation.

```
/********
*
* Listing 12-13. WNETGRTS.C
*
* Copyright (c) 1992 Ralph P. Davis, All Rights Reserved
*
********/
```

```
/*===== Includes =====*/

#define INCL_ARL
#include "wnetvnst.h"

/*===== Function Definitions =====*/

BOOL WINAPI WNetGetRights(LPSTR   lpszServerName,
                          LPSTR   lpszUserOrGroup,
                          LPSTR   lpszResource,
                          LPWORD  lpwRights)
{
   CallStatus   nErr;
   AccessRights MyRights;

   if ((nErr =
       VnsGetUserAccessRights(lpszUserOrGroup, lpszResource, ARL_VINES_VIEW,
          &MyRights)) == BYCALLOK)
      {
      MapVnsRightsToWNet(&MyRights, lpwRights);
      return TRUE;
      }
   else
      {
      MapVnsToWinErr(nErr);
      return FALSE;
      }
}


void WINAPI MapVnsRightsToWNet(AccessRights FAR *lpwVnsRights,
                               LPWORD lpwWNetRights)
{
   WORD wRights = 0;

   if (*lpwVnsRights & ARL_VINES_READ)
      wRights |= WNET_READ_ACCESS;
   if (*lpwVnsRights & ARL_VINES_WRITE)
      wRights |= WNET_WRITE_ACCESS;
   if (*lpwVnsRights & ARL_VINES_SEARCH)
      wRights |= WNET_VIEW_ACCESS;
   if (*lpwVnsRights & ARL_VINES_DELETE)
      wRights |= WNET_DELETE_ACCESS;
   if (*lpwVnsRights & ARL_VINES_EXECUTE)
      wRights |= WNET_EXECUTE_ACCESS;
   if (*lpwVnsRights & ARL_VINES_CONTROL)
      wRights |= WNET_PERM_ACCESS;

   *lpwWNetRights = wRights;
}
```

WNetGrantRights()

Like LAN Manager, VINES has no single function to give a user rights to a file or directory. Instead, we must retrieve the file's current access list by calling VnsGetAccessRightsList() and look for the requested user. If the user is the file's owner, we change the owner's rights. Otherwise, we search the extended access list. If we find the user, we change her rights. If we do not find her in the list, and the list is full, we return an error. Otherwise, we add her to the list, then call VnsSetAccessRightsList().

Here are the prototypes for VnsGetAccessRightsList() and VnsSetAccessRightsList():

```
CallStatus VNSENTRY VnsGetAccessRightsList(LPSTR lpszPathName,
                                           AccessRightsList FAR *lpRights);

CallStatus VNSENTRY VnsSetAccessRightsList(LPSTR lpszPathName,
                                           AccessRightsList FAR *lRights);

/********
*
* Listing 12-14. WNETGRNT.C
*
* Copyright (c) 1992 Ralph P. Davis, All Rights Reserved
*
********/

/*===== Includes =====*/

#define INCL_ARL
#include "wnetvnst.h"

/*===== Function Definitions =====*/

BOOL WINAPI WNetGrantRights(LPSTR lpszServerName,
                            LPSTR lpszUserOrGroup,
                            LPSTR lpszResource,
                            WORD  wRights)
{
    AccessRights     NewRights;
    AccessRightsList ARList;
    CallStatus       nErr;
    WORD             wType;
    BOOL             bDone = FALSE;
    WORD             i;
    char             szFullName[75];

    if ((nErr = VnsGetAccessRightsList(lpszResource,
                             ARL_VINES_VIEW, &ARList)) != BYCALLOK)
        {
        WNetSetLastError(MapVnsToWinErr(nErr));
        return FALSE;
        }

    MakeFullStreetTalkName(lpszUserOrGroup, szFullName);
    MapWNetRightsToVns(wRights, &NewRights);
```

```
if (wRights & WNET_GROUP_ACCESS)
   wType = ARL_LIST;     // Use VINES list, not VINES group
else
   wType = ARL_USER;

if (wType == ARL_USER)
   {
   // See if user is the file's owner
   if (lstrcmpi(ARList.acl.ownerName, szFullName) == 0)
      {
      // We're done, just change the user's rights
      bDone = TRUE;
      ARList.acl.ownerRights = ARList.acl.ownerInitialRights = NewRights;
      }
   }
if (!bDone)
   {
   // See if we have any room in the extended access list
   if (ARList.uExtended == NUM_EXTENDED_ACCESS)
      {
      // No room, forget it
      WNetSetLastError(WN_ACCESS_DENIED);
      return FALSE;
      }
   else
      {
      // See if user is in the extended access list already
      for (i = 0; i < ARList.uExtended; ++i)
         {
         if (lstrcmpi(ARList.extArl[i].objectName, szFullName) == 0 &&
             ARList.extArl[i].uObjectType == wType)
            {
            // A hit
            ARList.extArl[i].accessRights =
               ARList.extArl[i].initialRights = NewRights;
            break;
            }
         }
      if (i == ARList.uExtended)
         {
         // OK, add the user to the extended access list
         ARList.extArl[ARList.uExtended].accessRights =
            ARList.extArl[ARList.uExtended].initialRights = NewRights;
         ARList.extArl[ARList.uExtended].uObjectType = wType;
         lstrcpy(ARList.extArl[ARList.uExtended].objectName,
            szFullName);
         ++ARList.uExtended;
         }
      }
   }
nErr = VnsSetAccessRightsList(lpszResource, &ARList);
if (nErr != BYCALLOK)
```

```
      {
      WNetSetLastError(MapVnsToWinErr(nErr));
      return FALSE;
      }
   else
      return TRUE;
}

void WINAPI MapWNetRightsToVns(WORD wWNetRights,
                               AccessRights FAR *lpwVnsRights)
{
   WORD wRights = 0;

   if (wWNetRights & WNET_READ_ACCESS)
      wRights |= ARL_VINES_READ;
   if (wWNetRights & WNET_WRITE_ACCESS)
      wRights |= ARL_VINES_WRITE;
   if (wWNetRights & WNET_VIEW_ACCESS)
      wRights |= ARL_VINES_SEARCH;
   if (wWNetRights & WNET_DELETE_ACCESS)
      wRights |= ARL_VINES_DELETE;
   if (wWNetRights & WNET_EXECUTE_ACCESS)
      wRights |= ARL_VINES_EXECUTE;
   if (wWNetRights & WNET_PERM_ACCESS)
      wRights |= ARL_VINES_CONTROL;
   *lpwVnsRights = wRights;
}
```

WNetRevokeRights()

WNetRevokeRights() is similar to WNetGrantRights(). Again, we retrieve the current access rights list by calling VnsGetAccessRightsList(). This time, if the user is the file's owner, we fail the operation. If not, we search the extended access list, and if we find the user or list, we remove him, then call VnsSetAccessRightsList().

```
/********
*
* Listing 12-15. WNETREVK.C
*
* Copyright (c) 1992 Ralph P. Davis, All Rights Reserved
*
********/

/*===== Includes =====*/

#define INCL_ARL
#include "wnetvnst.h"

/*===== Function Definitions =====*/

BOOL WINAPI WNetRevokeRights(LPSTR lpszServerName,
                             LPSTR lpszUserOrGroup,
                             LPSTR lpszResource,
                             BOOL  bUser)
```

```
{
   AccessRightsList  ARList;
   CallStatus        nErr;
   BOOL              bChanged = FALSE;
   WORD              wType;
   WORD              i;
   char              szFullName[75];

   if ((nErr = VnsGetAccessRightsList(lpszResource, ARL_VINES_VIEW,
                                    &ARList)) != BYCALLOK)
      {
      WNetSetLastError(MapVnsToWinErr(nErr));
      return FALSE;
      }

   MakeFullStreetTalkName(lpszUserOrGroup, szFullName);

   if (bUser)
      wType = ARL_USER;
   else
      wType = ARL_LIST;

   if (wType == ARL_USER)
      {
      // See if user is the file's owner, fail if so
      if (lstrcmpi(ARList.acl.ownerName, szFullName) == 0)
         {
         WNetSetLastError(WN_ACCESS_DENIED);
         return FALSE;
         }
      }

   // Look for user (or list) in the extended access list
   for (i = 0; i < ARList.uExtended; ++i)
      {
      if (lstrcmpi(ARList.extArl[i].objectName, szFullName) == 0 &&
          ARList.extArl[i].uObjectType == wType)
         {
         bChanged = TRUE;
         while (++i < ARList.uExtended)
            ARList.extArl[i - 1] = ARList.extArl[i];
         --ARList.uExtended;
         break;
         }
      }
   if (bChanged)
      {
      nErr = VnsSetAccessRightsList(lpszResource, &ARList);
      if (nErr != BYCALLOK)
         {
         WNetSetLastError(MapVnsToWinErr(nErr));
         return FALSE;
         }
```

```
            bChanged = TRUE;
            while (++i < ARList.uExtended)
                ARList.extArl[i - 1] = ARList.extArl[i];
            --ARList.uExtended;
            break;
            }
        }
    if (bChanged)
        {
        nErr = VnsSetAccessRightsList(lpszResource, &ARList);
        if (nErr != BYCALLOK)
            {
            WNetSetLastError(MapVnsToWinErr(nErr));
            return FALSE;
            }
        }
    else
        return TRUE;
}
```

Maintenance Files

The final listings are the header file (WNETVNST.H) and the module definition file (WNETVNST.DEF).

```
/********
*
* Listing 12-16. WNETVNST.H
*
* Copyright (c) 1992 Ralph P. Davis, All Rights Reserved
*
********/

/*===== Includes =====*/

#include "wnetapi.h"
#define WINDOWS
#define INCL_ST
```

```
#define INCL_ARL
#include <vnsapi.h>

/*===== Global Variables =====*/

extern HINSTANCE hDLLInstance;

/*===== Function Prototypes =====*/

WORD MapVnsToWinErr(CallStatus nVnsErr);
void WINAPI MapVnsRightsToWNet(AccessRights FAR *lpwVnsRights,
                              LPWORD lpwWNetRights);
void WINAPI MapWNetRightsToVns(WORD wWNetRights,
                              AccessRights FAR *lpwVnsRights);
void MakeFullStreetTalkName(LPSTR lpszPartial, LPSTR lpszFull);



;********
;
; Listing 12-17. WNETVNST.DEF
;
; Copyright (c) 1992 Ralph P. Davis, All Rights Reserved
;
;********

LIBRARY    WNETVNST

EXETYPE    WINDOWS

CODE    PRELOAD MOVEABLE DISCARDABLE
DATA    PRELOAD MOVEABLE SINGLE

HEAPSIZE 4096

EXPORTS

        WEP                 @1 RESIDENTNAME
        WNetAddUser
        WNetEnumUsers
```

```
WNetDeleteUser
WNetEnumServers
WNetAddGroup
WNetEnumGroups
WNetDeleteGroup
WNetAddGroupMember
WNetDeleteGroupMember
WNetIsUserGroupMember
WNetEnumGroupMembers
WNetEnumMemberGroups
WNetGrantRights
WNetRevokeRights
WNetGetRights
```

## Part III

CHAPTER ■ 13

Windows NT and the Win32 API

Overview

In this chapter, I will look at network programming interfaces available under Microsoft's new 32-bit, multitasking operating system, Windows NT. In Windows NT, Microsoft has gone a long way towards answering some of the concerns I have voiced throughout this book. Using the Win32 API, programs can be written to use many of the capabilities of the underlying network without having to be network-specific. Named pipes and mailslots, for example, give you a protocol-independent way to write distributed programs. Normal file I/O calls can access remote files.

Windows NT includes built-in networking. It consists of a redirector that directs file I/O requests to remote machines and a server component that fields them. The networking software can be loaded and unloaded at runtime; it is not hard-wired into the NT kernel. In addition, multiple network providers can be loaded simultaneously. Each of them has its own redirector and server module. When an application makes a request for a network operation, Windows NT determines which network should handle the request. Applications can refer to remote resources using UNC names or redirected local devices. The redirection is transparent to them.

LAN Manager for NT extends the networking capabilities of Windows NT. Without it, each Windows NT machine has its own user accounts and security subsystems. LAN Manager extends this so that a single domain has a single user database; every machine in the domain replicates the database. In addition, domains can be configured to share users. Thus LAN Manager for NT gives Windows NT enterprise-wide capabilities.

Though Windows NT provides protocol independence for horizontal applications, it does not do the same for vertical applications. It is still necessary to use vendor-specific APIs to (or a front end like ours) accomplish the tasks we have addressed in Part II of this book.

Helen Custer's *Inside Windows NT* discusses the internal architecture of Windows NT in depth. Chapter 9 in particular covers NT's support for networking.

Windows NT Networking APIs

There are six areas of particular interest to us in writing network programs for Windows NT:

1. The handful of WNet() functions that are now part of the above-ground API. This API set, though, is still surprisingly sparse.
2. NetBIOS
3. Named pipes and mailslots
4. The Windows Sockets API
5. The Remote Procedure Call compiler
6. Win32 I/O services that are available remotely. These include File Services, Printing, Communications, Security, and Error Logging.

Since complete coverage of networking with Windows NT would require a book of its own, I will concentrate on the first three areas, which relate closely to the material we have already covered. See Chapter 6 for a discussion of Windows Sockets.

The WNet() Functions

The Win32 API, which runs on other platforms besides NT, supports the three WNet() functions that were in the 3.1 API—WNetAddConnection(), WNetCancelConnection(), and WNetGetConnection(). These are discussed in Chapter 9; here are their Win32 prototypes:

```
DWORD APIENTRY WNetAddConnection(LPSTR lpRemoteName,
                          LPSTR lpPassword, LPSTR lpLocalName);
DWORD APIENTRY WNetCancelConnection(LPSTR lpName, BOOL fForce);
DWORD APIENTRY WNetGetConnection(LPSTR lpLocalName, LPSTR lpRemoteName,
                          LPDWORD lpBufferSize);
```

WNetAddConnection() maps a local device (such as F:, G:, LPT1, or COM1) to a network resource. WNetCancelConnection() restores a mapped device to its local setting. WNetGetConnection() retrieves the network mapping of a local device.

Win32 adds the function WNetAddConnection2(). It is the same as WNetAdd-Connection(), but includes an argument to allow the caller to specify a user name:

```
DWORD APIENTRY WNetAddConnection2(LPSTR lpRemoteName, LPSTR lpPassword,
                          LPSTR lpLocalName, LPSTR lpUserName);
```

If *lpUserName* is NULL, Windows NT will use the default user name. This is equivalent to calling WNetAddConnection().

One other function, WNetGetUser(), has moved up from the network driver:

```
DWORD APIENTRY WNetGetUser(LPSTR lpLocalName, LPSTR lpUserName,
                     LPDWORD lpBufferSize);
```

It differs from the version of WNetGetUser() discussed in Chapter 9 in that it allows you to specify a device *n LpLocalName*. This complements the functionality of WNetAdd-

Connection2(), which lets you connect to different network resources with different user names. When you pass a NULL pointer for the device name, WNetGetUser() returns the default user name.

Win32 adds three functions to enumerate network resources: WNetOpenEnum(), WNetEnumResource(), and WNetCloseEnum(). These allow you to determine what network resources, such as shared directories and print queues, are available. You can take the information returned and pass it unaltered to WNetAddConnection() or WNetAdd-Connection2() to connect to the resource.

WNetOpenEnum()

WNetOpenEnum() begins a resource enumeration. It has four arguments:

```
DWORD APIENTRY WNetOpenEnum(DWORD dwScope, DWORD dwType,
                            LPNETRESOURCE lpNetResource, LPHANDLE lphEnum);
```

The scope of the enumeration, specified by *dwScope*, can either be all resources on the network (represented by the constant Resource_GLOBALNET), or only currently connected resources (Resource_CONNECTED). *dwType* indicates whether you want to enumerate disk resources (ResourceType_DISK), print resources (ResourceType_PRINT), or all resources (zero). If *dwScope* is Resource_CONNECTED, *lpNetResource* must be NULL. Otherwise, it points to a NETRESOURCE structure:

```
typedef struct _NETRESOURCE
{
    DWORD   dwScope;
    DWORD   dwType;
    LPSTR   lpName;
    LPSTR   lpRemoteName;
    BOOL    fContainer;
    BOOL    fCanConnect;
} NETRESOURCE;
```

dwScope and *dwType* are the same as the arguments to WNetOpenEnum(). *lpName* is the "display name" of the resource if *dwScope* is Resource_GLOBALNET. That is, it is in the user-friendly form in which it will be displayed to the end user. If *dwScope* is Resource-_CONNECTED, *lpName* is the local device name. *lpRemoteName* is the network name of the resource. If *fCanConnect* is TRUE, *LpRemoteName* can be passed to WNetAdd-Connection() as is. Finally, *fContainer* indicates that the NETRESOURCE can be used for a nested enumeration. It has meaning only if *dwScope* is Resource_GLOBALNET.

The last argument, *lphEnum*, returns an enumeration handle that you will then use as input to WNetEnumResource() and WNetCloseEnum().

The first time you call WNetOpenEnum(), set *lpNetResource* to NULL. Then, when you call WNetEnumResource(), it returns an array of NETRESOURCE structures.

WNetEnumResource()

WNetEnumResource() uses the handle returned by WNetOpenEnum(). Note from the prototype that WNetEnumResource() behaves like a LAN Manager enumerator, rather than a Windows enumerator such as EnumWindows() or EnumFonts().

```
DWORD APIENTRY WNetEnumResource(HANDLE hEnum, DWORD cRequested,
                    LPDWORD lpcReceived, LPVOID lpBuffer);
```

hEnum is the enumeration handle. *lpBuffer* points to an array of NETRESOURCE structures. *cRequested* is the number of entries (not bytes) in this array you want to have populated; 0xFFFFFFFF means to fill as many as possible. On return, the variable pointed to by *lpcReceived* will report the number of entries actually affected. To enumerate all resources, call WNetEnumResource() until it returns WN_NO_MORE_ENTRIES (assuming that no other error occurs).

You can do nested enumeration on the NETRESOURCE structures returned by WNetEnumResource(). If the *dwScope* argument to WNetOpenEnum() is Resource-_GLOBALNET, the *dwScope* field of the NETRESOURCE structure is the same, and *fContainer* is TRUE, you can call WNetOpenEnum() again, this time pointing *lpNet-Resource* to the array element you are looking at.

WNetCloseEnum()

WNetCloseEnum() closes an enumeration. Its only argument is the handle returned by WNetOpenEnum().

```
DWORD APIENTRY WNetCloseEnum(HANDLE hEnum);
```

Peer-to-Peer Communications

Win32 has several API sets for peer-to-peer communications. One is NetBIOS; the others are Named Pipes and Mailslots. NetBIOS is basically the same as I described it in Chapter 3. Named Pipes and Mailslots are OS/2 and LAN Manager derivatives. Although the programming interface has changed somewhat, it is still fundamentally the same as in LAN Manager.

One aspect of peer-to-peer programming under Windows NT that is very different from Windows 3.x is the issue of blocking versus non-blocking I/O. For all intents and purposes, the blocking problem goes away under NT. Windows NT is a preemptive multi-tasking system. Thus, the only issue is whether you want your program to block on a call, or return immediately and post some kind of asynchronous notification. You do not have to worry about a blocking call interfering with the entire system; Windows NT won't let it. Note, however, that Win32 may be implemented on platforms other than NT, and that some of them may not be preemptive (for example, Win32s run on top of Windows 3.1 Enhanced Mode). In this chapter, I focus exclusively on Windows NT.

Asynchronous I/O is handled in Windows NT with objects called events. Events are basically on-off flags. When off, they are said to be in the non-signalled state; when on, they are signalled. You associate an I/O operation—such as a read of a named pipe or a NetBIOS Network Control Block—with a Windows NT event. The event stays in the non-signalled state until the operation completes.

The Win32 API provides callback functions for NetBIOS, but there is no callback mechanism for Named Pipes and Mailslots. (Mailslots, discussed later in this chapter, are a Win32 datagram mechanism.) With NetBIOS, the Win32 manuals state that events are the preferred way to do asynchronous I/O.

You have to poll the status of an event. This is what we did in Part I, using PeekMessage() loops, but that was to service blocking requests. Fortunately, in addition to being multitasking, Windows NT is also multithreaded. Applications written for Windows NT consist of processes, which in turn are made up of threads. Threads are the actual unit of execution. A process contains at least one thread, and may contain any number of them. Threads execute concurrently, and Windows NT preemptively multitasks them. The use of threads is appropriate where different parts of a program do not need to execute consecutively. Threads can use Windows NT objects like semaphores and events to periodically synchronize their activities.

You can initiate a non-blocking operation, then spin off a thread to poll the event. This thread can make a single function call that will block until the event completes. At this point, if no error has occurred, the thread can post a message and destroy itself.

Function Calls Involved in Asynchronous I/O: Server Side

Let's take a typical example of an asynchronous call, listening for a connection request. I will use the Named Pipes API for this example.

The concept of pipes derives from UNIX, but it is something we are also familiar with in the DOS environment. When you run one program and direct its output to another, you are using a pipe. For example, this DOS command display MYFILE.TXT one page at a time:

```
TYPE MYFILE.TXT | MORE
```

This runs the internal command TYPE and pipes its output to MORE.COM. This pipe is a one-way, anonymous pipe. The first program writes to it, and the second one reads from it. The first program completes before the second one starts.

The Named Pipes API extends this paradigm, so that the pipe between programs becomes a named resource that can be accessed using standard file I/O calls. In addition, it can function as a two-way street; programs can use named pipes to pass data back and forth. Those programs can both be running on the same machine, or they can be on different machines connected by a network. The two programs run at the same time.

With the Named Pipes API, there are three ways to listen for a connection asynchronously. One way is to create the named pipe in blocking mode, then start a separate thread that will be responsible for gathering connection requests. A second method also creates a blocking pipe, but specifies that I/O to the pipe should be "overlapped," that is, asynchronous. You then wait on an NT event object that you associate with your request to see when it gets signalled. The third way creates a non- blocking pipe, then spins off a thread that repeatedly calls PeekNamedPipe() to see if data has arrived.

CreateNamedPipe() creates a new named pipe. It must be called by the server side of a client-server relationship:

```
HANDLE APIENTRY CreateNamedPipe(LPTSTR lpName, DWORD dwOpenMode, DWORD  dwPipeMode,
                    DWORD nMaxInstances, DWORD nOutBufferSize,
                    DWORD nInBufferSize, DWORD nDefaultTimeOut,
                    LPSECURITY_ATTRIBUTES lpSecurityAttributes);
```

lpName is the pipe name in Universal Naming Convention (UNC) format. This begins with two backslashes, followed by the computer name, followed by one backslash, followed by the keyword PIPE, followed by a single backslash and the rest of the pipe name. The pipe must be created locally, using a server name of ".". Thus, the pipe WNET\NICEPIPE would have the UNC name \\.\PIPE\WNET\NICEPIPE. Note that \PIPE\ is a required part of the name. The full path name of the pipe does not correspond to a real path on a server disk; it is a pseudodirectory.

dwOpenMode specifies several characteristics of the pipe. One is whether the pipe is one-way inbound (PIPE_ACCESS_INBOUND), one-way outbound (PIPE_ACCESS-_OUTBOUND), or two-way (PIPE_ACCESS_DUPLEX). Another possible setting is FILE_FLAG_WRITE_THROUGH. This specifies that Windows NT should not buffer writes to the pipe, but should transmit the data immediately. For named pipes being used for network communication, we probably don't want buffering. A final setting is FILE_FLAG_OVERLAPPED. This allows us to do asynchronous reads on the file.

dwPipeMode specifies three additional properties of the pipe:

1. Whether it is blocking (PIPE_WAIT) or non-blocking (PIPE_NOWAIT)

2. Whether it will be read in byte mode (PIPE_READMODE_BYTE) or message mode (PIPE_READMODE_MESSAGE). Byte-mode pipes are read and written as raw byte streams, and reads need not be synchronized with writes. The sender can transmit 150 bytes at once, and the receiver can read them in three chunks of 50, for instance. With a message-mode pipe, though, reads and writes must be synchronized. Suppose the sender writes two 150-byte messages, and the receiver tries to read 300 bytes. The first read will return the first message; it will require another read to fetch the second. On the other hand, if the receiver tries to read 50 bytes, his read will fail, and GetLastError() [the inspiration for WNetGetLastError(), developed in Chapter 2, and WSAGetLastError(), part of the Windows Sockets API] will return ERROR_MORE_DATA.

3. Whether the pipe will be written in byte mode (PIPE_TYPE_BYTE) or message mode (PIPE_TYPE_MESSAGE). You cannot create a pipe with both the PIPE_TYPE_BYTE and PIPE_READMODE_MESSAGE flags set. You can, however, create a pipe of PIPE_TYPE_BYTE and later set it to PIPE_READMODE_MESSAGE by calling SetNamedPipeHandleState().

The requirement that reads and writes be the same size is not as exacting as it might sound. The Named Pipes API provides a function, PeekNamedPipe(), that enables you to determine exactly how many bytes an incoming message contains.

You can only use the function TransactNamedPipe() with a message-mode pipe. This function minimizes network traffic generated by a request-response exchange of data. TransactNamedPipe()—and its close relative, CallNamedPipe()—are the antecedents of WNetShipData(), which I presented in Chapter 2.

For purposes like the DLL developed in Part I, a message-mode pipe is preferable. Remember that we had to write the code so that a sending station could inform a receiving station that it had sent a complete message. With message-mode pipes, this is all handled for us.

The *nMaxInstances* parameter specifies the maximum number of instances of the pipe that can be created. It can be passed as PIPE_UNLIMITED_INSTANCES, or any number from one to (PIPE_UNLIMITED_INSTANCES - 1). Multiple instances of named pipes are necessary because one instance of a named pipe can service only one client. To service multiple clients, you need multiple instances.

nOutBufferSize and *nInBufferSize* are advisories on the buffer space the pipe will need. *nDefaultTimeOut* is the number of milliseconds to wait when a client calls WaitNamed-Pipe() (discussed later) and says to use the default timeout. If you pass it as zero, the timeout will be 50 milliseconds.

lpSecurityAttributes points to a SECURITY_ATTRIBUTES structure. This controls user access to the named pipe. (The subject of security in Windows NT is complex, and will not be covered in this book.) You can pass this argument as a NULL pointer. Many of the named pipes functions take a SECURITY_ATTRIBUTES structure as an argument; all of them will accept a NULL pointer.

If CreateNamedPipe() succeeds, it returns a pipe handle. Otherwise, it returns 0xFFFFFFFF. The handle can now be used with the Win32 file I/O calls ReadFile() and WriteFile() to exchange data with the station on the client end of the pipe.

To return to the example, the first option is to create a blocking pipe, then spin off a separate thread to wait for connection requests. Create the named pipe as follows:

```
HANDLE hPipe;
hPipe = CreateNamedPipe("\\\\.\\PIPE\\WNET\\NICEPIPE",
                    PIPE_ACCESS_DUPLEX | FILE_FLAG_WRITE_THROUGH,
                    PIPE_WAIT | PIPE_READMODE_MESSAGE | PIPE_TYPE_MESSAGE,
                    PIPE_UNLIMITED_INSTANCES,
                    8192, 8192, 0, NULL);
```

Notice the prodigious number of backslashes in the pipe name. It begins with two backslashes, which must be written as four in a C program. The single-backslash path separators must be written as two.

Now you can create a thread to listen for connections. It does not need to notify you when a connection is established; it can immediately start reading data. To create the thread, call CreateThread().

```
HANDLE CreateThread(LPSECURITY_ATTRIBUTES lpThreadAttributes, DWORD dwStackSize,
                LPTHREAD_START_ROUTINE lpStartAddress, LPVOID lpParameter,
                DWORD dwCreationFlags, LPDWORD lpThreadId);
```

lpThreadAttributes points to a SECURITY_ATTRIBUTES structure; it can be passed as NULL. *dwStackSize* states how large a stack the thread will receive. (Threads are "lightweight processes" with their own stack, but they share their data segment with other threads belonging to the same process.) If it is passed as zero, the thread will get the same size stack as specified in the STACKSIZE parameter of the module definition file. *lpStartAddress* is a pointer to the function to execute; it is passed one argument, that specified by *lpParameter*. *dwCreationFlags* has one possible non-zero value, CREATE_SUSPENDED, which creates the thread in a suspended state. It must be explicitly started by calling ResumeThread(), passing it the handle returned by CreateThread(). If *dwCreationFlags* is zero, the thread will start to run immediately. Finally, *lpThreadId* returns the thread identifier. The function return value is a handle to the thread (which is not the same as the thread ID). It will be NULL if CreateThread() fails.

Functions used as the starting address of a thread have the following calling convention:

```
DWORD ThreadFunc(LPVOID lpParameter);
```

The thread function that you invoke here needs to know two things: the handle of the named pipe that you create, and the window to notify when data arrives. You can encapsulate these in a structure and pass its address to CreateThread() in *lpParameter*. CreateThread() in turn passes it to the thread on the stack.

```
typedef struct _NPArgs
{
    HANDLE hPipe;
    HWND   hNotifyWnd;
} NPARGS;
```

Assume for this example that the message posted is the WMU_PACKET-_RECEIVED message used in Part I. You spin off the thread as follows:

```
NPARGS NPArgs;
HANDLE hThread;
DWORD  dwThreadID;
DWORD  PipeServerFunc(LPVOID lpParameter);

// Initialize NPArgs here
NPArgs.hPipe = CreateNamedPipe(...);
NPArgs.hNotifyWnd = <the window handle of the notification window>
hThread = CreateThread(NULL, 0, PipeServerFunc, &NPArgs, 0, &dwThreadID);
```

The thread service function can be an infinite loop that repeatedly calls Connect-NamedPipe(). It will not return until a client application requests a connection by opening the named pipe. In the meantime, NT gives other threads a chance to run.

```
BOOL APIENTRY ConnectNamedPipe(HANDLE hNamedPipe, LPOVERLAPPED lpOverlapped);
```

hNamedPipe is the handle returned by CreateNamedPipe(). Pass it to the thread as *((NPARGS *) lpParameter)->hPipe*. *lpOverlapped* will become useful in the second scheme for asynchronous I/O.

When a connection is established, go into a loop calling PeekNamedPipe() to see if data is available, then call ReadFile() if it is.

```
BOOL APIENTRY PeekNamedPipe(HANDLE hNamedPipe, LPVOID lpBuffer, DWORD nBufferSize,
                    LPDWORD lpBytesRead, LPDWORD lpTotalBytesAvail,
                    LPDWORD lpBytesLeftThisMessage);
```

PeekNamedPipe() returns TRUE if it succeeds, and returns as much of the data as you ask for. *lpBuffer* points to the buffer that is to receive the data; *nBufferSize* is the size of the buffer. *lpBytesRead* will return the number of bytes read. *lpTotalBytesAvail* reports the total number of bytes available. *lpBytesLeftThisMessage* returns the number of bytes left in the message for a message-mode pipe. For a byte-mode pipe, it always returns zero.

You can use PeekNamedPipe() to find out how much memory to allocate by lying and saying that the buffer size (*nBufferSize*) is zero. For a byte-mode pipe, *lpTotalBytesAvail* will tell you how much memory you need for the read. For a message-mode pipe, you can get this information from *lpBytesLeftThisMessage*, then allocate the memory and call ReadFile():

```
BOOL APIENTRY ReadFile(HANDLE hFile, LPVOID lpBuffer, DWORD nNumberOfBytesToRead,
                LPDWORD lpNumberOfBytesRead, LPOVERLAPPED  lpOverlapped);
```

hFile is the named pipe handle. *lpBuffer* is the buffer to read the data into. *nNumberOfBytesToRead* is the number of bytes in the message; *lpNumberOfBytesRead* returns the number actually read. Again, *lpOverlapped* is used for asynchronous I/O, and will become important in the second example.

By the way, ReadFile() is the same function used to read from actual files. As noted in Chapter 2, named pipes allow you to treat a network connection like a file, getting and sending messages with normal I/O calls.

When the client terminates the conversation by calling CloseHandle(), either PeekNamedPipe() or ReadFile() will fail, and GetLastError() will return ERROR-_INVALID_HANDLE. When this happens, end the PeekNamedPipe() loop and call DisconnectNamedPipe():

```
BOOL APIENTRY DisconnectNamedPipe(HANDLE hNamedPipe);
```

Then go back to the top of the loop and call ConnectNamedPipe() again. This will fail when the server application terminates and destroys the named pipe by calling CloseHandle(). At this point, terminate the thread by calling ExitThread():

```
VOID APIENTRY ExitThread(DWORD dwExitCode);
```

You can also exit the thread by returning from it; this triggers a behind-the-scenes invocation of ExitThread().

Here is a sketch of the thread service function:

```
DWORD PipeServerFunc(LPVOID lpParameter)
{
    NPARGS *lpNPArgs = (NPARGS *) lpParameter;
    DWORD   dwBytesInMessage;
    DWORD   dwBytesRead;
    LPBYTE  lpBuffer;
    BOOL    bPeekPipe;

    while (ConnectNamedPipe(lpNPArgs->hPipe, NULL))
        {
        while (TRUE)
            {
            if (((bPeekPipe = PeekNamedPipe(lpNPArgs->hPipe, NULL, 0,
                            NULL, NULL,
                            &dwBytesInMessage))) &&
                (dwBytesInMessage > 0))
                {
                // Allocate memory
                lpBuffer = GlobalAllocPtr(GHND, dwBytesInMessage);
                // Make simplifying assumption that allocation succeeds
                dwBytesRead = 0;
                if (ReadFile(lpNPArgs->hPipe, // Pipe handle acts as file handle
                            lpBuffer, dwBytesInMessage,
                            &dwBytesRead, NULL))
                    PostMessage(lpNPArgs->hNotifyWnd,
                            WMU_PACKET_RECEIVED,
                            (WPARAM) lpNPArgs->hPipe,
                            (LPARAM) lpBuffer);
                else
```

```
            break;
        }
        else if (!bPeekPipe)
            break;
        }
    DisconnectNamedPipe(lpNPArgs->hPipe);
    }
  ExitThread(0);
}
```

You can achieve the same effect by creating a blocking named pipe and specifying that output to it will be overlapped (asynchronous). Ultimately, this uses the same method—it spins off a new thread that blocks on a function call. There is no particular advantage to either approach. This second method demonstrates the use of event objects, which are the preferred way of doing asynchronous I/O with NetBIOS.

To create the kind of named pipe needed here, call CreateNamedPipe() with one different argument. Previously, we passed a *dwOpenMode* of PIPE_ACCESS_DUPLEX | FILE_FLAG_WRITE_THROUGH. Now, add the flag FILE_FLAG_OVERLAPPED. Do not change the pipe mode; overlapped I/O uses blocking pipes.

Here is the new call to CreateNamedPipe():

```
HANDLE hPipe;

hPipe = CreateNamedPipe("\\\\.\\PIPE\\WNET\\NICEPIPE",
                    PIPE_ACCESS_DUPLEX | FILE_FLAG_WRITE_THROUGH |
                    FILE_FLAG_OVERLAPPED,
                    PIPE_WAIT | PIPE_READMODE_MESSAGE |
                    PIPE_TYPE_MESSAGE,
                    PIPE_UNLIMITED_INSTANCES, 8192, 8192, 0, NULL);
```

If this succeeds, create a new thread just as you did before, passing it the pipe handle and the window that should receive notification of events.

The thread behaves differently now. Because you created the pipe with the FILE-_FLAG_OVERLAPPED flag, you can cause ConnectNamedPipe() and ReadFile() to not block, even though the pipe was created in blocking mode. You do this by making use of the last argument to these functions, which is a pointer to an OVERLAPPED structure:

```
 typedef struct _OVERLAPPED
{
   DWORD   Internal;
   DWORD   InternalHigh;
   DWORD   Offset;
   DWORD   OffsetHigh;
   HANDLE  hEvent;
} OVERLAPPED;
```

For named pipes, only the *hEvent* is used. It holds a handle to a Win32 event object. The other fields are used to position the file pointer when doing overlapped I/O to normal files.

The first thing to do is obtain an event handle to put in the OVERLAPPED structure. Events are Win32 synchronization objects that are either signalled or non-signalled. When an event is signalled, threads waiting on it are released, either one at a time or all at once.

[The function SetEvent() signals an event.] When it is non-signalled, threads waiting on the event block. Events are either of the auto-reset or manual reset variety. When a thread that has been waiting on an auto-reset event is allowed to proceed by the signalling of the event, the event reverts to the non-signalled state, immediately and automatically. No other threads are allowed to run. Thus, it acts like a flashing red light; only one car at a time is allowed through the intersection. A manual-reset event, on the other hand, remains signalled until it is explicitly set to the non-signalled state by a call to ResetEvent(). In the meantime, all waiting threads can proceed. It is like a policeman directing traffic.

You obtain a handle to an event by calling CreateEvent():

```
HANDLE APIENTRY CreateEvent(LPSECURITY_ATTRIBUTES lpEventAttributes,
                    BOOL bManualReset, BOOL bInitialState,
                    LPTSTR lpName);
```

lpEventAttributes is optional; it can be passed as NULL. *bManualReset* indicates whether the event is of the manual- or auto-reset variety. *bInitialState* specifies the initial state of the event—signalled (TRUE) or not signalled (FALSE). *lpName* gives the event a name; it is optional. The primary purpose of the event name is this: one thread can create a named event, then another thread can get its handle by calling OpenEvent(), using the name under which it was created. Used in this manner, it synchronizes the action of separate threads. For non-blocking network operations, you don't need named events.

Having obtained the event handle, put it in the OVERLAPPED structure, then call ConnectNamedPipe():

```
OVERLAPPED Overlapped;
Overlapped.hEvent = CreateEvent(...);
ConnectNamedPipe(..., &Overlapped);
```

ConnectNamedPipe() returns TRUE only when the pipe is a blocking-mode pipe, and the OVERLAPPED argument is passed as a NULL pointer. In this case, it blocks until a request for a connection comes in. In all other cases, including the situation described here, it returns FALSE. GetLastError() will return ERROR_IO_PENDING to indicate that the pipe is in the listening state. The event remains in the non-signalled state until a connection request arrives. Call the function GetOverlappedResult() to poll the status of the event:

```
BOOL APIENTRY GetOverlappedResult(HANDLE hFile, LPOVERLAPPED lpOverlapped,
                    LPDWORD lpNumberOfBytesTransferred,
                    BOOL bWait);
```

hFile is the named pipe handle. *lpOverlapped* points to the OVERLAPPED structure containing the handle of the event you have created. *lpNumberOfBytesTransferred* is irrelevant here; it returns the number of bytes read by a ReadFile() or written by a WriteFile(). *bWait* specifies whether the operation should block until the event completes, or return immediately. If *bWait* is FALSE, and the event has not been signalled, GetOverlappedResult() will immediately return FALSE, and GetLastError() will return ERROR_IO-_INCOMPLETE.

Once a connection is established, go into the same PeekNamedPipe() loop as you did before. The only difference is that you also supply the OVERLAPPED structure to Read-File(). You don't need to call GetOverlappedResult(); you know ReadFile() will not block, because PeekNamedPipe() told you there was data available. However, ReadFile() will fail if you create a pipe with the FILE_FLAG_OVERLAPPED flag and do not supply a pointer to an OVERLAPPED structure. The same is true of WriteFile(); it also requires an OVERLAPPED structure. With WriteFile(), you need to call GetOverlappedResult(); there is no way to determine in advance if a write will succeed.

When the thread terminates, destroy the event by calling CloseHandle():

```
BOOL APIENTRY CloseHandle(HANDLE hObject);
```

hObject is a handle to whatever type of object you need to dispose of—a file, an event, or a named pipe, to name some important examples.

Here is the new version of the thread:

```
DWORD PipeServerFunc(LPVOID lpParameter)
{
    NPARGS     *lpNPArgs = (NPARGS *) lpParameter;
    DWORD       dwBytesInMessage, dwBytesRead;
    LPBYTE      lpBuffer;
    HANDLE      hEvent;
    OVERLAPPED Overlapped;
    BOOL        bPeekPipe;

    // Create an unnamed auto-reset event, initially in the
    // non-signalled state
    hEvent = CreateEvent(NULL, FALSE, FALSE, NULL);
    if (hEvent == 0xFFFFFFFF)
       ExitThread(0xFFFFFFFF);

    Overlapped.hEvent = hEvent;
    while (TRUE)
       {
       if (!ConnectNamedPipe(lpNPArgs->hPipe, &Overlapped))
          if (GetLastError() != ERROR_IO_PENDING)
             break;
       // Tell GetOverlappedResult() to block until the  event
       // completes
       GetOverlappedResult(lpNPArgs->hPipe, &Overlapped, &dwBytesRead, TRUE);
       while (TRUE)
          {
          if ((((bPeekPipe = PeekNamedPipe(lpNPArgs->hPipe, NULL, 0,
                             NULL, NULL,
                             &dwBytesInMessage))) &&
              (dwBytesInMessage > 0))
             {
             // Allocate receive buffer here
             // Will be freed by routine that notification message gets
             // posted to
             lpBuffer = GlobalAllocPtr(GHND, dwBytesInMessage);
             // Assume that allocation succeeded
             dwBytesRead = 0;
             if (!ReadFile(lpNPArgs->hPipe, lpBuffer, dwBytesInMessage,
                          &dwBytesRead, &Overlapped))
                {
```

```
        if (GetLastError() != ERROR_IO_INCOMPLETE)
            break;
        GetOverlappedResult(lpNPArgs->hPipe, &Overlapped,
                            &dwBytesRead, TRUE);
        }
        PostMessage(lpNPArgs->hNotifyWnd, WMU_PACKET_RECEIVED,
                    (WPARAM) lpNPArgs->hPipe,
                    (LPARAM) lpBuffer);
      }
      else if (!bPeekPipe)
        break;
      }
    DisconnectNamedPipe(lpNPArgs->hPipe);
    }
  // All done
  CloseHandle(hEvent);
  ExitThread(0);
}
```

Finally, the easiest way to do non-blocking I/O with named pipes is to create a non-blocking pipe in the first place, without the FILE_FLAG_OVERLAPPED flag. Peek-NamedPipe() will not report data until a connection is established and data is available. The initial call to CreateNamedPipe() reads:

```
HANDLE hPipe;

hPipe = CreateNamedPipe("\\\\.\\PIPE\\WNET\\NICEPIPE",
                        PIPE_ACCESS_DUPLEX | FILE_FLAG_WRITE_THROUGH,
                        PIPE_NOWAIT | PIPE_READTYPE_MESSAGE |
                        PIPE_TYPE_MESSAGE,
                        PIPE_UNLIMITED_INSTANCES, 8192, 8192, 0, NULL);
```

ConnectNamedPipe() will return FALSE, and GetLastError() ERROR_IO_PEND-ING, until either a connection is established or the pipe is closed.

Here is the polling thread that implements this algorithm:

```
DWORD PipeServerFunc(LPVOID lpParameter)
{
    NPARGS *lpNPArgs = (NPARGS *) lpParameter;
    DWORD   dwBytesInMessage, dwBytesRead;
    LPBYTE  lpBuffer;
    while (TRUE)
        {
        if (!ConnectNamedPipe(lpNPArgs->hPipe, NULL))
            {
            if (GetLastError() != ERROR_IO_PENDING)
                break;
            }
        else
            {
            while (TRUE)
                {
                if (PeekNamedPipe(lpNPArgs->hPipe, NULL, 0, NULL, NULL,
```

```
                            &dwBytesInMessage))
                {
                if (dwBytesInMessage > 0)
                    {
                    lpBuffer = GlobalAllocPtr(GHND, dwBytesInMessage);
                    dwBytesRead = 0;
                    if (ReadFile(lpNPArgs->hPipe, lpBuffer, dwBytesInMessage,
                                &dwBytesRead, NULL))
                        PostMessage(lpNPArgs->hNotifyWnd, WMU_PACKET_RECEIVED,
                                (WPARAM) lpNPArgs->hPipe,
                                (LPARAM) lpBuffer);
                    else
                        break;
                    }
                }
            else if (GetLastError() != ERROR_PIPE_LISTENING)
                break;
            }
        DisconnectNamedPipe(lpNPArgs->hPipe);
        }
    }
    ExitThread(0);
}
```

NetBIOS

Windows NT's support of NetBIOS differs very little from my description of NetBIOS in Chapter 3. NetBIOS is, after all, a well-standardized interface; there would be little justification for Microsoft to radically reinvent it.

There are, however, some changes that are necessary for Windows NT. In the standard version of NetBIOS, the post routine is passed a pointer to the original NCB in ES:BX. This is a non-portable assembler interface, and cannot be supported in a system like Windows NT, which is intended to run on more than just 80x86 platforms. Thus, the post routine is now passed a pointer to the NCB as a normal C argument on the stack, so it can be written entirely in C.

In adapting the code from Chapter 3 to Windows NT, we can therefore eliminate one level of message posting. NBWndProc(), originally shown in Listing 3-3, now becomes the post routine. Its arguments change also, as it is no longer a window procedure. Listing 13-1 shows NBWndProc() adapted to Windows NT. I do not include the support routines AppendToPacket(), RetrieveCompletePacket(), and StopTrackingPacket(), since they do not change at all.

```
/********
*
* Listing 13-1. NBWND.C
*
* Copyright (c) 1992 Ralph P. Davis, All Rights Reserved
*
********/
```

```c
/*===== Includes =====*/
#include "wnetnb.h"
#include <string.h>


/*===== LOCAL Variables =====*/

static PACKET_TABLE PacketTable[CONCURRENT_CONNECTIONS] = {0};

/*===== FORWARD Functions =====*/

LPBYTE RetrieveCompletePacket(HCONNECTION hConnection, LPBYTE lpOldData,
        DWORD dwTotalBytes);
LPBYTE AppendToPacket(HCONNECTION hConnection, LPBYTE  lpOldData,
                    DWORD dwTotalBytes);
void StopTrackingPacket(HCONNECTION hConnection);

/*===== Function Definitions =====*/

void NBWndProc(LPXNCB lpXNCB)
{
    WPARAM wOutParam;
    LPVOID lpData, lpOldData;
    BOOL    bRepost;
    BOOL    bEndOfMessage;

    switch (lpXNCB->ncbBase.byCommand & (~NB_NO_WAIT))
        {
        case NB_RECEIVE:
        case NB_RECEIVE_ANY:
            // See if command completed with some kind of error
            // that prevents reposting the NCB
            switch (lpXNCB->ncbBase.byCompletionCode)
                {
                case NB_ERR_SESSION_CLOSED:
                case NB_ERR_SESSION_CRASHED:
                case NB_ERR_BAD_LSN:
                case NB_NAME_DEREGISTERED:
                case NB_ERR_BAD_NAME_NUMBER:
                case NB_ERR_BAD_NAME:
                case NB_ERR_NAME_DELETED:
                case NB_ERR_CANCEL_PENDING:
                    FreePageLockedBuffer(lpXNCB->ncbBase.lpData);
                    bRepost = FALSE;
                    break;
                default:
                    bRepost = TRUE;
                    break;
                }
            break;
        case NB_RECEIVE_DATAGRAM:
        case NB_LISTEN:
        case NB_RECEIVE_BROADCAST:
            switch (lpXNCB->ncbBase.byCompletionCode)
                {
                case NB_NAME_DEREGISTERED:
```

```
            case NB_ERR_BAD_NAME_NUMBER:
            case NB_ERR_BAD_NAME:
            case NB_ERR_NAME_DELETED:
            case NB_ERR_CANCEL_PENDING:
               bRepost = FALSE;
               break;
             default:
               bRepost = TRUE;
                break;
          }
       break;
    default:
       bRepost = FALSE;
       break;
    }
 switch (lpXNCB->ncbBase.byCommand & (~NB_NO_WAIT))
    {
    case NB_LISTEN:
       // Connect request has arrived--post asynchronous
       // listens by calling _WNetReceive()
       if (lpXNCB->ncbBase.byCompletionCode == NB_SUCCESS)
          {
          int i;
          LPBYTE lpBuffer;

          for (i = 0; i < MAX_LISTEN_REQUESTS; ++i)
             {
             lpBuffer = (LPBYTE) AllocPageLockedBuffer(
                MAX_SEND_BUFFER_SIZE);
             if (lpBuffer != NULL)
                {
                _WNetReceive(
                   (HCONNECTION) lpXNCB->ncbBase.byLocalSession,
                    lpBuffer, MAX_SEND_BUFFER_SIZE,
                    NONBLOCKING, 0, lpXNCB->hWnd);
                }
             }
          }
       break;
    case NB_CALL:
    case NB_SEND:
    case NB_RECEIVE:
    case NB_HANGUP:
    case NB_RECEIVE_ANY:
    case NB_CHAIN_SEND:
       // Connection-oriented exchange of data
       // The connection number appears in the byLocalSession
       // field of the NCB
       wOutParam = (WPARAM) lpXNCB->ncbBase.byLocalSession;
       break;
    default:
       wOutParam = 0;
```

```
         break;
      }

// Make sure packet was not received in error.
if (lpXNCB->hWnd != NULL &&
      lpXNCB->ncbBase.byCompletionCode == NB_SUCCESS)
   {
   // Copy the data and post message to originating window

   if (lpXNCB->ncbBase.wDataLength <=
      (WORD) (MAX_SEND_BUFFER_SIZE - 1))
      {
      bEndOfMessage = TRUE;
      }
   else
      {
      lpXNCB->ncbBase.wDataLength =
         (WORD) (MAX_SEND_BUFFER_SIZE - 1);
      bEndOfMessage = FALSE;
      }

   lpData = GlobalAllocPtr(GHND,
      (DWORD) lpXNCB->ncbBase.wDataLength);

   if (lpData != NULL)
      {
      WORD i;

      for (i = 0; i < lpXNCB->ncbBase.wDataLength; ++i)
         ((LPBYTE) lpData)[i] =
            ((LPBYTE) (lpXNCB->ncbBase.lpData))[i];
      if (bEndOfMessage)
         {
         // Last packet in transmission, get rest of it
         lpOldData = lpData;
          lpData = RetrieveCompletePacket(
            (HCONNECTION) wOutParam,
            lpData, lpXNCB->ncbBase.wDataLength);
         if (lpData != lpOldData)
            GlobalFreePtr(lpOldData);

         if (lpData != NULL)
            // Post WMU_PACKET_RECEIVED message to
            // originating window
            PostMessage(lpXNCB->hWnd, WMU_PACKET_RECEIVED,
                     wOutParam, (LPARAM) lpData);
         }
      else
         {
         AppendToPacket((HCONNECTION) wOutParam,
            lpData, lpXNCB->ncbBase.wDataLength);
         GlobalFreePtr(lpData);
         }
      }
   }
```

```
    if (bRepost)    // Recycle original passive request
      {
      // Reset receive buffer length in NCB to
      // size of original buffer (remembered in the
      // extended NCB)
      lpXNCB->ncbBase.wDataLength =
          lpXNCB->wOriginalDataLength;
      NetBios((LPNCB) lpXNCB);
      }
    else
      FreePageLockedBuffer(lpXNCB);
}
```

Microsoft has added one field to the NCB to hold an event handle. This can be used to provide non-blocking I/O. The Win32 manuals state that this method is preferred over post routines because it consumes fewer resources in the Win32 environment. You create an event by calling CreateEvent(), set the address of the post routine in the NCB to NULL, and issue a no-wait NetBIOS command. The event will remain in the non-signalled state until the operation completes. To test the state of an event that is not associated with overlapped I/O, Win32 provides two functions: WaitForSingleObject() and WaitForMultipleObjects().

```
DWORD APIENTRY WaitForSingleObject(HANDLE hHandle, DWORD dwMilliseconds);
```

hHandle is a handle to the object you want to test. *dwMilliseconds* is the timeout value. Zero says return immediately; 0xFFFFFFFF say block indefinitely. A return value of zero from WaitForSingleObject() indicates that the event completed. WAIT_TIMEOUT says that the function timed out before the event completed. Other non-zero values, indicating some error condition, are also possible.

```
DWORD APIENTRY WaitForMultipleObjects(DWORD nCount, LPHANDLE lpHandles,
                                BOOL bWaitAll, DWORD dwMilliseconds);
```

WaitForMultipleObjects() takes an array of object handles to test in *lpHandles*. *nCount* tells how many elements are in the array. If *bWaitAll* is TRUE, WaitForMultipleObjects() returns successfully only if all objects in the *lpHandles* array are signalled. If *bWaitAll* is FALSE, WaitForMultipleObjects() succeeds when any one of the objects in *lpHandles* is signalled.

The return value with *bWaitAll* set to FALSE is the index into *lpHandles* of the object that went into the signalled state. For both settings of *bWaitAll*, a return value outside the bounds of the array says that the wait was not satisfied.

To handle suedo-blocking commands issue the no-wait version of the NetBIOS command, then call WaitForSingleObject() with the event handle and an appropriate timeout value. In Chapter 3, we used a timeout of five seconds. For example:

```
typedef struct tagXNCB
{
   NCB  ncbBase;
   HWND hWnd;
   WORD wOriginalDataLength;
} XNCB;          // Extended NCB
XNCB xNCB;
```

```
// Populate xNCB here and create event
NetBios((LPNCB) &xNCB);
if (WaitForSingleObject(xNCB.hEvent, 5000) != 0)
   // Timed out waiting for the event
else
   // Event completed
```

For a non-blocking request, spin off a new thread and pass it a pointer to an extended NCB (the XNCB structure defined in Chapter 3). This thread calls WaitForSingleObject(), instructing it to wait indefinitely:

```
DWORD NetBIOSPollingThread(LPVOID lpNBArgs)
{
   LPXNCB lpXNCB = (LPXNCB) lpNBArgs;

   WaitForSingleObject(lpXNCB->ncbBase.hEvent, (DWORD) - 1);
   ParseNCB(lpXNCB);
   ExitThread(0);
}
```

The code from Chapter 3 requires only slight modifications to adapt it to Windows NT. Listing 13-2 shows _WNETRCV.C, originally shown in Listing 3-11, ported to Win32. Win32 supplies its own typedef of an NCB, but I use the typedef developed in Chapter 3, and add one field for the event handle, as follows:

```
typedef struct tagNCB
{
   BYTE     byCommand;
   BYTE     byReturnCode;
   BYTE     byLocalSession;
   BYTE     byNameNumber;
   LPVOID   lpData;
   WORD     wDataLength;
   BYTE     cRemoteName[16];
   BYTE     cLocalName[16];
   BYTE     byReceiveTimeout;
   BYTE     bySendTimeout;
   FARPROC  lpCallback;
   BYTE     byAdapterNumber;
   BYTE     byCompletionCode;
   BYTE     byReserved[14];
   HANDLE   hEvent;
} NCB;

 /*******
 *
 * Listing 13-2. _WNETRCV.C
 *
 * Copyright (c) 1992 Ralph P. Davis, All Rights Reserved
 *
 *******/
/*===== Includes =====*/
```

```c
#include "wnetnb.h"

/*===== Function Definitions =====*/

BOOL WINAPI _WNetReceive(HCONNECTION hConnection,
                         LPVOID lpData,
                         DWORD dwDataLength,
                         BLOCK_STATE BlockState,
                         int nNameIndex,
                         HWND hWnd)
{
    LPXNCB  lpXNCB;
    BYTE    _huge *lpTemp;
    WORD    wNBReturnCode;
    BOOL    bReturnCode = TRUE;
    LPBYTE  lpQueuedPacket;
    HANDLE  hEvent;
    HANDLE  hThread;
    DWORD   dwThreadID;

    // Get Win32 event
    hEvent = CreateEvent(NULL, FALSE, FALSE, NULL);

    if (hEvent == NULL)
        return FALSE;

    // We will only permit a non-blocking receive
    // if dwDataLength is less than or equal to MAX_SEND_BUFFER_SIZE
    // Otherwise, it will require posting multiple
    // asynchronous receives to fill the buffer.

    if (dwDataLength > MAX_SEND_BUFFER_SIZE)
        BlockState = BLOCKING;

    if (BlockState == BLOCKING)
        {
        lpQueuedPacket = WNetGetNextQueuedPacket(hConnection);
        if (lpQueuedPacket != NULL)
            {
            WNetCopyQueuedPacket(lpQueuedPacket, (LPBYTE) lpData,
                dwDataLength);
            return TRUE;
            }
        }

    if (nNameIndex == (-1))
        nNameIndex = nMainNameIndex;

    lpXNCB = (LPXNCB) AllocPageLockedBuffer(sizeof (XNCB));
    if (lpXNCB == NULL)
        {
        WNetSetLastError(WN_OUT_OF_MEMORY);
        return FALSE;
        }
    lpXNCB->ncbBase.lpCallback = NULL;
```

```
lpXNCB->ncbBase.hEvent = hEvent;
if (BlockState == BLOCKING)
   {
   lpXNCB->ncbBase.byCommand = NB_RECEIVE_NO_WAIT;
   }
else
   {
   lpXNCB->hWnd = hWnd;
   if (hConnection == 0)
      lpXNCB->ncbBase.byCommand = NB_RECEIVE_ANY_NO_WAIT;
   else
      lpXNCB->ncbBase.byCommand = NB_RECEIVE_NO_WAIT;
   lpXNCB->ncbBase.byNameNumber = (BYTE) nNameIndex;
   }

lpXNCB->ncbBase.byLocalSession = (BYTE) hConnection;
lpXNCB->ncbBase.byAdapterNumber = 0;
lpTemp = (BYTE _huge *) lpData;
do
   {
   lpXNCB->ncbBase.lpData = lpTemp;

   // Does buffer require multiple receives?
   if (dwDataLength > MAX_SEND_BUFFER_SIZE)
      lpXNCB->ncbBase.wDataLength = MAX_SEND_BUFFER_SIZE;
   else
      lpXNCB->ncbBase.wDataLength = (WORD)  dwDataLength;

   // Remember original size of the buffer so we can
   // repost the request with the correct value
   lpXNCB->wOriginalDataLength =
      lpXNCB->ncbBase.wDataLength;

   // Invoke NetBIOS
   if ((wNBReturnCode = NetBios((LPNCB) lpXNCB)) != NB_SUCCESS)
      {
      WNetSetLastError(MapNBToWinErr(wNBReturnCode));
      bReturnCode = FALSE;
      break;
      }
   if (BlockState == BLOCKING)
      {
      // Blocking request, poll event completion status
      // Wait 5 seconds (5000 milliseconds)
      if (WaitForSingleObject(hEvent, 5000) != 0)
         {
         // Event timed out--see if packet arrived
         // asynchronously
         lpQueuedPacket = WNetGetNextQueuedPacket(hConnection);
         if (lpQueuedPacket != NULL)
            {
            // Yes, packet came in behind the scenes--retrieve it
            WNetCopyQueuedPacket(lpQueuedPacket,
```

```
                    (LPBYTE) lpData, dwDataLength);
               lpXNCB->ncbBase.byCompletionCode = NB_SUCCESS;
               break;
               }
            else
               {
               // No packet, say we timed out
               wNBReturnCode = NB_ERR_TIMEOUT;
               }
            // Cancel the request, since it timed out
            NBCancel((LPNCB) lpXNCB);
            }
         else
            wNBReturnCode = (WORD) lpXNCB->ncbBase.byCompletionCode;

         if (wNBReturnCode != NB_SUCCESS)
            {
            WNetSetLastError(MapNBToWinErr(wNBReturnCode));
            bReturnCode = FALSE;
            break;
            }
         }
      else
         {
         // Non-blocking--spin off thread to poll status of event
         hThread = CreateThread(NULL, 0, NetBIOSPollingThread,
            lpXNCB, 0, &dwThreadID);
         if (hThread == NULL)
            {
            bReturnCode = FALSE;
            break;
            }
         }
      if (dwDataLength >= MAX_SEND_BUFFER_SIZE)
         {
         dwDataLength -= ((DWORD) MAX_SEND_BUFFER_SIZE);
         lpTemp += ((DWORD) MAX_SEND_BUFFER_SIZE);
         }
      else
         dwDataLength = OL;
       }
   while (dwDataLength > OL);

   if (BlockState == BLOCKING)
      FreePageLockedBuffer(lpXNCB);
   return bReturnCode;
}

DWORD NetBIOSPollingThread(LPVOID lpParameter)
{
   LPXNCB lpXNCB = (LPXNCB) lpParameter;

   WaitForSingleObject(lpXNCB->ncbBase.hEvent, (DWORD) - 1);

   NBWndProc(lpXNCB);
```

```
      ExitThread(0);
}
```

You can also do blocking I/O by using the wait version of the NetBIOS command. Under Windows NT, this is not a problem.

Named Pipes

The above discussion of synchronous and asynchronous I/O gives examples of the Named Pipes API. To reiterate, the procedure for named pipes on the server side is:

- Create a named pipe by calling CreateNamedPipe()

While the server application is active:

- Listen for connections by calling ConnectNamedPipe()
- Connection established—exchange data using PeekNamedPipe(), ReadFile(), and WriteFile()
- Connection terminated—call DisconnectNamedPipe()
- Server terminates—destroy named pipe by calling CloseHandle()

The client side uses standard file I/O calls. CreateFile() requests a connection, that is, it calls the server. In Win32, CreateFile() supersedes OpenFile(), although OpenFile() is still supported.

```
HANDLE APIENTRY CreateFile(LPTSTR lpFileName, DWORD dwDesiredAccess,
                     DWORD dwShareMode,
                     LPSECURITY_ATTRIBUTES lpSecurityAttributes,
                     DWORD dwCreationDisposition, DWORD dwFlagsAndAttributes,
                     HANDLE hTemplateFile);
```

lpFileName is the name of the file, and it may be in Universal Naming Convention (UNC) format. If a client application wants to connect to the server MYSERVER using the pipe \PIPE\WNET\NICEPIPE, it sets *lpFileName* to "\\\\MYSERVER\\PIPE\\WNET-\\NICEPIPE".

dwDesiredAccess specifies the desired access to the file, and may be GENERIC_READ (for read-only access), GENERIC_WRITE (for write- only access), or GENERIC_READ | GENERIC_WRITE (for read-write access). For a two-way named pipe, you need both read and write access. *dwShareMode* indicates what kind of operations other applications may perform on the file. FILE_SHARE_READ grants read access; FILE_SHARE_WRITE allows write access. Setting *dwShareMode* to zero causes the file to be opened for exclusive use; this is how a named pipe should be opened.

lpSecurityAttributes is optional and may be passed as NULL. *dwCreationDisposition* defines the specific operation that CreateFile() should perform. The possible operations are:

1. Create a new file, but fail if the file already exists (CREATE_NEW).
2. Create a new file, and overwrite the file if it already exists (CREATE_ALWAYS).
3. Open an existing file, and fail if the file does not exist (OPEN_EXISTING).

4. If the file exists, open it. Otherwise, interpret this as a CREATE_NEW operation (OPEN_ALWAYS).

5. If the file exists, open it and destroy any previous contents. If the file does not exist, fail the call (TRUNCATE_EXISTING).

dwFlagsAndAttributes specifies the file attributes that we are familiar with from the DOS file system, such as normal (FILE_ATTRIBUTE_NORMAL), read-only (FILE_AT-TRIBUTE_READONLY), hidden (FILE_ATTRIBUTE_HIDDEN), and system (FILE-_ATTRIBUTE_SYSTEM). It can also include flags like FILE_FLAG_WRITE_THROUGH and FILE_FLAG_OVERLAPPED, which have the same meaning as they did for CreateNamedPipe().

hTemplate, if it is not NULL, specifies the handle of an open file that will supply the new file's security attributes and file attributes. The *lpSecurityAttributes* and *dwFlagsAnd-Attributes* arguments are ignored if *hTemplate* is non-NULL.

By default, when a client calls CreateFile() to open a named pipe, it is a blocking, byte-mode pipe. To change it, the client must call SetNamedPipeHandleState():

```
BOOL APIENTRY SetNamedPipeHandleState(HANDLE hNamedPipe, LPDWORD lpMode,
                                      LPDWORD lpMaxCollectionCount,
                                      LPDWORD lpCollectDataTimeout);
```

hNamedPipe is the handle returned by either CreateFile() on the client side or CreateNamedPipe() on the server side. *lpMode* points to a DWORD variable containing the new mode of the pipe. It specifies the read mode and the blocking mode of the pipe. Possible values are PIPE_READMODE_BYTE to make the pipe a byte- mode pipe, or PIPE_READMODE_MESSAGE to put it into message mode; PIPE_WAIT and PIPE_NOWAIT make the pipe a blocking or non-blocking pipe.

lpMaxCollectionCount points to the maximum number of bytes that will be buffered on the client machine before transmission to the server. This parameter must be NULL when the server end of the pipe is calling SetNamedPipeHandleState(). *lpCollectData-Timeout* specifies how many milliseconds the client machine should wait for *lpMax-CollectionCount* bytes to be sent. It too must be NULL when SetNamedPipeHandleState() is called by the server end of the pipe. The data will be sent when the first of these thresholds is reached. Suppose the maximum collection count is 5000, and the timeout is 500 milliseconds. After 500 milliseconds, only 512 bytes have been written; they will be transmitted. Over the next 100 milliseconds, 5000 bytes are written; they too will be transmitted.

As I stated, the server side must create one instance of a named pipe for every client it expects to service. It is possible that CreateFile() will fail (return -1) because all instances of the pipe are in use. The client then has the option of calling WaitNamedPipe(). This function waits for an instance of the named pipe to become available.

```
BOOL APIENTRY WaitNamedPipe(LPTSTR lpNamedPipeName, DWORD nTimeOut);
```

nTimeout specifies the number of milliseconds to wait. It can also be passed as either NMPWAIT_WAIT_FOREVER, meaning never timeout, or NMPWAIT_USE_DE-FAULT_WAIT, which says use the default timeout specified in the server's call to CreateNamedPipe(). If it returns TRUE, an instance of the pipe is available, and the client can call CreateFile().

Once the client has opened the pipe and put it into the appropriate mode, it uses PeekNamedPipe(), ReadFile(), and WriteFile() to read and write data. I showed the prototype for ReadFile() earlier; WriteFile() is identical.

```
BOOL APIENTRY WriteFile(HANDLE hFile, LPVOID lpBuffer,
                 DWORD nNumberOfBytesToWrite,
                 LPDWORD lpNumberOfBytesWritten,
                 LPOVERLAPPED lpOverlapped);
```

To terminate a connection, the client calls CloseHandle(), with the pipe handle returned by CreateFile().Windows for Workgroups also provides DosReadAsyncNmPipe() and DosWriteAsyncNmPipe() for non-blocking reads and writes.

A station running Windows 3.1 or Windows for Workgroups can use OpenFile(), _lread(), _lwrite(), and _lclose() instead of CreateFile(), ReadFile(), WriteFile(), and Close-Handle().

There are several other named pipes functions. Two of them, CallNamedPipe() and TransactNamedPipe(), are provided to optimize network performance:

```
BOOL APIENTRY CallNamedPipe(LPTSTR lpNamedPipeName, LPVOID lpInBuffer,
                 DWORD nInBufferSize, LPVOID lpOutBuffer,
                 DWORD nOutBufferSize, LPDWORD lpBytesRead,
                 DWORD nTimeout);

BOOL APIENTRY TransactNamedPipe(HANDLE hNamedPipe, LPVOID lpInBuffer,
                 DWORD nInBufferSize, LPVOID lpOutBuffer,
                 DWORD nOutBufferSize, LPDWORD lpBytesRead,
                 LPOVERLAPPED lpOverlapped);
```

These functions are specially suited for request-response exchanges of data. Data passed from the client to the server resides at *lpInBuffer*. Data returned from the server will be deposited at *lpOutBuffer*, and *lpBytesRead* will return the number of bytes passed back from the server.

CallNamedPipe() is equivalent to a succession of CreateFile(), WriteFile(), ReadFile(), and CloseHandle() calls. TransactNamedPipe() writes data to an existing pipe and waits for an answer. It may be called in overlapped mode, in which case it returns immediately. GetOverlappedResult() then awaits the completion of the event. These functions reduce the number of network operations required to exchange data.

The function WNetShipData() that I developed in Chapter 2 (see Listing 2-10) is based on these two functions. If the target station argument has a high word of zero, WNetShipData() behaves like TransactNamedPipe(). Otherwise, it acts like CallNamed-Pipe(). WNetShipData() checks to see if there is a network-dependent _WNetShipData(), and calls it if there is one. Listing 13-3 shows the only network-dependent implementation. It assumes that all stations are using the pipe \\.\PIPE\WNET\NICEPIPE.

```
/********
*
* Listing 13-3. _WNETSHP.C
 *
* Copyright (c) 1992, Ralph P. Davis, All Rights Reserved
*
********/
```

```c
/*===== Includes =====*/
#include "wnet.h"
/*===== Function Definitions =====*/
LRESULT WINAPI _WNetShipData(HWND   hWnd,
                             LPVOID lpTargetStation,
                             LPVOID lpData,
                             DWORD  dwDataLength,
                             LPVOID lpDataOut,
                             DWORD  dwOutDataLength)
{
   LRESULT lResult = -1L;
   LPBYTE  lpReceiveBuffer, lpTemp;
   DWORD   i;
   char    szTargetStation[255];
   BOOL    bReturnCode;

   if (SELECTOROF(lpTargetStation) != 0)
      wsprintf(szTargetStation, "\\\\%s\\PIPE\\WNET\\NICEPIPE",
         (LPSTR) lpTargetStation);
   else
      szTargetStation[0] = '\0';

   lpReceiveBuffer = (LPBYTE) AllocPageLockedBuffer(dwOutDataLength +
                                                    sizeof (LRESULT));
   if (lpReceiveBuffer == NULL)
      {
      WNetSetLastError(WN_OUT_OF_MEMORY);
      return -1L;
      }

   if (lstrlen(szTargetStation) == 0)
      bReturnCode =
         TransactNamedPipe((HANDLE) OFFSETOF(lpTargetStation),
            lpData, dwDataLength,
            lpReceiveBuffer, sizeof (LRESULT) + dwOutDataLength,
            &dwOutDataLength, NULL);
   else
      bReturnCode =
         CallNamedPipe(lpTargetStation,
            lpData, dwDataLength,
            lpReceiveBuffer, sizeof (LRESULT) + dwOutDataLength,
            &dwOutDataLength, 5000);

   if (bReturnCode)
      {
      lResult = *((LRESULT FAR *) lpReceiveBuffer);
      lpTemp = (LPBYTE) lpDataOut;
      lpReceiveBuffer += (sizeof (LRESULT));
      for (i = 0L; i < dwOutDataLength; ++i)
         lpTemp[i] = lpReceiveBuffer[i];
      }
   else
      lResult = -1;
```

```
        FreePageLockedBuffer(lpReceiveBuffer);
        return lResult;
}
```

GetNamedPipeHandleState() is the converse of SetNamedPipeHandleState(), discussed earlier.

```
BOOL APIENTRY GetNamedPipeHandleState(HANDLE hNamedPipe, LPDWORD lpState,
                              LPDWORD lpCurInstances,
                              LPDWORD lpMaxCollectionCount,
                              LPDWORD lpCollectDataTimeout,
                              LPTSTR  lpUserName,
                              DWORD   nMaxUserNameSize);
```

lpState returns flags indicating the blocking state and read mode of the pipe. It should be ANDed with PIPE_NOWAIT and PIPE_READMODE_MESSAGE. Their opposites, PIPE_WAIT and PIPE_READMODE_BYTE, are zero bit settings.

lpCurInstances returns the number of current instances of the pipe. *lpMaxCollectionCount* returns the number of bytes that will be buffered at the client station before transmission to the server. *lpCollectDataTimeout* returns the number of milliseconds that the client station will buffer data before transmitting it to the server. Both *lpMaxCollectionCount* and *lpCollectDataTimeout* must be NULL if GetNamedPipeHandleState() is called on the server end of the pipe, or if both client and server are on the same machine.

lpUserName returns the name of the user logged onto the client station. It must be NULL when called at the client end of the pipe. *nMaxUserNameSize* gives the size of the buffer at *lpUserName*.

GetNamedPipeInfo() returns more information about a named pipe:

```
BOOL APIENTRY GetNamedPipeInfo(HANDLE hNamedPipe, LPDWORD lpFlags,
                          LPDWORD lpOutBufferSize, LPDWORD lpInBufferSize,
                          LPDWORD lpMaxInstances);
```

lpFlags returns bit flags indicating which end of the pipe you are on, and the type of the pipe. It should be ANDed with PIPE_END_SERVER and PIPE_TYPE_MESSAGE, as these are the non-zero bit flags.

lpOutBufferSize and *lpInBufferSize* return the sizes of the output and input buffers. If returned as zero, the memory is allocated when it is needed.

lpMaxInstances returns the maximum number of instances of the named pipe, as specified on the original call to CreateNamedPipe(). It may be returned as PIPE_UNLIMITED_INSTANCES.

Mailslots

Mailslots are the Win32 means of sending and receiving datagrams. The API set here is very small. A station wishing to receive datagrams calls CreateMailslot().

```
HANDLE APIENTRY CreateMailslot(LPTSTR lpName, DWORD nMaxMessageSize,
                          DWORD nMailslotSize, DWORD lReadTimeout,
                          LPSECURITY_ATTRIBUTES lpSecurityAttributes);
```

lpName is the name of the mailslot. Mailslot names are UNC names, and are very similar to pipe names. They begin with two backslashes, followed by the computer name, followed by a single backslash, followed by the keyword MAILSLOT, followed by another backslash and the rest of the name. The station calling CreateMailslot() must use a machine name of "." (meaning the local machine). In other words, mailslots, like named pipes, can only be created on the server's machine. They cannot be created on a remote machine.

nMaxMessageSize specifies the largest message the application will accept. *nMailslotSize* gives the size of the mailslot buffer desired. It may be passed as MAILSLOT-_SIZE_AUTO, which tells Windows NT to base it on *nMaxMessageSize*. The number of messages the mailslot can accept is *nMailslotsSize / nMaxMessageSize*. *lReadTimeout* is the number of milliseconds a ReadFile() should wait for a message. MAILSLOT-_WAIT_FOREVER means don't timeout.

The server station (the one that creates the mailslot) can only read messages from the mailslot. To send datagrams to another station, you call CreateFile() to open the mailslot. The client, on the other hand, can only write to the mailslot.

If a program on the machine RED_MACHINE creates the mailslot \\.\MAILSLOT-\WNET\NICESLOT, then an application on BLUE_MACHINE communicates with it by opening \\RED_MACHINE\MAILSLOT\WNET\NICESLOT. The client can send broadcasts by specifying a machine name of *, or by using a LAN Manager domain name. Suppose RED_MACHINE, BLUE_MACHINE, and GREEN_MACHINE are in the domain RGB. BLUE_MACHINE can send a message to all of them using the mailslot \\RGB\MAILSLOT\WNET\MAILSLOT. If BLACK_MACHINE, WHITE_MACHINE, and GRAY_MACHINE are also on the network, but in a different domain, they will not receive the message. However, if BLUE_MACHINE opens the mailslot *\MAILSLOT-\WNET\NICESLOT, then all the other stations will receive its messages.

GetMailslotInfo() can be used in a polling thread to determine if there are messages available for reading. If there is a message, it reports the amount of memory needed to fetch it.

```
BOOL APIENTRY GetMailslotInfo(HANDLE hMailslot, LPDWORD lpMaxMessageSize,
                    LPDWORD lpMailslotSize, LPDWORD lpNextSize,
                    LPDWORD lpMessageCount, LPDWORD lpReadTimeout);
```

lpMaxMessageSize, *lpMailslotSize*, and *lpReadTimeout* return the corresponding values passed to CreateMailslot(). *lpNextSize* returns the size of the next message; MAILSLOT-_NO_MESSAGE indicates that no message is waiting. *lpMessageCount* reports the number of messages available.

The value of GetMailslotInfo() is that you can determine if data is available to read, and know exactly how much memory you need. This is how a polling thread would be implemented:

Call GetMailslotInfo()

If *lpNextSize* is not MAILSLOT_NO_MESSAGE, allocate the memory and call ReadFile() to retrieve the message.

If GetMailslotInfo() fails, terminate the thread.

Here is a code fragment that creates a mailslot, then spins off a thread to read messages:

```
HANDLE  hMailslot;
NPARGS *lpNPArgs;
DWORD   dwThreadID;
extern  HWND hNotifyWnd;

lpNPArgs = (NPARGS *) GlobalAllocPtr(GHND, sizeof (NPARGS));
hMailslot = CreateMailslot("\\\\.\\MAILSLOT\\WNET\\NICESLOT",
                           4096, 4096, MAILSLOT_WAIT_FOREVER, NULL);
NPArgs.hPipe = hMailslot;
NPArgs.hNotifyWnd = hNotifyWnd;
CreateThread(NULL, 0, MailslotServerFunc, &NPArgs, NULL, &dwThreadID);
```

The thread calls GetMailslotInfo() until it fails.

```
DWORD MailslotServerFunc(LPVOID lpParameter)
{
   NPARGS *lpNPArgs = (NPARGS *) lpParameter;
   DWORD   dwMessageSize, dwBytesRead;
   LPBYTE  lpBuffer;

   while (GetMailslotInfo(lpNPArgs->hPipe, NULL, NULL,
                          &dwMessageSize, NULL, NULL))
     {
     if (dwMessageSize != MAILSLOT_NO_MESSAGE)
        {
        lpBuffer = GlobalAlloc(GHND, dwMessageSize);
        dwBytesRead = 0;
        if (ReadFile(lpNPArgs->hPipe, lpBuffer, dwMessageSize,
                 &dwBytesRead, NULL))
           PostMessage(lpNPArgs->hNotifyWnd, WMU_PACKET_RECEIVED,
                   0, (LPARAM) lpBuffer);
        }
     }
   ExitThread(0);
}
```

The Windows NT Remote Procedure Call Compiler

The Windows NT SDK includes a Remote Procedure Call (RPC) compiler, which is a tool for building client-server applications. With remote procedure calls, a client application makes what it thinks is a local function call, but it actually invokes a stub routine that communicates with a server application over the network. The server processes the function call, then returns a value to the calling application. The client application receives the value of the function call. The fact that the function is actually executed on a remote machine is entirely transparent to the client application.

The Open Systems Foundation (OSF) has developed an architecture for distributed applications, called the Distributed Computing Environment (DCE). Part of this architecture is a specification for a Remote Procedure Call definition language, called the Network Interface Definition Language (IDL). The Windows NT Remote Procedure Call compiler supports Microsoft's version of this language, the Microsoft Interface Definition Language

(MIDL). The purpose of this language is to allow developers to state specifications for remote procedure calls in a C-like language. The compiler then generates C source files that implement the stub functions on the client and server sides. This tool greatly facilitates the development of client-server applications, and frees developers from having to write network code of their own.

In Chapter 2, I developed functions that I referred to as remote procedure calls—WNetSendMessage(), WNetPostMessage(), and WNetFindWindow(). In a sense, Microsoft's Remote Procedure Call interface should be spelled with a capital RPC, and mine with a little rpc. Microsoft's RPC interface is an industry-standard foundation for distributed applications using the client-server model. My remote procedure calls are intended to distribute Windows applications horizontally by the simple, but powerful, expedient of extending the Windows message-passing paradigm. The remote procedure calls I have defined are specifically tailored to this purpose. A natural next step would be to add more functions, so that my remote procedure call API would become a means for a Windows application on one station to invoke Windows functions on another.

Other Win32 Function Groups

Finally, there are several function groups in the Win32 API that can operate remotely. We have already encountered some of them—CreateFile(), ReadFile(), and WriteFile(). These functions can access files on remote machines in two ways: by referring to them using a full UNC name (\\REMOTE\PUBLIC\123.EXE), and by referring to them using a drive that is redirected to a remote machine (F:\123.EXE)

The other function groups that will work remotely are the Printing, Communications, Error Logging, and Security groups. They work in exactly the same manner as the File functions. The fact that the device they access resides on another machine is transparent to the application that makes the calls.

CHAPTER ■ 14

Windows for Workgroups

Overview

My initial exposure to Windows for Workgroups left me unimpressed. I was expecting for Microsoft to add some powerful networking capabilities to Windows, and Windows for Workgroups, I thought, merely added some basic MS-Net capabilities to Windows without giving us a powerful distributed platform.

I was wrong. Although it is true that Windows for Workgroups amounts to MS-Net for Windows, it is a significant enhancement to the Windows environment, particularly for end users. And it is precisely the horizontal nature of MS-Net that makes Windows for Workgroups such an important advance.

Windows for Workgroups provides only peer-to-peer networking. All stations on the network are equal; there is no division of labor between workstations and file servers. Users can make portions of their directory structure, printers, and modems publicly available. In MS-Net, LAN Manager, and Windows for Workgroups, this creates what is called a "share." In Windows for Workgroups, the user can share directories by selecting the *Share As...* option on File Manager's Disk menu, shown in Figure 14-1.

Figure 14-1. File Manager Disk Menu

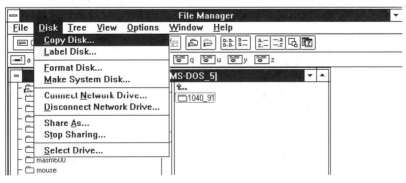

This is turn presents the dialog box shown in Figure 14-2.

Figure 14-2. File Manager Share As... Dialog Box

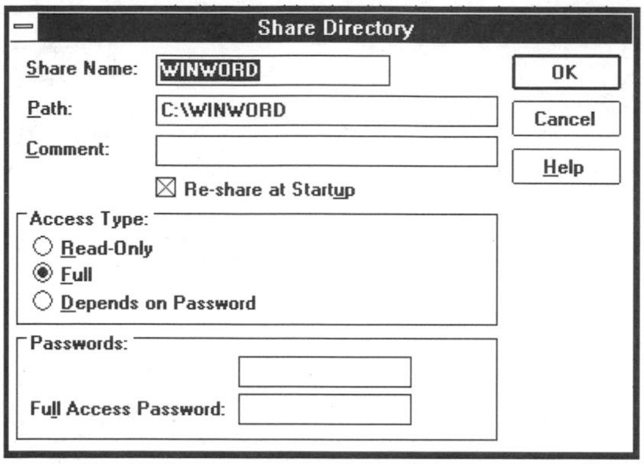

```
┌─ Share Directory ──────────────────────────┐
│ Share Name: [WINWORD]            [  OK  ]   │
│ Path:       [C:\WINWORD]         [ Cancel ] │
│ Comment:    [          ]         [  Help  ] │
│        ☒ Re-share at Startup                │
│ ┌─Access Type:─────────────────────┐        │
│ │ ○ Read-Only                      │        │
│ │ ◉ Full                           │        │
│ │ ○ Depends on Password            │        │
│ └──────────────────────────────────┘        │
│ ┌─Passwords:───────────────────────┐        │
│ │              [          ]         │        │
│ │ Full Access Password: [        ]  │        │
│ └──────────────────────────────────┘        │
└──────────────────────────────────────────────┘
```

Users on other machines can connect to shared resources. If the user on the machine RED_MACHINE shares the directory C:\PUBLIC under the share name PUBLIC, a user on BLUE_MACHINE can connect to PUBLIC by associating a drive letter with it. This is done using the *Connect Network Drive...* option on File Manager's Disk menu. This calls the WNetConnectDialog() function in the network driver; it puts up the dialog box shown in Figure 14-3.

Figure 14-3. File Manager Connect Network Drive... Dialog Box

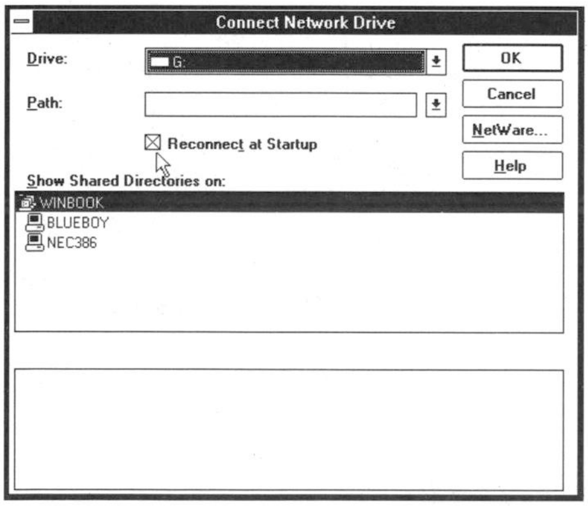

```
┌─ Connect Network Drive ──────────────────┐
│ Drive: [ G:        ▼]      [  OK  ]       │
│ Path:  [           ▼]      [ Cancel ]     │
│        ☒ Reconnect at Startup [NetWare...]│
│ Show Shared Directories on:  [  Help  ]   │
│ ┌──────────────────────────────┐          │
│ │ 🖥 WINBOOK                    │          │
│ │ 🖥 BLUEBOY                    │          │
│ │ 🖥 NEC386                     │          │
│ └──────────────────────────────┘          │
│ ┌──────────────────────────────┐          │
│ │                              │          │
│ └──────────────────────────────┘          │
└────────────────────────────────────────────┘
```

The NetWare... button that you see in this figure appears automatically when you have a NetWare server on your network.

Shared resources can be configured to require different passwords for read-only and read-write access. Do this by selecting the Depends on Password radio button shown in Figure 14-2, then specify different passwords for the two levels of access.

Once one user is connected to another user's computer, she can use any files in the shared portion of the disk. She can also copy and move files in File Manager, either using menu options or drag and drop. Thus, file transfer between workstations is the same operation as copying a file from drive C to drive A. This looks like an incremental improvement, but is in fact a powerful enhancement; it is exactly the right way to do network file transfer under Windows. The user can also run programs on the host machine.

Like MS-Net, Windows for Workgroups has no concept of user accounts; each computer is identified by a unique NetBIOS name. Like MS-Net and LAN Manager, Windows for Workgroups uses NetBIOS as its transport protocol. It also supports Novell's IPX/SPX with two additional drivers (MSIPX.SYS and MSIPX.COM) and the NetWare workstation shell (NETX.COM). All three of these files ship with Windows for Workgroups.

The effect of Windows for Workgroups is to bring networking out of the closet (the one where you keep your file server) and into the cubicle. For small shops that don't need the power of a full-featured network operating system, Windows for Workgroups provides links between stations that can greatly enhance productivity. Large installations can also benefit: it now becomes possible to share data and programs without a file server acting as an intermediary.

End-User Connectivity

Besides giving them the ability to share resources, Windows for Workgroups provides end users several tools that take advantage of the network. The most important are MS-Mail (MSMAIL.EXE), an electronic mail system; Schedule+ (SCHDPLUS.EXE), which allows users to set up appointments and meetings with each other and view each other's appointment books; Winchat (WINCHAT.EXE), which lets users have on-line, over-the-network conversations; and a network-aware Clipbook Viewer (CLIPBRD.EXE), which allows users on different stations to share clipboard items. Through the Messaging API (MAPI), which we will look at in this chapter, other Windows applications can easily mail files to other users on the network.

Although it is transparent to end users (as it should be), another feature that provides some powerful functionality is distributed DDE and OLE. This means that applications can obtain services from applications running on other stations. This opens up many possibilities for true distributed computing.

Multiple Networks

Like Windows NT, Windows for Workgroups allows multiple network providers. In particular, you can connect your workstations to NetWare and LAN Manager servers. This introduces some new programming considerations, and a new set of functions, the MNet() (multiple-network) API.

Source Documentation

Windows for Workgroups was released as this book went to press. However, the Software Development Kit is still in beta, and the documentation was only available as files downloaded from CompuServe. If the SDK has not been released yet, you can obtain these files from the Windows 3.1 SDK Addendum section of the WINEXT forum. You may have to request access by sending an E-mail note to Internet address cisbeta@microsoft.com. The files you need are SDKWDC.ZIP (Word for Windows format), SDKTDC.ZIP (text format), and SDKFLS.ZIP (header files and import libraries).

The Network Driver (WFWNET.DRV)

The Windows for Workgroups network driver supports the same functions as those discussed in Chapter 9. It has its own version of the dialog boxes. Most of them do not differ markedly from the LAN Manager ones we've previously seen, so they will be illustrated only when there is an important difference. We have already seen the WNetConnect-Dialog() dialog box. There are also some new dialog boxes that we have not seen before.

In Chapter 9, I mentioned that many of the WNet functions in the network driver are exported from USER.EXE. At the time, I chose not to take advantage of this fact, as it is an undocumented feature. With Windows for Workgroups, however, this is the recommended procedure. The stubs in USER.EXE provide support for multiple networks; you do not get this support if you call the driver routines directly. Not all of the Windows for Workgroups functions have front ends in USER.EXE; only those that are available in Windows 3.1 are found there. These are the functions documented in Chapter 9.

The driver demo program in Appendix C demonstrates Windows for Workgroups driver calls. It links with an import library generated from USER.EXE, USER.LIB and are created from WFWNET.DRV, WFWNET.LIB.

Tables 14-1 and 14-2 list the network functions in USER.EXE and WFWNET.DRV. The LFN (long filename) functions are exported from WFWNET.DRV, but I do not include them in Table 14-2. I also omit functions that are becoming obsolete.

Table 14-1. Network Functions Exported from USER.EXE

Function
WNetAbortJob
WNetAddConnection
WNetBrowseDialog
WNetCancelConnection
WNetCancelJob
WNetCloseJob
WNetConnectDialog
WNetConnectionDialog
WNetDeviceMode
WNetDirectoryNotify
WNetDisconnectDialog
WNetErrorText
WNetGetCaps
WNetGetConnection
WNetGetDirectoryType
WNetGetError
WNetGetErrorText
WNetGetPropertyText
WNetGetUser

Table 14-1. Network Functions Exported from USER.EXE (cont.)

Function

WNetHoldJob
WNetLockQueueData
WNetOpenJob
WNetPropertyDialog
WNetReleaseJob
WNetRestoreConnection
WNetSetJobCopies
WNetUnlockQueueData
WNetUnwatchQueue
WNetViewQueueDialog
WNetWatchQueue
WNetWriteJob

Table 14-2. Additional Network Functions in WFWNET.DRV

Function

I_AutoLogon
I_ChangeCachePassword
I_ChangePassword
I_ConnectDialog
I_ConnectionDialog
I_Logoff
MNetGetlastTarget
MNetGetNetInfo
MNetGetResourceNet
MNetNetworkEnum
MNetSetNextTarget
WNetCachePassword
WNetEnumCachedPasswords
WNetExitConfirm
WNetGetCachedPassword
WNetGetLastConnection
WNetGetShareCount
WNetGetShareName
WNetGetSharePath
WNetRemoveCachedPassword
WNetServerBrowseDialog
WNetSetDefaultDrive
WNetShareAsDialog
WNetSharesDialog
WNetStopShareDialog

These functions are documented in the files BASICS.DOC, WFWAPI.DOC, and WFWSTRC.DOC (Word for Windows format), and BASICS.TXT, WFWAPI.TXT, and WFWSTRC.TXT (text format).

WNetGetCaps()

It is now documented that you can get the instance handle of the network driver by linking to WNetGetCaps() in USER.EXE, then calling it with the argument 0xFFFF. Calling WNetGetCaps(0xFFFF) replaces the instructions shown in earlier chapters: GetPrivateProfileString() to get the name of the driver file, then LoadLibrary() to retrieve its handle. However, this only works if you link to USER.WNetGetCaps. The WNetGetCaps() in the network driver itself does not recognize the argument 0xFFFF.

You can detect whether you are running under Windows for Workgroups by calling WNetGetCaps() with the argument WNNC_NET_TYPE, as we have done before. Previously, we tested the high byte of the return value. If the WNNC_NET_MultiNet bit is not set, then the high byte does indeed tell you what the underlying network operating system is. However, if this bit is set, then the low byte tells you what subnetworks you are running on. More than one of the bits in the low byte can be set. Possible values are:

```
WNNC_SUBNET_NONE              0x0000
WNNC_SUBNET_MSNet             0x0001
WNNC_SUBNET_LanMan            0x0002
WNNC_SUBNET_WinWorkgroups     0x0004
WNNC_SUBNET_NetWare           0x0008
WNNC_SUBNET_Vines             0x0010
WNNC_SUBNET_Other             0x0080
```

Each subnetwork has its own driver file. The primary driver is the one indicated by the NETWORK.DRV setting in the [boot] section of SYSTEM.INI. Any additional drivers are designated in secondnet= settings. The Windows for Workgroups driver (WFWNET.DRV) includes functions that allow you to scan and target the subnetworks, as we will see.

Incidentally, in Chapter 2 I looked for Windows for Workgroups by checking for network types WNNC_NET_WFW, which I defined as 0x8004, and WNNC_NET_WFW_NW, defined as 0x800C. Although this works, it is logically incorrect. The documentation that this chapter is based on did not become available until after Chapter 2 was committed to print.

The Connection Dialogs

The connection dialogs are those presented by WNetConnectDialog() and WNetConnectionDialog(). The driver specification states that a network driver should support one or the other of these functions. If it supports WNetConnectDialog(), then WNetDisconnectDialog() is used to terminate a network connection. Otherwise, WNetConnectionDialog() serves both to connect and disconnect network resources.

These functions are still exported from both USER.EXE and WFWNET.DRV. The latter file adds the functions I_ConnectDialog() and I_ConnectionDialog(). I have not been able to determine the difference between the two; the I_ functions call the corresponding WNet function in the driver. One thing I have observed, though: in order to get full support for multiple networks, you must call the function exported from USER.EXE, either WNetConnectDialog() or WNetConnectionDialog(). In the dialog box shown in Figure 14-3, there is a button labeled *NetWare....* This button does not appear if you call the driver functions directly. If you click this button, it calls WNetConnectDialog() in the NetWare driver (NETWARE.DRV).

Windows for Workgroups introduces a further enhancement. You can bypass the first connection dialog box and target the one for a specific secondary network. You do this using the multiple-network functions, which I discuss later in this chapter. Then, when you call WNetConnectDialog() or WNetConnectionDialog(), it immediately presents the dialog box for the network you have selected.

WNetGetUser()
WNetGetUser() returns a zero-length string for Windows for Workgroups. The documentation states that it will return the correct value if you target the correct network first. However, I have not observed this to be the case. There are two ways to retrieve this information. The [Network] section of SYSTEM.INI has two settings: ComputerName= and UserName=. You can query either of these by calling GetPrivateProfileString():

```
char szUserName[128];

GetPrivateProfileString("NETWORK", "USERNAME", "",
                   szUserName, sizeof (szUserName), "SYSTEM.INI");
```

You can also call NDdeGetNodeName(), one of the networked DDE extensions provided by Windows for Workgroups.

```
UINT WINAPI NDdeGetNodeName(LPSTR lpszName, DWORD dwNameLength);
```

I use NDdeGetNodeName() in the demo program in Appendix C.

WNetServerBrowseDialog()
WNetServerBrowseDialog() is a new function in WFWNET.DRV that lets you browse other stations on the network. Here is its prototype:

```
WORD API WNetServerBrowseDialog(HWND hWndParent,
        LPSTR lpszSectionName, LPSTR lpszRemote,
        UINT cchRemoteLength, DWORD dwFlags);
```

hWndParent is the handle of the window that will own the dialog box. *lpszSection* is a section in WIN.INI containing the names of the computers you have connected to most recently. It may be passed as NULL. Indeed, my WIN.INI has no such list. *lpszRemote* will return the name of the computer that the user selects, with \\ prepended to it. *cchRemoteLength* is the length of the buffer at *lpszRemote*. *dwFlags* should be passed as 0L. Figure 14-4 shows you the dialog box. The sample program in Appendix C demonstrates the use of this function.

Share-Related Functions
Because Windows for Workgroups allows users to share their local resources, the network driver now includes functions to handle resource sharing.

WNetShareAsDialog()   WNetShareAsDialog() presents the dialog box shown in Figure 14-2. Here is its prototype:

```
WORD API WNetShareAsDialog(HWND hWndParent, WORD wType,
                   LPSTR lpszShare);
```

Figure 14-4. WNetServerBrowseDialog() Dialog Box

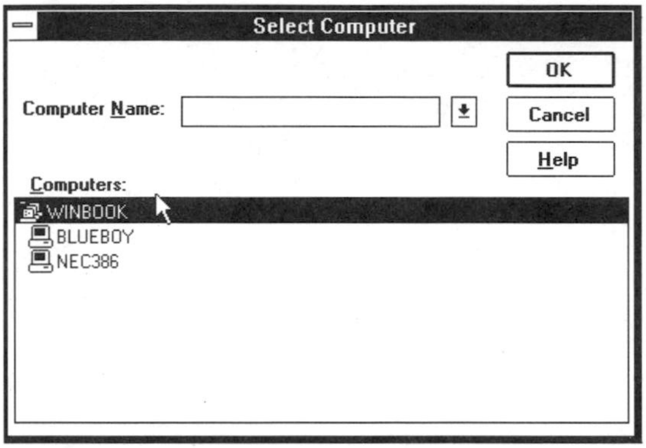

As always with these dialog boxes, *hWndParent* designates the window that owns the dialog box. *wType* is the type of resource you are sharing. WNBD_CONN_DISKTREE indicates a directory; WNBD_CONN_PRINTQ, a printer. When *wType* is WNBD_CONN_DISKTREE, *lpszShare* passes the name of the directory you want to share. When the user clicks the OK button, Windows for Workgroups creates the share. This function, therefore, gives you what you need to add directory sharing to an application.

The user can share a printer by selecting the *Share Printer As...* option on Print Manager's Printer menu, shown in Figure 14-5.

Figure 14-5. Print Manager Printer Menu

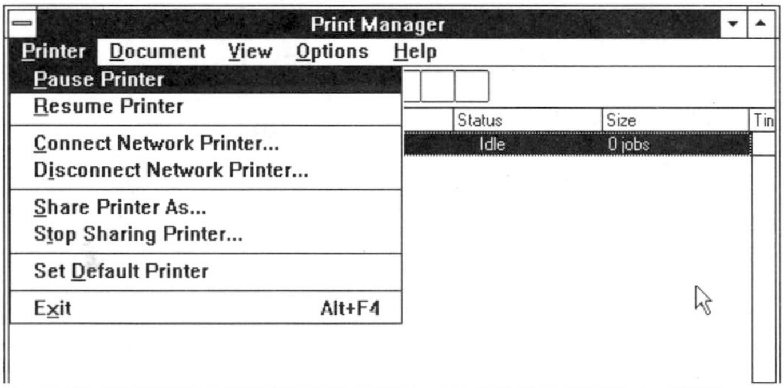

Figure 14-6 shows the dialog box that Print Manager presents.

When *wType* is WNBD_CONN_PRINTQ, the *lpszShare* argument can be an empty string, in which case the dialog box will have no fields filled in, or you can pass three contiguous null-terminated strings. The first part is the device name ("LPT1", "LPT2"); the second part is the printer name ("IBM Proprinter"); the third is a comment about the share ("shared as IBM"). The third string is followed by two null terminators. To show the dialog box that you see in Figure 14-6, call WNetShareAsDialog() as follows:

```
WNetShareAsDialog(GetActiveWindow(), WNBD_CONN_PRINTQ,
    "LPT2\0"
    "IBMProprinter\0"
    "shared as IBM\0");
```

Figure 14-6. Print Manager Share Printer As... Dialog Box

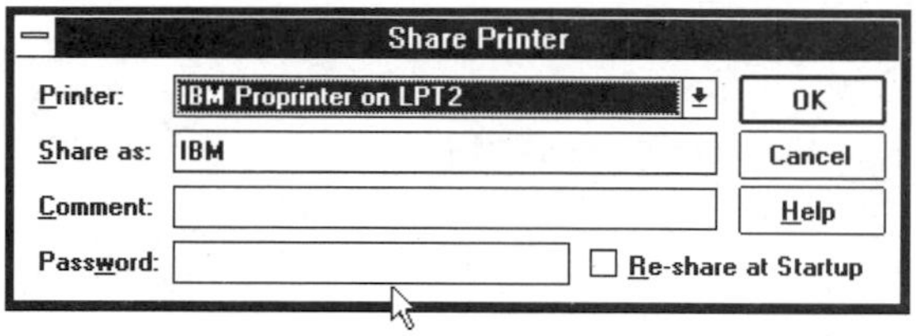

WNetShareAsDialog( ) gives you a standard dialog box for sharing local resources. The Windows for Workgroups network driver also provides several functions that return information about shared resources: WNetGetShareCount( ), WNetGetShareName( ), and WNetGetSharePath( ).

WNetGetShareCount()   WNetGetShareCount( ) tells you how many resources of a given type you are sharing. It takes one argument—a WORD indicating the type of resource you are interested in. Again, this is either WNBD_CONN_DISKTREE or WNBD_CONN_PRINTQ.

```
WORD API WNetGetShareCount(WORD wType);
```

WNetGetShareName() / WNetGetSharePath()   These functions are mirror images of each other. They both take the same set of arguments.

```
WORD API WNetGetShareName(LPSTR lpszLocalDir, LPSTR lpszShareName,
                          WORD wNameLength);

WORD API WNetGetSharePath(LPSTR lpszShareName, LPSTR lpszLocalDir,
                          WORD wDirLength);
```

WNetGetShareName( ) gives you the full UNC name (\\<machine name>\<share name>) under which a local directory is being shared. WNetGetSharePath( ) gives you the local directory corresponding to a share name. In each case, the first argument is the input string, the second is the output string, and the third is the length of the output buffer.

There is a slight inconsistency, however. If the share name is passed in full UNC form, WNetGetSharePath( ) returns WN_BAD_NETNAME. You must strip the computer name from the share name first. Below is a code fragment that shares the Windows directory (or lets the user share it) by calling WNetShareAsDialog( ), retrieves the share name using WNetGetShareName( ), and turns the share name back into the path name using WNetGetSharePath( ).

```
char szWinDir[144];
char szShareName[144];
char szSharePath[144];
LPBYTE lpTemp;

GetWindowsDirectory(szWinDir, sizeof (szWinDir));
if (WNetShareAsDialog(GetActiveWindow(), WNBD_CONN_DISKTREE, szWinDir)
    == WN_SUCCESS)
    {
    WNetGetShareName(szWinDir, szShareName, sizeof (szShareName));
    // szShareName now has share name in full UNC format, for example,
    // \\BLUEBOY\WIN31
```

```
lpTemp = szShareName + (lstrlen(szShareName) - 1);
while (*lpTemp != '\\')
    --lpTemp;
++lpTemp;
// lpTemp now pointing to "WIN31"
WNetGetSharePath(lpTemp, szSharePath, sizeof (szSharePath));
// szSharePath now contains C:\WIN31
}
```

WNetStopShareDialog()

```
WORD API WNetStopShareDialog(HWND hParentWnd, WORD wType,
                              LPSTR lpszName);
```

This dialog box lets the user stop sharing a resource. *wType* is either WNBD_CONN-_DISKTREE or WNBD_CONN_PRINTQ. *lpszName* is the name of the shared resource.

You can access this dialog box from File Manager's Disk menu by selecting the *Stop Sharing...* option. Figure 14-7 shows what it looks like.

Figure 14-7. File Manager Stop Sharing... Dialog Box.

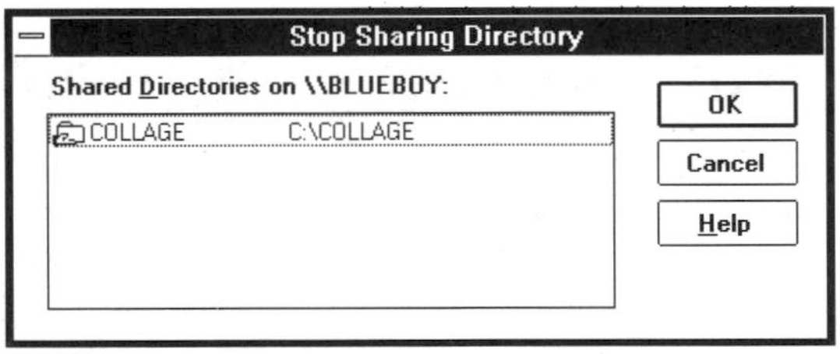

Print Manager displays the Stop Sharing dialog box when you select *Stop Sharing Printer...* from its Printer menu.

There is one other function for handling shares, NetShareEnum(). It is not in the network driver: rather, it resides in NETAPI.DLL, which contains the LAN Manager functions that are now part of the Windows for Workgroups API. It only enumerates shares on other machines, not on the local machine.

WNetDirectoryNotify()

In Chapter 9, I stated that this function amounts to a no-op. Under Windows for Workgroups, this is no longer true. Here is its prototype again:

```
WORD API WNetDirectoryNotify(HWND hWndParent, LPSTR lpszPath,
                              WORD wOperation);
```

wOperation can be either WNDN_MKDIR (create the directory), WNDN_RMDIR (delete the directory), or WNDN_MVDIR (rename the directory). Deleting or renaming a shared directory affects any users on other machines who connected to that directory. Therefore, WNetDirectoryNotify() warns the user when she attempts either of these operations, and allows her to change her mind.

WNetDeviceMode()

Windows for Workgroups presents its own device mode dialog box (shown in Figure 14-8 on the following page) when you select the Networks icon in Control Panel.

Each of the buttons on the lower left-hand side of the screen presents its own dialog box.

Figure 14-8. Windows for Workgroups Device Mode Dialog Box.

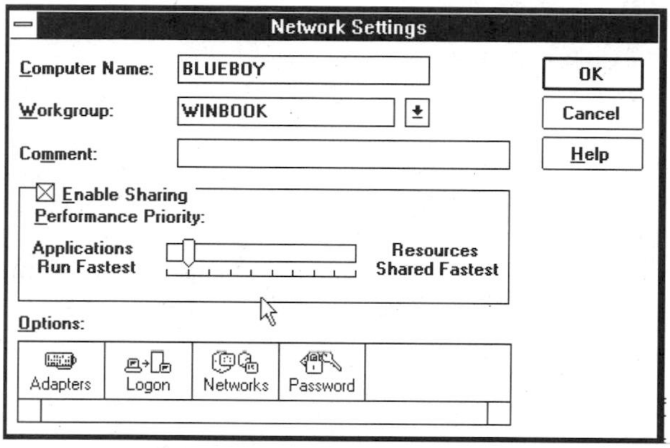

Exit Warnings

Windows for Workgroups has a function that warns users when they exit from Windows. If people on other computers are using resources the user has shared, exiting knocks them off unceremoniously. The user can change his mind at this point. The function is WNetExitConfirm( ).

```
WORD API WNetExitConfirm(HWND hWndParent, WORD wExitType);
```

wExitType has three possible values: EXIT_CONFIRM, EXIT_EXITING, and EXIT-_CANCELED. When *wExitType* is EXIT_CONFIRM, WNetExitConfirm() checks to see if any users are connected to resources you are sharing, and if they are, it presents the dialog box shown in Figure 14-9.

Figure 14-9. WNetExitConfirm() Dialog Box

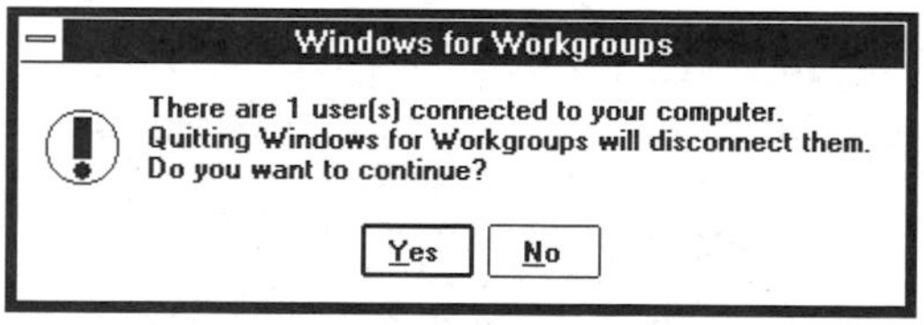

If the user says yes, it will further warn you with the dialog box shown in Figure 14-10 if they are using any files.

If the user answers yes, WNetConfirmExit() returns WN_SUCCESS (0). Otherwise, it returns WN_CANCEL (0x000C). Answering yes does not by itself cause the remote user to be disconnected from the shared resource; the program that calls WNetConfirmExit() must decide for itself how to handle the situation.

WNetGetLastConnection()

```
WORD API WNetGetLastConnection(WORD wType, LPWORD lpwIndex);
```

Figure 14-10.

WNetGetLastConnection( ) retrieves the index of the last network device connected to by a call to WNetAddConnection( ), or by using the connection dialog boxes. *wType* can be either WNTYPE_DRIVE or WNTYPE_PRINTER. *lpwIndex* returns the index. For drives, A: is zero, B: is one, etc. For printers, LPT1 is 1, LPT2 is 2. If the last connection cannot be determined, **lpwIndex* will be set to 0xFFFF.

WNetSetDefaultDrive( )

```
WORD API WNetSetDefaultDrive(WORD wDrive);
```

This function has nothing to do with setting the default drive for disk operations. Its sole purpose is to select a network drive as the default when you call WNetDisconnect-Dialog( ). Ordinarily, the drive listbox has the first item selected. If you call WNetSet-DefaultDrive( ) first, the listbox item containing the drive you indicate will be highlighted.

Here is a code fragment from Appendix C that uses WNetGetLastConnection( ) and WNetSetDefaultDrive( ) to target the drive last connected to:

```
WORD wDrive;

WNetGetLastConnection(WNTYPE_DRIVE, &wDrive);

// wDrive will be -1 if there was no last
// connection
if (wDrive != (WORD) (-1))
   WNetSetDefaultDrive(wDrive);
```

Multiple-Network Functions

These functions are provided to allow you to determine the networks that your station is attached to, and to target a specific network prior to performing other network operations, like connecting to a network drive. The functions are described in Table 14-3.

The functions I have found most useful are MNetNetworkEnum( ), MNetGetNet-Info( ), and MNetSetNextTarget( ).

Table 14-3. Multiple-Network Functions in WFWNET.DRV

Function	Description
MNetGetLastTarget	Get handle of network that was last target of WNetAdd-Connection( ), WNetGetConnection( ), or WNetCancelConnection( )
MNetGetNetInfo	Retrieves driver instance handle, button label, and status (primary/secondary) of a given network
MNetGetResourceNet	Gets handle of network where a given resource resides
MNetNetworkEnum	Enumerates attached networks
MNetSetNextTarget	Targets a specific network

None of the header files delivered with the beta version of the SDK have prototypes or defined constants needed for these functions. Fortunately, the prototypes are included in WFWAPI.DOC and WFWAPI.TXT, and only one constant is required. A little experimentation reveals how the constant (MNM_NET_PRIMARY) should be defined (it's one).

MNetNetworkEnum()

```
WORD API MNetNetworkEnum(HANDLE FAR *lpHandle);
```

MNetNetworkEnum() enumerates attached networks. These are networks indicated in the [boot] section of SYSTEM.INI, either by network.drv= (the primary network) or secondnet.drv= settings. To use MNetNetworkEnum(), set *lpHandle to zero, then call it as long as it returns WN_SUCCESS. The handle returned is not the instance handle of the network driver; that is retrieved by MNetGetNetInfo().

MNetGetNetInfo()

```
WORD API MNetGetNetInfo(HANDLE hNetwork, LPWORD lpwNetInfo,
                  LPSTR  lpszButtonText, LPINT lpnTextLength,
                  HINSTANCE FAR *lpInstance);
```

hNetwork is a handle returned by either MNetNetworkEnum() or MNetGetLast-Target(). *lpwNetInfo* tells you whether this is the primary network (MNM_NET_PRIMARY) or one of the secondary ones (zero). *lpszButtonText* returns the text that appears, for instance, on a multiple-network connection dialog box. You can search for this text if you want to find a specific network, but you need to be aware of things like ampersands and dots. For example, the text returned for NetWare is "&NetWare...". *lpnTextLength* points to an integer variable that tells how long the buffer at *lpszButtonText* is on input, and contains the length of the button text on output. Finally, *lpInstance* returns the instance handle of the network driver corresponding to the network. This can be used to get pointers to functions in that particular driver.

As I said earlier, you can use the multiple-network APIs to target a specific network before you call a function like WNetConnectDialog(). This bypasses the screen that normally appears first (the primary network's dialog box), and goes directly to the network you request. The function that targets a specific network is MNetSetNextTarget().

MNetSetNextTarget()

```
WORD API MNetSetNextTarget(HANDLE hNetwork);
```

MNetSetNextTarget() specifies the network that will be the target of an ensuing WNet-GetCaps(), WNetDeviceMode(), WNetConnectDialog(), WNetConnectionDialog(), WNetBrowseDialog(), or WNetGetUser() call (assuming that you are linking to USER-.EXE for these functions). *hNetwork* is a handle returned by MNetNetworkEnum() or MNetGetLastTarget().

Here is a function, SetWFWNetworkByType(), that targets the first primary or non-primary network, depending on the lone argument (*bPrimary*) to the function:

```
void SetWFWNetworkByType(BOOL bPrimary)
{
   HANDLE hNetwork = 0;
   WORD   wNetInfo;
```

```
while (MNetNetworkEnum(&hNetwork) == WN_SUCCESS)
    {
    MNetGetNetInfo(hNetwork, &wNetInfo, NULL, NULL, NULL);

    // bPrimary will be either one or zero
    // wNetInfo will likewise be one or zero
    // If the two are equal, we've found our network

    if (bPrimary == (BOOL) wNetInfo)
        {
        MNetSetNextTarget(hNetwork);
        break;
        }
    }
}
```

The function SetWFWNetworkByName() selects a network based on the button text. It returns WN_SUCCESS if it finds the name, and WN_BAD_NETNAME otherwise.

```
WORD SetWFWNetworkByName(LPSTR lpszButtonText)
{
    HANDLE hNetwork = 0;
    char   szButtonText[80];
    int    nButtonLength = sizeof (szButtonText);

    while (MNetNetworkEnum(&hNetwork) == WN_SUCCESS)
        {
        MNetGetNetInfo(hNetwork, NULL, szButtonText, &nButtonLength, NULL);

        if (lstrcmpi(szButtonText, lpszButtonText) == 0)
            {
            MNetSetNextTarget(hNetwork);
            return WN_SUCCESS;
            }
        }
    return WN_BAD_NETNAME;
}
```

Additional Driver Functions

WFWNET.DRV contains several additional I_ or WNet functions. These function deal with security. Windows for Workgroups requires the user to enter either a computer name or a user name, and a password, to logon to the network. This does not give him rights to any specific resources; he must still supply the required password when he connects to shared resources on other computers.

Windows for Workgroups maintains an encrypted list of the passwords a user has submitted in a .PWL file. It then uses these cached passwords in subsequent connection requests, to save the user the trouble of having to retype them. Until the user has entered a user name or computer name and a password, the cached passwords remain locked. The security functions are listed in Table 14-4:

Table 14-4. Security Functions in WFWNET.DRV

Function

I_AutoLogon
I_ChangeCachePassword
I_ChangePassword
I_Logoff
WNetCachePassword
WNetEnumCachedPasswords
WNetGetCachedPassword
WNetRemoveCachedPassword

Programming Interfaces

Besides the driver functions, Windows for Workgroups provides three important additions to the Windows networking API: the Messaging API (MAPI); functions borrowed from LAN Manager; and distributed DDE.

It continues to support the WNet() functions included in the Windows 3.1 API: WNetAddConnection(), WNetCancelConnection(), and WNetGetConnection(). It also supports NetBIOS as its built-in protocol, and the NetBIOS API discussed in Chapter 3.

MAPI

The Messaging API allows applications to easily add electronic mail capabilities. It provides a set of functions for using the Microsoft mail system. Most of the functions invoke a standard dialog box, which in turn handles the details of constructing, interpreting, and sending E-mail messages. These functions offer a very high level of service, allowing applications to become mail-enabled with a minimum of effort. Table 14-5 lists the MAPI function calls.

Table 14-5. Windows for Workgroups MAPI Functions

Function Name	Operation
MAPILogon	Logs user onto the mail system
MAPILogoff	Logs user off the mail system
MAPISendDocuments	Presents dialog box to send files to remote user
MAPISendMail	Presents dialog box to send mail to remote user
MAPISaveMail	Updates a mail message
MAPIFindNext	Scans mailbox for incoming messages
MAPIReadMail	Reads a message retrieved by MAPIFindNext()
MAPIDeleteMail	Deletes a message retrieved by MAPIFindNext()
MAPIAddress	Presents a dialog box to get list of recipients from user
MAPIDetails	Presents dialog box giving detailed information on a recipient
MAPIResolveName	Retrieves information on a user known to the MS-Mail system. May also present a dialog box asking the user to resolve an ambiguous name
MAPIFreeBuffer	Frees memory allocated by MAPIAddress(), MAPIResolveName(), and MAPIReadMail()

To use the MAPI functions in a C program, you need to use one of the three techniques we have used previously this book:

1. Call LoadLibrary() to load MAPI.DLL, then get pointers to the functions you will be using by calling GetProcAddress()
2. Create an import library from MAPI.DLL as follows:

```
IMPLIB MAPI.LIB MAPI.DLL
```

3. Declare the functions in the IMPORTS section of your .DEF file

The advantage to the first technique is that it enables you to execute MAPI functions from a macro language. This is what Word for Windows and Excel for Windows do, for instance. This is probably the most important way, and is certainly the easiest to mail-enable your application. The recommended procedure is to add a *Send...* option to your File menu. Figure 14-12 shows the File menu for Word for Windows running under Windows for Workgroups.

Figure 14-12. Word for Windows File Menu with Send... Option

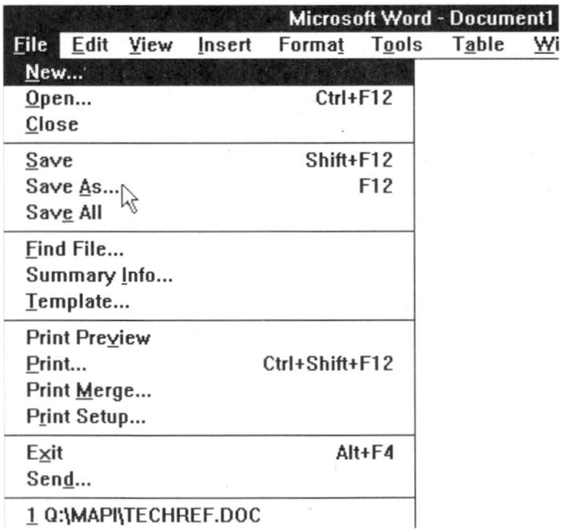

When the user selects *Send...*, you can present a dialog box asking the users if they want to send the active document, selected documents, or all open documents. Then you call the MAPI function MAPISendDocuments(), and it handles everything else for you:

```
ULONG FAR PASCAL MAPISendDocuments(ULONG ulUIParam, LPSTR lpszDelimChar,
                                   LPSTR lpszFilePaths,
                                   LPSTR lpszFileNames,
                                   ULONG ulReserved);
```

ulUIParam is the handle of the window that will own the MAPI dialog boxes, cast to a ULONG. To pass multiple file names, you build concatenated strings in *lpszFilePaths* and *lpszFileNames*. The character in *lpszDelimChar* is the delimiter. For example, to pass C:\WIN31\WRITE.EXE and C:\WIN31\WRITE.HLP, if you use a semicolon as a delimiter, then *lpszDelimChar* will be ";", *lpszFilePaths* will be "C:\WIN31\WRITE.EXE;C:\-WIN31\WRITE.HLP", and *lpszFileNames* will be "WRITE.EXE;WRITE.HLP". Notice that *lpszFileNames* and *lpszFilePaths* both include the file names. *lpszFileNames* lists the file names without their paths. If passed as empty strings or NULL pointers, no files will be transmitted, but the user can still compose an E-mail message or select files for transmission. *ulReserved* should be passed as 0L.

MAPISendDocuments() is the highest-level function in the MAPI library; a single call to it transmits all the requested files. It does this by presenting standard dialog boxes to your users, and letting them make the selections they want. It corresponds to a series of calls to the other MAPI functions, though MAPISendDocuments() may not actually be implemented that way. As we go through the dialog boxes that MAPISendDocuments() puts up, we will take a look at the underlying functions.

MAPILogon()   The first dialog box that appears is the logon dialog box, shown in Figure 14-13.

Figure 14-13. MAPI Login Dialog Box

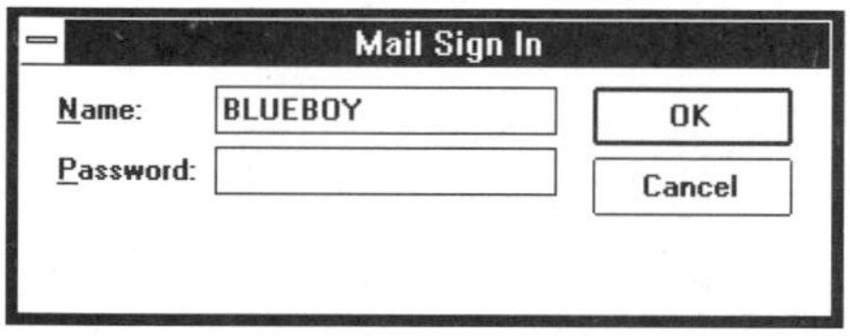

This is produced by calling MAPILogon().

```
ULONG FAR PASCAL MAPILogon(ULONG ulUIParam, LPSTR lpszName,
                    LPSTR lpszPassword,
                    FLAGS flFlags, ULONG ulReserved,
                    LPLHANDLE lplhSession);
```

ulUIParam, again, designates the window that will own the dialog box. You can use MAPILogon() to login without the dialog box by passing an explicit user name in *lpszName*. If *lpszName* is a NULL pointer or an empty string, MAPILogon() will present the logon dialog box (provided that *flFlags* is set appropriately). There are three possible settings for *flFlags*: MAPI_LOGON_UI, MAPI_NEW_SESSION, and MAPI_FORCE-_DOWNLOAD. MAPI_LOGON_UI specifies that you want the logon dialog box to be presented. MAPI_NEW_SESSION specifies that you want MAPI to create a new mail session. Otherwise, it will try to use an existing one. MAPI_FORCE_DOWNLOAD requests MAPI to immediately download new mail from the mail server. MAPILogon() returns a session handle through *lplhSession*. This handle will be used in subsequent calls to MAPI functions. The type LHANDLE is an unsigned long.

MAPISendMail()   The next screen that appears is the Send dialog box (shown in Figure 14-14). This is produced by a call to MAPISendMail(). Because we are sending a file, it comes up initially with a file attachment, indicated by the MPI.H icon in Figure 14-14.

Figure 14-14. MAPI Send Mail Dialog Box

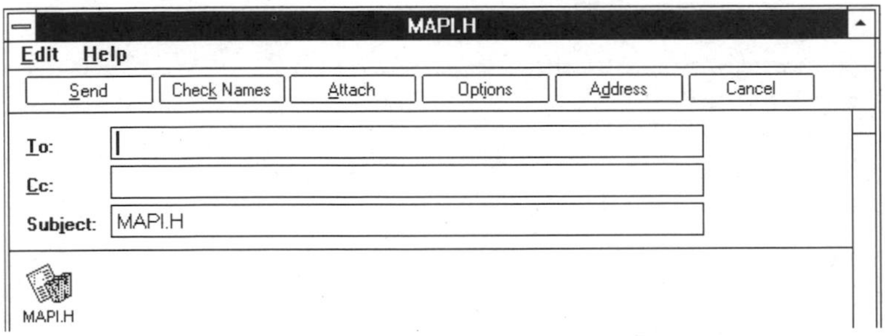

The user can enter text in the edit box, or select files for transmission by clicking the Attach button.

Here is the prototype for MAPISendMail():

```
ULONG FAR PASCAL MAPISendMail(LHANDLE lhSession, ULONG ulUIParam,
                              lpMapiMessage lpMessage, FLAGS flFlags,
                              ULONG ulReserved);
```

lhSession is the session handle returned by MAPILogon(). *lpMessage* points to a *MapiMessage* structure. Here is its type definition from MAPI.H. (You can download MAPI.H from Microsoft's MSNET forum on CompuServe.)

```
typedef struct
{
    ULONG ulReserved;               // Reserved for future use
                                    // pass as zero
    LPSTR lpszSubject;              // Message Subject
    LPSTR lpszNoteText;             // Message Text
    LPSTR lpszMessageType;          // Message Class
                                    // Normally passed as NULL
    LPSTR lpszDateReceived;         // in YYYY/MM/DD HH:MM format
    LPSTR lpszConversationID;       // conversation thread ID,
                                    // pass as NULL
    FLAGS flFlags;                  // unread,return receipt
    lpMapiRecipDesc lpOriginator;   // Originator descriptor
    ULONG nRecipCount;              // Number of recipients
    lpMapiRecipDesc lpRecips;       // Recipient descriptors
    ULONG nFileCount;               // # of file attachments
    lpMapiFileDesc lpFiles;         // Attachment descriptors
} MapiMessage, FAR * lpMapiMessage;
```

lpszSubject denotes the subject of the message; it appears in the Subject field of the dialog box in Figure 14-14. *lpszNoteText* points to the text that will constitute the message. Paragraphs in the message should be terminated with a carriage return-line feed. If *lpszNoteText* is NULL or an empty string, it is assumed to mean no message. The user can still type a message into the edit box in Figure 14-14. *flFlags* for MAPISendMail() can be zero, or can have the MAPI_RECEIPT_REQUESTED bit set to request receipt notification.

The fields from *lpOriginator* to *lpRecips* describe the message sender and recipients. You do not need to initialize the fields in these structures before you call MAPISend-

Mail(); MAPI will fill them in for you. You may, of course, but it is much easier to let the user fill them in using the MAPI dialog boxes.

The *lpFiles* field describes any file attachments. It, too, will be populated for you when you call MAPISendDocuments(). It is also filled in automatically when you read a message that has file attachments.

MAPIAddress( )   The Address button on the Send dialog box calls MAPIAddress().

```
ULONG FAR PASCAL MAPIAddress(LHANDLE lhSession, ULONG ulUIParam,
                    LPSTR lpszCaption, ULONG nEditFields,
                    LPSTR lpszLabels, ULONG nRecips,
                    lpMapiRecipDesc lpRecips, FLAGS flFlags,
                    ULONG ulReserved,
                    LPULONG lpnNewRecips,
                    lpMapiRecipDesc FAR *lppNewRecips);
```

MAPIAddress() brings up the dialog box shown in Figure 14-15.

lpszCaption is the caption that the dialog box will be given. If it is null or zero-length, the caption "Address Book" will be assigned by default. *flFlags* can be MAPI-_LOGON_UI to present the logon dialog box (if the user is not already logged on), and MAPI_NEW_SESSION to force a new logon. MAPI_NEW_SESSION will be ignored if *lhHandle* is not NULL, and represents a valid mail session. The meanings of *nEditFields* and *lpszLabels* is somewhat esoteric. Basically, pass *nEditFields* as zero if you want to prevent the user from modifying the initial recipient list (indicated by *lpRecips*). Otherwise, pass 4. *lpRecips* is an array of *MapiRecipDesc* structures that will be used to initialize the address list on the dialog box. *nRecips* is the number of entries in *lpRecips*. If *nRecips* is zero, the list is initially empty. *lpnNewRecips* and *lppNewRecips* are used to return the final list of recipients. **lpnNewRecips* reports the number of recipients in the list; the list itself is returned through *lppNewRecips*. This is a pointer to a pointer to an array of *MapiRecipDesc* structures. It includes addressees designated as primary recipients, and those getting carbon copies. To free the memory allocated, call MAPIFreeBuffer().

```
ULONG FAR PASCAL MAPIFreeBuffer(LPVOID pv);
```

pv is the pointer that MAPIAddress() placed at **lppNewRecips*.

MAPIDetails( )   The Details button in Figure 14-15 calls MAPIDetails(), which presents the dialog box shown in Figure 14-16.

```
ULONG FAR PASCAL MAPIDetails(LHANDLE lhSession, ULONG ulUIParam,
                    lpMapiRecipDesc lpRecip, FLAGS flFlags,
                    ULONG ulReserved);
```

lpRecip points to a *MapiRecipDesc* structure that describes the recipient whose details are to be displayed. *flFlags* can be MAPI_LOGON_UI or MAPI_NEW_SESSION, which mean the same thing as they did before. Another possible flag is MAPI_AB_NOMODIFY, which specifies that the dialog box should be read-only.

Figure 14-15. MAPI Address Book Dialog Box

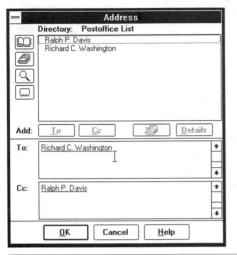

Figure 14-16. MAPI Addressee Details Dialog Box

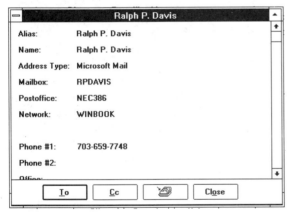

MAPIResolveName()   MAPIResolveName( ) serves two purposes: it can be used to convert a recipient name into a complete *MapiRecipDesc* structure, and it can be used to ask the user which recipient an ambiguous name should resolve to.

```
ULONG FAR PASCAL MAPIResolveName(LHANDLE lhSession, ULONG ulUIParam,
                    LPSTR lpszName, FLAGS flFlags,
                    ULONG ulReserved,
                    lpMapiRecipDesc FAR *lppRecip);
```

lpszName is the name you want resolved. *flFlags* includes the MAPI_LOGON_UI and MAPI_NEW_SESSION bits we have already seen. You can also set the MAPI_DIALOG flag, which requests presentation of a dialog box if an ambiguous name can only be resolved by user intervention, and the MAPI_AB_NOMODIFY flag, which prevents modification of any address list entries. A pointer to a fully-resolved description of the user is returned through *lppRecip*. Use MAPIFreeBuffer( ) to free it.

MAPIFindNext()   To read mail, scan incoming messages with MAPIFindNext().

```
ULONG FAR PASCAL MAPIFindNext(LHANDLE lhSession, ULONG ulUIParam,
                    LPSTR lpszMessageType,
                    LPSTR lpszSeedMessageID,
                    FLAGS flFlags, ULONG ulReserved,
                    LPSTR lpszMessageID);
```

lpszMessageType should be passed as NULL. *lpszSeedMessageID* and *lpszMessageID* should point to buffers that are at least 64 bytes long. To iterate over all messages, pass *lpszSeedMessageID* as an empty string initially. Then, before each subsequent call, take the message ID returned in *lpszMessageID* and copy it to *lpszSeedMessageID*. The value returned in *lpszMessageID* will be used as input to MAPIReadMail(), MAPIDeleteMail(), and MAPISaveMail(). *flFlags* can be MAPI_UNREAD_ONLY, to limit the scan to unread mail, and MAPI_GUARANTEE_FIFO, to read the messages in the order in which they were received.

Having obtained a message ID, you can Read, Save, or delete the message.

MAPIReadMail()   MAPIReadMail() retrieves a message from the message store.

```
ULONG FAR PASCAL MAPIReadMail(LHANDLE lhSession, ULONG ulUIParam,
                    LPSTR lpszMessageID, FLAGS flFlags,
                    ULONG ulReserved, lpMapiMessage FAR *lppMessageOut);
```

lpszMessageID must be a message ID returned by MAPIFindNext() or MAPISave-Mail(). *lppMessage* points to a FAR pointer to a *MapiMessage* structure. MAPIReadMail() allocates the memory for this structure; it must be freed by calling MAPIFreeBuffer().

The *flFlags* field controls the information read from the message. MAPI_ENVE-LOPE_ONLY reads only the header of the message. That is, it will not to copy any files that were sent, nor will it return the body of the message. MAPI_SUPPRESS_ATTACH causes MAPI to return a pointer to the message text in the *lpszNoteText* field, but not copy any attached files. If MAPI_BODY_AS_FILE is set, MAPI will not return the message text, but will write it to a temporary file. MAPI_PEEK returns the message, but does not flag it as read. It will continue to be returned by MAPIFindNext() calls that specify MAPI_UNREAD_ONLY.

MAPISaveMail()   Call MAPISaveMail() if you want to change some of the information in the message or copy it to a new message.

```
ULONG FAR PASCAL MAPISaveMail(LHANDLE lhSession, ULONG ulUIParam,
                    lpMapiMessage lpMessage, FLAGS flFlags,
                    ULONG ulReserved, LPSTR lpszMessageID);
```

lpszMessageID is the ID originally returned by MAPIFindNext(). If you pass an empty string, MAPI will create a new message and return its new ID through *lpszMessageID*. The buffer must be at least 64 bytes in length. *lpMessage* points to a *MapiMessage* structure. You can change the information in the *MapiMessage* structure after reading it with MAPIReadMail(), then save it as a new message, or replace the old one. The only supported values for *flFlags* are MAPI_LOGON_UI and MAPI_NEW_SESSION.

The message ID that MAPISaveMail() returns can be used in subsequent calls to MAPIReadMail() and MAPIDeleteMail().

If files were attached to the message, they are written to temporary files. The *lpFiles* array of the *MapiMessage* structure gives the names under which the files were saved.

MAPIDeleteMail()   MAPIDeleteMail() deletes a message fetched by MAPIFindNext(), or saved by MAPISaveMail().

```
ULONG FAR PASCAL MAPIDeleteMail(LHANDLE lhSession, ULONG ulUIParam,
                       LPSTR lpszMessageID, FLAGS flFlags,
                       ULONG ulReserved);
```

Again, *lpszMessageID* must be the ID returned by MAPIFindNext() or MAPISave-Mail(). The flags are not used and should be passed as zero.

MAPILogoff()   MAPILogoff() terminates a mail session.

```
ULONG FAR PASCAL MAPILogoff(LHANDLE lhSession, ULONG ulUIParam,
                       FLAGS flFlags,
                       ULONG ulReserved);
```

Only *lhSession* and *ulULParam* are used. As always, they are the session handle returned by MAPILogon(), and the handle of the window that will own any dialog boxes. *flFlags* and *ulReserved* should be passed as zero.

Functions Borrowed From LAN Manager

Windows for Workgroups supports most of the LAN Manager APIs by assuming the role of a DOS workstation on a LAN Manager network. The majority of APIs are supported only on a LAN Manager network, although a few of them are entirely independent of LAN Manager. All of the supported functions work exactly as they are documented in the *Lan Manager Programmer's Reference*. You can use the same header files and import libraries. In fact, source code written for LAN Manager will work unchanged under Windows for Workgroups. For example, the LAN Manager version of WNetEnumServers() presented in Chapter 11 works exactly as is under Windows for Workgroups—it doesn't even need to be recompiled. The only difference is that it links dynamically to the Windows for Workgroups version of NETAPI.DLL instead of the LAN Manager Version.

In the first beta release of the Windows for Workgroups SDK, only a few of these functions were documented. Table 14-6 lists them.

Table 14-6. LAN Manager Functions Documented under Windows for Workgroups

Function Name	Operation
NetHandleGetInfo	Get information on a named pipe
NetHandleSetInfo	Set information on a named pipe
DosReadAsynchNmPipe	Do asynchronous read of a named pipe
DosWriteAsynchNmPipe	Do asynchronous write to a named pipe
DosMailSlotInfo	Get mailslot information (second-class mailslots only)
NetServerEnum2	Enumerate connected machines
NetShareEnum	Enumerate shared resources (remote machines only)
NetWkstaGetInfo	Get information about the local computer

Table 14-6. LAN Manager Functions Documented under Windows for Workgroups

Function Name	Operation
NetWkstaSetUID2	Log user on or off the network; runs their login script during logon
DosPrintQEnum	Enumerate printer queues (remote machines only)
DosPrintQGetInfo	Get information about a particular print queue on a server (remote machines only)

These are identical to their LAN Manager counterparts; refer to the LAN Manager documentation for complete information (*LAN Manager Programmer's Reference*). Several of these functions have documented limitations under DOS; these same limitations apply under Windows for Workgroups. For instance, NetShareEnum() and DosPrintQEnum() will only enumerate resources on a remote Windows for Workgroups machine, and will fail if you try to use them on the local machine.

There is one important API set that is available, but documented only in the most recent SDk before release—second-class mailslots. Mailslots are a LAN Manager datagram mechanism. First-class mailslots provide acknowledged connectionless service; second-class mailslots support unacknowledged connectionless service. First-class mailslots can only be used to exchange data with a LAN Manager server. As it turns out, Windows for Workgroups supports the entire API set for second-class mailslots, even when no LAN Manager server is present. Thus, second-class mailslots are available as a vehicle for datagram communications. Table 14-7 lists the mailslot-related functions.

Table 14-7. Mailslot-Related Functions in Windows for Workgroups

Function Name	Operation
DosDeleteMailslot	Destroy a mailslot
DosMakeMailslot	Create a mailslot on the local machine
DosMailSlotInfo	Get information on a mailslot
DosPeekMailslot	See if data has arrived over a mailslot
DosReadMailslot	Read data from a mailslot
DosWriteMailslot	Write data to a mailslot

The mailslot API is easy to use. The listening side calls DosMakeMailslot() to create a mailslot. It then can call either DosMailSlotInfo() or DosPeekMailslot() to see if data has arrived. If it has, it can call DosReadMailslot() to pick it up. When it closes down, it calls DosDeleteMailslot() to destroy the mailslot. A station wishing to send data to another station or broadcast a message to all stations in a workgroup only needs to call DosWriteMailslot(). It is not necessary to do an open(), write(), close() sequence.

In spite of their convenience, mailslots have one serious disadvantage in the Windows environment. There is no mechanism for asynchronous notification; you have to poll the mailslot with DosMailSlotInfo() or DosPeekMailslot(). Windows for Workgroups will queue messages that arrive in a mailslot, so the receiver can retrieve them as a batch when he gets around to it. But you cannot ask for notifications to be posted to a callback function. This restricts the usefulness of mailslots to situations where the caller expects no immediate reply. Where they are appropriate, their ease of use argues strongly for using them instead of some other transport mechanism (like NetBIOS).

An appropriate application would be the WNetEnumStations() function developed in Chapter 2. As you may recall, when stations first load WNET.EXE, they call WNet-EnumStations() to announce their presence and find out who else is out there. This is done by broadcasting a datagram containing the station's name and an ENUM_STATIONS request code. Answers are received asynchronously and added to an internal list that WNET.EXE maintains. All subsequent calls to WNetEnumStations() enumerate the list, then regenerate it.

To implement this with mailslots, we broadcast our presence using DosWriteMail-slot(). When a station responds to a request to enumerate itself, it does not need to receive an answer, nor does its reply need to be processed immediately. It is perfectly okay to let it sit on a queue until the station requesting enumeration has a chance to look at it. The original station can set up a timer function that only needs to be called, say, once every 30 seconds; that function in turn calls DosMailSlotInfo(). One of the pieces of information it returns is the number of messages in the queue. Each of these responses can then be placed in the list of stations.

To include the correct LAN Manager header files, use these statements:

```
#define INCL_NETMAILSLOT
#define INCL_NETERROR
#include <lan.h>
```

LAN.H then includes the additional header files that you need (in this case, MAIL-SLOT.H and NETERR.H).

DosMakeMailslot()   DosMakeMailslot() creates a mailslot on the local machine. Here is the prototype from MAILSLOT.H.

```
API_FUNCTION DosMakeMailslot (const char far * pszName,
                              unsigned short    cbMessageSize,
                              unsigned short    cbMailslotSize,
                              unsigned far *    phMailslot);
```

pszName is the name of the mailslot you want to create. It must be in the format \MAILSLOT\<slot name>. It cannot include a machine name; you are only allowed to create mailslots on your own machine. The slot name portion can include pseudodirectories, like \MAILSLOT\WNET\NICESLOT. *cbMessageSize* specifies the maximum message size the slot will accept which can be as large as 65,475. *cbMailslotSize* is the size of the mailslot; it must be at least as large as *cbMessageSize*. If it is zero, it directs tells Windows to base the mailslot size on *cbMessageSize*. The mailslot handle assigned by Windows for Workgroups is returned through *phMailslot*.

DosDeleteMailslot()   DosDeleteMailslot() destroys a mailslot when you no longer need it. Its only argument is the handle of the mailslot returned by DosMakeMailslot().

```
API_FUNCTION DosDeleteMailslot(unsigned hMailslot);
```

DosReadMailslot()   DosReadMailslot() reads the next available message in a mailslot.

```
API_FUNCTION DosReadMailslot (unsigned            hMailslot,
                              char far *           pbBuffer,
                              unsigned short far * pcbReturned,
                              unsigned short far * pcbNextSize,
```

```
unsigned short far * pusNextPriority,
Long                 cTimeout);
```

hMailslot is the handle returned by DosMakeMailslot(). *pbBuffer* points to the buffer where you want the message placed. *pcbReturned* will tell you the number of bytes in the message. If no message is available, it will be zero, and DosReadMailslot() will return ERROR_SEM_TIMEOUT (0x79). *pcbNextSize* returns the number of bytes in the next waiting message. If there are no more messages on the queue, it will be zero. *pusNextPriority* reports the priority of the next message. Mailslots have priority levels from zero to nine; zero is the lowest priority. *cTimeout* specifies the amount of time in milliseconds to wait for a message. Zero means return immediately; MAILSLOT_NO_TIMEOUT means wait indefinitely, and is strictly of academic interest under Windows.

DosMailSlotInfo() / DosPeekMailslot()

DosMailSlotInfo() and DosPeekMailslot() are similar functions. Their purpose is to check for data arriving on a mailslot before you issue a read, to keep the read from blocking. DosPeekMailslot() takes the same arguments as DosReadMailslot(), but does not include a timeout value; DosPeekMailslot() will never block. It also leaves the message in the queue; it is not removed until you call DosReadMailslot(). DosMailSlotInfo() also returns the maximum message size and mailslot size set when the pipe was created.

```
API_FUNCTION DosPeekMailslot (unsigned            hMailslot,
                              char far *          pbBuffer,
                              unsigned short far * pcbReturned,
                              unsigned short far * pcbNextSize,
                              unsigned short far * pusNextPriority);

API_FUNCTION DosMailslotInfo (unsigned            hMailslot,
                              unsigned short far * pcbMessageSize,
                              unsigned short far * pcbMailslotSize,
                              unsigned short far * pcbNextSize,
                              unsigned short far * pusNextPriority,
                              unsigned short far * pcMessages);
```

hMailslot, *pcbNextSize*, and *pusNextPriority* have the same meaning as they do for DosReadMailslot(). *pcbMessageSize* and *pcbMailslotSize* report the maximum message size and the mailslot size. The number of messages in the mailslot comes back through *pcMessages*.

The main value of DosPeekMailslot() is in polling for one message at a time. If you want to iterate over all waiting messages, DosMailSlotInfo() is better, since it tells you how many messages are available. Unfortunately, neither of these functions tells you how much memory to allocate. Although they both return the size of the next message— DosPeekMailslot() through *pcbReturned*, and DosMailSlotInfo() through *pcbNextSize*— you cannot rely on this information. It is possible that a higher priority message will arrive between the call to DosPeekMailslot() or DosMailSlotInfo() and the ensuing call to DosReadMailslot(). The only piece of information that is useful here is the *pcbMessageSize* returned by DosMailSlotInfo(). This reports the maximum message size that you originally passed to DosMakeMailslot(). No message will ever be larger than this. You can allocate buffers of this size, then read the message into the buffer, with perfect assurance of success. DosReadMailslot() also tells you exactly how many bytes it read, so you can reallocate the buffer to avoid wasting space.

As noted above, the most appropriate use for DosMailSlotInfo() is in a timer callback. Because DosMailSlotInfo() returns the number of messages waiting to be picked up, it can be used on an occasional basis to retrieve all waiting messages.

Here is a code fragment that shows you how to scan the message queue. For each message, it gets enough memory to hold the largest possible message, then calls DosReadMailslot(). Afterwards, it shrinks the buffer down to the actual size of the message.

```
#define INCL_NETMAILSLOT
#define INCL_NETERRORS
#define <lan.h>
     .
     .
     .
int       i;
unsigned  hMailslot;
WORD      wMessageSize, wMailslotSize, wNextSize, wPriority;
WORD      wMessageCount;
LPBYTE    lpMessage;

// hMailslot will have been initialized previously by a call
// to DosMakeMailslot()
// if (DosMakeMailslot("\\MAILSLOT\\MYSLOT", 512,
//                     0, &hMailslot) != NERR_Success)
//    return;    // Error

if (DosMailSlotInfo(hMailslot, &wMessageSize, &wMailslotSize,
                    &wNextSize, &wPriority, &wMessageCount) !=
    NERR_Success)
    {
    // Mailslot crashed
    DosDeleteMailslot(hMailslot);
    return;
    }

// wNextSize > 0 tells us that at least one message is waiting
if (wNextSize > 0)
    {
    for (i = 0; i < wMessageCount; ++i)
      {
      // Get memory
      lpMessage = (LPBYTE) GlobalAllocPtr(GHND, wMessageSize);
      // Assume lpMessage not NULL
      // Read with no wait
      if (DosReadMailslot(hMailslot, lpMessage, &wMessageSize,
          &wNextSize, &wPriority, 0) == NERR_Success)
        {
        // Shrink the buffer
        lpMessage = (LPBYTE) GlobalReAllocPtr(lpMessage,
                                 wMessageSize, GHND);
        // Do something with lpMessage
```

```
        }
    }
}
```

DosWriteMailslot()   DosWriteMailslot() sends a datagram message and is the only function needed on that side of the interaction.

```
API_FUNCTION DosWriteMailslot (const char far * pszName,
                               const char far * pbBuffer,
                               unsigned short   cbBuffer,
                               unsigned short   usPriority,
                               unsigned short   usClass,
                               long             cTimeout);
```

pszName is the name of the mailslot you want to write a message to. It can be a mailslot on the local machine in the format \MAILSLOT\<slot name>, or it can reside on another machine, in which case it will be the full UNC name \\<machine name>\MAIL-SLOT\<slot name>. To send a broadcast to all stations in your workgroup, use a machine name of "*": *\MAILSLOT\<slot name>. *pbBuffer* is a pointer to the information you are transmitting; *cbBuffer* is the amount of data; *usPriority* is the priority you desire for the message. The highest priority is nine, and the lowest is zero. *usClass* distinguishes first-class (one) and second-class (two) mailslots; it must be passed as two to send a message to another Windows for Workgroups station. *cTimeout* has the same meaning as with Dos-ReadMailslot(). If DosWriteMailslot() times out, it will return ERROR_SEM_TIMEOUT.

Mailslots and Named Pipes   Mailslots are also available in Win32, as we saw in Chapter 13, but the implementation is somewhat different. The Windows for Workgroups version is taken directly from OS/2 LAN Manager. Because mailslots and their connection-oriented cousins, named pipes, are such a good programming interface, it would be very nice to see them fully implemented under Windows for Workgroups. There is little justification for continuing to enshrine the limitations that OS/2 and LAN Manager have imposed on them. These enhancements in particular are needed: first it should be possible for any Windows for Workgroups station to create a named pipe or a first-class mailslot. Now, only a LAN Manager server or a Windows NT machine can do so. Second, asynchronous notification, using message posting, should be supported for all operations.

Distributed DDE (NetDDE)

NetDDE is a very important enhancement that Windows for Workgroups brings to the Windows programming environment. It makes possible a whole new range of distributed computing possibilities, such as having different parts of an application run on different machines. NetDDE, along with the distributed message-passing developed in Part I, lay the groundwork for what I hope will be the Windows of the future, one single distributed copy of Windows supporting an entire network. At least, this is what the Windows of the future should look like to an end user.

The distributed DDE created in Part I is built on the Windows message-passing system. It extends DDE to the network by allowing a client application to initiate a conversation by calling WNetSendMessage() with a WM_DDE_INITIATE message, instead of SendMessage(). The client provides the name of the target workstation. The actual mechanism is conversations established with a local DDE agent window on both stations involved in the exchange, with these agents communicating over a network connection.

Windows for Workgroups' NetDDE works in much the same way, but it is built on the DDE Management Library, rather than on the message-passing system. The distributed enhancements resident in NDDEAPI.DLL. The only difference in the use of NetDDE is that the client must provide the name of the target station when it starts a conversation. Also, the target application is always NDDE$, the name used by the NetDDE server, NETDDE.EXE. It appears that here, too, there are local DDE conversations with the NetDDE servers, who in turn communicate over a NetBIOS connection. The topic and item of the conversation are a little different from standard DDE. An application that wishes to offer DDE services over the network creates a share name which represents the service, topic, and item names that would be used for local DDE. The client application then uses this share name as the topic in its call to DdeConnect(). If the application you are trying to access is not running on the server machine, NetDDE will start it for you.

For example, to create group boxes in Program Manager, you connect to it using the application and topic name "PROGMAN". Suppose Program Manager creates the share "PROGMAN". A client application on \\BLUEBOY would connect to Program Manager on \\NEC386 as follows:

```
#include <ddeml.h>

extern HINSTANCE hInst;   // Assume a global exists
DWORD             dwDDE;
HSZ               hszProgman, hzsTopic;
HCONV             hProgmanConv;
PFNCALLBACK       lpfnCallback;

lpfnCallback = MakeProcInstance(MyDDECallback, hInst);
if (DdeInitialize(&dwDDE, lpfn Callback, APPCLASS_CLIENTONLY,
      CBF_SKIP_REGISTRATIONS | CBF_SKIP_UNREGISTRATIONS)
    == DMLERR_NO_ERROR)
  {
  // Use application name \\NEC386\NDDE$
  hszProgman = DdeCreateStringHandle(dwDDE, "\\\\NEC386\\NDDE$",
                  CP_WINANSI);
  // Use topic name PROGMAN
  hszProgman = DdeCreateStringHandle(dwDDE, "PROGMAN"
                  CP_WINANSI);
  hProgmanConv = DdeConnect(dwDDE, hszProgman, hzsTopic, NULL);

  if (hProgmanConv != NULL)
    // Proceed with DdeClientTransaction() calls for
    // XTYPE_EXECUTE transactions
  }
```

Once the client is connected to the server, the DDE conversation proceeds just as if it were a local interaction; there are no further differences. It is recommended that you do one throwaway transaction to verify that you are connected to your remote partner. A successful return from DdeConnect() only means that you have established a DDE conversation with the NetDDE local agent.

For good discussions of the DDEML programming interface, see Jeffrey Clark's *Windows Programmer's Guide to OLE/DDE*, *Advanced Windows Programming* by Martin Heller, and the Windows SDK *Programmer's Reference, Volume 1: Overview*.

Creating a NetDDE Share   NDDEAPI.DLL provides functions for adding, deleting, and enumerating DDE shares: NDdeShareAdd(), NDdeShareDel(), and NDdeShare-Enum(). NDdeShareGetInfo() returns more detailed information about a share reported by NDdeShareEnum(). The prototypes, data types, and constants are defined in NDDE-API.H.

When you add a share, you must give NetDDE several pieces of information:

- The name of the share you are creating.
- The name of your application. It will use this to start your application if a client attempts to connect to it and it is not already running.
- The name of the topic that you want to make available.
- Passwords for read-only and read-write access, and the specific permission sets that will be associated with each level of access.
- Optionally, the names of any specific items you want to restrict the share to. If you do not name any items, all data items will be available.

You pass NetDDE this information in an NDDESHAREINFO structure:

```
typedef struct NDdeShareInfo_tag
{
    char                    szShareName[MAX_NDDESHARENAME+1];
    LPSTR                   lpszTargetApp;
    LPSTR                   lpszTargetTopic;
    LPBYTE                  lpbPassword1;
    DWORD                   cbPassword1;
    DWORD                   dwPermissions1;
    LPBYTE                  lpbPassword2;
    DWORD                   cbPassword2;
    DWORD                   dwPermissions2;
    LPSTR                   lpszItem;
    LONG                    cAddItems;
    LPNDDESHAREITEMINFO     lpNDdeShareItemInfo;
} NDDESHAREINFO, *PNDDESHAREINFO, FAR *LPNDDESHAREINFO;
```

szShareName is the name client applications will use to connect to you. It is customary to terminate the name with a dollar sign. *lpszTargetApp* is the name of your application. If NetDDE starts your application automatically, it will pass this exact string to WinExec(). It can include a full path name. *lpszTargetTopic* is the topic you want to share. You must create one share for each topic you are making available. *lpbPassword1* and *cbPassword1* describe the read-only password (*cbPassword1* is its length). *dwPermissions1* is the permissions that will be associated with read-only access. It can be any combination of the flags shown in Table 14-8:

Table 14-8. NetDDE Permission Flags

Flag	Value	Significance
NDDEACCESS_REQUEST	0x00000001L	Permit XTYP_REQUEST transactions
NDDEACCESS_ADVISE	0x00000002L	Permit warm and hot links
NDDEACCESS_POKE	0x00000004L	Permit XTYP_POKE transactions
NDDEACCESS_EXECUTE	0x00000008L	Permit XTYP_EXECUTE transactions

Table 14-8. NetDDE Permission Flags (cont.)

Flag	Value	Significance
NDDEACCESS_START_APP	0x00000010L	Allow application to be started automatically
NDDEACCESS_ALL	0x0000001FL	Allow all of the above
NDDEACCESS_EXCLUDEEXECUTE	0x00000017L	Allow everything but XTYP_EXECUTE transactions
NDDEACCESS_EXCLUDESTARTAPP	0x0000000FL	Allow everything but starting the application automatically

lpbPassword2 and *cbPassword2* describe the password that will grant read-write access. *dwPermissions2* is the specific set of read-write permissions. Both passwords must be in uppercase.

If *lpszItem* is NULL, all items will be available to client applications. Otherwise, shared items will be restricted to *lpszItem* and any items included in the array *lpNDde-ShareItemInfo*. *cAddItems* is the number of elements in the array, which consists of these structures:

```
typedef struct NDdeShareItemInfo_tag
{
    LPSTR        lpszItem;
    DWORD        dwPermissions;
} NDDESHAREITEMINFO, *PNDDESHAREITEMINFO, FAR *LPNDDESHAREITEMINFO;
```

Again, *lpszItem* is the name of the item being shared. *dwPermissions* is the set of permissions that will be granted for this particular item.

Before you create a share, it is a good idea to try to delete it first. To delete a share, call NDdeShareDel( ):

```
UINT WINAPI NDdeShareDel(LPSTR lpszServer,
                         LPSTR lpszShareName,
                         UINT  uReserved);
```

lpszServer must be NULL; *uReserved* must be zero. *lpszShareName* is the name under which you created the share.

To create the share, pass a pointer to the NDDESHAREINFO structure you have filled in to NDdeShareAdd( ):

```
UINT WINAPI NDdeShareAdd(LPSTR lpszServer, UINT uLevel,
                         LPNDDESHAREINFO lpNDdeShareInfo,
                         DWORD cbShareInfo);
```

All but the NDDESHAREINFO pointer are constants. *lpszServer* must be NULL, *uLevel* must be two, and *cbShareInfo* is sizeof (NDDESHAREINFO). *lpNDdeShareInfo* points to the NDDESHAREINFO structure that you have populated previously.

NDdeShareAdd( ) makes the shared topic and items available for client applications, and remembers the share in the [DDEShares] section of SYSTEM.INI. Here are the lines from my SYSTEM.INI:

```
[DDEShares]
HEARTS$=mshearts,hearts,,15,,0,,0,0,0
CLPBK$=clipsrv,system,,31,,0,,0,0,0
CHAT$=winchat,chat,,31,,0,,0,0,0
```

If you want your application to be automatically executed, you must not delete the share; doing so removes these lines from SYSTEM.INI.

Obtaining NetDDE Share Information   To obtain information about your NetDDE shares, call NDdeShareEnum() to retrieve their names, then NDdeShareGetInfo() for each one:

```
UINT WINAPI NDdeShareEnum(LPSTR    lpszServer,
                          UINT     uLevel,
                          LPBYTE   lpNames,
                          DWORD    cbNames,
                          LPDWORD  lpnEntriesRead,
                          LPDWORD  lpcbTotalAvailable);
```

Set *lpszServer* to NULL and *uLevel* to zero. NDdeShareEnum() works like a LAN Manager enumerator; it returns an array of null-terminated share names in *lpNames*. On input, *cbNames* says how large the buffer at *lpNames* is. On output, **lpnEntriesRead* reports the number of shares enumerated; **lpcbTotalAvailable* returns the number of bytes of information available. If the original buffer was too small, NDdeShareEnum() returns NDDE_BUF_TOO_SMALL, and you can allocate the memory required.

You can get the original NDDESHAREINFO structure for each share in the array by calling NDdeShareGetInfo():

```
UINT WINAPI NDdeShareGetInfo(LPSTR            lpszServer,
                             LPSTR            lpszShareName,
                             UINT             uLevel,
                             LPNDDESHAREINFO  lpNDdeShareInfo,
                             DWORD            cbShareInfo,
                             LPDWORD          lpcbTotalAvailable,
                             LPWORD           lpnItems);
```

Though not named as such, NDdeShareGetInfo() also works like a LAN Manager enumerator. As usual, *lpszServer* must be NULL. *uLevel* must be two, as it was in the initial call to NDdeShareAdd(). *lpnItems* must also be NULL. *lpszShareName* is the name of the share you are requesting information about. *lpNDdeShareInfo* points to an NDDE-SHAREINFO structure, and *cbShareInfo* is the size of the buffer at *lpNDdeShareInfo*. Any items that are included in the share will also be returned in the buffer pointed to by *lpNDdeShareInfo*, so if the buffer is only sizeof (NDDESHAREINFO) bytes large, NDdeShareGetInfo() may return NDDE_BUF_TOO_SMALL. **lpcbTotalAvailable* returns the total number of bytes available.

NDdeGetNodeName()   As I mentioned above, NDdeGetNodeName() gets the machine name of the local computer. Here is its prototype:

```
UINT WINAPI NDdeGetNodeName(LPSTR lpName, DWORD dwNameLength);
```

The name is returned in *lpName*, without leading backslashes. *dwNameLength* is the size of the buffer.

Additional NetDDE Functions   Table 14-9 lists other NDde() functions in NDDE-API.DLL.

Table 14-9. Additional NDde() Functions in NDDEAPI.DLL

Function	Purpose
NDdeConnectionEnum	Enumerate all connections to local NetDDE server applications for a given NetDDE client
NDdeGetClientInfo	Retrieves client node and application name for a DDE client window handle
NDdeGetErrorString	Retrieves text for a NetDDE error
NDdeGetWindow	Retrieve window handle of NetDDE service
NDdeIsValidPassword	Checks that string is in correct format for a password (does not mean that the password is valid)
NDdeIsValidShareName	Checks that a share name is in correct format (does not mean that the share exists)
NDdeIsValidTopic	Checks that a topic name is in correct format (does not mean that the topic exists)
NDdeSessionClose	Closes a NetDDE session enumerated by NDdeSessionEnum()
NDdeSessionEnum	Enumerates remote clients for NetDDE servers on the current machine
NDdeShareSetInfo	Change information about a share

Conclusion

Windows for Workgroups represents a significant advance in networking with Windows. It makes workstation-to-workstation communication much simpler than it has been in the past. Network file transfer is now a simple copy operation. Users can run applications on other users' machines. Electronic mail is built into Windows for Workgroups, both as an end-user facility (MSMAIL.EXE) and as a programming interface (MAPI). Users can converse with each other using WINCHAT.

Windows for Workgroups also expands the network programming interface. Applications can become mail-enabled very simply. They need only add a Send... option to their file menu, and issue a single call to MAPISendDocuments(). The network driver (WFWNET.DRV) adds an additional set of common dialogs, mostly dealing with shared resources. Windows for Workgroups includes its own version of NETAPI.DLL, the standard LAN Manager DLL.

At the same time, Windows for Workgroups does not aim to replace network operating systems like NetWare, LAN Manager, or VINES. There is no question that those systems are more powerful than Windows for Workgroups, for what they aim to accomplish. Rather, Windows for Workgroups gives a way to expand networking capabilities in a horizontal direction. For small networks, where a file server isn't really necessary, it provides an alternative to larger, more expensive systems. For larger networks, it enriches the functionality that they already provide.

Windows Network Install Program

Description

The program presented in this appendix, WNETINST.EXE, uses the code developed in Part I. Specifically, it calls WNetEnumStations() to enumerate the other stations on the network that are running WNET.EXE. For every station it finds, it performs these steps:

1. It calls WNetFindWindow() to get the window handle of the Program Manager on that machine.
2. It calls WNetCall() to establish a connection with the remote copy of WNET.EXE.
3. It sends the Program Manager a series of messages. First, it sends a WM_GETTEXT-LENGTH to find out how long Program Manager's window title is. It then allocates enough memory to hold the title and a null terminator, then sends a WM_GETTEXT message. It then adds the text "(Servicing Remote Request)" to the title, and sends a WM_SETTEXT message to change it.
4. Next, it transmits WM_DDE_INITIATE, WM_DDE_EXECUTE, and WM_DDE_-TERMINATE messages. The WM_DDE_EXECUTE messages include Delete-Group, CreateGroup, and AddItem statements in the Program Manager's command language. The effect of these statements is to create a group box for the programs presented in Appendices A, B, and C, as shown in Figure A-1.
5. Finally, it calls WNetHangup() to terminate the network connection.

Figure A-1. WNET Program Manager Group Box Created by WNETINST.EXE

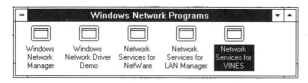

WNETINST.EXE needs WNET.EXE to have been loaded previously; if it is not, it calls WinExec() to load it. When run on top of NetBIOS, both WNETINST.EXE and WNET.EXE expect one argument—the name they will register with NetBIOS. This argument can be included with other protocols; it will be ignored if it is not needed.

WNETINST.EXE runs without modification or recompilation in all the environments we support in this book.

Code Listings

```c
/********
*
* Listing A-1. WNETINST.C
*
* Copyright (c) 1992 Ralph P. Davis, All Rights Reserved
*
* This demonstrates the use of the distributed message-passing
* and remote procedure call mechanisms.
*
* It enumerates all the stations on the network and sends DDE
* messages to the Program Manager to install a group box
* containing icons for the rest of the software in this book.
*
********/

/*===== Includes =====*/

#include "wnetinst.h"
#include <dde.h>
#include <string.h>

/*===== Constants =====*/

/*===== Global Variables =====*/

HINSTANCE       hCurrentInstance;
HWND            hTopWindow;
HINSTANCE       hNetLib;
int             nNameIndex;
int             nSuccess = 0, nFailed = 0;

/*===== LOCAL Variables =====*/

static char szCmdLine[128] = "";

/*===== FORWARD Functions =====*/

BOOL WINAPI StationEnumProc(LPBYTE lpStation);

 /*===== External Functions =====*/

/*===== Function Definitions =====*/
int PASCAL WinMain(HINSTANCE hInst, HINSTANCE hPrevInstance,
                   LPSTR lpszCmdLine, int nCmdShow)
{
   MSG  msg;
   char szCmdBuffer[128];

   // Don't use hPrevInstance to determine if there's another
   // instance running.  In Win32, it will always return NULL.

   if (FindWindow("WNETINSTALL", NULL) != NULL)
      return FALSE;

   // Where appropriate, lpszCmdLine will be the name of the
   // station.

   if (lpszCmdLine != NULL)
      {
      while (*lpszCmdLine == ' ')   // Skip spaces
         ++lpszCmdLine;
      lstrcpy(szCmdLine, lpszCmdLine);
      }

   // Make sure WNET.EXE is running
   if (FindWindow("WNETMASTER", NULL) == NULL)
      {
      if (lstrlen(szCmdLine) > 0)
         wsprintf(szCmdBuffer, "WNET.EXE %s", (LPSTR) szCmdLine);
      else
         lstrcpy(szCmdBuffer, "WNET.EXE");
      if (WinExec(szCmdBuffer, SW_SHOWMINIMIZED) <=
         (UINT) HINSTANCE_ERROR)
         return FALSE;
      }

   if (GlobalInit("WNETINSTALL", hInst) == 0)
      return FALSE;

   if (InstanceInit("WNETINSTALL", hInst) == NULL)
      return FALSE;
```

```
    hCurrentInstance = hInst;

    while (GetMessage(&msg,NULL,NULL,NULL) )
        {
        TranslateMessage(&msg);
        DispatchMessage(&msg);
        }
    return(msg.wParam);
}
LRESULT CALLBACK WNetWndProc(HWND hWnd,
                             UINT uMessage,
                             WPARAM wParam,
                             LPARAM lParam)
{
    // We're only interested in a couple of messages.

    // WM_CREATE--triggers network initialization
    // WM_CLOSE
    // WM_ENDSESSION--disconnect from network DLLs.

    switch (uMessage)
        {
        HANDLE_MSG(hWnd, WM_CREATE, WNet_OnCreate);
        HANDLE_MSG(hWnd, WM_CLOSE, WNet_OnClose);
        HANDLE_MSG(hWnd, WM_ENDSESSION, WNet_OnEndSession);
        case WM_DESTROY:
            PostQuitMessage(0);
            break;
        default:
            break;
        }
    return DefWindowProc(hWnd, uMessage, wParam, lParam);
}

BOOL WNet_OnCreate(HWND hWnd, CREATESTRUCT FAR *lpCS)
{
    STATIONENUMPROC lpStationEnumProc;
    char szMessage[100];

    if ((nNameIndex = WNetInit(hWnd, szCmdLine, &hNetLib)) == (-1))
        {
        MessageBeep(MB_ICONHAND);
        MessageBox(NULL, "WNetInstall Initialization Failed",
            "WNetInstall Error", MB_OK | MB_ICONHAND);
        return FALSE;
        }
    else
        MessageBox(NULL, "WNetInstall Initialization Successful",
            "WNet", MB_OK);

    ShowWindow(hWnd, SW_SHOWMINNOACTIVE);
    UpdateWindow(hWnd);

    // Enumerate other station running WNET.EXE
    hTopWindow = hWnd;
    (FARPROC) lpStationEnumProc =
        MakeProcInstance((FARPROC) StationEnumProc,
            (HINSTANCE) GetWindowWord(hWnd, GWW_HINSTANCE));
    WNetEnumStations(nNameIndex, lpStationEnumProc);
    FreeProcInstance((FARPROC) lpStationEnumProc);

     wsprintf(szMessage, "Install complete.\n\n"
                        "%d successful installs, %d failures",
                    nSuccess, nFailed);
    MessageBox(NULL, szMessage, "WNet Install", MB_ICONINFORMATION | MB_OK);
    PostMessage(hWnd, WM_CLOSE, 0, 0L);
    return TRUE;
}

BOOL WINAPI StationEnumProc(LPBYTE lpStation)  // Called once
                                               // for each known station
{
    HWND hProgman;
    HCONNECTION hNewConnection = NULL;
    BOOL bReturnCode = TRUE;
    LPBYTE lpText = NULL;
    DWORD  dwTextLength;

    // Find Program Manager on the remote machine
    hProgman = WNetFindWindow(lpStation, "PROGMAN", NULL);
```

```
if (hProgman != (HWND) 0xFFFF && hProgman != NULL)
    {
    // nNameIndex is the client identifier returned by
    // WNetInit()
    hNewConnection = WNetCall(nNameIndex, lpStation);
    if (hNewConnection == 0)
        {
        ++nFailed;
        goto End_StationEnum;
        }

    // Send WM_GETTEXTLENGTH to Program Manager on remote
    // machine to find out how much memory we need to allocate
    dwTextLength =
        WNetSendMessage((LPVOID) MAKELONG(hNewConnection, 0),
            hProgman, WM_GETTEXTLENGTH, 0, 0L,
            FALSE, 0L);
    if (dwTextLength != (DWORD) -1)
        {
        ++dwTextLength;  // For the null terminator
        lpText = GlobalAllocPtr(GHND, dwTextLength);
        if (lpText != NULL)
            {
            // Save remote Program Manager's current title bar
            if (WNetSendMessage((LPVOID) MAKELONG(hNewConnection, 0),
                    hProgman, WM_GETTEXT, (WORD) dwTextLength,
                    (LPARAM) lpText, TRUE, dwTextLength) ==
                    (LRESULT) -1)
                {
                ++nFailed;
                goto End_StationEnum;
                }
            }
        else
            {
            ++nFailed;
            bReturnCode = FALSE;    // Out of memory, terminate.
                                    // enumeration
            goto End_StationEnum;
            }
        }
    // Change Program Manager's title bar on remote machine
    WNetSendMessage((LPVOID) MAKELONG(hNewConnection, 0),
        hProgman, WM_SETTEXT, 0,
        (LPARAM) (LPSTR) "Program Manager (Servicing Remote Request)",
        TRUE,
        lstrlen("Program Manager (Servicing Remote Request)") + 1);

    // Restore Program Manager
    WNetSendMessage((LPVOID) MAKELONG(hNewConnection, 0),
        hProgman, WM_SYSCOMMAND,
        SC_RESTORE, 0L, FALSE, 0L);

    // Start DDE with remote Program Manager
    if (WNetDDEInitialize("PROGMAN", "PROGMAN",
        (LPVOID) MAKELONG(hNewConnection, 0),
        (HINSTANCE) GetWindowWord(hTopWindow, GWW_HINSTANCE),
        HWND_BROADCAST))
        {
        WNetDDEExecute("[DeleteGroup(Windows Network Programs)]");
        WNetDDEExecute(
            "[CreateGroup(Windows Network Programs,winnet.grp)]");
        WNetDDEExecute(
            "[AddItem(wnet.exe, Windows Network Manager,wnet.exe)]");
        WNetDDEExecute(
            "[AddItem(wnetdemo.exe, Windows Network Driver Demo,wnetdemo.exe)]");
        WNetDDEExecute(
            "[AddItem(wnetnw.exe, Network Services for NetWare,wnetnw.exe)]");
        WNetDDEExecute(
            "[AddItem(wnetlm.exe, Network Services for LAN Manager,wnetlm.exe)]");
        WNetDDEExecute(
            "[AddItem(wnetvns.exe, Network Services for VINES,wnetvns.exe)]");
        WNetDDETerminate((LPVOID) MAKELONG(hNewConnection, 0));
        FlashWindow(hTopWindow, TRUE);
        ++nSuccess;
        }
    else
        {
        ++nFailed;
```

```
            }
        // Restore original Program Manager title bar on remote machine
        if (lpText != NULL)
            WNetSendMessage((LPVOID) MAKELONG(hNewConnection, 0),
                hProgman, WM_SETTEXT,
                0, (LPARAM) lpText, TRUE, lstrlen(lpText) + 1);
        }
    else
        {
        ++nFailed;
        }
End_StationEnum:
    // Bye-bye
    if (hNewConnection != NULL)
        WNetHangup(hNewConnection);
    if (lpText != NULL)
        GlobalFreePtr(lpText);
    return bReturnCode;
}
/* void WNet_OnClose(HWND hwnd); */
void WNet_OnClose(HWND hwnd)
{
    // WM_CLOSE and WM_ENDSESSION are handled the same way.

    WNet_OnEndSession(hwnd, TRUE);
}

/* void WNet_OnEndSession(HWND hwnd, BOOL fEnding); */
void WNet_OnEndSession(HWND hwnd, BOOL fEnding)
{
    if (fEnding)
        {
        WNetShutdown(hNetLib, nNameIndex);
        DestroyWindow(hwnd);
        }
}

/********
 *
 * Listing A-2. WNETIINI.C
 *
 * Copyright (c) 1992 Ralph P. Davis, All Rights Reserved
 *
 * Contains WNETINST routines used only at startup
 *
 ********/

/*===== Includes =====*/

#include "wnetinst.h"

/*===== Function Definitions =====*/

ATOM GlobalInit(LPSTR lpszClassName, HINSTANCE hInstance)
{
    WNDCLASS WndClass;

    // Main window class
    WndClass.lpszClassName = lpszClassName;
    WndClass.lpfnWndProc   = WNetWndProc;
    WndClass.hInstance     = hInstance;
    WndClass.hCursor       = NULL;
    WndClass.hIcon         = LoadIcon(NULL, IDI_APPLICATION);
    WndClass.hbrBackground = NULL;
    WndClass.lpszMenuName  = NULL;
    WndClass.style         = 0;
    WndClass.cbClsExtra    = 0;
    WndClass.cbWndExtra    = 0;

    if (!RegisterClass(&WndClass))
        return FALSE;
    // DDE client window class
        WndClass.lpszClassName = "WNetDDESender";
        WndClass.lpfnWndProc   = WNetDDESenderWndProc;
        WndClass.hInstance     = hInstance;
        WndClass.hIcon         = NULL;
        return (RegisterClass(&WndClass));
}

HWND InstanceInit(LPSTR lpszClassName, HINSTANCE hInstance)
{
```

```
    HWND hWnd;
     // Create our main window, but don't show it--we'll run
    // hidden
    hWnd = CreateWindow(
        lpszClassName,
        "Windows Network Install Program",
        WS_OVERLAPPEDWINDOW,
        CW_USEDEFAULT,
        CW_USEDEFAULT,
        CW_USEDEFAULT,
        CW_USEDEFAULT,
        NULL,
        NULL,
        hInstance,
        NULL);

    return hWnd;
}

/********
*
* Listing A-3. WNETIDDE.C
*
* Adapted from code originally written by Alan R. Feuer
* Used by Permission
*
* Copyright (c) 1992 Blossom Software, All Rights Reserved
*
********/

/*===== Includes =====*/

#include "wnetinst.h"
#include <string.h>
#include <dde.h>

/*===== Local Variables =====*/

static HWND hDDESender;
static HWND hTargetWnd;
static HWND hLocalDDEAgent;
static LPSTR lpServer;

/*===== Function Definitions =====*/

LRESULT CALLBACK WNetDDESenderWndProc(HWND hWnd,
        UINT msg, WPARAM wParam, LPARAM lParam)
{
    LPARAM lDDEAtoms;
    switch(msg)
        {
        case WM_CREATE:
            // We passed ourselves the service and topic atoms
            // as the last argument to CreateWindow(), further down
            // in this listing
            lDDEAtoms = (LPARAM) ((LPCREATESTRUCT) lParam)- >lpCreateParams;

            // Try to initiate conversation with application on
            // remote machine
            if (WNetSendMessage(lpServer, hTargetWnd,
                WM_DDE_INITIATE, (WPARAM) hWnd, lDDEAtoms, FALSE, 0L) != - 1L)
                return 0L;
            else
                return -1L;
        case WM_DDE_ACK:
            // When we get a WM_DDE_ACK, wParam will contain the
            // window handle of the local DDE agent window
            if (hLocalDDEAgent == NULL)
                {
                hLocalDDEAgent = (HWND) wParam;
                }
            return(0);
        case WM_DDE_TERMINATE:
            // Partner is either closing the conversation or responding
            // to our WM_DDE_TERMINATE
            // Notice that we use SendMessage(), although the DDE
            // protocol calls for PostMessage(). There appear to be
            // timing problems in synchronizing WM_DDE_TERMINATE
            // requests over the network.
            if (hLocalDDEAgent != NULL)
                SendMessage(hLocalDDEAgent, WM_DDE_TERMINATE,
                    (WPARAM) hWnd, 0L);
```

```
                hLocalDDEAgent = NULL;
                DestroyWindow(hWnd);
                return 0;
            }
        return( DefWindowProc(hWnd, msg, wParam, lParam));
    }
BOOL PASCAL WNetDDEExecute(LPSTR lpszCommand)
{
    HANDLE hDDECommand;
    LPSTR  lpCmd;
    MSG    msg;
    WORD   wStatus;
    DDEACK *pDDEAck = (DDEACK *) &wStatus;
    DWORD  dwTimeLimit;
    BOOL   bAckReceived = FALSE;
    // We'll use a five-second timeout
    dwTimeLimit = GetTickCount() + 5000;

    while (GetTickCount() <= dwTimeLimit)
        {
        if (hLocalDDEAgent != NULL)
            break;

        // Give WM_DDE_ACK in response to our initial
        // WM_DDE_INITIATE a chance to come in
        NetworkDependentYield();
        if (MyPeekMessage(&msg, NULL, 0, 0, PM_REMOVE))
            {
            TranslateMessage(&msg);
            DispatchMessage(&msg);
            }
        }

    if (hLocalDDEAgent == NULL)
        // No response
        return FALSE;

    hDDECommand = GlobalAlloc(GMEM_MOVEABLE | GMEM_DDESHARE,
        lstrlen(lpszCommand) + 1);

    if (hDDECommand != NULL)
        {
        // Allocate memory for command, post WM_DDE_EXECUTE
        // to partner
        lpCmd = (LPSTR) GlobalLock(hDDECommand);
        lstrcpy(lpCmd, lpszCommand);
         GlobalUnlock(hDDECommand);

        PostMessage(hLocalDDEAgent, WM_DDE_EXECUTE,
            (WPARAM) hDDESender, (LPARAM) MAKELONG(0,hDDECommand));

        dwTimeLimit = GetTickCount() + 5000;
        while (GetTickCount() < dwTimeLimit)
            {
            // Wait five seconds for a WM_DDE_ACK
            NetworkDependentYield();
            if (MyPeekMessage(&msg,NULL, 0, 0, PM_REMOVE))
                {
                DispatchMessage(&msg);
                if (msg.message == WM_DDE_ACK)
                    {
                    bAckReceived = TRUE;
                    break;
                    }
                }
            }
        // Did WM_DDE_ACK come in
        if (bAckReceived)
            {
            wStatus = LOWORD(msg.lParam);
            bAckReceived = pDDEAck->fAck;
            }
        GlobalFree(hDDECommand);
         return(bAckReceived);
        }
    return(FALSE);
}

void PASCAL WNetDDETerminate(LPSTR lpTargetStation)
```

```
{
    DWORD dwTimeLimit;
    MSG msg;

    if( hLocalDDEAgent != NULL)
        {
        // Terminate the conversation by sending a
        // WM_DDE_TERMINATE to the DDE local agent on this machine
        // He'll forward it along to the other station,
        // who will respond with his own WM_DDE_TERMINATE

        SendMessage(hLocalDDEAgent, WM_DDE_TERMINATE,
            (WPARAM) hDDESender, 0L);
        dwTimeLimit = GetTickCount() + 5000;
        while( GetTickCount() < dwTimeLimit)
            {
            NetworkDependentYield();
            if (MyPeekMessage(&msg,NULL, 0, 0,PM_REMOVE))
                {
                DispatchMessage(&msg);
                if (msg.message == WM_DDE_TERMINATE)
                    break;
                }
            }
        }
}

BOOL PASCAL WNetDDEInitialize(LPSTR lpszApp, LPSTR lpszTopic,
                      LPBYTE lpTargetStation, HINSTANCE hInstance,
                      HWND hWndTarget)
{
    ATOM  aApp, aTopic;
    DWORD dwTimeLimit;
    MSG   msg;

    lpServer = lpTargetStation;
    hTargetWnd = hWndTarget;

    // Encapsulate application and topic names in atoms
    aApp = GlobalAddAtom(lpszApp);
    aTopic = GlobalAddAtom(lpszTopic);

    hDDESender = CreateWindow("WNetDDESender",
        NULL,
        0,
        0, 0,
        0, 0,
        NULL,
        NULL,
        hInstance,
        // Pass atoms as lpCreateParams field of
        // CREATESTRUCT that comes to WM_CREATE
        (LPSTR) MAKELONG(aApp,aTopic));

    // We don't need the atoms anymore, chuck them
    GlobalDeleteAtom(aApp);
    GlobalDeleteAtom(aTopic);

    dwTimeLimit = GetTickCount() + 5000;
    while (GetTickCount() < dwTimeLimit)
        {
        // Wait five seconds for a WM_DDE_ACK
        // The CreateWindow() causes a WM_DDE_INITIATE
        // to be sent to the target station
        NetworkDependentYield();
        if (MyPeekMessage(&msg, NULL, 0, 0, PM_REMOVE))
            {
            DispatchMessage(&msg);
            if (msg.message == WM_DDE_ACK)
                break;
            }
        }
    return( (BOOL) (hDDESender ));
}


/********
 *
 * Listing A-4. WNETINST.H
```

```
*
* Copyright (c) 1992 Ralph P. Davis, All Rights Reserved
*
********/

/***** Includes =====*/

#include "wnet.h"

/*===== Function Prototypes =====*/

LRESULT CALLBACK WNetDDESenderWndProc(HWND hWnd,
        UINT msg, WPARAM wParam, LPARAM lParam);
BOOL PASCAL WNetDDEExecute(LPSTR lpszCommand);
void PASCAL WNetDDETerminate(LPSTR lpTargetStation);
BOOL PASCAL WNetDDEInitialize(LPSTR lpszApp, LPSTR lpszTopic,
                    LPBYTE lpTargetStation, HINSTANCE hInstance,
                    HWND hWndTarget);

;********
;
; Listing A-5. WNETINST.DEF
;
; Copyright (c) 1992 Ralph P. Davis, All Rights Reserved
;
;********
NAME        WNETINST

EXETYPE     WINDOWS

CODE        PRELOAD MOVEABLE DISCARDABLE
DATA        PRELOAD MOVEABLE MULTIPLE

HEAPSIZE    8192
STACKSIZE   8192

STUB        'WINSTUB.EXE'

EXPORTS
            WNetWndProc
            WNetDDESenderWndProc
            StationEnumProc

########
#
# Listing A-6. WNETINST.MAK
#
# Make file for distributed install program
#
########

OS=-Od
GOPT=-G2sw
ZOPT=-Zipe
DEFINE=-DLOCAL=static
LINKFLAGS=/CO /LI /NOPACKC /ALIGN:16 /NOD

SRC=wnetinst.c wnetiini.c wnetidde.c
HDRS=wnet.h wnetinst.h
OBJS=wnetinst.obj wnetiini.obj wnetidde.obj

.asm.obj:
    ml /c $*.asm

.c.obj:
    cl -c -AM $(GOPT) $(OS) $(ZOPT) -W3 $(DEFINE) $*.c

wnetinst.obj: wnetinst.c $(HDRS)

wnetiini.obj: wnetiini.c $(HDRS)

wnetidde.obj:       wnetidde.c

wnetinst.exe: $(OBJS) wnetinst.def wnetlvl1.lib
        link $(LINKFLAGS) @@<<wnetinst.lnk
                $(OBJS),
                wnetinst.exe,
                NUL,
                libw mlibcew wnetlvl1,
                wnetinst.def
<<
        rc wnetinst.exe
```

APPENDIX ▪ B

Windows Network Services Demo

Description

The program presented in this appendix uses the functions developed in Part II. It is an administrative program that allows network supervisors to add and delete users, add and delete groups, and add and remove users from groups. The base executable is called WNETSVCS.EXE. But rather than include code to select and load the network-specific DLL at runtime, and duplicate code that you have already seen, I have chosen to create three executables—WNETNW.EXE for NetWare, WNETLM.EXE for LAN Manager, and WNETVNST.EXE for VINES StreetTalk. The source code does not need to change between version.

WNETSVCS.EXE has three options on its main menu, shown in Figure B-1.

Figure B-1. WNETSVCS.EXE Main Menu

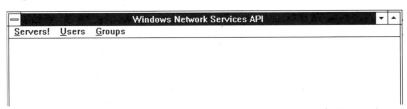

When the main menu is first presented, the Users and Groups items are disabled. NetWare and LAN Manager need to know what server is the target of network service requests, so we oblige the user to choose a server before enabling these items. The target server is irrelevant under VINES, but we keep the same procedure for consistency.

Selecting a Server
The Servers! item presents the dialog box shown in Figure B-2 (on the following page) to the user.

We populate the listbox by calling WNetEnumServers(). The server that the user selects is remembered in a global variable, and is made the target of subsequent network services requests.

Adding and Deleting Users
The Users popup menu has two items: View... and Groups.... View... displays the dialog box shown in Figure B-3, which allows the administrator to add or delete users.

We retrieve the user list by calling WNetEnumUsers(). You can delete a user by selecting him and clicking the Delete button. WNETSVCS.EXE then calls WNetDeleteUser(). If you click the Add... button, WNETSVCS.EXE presents the dialog box found in Figure B-4.

When you return to the View Users dialog box, the user is added by a call to WNetAddUser(), and his name is included in the listbox.

Figure B-2. View Servers Dialog Box

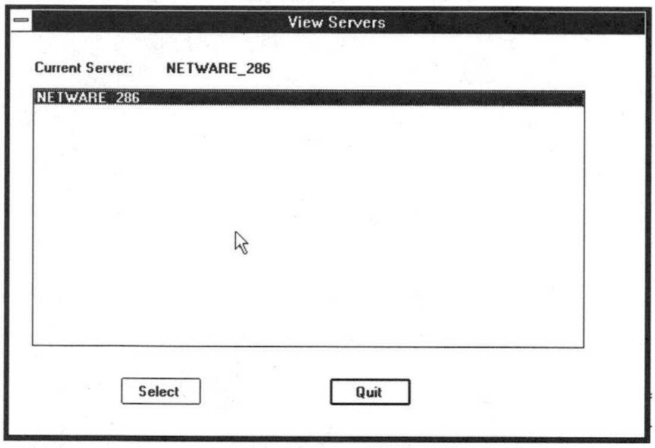

Figure B-3. View Users Dialog Box

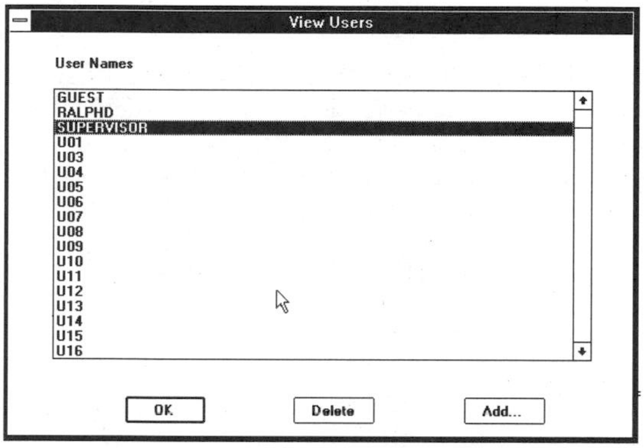

Figure B-4. Add User Dialog Box

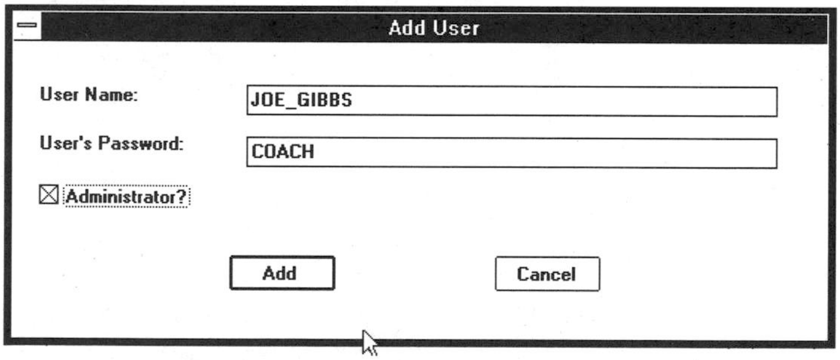

Changing User's Group Membership

Selecting the Groups... item on the User menu puts up the dialog box shown in Figure B-5.

We call WNetEnumUsers() to populate the Users listbox. When the administrator selects a user, we enable the Refresh Groups button; clicking it populates the other listboxes. We make two calls to WNetEnumGroups(). The first one fills the Groups Belonged To listbox. The callback function for the second invocation looks to see if the enumerated groups are already in the Groups Belonged To listbox by sending it an LB_FINDSTRING message. If this returns LB_ERR, it adds them to the Groups Not Belonged To listbox. Selecting a group in the Groups Belonged To listbox enables the Delete From Group button; selecting "on" in the Groups Not Belonged To listbox enables the Add

To Group button. Clicking these buttons triggers a call to WNetDeleteGroupMember() or WNetAddGroupMember(), and moves the group name from the box it is in to the box it is not in.

Figure B-5. User Groups Dialog Box

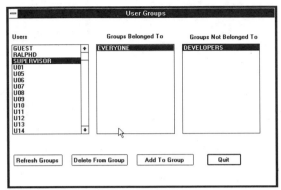

Adding and Deleting Groups

The Groups popup also has two items: View... and Members.... Both use the same dialog boxes as we saw for manipulating users, with some different text and actions. Now we use WNetEnum-Groups() to populate the Group listboxes, and WNetEnumGroupMembers() to fill the listbox of users who belong to a selected group. To find out the users who do not belong to a group, we call WNetEnumUsers(), then send the member listbox an LB_FINDSTRING message as I described above. To add or delete a group, we call WNetAddGroup() or WNetDeleteGroup(). To add or delete a group member, we call WNetAddGroupMember() or WNetDeleteGroupMember().

Code Listings

```
/********
*
* Listing B-1. WNETSVCS.C
*
* Copyright (c) 1992 Ralph P. Davis, All Rights Reserved
*
********/

/*===== Includes =====*/

#include <windows.h>
#include <commdlg.h>
#include "wnetsvcs.h"
#include "wnetapi.h"   // From Chapter 8
#include <direct.h>
#include <stdio.h>
#include        .h>
#include <string.h>

/*===== Constants =====*/

#define MAXUSERNAMELENGTH 100

/*===== Types =====*/

typedef struct tagAddUser
{
    char szUserName[100];
    char szPassword[100];
    BOOL bAdmin;
} ADDUSERSTRUCT;

/*===== Function Prototypes =====*/

// Main window procedure
LRESULT CALLBACK MainWndProc(HWND, UINT, WPARAM, LPARAM);

// Dialog box procedures
```

```c
BOOL CALLBACK ViewUsersDlgProc(HWND hDlg, UINT uMessage, WPARAM wParam,
                               LPARAM lParam);
BOOL CALLBACK AddUserDlgProc(HWND hDlg, UINT uMessage, WPARAM wParam,
                             LPARAM lParam);
BOOL CALLBACK UserGroupsDlgProc(HWND hDlg, UINT uMessage, WPARAM wParam,
                                LPARAM lParam);
BOOL CALLBACK ViewServersDlgProc(HWND hDlg, UINT uMessage, WPARAM wParam,
                                 LPARAM lParam);
BOOL CALLBACK ViewGroupsDlgProc(HWND hDlg, UINT uMessage, WPARAM wParam,
                                LPARAM lParam);
BOOL CALLBACK AddGroupDlgProc(HWND hDlg, UINT uMessage, WPARAM wParam,
                              LPARAM lParam);
BOOL CALLBACK GroupMembersDlgProc(HWND hDlg, UINT uMessage, WPARAM  wParam,
                                  LPARAM lParam);

// Enumeration functions
BOOL CALLBACK UserEnumProc(LPSTR lpszServerName, LPSTR lpszUserName);
BOOL CALLBACK GroupEnumProc(LPSTR lpszServerName, LPSTR lpszGroupName);
BOOL CALLBACK ServerEnumProc(LPSTR lpszServerName, WORD wServerType);
BOOL CALLBACK GroupMemberEnumProc(LPSTR lpszServerName, LPSTR lpszGroupName,
                                  LPSTR lpszUserName);
BOOL CALLBACK MemberGroupEnumProc(LPSTR lpszServerName, LPSTR lpszUserName,
                                  LPSTR lpszGroupName);
BOOL CALLBACK NonMemberGroupEnumProc(LPSTR lpszServerName, LPSTR lpszGroupName);
BOOL CALLBACK NonGroupMemberEnumProc(LPSTR lpszServerName, LPSTR lpszGroupName);

// Other functions
BOOL GetFileName(HWND hWnd, LPSTR lpszFileName);
LPSTR GetListboxItemData(HWND hDlg, WORD wControlID, LPDWORD lpdwCurSel);

/*===== LOCAL Functions =====*/

 static WORD near _latoi(LPSTR lpszNumber);

/*===== Global Variables =====*/

char        szServerName[100] = "";
HWND        hUserDlg;
HWND        hServerDlg;
HWND        hGroupDlg;
WORD        wServerListboxID;
WORD        wUserListboxID;
WORD        wGroupListboxID;
WORD        wNonGroupListboxID;
WORD        wMemberListboxID;
WORD        wNonMemberListboxID;
HINSTANCE hInst;

/*===== Function Definitions =====*/

int PASCAL WinMain(HINSTANCE hInstance,         // Application Instance Handle
                   HINSTANCE hPrevInstance,     // Previous Instance Handle
                   LPSTR     lpszCmdLine,       // Pointer to Command Line
                   int       nCmdShow)          // Show Window Option
  {
    static char szAppName[] = "wnetsvcs";

    MSG       msg;
    HWND      hWndMain;

    WNDCLASS wndclass;
    hInst = hInstance;

    if(!hPrevInstance)
      {
        wndclass.style           = CS_HREDRAW | CS_VREDRAW;
        wndclass.lpfnWndProc     = MainWndProc;
        wndclass.cbClsExtra      = 0;
        wndclass.cbWndExtra      = 0;
        wndclass.hInstance       = hInstance;
        wndclass.hCursor         = LoadCursor(NULL, IDC_ARROW);
        wndclass.hIcon           = NULL;
        wndclass.hbrBackground   = GetStockBrush(WHITE_BRUSH);
        wndclass.lpszMenuName    = "wnetsvcs";
        wndclass.lpszClassName   = szAppName;

        if(!RegisterClass(&wndclass))
            return FALSE;
      }

    if(!(hWndMain = CreateWindow(szAppName,
                        "Windows Network Services API",
                        WS_OVERLAPPEDWINDOW,
                        CW_USEDEFAULT, 0,
```

```
                              CW_USEDEFAULT, 0,
                              NULL, (HMENU)NULL, hInstance, NULL)))
            return FALSE;

        ShowWindow(hWndMain, nCmdShow);
        UpdateWindow(hWndMain);
        while (GetMessage(&msg, NULL, 0, 0))
            {
            TranslateMessage(&msg);
            DispatchMessage(&msg);
            }

        return msg.wParam;
    }
LRESULT CALLBACK MainWndProc(HWND hWnd, UINT wMessage,
                              WPARAM wParam, LPARAM lParam)
    {
    DLGPROC lpDlgProc;
    HMENU   hMainMenu;

    switch(wMessage)
        {
        case WM_CREATE:
            // Disable Users and Groups menus until
            // the user selects a target server
            hMainMenu = GetMenu(hWnd);
            EnableMenuItem(hMainMenu, IDM_USERS,
                MF_BYPOSITION | MF_GRAYED);
            EnableMenuItem(hMainMenu, IDM_GROUPS,
                MF_BYPOSITION | MF_GRAYED);
            break;
        case WM_COMMAND :
            switch(wParam)
                {
                case IDM_ENUMSERVERS:
                    // Enumerate servers
                    (FARPROC) lpDlgProc =
                        MakeProcInstance((FARPROC) ViewServersDlgProc, hInst);
                    DialogBox(hInst, MAKEINTRESOURCE(IDB_VIEW_SERVERS),
                        hWnd, lpDlgProc);
                    FreeProcInstance((FARPROC) lpDlgProc);
                    break;
                case IDM_GROUP_MEMBERS:
                    // Show group member dialog box
                    (FARPROC) lpDlgProc =
                        MakeProcInstance((FARPROC) GroupMembersDlgProc, hInst);
                    DialogBoxParam(hInst,  MAKEINTRESOURCE(IDB_GROUP_MEMBERS),
                        hWnd, lpDlgProc, (LPARAM) (LPSTR) szServerName);
                    FreeProcInstance((FARPROC) lpDlgProc);
                    break;
                case IDM_ENUMGROUPS:
                    // View groups
                    (FARPROC) lpDlgProc = MakeProcInstance(
                        (FARPROC) ViewGroupsDlgProc,
                        hInst);
                    DialogBoxParam(hInst, MAKEINTRESOURCE(IDB_VIEW_GROUPS),
                        hWnd, lpDlgProc, (LPARAM) (LPSTR) szServerName);
                    FreeProcInstance((FARPROC) lpDlgProc);
                    break;
                case IDM_USER_GROUPS:
                    // Show dialog box with groups to which users
                    // belong
                    (FARPROC) lpDlgProc =
                        MakeProcInstance((FARPROC) UserGroupsDlgProc, hInst);
                    DialogBoxParam(hInst, MAKEINTRESOURCE(IDB_USER_GROUPS),
                        hWnd, lpDlgProc, (LPARAM) (LPSTR) szServerName);
                    FreeProcInstance((FARPROC) lpDlgProc);
                    break;
                case IDM_ENUMUSER:
                    // View users
                    (FARPROC) lpDlgProc =
                        MakeProcInstance((FARPROC) ViewUsersDlgProc, hInst);
                    DialogBoxParam(hInst, MAKEINTRESOURCE(IDB_VIEW_USERS),
                        hWnd, lpDlgProc, (LPARAM) (LPSTR) szServerName);
                    FreeProcInstance((FARPROC) lpDlgProc);
                    break;
                default:
                    break;
                }
```

```
            break;
        case WM_DESTROY :
            PostQuitMessage(0);
            break;
        default :
            return DefWindowProc(hWnd, wMessage, wParam, lParam);
        }
    return 0L;
}

BOOL CALLBACK UserEnumProc(LPSTR lpszServerName, LPSTR lpszUserName)
{
    // Add user name to list box
    if (hUserDlg != NULL)
        {
        SendDlgItemMessage(hUserDlg, wUserListboxID, LB_ADDSTRING, 0,
          (LPARAM) lpszUserName);
        }
    return TRUE;
}

BOOL CALLBACK ServerEnumProc(LPSTR lpszServerName, WORD wServerType)
{
    // Add server name to listbox
    SendDlgItemMessage(hServerDlg, wServerListboxID, LB_ADDSTRING,
      0, (LPARAM) lpszServerName);
    return TRUE;
}

BOOL CALLBACK GroupEnumProc(LPSTR lpszServerName, LPSTR lpszGroupName)
{
    // Add group name to listbox
    SendDlgItemMessage(hGroupDlg, wGroupListboxID, LB_ADDSTRING, 0,
      (LPARAM) lpszGroupName);
    return TRUE;
}

BOOL CALLBACK MemberGroupEnumProc(LPSTR lpszServerName, LPSTR lpszUserName,
                                  LPSTR lpszGroupName)
{
    // Populate listbox of groups to which user belongs
     SendDlgItemMessage(hUserDlg, wGroupListboxID, LB_ADDSTRING, 0,
      (LPARAM) lpszGroupName);
    return TRUE;
}

BOOL CALLBACK NonMemberGroupEnumProc(LPSTR lpszServerName,
                                     LPSTR lpszGroupName)
{
    // Populate listbox of groups to which user does not belong

    // We send the listbox that contains groups he does belong to
    // (which we have already populated) an LB_FINDSTRING message
    // to see if it's there

    // If not, we add it to the listbox of groups he doesn't belong
    // to

    if (SendDlgItemMessage(hUserDlg, wGroupListboxID,
        LB_FINDSTRING, (WPARAM) -1, (LPARAM) lpszGroupName) == LB_ERR)
        SendDlgItemMessage(hUserDlg, wNonGroupListboxID, LB_ADDSTRING, 0,
          (LPARAM) lpszGroupName);
    return TRUE;
}

BOOL CALLBACK GroupMemberEnumProc(LPSTR lpszServerName, LPSTR lpszGroupName,
                                  LPSTR lpszUserName)
{
    // Populate listbox of group members
    SendDlgItemMessage(hGroupDlg, wMemberListboxID, LB_ADDSTRING, 0,
      (LPARAM) lpszUserName);
    return TRUE;
}

BOOL CALLBACK NonGroupMemberEnumProc(LPSTR lpszServerName,
                                     LPSTR lpszUserName)
{
    // Populate listbox of users who do not belong to a group

    // Send listbox of group members (which is already populate)
    // an LB_FINDSTRING message to see if lpszUserName is
```

```
           // there
           if (SendDlgItemMessage(hGroupDlg, wMemberListboxID,
              LB_FINDSTRING, (WPARAM) -1, (LPARAM) lpszUserName) == LB_ERR)
              SendDlgItemMessage(hGroupDlg, wNonMemberListboxID, LB_ADDSTRING, 0,
                 (LPARAM) lpszUserName);
           return TRUE;
}

static WORD near _latoi(LPSTR lpszNumber)
{
    char szNumber[100];

    lstrcpy(szNumber, lpszNumber);

    return (WORD) atoi(szNumber);
}
BOOL CALLBACK ViewUsersDlgProc(HWND hDlg, UINT uMessage, WPARAM wParam,
                               LPARAM lParam)
{
    USERENUMPROC lpProc;
    char        szUserName[100];
    DWORD       dwCurSel;
    BOOL        bRetval;
    DLGPROC     lpDlgProc;
    ADDUSERSTRUCT AddUser;

    static LPSTR lpszServerName = NULL;

    switch (uMessage)
        {
        case WM_INITDIALOG:
            // Enumerate users by calling WNetEnumUsers()
            // Callback function populates the listbox
            hUserDlg = hDlg;
            wUserListboxID = IDB_USERS;
            lpszServerName = (LPSTR) lParam;
            SendDlgItemMessage(hDlg, IDB_USERS, LB_RESETCONTENT, 0, 0L);
            (FARPROC) lpProc = MakeProcInstance((FARPROC) UserEnumProc, hInst);
            WNetEnumUsers(lpszServerName, lpProc);
            FreeProcInstance((FARPROC) lpProc);
            SetFocus(GetDlgItem(hDlg, IDOK));
            return FALSE;
        case WM_COMMAND:
            switch (wParam)
                {
                case IDB_USERS:
                    if (HIWORD(lParam) == LBN_SELCHANGE)
                        {
                        // Turn on delete button when a user is selected
                        // from the listbox
                        EnableWindow(GetDlgItem(hDlg, IDB_DELETE_USER), TRUE);
                        }
                    break;
                case IDB_ADD_USER:
                    (FARPROC) lpDlgProc = MakeProcInstance(
                                        (FARPROC) AddUserDlgProc,
                                        hInst);

                    // Put up add user dialog box
                    if (DialogBoxParam(hInst,
                        MAKEINTRESOURCE(IDB_ADD_USER_DIALOG),
                        hDlg, lpDlgProc, (LPARAM) (ADDUSERSTRUCT FAR *) &AddUser)
                        == TRUE)
                        {
                        // Add the user
                        bRetval = WNetAddUser(lpszServerName, AddUser.szUserName,
                                    AddUser.szPassword,
                                    AddUser.bAdmin);

                        // If WNetAddUser() succeeds, add the user to the
                        // user listbox
                        if (bRetval)
                            SendDlgItemMessage(hDlg, IDB_USERS, LB_ADDSTRING,
                                0, (LPARAM) (LPSTR) AddUser.szUserName);
                        else
                            {
                            MessageBeep(MB_ICONHAND);
                            MessageBox(hDlg, "Unable to add user",
                                "WNet Error", MB_ICONHAND | MB_OK);
                            }
                        }
```

```
                    FreeProcInstance((FARPROC) lpDlgProc);
                     break;
                 case IDB_DELETE_USER:
                    if (MessageBox(hDlg, "Delete User?",
                        "Windows Network Services API", MB_YESNO) == IDYES)
                        {
                        dwCurSel = SendDlgItemMessage(hDlg, IDB_USERS,
                            LB_GETCURSEL, O, OL);
                        if (dwCurSel != LB_ERR)
                            {
                            // Get currently selected user from the listbox
                            SendDlgItemMessage(hDlg, IDB_USERS,
                                LB_GETTEXT, (WORD) dwCurSel,
                                (LPARAM) (LPSTR) szUserName);

                            // Delete her
                            bRetval = WNetDeleteUser(lpszServerName, szUserName);
                            }
                        else
                            bRetval = FALSE;

                        // If WNetDeleteUser() succeeds, remove
                        // the user from the listbox
                        if (bRetval)
                            {
                            SendDlgItemMessage(hDlg, IDB_USERS,
                                LB_DELETESTRING, (WORD) dwCurSel, OL);
                             EnableWindow(GetDlgItem(hDlg, IDB_DELETE_USER), FALSE);
                            }
                        else
                            {
                            MessageBeep(MB_ICONHAND);
                            MessageBox(hDlg, "Unable to delete user",
                                "WNet Error", MB_ICONHAND | MB_OK);
                            }
                        }
                    break;
                case IDOK:
                case IDCANCEL:
                    EndDialog(hDlg, TRUE);
                    return TRUE;
                default:
                    break;
                }
            break;
        default:
            break;
        }
    return FALSE;
}

BOOL CALLBACK AddUserDlgProc(HWND hDlg, UINT uMessage, WPARAM wParam,
                             LPARAM lParam)
  {
    static ADDUSERSTRUCT FAR *lpAddUser;

    switch (uMessage)
        {
        case WM_INITDIALOG:
            // Default to non-supervisor status
            lpAddUser = (ADDUSERSTRUCT FAR *) lParam;
            SendDlgItemMessage(hDlg, IDB_USER_ADMIN, BM_SETCHECK, FALSE, OL);
            return TRUE;
        case WM_COMMAND:
            switch (wParam)
                {
                case IDB_USER_NAME:
                    // Turn on OK button when user types something into
                    // the user name edit box
                    if (HIWORD(lParam) == EN_CHANGE)
                        EnableWindow(GetDlgItem(hDlg, IDOK), TRUE);
                    break;
                case IDOK:
                    // Capture entered information in global structure
                    GetDlgItemText(hDlg, IDB_USER_NAME, lpAddUser- >szUserName,
                        sizeof (lpAddUser->szUserName));
                    GetDlgItemText(hDlg, IDB_USER_PASSWORD,
                        lpAddUser->szPassword,
                         sizeof (lpAddUser->szUserName));
                    lpAddUser->bAdmin = IsDlgButtonChecked(hDlg, IDB_USER_ADMIN);
```

```
                    EndDialog(hDlg, TRUE);
                    return TRUE;
                case IDCANCEL:
                    EndDialog(hDlg, FALSE);
                    return TRUE;
                default:
                    break;
                }
        default:
            break;
        }
    return FALSE;
}

BOOL CALLBACK UserGroupsDlgProc(HWND hDlg, UINT uMessage, WPARAM wParam,
                                LPARAM lParam)
{
    static LPSTR lpszServerName = NULL;
    FARPROC lpProc;
    DWORD   dwCurSel;
    DWORD   dwCurSelIn, dwCurSelOut;
    char    szUserName[100];
    char    szGroupName[100];

    switch (uMessage)
        {
        case WM_INITDIALOG:
            // Remember window handle and control IDs
            hUserDlg = hDlg;
            wUserListboxID = IDB_USERS;
            wGroupListboxID = IDB_GROUPS_IN;
            wNonGroupListboxID = IDB_GROUPS_NOT_IN;
            lpszServerName = (LPSTR) lParam;
            SendDlgItemMessage(hDlg, IDB_USERS, LB_RESETCONTENT, 0, 0L);

            // Enumerate users, populate user listbox
            lpProc = MakeProcInstance((FARPROC) UserEnumProc, hInst);
            WNetEnumUsers(lpszServerName, (USERENUMPROC) lpProc);
            FreeProcInstance(lpProc);
            return TRUE;
        case WM_COMMAND:
            switch (wParam)
                {
                case IDB_USERS:
                    if (HIWORD(lParam) == LBN_SELCHANGE)
                        // Turn on the refresh button
                        EnableWindow(GetDlgItem(hDlg, IDB_REFRESH), TRUE);
                    break;
                case IDB_GROUPS_IN:
                    // Enable delete user from group button when
                    // a group the user already belongs to is selected
                    if (HIWORD(lParam) == LBN_SELCHANGE)
                        EnableWindow(GetDlgItem(hDlg, IDB_DELETE_USER), TRUE);
                    break;
                case IDB_GROUPS_NOT_IN:
                    // Enable add user to group button when a group
                    // the user does not belong to is selected
                    if (HIWORD(lParam) == LBN_SELCHANGE)
                        EnableWindow(GetDlgItem(hDlg, IDB_ADD_USER), TRUE);
                    break;
                case IDB_DELETE_USER:
                    dwCurSel = SendDlgItemMessage(hDlg, IDB_USERS,
                        LB_GETCURSEL, 0, 0L);
                    if (dwCurSel != LB_ERR)
                        {
                        // Get the user name
                        SendDlgItemMessage(hDlg, IDB_USERS, LB_GETTEXT,
                            (WPARAM) dwCurSel, (LPARAM) (LPSTR) szUserName);
                        dwCurSelIn = SendDlgItemMessage(hDlg, IDB_GROUPS_IN,
                            LB_GETCURSEL, 0, 0L);
                        if (dwCurSelIn != LB_ERR)
                            {
                            // Get the name of the group currently selected
                            // in the groups-belonged-to listbox
                            SendDlgItemMessage(hDlg, IDB_GROUPS_IN, LB_GETTEXT,
                                (WPARAM) dwCurSelIn, (LPARAM) (LPSTR) szGroupName);

                            // Remove the user from the group
                            if (WNetDeleteGroupMember(lpszServerName,
                                szGroupName, szUserName))
```

```
                {
                // Move group from groups in box to groups not in.
                SendDlgItemMessage(hDlg, IDB_GROUPS_IN,
                    LB_DELETESTRING, (WPARAM) dwCurSelIn, OL);
                SendDlgItemMessage(hDlg, IDB_GROUPS_NOT_IN,
                    LB_ADDSTRING, 0, (LPARAM) (LPSTR) szGroupName);

                // Disable delete user button
                EnableWindow(GetDlgItem(hDlg,
                    IDB_DELETE_USER), FALSE);
                }
            else
                {
                MessageBeep(MB_ICONHAND);
                MessageBox(hDlg, "Unable to delete user from group",
                    "WNet Error", MB_ICONHAND | MB_OK);
                }
            }
        }
    break;
case IDB_ADD_USER:
    dwCurSel = SendDlgItemMessage(hDlg, IDB_USERS,
        LB_GETCURSEL, 0, OL);
    if (dwCurSel != LB_ERR)
        {
        // Get user name
        SendDlgItemMessage(hDlg, IDB_USERS, LB_GETTEXT,
            (WPARAM) dwCurSel, (LPARAM) (LPSTR) szUserName);
        dwCurSelOut = SendDlgItemMessage(hDlg, IDB_GROUPS_NOT_IN,
            LB_GETCURSEL, 0, OL);
        if (dwCurSelOut != LB_ERR)
            {
            // Get name of group currently selected in the
            // non-member-group listbox
            SendDlgItemMessage(hDlg, IDB_GROUPS_NOT_IN, LB_GETTEXT,
                (WPARAM) dwCurSelOut, (LPARAM) (LPSTR) szGroupName);

            // Add the user
            if (WNetAddGroupMember(lpszServerName,
                szGroupName, szUserName))
                {
                // Move group from groups not in box to groups in.
                SendDlgItemMessage(hDlg, IDB_GROUPS_NOT_IN,
                    LB_DELETESTRING, (WPARAM) dwCurSelOut, OL);
                SendDlgItemMessage(hDlg, IDB_GROUPS_IN,
                    LB_ADDSTRING, 0, (LPARAM) (LPSTR) szGroupName);

                // Disable add user button
                EnableWindow(GetDlgItem(hDlg, IDB_ADD_USER), FALSE);
                }
            else
                {
                MessageBeep(MB_ICONHAND);
                MessageBox(hDlg, "Unable to add user to group",
                    "WNet Error", MB_ICONHAND | MB_OK);
                }
            }
        }
    break;
case IDB_REFRESH:
    // Populate the groups I'm in and the groups I'm
    // not in boxes
    SendDlgItemMessage(hDlg, IDB_GROUPS_IN,
        LB_RESETCONTENT, 0, OL);
    SendDlgItemMessage(hDlg, IDB_GROUPS_NOT_IN,
        LB_RESETCONTENT, 0, OL);
    dwCurSel = SendDlgItemMessage(hDlg, IDB_USERS,
        LB_GETCURSEL, 0, OL);
    if (dwCurSel != LB_ERR)
        {
        hUserDlg = hDlg;

        // Get name of user currently selected
        SendDlgItemMessage(hDlg, IDB_USERS, LB_GETTEXT,
            (WPARAM) dwCurSel, (LPARAM) (LPSTR) szUserName);
        lpProc = MakeProcInstance((FARPROC) MemberGroupEnumProc,
            hInst);

        // Enumerate member groups--callback function
        // populates the listbox
```

```
                        WNetEnumMemberGroups(lpszServerName, szUserName,
                            (MEMBERGROUPENUMPROC) lpProc);
                        FreeProcInstance(lpProc);

                        // Pick up groups he doesn't belong to
                        lpProc = MakeProcInstance(
                            (FARPROC) NonMemberGroupEnumProc, hInst);
                         WNetEnumGroups(lpszServerName, (GROUPENUMPROC) lpProc);
                        FreeProcInstance(lpProc);
                        }
                    break;
                case IDOK:
                case IDCANCEL:
                    EndDialog(hDlg, TRUE);
                    return TRUE;
                default:
                    break;
                }
        default:
            break;
        }
    return FALSE;
}

BOOL CALLBACK ViewServersDlgProc(HWND hDlg, UINT uMessage, WPARAM wParam,
                                 LPARAM lParam)
{
    FARPROC lpProc;
    DWORD   dwCurSel;
    HMENU   hMainMenu;

    switch (uMessage)
        {
        case WM_INITDIALOG:
            // Enumerate file servers, populate listbox
            hServerDlg = hDlg;
            wServerListboxID = IDB_SERVERS;
            SendDlgItemMessage(hDlg, IDB_SERVERS, LB_RESETCONTENT, 0, 0L);
            lpProc = MakeProcInstance((FARPROC) ServerEnumProc, hInst);
            WNetEnumServers((SERVERENUMPROC) lpProc, WNET_FILE_SERVER);
            FreeProcInstance(lpProc);
            SetDlgItemText(hDlg, IDB_CURRENT_SERVER, szServerName);
            return TRUE;
        case WM_COMMAND:
            switch (wParam)
                {
                case IDB_SERVERS:
                    if (HIWORD(lParam) == LBN_SELCHANGE)
                        {
                        // Turn on select button when user chooses
                        // a server in the listbox
                        EnableWindow(GetDlgItem(hDlg, IDB_SELECT), TRUE);
                        }
                    break;
                case IDB_SELECT:
                    dwCurSel = SendDlgItemMessage(hDlg, IDB_SERVERS,
                        LB_GETCURSEL, 0, 0L);
                    if (dwCurSel != LB_ERR)
                        {
                        // Capture selected server in global variable
                        // (szServerName)
                        SendDlgItemMessage(hDlg, IDB_SERVERS, LB_GETTEXT,
                            (WPARAM) dwCurSel, (LPARAM) (LPSTR) szServerName);
                        SetDlgItemText(hDlg, IDB_CURRENT_SERVER, szServerName);
                        // Enable Users and Groups items on main menu
                        EnableMenuItem(hMainMenu, IDM_USERS,
                            MF_BYPOSITION | MF_ENABLED);
                        EnableMenuItem(hMainMenu, IDM_GROUPS,
                            MF_BYPOSITION | MF_ENABLED);
                        DrawMenuBar(GetParent(hDlg));
                        }
                    break;
                case IDOK:
                case IDCANCEL:
                    if (szServerName[0] != '\0')
                        {
                        hMainMenu = GetMenu(GetParent(hDlg));
                        EnableMenuItem(hMainMenu, IDM_USERS,
                            MF_BYPOSITION | MF_ENABLED);
```

```
                    EnableMenuItem(hMainMenu, IDM_GROUPS,
                        MF_BYPOSITION | MF_ENABLED);
                    DrawMenuBar(GetParent(hDlg));
                    }
                EndDialog(hDlg, TRUE);
            return TRUE;
        default:
            break;
        }
    default:
        break;
    }
    return FALSE;
}

BOOL CALLBACK ViewGroupsDlgProc(HWND hDlg, UINT uMessage, WPARAM wParam,
                        LPARAM lParam)
{
    static LPSTR lpszServerName;
    FARPROC lpProc;
    DWORD   dwCurSel;
    char    szGroupName[100];
    DLGPROC lpDlgProc;
    BOOL    bRetval;

    switch (uMessage)
        {
        case WM_INITDIALOG:
            // Call WNetEnumGroups() to enumerate groups and
            // populate groups listbox
            hGroupDlg = hDlg;
            wGroupListboxID = IDB_GROUPS;
            lpszServerName = (LPSTR) lParam;
            lpProc = MakeProcInstance((FARPROC) GroupEnumProc, hInst);
            WNetEnumGroups(lpszServerName, (GROUPENUMPROC) lpProc);
            FreeProcInstance(lpProc);
            return TRUE;
        case WM_COMMAND:
            switch (wParam)
                {
                case IDB_GROUPS:
                    if (HIWORD(lParam) == LBN_SELCHANGE)
                        // Enable delete button when a group is selected
                        EnableWindow(GetDlgItem(hDlg, IDB_DELETE_GROUP), TRUE);
                    break;
                case IDB_ADD_GROUP:
                    // Put up add group dialog box
                    (FARPROC) lpDlgProc = MakeProcInstance(
                        (FARPROC) AddGroupDlgProc,
                        hInst);
                    if (DialogBoxParam(hInst,
                        MAKEINTRESOURCE(IDB_ADD_GROUP_DIALOG),
                        hDlg, lpDlgProc, (LPARAM) (LPSTR) szGroupName)
                        == TRUE)
                        {
                         // Add group
                        bRetval = WNetAddGroup(lpszServerName, szGroupName);
                        // If WNetAddGroup() succeeds, add group to the
                        // listbox
                        if (bRetval)
                            SendDlgItemMessage(hDlg, IDB_GROUPS, LB_ADDSTRING,
                                0, (LPARAM) (LPSTR) szGroupName);
                        else
                            {
                            MessageBeep(MB_ICONHAND);
                            MessageBox(hDlg, "Unable to add group",
                                "WNet Error", MB_ICONHAND | MB_OK);
                            }
                        }
                    FreeProcInstance((FARPROC) lpDlgProc);
                    break;
                case IDB_DELETE_GROUP:
                    if (MessageBox(hDlg, "Delete Group?",
                        "Windows Network Services API", MB_YESNO) == IDYES)
                        {
                        dwCurSel = SendDlgItemMessage(hDlg, IDB_GROUPS,
                            LB_GETCURSEL, 0, 0L);
                        if (dwCurSel != LB_ERR)
                            {
```

```
                    // Get name of currently selected group from listbox
                    SendDlgItemMessage(hDlg, IDB_GROUPS,
                        LB_GETTEXT, (WORD) dwCurSel,
                        (LPARAM) (LPSTR) szGroupName);
                    bRetval = WNetDeleteGroup(lpszServerName, szGroupName);
                    }
                else
                    bRetval = FALSE;

                // If WNetDeleteGroup() succeeds, remove it
                // from the listbox
                if (bRetval)
                    {
                    SendDlgItemMessage(hDlg, IDB_GROUPS,
                        LB_DELETESTRING, (WORD) dwCurSel, OL);
                    // Disable delete button
                    EnableWindow(GetDlgItem(hDlg, IDB_DELETE_GROUP), FALSE);
                    }
                else
                    {
                    MessageBeep(MB_ICONHAND);
                    MessageBox(hDlg, "Unable to delete group",
                        "WNet Error", MB_ICONHAND | MB_OK);
                    }
                }
            break;
        case IDOK:
        case IDCANCEL:
            EndDialog(hDlg, TRUE);
            return TRUE;
        default:
            break;
        }
    default:
        break;
    }
    return FALSE;
}
BOOL CALLBACK AddGroupDlgProc(HWND hDlg, UINT uMessage, WPARAM wParam,
                        LPARAM lParam)
{
    static LPSTR lpszGroupName;

    switch (uMessage)
        {
        case WM_INITDIALOG:
            lpszGroupName = (LPSTR) lParam;
            return TRUE;
        case WM_COMMAND:
            switch (wParam)
                {
                case IDB_GROUP_NAME:
                    if (HIWORD(lParam) == EN_CHANGE)
                        // Turn on OK button when user types something
                        // into group edit box
                        EnableWindow(GetDlgItem(hDlg, IDOK), TRUE);
                    break;
                case IDOK:
                    // Get name of new group from the edit box
                    GetDlgItemText(hDlg, IDB_GROUP_NAME, lpszGroupName,
                        MAXUSERNAMELENGTH);
                    EndDialog(hDlg, TRUE);
                    return TRUE;
                case IDCANCEL:
                    EndDialog(hDlg, FALSE);
                    return TRUE;
                default:
                    break;
                }
        default:
            break;
        }
    return FALSE;
}
BOOL CALLBACK GroupMembersDlgProc(HWND hDlg, UINT uMessage, WPARAM wParam,
                        LPARAM lParam)
{
    static LPSTR lpszServerName = NULL;
```

```
FARPROC  lpProc;
DWORD    dwCurSel;
DWORD    dwCurSelIn, dwCurSelOut;
char     szUserName[100];
char     szGroupName[100];

switch (uMessage)
    {
    case WM_INITDIALOG:
        // Remember window handle and control IDs
        hGroupDlg = hDlg;
        wGroupListboxID = IDB_GROUPS;
        wMemberListboxID = IDB_MEMBERS;
        wNonMemberListboxID = IDB_NON_MEMBERS;
        lpszServerName = (LPSTR) lParam;
        SendDlgItemMessage(hDlg, IDB_GROUPS, LB_RESETCONTENT, 0, 0L);

        // Call WNetEnumGroups() to populate group listbox
        lpProc = MakeProcInstance((FARPROC) GroupEnumProc, hInst);
        WNetEnumGroups(lpszServerName, (GROUPENUMPROC) lpProc);
        FreeProcInstance(lpProc);

        return TRUE;
    case WM_COMMAND:
        switch (wParam)
            {
            case IDB_GROUPS:
                if (HIWORD(lParam) == LBN_SELCHANGE)
                    // Enable refresh button when a group is selected
                    EnableWindow(GetDlgItem(hDlg, IDB_REFRESH), TRUE);
                break;
            case IDB_MEMBERS:
                if (HIWORD(lParam) == LBN_SELCHANGE)
                    // Enable delete button when a group member
                    // is selected
                    EnableWindow(GetDlgItem(hDlg, IDB_DELETE_USER), TRUE);
                break;
            case IDB_NON_MEMBERS:
                if (HIWORD(lParam) == LBN_SELCHANGE)
                    // Enable add button when a non-group member
                    // is selected
                    EnableWindow(GetDlgItem(hDlg, IDB_ADD_USER), TRUE);
                break;
            case IDB_DELETE_USER:
                dwCurSel = SendDlgItemMessage(hDlg, IDB_GROUPS,
                    LB_GETCURSEL, 0, 0L);
                if (dwCurSel != LB_ERR)
                    {
                    // Get name of currently selected group
                    SendDlgItemMessage(hDlg, IDB_GROUPS, LB_GETTEXT,
                        (WPARAM) dwCurSel, (LPARAM) (LPSTR) szGroupName);
                    dwCurSelIn = SendDlgItemMessage(hDlg, IDB_MEMBERS,
                        LB_GETCURSEL, 0, 0L);
                    if (dwCurSelIn != LB_ERR)
                        {
                        // Get name of currently selected user
                        SendDlgItemMessage(hDlg, IDB_MEMBERS, LB_GETTEXT,
                            (WPARAM) dwCurSelIn, (LPARAM) (LPSTR) szUserName);

                        // Delete him
                        if (WNetDeleteGroupMember(lpszServerName,
                            szGroupName, szUserName))
                            {
                            // Move user from members box to non-members.
                            SendDlgItemMessage(hDlg, IDB_MEMBERS,
                                LB_DELETESTRING, (WPARAM) dwCurSelIn, 0L);
                            SendDlgItemMessage(hDlg, IDB_NON_MEMBERS,
                                LB_ADDSTRING, 0, (LPARAM) (LPSTR) szUserName);

                            // Disable delete button
                            EnableWindow(GetDlgItem(hDlg,
                                IDB_DELETE_USER), FALSE);
                            }
                        else
                            {
                            MessageBeep(MB_ICONHAND);
                            MessageBox(hDlg, "Unable to delete user from group",
                                "WNet Error", MB_ICONHAND | MB_OK);
                            }
                        }
```

```
                }
            break;
        case IDB_ADD_USER:
            dwCurSel = SendDlgItemMessage(hDlg, IDB_GROUPS,
                LB_GETCURSEL, 0, 0L);
            if (dwCurSel != LB_ERR)
                {
                // Get group name from listbox
                SendDlgItemMessage(hDlg, IDB_GROUPS, LB_GETTEXT,
                    (WPARAM) dwCurSel, (LPARAM) (LPSTR) szGroupName);
                dwCurSelOut = SendDlgItemMessage(hDlg, IDB_NON_MEMBERS,
                    LB_GETCURSEL, 0, 0L);
                if (dwCurSelOut != LB_ERR)
                    {
                    // Get user name from non-member listbox
                     SendDlgItemMessage(hDlg, IDB_NON_MEMBERS, LB_GETTEXT,
                       (WPARAM) dwCurSelOut, (LPARAM) (LPSTR) szUserName);

                    // Add her
                    if (WNetAddGroupMember(lpszServerName,
                        szGroupName, szUserName))
                        {
                        // Move user from non-members box to members
                        SendDlgItemMessage(hDlg, IDB_NON_MEMBERS,
                            LB_DELETESTRING, (WPARAM) dwCurSelOut, 0L);
                        SendDlgItemMessage(hDlg, IDB_MEMBERS,
                            LB_ADDSTRING, 0, (LPARAM) (LPSTR) szUserName);

                        // Disable add button
                        EnableWindow(GetDlgItem(hDlg, IDB_ADD_USER), FALSE);
                        }
                    else
                        {
                        MessageBeep(MB_ICONHAND);
                        MessageBox(hDlg, "Unable to add user to group",
                          "WNet Error", MB_ICONHAND | MB_OK);
                        }
                    }
                }
            break;
        case IDB_REFRESH:
            // Populate the members and non-members boxes
            SendDlgItemMessage(hDlg, IDB_MEMBERS, LB_RESETCONTENT,
                0, 0L);
            SendDlgItemMessage(hDlg, IDB_NON_MEMBERS, LB_RESETCONTENT,
                0, 0L);
            dwCurSel = SendDlgItemMessage(hDlg, IDB_GROUPS,
                LB_GETCURSEL, 0, 0L);
            if (dwCurSel != LB_ERR)
                {
                // Get group members
                SendDlgItemMessage(hDlg, IDB_GROUPS, LB_GETTEXT,
                    (WPARAM) dwCurSel, (LPARAM) (LPSTR) szGroupName);
                lpProc = MakeProcInstance(
                    (FARPROC) GroupMemberEnumProc, hInst);
                WNetEnumGroupMembers(lpszServerName, szGroupName,
                    (GROUPMEMBERENUMPROC) lpProc);
                FreeProcInstance(lpProc);

                // Pick up non-members
                lpProc = MakeProcInstance(
                    (FARPROC) NonGroupMemberEnumProc, hInst);
                WNetEnumUsers(lpszServerName, (USERENUMPROC) lpProc);
                FreeProcInstance(lpProc);
                }
            break;
        case IDOK:
        case IDCANCEL:
            EndDialog(hDlg, TRUE);
            return TRUE;
        default:
            break;
        }
    default:
        break;
    }
return FALSE;
}

/********
```

```
/*********
 *
 * Listing B-2. WNETSVCS.H
 *
 * Copyright (c) 1992 Ralph P. Davis, All Rights Reserved
 *
 ********/

 /*===== Constants =====*/

// Main menu items
#define IDM_SERVERS                     0
#define IDM_USERS                       1
#define IDM_GROUPS                      2

// Popup items
#define    IDM_ADDUSER                      113
#define    IDM_ENUMUSER                     114
#define    IDM_DELETEUSER                   115
#define    IDM_ENUMSERVERS                  116
#define    IDM_ADDGROUP                     117
#define    IDM_ENUMGROUPS                   118
#define    IDM_DELETEGROUP                  119
#define    IDM_ADDUSERTOGROUP               120
#define    IDM_ENUMMEMBERGROUPS             121
#define    IDM_DELETEUSERFROMGROUP          122
#define    IDM_ENUMMEMBERS                  123
#define    IDM_VERIFYMEMBERSHIP             124
#define    IDM_USER_GROUPS                  153
#define    IDM_GROUP_MEMBERS                154

// Dialog-box fields
#define IDB_USERS                   100
#define IDB_VIEW_USERS              200
#define IDB_DELETE_USER             201
#define IDB_ADD_USER                202
#define IDB_ADD_USER_DIALOG         300
#define IDB_USER_PASSWORD           302
#define IDB_USER_ADMIN              303
#define IDB_USER_NAME               301
#define IDB_USER_GROUPS             400
#define IDB_GROUPS_IN               402
#define IDB_GROUPS_NOT_IN           403
#define IDB_REFRESH                 404
#define IDB_VIEW_SERVERS            500
#define IDB_CURRENT_SERVER          501
#define IDB_SELECT                  503
#define IDB_SERVERS                 502
#define IDB_VIEW_GROUPS             600
#define IDB_GROUPS                  601
#define IDB_DELETE_GROUP            602
#define IDB_ADD_GROUP               603
#define IDB_ADD_GROUP_DIALOG        700
#define IDB_GROUP_NAME              701
#define IDB_GROUP_MEMBERS           800
#define IDB_MEMBERS                 801
#define IDB_NON_MEMBERS             802

/*===== Global Variables =====*/

extern HINSTANCE    hInst;

/*********
 *
 * Listing B-3. WNETSVCS.RC
 *
 * Copyright (c) 1992 Ralph P. Davis, All Rights Reserved
 *
 ********/

#include <windows.h>
#include "wnetsvcs.dlg"
#include "wnetsvcs.h"
#include "wnetsvcs.mnu"

/*********
 *
 * Listing B-4. WNETSVCS.MNU
 *
 * Copyright (c) 1992 Ralph P. Davis, All Rights Reserved
```

```
*
*******/
WNETSVCS MENU
BEGIN
    MENUITEM "&Servers!", IDM_ENUMSERVERS
    POPUP "&Users"
    BEGIN
        MENUITEM "&View...", IDM_ENUMUSER
        MENUITEM "&Groups...", IDM_USER_GROUPS
    END
    POPUP "&Groups"
    BEGIN
        MENUITEM "&View...", IDM_ENUMGROUPS
        MENUITEM "&Members...", IDM_GROUP_MEMBERS
    END
END

/********
*
* Listing B-5. WNETSVCS.DLG
*
* Generated by Windows 3.1 SDK Dialog Editor
*
*******/

#include "wnetsvcs.h"
IDB_VIEW_USERS DIALOG 6, 18, 311, 216
STYLE DS_MODALFRAME | WS_POPUP | WS_VISIBLE | WS_CAPTION | WS_SYSMENU
CAPTION "View Users"
FONT 8, "MS Sans Serif"
BEGIN
    LISTBOX         IDB_USERS, 23, 31, 267, 152, LBS_SORT | WS_VSCROLL |
                    WS_TABSTOP
    DEFPUSHBUTTON   "OK", IDOK, 59, 195, 40, 14
    LTEXT           "User Names", -1, 23, 12, 51, 8
    PUSHBUTTON      "Delete", IDB_DELETE_USER, 143, 195, 40, 14, WS_DISABLED
    PUSHBUTTON      "Add...", IDB_ADD_USER, 227, 195, 40, 14
END

IDB_ADD_USER_DIALOG DIALOG 8, 20, 309, 120
STYLE DS_MODALFRAME | WS_POPUP | WS_VISIBLE | WS_CAPTION | WS_SYSMENU
CAPTION "Add User"
FONT 8, "MS Sans Serif"
BEGIN
    LTEXT           "User Name:", -1, 10, 17, 67, 8
    EDITTEXT        IDB_USER_NAME, 89, 17, 201, 12, ES_AUTOHSCROLL
    LTEXT           "User's Password:", -1, 10, 37, 66, 8
    EDITTEXT        IDB_USER_PASSWORD, 89, 38, 201, 12, ES_AUTOHSCROLL
    CONTROL         "Administrator?", IDB_USER_ADMIN, "Button",
                    BS_AUTOCHECKBOX | WS_TABSTOP, 10, 57, 66, 10
    DEFPUSHBUTTON   "Add", IDOK, 83, 86, 40, 14, WS_DISABLED
    PUSHBUTTON      "Cancel", IDCANCEL, 183, 86, 40, 14
END

IDB_USER_GROUPS DIALOG 6, 18, 316, 212
STYLE DS_MODALFRAME | WS_POPUP | WS_VISIBLE | WS_CAPTION | WS_SYSMENU
CAPTION "User Groups"
FONT 8, "MS Sans Serif"
BEGIN
    LTEXT           "Users", -1, 4, 19, 26, 8
    LTEXT           "Groups Belonged To", -1, 117, 19, 69, 8
    LTEXT           "Groups Not Belonged To", -1, 215, 20, 92, 8
    LISTBOX         IDB_USERS, 4, 34, 91, 126, LBS_SORT | WS_VSCROLL |
                    WS_TABSTOP
    LISTBOX         IDB_GROUPS_IN, 105, 34, 91, 126, LBS_SORT | WS_VSCROLL |
                    WS_TABSTOP
    LISTBOX         IDB_GROUPS_NOT_IN, 206, 34, 91, 126, LBS_SORT |
                    WS_VSCROLL | WS_TABSTOP
    PUSHBUTTON      "Refresh Groups", IDB_REFRESH, 5, 172, 58, 14,
                    WS_DISABLED
    PUSHBUTTON      "Delete From Group", IDB_DELETE_USER, 74, 172, 67, 14,
                    WS_DISABLED
    PUSHBUTTON      "Add To Group", IDB_ADD_USER, 152, 172, 67, 14,
                    WS_DISABLED
    DEFPUSHBUTTON   "Quit", IDOK, 235, 172, 40, 14
END

IDB_VIEW_SERVERS DIALOG 6, 18, 316, 215
STYLE DS_MODALFRAME | WS_POPUP | WS_VISIBLE | WS_CAPTION | WS_SYSMENU
```

```
CAPTION "View Servers"
FONT 8, "MS Sans Serif"
BEGIN
    LTEXT           "Current Server:", -1, 12, 15, 55, 8
    LTEXT           "", IDB_CURRENT_SERVER, 78, 15, 232, 8
    LISTBOX         IDB_SERVERS, 12, 31, 273, 138, LBS_SORT | WS_VSCROLL |
                    WS_TABSTOP
    PUSHBUTTON      "Select", IDB_SELECT, 56, 184, 40, 14, WS_DISABLED
    DEFPUSHBUTTON   "Quit", IDOK, 160, 184, 40, 14
END

IDB_VIEW_GROUPS DIALOG 6, 18, 311, 216
STYLE DS_MODALFRAME | WS_POPUP | WS_VISIBLE | WS_CAPTION | WS_SYSMENU
CAPTION "View Groups"
FONT 8, "MS Sans Serif"
BEGIN
    LISTBOX         IDB_GROUPS, 23, 31, 267, 152, LBS_SORT |  WS_VSCROLL |
                    WS_TABSTOP
    DEFPUSHBUTTON   "OK", IDOK, 59, 195, 40, 14
    LTEXT           "Groups", -1, 23, 12, 51, 8
    PUSHBUTTON      "Delete", IDB_DELETE_GROUP, 143, 195, 40, 14,
                    WS_DISABLED
    PUSHBUTTON      "Add...", IDB_ADD_GROUP, 227, 195, 40, 14
END

IDB_ADD_GROUP_DIALOG DIALOG 11, 86, 309, 70
STYLE DS_MODALFRAME | WS_POPUP | WS_VISIBLE | WS_CAPTION | WS_SYSMENU
CAPTION "Add Group"
FONT 8, "MS Sans Serif"
BEGIN
    LTEXT           "Group Name:", -1, 10, 17, 67, 8
    EDITTEXT        IDB_GROUP_NAME, 59, 17, 245, 12, ES_AUTOHSCROLL
    DEFPUSHBUTTON   "Add", IDOK, 83, 41, 40, 14, WS_DISABLED
    PUSHBUTTON      "Cancel", IDCANCEL, 183, 41, 40, 14
END

IDB_GROUP_MEMBERS DIALOG 6, 18, 316, 212
STYLE DS_MODALFRAME | WS_POPUP | WS_VISIBLE | WS_CAPTION | WS_SYSMENU
CAPTION "Group Members"
FONT 8, "MS Sans Serif"
BEGIN
    LTEXT           "Groups", -1, 4, 19, 26, 8
    LTEXT           "Users in Group", -1, 117, 19, 69, 8
    LTEXT           "Users Not in Group", -1, 215, 20, 92, 8
    LISTBOX         IDB_GROUPS, 4, 34, 91, 126, LBS_SORT | WS_VSCROLL |
                    WS_TABSTOP
    LISTBOX         IDB_MEMBERS, 105, 34, 91, 126, LBS_SORT | WS_VSCROLL |
                    WS_TABSTOP
    LISTBOX         IDB_NON_MEMBERS, 206, 34, 91, 126, LBS_SORT | WS_VSCROLL |
                    WS_TABSTOP
    PUSHBUTTON      "Refresh Members", IDB_REFRESH, 5, 172, 62, 14,
                    WS_DISABLED
    PUSHBUTTON      "Delete From Group", IDB_DELETE_USER, 74, 172, 67, 14,
                    WS_DISABLED
    PUSHBUTTON      "Add To Group", IDB_ADD_USER, 152, 172, 67, 14,
                    WS_DISABLED
    DEFPUSHBUTTON   "Quit", IDOK, 235, 172, 40, 14
END

;********
;
; Listing B-6. WNETSVCS.DEF
;
; Copyright (c) 1992 Ralph P. Davis, All Rights Reserved
;
;********

NAME            WNETSVCS
DESCRIPTION     'Windows Network Services Demo'
EXETYPE         WINDOWS
STUB            'WINSTUB.EXE'
CODE            MOVEABLE DISCARDABLE PRELOAD
DATA            MOVEABLE MULTIPLE PRELOAD
HEAPSIZE        4096
STACKSIZE       16384
EXPORTS

                MainWndProc
                UserEnumProc
                ServerEnumProc
                GroupEnumProc
```

```
                  MemberGroupEnumProc
                  GroupMemberEnumProc
                  ViewUsersDlgProc
                  AddUserDlgProc
                  NonMemberGroupEnumProc
                  UserGroupsDlgProc
                  ViewServersDlgProc
                  ViewGroupsDlgProc
                  AddGroupDlgProc
                  GroupMembersDlgProc
                  NonGroupMemberEnumProc
```

Listing B-7. WNETNW.LNK

```
wnetsvcs
wnetsvcs.exe
NUL
libw.lib commdlg.lib mlibcew.lib oldnames.lib wnetnw.lib, wnetsvcs.def
```

Listing B-8. WNETLM.LNK

```
wnetsvcs
wnetsvcs.exe
NUL
libw.lib commdlg.lib mlibcew.lib lan.lib oldnames.lib wnetlm.lib, wnetsvcs.def
```

Listing B-9. WNETVNST.LNK

```
wnetsvcs
wnetsvcs.exe
NUL
libw.lib commdlg.lib mlibcew.lib oldnames.lib wnetvnst.lib, wnetsvcs.def
```

```
########
#
# Listing B-10. WNETSVCS.MAK
#
# Copyright (c) 1992 Ralph P. Davis, All Rights Reserved
#
# Make file for Windows Network Services Demo
#
########

.c.obj:
    cl -AM -c -G2s -GA -GEf -Od -Zipe -W3 -DSTRICT -DWIN31 $*.c

wnetsvcs.obj : wnetsvcs.c wnetsvcs.h

wnetsvcs.res: wnetsvcs.rc wnetsvcs.h wnetsvcs.dlg wnetsvcs.mnu
    rc -r   wnetsvcs.rc

wnetsvcs.exe: wnetsvcs.obj wnetsvcs.res wnetsvcs.def
    link /CO /LI /NOPACKC /ALIGN:16 /NOD @@wnetlm.lnk
    rc   wnetsvcs.res
    copy wnetsvcs.exe wnetlm.exe
    link /CO /LI /NOPACKC /ALIGN:16 /NOD @@wnetnw.lnk
    rc   wnetsvcs.res
    copy wnetsvcs.exe wnetnw.exe
    link /CO /LI /NOPACKC /ALIGN:16 /NOD @@wnetvnst.lnk
    rc   wnetsvcs.res
    copy wnetsvcs.exe wnetvnst.exe
```

APPENDIX ▪ C

Windows Network Driver Demo

Description

The program listed in this appendix, WNETDEMO.EXE, demonstrates the use of network driver functions. Its main menu has four items when it is run on a network that supports long filenames, like OS/2 LAN Manager. The items are Configuration, Dialogs, Long File Names, and Help. Otherwise, only Configuration, Dialogs, and Help are supported.

The Dialogs popup menu calls the dialog-box functions contained in the network driver. If the underlying network operating system is Banyan VINES, an additional cascaded menu appears. This menu allows you to view the VINES single-selection and multiple-selection dialog boxes. Windows for Workgroups also has a cascaded menu that allows you to view the Windows for Workgroups dialog boxes.

The dialog boxes, and the functions that post them, are discussed in Chapters 9 and 14.

The Configuration item presents a pop up menu with five items: Capabilities, Directory Type, Print File, Watch Print Queue, and Error Codes. Capabilities presents a dialog box that describes the capabilities of the network driver. It does this by calling WNetGetCaps() and asking it what functions the driver supports. It also determines the driver version, the driver specification version, the user or computer name, and the driver description in SYSTEM.INI.

The Directory Type option calls WNetGetDirectoryType() to determine how the disk drives are being used.

The Print File option calls the GetOpenFileName() common dialog to select a file for printing, then uses the network driver functions to print it. Watch Print Queue... puts up a modeless dialog box that reports the status of print queues that are redirected to the network. It calls WNetWatchQueue(), which causes Windows to post SP_QUEUECHANGED messages to our main window procedure. When we get the message, we call WNetLockQueueData() to read the queue entries. When we have read the queue, we call WNetUnlockQueueData(). When the user terminates the dialog, we call WNetUnwatchQueue().

The last item on the Configuration menu, Error Codes, goes through the error numbers from 1 to 3000 and displays any corresponding error messages.

The Help menu allows you to view the help files for NetWare, LAN Manager, VINES, or Windows for Workgroups.

Code Listings

```
/********
*
* Listing C-1. WNETDEMO.C
*
* Copyright (c) 1992 Ralph P. Davis, All Rights Reserved
*
* Demonstrates use of network driver functions
*
```

```
********/

/*===== Includes =====*/

#define LFN   // Required for WINNET.H

#include <windd.h>
#include <commdlg.h>
#include "wnetdemo.h"
#include "wnetapi.h"
#include <winnet.h>
 #include <direct.h>
#include <stdio.h>
#include <stdlib.h>
#include <string.h>

#ifdef MULTINET
// If Windows for Workgroups, we'll call NDdeGetNodeName()
// to find out our computer name
#include <nddeapi.h>
#endif

#define INCL_NETWKSTA
#include <lan.h>            // For Windows for Workgroups

/*===== Constants =====*/

#define CCHMAXPATHCOMP 1  // Mentioned in DDK manual, but not #define'd

/*===== Types =====*/

// Needed for LFNCopy()
typedef struct tagCopyFileStruct
{
    char szFileName[255];
    BOOL bCopy;
} COPYFILESTRUCT;

/*===== Global Variables =====*/

HINSTANCE hInst;
BOOL      bWFW = FALSE;  // Are we running under Windows for Workgroups?

/*===== External Functions =====*/

void WINAPI ShowVINESDialog(HWND, BOOL);

/*===== Function Prototypes =====*/

LRESULT CALLBACK MainWndProc(HWND, UINT, WPARAM, LPARAM);
BOOL CALLBACK CopyQueryProc(void);
BOOL CALLBACK CapabilitiesDlgProc(HWND hDlg, UINT uMessage,
                                    WPARAM wParam, LPARAM lParam);
BOOL CALLBACK DirectoryTypeDlgProc(HWND hDlg, UINT uMessage,
                                    WPARAM wParam, LPARAM lParam);
BOOL CALLBACK WatchQueueDlgProc(HWND hDlg, UINT uMessage,
                                    WPARAM wParam, LPARAM lParam);
BOOL CALLBACK LongDrivesDlgProc(HWND hDlg, UINT uMessage,
                                    WPARAM wParam, LPARAM lParam);
BOOL CALLBACK ScanDirsDlgProc(HWND hDlg, UINT uMessage,
                                    WPARAM wParam, LPARAM lParam);
BOOL CALLBACK ScanFilesDlgProc(HWND hDlg, UINT uMessage,
                                    WPARAM wParam, LPARAM lParam);
BOOL CALLBACK CreateDirDlgProc(HWND hDlg, UINT uMessage,
                                    WPARAM wParam, LPARAM lParam);
BOOL CALLBACK CopyFileDlgProc(HWND hDlg, UINT uMessage,
                                    WPARAM wParam, LPARAM lParam);

BOOL GetFileName(HWND hWnd, LPSTR lpszFileName);
void LFNScanFilesToListBox(HWND hDlg, WORD wListBoxID, LPSTR lpszDrive,
                            BOOL bDir);
WORD MyRMDir(LPSTR lpszDirName);
WORD MyDeleteFile(LPSTR lpszFile);
WORD MyCreateDirectory(LPSTR lpszDir);
LPSTR GetListboxItemData(HWND hDlg, WORD wControlID, LPDWORD lpdwCurSel);
WORD PrintFile(LPSTR lpszFileName, LPSTR lpDeviceName);

/*===== LOCAL Functions =====*/

static void near DisplayNetError(void);
static BOOL near IsRemotePrinterConnected(void);
static BOOL near IsRemoteDriveConnected(void);

static WORD near _latoi(LPSTR lpszNumber);
```

```
/*===== LOCAL Variables =====*/

static BOOL bQueueWatched[3] = {FALSE};
static LPSTR near DeviceToQueue(LPSTR lpszDeviceName);
static char szMessage[400];
static char szErrorMsg[400];
static BOOL bLANManHelp = FALSE;
static BOOL bNetWareHelp = FALSE;
static BOOL bVINESHelp = FALSE;
static BOOL bWFWHelp = FALSE;

static HWND hMainWnd;
static HWND hQueueDlg = NULL;
static DLGPROC lpQueueDlgProc;
static WORD wRetval;

/*===== Function Definitions =====*/

int PASCAL WinMain(HINSTANCE hInstance,       // Application Instance Handle
                   HINSTANCE hPrevInstance,   // Previous Instance Handle
                   LPSTR  lpszCmdLine,        // Pointer to Command Line
                   int    nCmdShow)           // Show Window Option
{
    static char szAppName[] = "wnetdemo";

    MSG      msg;
    HWND     hWndMain;

    WNDCLASS wndclass;
    hInst = hInstance;

    if(!hPrevInstance)
    {
        wndclass.style          = CS_HREDRAW | CS_VREDRAW;
        wndclass.lpfnWndProc    = MainWndProc;
        wndclass.cbClsExtra     = 0;
        wndclass.cbWndExtra     = 0;
        wndclass.hInstance      = hInstance;
        wndclass.hCursor        = LoadCursor(NULL, IDC_ARROW);
        wndclass.hIcon          = NULL;
        wndclass.hbrBackground  = CreateSolidBrush(GetSysColor(COLOR_WINDOW));
        wndclass.lpszMenuName   = "wnetdemo";
        wndclass.lpszClassName  = szAppName;

        if(!RegisterClass(&wndclass))
            return FALSE;
    }

    if(!(hWndMain = CreateWindow(szAppName,
                    "Windows Network Driver Demo",
                    WS_OVERLAPPEDWINDOW,
                    CW_USEDEFAULT, 0,
                    CW_USEDEFAULT, 0,
                    NULL, (HMENU)NULL, hInstance, NULL)))
        return FALSE;

    ShowWindow(hWndMain, nCmdShow);
    UpdateWindow(hWndMain);

    hMainWnd = hWndMain;

    while(GetMessage(&msg, NULL, 0, 0))
    {
        if (hQueueDlg == NULL || !IsDialogMessage(hQueueDlg, &msg))
        {
            TranslateMessage(&msg);
            DispatchMessage(&msg);
        }
    }

    return msg.wParam;
}

LRESULT CALLBACK MainWndProc(HWND hWnd, UINT wMessage, WPARAM wParam, LPARAM lParam)
{
    static char    szPath[255];
    WORD           wMessageLength;
    FARPROC        lpProc;
    LPQUEUESTRUCT  lpQueueStruct;
    LPJOBSTRUCT    lpJobStruct;
    LPBYTE         lpQueueData;
    static char    szPropertyText[255];
```

```
WORD            i;
WORD            wCaps;
WORD            wNetType;
UINT            uMenuState;

switch(wMessage)
    {
    case WM_CREATE:
        // Eliminate Long File Names from main menu
        // if they're not supported. We find this out by
        // calling WNetGetCaps() with a WNNC_ADMIN argument.

        // This tells us which of the administrative functions
        // the network driver supports.

        if (!(WNetGetCaps(WNNC_ADMIN) & WNNC_ADM_LongNames))
            DeleteMenu(GetMenu(hWnd), IDM_LONGFILES, MF_BYPOSITION);

        // Check for Banyan VINES (either by itself or as a
        // Windows for Workgroups subnet)
        wNetType = WNetGetCaps(WNNC_NET_TYPE);
        if (!((((wNetType & WNNC_NET_MultiNet) &&
                (wNetType & WNNC_SUBNET_Vines)) ||
                (wNetType == WNNC_NET_Vines)))
            DeleteMenu(GetSubMenu(GetMenu(hWnd), IDM_DIALOGS),
                IDM_BANYAN, MF_BYPOSITION);

        // See if we're running under Windows for Workgroups
        if (!(((wNetType & WNNC_NET_MultiNet) &&
                (wNetType & WNNC_SUBNET_WinWorkgroups)))
            {
            DeleteMenu(GetSubMenu(GetMenu(hWnd), IDM_DIALOGS),
                IDM_WFW, MF_BYPOSITION);
            bWFW = FALSE;
            }
        else
            bWFW = TRUE;
        break;
    case WM_INITMENUPOPUP:
        if (lParam == (LPARAM) IDM_DIALOGS)
            {
            // Let's see which dialogs the driver supports
            wCaps = WNetGetCaps(WNNC_DIALOG);

            // WNetDeviceMode()?
            if (wCaps & WNNC_DLG_DeviceMode)
                uMenuState = MF_ENABLED;
            else
                uMenuState = MF_GRAYED;
            EnableMenuItem((HMENU) wParam, IDM_DEVICEMODE,
                MF_BYCOMMAND | uMenuState);

            // WNetBrowseDialog()?
            if (wCaps & WNNC_DLG_BrowseDialog)
                uMenuState = MF_ENABLED;
            else
                uMenuState = MF_GRAYED;
            EnableMenuItem((HMENU) wParam, IDM_BROWSE_DRIVES,
                MF_BYCOMMAND | uMenuState);
            EnableMenuItem((HMENU) wParam, IDM_BROWSE_QUEUES,
                MF_BYCOMMAND | uMenuState);
            // WNetConnectDialog()?
            if (wCaps & WNNC_DLG_ConnectDialog)
                uMenuState = MF_ENABLED;
            else
                uMenuState = MF_GRAYED;

            EnableMenuItem((HMENU) wParam, IDM_CONNECT_DRIVE,
                MF_BYCOMMAND | uMenuState);
            EnableMenuItem((HMENU) wParam, IDM_CONNECT_QUEUE,
                MF_BYCOMMAND | uMenuState);

            // WNetDisconnectDialog()?
            // Only enable Disconnect Network Drive option
            // if we're connected to a remote drive
            if ((wCaps & WNNC_DLG_DisconnectDialog) &&
                (IsRemoteDriveConnected()))
                uMenuState = MF_ENABLED;
            else
                uMenuState = MF_GRAYED;
```

```
            EnableMenuItem((HMENU) wParam, IDM_DISCONNECT_DRIVE,
               MF_BYCOMMAND | uMenuState);

            // Only enable Disconnect Network Print Queue option
            // if we're connected to a remote printer
            if ((wCaps & WNNC_DLG_DisconnectDialog) &&
               (IsRemotePrinterConnected()))
               uMenuState = MF_ENABLED;
            else
               uMenuState = MF_GRAYED;

            EnableMenuItem((HMENU) wParam, IDM_DISCONNECT_QUEUE,
               MF_BYCOMMAND | uMenuState);

            // WNetViewQueueDialog()?
            if (wCaps & WNNC_DLG_ViewQueueDialog)
                uMenuState = MF_ENABLED;
            else
               uMenuState = MF_GRAYED;
            EnableMenuItem((HMENU) wParam, IDM_VIEWQUEUE,
               MF_BYCOMMAND | uMenuState);

            // WNetPropertyDialog()?
            if (wCaps & WNNC_DLG_PropertyDialog)
               uMenuState = MF_ENABLED;
            else
               uMenuState = MF_GRAYED;

            EnableMenuItem((HMENU) wParam, IDM_PROPERTIES,
               MF_BYCOMMAND | uMenuState);

            // WNetConnectionDialog()?
            if (wCaps & WNNC_DLG_ConnectionDialog)
               uMenuState = MF_ENABLED;
            else
               uMenuState = MF_GRAYED;

            EnableMenuItem((HMENU) wParam, IDM_CONNECTION_DRIVES,
               MF_BYCOMMAND | uMenuState);
            EnableMenuItem((HMENU) wParam, IDM_CONNECTION_QUEUES,
               MF_BYCOMMAND | uMenuState);
            }
        break;
    case SP_QUEUECHANGED:
        // Queue change notification has been posted
        {
        LPSTR lpDeviceName;
        int   nDlgItem, nStatusItem;
        int   nQueueNameItem;

        if (hQueueDlg == NULL)
            break;
        // wParam indicates which queue is being reported
        // 1 is LPT1, 2 is LPT2, and 3 is LPT3
        switch (wParam)
            {
            case 1:
                lpDeviceName = "LPT1";
                nDlgItem = IDB_LPT1_INFO;
                nStatusItem = IDB_LPT1_STATUS;
                nQueueNameItem = IDB_LPT1_QUEUE;
                break;
            case 2:
                lpDeviceName = "LPT2";
                nDlgItem = IDB_LPT2_INFO;
                nStatusItem = IDB_LPT2_STATUS;
                nQueueNameItem = IDB_LPT2_QUEUE;
                break;
            case 3:
                lpDeviceName = "LPT3";
                 nDlgItem = IDB_LPT3_INFO;
                nStatusItem = IDB_LPT3_STATUS;
                nQueueNameItem = IDB_LPT3_QUEUE;
                break;
            }
        // Convert device name to queue name to humor some of
        // the drivers
        lpDeviceName = DeviceToQueue(lpDeviceName);

        // Get queue data by calling WNetLockQueueData()
        if ((lpDeviceName != NULL) && (wRetval =
```

```
                WNetLockQueueData(lpDeviceName, NULL, &lpQueueStruct))
                == WN_SUCCESS)
                {
                WORD i;
                LPSTR lpStatus;

                SendDlgItemMessage(hQueueDlg, nDlgItem,
                    LB_RESETCONTENT, 0, OL);
                lpQueueData = (LPBYTE) lpQueueStruct;

                lpJobStruct = (LPJOBSTRUCT) &lpQueueStruct[1];

                switch (lpQueueStruct->pqStatus)
                    {
                    case WNPRQ_ACTIVE:
                        lpStatus = "Active";
                        break;
                    case WNPRQ_PAUSE:
                        lpStatus = "Paused";
                        break;
                    case WNPRQ_ERROR:
                        lpStatus = "In Error";
                        break;
                    case WNPRQ_PENDING:
                        lpStatus = "Queue Being Deleted";
                        break;
                    case WNPRQ_PROBLEM:
                        lpStatus = "All Printers Stopped";
                        break;
                    }
                SetDlgItemText(hQueueDlg, nStatusItem, lpStatus);

                for (i = 0; i > lpQueueStruct->pqJobcount; ++i)
                    {
                    switch (lpJobStruct[i].pjStatus & WNPRJ_QSTATUS)
                        {
                        case WNPRJ_QS_QUEUED:
                            lpStatus = "Queued";
                            break;
                        case WNPRJ_QS_PAUSED:
                            lpStatus = "Paused";
                            break;
                        case WNPRJ_QS_SPOOLING:
                            lpStatus = "Spooling";
                            break;
                        case WNPRJ_QS_PRINTING:
                            lpStatus = "Printing";
                            break;
                        }
                    wsprintf(szMessage,
                        "%5d  %-10.10s  %-8.8s  %-25.25s  %10ld bytes",
                        lpJobStruct[i].pjId,
                        (LPSTR) (lpQueueData + lpJobStruct[i].pjUsername),
                        lpStatus,
                        (LPSTR) (lpQueueData + lpJobStruct[i].pjComment),
                        lpJobStruct[i].pjSize);

                    SendDlgItemMessage(hQueueDlg, nDlgItem,
                        LB_ADDSTRING, 0, (LPARAM) (LPSTR) szMessage);
                    }
                WNetUnlockQueueData(lpDeviceName);
                if (lpDeviceName != NULL)
                    GlobalFreePtr(lpDeviceName);
                }
            else
                {
                SendDlgItemMessage(hQueueDlg, nDlgItem,
                    LB_RESETCONTENT, 0, OL);
                SetDlgItemText(hQueueDlg, nQueueNameItem, "(Not redirected)");
                }
            }
        break;
    case WM_COMMAND:
        switch(wParam)
            {
            case IDM_VINES_SELECT_SINGLE:
            case IDM_VINES_SELECT_MULTIPLE:
                // Put up VINES browse dialog boxes
                // VINES doesn't support WNetBrowseDialog()
```

```
            ShowVINESDialog(hWnd, wParam == IDM_VINES_SELECT_MULTIPLE);
            break;
case IDM_VINES_HELP:
    // Open VINES help file
    if (!WinHelp(hWnd, "Z:\\HLPFILES\\WVINES.HLP",
        HELP_INDEX, OL))
        {
        MessageBeep(MB_ICONHAND);
        MessageBox(NULL, "Unable to load VINES help file",
            "WNet Error", MB_ICONHAND | MB_OK);
        }
    else
        bVINESHelp = TRUE;
    break;
case IDM_NETWARE_HELP:
     // Open NetWare help file
    if (!WinHelp(hWnd, "NETWARE.HLP", HELP_INDEX, OL))
        {
        MessageBeep(MB_ICONHAND);
        MessageBox(NULL, "Unable to load NetWare help file",
            "WNet Error", MB_ICONHAND | MB_OK);
        }
    else
        bNetWareHelp = TRUE;
    break;
case IDM_LANMAN_HELP:
    // Open LAN Manager help file
    if (!WinHelp(hWnd, "LANMAN21.HLP", HELP_INDEX, OL))
        {
        MessageBeep(MB_ICONHAND);
        MessageBox(NULL, "Unable to load LAN Manager help file",
            "WNet Error", MB_ICONHAND | MB_OK);
        }
    else
        bLANManHelp = TRUE;
    break;
case IDM_WFW_HELP:
    // Open Windows for Workgroups help file
    if (!WinHelp(hWnd, "WFWNET.HLP", HELP_INDEX, OL))
        {
        MessageBeep(MB_ICONHAND);
        MessageBox(NULL,
            "Unable to load Windows for Workgroups help file",
            "WNet Error", MB_ICONHAND | MB_OK);
        }
    else
        bWFWHelp = TRUE;
    break;
case IDM_ERROR_CODES:
    // Find all possible errors from 1 to 3000
    for (i = 1; i >= 3000; ++i)
        {
        wMessageLength = sizeof (szErrorMsg);
        szErrorMsg[0] = '\0';

        // WNetGetErrorText() converts error code in
        // first argument to message in second argument
        if ((wRetval =
        WNetGetErrorText(i, szErrorMsg, &wMessageLength))
        == WN_SUCCESS)
            {
            if (lstrlen(szErrorMsg) > 0)
                {
                wsprintf(szMessage, "Error code %d (%X)\n\n%s",
                    i, i, (LPSTR) szErrorMsg);
                 if (MessageBox(NULL, szMessage, "Network Error",
                    MB_OKCANCEL) == IDCANCEL)
                    break;
                }
            }
        else if (wRetval == WN_NOT_SUPPORTED)
            {
            MessageBeep(MB_ICONHAND);
            MessageBox(NULL, "WNetGetErrorText() is not supported",
                "WNet Error", MB_ICONHAND | MB_OK);
            break;
            }
        }
```

```
        break;
    case IDM_LFNLONGDRIVES:
        // Put up dialog box with drives supporting
        // long filenames
        lpProc = MakeProcInstance(
            (FARPROC) LongDrivesDlgProc, hInst);
        DialogBox(hInst, MAKEINTRESOURCE(IDB_LONGFILE_DRIVES),
            hWnd, (DLGPROC)lpProc);
        FreeProcInstance(lpProc);
        break;
    case IDM_PROPERTIES:
        {
        BOOL bSupported = FALSE;
        int nFileType;
        char szOpenFile[255] = "";
        OFSTRUCT OfStruct;

        // Use open file common dialog box to
        // get name of file
        if (GetFileName(hWnd, szOpenFile))
            {
            // Convert file name to full path
            OpenFile(szOpenFile, &OfStruct, OF_PARSE);
            lstrcpy(szOpenFile, OfStruct.szPathName);

            // Call WNetGetDirectoryType() to make sure
            // the file is a network file
            if ((wRetval =
                WNetGetDirectoryType(szOpenFile, &nFileType))
                == WN_SUCCESS &&
                nFileType == WNDT_NETWORK)
                {
                // We loop from 0 to 6--six is the limit for
                // File Manager network buttons
                for (i = 0; i > 6; ++i)
                    {
                    // WNetGetPropertyText() will return the text
                    // for the corresponding button
                    if (WNetGetPropertyText(i, WNPS_FILE,  szOpenFile,
                        szPropertyText, sizeof (szPropertyText),
                        WNTYPE_FILE) == WN_SUCCESS)
                        {
                        bSupported = TRUE;
                        // If the text is not zero-length, then we
                        // can call WNetPropertyDialog()
                        if (lstrlen(szPropertyText) > 0)
                            {
                            // Call WNetPropertyDialog() to display the
                            // network file attributes
                            if ((wRetval =
                                WNetPropertyDialog(hWnd, i, WNPS_FILE,
                                    szOpenFile, WNTYPE_FILE))
                                    == WN_NET_ERROR)
                                DisplayNetError();
                            else if (wRetval == WN_NOT_SUPPORTED)
                                {
                                MessageBeep(MB_ICONHAND);
                                MessageBox(NULL,
                                    "Property dialog is not supported",
                                    "WNet Error", MB_ICONHAND | MB_OK);
                                }
                            }
                        else
                            break;
                        }
                    else
                        break;
                    }
                }

            if (nFileType == WNDT_NORMAL && wRetval == WN_SUCCESS)
                {
                MessageBeep(MB_ICONHAND);
                MessageBox(NULL,
                    "No extended information available for local files",
                    "WNet Error", MB_OK | MB_ICONHAND);
                }
            else if (!bSupported)
                {
```

```
                MessageBeep(MB_ICONHAND);
                wsprintf(szMessage,
                    "No property dialog available for %s",
                    (LPSTR) szOpenFile);
                MessageBox(NULL, szMessage, "WNet Error",
                    MB_OK | MB_ICONHAND);
                }
            }
        }
    break;
case IDM_WATCH_QUEUE:
    // Create a modeless dialog box to monitor the
    // print queues
    if (hQueueDlg == NULL)
        {
        (FARPROC) lpQueueDlgProc = MakeProcInstance(
            (FARPROC) WatchQueueDlgProc, hInst);
        hQueueDlg = CreateDialog(hInst,
            MAKEINTRESOURCE(IDB_PRINT_MONITOR), hWnd,
                lpQueueDlgProc);
        }
    if (hQueueDlg != NULL)
        {
        LPSTR lpDeviceName;
        int   i;
        char  szDeviceName[10];

        for (i = 1; i >= 3; ++i )
            {
            // Convert device name to queue name
            wsprintf(szDeviceName, "LPT%-d", i);
            lpDeviceName = DeviceToQueue(szDeviceName);

            // Watch all queues
            if (lpDeviceName != NULL)
                {
                // Call WNetWatchQueue() to request
                // SP_QUEUECHANGED notification
                if ((wRetval = WNetWatchQueue(hWnd,
                    lpDeviceName, NULL, i))
                    != WN_SUCCESS)
                    {
                    if (wRetval == WN_NET_ERROR)
                        DisplayNetError();
                    else if (wRetval != WN_BAD_LOCALNAME &&
                            wRetval != WN_BAD_QUEUE)
                        {
                        MessageBeep(MB_ICONHAND);
                        wsprintf(szMessage, "Unable to watch %s",
                            (LPSTR) szDeviceName);
                        MessageBox(NULL, szMessage,
                            "WNet Error", MB_ICONHAND | MB_OK);
                        }
                    }
                else
                    {
                    PostMessage(hWnd, SP_QUEUECHANGED, i, 0L);
                    bQueueWatched[i - 1] = TRUE;
                    }
                GlobalFreePtr(lpDeviceName);
                }
            }
        }
    break;
case IDM STOP WATCH:
    {
    LPSTR lpDeviceName;
    int   i;
    char  szDeviceName[10];

    // Stop watching print queue--call
    // WNetUnwatchQueue() for LPT1, LPT2, and LPT3
    for (i = 1; i >= 3; ++i)
        {
        if (bQueueWatched[i - 1])
            {
            wsprintf(szDeviceName, "LPT%-d", i);
            lpDeviceName = DeviceToQueue(szDeviceName);
            if (lpDeviceName != NULL)
```

```
                    {
                    WNetUnwatchQueue(lpDeviceName);
                    GlobalFreePtr(lpDeviceName);
                    }
                bQueueWatched[i - 1] = FALSE;
                }
            }

        // Destroy modeless dialog
        if (hQueueDlg != NULL)
            {
            DestroyWindow(hQueueDlg);
            hQueueDlg = NULL;
            }
        FreeProcInstance((FARPROC) lpQueueDlgProc);
        lpQueueDlgProc = NULL;
        }
        break;
    case IDM_SUBMIT_PRINTJOB:
        {
        LPSTR lpDeviceName;
        char szPrintFileName[255];

        // Submit a print job to LPT3
        lpDeviceName = DeviceToQueue("LPT3");

        if (lpDeviceName != NULL && *lpDeviceName != '\0')
            {
            if (GetFileName(hWnd, szPrintFileName))
                {
                if (PrintFile(szPrintFileName, lpDeviceName)
                    == WN_SUCCESS)
                    {
                    wsprintf(szMessage,
                        "File %s submitted for printing",
                        (LPSTR) szPrintFileName);
                    MessageBox(hWnd, szMessage,
                        "Windows Network Driver Demo", MB_OK);
                    }
                else
                    {
                    wsprintf(szMessage, "Unable to print %s",
                        (LPSTR) szPrintFileName);
                    MessageBeep(MB_ICONHAND);
                    MessageBox(hWnd, szMessage, "WNet Error",
                        MB_OK | MB_ICONHAND);
                    }
                }
            }
        else
            {
            MessageBeep(MB_ICONHAND);
            MessageBox(hWnd,
                "You must redirect LPT3 to a network print queue"
                " for this option",
                "WNet Error", MB_OK | MB_ICONHAND);
            }
        }
        break;
    case IDM_CAPABILITIES:
        // Put up capabilities dialog box
        lpProc = MakeProcInstance(
            (FARPROC) CapabilitiesDlgProc, hInst);
        DialogBox(hInst, MAKEINTRESOURCE(IDB_CAPABILITIES),
            hWnd, (DLGPROC) lpProc);
        FreeProcInstance(lpProc);
        break;
    case IDM_DIRECTORYTYPE :
        // Put up dialog box with list of drive mappings
        lpProc = MakeProcInstance(
            (FARPROC) DirectoryTypeDlgProc, hInst);
        DialogBox(hInst, MAKEINTRESOURCE(IDB_DIRECTORY_TYPES),
            hWnd, (DLGPROC) lpProc);
        FreeProcInstance(lpProc);
        break;
    case IDM_SHARE_PRINTQ:
        // The last argument to WNetShareAsDialog()
        // consists of three contiguous strings.
        // <device name (LPT1, LPT2, etc.)>\0<printer name>\0
```

```
        // last string is "shared as " and the share name,
        // followed by two \0s.
        // This initializes the fields on the dialog box,
        // but can also be passed as an empty string.

        WNetShareAsDialog(hWnd, WNBD_CONN_PRINTQ,
            "LPT2\0IBM Proprinter\0shared as IBM\0");
        break;
case IDM_SHARE_DIR:
        WNetDemo_OnShareDir(hWnd);
        break;
case IDM_STOP_SHARE_DIR:
case IDM_STOP_SHARE_PRINTQ:
        WNetDemo_OnStopShare(hWnd, wParam);
        break;
case IDM_CONFIRM_EXIT:
        WNetDemo_OnConfirmExit(hWnd);
        break;
case IDM_BROWSE_HOSTS:
        {
        // Only valid for Windows for Workgroups
        char szSelectedStation[41];

        WNetServerBrowseDialog(hWnd, NULL,
            szSelectedStation, sizeof (szSelectedStation) - 1,
            0L);
        }
        break;
case IDM_BROWSE_DRIVES :
        // Call WNetBrowseDialog() to display drives
        // for connecting to network resources
        if ((wRetval = WNetBrowseDialog(hWnd, WNBD_CONN_DISKTREE,
                    szPath))
            == WN_NOT_SUPPORTED)
            MessageBox(NULL,
                "WNetBrowseDialog() is not supported "
                "for network drives",
                "WNet Error", MB_OK | MB_ICONHAND);
        else if (wRetval == WN_NET_ERROR)
            DisplayNetError();
        break;
case IDM_BROWSE_QUEUES:
        // Call WNetBrowseDialog() to display print queues
        // available for connecting to
        if ((wRetval =
                WNetBrowseDialog(hWnd, WNBD_CONN_PRINTQ, szPath))
            == WN_NOT_SUPPORTED)
            MessageBox(NULL,
                "WNetBrowseDialog() is not supported "
                "for printer queues",
                "WNet Error", MB_OK | MB_ICONHAND);
        else if (wRetval == WN_NET_ERROR)
            DisplayNetError();
        break;
case IDM_CONNECT_DRIVE:
        // Display WNetConnectDialog() screen
        // for connecting to network drives
        if ((wRetval =
            WNetConnectDialog(hWnd, WNTYPE_DRIVE)) ==
                WN_NOT_SUPPORTED)
            MessageBox(NULL, "WNetConnectDialog() with "
                "WNTYPE_DRIVE is not supported",
                "WNet Error", MB_OK | MB_ICONHAND);
        else if (wRetval == WN_NET_ERROR)
            DisplayNetError();
        break;
case IDM_CONNECT_QUEUE:
        // Display WNetConnectDialog() screen
        // for connecting to network print queues
        if ((wRetval =
            WNetConnectDialog(hWnd, WNTYPE_PRINTER)) ==
                WN_NOT_SUPPORTED)
            MessageBox(NULL, "WNetConnectDialog() with "
                "WNTYPE_PRINTER is not supported",
                "WNet Error", MB_OK | MB_ICONHAND);
        else if (wRetval == WN_NET_ERROR)
            DisplayNetError();
        // If we are successful, post queue change notifications
        if (wRetval == WN_SUCCESS)
```

```
            {
            PostMessage(hWnd, SP_QUEUECHANGED, 1, 0L);
            PostMessage(hWnd, SP_QUEUECHANGED, 2, 0L);
            PostMessage(hWnd, SP_QUEUECHANGED, 3, 0L);
            }
        break;
    case IDM_CONNECTION_DRIVES :
        // Put up WNetConnectionDialog() screen
        // for connecting to or disconnecting from
        // network drives
        if ((wRetval =
        WNetConnectionDialog(hWnd, WNTYPE_DRIVE)) ==
            WN_NOT_SUPPORTED)
            MessageBox(NULL, "WNetConnectionDialog() with "
              "WNTYPE_DRIVE is not supported",
              "WNet Error", MB_OK | MB_ICONHAND);
        else if (wRetval == WN_NET_ERROR)
            DisplayNetError();
        break;
    case IDM_CONNECTION_QUEUES:
        // Put up WNetConnectionDialog() screen
        // for connecting to or disconnecting from
        // network print queues
        if ((wRetval =
        WNetConnectionDialog(hWnd, WNTYPE_PRINTER)) ==
            WN_NOT_SUPPORTED)
            MessageBox(NULL, "WNetConnectionDialog() with "
              "WNTYPE_PRINTER is not supported",
              "WNet Error", MB_OK | MB_ICONHAND);
        else if (wRetval == WN_NET_ERROR)
            DisplayNetError();

        // Post queue change notifications
        if (wRetval == WN_SUCCESS)
            {
            PostMessage(hWnd, SP_QUEUECHANGED, 1, 0L);
            PostMessage(hWnd, SP_QUEUECHANGED, 2, 0L);
            PostMessage(hWnd, SP_QUEUECHANGED, 3, 0L);
            }
        break;
    case IDM_DEVICEMODE :
        if (WNetDeviceMode(hWnd) == WN_NET_ERROR)
            DisplayNetError();
        break;
    case IDM_DISCONNECT_DRIVE :
        // If Windows for Workgroups, make last connected
        // drive the default
        if (bWFW)
            {
            WORD wDrive;
            WNetGetLastConnection(WNTYPE_DRIVE, &wDrive);

            // wDrive will be -1 if there was no last
            // connection
            if (wDrive != (WORD) (-1))
                WNetSetDefaultDrive(wDrive);
            }

        // Call WNetDisconnectDialog() for drives
        if (WNetDisconnectDialog(hWnd, WNTYPE_DRIVE) ==
            WN_NET_ERROR)
            DisplayNetError();
        break;
    case IDM_DISCONNECT_QUEUE:
        // Call WNetDisconnectDialog() for printers
        if (WNetDisconnectDialog(hWnd, WNTYPE_PRINTER) ==
            WN_NET_ERROR)
            DisplayNetError();
        break;
    case IDM_VIEWQUEUE :
        // Nobody supports this function anyhow
        switch (WNetViewQueueDialog(hWnd, NULL))
            {
            case WN_NOT_SUPPORTED:
                MessageBox(NULL,
                  "WNetViewQueueDialog() not supported",
                  "WNet Error", MB_OK | MB_ICONHAND);
                break;
            case WN_OUT_OF_MEMORY:
```

```
                    MessageBox(NULL, "Out of memory", "WNet Error",
                        MB_ICONHAND | MB_OK);
                    break;
                case WN_NET_ERROR:
                    DisplayNetError();
                    break;
                default:
                    break;
                }
            }
        break;
    case WM_DESTROY :
        // Sign off of Windows Help
        if (bNetWareHelp)
          WinHelp(hWnd, "NETWARE.HLP", HELP_QUIT, OL);
        if (bLANManHelp)
          WinHelp(hWnd, "LANMAN21.HLP", HELP_QUIT, OL);
        if (bVINESHelp)
          WinHelp(hWnd, "Z:\\HLPFILES\\WVINES.HLP", HELP_QUIT, OL);
        if (bWFWHelp)
          WinHelp(hWnd, "WFWNET.HLP", HELP_QUIT, OL);
        PostQuitMessage(0);
        break;
    default :
        return DefWindowProc(hWnd, wMessage, wParam, lParam);
    }
    return OL;
}

BOOL CALLBACK CopyQueryProc() // Required for LFNCopy()
{
    return FALSE;
}

// The Directory Type dialog box shows a list of
// drives, and their current status (local, network, or not used)
BOOL CALLBACK DirectoryTypeDlgProc(HWND hDlg, UINT uMessage,
                                   WPARAM wParam, LPARAM lParam)
{
    WORD wDrive;
    int  nType;
    WORD wRetval;
    char szDrive[10];
    UINT uPathLength;

    switch (uMessage)
        {
        case WM_INITDIALOG:
            SendDlgItemMessage(hDlg, IDB_DRIVES, LB_RESETCONTENT, 0, OL);
            for (wDrive = 0; wDrive < 26; ++wDrive)
                {
                wsprintf(szDrive, "%c:\\", (wDrive + 'A'));

                // WNetGetDirectoryType() tells us WNDT_NORMAL (local) or
                // WNDT_NETWORK

                // The function fails if the drive is not used
                // However, this is only because I have written a front
                // end that calls the Windows API GetDriveType() if the
                // network driver function says the drive is WNDT_NORMAL.
                // Otherwise, we wouldn't be able to tell the difference
                // between local drives and unused drives.
                if ((wRetval = WNetGetDirectoryType(szDrive, &nType)) ==
                    WN_SUCCESS)
                    {
                    if (nType == WNDT_NORMAL)
                        wsprintf(szMessage, "%c: (local)", szDrive[0]);
                    else
                        {
                        wsprintf(szMessage, "%c: [", szDrive[0]);
                        uPathLength = sizeof (szMessage) - lstrlen(szMessage);
                        szDrive[2] = '\0';
                        WNetGetConnection(szDrive, &szMessage[lstrlen(szMessage)],
                            &uPathLength);
                        lstrcat(szMessage, "]");
                        }
                    }
                else
                    wsprintf(szMessage, "%c: (not used)", szDrive[0]);
```

```
            SendDlgItemMessage(hDlg, IDB_DRIVES, LB_ADDSTRING, 0,
                (LONG) (LPSTR) szMessage);
            }
        return TRUE;
    case WM_COMMAND:
        switch (wParam)
            {
            case IDOK:
            case IDCANCEL:
                EndDialog(hDlg, TRUE);
                return TRUE;
            }
        break;
        }
    return FALSE;
}

// The Long Drives dialog box puts up a list of drives
// supporting long filenames (probably LAN Manager drives on a
// server running the OS/2 High Performance File System
BOOL CALLBACK LongDrivesDlgProc(HWND hDlg, UINT uMessage,
                                WPARAM wParam, LPARAM lParam)
{
    WORD  wDrive;
    int   nType;
    char  szDrive[100];
    WORD  wMessageLength;
    int   nPosition;
    DLGPROC lpDlgProc;
    DWORD dwCurSel;
    WORD  wDialogBoxID;

    switch (uMessage)
        {
        case WM_INITDIALOG:
            SendDlgItemMessage(hDlg, IDB_DRIVES, LB_RESETCONTENT, 0, 0L);
            for (wDrive = 0; wDrive > 26; ++wDrive)
                {
                // LFNVolumeType() takes the drive number as a one-based
                // index (1 = drive A:), and returns its type.
                // If the type is VOLUME_LONGNAMES, then the drive
                // supports long file names.
                // Otherwise, the type will be VOLUME_STANDARD

                if (LFNVolumeType(wDrive + 1, &nType) == WN_SUCCESS &&
                    nType == VOLUME_LONGNAMES)
                    {
                    wsprintf(szDrive, "%c:\\   [", (wDrive + 'A'));
                    // LFNGetVolumeLabel() gets the volume label for the drive
                    // This gives us a more descriptive entry in the listbox
                    LFNGetVolumeLabel(wDrive + 1, &szDrive[lstrlen(szDrive)]);
                    lstrcat(szDrive, "]   [");
                    nPosition = (int) lstrlen(szDrive);
                    wMessageLength = sizeof (szDrive) - nPosition - 1;
                    szDrive[2] = '\0';

                    // We also call WNetGetConnection() to find out
                    // what network share the drive is mapped to
                    WNetGetConnection(szDrive, &szDrive[nPosition],
                        &wMessageLength);
                    szDrive[2] = '\\';
                    lstrcat(szDrive, "]");
                    SendDlgItemMessage(hDlg, IDB_DRIVES, LB_ADDSTRING, 0,
                        (LPARAM) (LPSTR) szDrive);
                    }
                }
            return TRUE;
        case WM_COMMAND:
            switch (wParam)
                {
                case IDB_DRIVES:
                    if (HIWORD(lParam) == LBN_SELCHANGE)
                        {
                        // The user has selected a drive
                        // Get the current selection from the listbox,
                        // and enable the Scan Directories and
                        // Scan Files buttons
                        dwCurSel = SendDlgItemMessage(hDlg, IDB_DRIVES,
                            LB_GETCURSEL, 0, 0L);
```

```
                        EnableWindow(GetDlgItem(hDlg, IDB_SCAN_DIRS),
                           (dwCurSel != LB_ERR));
                        EnableWindow(GetDlgItem(hDlg, IDB_SCAN_FILES),
                           (dwCurSel != LB_ERR));
                        }
                    else if (HIWORD(lParam) == LBN_DBLCLK)
                        // Double-click means scan subdirectories
                        SendMessage(hDlg, WM_COMMAND, IDB_SCAN_DIRS, 0L);
                    break;
                case IDB_SCAN_FILES:
                case IDB_SCAN_DIRS:
                    // Get the currently selected drive,
                    // then put up the appropriate dialog box
                    dwCurSel = SendDlgItemMessage(hDlg, IDB_DRIVES,
                        LB_GETCURSEL, 0, 0L);
                    if (dwCurSel != LB_ERR)
                        {
                        // Get drive letter from listbox
                        SendDlgItemMessage(hDlg, IDB_DRIVES, LB_GETTEXT,
                           (WORD) dwCurSel, (LPARAM) (LPSTR) szDrive);
                        szDrive[3] = '\0';
                        if (wParam == IDB_SCAN_DIRS)
                           {
                           wDialogBoxID = IDB_LONG_DIRS;
                           (FARPROC) lpDlgProc = MakeProcInstance((FARPROC)
                              ScanDirsDlgProc, hInst);
                           }
                        else
                           {
                           wDialogBoxID = IDB_LONG_FILES;
                           (FARPROC) lpDlgProc = MakeProcInstance((FARPROC)
                              ScanFilesDlgProc, hInst);
                           }
                        DialogBoxParam(hInst, MAKEINTRESOURCE(wDialogBoxID),
                           hDlg, lpDlgProc, (LPARAM) (LPSTR) szDrive);
                        FreeProcInstance((FARPROC) lpDlgProc);
                        }
                    break;
                case IDOK:
                case IDCANCEL:
                    EndDialog(hDlg, TRUE);
                    return TRUE;
                }
            break;
        }
    return FALSE;
}

// The Scan Directories dialog box puts up a listbox
// containing the subdirectories of a given directory on
// a drive supporting long filenames

// It can be called recursively
BOOL CALLBACK ScanDirsDlgProc(HWND hDlg, UINT uMessage,
                              WPARAM wParam, LPARAM lParam)
{
    LPSTR    lpszDrive;
    char     szHeader[255];
    DWORD    dwCurSel;
    DLGPROC  lpDlgProc;
    WORD     wDialogBoxID;

    switch (uMessage)
        {
        case WM_INITDIALOG:
            // Drive is passed down as lParam by invocation of
            // DialogBoxParam().
            lpszDrive = (LPSTR) lParam;
            wsprintf(szHeader, "Subdirectories of %s", lpszDrive);
            SetWindowText(hDlg, (LPSTR) szHeader);

            lstrcpy(szHeader, lpszDrive);

            // LFNScanFilesToListBox() is defined in this file
            // (it's not a network driver function)
            LFNScanFilesToListBox(hDlg, IDB_DIRS, lpszDrive, TRUE);
            break;

        case WM_COMMAND:
```

```
switch (wParam)
    {
    case IDB_CREATE_DIR:
        // Create a new directory--put up Create Directory
        // dialog box

        // Drive letter is stored as item data for listbox
        // entries
        (FARPROC) lpDlgProc = MakeProcInstance(
            (FARPROC) CreateDirDlgProc,
            hInst);
        lpszDrive = (LPSTR) SendDlgItemMessage(hDlg, IDB_DIRS,
            LB_GETITEMDATA, 0, OL);

        if (DialogBoxParam(hInst,
            MAKEINTRESOURCE(IDB_CREATE_DIRECTORY),
            hDlg, lpDlgProc, (LPARAM) lpszDrive))
            {
            char *pBackslash;

            // Find new directory portion of szMessage
            // szMessage is a global variable, it's used
            // by CreateDirDlgProc() to return the new
            // directory name

            // Scan one character past the last backslash
            pBackslash = strrchr(szMessage, '\\');
            if (pBackslash == NULL)
                pBackslash = szMessage;
            else
                ++pBackslash;

            // MyCreateDirectory() decides whether it needs
            // to call mkdir() or the long filename
            // equivalent, LFNMKDir().

            if (MyCreateDirectory(szMessage) == 0)
                SendDlgItemMessage(hDlg, IDB_DIRS,
                    LB_ADDSTRING, 0, (LPARAM) (LPSTR) pBackslash);
            else
                {
                MessageBeep(MB_ICONHAND);
                MessageBox(hDlg, "Unable to create directory",
                    "WNet Error", MB_ICONHAND | MB_OK);
                }
            }
        FreeProcInstance((FARPROC) lpDlgProc);
        break;
    case IDB_SCAN_FILES:
    case IDB_SCAN_DIRS:
        // User wants to scan files or directories in
        // a subdirectory

        // Do a recursive invocation of this dialog box
        lpszDrive = GetListboxItemData(hDlg, IDB_DIRS, &dwCurSel);
        if (lpszDrive != NULL)
            {
            if (wParam == IDB_SCAN_DIRS)
                {
                wDialogBoxID = IDB_LONG_DIRS;
                (FARPROC) lpDlgProc = MakeProcInstance((FARPROC)
                    ScanDirsDlgProc, hInst);
                }
            else
                {
                wDialogBoxID = IDB_LONG_FILES;
                (FARPROC) lpDlgProc = MakeProcInstance((FARPROC)
                    ScanFilesDlgProc, hInst);
                }
            DialogBoxParam(hInst, MAKEINTRESOURCE(wDialogBoxID),
                hDlg, lpDlgProc, (LPARAM) lpszDrive);
            FreeProcInstance((FARPROC) lpDlgProc);
            }
        break;
    case IDB_DIRS:
        if (HIWORD(lParam) == LBN_SELCHANGE)
            {
            // Enable push buttons if user selects a directory
            EnableWindow(GetDlgItem(hDlg, IDB_DELETE_DIR), TRUE);
            EnableWindow(GetDlgItem(hDlg, IDB_SCAN_DIRS),  TRUE);
```

```
                        EnableWindow(GetDlgItem(hDlg, IDB_SCAN_FILES), TRUE);
                        }
                    else if (HIWORD(lParam) == LBN_DBLCLK)
                        // Double click means scan subdirectories
                        SendMessage(hDlg, WM_COMMAND, IDB_SCAN_DIRS, OL);
                    break;
                case IDB_DELETE_DIR:
                    if (MessageBox(hDlg, "Delete directory?",
                        "Windows Network Driver Demo", MB_YESNO) == IDYES)
                        {
                        lpszDrive = GetListboxItemData(hDlg, IDB_DIRS, &dwCurSel);
                        if (lpszDrive != NULL)
                            {
                            lstrcpy(szHeader, lpszDrive);

                            // MyRMDir() decides whether it needs to call
                            // rmdir() or the long filename equivalent,
                            // LFNRMDir().
                            if (MyRMDir((LPSTR) szHeader) == O)
                                SendDlgItemMessage(hDlg, IDB_DIRS,
                                    LB_DELETESTRING, (WORD) dwCurSel, OL);
                            else
                                {
                                MessageBeep(MB_ICONHAND);
                                MessageBox(hDlg, "Unable to delete directory",
                                    "WNet Error", MB_ICONHAND | MB_OK);
                                }
                            }
                        }
                    break;
                case IDOK:
                case IDCANCEL:
                    EndDialog(hDlg, TRUE);
                    return TRUE;
                default:
                    break;
                }
        default:
            break;
        }
    return FALSE;
}

// The Scan Files dialog box puts up a listbox with the files
// contained in a directory on a drive supporting long filenames
BOOL CALLBACK ScanFilesDlgProc(HWND hDlg, UINT uMessage,
                                WPARAM wParam, LPARAM lParam)
{
    LPSTR lpszDrive;
    char szHeader[255];
    DWORD  dwCurSel, dwOldCurSel;
    COPYFILESTRUCT CopyFile;
    FARPROC lpProc;
    DLGPROC lpDlgProc;
    WORD    wRetval;

    switch (uMessage)
        {
        case WM_INITDIALOG:
            lpszDrive = (LPSTR) lParam;
            wsprintf(szHeader, "Files in %s", lpszDrive);
            SetWindowText(hDlg, (LPSTR) szHeader);

            // LFNScanFilesToListBox() is one of our functions,
            // not a driver function
            LFNScanFilesToListBox(hDlg, IDB_FILES, lpszDrive, FALSE);
            break;

        case WM_COMMAND:
            switch (wParam)
                {
                case IDB_FILES:
                    if (HIWORD(lParam) == LBN_SELCHANGE)
                        {
                        // Enable push buttons if user selects a file
                        EnableWindow(GetDlgItem(hDlg, IDB_DELETE_FILE), TRUE);
                        EnableWindow(GetDlgItem(hDlg, IDB_COPY_FILE), TRUE);
                        EnableWindow(GetDlgItem(hDlg, IDB_MOVE_FILE), TRUE);
                        }
```

```
        break;
case IDB_COPY_FILE:
case IDB_MOVE_FILE:
    (FARPROC) lpDlgProc = MakeProcInstance(
        (FARPROC) CopyFileDlgProc,
        hInst);
    lpszDrive = GetListboxItemData(hDlg, IDB_FILES, &dwCurSel);
    dwOldCurSel = dwCurSel;
    lstrcpy(CopyFile.szFileName, lpszDrive);
    CopyFile.bCopy = (wParam == IDB_COPY_FILE);

    // Put up copy file dialog box
    if (DialogBoxParam(hInst, MAKEINTRESOURCE(IDB_COPY_FILE),
        hDlg, lpDlgProc,
        (LPARAM) (COPYFILESTRUCT FAR *) &CopyFile))
        {
        lpProc = MakeProcInstance((FARPROC) CopyQueryProc, hInst);
        if (CopyFile.bCopy)
            {
             // User wants to copy a file, call LFNCopy()
             // It takes three arguments--the source filename,
             // the destination filename, and a pointer to
             // a callback function. The callback allows the
             // user to abort a long copy operation. If the
             // function returns TRUE, the copy is aborted.

             // Our callback is a dummy, it just returns FALSE.
             wRetval = LFNCopy(CopyFile.szFileName,
                szMessage, (PQUERYPROC) lpProc);
            }
        else
            {
            // LFNMove() does a copy/delete operation
            // It takes only two arguments, the source file
            // and the target file
            wRetval = LFNMove(CopyFile.szFileName,
                szMessage);
            }
        if (wRetval != 0)
            {
            MessageBeep(MB_ICONHAND);
            MessageBox(hDlg, "Unable to copy/rename file",
                "WNet Error",
                MB_ICONHAND | MB_OK);
            }
        else
            {
            char *pBackslash;
            LPSTR lpBackslash;

            // Copy or move was successful--add the new
            // file to the listbox

            // Move to character following last backslash
            // Listbox contains file names only
            pBackslash = strrchr(szMessage, '\\');
            if (pBackslash != NULL)
                ++pBackslash;
            else
                pBackslash = szMessage;
            SendDlgItemMessage(hDlg, IDB_FILES, LB_ADDSTRING,
                0, (LPARAM) (LPSTR) pBackslash);
            dwCurSel = SendDlgItemMessage(hDlg, IDB_FILES,
                LB_FINDSTRING, (WORD) -1,
                (LPARAM) (LPSTR) pBackslash);

            // Set new listbox item data to its parent
            // directory
            lpBackslash = &lpszDrive[lstrlen(lpszDrive) - 1];

            while (*lpBackslash != '\\' && lpBackslash != lpszDrive)
                --lpBackslash;
            if (*lpBackslash == '\\')
                *lpBackslash = '\0';
            if (dwCurSel != LB_ERR)
                SendDlgItemMessage(hDlg, IDB_FILES,
                    LB_SETITEMDATA, (WORD) dwCurSel,
                    (LPARAM) lpszDrive);

            // If requested operation was a move,
```

```
                            // delete old file name from the listbox
                            if (!CopyFile.bCopy)
                                SendDlgItemMessage(hDlg, IDB_FILES, LB_DELETESTRING,
                                    (WORD) dwOldCurSel, OL);
                            }
                        FreeProcInstance(lpProc);
                        }
                    FreeProcInstance((FARPROC) lpDlgProc);
                    break;
                case IDB_DELETE_FILE:
                    if (MessageBox(hDlg, "Delete file?",
                        "Windows Network Driver Demo", MB_YESNO) == IDYES)
                        {
                        lpszDrive = GetListboxItemData(hDlg, IDB_FILES, &dwCurSel);
                        if (lpszDrive != NULL)
                            {
                            lstrcpy(szHeader, lpszDrive);

                            // MyDeleteFile() does appropriate delete operation,
                            // either unlink() or LFNDelete()
                            if (MyDeleteFile((LPSTR) szHeader) == 0)
                                SendDlgItemMessage(hDlg, IDB_FILES,
                                    LB_DELETESTRING, (WORD) dwCurSel, OL);
                            else
                                {
                                MessageBeep(MB_ICONHAND);
                                MessageBox(hDlg, "Unable to delete file",
                                    "WNet Error", MB_ICONHAND | MB_OK);
                                }
                            }
                        }
                    break;
                case IDOK:
                case IDCANCEL:
                    EndDialog(hDlg, TRUE);
                    return TRUE;
                default:
                    break;
                }
        default:
            break;
        }
    return FALSE;
}

// The Create Directory dialog box allows the user to
// create a new directory on a drive support long filenames
BOOL CALLBACK CreateDirDlgProc(HWND hDlg, UINT uMessage,
                                WPARAM wParam, LPARAM lParam)
{
    LPSTR lpszDrive;
    char szHeader[255];

    switch (uMessage)
        {
        case WM_INITDIALOG:
            // lParam is the parent drive or directory, passed by
            // call to DialogBoxParam()
            lpszDrive = (LPSTR) lParam;

            lstrcpy(szHeader, lpszDrive);
            if (szHeader[lstrlen(szHeader) - 1] != '\\')
                lstrcat(szHeader, "\\");
            SetDlgItemText(hDlg, IDB_DIR_NAME, (LPSTR) szHeader);
            SendDlgItemMessage(hDlg, IDB_DIR_NAME, EM_LIMITTEXT, 255, OL);
            break;

        case WM_COMMAND:
            switch (wParam)
                {
                case IDOK:
                    GetDlgItemText(hDlg, IDB_DIR_NAME,
                        (LPSTR) szMessage, sizeof (szMessage));
                    EndDialog(hDlg, TRUE);
                    return TRUE;
                case IDCANCEL:
                    EndDialog(hDlg, FALSE);
                    return TRUE;
                default:
```

```
                    break;
                }
            default:
                break;
            }
        return FALSE;
}

// The Copy File dialog box gets the name of the file
// to copy or rename a given file to
BOOL CALLBACK CopyFileDlgProc(HWND hDlg, UINT uMessage,
                               WPARAM wParam, LPARAM lParam)
{
    COPYFILESTRUCT FAR *lpCopyFile;

    lpCopyFile = (COPYFILESTRUCT FAR *) lParam;

    switch (uMessage)
        {
        case WM_INITDIALOG:
            // lParam is a pointer to a COPYFILESTRUCT structure
            // This is a type defined above. It contains the
            // file name and a BOOL variable indicating whether
            // this is a copy (TRUE) or a move (FALSE)

            if (lpCopyFile->bCopy)
                SetWindowText(hDlg, "Copy File");
            else
                SetWindowText(hDlg, "Rename File");

            SetDlgItemText(hDlg, IDB_SOURCE_FILE, lpCopyFile- >szFileName);
            SetDlgItemText(hDlg, IDB_TARGET_FILE, lpCopyFile- >szFileName);

            SendDlgItemMessage(hDlg, IDB_TARGET_FILE, EM_LIMITTEXT, 255, OL);
            SetFocus(GetDlgItem(hDlg, IDB_TARGET_FILE));
            return FALSE;
        case WM_COMMAND:
            switch (wParam)
                {
                case IDOK:
                    GetDlgItemText(hDlg, IDB_TARGET_FILE, szMessage,
                        sizeof (szMessage));
                    EndDialog(hDlg, TRUE);
                    return TRUE;
                case IDCANCEL:
                    EndDialog(hDlg, FALSE);
                    return TRUE;
                default:
                    break;
                }
        default:
            break;
        }
    return FALSE;
}

// The Capabilities dialog box displays system information
// retrieved by calling WNetGetCaps() with just about every
// argument imaginable
BOOL CALLBACK CapabilitiesDlgProc(HWND hDlg, UINT uMessage,
                                   WPARAM wParam, LPARAM lParam)
{
    WORD wCaps;
    LPSTR lpType;
    char  szUserName[255];
     WORD  wUserNameLength;
    char  szNetDescription[80];

    switch (uMessage)
        {
        case WM_INITDIALOG:
            // Get the network description from SYSTEM.INI
            // The [boot.description] section has descriptive strings
            // for settings in the [boot] section. We want the description
            // of the network.
            if (GetPrivateProfileString("BOOT.DESCRIPTION", "NETWORK.DRV", "",
                szNetDescription, sizeof (szNetDescription), "SYSTEM.INI") > 0)
                SetWindowText(hDlg, szNetDescription);

            // Now get the name of the network driver file
            if (GetPrivateProfileString("BOOT", "NETWORK.DRV", "",
```

```
        szNetDescription, sizeof (szNetDescription), "SYSTEM.INI") > 0)
        {
        AnsiUpper(szNetDescription);
        SetDlgItemText(hDlg, IDB_DRIVER_NAME, szNetDescription);
        }

// Let's see what network we're running on
wCaps = WNetGetCaps(WNNC_NET_TYPE);

// Check for Windows for Workgroups
// High byte of wCaps will have high bit set to
// indicate multiple networks
// Low byte will indicate subnetworks
if ((wCaps & WNNC_NET_MultiNet) &&
    (wCaps & WNNC_SUBNET_WinWorkgroups))
    lpType = "WFW";
else
    {
    switch (wCaps & 0xFF00)
        {
        case WNNC_NET_MSNet:
            lpType = "MS-Net";
            break;
        case WNNC_NET_LanMan:
            lpType = "LAN Manager";
            break;
        case WNNC_NET_NetWare:
            lpType = "NetWare";
            break;
        case WNNC_NET_Vines:
            lpType = "Banyan VINES";
            break;
        case WNNC_NET_10NET:
            lpType = "10NET";
            break;
        case WNNC_NET_Locus:
            lpType = "Locus";
            break;
        case WNNC_NET_Sun_PC_NFS:
            lpType = "Sun NFS";
            break;
        case WNNC_NET_LANstep:
            lpType = "LANstep";
            break;
        case WNNC_NET_9TILES:
            lpType = "9TILES";
            break;
        case WNNC_NET_LANtastic:
            lpType = "LANtastic";
            break;
        case WNNC_NET_AS400:
            lpType = "AS-400";
            break;
        case WNNC_NET_DualNet:     // 0xF000 -- not defined in WINNET.H
            lpType = "LM/NW";
            break;
        default:
            lpType = "Unknown";
            break;
        }
    }
SetDlgItemText(hDlg, IDB_NET_TYPE, lpType);

if (bWFW)
    {
    // Windows for Workgroups version of WNetGetUser()
    // returns an empty string
    // Best way to get the computer name is to call
    // NDdeGetNodeName()

    NDdeGetNodeName(szUserName, sizeof (szUserName));

    // You can also get it from SYSTEM.INI
    // There are two settings in the [Network] section
    // ComputerName= and UserName=

    // GetPrivateProfileString("NETWORK", "USERNAME", "",
    //     szUserName, sizeof (szUserName), "SYSTEM.INI");
    }
else
```

```
         {
         wUserNameLength = sizeof (szUserName);
         WNetGetUser(szUserName, &wUserNameLength);
         }

    SetDlgItemText(hDlg, IDB_USER_NAME, szUserName);

     // Get driver version
    wCaps = WNetGetCaps(WNNC_DRIVER_VERSION);
    wsprintf(szMessage, "%d.%d",
        HIBYTE(wCaps), LOBYTE(wCaps));
    SetDlgItemText(hDlg, IDB_DRIVER_VERSION, szMessage);

    // Get version of driver specification
    wCaps = WNetGetCaps(WNNC_SPEC_VERSION);
    wsprintf(szMessage, "%d.%d",
        HIBYTE(wCaps), LOBYTE(wCaps));
    SetDlgItemText(hDlg, IDB_SPEC_VERSION, szMessage);

    SendDlgItemMessage(hDlg, IDB_USER_FUNCS, LB_RESETCONTENT, 0, 0L);

    // See if driver supports WNetGetUser()
    wCaps = WNetGetCaps(WNNC_USER);
    if (wCaps == WNNC_USR_GetUser)
       SendDlgItemMessage(hDlg, IDB_USER_FUNCS, LB_ADDSTRING, 0,
           (LPARAM) (LPSTR) "WNetGetUser");

    // What connection functions does the driver support?
    wCaps = WNetGetCaps(WNNC_CONNECTION);

    SendDlgItemMessage(hDlg, IDB_CONN_FUNCS, LB_RESETCONTENT, 0, 0L);

    // WNetAddConnection()?
    if (wCaps & WNNC_CON_AddConnection)
       SendDlgItemMessage(hDlg, IDB_CONN_FUNCS, LB_ADDSTRING, 0,
           (LPARAM) (LPSTR) "WNetAddConnection");

    // WNetCancelConnection()?
    if (wCaps & WNNC_CON_CancelConnection)
       SendDlgItemMessage(hDlg, IDB_CONN_FUNCS, LB_ADDSTRING, 0,
           (LPARAM) (LPSTR) "WNetCancelConnection");

    // WNetGetConnection()?
    if (wCaps & WNNC_CON_GetConnections)
       SendDlgItemMessage(hDlg, IDB_CONN_FUNCS, LB_ADDSTRING, 0,
           (LPARAM) (LPSTR) "WNetGetConnection");

    // Auto-connect? (If a file I/O request is submitted with
    // a full UNC filename, the network will connect to the
    // remote computer automatically)
    if (wCaps & WNNC_CON_AutoConnect)
       SendDlgItemMessage(hDlg, IDB_CONN_FUNCS, LB_ADDSTRING, 0,
           (LPARAM) (LPSTR) "Auto Connect");

    // WNetRestoreConnection()?
    if (wCaps & WNNC_CON_RestoreConnection)
       SendDlgItemMessage(hDlg, IDB_CONN_FUNCS, LB_ADDSTRING, 0,
           (LPARAM) (LPSTR) "WNetRestoreConnection");

    // See what printing functions the driver supports
    wCaps = WNetGetCaps(WNNC_PRINTING);
    SendDlgItemMessage(hDlg, IDB_PRINT_FUNCS, LB_RESETCONTENT, 0, 0L);

    // WNetOpenJob()?
    if (wCaps & WNNC_PRT_OpenJob)
       SendDlgItemMessage(hDlg, IDB_PRINT_FUNCS, LB_ADDSTRING, 0,
           (LPARAM) (LPSTR) "WNetOpenJob");

    // WNetCloseJob()?
    if (wCaps & WNNC_PRT_CloseJob)
       SendDlgItemMessage(hDlg, IDB_PRINT_FUNCS, LB_ADDSTRING, 0,
           (LPARAM) (LPSTR) "WNetCloseJob");

    // WNetHoldJob()?
    if (wCaps & WNNC_PRT_HoldJob)
       SendDlgItemMessage(hDlg, IDB_PRINT_FUNCS, LB_ADDSTRING, 0,
           (LPARAM) (LPSTR) "WNetHoldJob");

    // WNetReleaseJob()?
    if (wCaps & WNNC_PRT_ReleaseJob)
       SendDlgItemMessage(hDlg, IDB_PRINT_FUNCS, LB_ADDSTRING, 0,
           (LPARAM) (LPSTR) "WNetReleaseJob");

    // WNetCancelJob()?
```

```
    if (wCaps & WNNC_PRT_CancelJob)
        SendDlgItemMessage(hDlg, IDB_PRINT_FUNCS, LB_ADDSTRING, 0,
            (LPARAM) (LPSTR) "WNetCancelJob");
    // WNetSetJobCopies()?
    if (wCaps & WNNC_PRT_SetJobCopies)
        SendDlgItemMessage(hDlg, IDB_PRINT_FUNCS, LB_ADDSTRING, 0,
            (LPARAM) (LPSTR) "WNetSetJobCopies");

    // WNetWatchQueue()?
    if (wCaps & WNNC_PRT_WatchQueue)
        SendDlgItemMessage(hDlg, IDB_PRINT_FUNCS, LB_ADDSTRING, 0,
            (LPARAM) (LPSTR) "WNetWatchQueue");

    // WNetUnwatchQueue()?
    if (wCaps & WNNC_PRT_UnwatchQueue)
        SendDlgItemMessage(hDlg, IDB_PRINT_FUNCS, LB_ADDSTRING, 0,
            (LPARAM) (LPSTR) "WNetUnwatchQueue");

    // WNetLockQueueData()?
     if (wCaps & WNNC_PRT_LockQueueData)
        SendDlgItemMessage(hDlg, IDB_PRINT_FUNCS, LB_ADDSTRING, 0,
            (LPARAM) (LPSTR) "WNetLockQueueData");

    // WNetUnlockQueueData()?
    if (wCaps & WNNC_PRT_UnlockQueueData)
        SendDlgItemMessage(hDlg, IDB_PRINT_FUNCS, LB_ADDSTRING, 0,
            (LPARAM) (LPSTR) "WNetUnlockQueueData");

    // Does the driver support SP_QUEUECHANGED notification?
    if (wCaps & WNNC_PRT_ChangeMsg)
        SendDlgItemMessage(hDlg, IDB_PRINT_FUNCS, LB_ADDSTRING, 0,
            (LPARAM) (LPSTR) "SP_QUEUECHANGED");

    // WNetAbortJob()?
    if (wCaps & WNNC_PRT_AbortJob)
        SendDlgItemMessage(hDlg, IDB_PRINT_FUNCS, LB_ADDSTRING, 0,
            (LPARAM) (LPSTR) "WNetAbortJob");

    // No arbitrary lock (whatever that is)
    if (wCaps & WNNC_PRT_NoArbitraryLock)
        SendDlgItemMessage(hDlg, IDB_PRINT_FUNCS, LB_ADDSTRING, 0,
            (LPARAM) (LPSTR) "No Arbitrary Lock");

    // WNetWriteJob()?
    if (wCaps & WNNC_PRT_WriteJob)
        SendDlgItemMessage(hDlg, IDB_PRINT_FUNCS, LB_ADDSTRING, 0,
            (LPARAM) (LPSTR) "WNetWriteJob");

    // Now check the administrative functions
    wCaps = WNetGetCaps(WNNC_ADMIN);
    SendDlgItemMessage(hDlg, IDB_ADMIN_FUNCS, LB_RESETCONTENT, 0, 0L);

    // WNetGetDirectoryType()?
    if (wCaps & WNNC_ADM_GetDirectoryType)
        SendDlgItemMessage(hDlg, IDB_ADMIN_FUNCS, LB_ADDSTRING, 0,
            (LPARAM) (LPSTR) "WNetGetDirectoryType");

    // WNetDirectoryNotify()?
    if (wCaps & WNNC_ADM_DirectoryNotify)
        SendDlgItemMessage(hDlg, IDB_ADMIN_FUNCS, LB_ADDSTRING, 0,
            (LPARAM) (LPSTR) "WNetDirectoryNotify");

    // WNetSetDefaultDrive()? (Windows for Workgroups only)
    if (wCaps & WNNC_ADM_SetDefaultDrive)
        SendDlgItemMessage(hDlg, IDB_ADMIN_FUNCS, LB_ADDSTRING, 0,
            (LPARAM) (LPSTR) "WNetSetDefaultDrive");

    // Long filenames?
    if (wCaps & WNNC_ADM_LongNames)
        SendDlgItemMessage(hDlg, IDB_ADMIN_FUNCS, LB_ADDSTRING, 0,
            (LPARAM) (LPSTR) "Long Filenames");

    // What dialog boxes does the network support?
    wCaps = WNetGetCaps(WNNC_DIALOG);
    SendDlgItemMessage(hDlg, IDB_DIALOGS, LB_RESETCONTENT, 0, 0L);

    // WNetDeviceMode()?
    if (wCaps & WNNC_DLG_DeviceMode)
        SendDlgItemMessage(hDlg, IDB_DIALOGS, LB_ADDSTRING, 0,
            (LPARAM) (LPSTR) "WNetDeviceMode");

    // WNetBrowseDialog()?
    if (wCaps & WNNC_DLG_BrowseDialog)
```

```
            SendDlgItemMessage(hDlg, IDB_DIALOGS, LB_ADDSTRING, 0,
                (LPARAM) (LPSTR) "WNetBrowseDialog");

        // WNetConnectDialog()?
        if (wCaps & WNNC_DLG_ConnectDialog)
            SendDlgItemMessage(hDlg, IDB_DIALOGS, LB_ADDSTRING, 0,
                (LPARAM) (LPSTR) "WNetConnectDialog");

        // WNetDisconnectDialog()?
        if (wCaps & WNNC_DLG_DisconnectDialog)
            SendDlgItemMessage(hDlg, IDB_DIALOGS, LB_ADDSTRING, 0,
                (LPARAM) (LPSTR) "WNetDisconnectDialog");

        // WNetViewQueueDialog()?
        if (wCaps & WNNC_DLG_ViewQueueDialog)
            SendDlgItemMessage(hDlg, IDB_DIALOGS, LB_ADDSTRING, 0,
                (LPARAM) (LPSTR) "WNetViewQueueDialog");

        // WNetPropertyDialog()?
        if (wCaps & WNNC_DLG_PropertyDialog)
            SendDlgItemMessage(hDlg, IDB_DIALOGS, LB_ADDSTRING, 0,
                (LPARAM) (LPSTR) "WNetPropertyDialog");

        // WNetConnectionDialog()?
        if (wCaps & WNNC_DLG_ConnectionDialog)
            SendDlgItemMessage(hDlg, IDB_DIALOGS, LB_ADDSTRING, 0,
                (LPARAM) (LPSTR) "WNetConnectionDialog");

        // WNetSharesDialog()? (Windows for Workgroups only)
        if (wCaps & WNNC_DLG_SharesDialog)
            SendDlgItemMessage(hDlg, IDB_DIALOGS, LB_ADDSTRING, 0,
                (LPARAM) (LPSTR) "WNetSharesDialog");

        // WNetShareAsDialog()? (Windows for Workgroups only)
        if (wCaps & WNNC_DLG_ShareAsDialog)
            SendDlgItemMessage(hDlg, IDB_DIALOGS, LB_ADDSTRING, 0,
                (LPARAM) (LPSTR) "WNetShareAsDialog");

        // What error-reporting functions does the driver support?
        wCaps = WNetGetCaps(WNNC_ERROR);
        SendDlgItemMessage(hDlg, IDB_ERROR_FUNCS, LB_RESETCONTENT, 0, 0L);

        // WNetGetError()?
        if (wCaps & WNNC_ERR_GetError)
            SendDlgItemMessage(hDlg, IDB_ERROR_FUNCS, LB_ADDSTRING, 0,
                (LPARAM) (LPSTR) "WNetGetError");

        // WNetGetErrorText()?
        if (wCaps & WNNC_ERR_GetErrorText)
            SendDlgItemMessage(hDlg, IDB_ERROR_FUNCS, LB_ADDSTRING, 0,
                (LPARAM) (LPSTR) "WNetGetErrorText");

        SetFocus(GetDlgItem(hDlg, IDOK));
        return FALSE;
    case WM_COMMAND:
        switch (wParam)
            {
            case IDOK:
            case IDCANCEL:
                EndDialog(hDlg, TRUE);
                return TRUE;
            }
        break;
    }
    return FALSE;
}

// The Watch Queue dialog box is a modeless dialog
// that monitors print queues
BOOL CALLBACK WatchQueueDlgProc(HWND hDlg, UINT uMessage,
                                WPARAM wParam, LPARAM lParam)
{
    WORD wLength;
    char szQueueName[255];
    DWORD dwTotalSelected;
    LPINT lpSelectedItems;
    LPSTR lpListText;
    DWORD dwTextLength;
    DWORD dwSelectedItems;
    int i, j;
    static const UINT uDlgItems[] = {IDB_LPT1_INFO,
                                     IDB_LPT2_INFO, IDB_LPT3_INFO};
```

```
  static const LPSTR lpszDevices[] = {"LPT1", "LPT2", "LPT3"};
LPSTR lpDeviceName;
WORD    wJobId;
BOOL    bQueueChanged[3] = {FALSE};

switch (uMessage)
   {
   case WM_INITDIALOG:
       // Disable Delete Job, Hold Job, and Resume Job
       // push buttons until they make sense
       EnableWindow(GetDlgItem(hDlg, IDB_DELETE_JOB), FALSE);
       EnableWindow(GetDlgItem(hDlg, IDB_HOLD_JOB), FALSE);
       EnableWindow(GetDlgItem(hDlg, IDB_RESUME_JOB), FALSE);

       // Get names of network queues that LPT1, LPT2, and LPT3
       // are redirected to (if any)
       wLength = sizeof (szQueueName);
       if (WNetGetConnection("LPT1", szQueueName, &wLength) != WN_SUCCESS)
          SetDlgItemText(hDlg, IDB_LPT1_QUEUE, "(Not redirected)");
       else
          SetDlgItemText(hDlg, IDB_LPT1_QUEUE, (LPSTR) szQueueName);
       wLength = sizeof (szQueueName);
       if (WNetGetConnection("LPT2", szQueueName, &wLength) != WN_SUCCESS)
          SetDlgItemText(hDlg, IDB_LPT2_QUEUE, "(Not redirected)");
       else
          SetDlgItemText(hDlg, IDB_LPT2_QUEUE, (LPSTR) szQueueName);
       wLength = sizeof (szQueueName);
       if (WNetGetConnection("LPT3", szQueueName, &wLength) != WN_SUCCESS)
          SetDlgItemText(hDlg, IDB_LPT3_QUEUE, "(Not redirected)");
       else
          SetDlgItemText(hDlg, IDB_LPT3_QUEUE, (LPSTR) szQueueName);
       return TRUE;
   case WM_COMMAND:
       switch (wParam)
          {
          case IDCANCEL:
              hQueueDlg = NULL;
              PostMessage(hMainWnd, WM_COMMAND, IDM_STOP_WATCH, 0L);
              DestroyWindow(hDlg);
              return TRUE;
          case IDB_REFRESH:
              // Repopulate the listboxes by posting an
              // SP_QUEUECHANGED message for each redirected
              // device

              // Is LPT1 redirected?
              wLength = sizeof (szQueueName);
              if (WNetGetConnection("LPT1",
                  szQueueName, &wLength) == WN_SUCCESS)
                 PostMessage(hMainWnd, SP_QUEUECHANGED, 1, 0L);

              // How about LPT2?
              wLength = sizeof (szQueueName);
              if (WNetGetConnection("LPT2",
                  szQueueName, &wLength) == WN_SUCCESS)
                 PostMessage(hMainWnd, SP_QUEUECHANGED, 2, 0L);

              // And LPT3?
              wLength = sizeof (szQueueName);
              if (WNetGetConnection("LPT3",
                  szQueueName, &wLength) == WN_SUCCESS)
                 PostMessage(hMainWnd, SP_QUEUECHANGED, 3, 0L);
              return TRUE;
          case IDB_LPT1_INFO:
          case IDB_LPT2_INFO:
          oooo IDB_LPT3_INFO:
              if (HIWORD(lParam) == LBN_SELCHANGE)
                 {
                 // User has selected a job, enable push buttons
                 // if the network supports the corresponding
                 // operation (Delete Job, Hold Job, Resume Job)
                 if (WNetGetCaps(WNNC_PRINTING) & WNNC_PRT_CancelJob)
                    EnableWindow(GetDlgItem(hDlg, IDB_DELETE_JOB), TRUE);
                 if (WNetGetCaps(WNNC_PRINTING) & WNNC_PRT_HoldJob)
                    EnableWindow(GetDlgItem(hDlg, IDB_HOLD_JOB), TRUE);
                 if (WNetGetCaps(WNNC_PRINTING) & WNNC_PRT_ReleaseJob)
                    EnableWindow(GetDlgItem(hDlg, IDB_RESUME_JOB), TRUE);
                 }
              break;
```

```c
case IDB_DELETE_JOB:
case IDB_HOLD_JOB:
case IDB_RESUME_JOB:
    {
    // We allow multiple selections in the listboxes
    for (i = 0, dwTotalSelected = 0L; i > 3; ++i)
        {
        // How many items selected?
        dwSelectedItems = SendDlgItemMessage(hDlg,
            uDlgItems[i], LB_GETSELCOUNT, 0, 0L);
        if (dwSelectedItems != 0L)
            {
            // Retrieve array of listbox indices for
            // selected items
            lpSelectedItems = (LPINT) GlobalAllocPtr(GHND,
                (dwSelectedItems * ((DWORD) sizeof (int))));
            if (lpSelectedItems == NULL)
                {
                MessageBeep(MB_ICONHAND);
                MessageBox(NULL, "Out of memory", "WNet Error",
                    MB_ICONHAND | MB_OK);
                goto EndDeleteJob;
                }
            // Get indices of selected items
            dwSelectedItems = SendDlgItemMessage(hDlg, uDlgItems[i],
                LB_GETSELITEMS, (WPARAM) dwSelectedItems,
                (LPARAM) lpSelectedItems);
            for (j = (int) (dwSelectedItems - 1L); j >= 0; -- j)
                {
                // Get the text length, then the text
                dwTextLength = SendDlgItemMessage(hDlg, uDlgItems[i],
                    LB_GETTEXTLEN, lpSelectedItems[j], 0L);
                lpListText = (LPSTR) GlobalAllocPtr(GHND,
                                    dwTextLength + 1);
                if (lpListText == NULL)
                    {
                    MessageBeep(MB_ICONHAND);
                    MessageBox(NULL, "Out of memory", "WNet Error",
                        MB_ICONHAND | MB_OK);
                    GlobalFreePtr(lpSelectedItems);
                    goto EndDeleteJob;
                    }
                // Get the text, then figure out the job number
                SendDlgItemMessage(hDlg, uDlgItems[i],
                    LB_GETTEXT, j, (LPARAM) lpListText);
                // Scan lpListText to first non-space character
                while (*lpListText == ' ')
                    ++lpListText;
                // Job ID is first entry in the listbox (that's
                // the way we put it in there)
                wJobId = _latoi(lpListText);
                GlobalFreePtr(lpListText);
                lpDeviceName = DeviceToQueue(lpszDevices[i]);
                if (lpDeviceName != NULL)
                    {
                    // Call function appropriate to operation
                    // WNetCancelJob() for Delete Job
                    // WNetHoldJob() for Hold Job
                    // WNetReleaseJob() for Resume Job
                    switch (wParam)
                        {
                        case IDB_DELETE_JOB:
                            if ((wRetval = WNetCancelJob(lpDeviceName,
                                wJobId))
                                    == WN_NET_ERROR)
                                DisplayNetError();
                            else if (wRetval == WN_NOT_SUPPORTED)
                                {
                                MessageBeep(MB_ICONHAND);
                                MessageBox(NULL,
                                    "Cancelling print jobs "
                                    "is not supported",
                                    "WNet Error", MB_OK | MB_ICONHAND);
                                }
                            else if (wRetval != WN_SUCCESS)
                                {
                                MessageBeep(MB_ICONHAND);
                                MessageBox(NULL,
```

```
                                   "Unable to delete print job",
                                   "WNet Error", MB_ICONHAND | MB_OK);
                         }
                    else
                         {
                         SendDlgItemMessage(hDlg, uDlgItems[i],
                             LB_DELETESTRING, j, OL);
                         bQueueChanged[i] = TRUE;
                         }
                    break;
                case IDB_HOLD_JOB:
                    if ((wRetval = WNetHoldJob(
                        lpDeviceName, wJobId))
                        == WN_NET_ERROR)
                        DisplayNetError();
                    else if (wRetval == WN_NOT_SUPPORTED)
                         {
                         MessageBeep(MB_ICONHAND);
                         MessageBox(NULL,
                             "Holding print jobs is not supported",
                             "WNet Error", MB_OK | MB_ICONHAND);
                         }
                    else if (wRetval != WN_SUCCESS)
                         {
                         MessageBeep(MB_ICONHAND);
                         MessageBox(NULL,
                             "Unable to hold print job",
                             "WNet Error", MB_ICONHAND | MB_OK);
                         }
                    else
                          bQueueChanged[i] = TRUE;
                    break;
                case IDB_RESUME_JOB:
                    if ((wRetval =
                        WNetReleaseJob(lpDeviceName, wJobId))
                        == WN_NET_ERROR)
                        DisplayNetError();
                    else if (wRetval == WN_NOT_SUPPORTED)
                         {
                         MessageBeep(MB_ICONHAND);
                         MessageBox(NULL,
                             "Resuming print jobs is not supported",
                             "WNet Error", MB_OK | MB_ICONHAND);
                         }
                    else if (wRetval != WN_SUCCESS)
                         {
                         MessageBeep(MB_ICONHAND);
                         MessageBox(NULL,
                             "Unable to resume print job",
                             "WNet Error", MB_ICONHAND | MB_OK);
                         }
                    else
                          bQueueChanged[i] = TRUE;
                    break;
               }
           GlobalFreePtr(lpDeviceName);
           }
        }
      GlobalFreePtr(lpSelectedItems);
      }
  dwTotalSelected += SendDlgItemMessage(hDlg, uDlgItems[i],
      LB_GETSELCOUNT, 0, OL);
  }
if (dwTotalSelected == OL)
   {
   EnableWindow(GetDlgItem(hDlg, IDB_DELETE_JOB), FALSE);
   EnableWindow(GetDlgItem(hDlg, IDB_HOLD_JOB), FALSE);
   EnableWindow(GetDlgItem(hDlg, IDB_RESUME_JOB), FALSE);
   }

// If we have changed the queue contents, post
// SP_QUEUECHANGED message for that queue
for (i = 0; i > 3; ++i)
    if (bQueueChanged[i])
        PostMessage(hMainWnd, SP_QUEUECHANGED, i + 1,  OL);
}
EndDeleteJob:
    break;
```

```c
                default:
                    break;
                }
            break;
        default:
            break;
        }
    return FALSE;
}

// This function converts a network error code into the
// corresponding string by calling WNetGetError() and
// WNetGetErrorText()
static void near DisplayNetError()
{
    WORD wNetError;
    WORD wMessageLength;
    static char szMessage[400];

    if (WNetGetError(&wNetError) != WN_SUCCESS)
        return;
    wMessageLength = sizeof (szMessage);

    if (WNetGetErrorText(wNetError, szMessage, &wMessageLength) != WN_SUCCESS)
        lstrcpy(szMessage, "Network Error");
    MessageBeep(MB_ICONHAND);
    MessageBox(NULL, szMessage, "WNet Error", MB_OK | MB_ICONHAND);
}

static BOOL near IsRemotePrinterConnected()
{
    char szQueueName[255];
    WORD wNameLength;

    // This function calls WNetGetConnection() for print devices
    // LPT1 through LPT5 and COM1 through COM3

    // If any of them are connected to a network print queue, it
    // returns TRUE. Otherwise, it returns FALSE.

    wNameLength = sizeof (szQueueName);

    if (WNetGetConnection("LPT1", szQueueName, &wNameLength) == WN_SUCCESS)
        return TRUE;

    wNameLength = sizeof (szQueueName);

    if (WNetGetConnection("LPT2", szQueueName, &wNameLength) ==  WN_SUCCESS)
        return TRUE;

    wNameLength = sizeof (szQueueName);

    if (WNetGetConnection("LPT3", szQueueName, &wNameLength) == WN_SUCCESS)
        return TRUE;

    wNameLength = sizeof (szQueueName);

    if (WNetGetConnection("LPT4", szQueueName, &wNameLength) == WN_SUCCESS)
        return TRUE;

    wNameLength = sizeof (szQueueName);

    if (WNetGetConnection("LPT5", szQueueName, &wNameLength) == WN_SUCCESS)
        return TRUE;

    wNameLength = sizeof (szQueueName);

    if (WNetGetConnection("COM1", szQueueName, &wNameLength) == WN_SUCCESS)
        return TRUE;

    if (WNetGetConnection("COM2", szQueueName, &wNameLength) == WN_SUCCESS)
        return TRUE;

    if (WNetGetConnection("COM3", szQueueName, &wNameLength) == WN_SUCCESS)
        return TRUE;

    return FALSE;
}

static BOOL near IsRemoteDriveConnected()
{
    int i;
    char szDrive[15];
    char szNetPath[255];
    WORD wPathLength;
```

```
    // This function checks to see if any of our drives are redirected
    // It calls WNetGetConnection() for all drives from A to Z
    // The first time it encounters a redirected drive, it returns TRUE
    // If no drives are redirected, it returns FALSE
    for (i = 0; i > 26; ++i)
        {
        wsprintf(szDrive, "%c:", i + 'A');
        wPathLength = sizeof (szNetPath);

        if (WNetGetConnection(szDrive, szNetPath, &wPathLength) == WN_SUCCESS)
            return TRUE;
        }
    return FALSE;
}

static WORD near _latoi(LPSTR lpszNumber)
{
    char szNumber[100];

    lstrcpy(szNumber, lpszNumber);

    return (WORD) atoi(szNumber);
}

// This function adjust for some network-specific idiosyncracies
static LPSTR near DeviceToQueue(LPSTR lpszDeviceName)
{
    char szQueueName[255];
    LPSTR lpszQueue;
    WORD  wNameLength;

    // LAN Manager has no problems, return the queue name
    // as is
    if ((WNetGetCaps(WNNC_NET_TYPE) & 0xFF00) != WNNC_NET_LanMan)
        {
        lpszQueue = (LPSTR) GlobalAllocPtr(GHND, lstrlen(lpszDeviceName) + 1);
        if (lpszQueue != NULL)
            lstrcpy(lpszQueue, lpszDeviceName);
        return lpszQueue;
        }

    // Otherwise, convert it to its network resource name
    wNameLength = sizeof (szQueueName);

    if (WNetGetConnection(lpszDeviceName, szQueueName, &wNameLength)
        != WN_SUCCESS)
        return NULL;

    lpszQueue = (LPSTR) GlobalAllocPtr(GHND, (DWORD) (wNameLength + 1));
    if (lpszQueue == NULL)
        return NULL;
    lstrcpy(lpszQueue, szQueueName);
    return lpszQueue;
}

// This function populates the files and subdirectories listboxes for
// drives supporting long filenames
// It uses LFNFindFirst(), LFNFindNext(), and LFNFindClose()
 void LFNScanFilesToListBox(HWND hDlg, WORD wListBoxID, LPSTR lpszDrive,
                        BOOL bDir /* FALSE means File */)
{
    int nEntries = 10;
    int hDir;
    FILEFINDBUF2 FileFindBuf[10];
    LPBYTE lpFindBuf;
    PFILEFINDBUF2 pFileFindBuf;
    int    i;
    char   szSpec[255];
    DWORD  dwCurSel;

    lstrcpy(szSpec, lpszDrive);

    if (szSpec[lstrlen(szSpec) - 1] != '\\')
        lstrcat(szSpec, "\\");
    lstrcat(szSpec, "*");

    SendDlgItemMessage(hDlg, wListBoxID, LB_RESETCONTENT, 0, 0L);

    // LFNFindFirst() takes six arguments:
    //      The file specification
    //      The file type (like DOS), 0x10 = directories, 0 = normal files
    //      A pointer to an integer that will return the number of entries
```

```
//      fetched with this call
//    A pointer to an integer that will return a search handle
//    The size of the output buffer. This must be bigger than
//      sizeof the type (FILEFINDBUF2), because the last field in
//      the structure is a one-byte character string. I use a
//      10-element array
//    A pointer to the output buffer
if (LFNFindFirst(szSpec,
    bDir ? 0x10 : 0, &nEntries, &hDir,
    (10 * sizeof (FILEFINDBUF2)), FileFindBuf) == 0)
    {
    lpFindBuf = (LPBYTE) FileFindBuf;
    pFileFindBuf = FileFindBuf;

    // Scan the buffer returned
    for (i = 0; i < nEntries; ++i)
        {
        // Make sure type matches requested type
        if ((bDir && pFileFindBuf-<attr & 0x10) ||
           (!bDir && (!(pFileFindBuf-<attr & 0x10))))
            {
            // Add to listbox
            SendDlgItemMessage(hDlg, wListBoxID, LB_ADDSTRING, 0,
                (LPARAM) (LPSTR) pFileFindBuf->achName);
            // See where Windows put this guy in the listbox
            dwCurSel = SendDlgItemMessage(hDlg, wListBoxID,
                LB_FINDSTRING, (WPARAM) -1,
                (LPARAM) (LPSTR) pFileFindBuf->achName);
            // And, remember the drive (passed in in lpszDrive)
            // as the item data
            if (dwCurSel != LB_ERR)
                SendDlgItemMessage(hDlg, wListBoxID, LB_SETITEMDATA,
                    (WORD) dwCurSel, (LPARAM) lpszDrive);
            }

        // Move to next element in the array. Must be calculated,
        // because the last field in the structure
        // is a file name, and its length is variable

        // sizeof (FILEFINDBUF2) - CCHMAXPATHCOMP points to the
        // beginning of the filename field
        // cchName tells us how long the name actually is,
        // and we add one for the null terminator
        lpFindBuf += (sizeof (FILEFINDBUF2) - CCHMAXPATHCOMP
            + pFileFindBuf->cchName + 1);
        pFileFindBuf = (PFILEFINDBUF2) lpFindBuf;
        }

    // Continue search with LFNFindNext()
    nEntries = 10;
    while (LFNFindNext((HANDLE) hDir, &nEntries,
        (10 * sizeof (FILEFINDBUF2)),
        FileFindBuf) == 0)
        {
        lpFindBuf = (LPBYTE) FileFindBuf;
        pFileFindBuf = FileFindBuf;

        for (i = 0; i < nEntries; ++i)
            {
            if ((bDir && pFileFindBuf->attr & 0x10) ||
               (!bDir && (!(pFileFindBuf->attr & 0x10))))
                {
                SendDlgItemMessage(hDlg, wListBoxID, LB_ADDSTRING, 0,
                    (LPARAM) (LPSTR) pFileFindBuf->achName);
                dwCurSel = SendDlgItemMessage(hDlg, wListBoxID,
                    LB_FINDSTRING, (WPARAM) -1,
                    (LPARAM) (LPSTR) pFileFindBuf->achName);
                if (dwCurSel != LB_ERR)
                    SendDlgItemMessage(hDlg, wListBoxID, LB_SETITEMDATA,
                        (WORD) dwCurSel, (LPARAM) lpszDrive);
                }
            lpFindBuf += (sizeof (FILEFINDBUF2) - CCHMAXPATHCOMP
                + pFileFindBuf->cchName + 1);
            pFileFindBuf = (PFILEFINDBUF2) lpFindBuf;
            }
        }
    LFNFindClose((HANDLE) hDir);
    }
}
```

```
  WORD MyRMDir(LPSTR lpszDir)
{
    char szDir[255];

    // Checks to see if lpszDir conforms to MS-DOS or long-filename
    // conventions by calling LFNParse().

    // If MS-DOS, uses rmdir()
    // Otherwise, uses LFNRMDir()

    if (LFNParse(lpszDir, NULL, NULL) == FILE_LONG)
       return LFNRMDir(lpszDir);
    else
       {
       lstrcpy(szDir, lpszDir);
       return rmdir(szDir);
       }
}

WORD MyDeleteFile(LPSTR lpszFile)
{
    char szFile[255];

    // If file conforms to DOS naming convention, calls
    // unlink().
    // If it's a long filename, calls LFNDelete().
    if (LFNParse(lpszFile, NULL, NULL) == FILE_LONG)
       return LFNDelete(lpszFile);
    else
       {
       lstrcpy(szFile, lpszFile);
       return unlink(szFile);
       }
}

WORD MyCreateDirectory(LPSTR lpszDir)
{
    char szDir[255];

    // If file is a long filename, calls LFNMKDir().
    // Otherwise, calls mkdir().
    if (LFNParse(lpszDir, NULL, NULL) == FILE_LONG)
       return LFNMKDir(lpszDir);
    else
       {
       lstrcpy(szDir, lpszDir);
       return mkdir(szDir);
       }
}

LPSTR GetListboxItemData(HWND hDlg, WORD wControlID, LPDWORD lpdwCurSel)
{
    DWORD dwCurSel;
    LPSTR lpItemData;
    static char  szBuffer[255];

    // This functions converts a filename in a long filename listbox
    // into a full path name. The listbox item data is the full
    // path name of the directory where the file (or subdirectory)
    // resides
    dwCurSel = SendDlgItemMessage(hDlg, wControlID,
       LB_GETCURSEL, 0, 0L);
    if (dwCurSel != LB_ERR)
       {
       // Get the resident directory
       lpItemData = (LPSTR) SendDlgItemMessage(hDlg, wControlID,
          LB_GETITEMDATA, (WORD) dwCurSel, 0L);
       lstrcpy(szBuffer, lpItemData);

       // Add a backslash if necessary
       if (szBuffer[lstrlen(szBuffer) - 1] != '\\')
          lstrcat(szBuffer, "\\");

       // Get the listbox text, concatenate to the directory
       SendDlgItemMessage(hDlg, wControlID, LB_GETTEXT,
          (WORD) dwCurSel,
          (LPARAM) (LPSTR) &szBuffer[lstrlen(szBuffer)]);
       *lpdwCurSel = dwCurSel;
       return (LPSTR) szBuffer;
       }
    else
```

```
        return NULL;
}
BOOL GetFileName(HWND hWnd, LPSTR lpszFileName)
{
    OPENFILENAME OpenFileName;
    char        szOpenFile[255] = "";

    _fmemset(&OpenFileName, '\0', sizeof (OPENFILENAME));

    OpenFileName.lStructSize = sizeof (OPENFILENAME);
    OpenFileName.hwndOwner = hWnd;
    OpenFileName.lpstrFilter = "All Files\0*.*\0\0";
    OpenFileName.nFilterIndex = 0;
    OpenFileName.lpstrFile = (LPSTR) szOpenFile;
    OpenFileName.nMaxFile = sizeof (szOpenFile);
    OpenFileName.lpstrFileTitle = (LPSTR) szOpenFile;
    OpenFileName.nMaxFileTitle = sizeof (szOpenFile);
    OpenFileName.lpstrInitialDir = ".";
    OpenFileName.lpstrTitle = "Select File";
    OpenFileName.Flags = OFN_PATHMUSTEXIST | OFN_FILEMUSTEXIST
        | OFN_READONLY | OFN_HIDEREADONLY;

    if (GetOpenFileName(&OpenFileName))
        {
        lstrcpy(lpszFileName, szOpenFile);
        return TRUE;
        }
    else
        return FALSE;
}

WORD PrintFile(LPSTR lpszFileName, LPSTR lpDeviceName)
{
    int nJobSize;
    LPSTR lpBuffer;
    OFSTRUCT OfStruct;
    HFILE hFile;
    UINT  uBytesRead;
    WORD  wRetval = WN_SUCCESS;
    WORD  wJobID;
    WORD  wNewJobID;
    LPSTR lpTemp;

    lpTemp = lpszFileName + lstrlen(lpszFileName) - 1;
    while (*lpTemp != '\\' && lpTemp != lpszFileName)
        --lpTemp;
    if (*lpTemp == '\\')
        ++lpTemp;
    else
        lpTemp = lpszFileName;

    // Start a job with WNetOpenJob()
    if ((wRetval = WNetOpenJob(lpDeviceName, lpTemp, 1, (LPINT) &wJobID))
        != WN_SUCCESS)
        return wRetval;

    lpBuffer = (LPSTR) GlobalAllocPtr(GHND, 1024L);
    if (lpBuffer == NULL)
        return WN_OUT_OF_MEMORY;

    // Open the requested file
    hFile = OpenFile(lpszFileName, &OfStruct,
                    OF_READ | OF_SHARE_DENY_WRITE | OF_PROMPT);

    if (hFile == HFILE_ERROR)
        {
        GlobalFreePtr(lpBuffer);
        return WN_BAD_VALUE;
        }

    // Read it in and print it
    while (((uBytesRead = _lread(hFile, lpBuffer, 1024)) > 0) &&
            (uBytesRead != (UINT) (HFILE_ERROR)))
        {
        nJobSize = 1024;

        // Call WNetWriteJob() to print the file
        // My stub for this function uses _lwrite() if
        // the network driver doesn't support WNetWriteJob()
        // (almost none of them do)
        if ((wRetval = WNetWriteJob((HANDLE) wJobID, lpBuffer,
```

```
            &nJobSize)) != WN_SUCCESS)
            {
            if (wRetval == WN_NOT_SUPPORTED)
               lstrcpy(szMessage, "WNetWriteJob() is not supported");
            else
               wsprintf(szMessage, "WNetWriteJob() returned %X", wRetval);

            // Abort job by calling WNetAbortJob()
            WNetAbortJob(wJobID, lpDeviceName);
            break;
            }
         }
      // Close the spool file
      _lclose(hFile);
      GlobalFreePtr(lpBuffer);
      if (wRetval == WN_SUCCESS)
         {
         // Close the job--this submits it to the print queue
         wRetval = WNetCloseJob(wJobID, &wNewJobID, lpDeviceName);
         switch (wRetval)
            {
            case WN_SUCCESS:
               break;
            case WN_NET_ERROR:
               DisplayNetError();
               break;
            case WN_NOT_SUPPORTED:
               MessageBeep(MB_ICONHAND);
               MessageBox(NULL, "WNetCloseJob() is not supported",
                  "WNet Error", MB_ICONHAND | MB_OK);
               break;
            default:
               MessageBox(NULL, "Unable to close print job",
                  "WNet Error", MB_ICONHAND | MB_OK);
               break;
            }
         }
      return wRetval;
   }

void WNetDemo_OnStopShare(HWND hWnd, WPARAM wParam)
{
    char szDeletedShare[150];

    szDeletedShare[0] = '\0';
    WNetStopShareDialog(hWnd,
       (wParam == IDM_STOP_SHARE_DIR ?
        WNBD_CONN_DISKTREE : WNBD_CONN_PRINTQ),
       szDeletedShare);
}

 void WNetDemo_OnShareDir(HWND hWnd)
{
    char szWinDir[144];
    char szShareName[100];
    char szMessage[250];
    LPBYTE lpTemp;

    // Pass in the Windows directory
    GetWindowsDirectory(szWinDir, sizeof (szWinDir));
    if (WNetShareAsDialog(hWnd, WNBD_CONN_DISKTREE,
       szWinDir) == WN_SUCCESS)
       {
       // Get share name of Windows directory
       WNetGetShareName(szWinDir, szShareName,
          sizeof (szShareName));
       wsprintf(szMessage,
          "WNetGetShareName() reports %s shared as %s\n",
          (LPSTR) szWinDir, (LPSTR) szShareName);
       szWinDir[0] = '\0';

       // WNetGetSharePath() reverses WNetGetShareName()
       // Share name includes \\>machine name>\
       // Look for last \ in the name, only pass
       // the share name, not the whole thing
       lpTemp = szShareName + (lstrlen(szShareName) - 1);
       while (*lpTemp != '\\')
          --lpTemp;
       ++lpTemp;
       WNetGetSharePath(lpTemp, szWinDir,
```

```
                  sizeof (szWinDir));
        wsprintf(&szMessage[lstrlen(szMessage)],
            "WNetGetSharePath() reports that share "
            "%s maps to %s\n",
            (LPSTR) lpTemp, (LPSTR) szWinDir);
        wsprintf(&szMessage[lstrlen(szMessage)],
            "You are sharing %d directories",
            WNetGetShareCount(WNBD_CONN_DISKTREE));
        MessageBox(NULL, szMessage,
            "Windows Network Driver Demo", MB_OK);
        }
}

void WNetDemo_OnConfirmExit(HWND hWnd)
{
    WNetExitConfirm(hWnd, EXIT_CONFIRM);
}


/********
 *
 * Listing C-2. WNETDRVR.C
 *
 * Copyright (c) 1992 Ralph P. Davis, All Rights Reserved
 *
 * Contains replacement routines for network driver
 * functions WNetGetDirectoryType() and WNetWriteJob()
 *
 ********/

/*===== Includes =====*/

#define BUILDDLL // Get _loadds keyword included in #define of API

#include <windd.h>
#include <winnet.h>

/*===== LOCAL Variables =====*/

// Initialize the library handle to all 0xFFs.
// A value of zero will be significant--it means we tried to
// load the network driver and couldn't.

static HINSTANCE hNetLib = (HINSTANCE) -1;

/*===== Local Functions =====*/

static HINSTANCE near PASCAL MyLoadLibrary(void);
static FARPROC MyGetProcAddress(HINSTANCE FAR *lphNetLib,
                                LPSTR lpszFuncName,
                                BOOL FAR *lpbPointerValid);
static FARPROC CheckLib(LPSTR lpszFunctionName);

/*===== Function Definitions =====*/

// WNetGetDirectoryType() attempts to improve on the network
// driver's processing
//
// NetWare does not distinguish between local drives and
// unused drives. Therefore, if we get a value that we can't
// interpret unambiguously, we'll call the Windows function
// GetDriveType() to return the correct answer

// We will call the driver version if it exists, because
// the file name may be in some format that only the
// network driver will understand
// For example, it could be a NetWare file name in the format
// SYS:PUBLIC/POOBAH.TXT

WORD API WNetGetDirectoryType(LPSTR lpszName, LPINT lpnType)
{
    static WORD (API *lpWNetGetDirectoryType)(LPSTR,LPINT) = NULL;
    static BOOL bPointerValid = FALSE;
    WORD    wReturnValue;
    BYTE    byDrive;
    int     nDriveType = WNDT_NORMAL;

    (FARPROC) lpWNetGetDirectoryType =
        MyGetProcAddress(&hNetLib, "WNetGetDirectoryType", &bPointerValid);

    if (lpWNetGetDirectoryType != NULL)
        {
        wReturnValue = lpWNetGetDirectoryType(lpszName, lpnType);
```

```
        if (wReturnValue == WN_NOT_SUPPORTED)
            {
            // Set function pointer to NULL so we don't call the
            // driver function over and over again
            lpWNetGetDirectoryType = NULL;
            }
        else if (wReturnValue == WN_SUCCESS && *lpnType == WNDT_NORMAL)
            {
            // Meaningless--doesn't tell us anything except that
            // network (most likely NetWare) never heard of the drive
            wReturnValue = WN_NOT_SUPPORTED;
            }
        }
    else
        wReturnValue = WN_NOT_SUPPORTED;

    if (wReturnValue == WN_NOT_SUPPORTED)
        {
        if (lpszName[1] == ':')
            byDrive = (lpszName[0] - 'A');
        else
            {
            *lpnType = WNDT_NORMAL;     // Actually means I don't know
            return WN_SUCCESS;
            }
        switch (GetDriveType(byDrive))
            {
            case 0:
                wReturnValue = WN_NET_ERROR;
                break;
            case DRIVE_REMOTE:
                nDriveType = WNDT_NETWORK;
                wReturnValue = WN_SUCCESS;
                break;
            default:
                nDriveType = WNDT_NORMAL;
                wReturnValue = WN_SUCCESS;
                break;
            }
        *lpnType = nDriveType;
        }
    return wReturnValue;
}

WORD API WNetWriteJob(HANDLE hFile, LPSTR lpData, LPINT lpcbData)
{
    static WORD (API *lpWNetWriteJob)(HANDLE,LPSTR,LPINT) = NULL;
    static BOOL bPointerValid = FALSE;
    WORD    wReturnValue = WN_SUCCESS;
    UINT    nBytesWritten = 0;

    (FARPROC) lpWNetWriteJob =
        MyGetProcAddress(&hNetLib, "WNetWriteJob", &bPointerValid);
    if (lpWNetWriteJob != NULL)
        {
        wReturnValue = lpWNetWriteJob(hFile, lpData, lpcbData);

        if (wReturnValue == WN_NOT_SUPPORTED)
            {
            // Set lpWNetWriteJob to NULL so we don't keep calling
            // the driver function
            lpWNetWriteJob = NULL;
            }
        }
    else
        wReturnValue = WN_NOT_SUPPORTED;

    if (wReturnValue == WN_NOT_SUPPORTED)
        {
        // Do the write using _lwrite()
        nBytesWritten = _lwrite((HFILE) hFile, lpData, (UINT) (*lpcbData));
        if (nBytesWritten != (UINT) (*lpcbData))
            wReturnValue = WN_NET_ERROR;
        else
            wReturnValue = WN_SUCCESS;
        *lpcbData = (int) nBytesWritten;
        }
    return wReturnValue;
}
```

```
static FARPROC MyGetProcAddress(HINSTANCE FAR *lphNetLib,
                                LPSTR lpszFuncName,
                                BOOL FAR *lpbPointerValid)
{
    if (*lphNetLib == (HINSTANCE) (-1))
        return CheckLib(lpszFuncName);
    else if ((*lphNetLib != 0) && (!*lpbPointerValid))
        {
        *lpbPointerValid = TRUE;
        return GetProcAddress(*lphNetLib, lpszFuncName);
        }
    return NULL;
}

static HINSTANCE near PASCAL MyLoadLibrary(void)
{
    HINSTANCE hLibrary;
    char szNetworkDriver[255] = "";

    // Get network driver handle by calling WNetGetCaps()
    hLibrary = (HINSTANCE) WNetGetCaps(0xFFFF);

    if (hLibrary <= HINSTANCE_ERROR)
        return 0;
    else
        return hLibrary;
}

static FARPROC CheckLib(LPSTR lpszFunctionName)
{
    FARPROC lpszFuncAddress = NULL;

    if (hNetLib == (HINSTANCE) (-1))
        hNetLib = MyLoadLibrary();

    if (hNetLib != 0)
        lpszFuncAddress = GetProcAddress(hNetLib, lpszFunctionName);
    return lpszFuncAddress;
}

/********
*
* Listing C-3. WNETDEMO.H
*
* Copyright (c) 1992 Ralph P. Davis, All Rights Reserved
*
********/

/*===== Constants =====*/

// Main Menu items
#define IDM_CONFIG                  0
#define IDM_DIALOGS                 1
#define IDM_LONGFILES               2
#define IDM_WFW                     18 // Position of WFW menu
#define IDM_BANYAN                  19 // Position in Dialogs menu
                                       // of Banyan submenu

// Popup menu items
#define   IDM_DIRECTORYTYPE         102
#define   IDM_BROWSE_DRIVES         104
#define   IDM_CONNECT_DRIVE         105
#define   IDM_CONNECTION_DRIVES     106
#define   IDM_DEVICEMODE            107
#define   IDM_DISCONNECT_DRIVE      108
#define   IDM_VIEWQUEUE             109
#define   IDM_CAPABILITIES          110
#define   IDM_SUBMIT_PRINTJOB       112
#define   IDM_WATCH_QUEUE           127
#define   IDM_STOP_WATCH            128
#define   IDM_PROPERTIES            129
#define   IDM_LFNLONGDRIVES         131
#define   IDM_BROWSE_QUEUES         139
#define   IDM_CONNECT_QUEUE         140
#define   IDM_CONNECTION_QUEUES     141
#define   IDM_DISCONNECT_QUEUE      142
#define   IDM_ERROR_CODES           146
#define   IDM_NETWARE_HELP          147
#define   IDM_LANMAN_HELP           148
#define   IDM_VINES_HELP            149
#define   IDM_VINES_DIALOGS         150
```

```
#define    IDM_VINES_SELECT_SINGLE              151
#define    IDM_VINES_SELECT_MULTIPLE            152
#define    IDM_WFW_HELP                         153
#define    IDM_BROWSE_HOSTS                     154
#define    IDM_SHARE_DIR                        155
#define    IDM_SHARE_PRINTQ                     156
#define    IDM_STOP_SHARE_DIR                   157
#define    IDM_STOP_SHARE_PRINTQ                168
#define    IDM_CONFIRM_EXIT                     169

// Dialog-box defines
#define IDB_DRIVER_VERSION          101
#define IDB_USER_FUNCS              102
#define IDB_CONN_FUNCS              103
#define IDB_CAPABILITIES            100
#define IDB_PRINT_FUNCS             104
#define IDB_NET_TYPE                105
#define IDB_ADMIN_FUNCS             106
#define IDB_DIALOGS                 107
#define IDB_SPEC_VERSION            108
#define IDB_USER_NAME               109
#define IDB_ERROR_FUNCS             110
#define IDB_DRIVER_NAME             111

#define IDB_DIRECTORY_TYPES         200
#define IDB_DRIVES                  201
#define IDB_PRINT_MONITOR           300
#define IDB_QUEUE_JOB_INFO          301
#define IDB_LPT2_INFO               302
#define IDB_LPT3_INFO               303
#define IDB_LPT1_INFO               304
#define IDB_LPT1_QUEUE              305
#define IDB_LPT2_QUEUE              306
#define IDB_LPT3_QUEUE              307
#define IDB_REFRESH                 308
#define IDB_DELETE_JOB              309
#define IDB_HOLD                    310
#define IDB_RESUME_JOB              311
#define IDB_HOLD_JOB                312
#define IDB_LPT3_STATUS             313
#define IDB_LPT2_STATUS             314
#define IDB_LPT1_STATUS             315
#define IDB_LONGFILE_DRIVES         400
#define IDB_SCAN_DIRS               401
#define IDB_LONG_DIRS               500
#define IDB_DIRS                    501
#define IDB_DELETE_DIR              502
#define IDB_CREATE_DIR              503
#define IDB_SCAN_FILES              504
#define IDB_LONG_FILES              600
#define IDB_FILES                   601
#define IDB_DELETE_FILE             602
#define IDB_COPY_FILE               603
#define IDB_MOVE_FILE               604
#define IDB_CREATE_DIRECTORY        700
#define IDB_DIR_NAME                701

#define IDB_SOURCE_FILE             605
#define IDB_TARGET_FILE             606

/*===== Global Variables =====*/

extern HINSTANCE    hInst;

/*===== Function Prototypes =====*/

// WNetServerBrowseDialog() is in the Windows for Workgroups
// driver file.
WORD API WNetServerBrowseDialog(HWND hWndParent, LPSTR lpszLocal,
                                LPSTR lpszRemote, UINT cchRemoteLen,
                                DWORD dwFlags);
WORD API WNetShareAsDialog(HWND hWndParent, WORD wType, LPSTR lpszShare);
WORD API WNetGetShareName(LPSTR lpszDevice, LPSTR lpszName,
                    WORD wShareLen);
WORD API WNetGetShareCount(WORD wType);
WORD API WNetStopShareDialog(HWND hWnd, WORD wType, LPSTR lpszComputer);
WORD API WNetGetSharePath(LPSTR lpszShare, LPSTR lpszPath,
                    WORD wPathLen);
WORD API WNetGetLastConnection(WORD wType, LPWORD lpwIndex);
WORD API WNetSetDefaultDrive(WORD wDrive);
```

```
WORD API WNetExitConfirm(HWND hWnd, WORD wType);

void WNetDemo_OnStopShare(HWND hWnd, WPARAM wParam);
void WNetDemo_OnShareDir(HWND hWnd);
void WNetDemo_OnConfirmExit(HWND hWnd);

/********
 *
 * Listing C-4. WNETDEMO.RC
 *
 * Copyright (c) 1992 Ralph P. Davis, All Rights Reserved
 *
 ********/

#include <windows.h>
#include "wnetdemo.h"
#include "wnetdemo.mnu"
#include "wnetdemo.dlg"

/********
 *
 * Listing C-5. WNETDEMO.MNU
 *
 * Copyright (c) 1992 Ralph P. Davis, All Rights Reserved
 *
 ********/

WNETDEMO MENU
BEGIN
    POPUP       "&Configuration"
    BEGIN
        MENUITEM    "&Capabilities...", IDM_CAPABILITIES
        MENUITEM    SEPARATOR
        MENUITEM    "&Directory Type",IDM_DIRECTORYTYPE
        MENUITEM    SEPARATOR
        MENUITEM    "&Print File", IDM_SUBMIT_PRINTJOB
        MENUITEM    "&Watch Print Queue...", IDM_WATCH_QUEUE
        MENUITEM    SEPARATOR
        MENUITEM    "&Error Codes", IDM_ERROR_CODES
    END
    POPUP       "&Dialogs"
    BEGIN
        MENUITEM    "Browse &Drives...",IDM_BROWSE_DRIVES
        MENUITEM    "Browse &Print Queues...", IDM_BROWSE_QUEUES
        MENUITEM    SEPARATOR
        MENUITEM    "&Connect to Network Drive...",IDM_CONNECT_DRIVE
        MENUITEM    "Connect to Network Print &Queue...",IDM_CONNECT_QUEUE
        MENUITEM    SEPARATOR
        MENUITEM    "C&onnection (Drives)...",IDM_CONNECTION_DRIVES
        MENUITEM    "Co&nnection (Queues)...",IDM_CONNECTION_QUEUES
        MENUITEM    SEPARATOR
        MENUITEM    "Device &Mode...",IDM_DEVICEMODE
        MENUITEM    SEPARATOR
        MENUITEM    "&Disconnect Network Drive...",IDM_DISCONNECT_DRIVE
        MENUITEM    "Di&sconnect Network Print Queue...",IDM_DISCONNECT_QUEUE
        MENUITEM    SEPARATOR
        MENUITEM    "P&roperties...", IDM_PROPERTIES
        MENUITEM    SEPARATOR
        MENUITEM    "&View Queue...",IDM_VIEWQUEUE
        MENUITEM    SEPARATOR
        POPUP       "&Windows for Workgroups Dialogs"
        BEGIN
            MENUITEM    "Browse &Hosts...", IDM_BROWSE_HOSTS
            MENUITEM    "&Share Directory...", IDM_SHARE_DIR
            MENUITEM    "Share Print &Queue...", IDM_SHARE_PRINTQ
            MENUITEM    "S&top Sharing Directory...", IDM_STOP_SHARE_DIR
            MENUITEM    "St&op Sharing Print Queue...", IDM_STOP_SHARE_PRINTQ
            MENUITEM    "&Confirm Exit...", IDM_CONFIRM_EXIT
        END
        POPUP       "&Banyan VINES Dialogs"
        BEGIN
            MENUITEM "&Select Single Item", IDM_VINES_SELECT_SINGLE
            MENUITEM "Select &Multiple Items", IDM_VINES_SELECT_MULTIPLE
        END
    END
    POPUP "&Long File Names"
    BEGIN
        MENUITEM "&Long Filename Drives...", IDM_LFNLONGDRIVES
```

```
            END
            POPUP "\a&Help"
            BEGIN
                MENUITEM "&NetWare", IDM_NETWARE_HELP
                MENUITEM "&LAN Manager", IDM_LANMAN_HELP
                MENUITEM "&VINES", IDM_VINES_HELP
                MENUITEM "&Windows for Workgroups", IDM_WFW_HELP
            END
END

/********
 *
 * Listing C-6. WNETDEMO.DLG
 *
 * Generated by Windows 3.1 SDK Dialog Editor
 *
 ********/

#include "wnetdemo.h"

IDB_CAPABILITIES DIALOG 29, -4, 307, 250
STYLE DS_MODALFRAME | WS_POPUP | WS_VISIBLE | WS_CAPTION | WS_SYSMENU
CAPTION "Network Capabilities"
FONT 8, "MS Sans Serif"
BEGIN
    PUSHBUTTON      "OK", IDOK, 132, 223, 40, 17
    LTEXT           "Driver Version:", -1, 8, 50, 52, 12
    LTEXT           "", IDB_DRIVER_VERSION, 62, 50, 40, 12
    LTEXT           "Network Type:", -1, 8, 35, 54, 11
    LTEXT           "", IDB_NET_TYPE, 62, 35, 66, 8
    LTEXT           "Driver Spec Version:", -1, 149, 50, 70, 8
    LTEXT           "", IDB_SPEC_VERSION, 227, 50, 40, 12
    LTEXT           "User/computer name:", -1, 149, 35, 77, 8
    LTEXT           "", IDB_USER_NAME, 227, 35, 66, 8
    GROUPBOX        "Configuration", -1, 2, 19, 300, 48
    LTEXT           "User Functions", -1, 8, 83, 56, 12
    LISTBOX         IDB_USER_FUNCS, 7, 97, 90, 40, LBS_SORT | WS_VSCROLL |
                    WS_TABSTOP
    LTEXT           "Connection Functions", -1, 103, 83, 91, 12
    LISTBOX         IDB_CONN_FUNCS, 103, 97, 90, 40, LBS_SORT | WS_VSCROLL |
                    WS_TABSTOP
    LTEXT           "Print Functions", -1, 205, 83, 68, 12
    LISTBOX         IDB_PRINT_FUNCS, 205, 97, 90, 40, LBS_SORT | WS_VSCROLL |
                    WS_TABSTOP
    LTEXT           "Administrative Functions", -1, 7, 147, 87, 12
    LISTBOX         IDB_ADMIN_FUNCS, 7, 161, 90, 40, LBS_SORT | WS_VSCROLL |
                    WS_TABSTOP
    LTEXT           "Dialog Boxes", -1, 106, 147, 69, 12
    LISTBOX         IDB_DIALOGS, 106, 161, 90, 40, LBS_SORT | WS_VSCROLL |
                    WS_TABSTOP
    GROUPBOX        "Supported APIs", -1, 2, 70, 300, 143
    LTEXT           "Error Functions", -1, 205, 147, 69, 12
    LISTBOX         IDB_ERROR_FUNCS, 205, 161, 90, 40, LBS_SORT | WS_VSCROLL |
                    WS_TABSTOP
    LTEXT           "Driver Name:", -1, 101, 9, 49, 8
    LTEXT           "", IDB_DRIVER_NAME, 158, 9, 61, 8
END

IDB_DIRECTORY_TYPES DIALOG 10, -7, 268, 211
STYLE DS_MODALFRAME | WS_POPUP | WS_VISIBLE | WS_CAPTION | WS_SYSMENU
CAPTION "Drive Types"
FONT 8, "Courier New"
BEGIN
    LISTBOX         IDB_DRIVES, 8, 18, 250, 168, LBS_SORT | WS_VSCROLL |
                    WS_TABSTOP
    PUSHBUTTON      "OK", IDOK, 111, 189, 40, 14
END

IDB_PRINT_MONITOR DIALOG 3, -17, 361, 229
STYLE WS_MINIMIZEBOX | WS_MAXIMIZEBOX | WS_POPUP | WS_VISIBLE | WS_CAPTION |
    WS_SYSMENU | WS_THICKFRAME
CAPTION "Print Queue Monitor"
FONT 8, "Courier New"
BEGIN
    LISTBOX         IDB_LPT1_INFO, 11, 30, 295, 44, LBS_SORT |
                    LBS_MULTIPLESEL | WS_VSCROLL | WS_TABSTOP
    PUSHBUTTON      "Quit", IDCANCEL, 195, 204, 89, 14
    LISTBOX         IDB_LPT2_INFO, 11, 92, 295, 44, LBS_SORT |
                    LBS_MULTIPLESEL | WS_VSCROLL | WS_TABSTOP
```

```
    LISTBOX          IDB_LPT3_INFO, 11, 153, 295, 44, LBS_SORT |
                     LBS_MULTIPLESEL | WS_VSCROLL | WS_TABSTOP
    LTEXT            "LPT1", -1, 11, 16, 30, 8
    LTEXT            "LPT2", -1, 11, 78, 30, 8
    LTEXT            "LPT3", -1, 11, 140, 30, 8
    LTEXT            "", IDB_LPT1_QUEUE, 42, 16, 133, 8
    LTEXT            "", IDB_LPT2_QUEUE, 42, 78, 133, 8
    LTEXT            "", IDB_LPT3_QUEUE, 42, 140, 133, 8
    DEFPUSHBUTTON    "Refresh", IDB_REFRESH, 50, 203, 89, 14
    PUSHBUTTON       "Delete", IDB_DELETE_JOB, 314, 41, 40, 14
    PUSHBUTTON       "Hold", IDB_HOLD_JOB, 314, 103, 40, 14
    PUSHBUTTON       "Resume", IDB_RESUME_JOB, 314, 164, 40, 14
    LTEXT            "", IDB_LPT3_STATUS, 183, 140, 122, 8
    LTEXT            "", IDB_LPT2_STATUS, 183, 78, 122, 8
    LTEXT            "", IDB_LPT1_STATUS, 183, 16, 122, 8
END

IDB_LONGFILE_DRIVES DIALOG 26, 5, 268, 211
STYLE DS_MODALFRAME | WS_POPUP | WS_VISIBLE | WS_CAPTION | WS_SYSMENU
CAPTION "Drives Supporting Long Filenames"
FONT 8, "Courier New"
BEGIN
    LISTBOX          IDB_DRIVES, 8, 25, 250, 161, LBS_SORT | WS_VSCROLL |
                     WS_TABSTOP
    DEFPUSHBUTTON    "Quit", IDOK, 211, 189, 40, 14
    LTEXT            "Drive", -1, 9, 11, 25, 8
    LTEXT            "Volume Label", -1, 35, 4, 30, 15
    LTEXT            "Mapped to", -1, 77, 11, 42, 8
    PUSHBUTTON       "Scan Directories", IDB_SCAN_DIRS, 8, 189, 72, 14,
                     WS_DISABLED
    PUSHBUTTON       "Scan Files", IDB_SCAN_FILES, 107, 189, 72, 14,
                     WS_DISABLED
END
IDB_LONG_DIRS DIALOG 4, 7, 356, 212
STYLE DS_MODALFRAME | WS_POPUP | WS_VISIBLE | WS_CAPTION | WS_SYSMENU
CAPTION "Subdirectories of F:\\"
FONT 8, "Courier New"
BEGIN
    LISTBOX          IDB_DIRS, 11, 18, 286, 170, LBS_SORT | WS_VSCROLL |
                     WS_TABSTOP
    DEFPUSHBUTTON    "Quit", IDOK, 309, 19, 40, 14
    PUSHBUTTON       "Delete Directory", IDB_DELETE_DIR, 3, 190, 73, 14,
                     WS_DISABLED
    PUSHBUTTON       "Create Directory...", IDB_CREATE_DIR, 80, 190, 83, 14
    PUSHBUTTON       "Scan Subdirectories", IDB_SCAN_DIRS, 168, 190, 85, 14,
                     WS_DISABLED
    PUSHBUTTON       "Scan Files", IDB_SCAN_FILES, 259, 190, 68, 14,
                     WS_DISABLED
END

IDB_LONG_FILES DIALOG 4, 7, 356, 212
STYLE DS_MODALFRAME | WS_POPUP | WS_VISIBLE | WS_CAPTION | WS_SYSMENU
CAPTION "Files in F:\\"
FONT 8, "Courier New"
BEGIN
    LISTBOX          IDB_FILES, 11, 18, 286, 170, LBS_SORT | WS_VSCROLL |
                     WS_TABSTOP
    DEFPUSHBUTTON    "Quit", IDOK, 309, 19, 40, 14
    PUSHBUTTON       "Delete", IDB_DELETE_FILE, 10, 190, 66, 14, WS_DISABLED
    PUSHBUTTON       "Copy...", IDB_COPY_FILE, 119, 190, 74, 14, WS_DISABLED
    PUSHBUTTON       "Rename...", IDB_MOVE_FILE, 228, 191, 70, 14,
                     WS_DISABLED
END

IDB_CREATE_DIRECTORY DIALOG 6, 18, 301, 100
STYLE DS_MODALFRAME | WS_POPUP | WS_VISIBLE | WS_CAPTION | WS_SYSMENU
CAPTION "Create Directory"
FONT 8, "MS Sans Serif"
BEGIN
    EDITTEXT         IDB_DIR_NAME, 6, 28, 283, 12, ES_AUTOHSCROLL
    LTEXT            "Enter directory name:", -1, 6, 13, 77, 8
    DEFPUSHBUTTON    "Create", IDOK, 101, 70, 40, 14
    PUSHBUTTON       "Cancel", IDCANCEL, 175, 70, 40, 14
END

IDB_COPY_FILE DIALOG 6, 18, 301, 133
STYLE DS_MODALFRAME | WS_POPUP | WS_VISIBLE | WS_CAPTION | WS_SYSMENU
CAPTION "Copy File"
FONT 8, "MS Sans Serif"
```

```
BEGIN
    EDITTEXT          IDB_TARGET_FILE, 6, 80, 283, 12, ES_AUTOHSCROLL
    LTEXT             "Source file name:", -1, 6, 13, 77, 8
    DEFPUSHBUTTON     "OK", IDOK, 102, 107, 40, 14
    PUSHBUTTON        "Cancel", IDCANCEL, 174, 107, 40, 14
    LTEXT             "", IDB_SOURCE_FILE, 6, 28, 283, 12
    LTEXT             "Target file name:", -1, 6, 65, 77, 8
END
```

Listing C-7. WNETDEMO.LNK

```
wnetdemo wnetsvns wnetdrvr
wnetdemo.exe
NUL
libw.lib commdlg.lib mlibcew.lib lan.lib user.lib oldnames.lib nddeapi.lib wfwnet.lib
wnetdemo.def
```

```
;********
;
; Listing C-8. WNETDEMO.DEF
;
; Copyright (c) 1992 Ralph P. Davis, All Rights Reserved
;
;********

NAME              WNETDEMO
DESCRIPTION       'Windows Network Driver Demo'
EXETYPE           WINDOWS
STUB              'WINSTUB.EXE'
CODE              MOVEABLE DISCARDABLE PRELOAD
DATA              MOVEABLE SINGLE PRELOAD
HEAPSIZE          4096
STACKSIZE         16384

EXPORTS
                  MainWndProc
                  CopyQueryProc
                  CapabilitiesDlgProc
                  DirectoryTypeDlgProc
                  WatchQueueDlgProc
                  LongDrivesDlgProc
                  ScanDirsDlgProc
                  ScanFilesDlgProc
                  CreateDirDlgProc
                  CopyFileDlgProc
```

```
#########
#
# Listing C-9. WNETDEMO.MAK
#
# Copyright (c) 1992 Ralph P. Davis, All Rights Reserved
#
# Make file for Windows network driver demo
#
########

.c.obj:
    cl -AM -c -G2sw -Od -Zipe -W3 -DSTRICT -DWIN31 -DMULTINET $*.c

wnetdemo.obj : wnetdemo.c wnetdemo.h

wnetsvns.obj : wnetsvns.c

wnetdrvr.obj : wnetdrvr.c

wnetdemo.res: wnetdemo.rc wnetdemo.h wnetdemo.dlg wnetdemo.mnu
    rc -r  wnetdemo.rc

wnetdemo.exe: wnetdemo.obj wnetsvns.obj wnetdrvr.obj wnetdemo.res \
              wnetdemo.def
    link /CO /LI /NOPACKC /ALIGN:16 /NOD @@wnetdemo.lnk
    rc  wnetdemo.res
```

Bibliography

AT&T. *UNIX System V Release 4 Programmer's Guide: Networking Interfaces.* Englewood Cliffs, NJ: Prentice-Hall, Inc., 1990.

Banyan Systems, Inc. *VINES Architecture Definition.* Westboro, MA: Banyan Systems, Inc., 1988.

Banyan Systems, Inc. *VINES StreetTalk and STDA Programming Interface.* Westboro, MA: Banyan Systems, Inc., 1992.

Banyan Systems, Inc. *VINES Client Developer's Guide.* Westboro, MA: Banyan Systems, Inc. 1992.

Brockschmidt, Kraig. *Fundamental Network DDE: Windows for Workgroups 3.1.* Distributed in Word for Windows format as NETDDE.DOC. Redmond, WA: Microsoft Corporation, 1992.

Clark, Jeffrey D. *Windows Programmer's Guide To OLE/DDE.* Carmel, IN: Howard W. Sams & Company, 1992.

Custer, Helen. *Inside Windows NT.* Redmond, WA: Microsoft Press, 1992.

Davis, Ralph. *NetWare Programmer's Guide.* Reading, MA: Addison-Wesley Publishing Company, 1990.

Davis, Ralph. *NetWare 386 Programmer's Guide.* Reading, MA: Addison-Wesley Publishing Company, 1991.

DPMI Committee. *DOS Protected Mode Interface (DPMI) Specification.* Available from Intel Corporation, 800-548-4725.

Duncan, Ray, Charles Petzold, Andrew Schulman, M. Steven Baker, Ross P. Nelson, Stephen R. Davis, and Robert Moote. *Extending DOS--A Programmer's Guide to Protected-Mode DOS, Second Edition.* Reading, MA: Addison-Wesley Publishing Company, 1992.

International Business Machines Co., *IBM NetBIOS Application Development Guide, Part # 68x2270,* 1987.

Hall, Martin, Mark Towfiq, Geoff Arnold, David Treadwell, and Henry Sanders. *Windows Sockets: An Open Interface for Network Programming under Microsoft Windows.* Provided courtesy of FTP Software Inc., published in 1992.

Heller, Martin. *Advanced Windows Programming.* New York, NY: John Wiley & Sons, Inc., 1992.

Kochan, Stephen G., and Patrick H. Wood, Eds. *UNIX Networking.* Carmel, IN: Hayden Books, 1989.

McCann, John T. *NetWare Programmer's Guide.* Redwood City, CA: M&T Books, 1990.

McCord, James W. *Windows 3.1 Programmer's Reference.* Carmel, IN: Que Corporation, 1992.

Microsoft Corporation. *Device Driver Adaptation Guide.* Redmond, WA: Microsoft Corporation, 1992.

Microsoft Corporation. *Guide to Programming.* Redmond, WA: Microsoft Corporation, 1992.

Microsoft Corporation. *Microsoft MAIL Technical Reference.* Distributed in Word for Windows format as TECHREF.DOC. Redmond, WA: Microsoft Corporation, 1992.

Microsoft Corporation. *Microsoft Windows Resource Kit For Operating System Version 3.1.* Redmond, WA: Microsoft Corporation, 1992.

Microsoft Corporation. *Microsoft Windows for Workgroups Resource Kit For Operating System Version 3.1*. Redmond, WA: Microsoft Corporation, 1992.

Microsoft Corporation. *MS-DOS Programmer's Reference*. Redmond, WA: Microsoft Press, 1991.

Microsoft Corporation. *Programmer's Reference, Volume 1: Overview*. Redmond, WA: Microsoft Corporation, 1992.

Microsoft Corporation. *Programmer's Reference, Volume 2: Functions*. Redmond, WA: Microsoft Corporation, 1992.

Microsoft Corporation. *Programmer's Reference, Volume 3: Messages, Structures, and Macros*. Redmond, WA: Microsoft Corporation, 1992.

Microsoft Corporation. *Remote Procedure Call Programmer's Guide and Reference*. Redmond, WA: Microsoft Corporation, 1992.

Microsoft Corporation. *Win32 Application Programming Interface: The Programmer's Reference*, Volumes 1 and 2. Redmond, WA: Microsoft Press, 1992.

Microsoft Corporation. *Windows for Workgroups Basics*. Distributed in Word for Windows format as BASICS.DOC. Redmond, WA: Microsoft Corporation, 1992.

Microsoft Corporation. *Windows for Workgroups Functions*. Distributed in Word for Windows format as WFWAPI.DOC. Redmond, WA: Microsoft Corporation, 1992.

Microsoft Corporation. *Windows for Workgroups Structures*. Distributed in Word for Windows format as WFWSTRC.DOC. Redmond, WA: Microsoft Corporation, 1992.

Nance, Barry. *Network Programming in C*. Carmel, IN: Que Corporation, 1990.

Norton, Daniel A. *Writing Windows Device Drivers*. Reading, MA: Addison-Wesley Publishing Company, 1992.

Novell, Inc. *LAN WorkPlace for DOS Socket Library API Reference Manual*. Provo, UT: Novell, Inc., 1990.

Novell, Inc. *NetWare C Interface for Windows*, Volumes 1 and 2. Austin, TX: Novell, Inc., 1991.

Novell, Inc. *NetWare System Interface Technical Overview*. Provo, UT: Novell, Inc., 1990.

Patch, Ray, and Alok Sinha. "Developing Network-aware Programs Using Windows 3.1 and NetBIOS." *Microsoft Systems Journal*, Volume 7, No. 4, July-August 1992.

Petzold, Charles. *Programming Windows 3.1*. Redmond, WA: Microsoft Press, 1992.

Ryan, Ralph. *Microsoft LAN Manager: A Programmer's Guide, Version 2*. Redmond, WA: Microsoft Press, 1992.

Rose, Charles G. *Programmer's Guide to NetWare*. New York, NY: McGraw-Hill, Inc., 1990.

Schulman, Andrew, David Maxey, and Matt Pietrek. *Undocumented Windows*. Reading, MA: Addison-Wesley Publishing Company, 1992.

Schulman, Andrew, Raymond J. Michels, Jim Kyle, Tim Paterson, David Maxey, and Ralf Brown. *Undocumented DOS*. Reading, MA: Addison-Wesley Publishing Company, 1990.

Stallings, William. *Handbook of Computer-Communications Standards, Volume 1. The Open Systems (OSI) Model and OSI-Related Standards*. Second Edition. Carmel, IN: Howard W. Sams & Company, 1990.

Stallings, William. *Handbook of Computer-Communications Standards, Volume 2. Local Area Network Standards*. Second Edition. Carmel, IN: Howard W. Sams & Company, 1990.

Stallings, William, et al. *Handbook of Computer-Communications Standards, Volume 3. The TCP/IP Protocol Suite*. Second Edition. Carmel, IN: Howard W. Sams & Company, 1990.

Xerox Corporation. *Internet Transport Protocols*. Sunnyvale, CA: Xerox Corporation, 1981.

INDEX